Getting the Message Through

A Branch History of the U.S. Army Signal Corps

ARMY HISTORICAL SERIES

Getting the Message Through

A Branch History of the U.S. Army Signal Corps

by

Rebecca Robbins Raines

MILITARY INSTRVCTION

CENTER OF MILITARY HISTORY
UNITED STATES ARMY
WASHINGTON, D.C., 1996

Library of Congress Cataloging-in-Publication Data

Raines, Rebecca Robbins, 1952–
    Getting the message through : a branch history of the U.S. Army
Signal Corps / by Rebecca Robbins Raines.
       p. cm. — (Army history series)
    Includes bibliographical references and index.
    1. United States. Army—Communication systems—History.
I. Title II. Series.
UG573.R35 1996
358'.24'0973—dc20   95–2393
                                                    CIP

CMH Pub 30–17–1

First Printing

For sale by the U.S. Government Printing Office
Superintendent of Documents, Mail Stop: SSOP, Washington, DC 20402-9328
ISBN 0-16-045351-8

Army Historical Series

Jeffrey J. Clarke, General Editor

v

Foreword

This book traces the history of the U.S. Army Signal Corps from its beginnings on the eve of the American Civil War through its participation in the Persian Gulf conflict during the early 1990s. Over the course of its 135 years of existence, the Signal Corps has often been at the forefront of the revolutionary changes that have taken place in communications technology. It contributed significantly, for example, to the development of radar and the transistor. In today's information age, the Signal Corps continues its tradition of leadership and innovation on the digitized battlefields of the twenty-first century.

While accounts of the branch's service during the Civil War, World War II, and Vietnam have been published, little has been written about the rest of the Signal Corps' accomplishments. This book fills out the picture. It shows today's signal soldiers where their branch has been and points the way to where it is going. The reader, whether military or civilian, can follow the growth and development of one of the Army's most sophisticated technical branches. By telling the Signal Corps' story in a comprehensive manner, this volume makes a significant contribution to the history of the Army.

DOUGLAS D. BUCHHOLZ   JOHN W. MOUNTCASTLE
Major General, USA   Brigadier General, USA
Chief of Signal   Chief of Military History

Washington, D.C.
13 November 1995

The Author

Rebecca Robbins Raines was born in Belfast, Maine, and grew up in nearby Searsport. She graduated from the University of Maine with a B.A. degree in history in 1974. From 1974 to 1977 she was employed by the Maine State Archives. She joined the Center of Military History in 1977 as a historian in the Organizational History Branch. In 1981 she received her M.A. degree in American history from Georgetown University. Mrs. Raines is the author of several articles on the history of the U.S. Army Signal Corps.

Preface

This volume was originally conceived as part of a larger series of popular histories about each branch of the Army. To produce this study in a relatively short time, I confined the research largely to published primary and secondary sources. The focus is upon an institutional, rather than an operational or organizational, history of the Signal Corps. While the coverage is by no means comprehensive, it is designed to provide an overview of the many and varied aspects of the Signal Corps' work during its first 130 years. These range from operating a national weather service from 1870 to 1891 to becoming responsible in the 1980s for the Army's automation program. I emphasized the branch's history up to approximately 1985 and have not dealt with more recent events at length. Because much of the material on contemporary operations, such as URGENT FURY in Grenada and JUST CAUSE in Panama, remains classified, published accounts provide only a cursory overview. Operations DESERT SHIELD and DESERT STORM took place just as the manuscript was being finished, and I included some coverage of the Signal Corps' participation in the Persian Gulf conflict. Only the passage of time and the declassification of records will enable historians to analyze fully these most recent episodes in the Corps' history and place them in proper perspective.

The intended audience for this volume is the men and women serving in the Signal Corps, particularly students attending the Signal School at Fort Gordon, Georgia. I trust that it will help to instill in them an appreciation of the Signal Corps' rich heritage. I also hope that individuals interested in military history in general and military communications in particular will find the volume useful.

The preparation of this volume would not have been possible without the support of the successive chiefs of military history, Maj. Gen. William A. Stofft, Brig. Gen. Harold W. Nelson, and Brig. Gen. John W. Mountcastle. The Center's chief historians, Morris J. MacGregor and his successor, Dr. Jeffrey J. Clarke, helped guide the manuscript to its completion. Lt. Col. Charles R. Shrader, while serving as chief of the Historical Services Division, originally proposed the branch history series and launched this volume.

Writing is a solitary task, but a writer never works alone. Any volume is a cooperative effort, and I owe many thanks to the people who have assisted me in preparing this book. From its inception, generous assistance for this project has been provided by the U.S. Army Signal Center and Fort Gordon, Georgia. My sincere thanks are owed to the following chiefs of signal who served during the course of this undertaking: Maj. Gen. Thurman D. Rodgers, Maj. Gen. Bruce R. Harris, Maj. Gen. Leo M. Childs, Maj. Gen. Peter A. Kind, Maj. Gen. Robert E. Gray, and Maj. Gen. Douglas D. Buchholz. The command historian at Fort Gordon, Dr. Carol

E. Stokes, and her former assistant, Dr. Kathy R. Coker, helped me tremendously. Working with them was a pleasure.

A historian's job would be impossible without librarians, archivists, reference persons, and other invaluable colleagues. Over the years the Center's librarians and their aides have performed yeoman service under often less than ideal conditions. These dedicated individuals include Carol I. Anderson, Esther Howard, James B. Knight, and Mary L. Sawyer. I particularly appreciate their patience with me regarding overdue interlibrary loan books. Hannah M. Zeidlik and the members of the Historical Resources Branch—especially Geraldine K. Harcarik—graciously provided copies of material from the Center's archival collections. The following individuals who reviewed the manuscript at various stages provided valuable guidance and many helpful comments: Dr. Graham A. Cosmas, Dr. Albert E. Cowdrey, Romana Danysh, Col. C. Reid Franks, Dr. Mary C. Gillett, Dr. Vincent C. Jones, Morris J. MacGregor, Janice E. McKenney, Lt. Col. Robert E. Morris, Col. Robert H. Sholly, and John B. Wilson. In addition, many of my colleagues at the Center, past and present, provided advice and encouragement along the way as well as the benefits of their own extensive knowledge. I particularly wish to mention Walter H. Bradford, Dr. Norman M. Cary, Terrence J. Gough, Dr. William M. Hammond, Mary L. Haynes, Dr. Charles E. Kirkpatrick, Dr. Edgar F. Raines, Jr., and Dr. Robert K. Wright, Jr.

I also wish to acknowledge the following individuals outside the Center who generously donated their time to read the manuscript and furnish excellent commentary: Col. Alexander W. Cameron, Lt. Gen. Thomas M. Rienzi, U.S. Army (Ret.), and Dr. John Y. Simon.

While writing about information systems, I was also learning how to use them as the Center made the transition to the computer age. I want to thank Sherell Fersner who typed the initial drafts of the first chapter in the days before each historian received a personal computer. I also extend a hearty round of applause to Lt. Col. Adrian G. Traas, U.S. Army (Ret.), for his technical assistance in directing the electrons along the correct paths.

I owe a huge debt of gratitude to the many individuals at other agencies and institutions for their assistance—Margaret Novinger and the staff of the Conrad Technical Library, Fort Gordon, Georgia; Theodore F. Wise of the U.S. Army Signal Corps and Fort Gordon Museum; Glenn Swan and colleagues in the Office, Chief of Signal; Linda Means in the Public Affairs Office, Fort Gordon; John Slonaker, Dennis Vetock, and Louise Arnold-Friend of the Historical Reference Branch, U.S. Army Military History Institute (MHI), who kindly let me borrow most of their library, or so it seemed; Dr. Richard Sommers of the Archives Branch, MHI; and Michael Winey and Randy Hackenburg of the Special Collections Branch, MHI. Richard L. Boylan and Wilbert B. Mahoney of the National Archives and Records Administration provided much-needed guidance in locating Signal Corps records, and the staff of the Still Picture Branch assisted greatly in securing illustrations for the volume. Thanks are also due Dr. Richard B. Bingham, command historian of the U.S. Army Communications-Electronics Command at Fort

Monmouth, New Jersey; Dr. John P. Finnegan of the U.S. Army Intelligence and Security Command; David W. Gaddy of the National Security Agency; Don E. McLeod, Elaine Pospishil, and Danny M. Johnson, who have served successively as command historian of the U.S. Army Information Systems Command at Fort Huachuca, Arizona; and the staffs of the Prints and Photographs Division of the Library of Congress and the Special Collections Division of the United States Military Academy Library.

My thanks are also extended to the following individuals who assisted me in my search for illustrations: Regina Burns of the U.S. Army Aviation Museum at Fort Rucker, Alabama; Mark Dunn of the history office at Fort Gordon; Robert Hansen of the National Oceanographic and Atmospheric Administration, Department of Commerce; Cynthia Hayden, Command Historian, XVIII Airborne Corps and Fort Bragg; Earle M. Levine of GTE; and Barbara Tuttle of the Fort Huachuca Museum.

I reserve a very special and heartfelt thank-you to Dr. Paul J. Scheips, formerly of the Signal Corps Historical Division and for many years a treasured colleague at the Center. Without his guidance, support, and generosity, I could never have attempted to write this volume. From my earliest days at the Center he helped me learn about the Signal Corps and spurred my interest in its history. The Signal Corps owes an enormous debt to this gentleman and scholar, whose dissertation on the first chief signal officer, Albert J. Myer, is an indispensable resource. His many published works relating to Signal Corps history make him the dean of Signal Corps historians.

I am especially grateful for the expert assistance provided by my editor, Susan Carroll. Her patience, professionalism, and good humor were greatly appreciated. I am also indebted to the Center's production staff for its skill and expertise: John W. Elsberg, Catherine A. Heerin, Diane Sedore Arms, Diane Donovan, Arthur S. Hardyman, Beth MacKenzie, Sherry L. Dowdy, and Howell C. Brewer, Jr.

Words alone cannot convey the thanks I owe to my family. First, my parents, Carl and Evelyn Robbins, who encouraged my interest in history from an early age. Throughout the course of this project, my husband Ed and son Eddie showed enormous patience and provided much-needed support. Ed's love and enthusiasm for military history, not to mention his voluminous library, helped me over many rough spots.

If I have overlooked anyone, it was not intentional. I am not organized enough to have kept all the notes I needed to write this essay, as anyone who has ever seen my desk can testify. Finally, despite the best efforts of the individuals cited above, any errors that remain in the text are my sole responsibility.

Washington, D.C.   REBECCA ROBBINS RAINES
13 November 1995

Contents

Illustrations courtesy of the following sources: *Frontispiece*, pp. 5, 392, U.S.
Army Signal Center and Fort Gordon; pp. 10, 12, 24, 28 (*left*), 43, 57, 60, 62, 94,
97, 101, 102, 107, 109 (*top/bottom*), 123, 125, 129, 130, 134, 146, 148, 151, 167,
169, 171, 176, 177, 181, 183, 185, 189, 192, 195, 221, 223 (*bottom*), 228 (*left*),
234 (*top*), 237 (*left/right*), 238, 242, 243, 257, 259, 261, 267, 269, 270, 272, 273,

278 (*top/bottom*), 291, 294, 296, 297, 300, 307, 309, 319, 320, 325, 326, 328, 329, 331, 336, 340 (*top/bottom*), 343, 344 (*left/right*), 347 (*left/right*), 361, 369, 372 (*top left/top right/bottom*), 374, 379 (*top/bottom*), 381, National Archives; p. 19, U.S. Army Signal Corps Museum; pp. 21, 22 (*left*), Brown, *The Signal Corps in the War of the Rebellion*; p. 22 (*right*), *Photographic History of the Civil War*, vol. 8; p. 26, *Battles and Leaders of the Civil War*, vol. 3, pt. 1; p. 28 (*right*), Valentine Museum; p. 48, *Annual Report of the Chief Signal Officer*, 1875; p. 50, National Oceanic and Atmospheric Administration; p. 53, *Annual Report of the Chief Signal Officer*, 1885; pp. 59, 137, 150, U.S. Army Military History Institute; p. 67, *Annual Report of the Chief Signal Officer*, 1888; p. 85, Chicago Public Library; pp. 92, 198, 228 (*right*), Library of Congress; p. 91, *Annual Report of the Chief Signal Officer*, 1899; pp. 220, 223 (*top*), 332, 335, 366, U.S. Army Communications-Electronics Command; pp. 234 (*bottom left/bottom right*), 289, U.S. Army Center of Military History; pp. 239, 265, U.S. Army Intelligence and Security Command; p. 303, Army Art Collection; pp. 308, 403, U.S. Army Information Systems Command; p. 367, U.S. Army Aviation Museum; pp. 395, 405 (*top*), GTE; p. 399, U.S. Army Visual Information Center; and pp. 404, 405 (*bottom*), XVIII Airborne Corps.

Getting the Message Through

A Branch History of the U.S. Army
Signal Corps

CHAPTER I

The Birth of the Signal Corps

Effective communications have always been vital to military forces. Commanders must be able to maintain control over their units in order to fight successfully. By the mid-nineteenth century the extended battlefields created by more powerful weapons posed new challenges for military signaling. As armies grew larger and more complex, it became increasingly difficult to integrate their various components. For the U.S. Army, a small organization spread across a vast continent, geography provided an added impetus for the development of a means of rapid, long-distance military communication. In this milieu, the United States Army became the first army in the world to establish a separate communications branch, beginning with the appointment in 1860 of a signal officer to the Army staff in the War Department. This event marked the official origin of the U.S. Army Signal Corps.

Early Military Signaling

A separate institution was not, of course, necessary for the act of communication. Armies had managed to transmit information throughout the millennia without the help of a signal corps. As long as military units remained relatively small and engaged in close-order combat, the commander's voice provided an adequate means for transmitting signals on the battlefield. From ancient times armies also used musical instruments, such as trumpets and bugles, as signaling devices. For long-distance communication commanders employed runners or mounted messengers. In 490 B.C. a Greek runner delivered the news of victory over the Persians at Marathon to Athens and then died from the exertion. (This heroic feat gave rise to the athletic event known as the marathon.) Other less strenuous signaling methods included the use of beacon fires and pigeons. With the development of gunpowder, firearms and cannon increased the size of the battlefield, but signaling techniques made few significant advances until the dawn of the electrical age.

During the American Revolution the Continental Army closely followed the organization and procedures of the British Army, including its signaling techniques. Fifers and drummers provided the field music—that is, the transmission of signals in battle. During the winter of 1777–1778 at Valley Forge, Baron Friedrich Wilhelm von Steuben instituted the Continental Army's first system of drill procedures, which included standardized signals.[1] After achieving independence, the U.S. Army's signaling methods remained virtually unchanged until the invention of the electric telegraph in the 1840s. The new and still unreliable device saw limited service during the Mexican War (1846–1848). The quartermaster general, Brig. Gen. Thomas S. Jesup, for example, used the telegraph to communicate from his Washington office with the quartermaster offices in Baltimore, Philadelphia, and New York. As a precautionary measure, however, he supplemented each telegram with a letter.[2]

European nations, meanwhile, moved more quickly to adopt new communication methods. In the 1790s Claude Chappe, a French engineer, invented a semaphore telegraph system that consisted of mechanical arms mounted on towers. The raising or lowering of the arms in the proper combinations indicated specific letters, words, or phrases. Using this system, messages could be exchanged over long distances in hours rather than days. The British, noting the success of the French system, constructed a telegraph employing pivoted shutters that were opened and closed by levers. Other countries, among them Germany, Sweden, and Russia, adopted their own optical telegraph systems.[3]

During the Crimean War (1854–1856) European armies moved a step closer to modern communication methods by using electric telegraphy. The French and British jointly built telegraph lines to communicate with their home governments, and a message could be relayed from Balaclava to London in about twenty-four hours. The British established some field lines, but they were of only limited value. Artillery rounds landing in the cable trenches damaged the lines, and mice nibbled at any exposed wires. The soldiers themselves sabotaged the system by using the insulation as a substitute for broken pipe stems.[4] The French used the telegraph to communicate between the several army headquarters and the detached corps to "insure the rapid transmission of orders and harmony of movement."[5] The Russians also communicated by telegraph between St. Petersburg and Sevastopol.

Maj. Richard Delafield, an American engineer officer sent to observe the conflict, commented at some length on the use of the telegraph. While acknowledging its usefulness for communicating with the home government, he also recognized that it introduced a new factor to warfare: for the first time, command and control could be exercised from afar. He reported that "orders were sometimes given that more circumstantial information, only to be gained in sight of the enemy, would have shown to be highly inexpedient."[6] The British government, in fact, overburdened its commanders with suggestions, recommendations, and requests for useless information.[7] The new technology, although expanding the scope of command and control, concomitantly limited field officers' freedom of action.

While European armies had not yet fully exploited the potential of electric telegraphy, the Crimean War provided a glimpse of its possibilities. By 1856 the Prussian Army had introduced the use of the telegraph. Meanwhile, a young doctor from New York who had recently entered the United States Army was destined to play a vital role in the further development of military communications.

Albert J. Myer—Father of the Signal Corps

Myer in 1854

Albert J. Myer was born in Newburgh, New York, on 20 September 1828.[8] After his mother's death when he was only six, Myer was raised by an aunt in Buffalo. At the early age of thirteen he enrolled at Geneva (later Hobart) College, located about one hundred miles east of Buffalo. Following his graduation in 1847, Myer returned to Buffalo, where he began the study of medicine. During this period he also worked in the office of the New York State Telegraph Company.[9] In 1854, three years after receiving his medical degree from the University of Buffalo, Myer joined the Army as an assistant surgeon and was ordered to Texas. There he developed a military signaling system based on his medical dissertation, "A New Sign Language for Deaf Mutes." Drawing on his experience as a telegraph operator, Myer had originally transformed the Bain telegraph code into a means of personal communication by which words could be spelled by tapping them out upon a person's cheek or hand or on an object, such as a table. In Texas he converted this sign language into the flag and torch signaling system that has become known as "wigwag." Unlike semaphore signaling, which employed two flags, wigwag required just one.[10]

While serving at Fort Duncan, Texas, in 1856, Myer wrote to Secretary of War Jefferson Davis and offered his signaling system to the War Department. Although he did not provide details as to the mechanics—perhaps because he had not yet fully worked them out—he did envision a means "to communicate between detachments of troops, marching or halted, or ships at sea in motion or at rest. . . ." Listing the general characteristics of his proposal, Myer explained that communication would be made "by day or by night, in wet or in dry weather, in fogs or in sunshine." The equipment would be "such as can be rapidly transported and used by one man mounted or on foot." As for personnel, only two men, a sender and a receiver, would ordinarily be required.[11] Myer hoped to receive a formal hearing, and he secured the support of the Army's chief of engineers, Col. Joseph G. Totten. Myer's lack of specificity, however, cost him the attention of Secretary Davis, who wrote on his letter: "In the absence of more full information no opinion can be formed of the plan proposed."[12]

Despite Davis' rebuff, Myer's cause was not lost. Totten remained interested, and when John B. Floyd replaced Davis as secretary of war in 1857, the chief of engineers reintroduced Myer's proposal.[13] Floyd was receptive, and in March 1859 Myer appeared before a board of examination in Washington, D.C. But this body, presided over by Lt. Col. Robert E. Lee of the 2d Cavalry, gave his system only a lukewarm acceptance. According to the board's report, "this system is limited in its application, to very short distances, ordinarily to one mile, but certainly, to not over three miles, and then under quite favorable circumstances of elevation of ground at the Signal Stations." The board considered that "such a system might be useful as an accessory to, in many circumstances, but not as a Substitute for the means now employed to convey intelligence by an Army in the Field, and especially on a Field of Battle."[14] It did, however, recommend further tests.

Myer began these trials in April 1859 at Fort Monroe, Virginia, later moving to New York Harbor; West Point, New York; and Washington, D.C. Several officers and enlisted men assisted him, chief of whom was 2d Lt. Edward Porter Alexander, who began working with Myer in October. By then Myer had developed a new code. A combination of numerals represented each letter of the alphabet, and he assigned numerical values to the movements of the flag or torch to each side of a central reference point. For example, a movement to the left could equal "1" and to the right, "2." To discern the message, the receiver interpreted the movements of the flag or torch in accordance with the code. The end of a word, sentence, or message was indicated by dipping the flag forward one or more times.[15] During their three months of working together, Myer and Alexander communicated at distances up to fifteen miles and made some modifications to the equipment. In late November Myer reported to the War Department that the tests had "exceeded anticipation." Myer also suggested that if the Army adopted his signaling system he should be placed in charge of it.[16] (*Figure 1*)

The fate of Myer's plans now rested with the War Department and Congress. Secretary Floyd provided some encouragement by devoting two paragraphs of his annual report for 1859 to Myer's system, stating that "the plan proposed appears to be ready and reliable."[17] Floyd subsequently recommended that Congress add a signal officer to the Army staff. As a result, Myer and Alexander appeared in February 1860 before the Senate Committee on Military Affairs. Jefferson Davis, now a senator from Mississippi, served as its chairman. While awaiting action by the Senate committee, Myer (who was proving to be a consummate behind-the-scenes politician) also received a hearing from the House Committee on Military Affairs, which unanimously recommended the appointment of a signal officer with the rank of major. On 29 March 1860 the House approved the Army appropriations bill for fiscal year 1861 with the following amendment attached:

FIGURE 1—FLAG POSITIONS OF MYER'S ORIGINAL TWO-ELEMENT CODE*

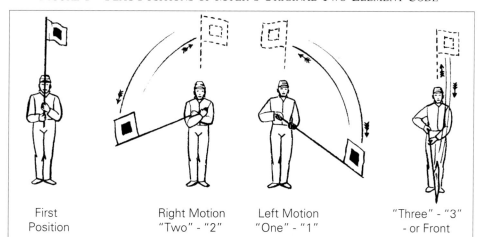

| First Position | Right Motion "Two" - "2" | Left Motion "One" - "1" | "Three" - "3" - or Front |

*Woods illustrates the General Service Code of 1872. In this illustration, the meaning of the right and left motions has been reversed to conform to Myer's original code.

Source: David L. Woods, *A History of Tactical Communication Techniques* (Orlando, Fla.: Martin-Marietta Corp., 1965), plate V–6.

For the manufacture or purchase of apparatus and equipment for field signals, $2000; and that there be added to the staff of the Army one signal officer, with the rank, pay, and allowance of a major of cavalry, who shall have charge, under the direction of the Secretary of War, of all signal duty, and all books, papers, and apparatus connected therewith.[18]

The bill then moved to the Senate where the amendment ran into opposition, notably that of Jefferson Davis. While Davis thought that Myer's signals should be used by the Army, he opposed the creation of the position of signal officer, believing that this appointment would lead to the establishment of a new department (which it ultimately did). Instead, signals should be placed within one of the existing departments. Despite Davis' objections, the Senate accepted the amendment, and President James Buchanan signed the appropriations bill into law on 21 June 1860. With this stroke of the pen, the U.S. Army Signal Corps was born.[19]

On 27 June 1860 the Senate confirmed Myer's appointment as signal officer with the rank of major.[20] He thus abandoned the practice of medicine for the uncertain future of a military communicator. Perhaps his marriage into a prominent Buffalo, New York, family, originally from Massachusetts—the Waldens of Walden Pond—made his career choice somewhat less risky. Nevertheless, within a month he received orders to report to the Department of New Mexico to test his signals in the field during a campaign against the Navajos. Myer requested the services of Lieutenant Alexander, but the young officer was serving elsewhere, and Myer could not get his assignment changed.[21] Consequently, Myer had to find and train a new assistant upon his arrival in New Mexico.[22] Before leaving for the Southwest, Myer applied for a patent on his signaling system, which he received in January 1861.

Arriving at Santa Fe in October 1860, Myer was assigned to the staff of the departmental commander, Col. Thomas T. Fauntleroy, and was further assigned to duty in the field with troops commanded by Maj. Edward R. S. Canby. Myer's signal party consisted of two detailed officers, an enlisted assistant for each officer, and a mounted escort. Among the officers who served under Myer was 2d Lt. William J. L. Nicodemus, later to become chief signal officer. Myer and his men accompanied troops on campaign, maintaining communication between the columns, performing reconnaissance, and reporting by signals. The simplicity of the Myer system, with its lightweight, portable equipment, made it well suited to use in the rugged terrain under winter conditions.

Major Canby became a strong supporter of Myer's signals, commending them on several occasions. In fact, Canby favored the formation of a specialized signal corps, to which Davis had objected, rather than the instruction of all officers in signaling, as then advocated by Myer.[23] With the surrender of the Navajos in February 1861, Myer was relieved from duty in the field and worked for a time on the departmental staff in Santa Fe where Colonel Fauntleroy also spoke highly of his work. The colonel reported that "the Services of the Signal Party have been valuable in the operations against the Navajoes and have conclusively demonstrated not only the practical usefulness of field signals but that they can be used under any of the contingencies of frontier warfare."[24] When relieved from duty in New Mexico in May 1861, Myer could feel confident that his efforts there had been successful.

Meanwhile, larger events were taking shape that would profoundly affect the future of Myer and his signals. By February 1861 seven southern states had seceded from the Union, and soon thereafter Jefferson Davis became the provisional president of the newly formed Confederate States of America. Shortly before Myer's relief from duty in New Mexico, the firing on Fort Sumter, South Carolina, by Confederate forces on 12 April 1861 proved to be the opening shots of the Civil War. Myer soon found himself back in Washington facing the challenge of his career: The time had come to test his signals in a full-scale conflict.

The Civil War—Organization and Training

Having worked out the basic mechanics of his system, Myer prepared to furnish communications in the various theaters of war. At first, however, the signal officer had no personnel because the June 1860 legislation had not allowed for any. Therefore, the various field commanders had to detail officers and men to signal duty from their regular units. The detailed officers were known as acting signal officers, and the corps was sometimes referred to as the "acting signal corps." The detail system, however, possessed serious drawbacks for both the branch and its personnel. Myer's primary concern was the fact that the men could be called back to their units at any time. On the other hand, soldiers considered signal duty detrimental to their careers because they were not eligible for promotion while on detail.

These problems prompted Myer in August 1861 to submit draft legislation to Secretary of War Simon Cameron "for the organization of a signal corps to serve during the present war, and to have the charge of all the telegraphic duty of the Army." Myer proposed that every officer of the corps be trained in both aerial and electrical signals. His plan, based on an Army of 500,000 men, called for a force consisting of seven assistant signal officers—two captains and five lieutenants—plus forty warrant officers and forty signal artificers who would serve as line builders and repairmen. Myer intended that each division "be accompanied by its corps of telegraphists or signal men, and that it be equipped with suitable apparatus and the appurtenances for both fixed and movable field telegraph and for the use of aerial and electric signals."[25] Myer, apparently influenced by Major Canby's arguments, now adopted the idea of a separate corps. Congress adjourned, however, before taking action, forcing the signal officer to continue his exertions to get the legislation passed.

Meanwhile, signal training had begun with Myer's assignment in early June 1861 to Fort Monroe, Virginia, where he set up a temporary school.[26] Although it existed only for the period that Myer served there, the school created the first nucleus of trained personnel who saw service in the initial engagements of the war. Several of the officers and men detailed for instruction soon applied their newly acquired skills to directing artillery fire upon the Confederate works at Sewall's Point, across Hampton Roads from Fort Monroe. Fire direction became a common function for Signal Corps officers during the Civil War, making them, in effect, forward observers.[27]

Early in the war Myer "wore two hats," for he was also assigned in August 1861 as chief signal officer of the Army of the Potomac commanded by Maj. Gen. George B. McClellan. As such he obtained officers and men from various regiments and sent them to signal training camps run by officers instructed at Fort Monroe. In late August Myer established a central training camp at Red Hill, Georgetown, D.C., in the area now occupied by the former Soviet embassy. The original class comprised soldiers detailed from regiments of the Pennsylvania Reserve Corps who were stationed nearby. Sgt. Luther C. Furst of the 10th Regiment was among the first to report there. In his diary he remarked upon the strict discipline maintained at the camp. "I suppose [we] will have a West Point life of it. . . . We are kept very busy drilling four hours a day in signalling besides attending to some 100 horses."[28] In September the students from outlying camps joined those at Red Hill, and signal training was consolidated there. For the officers this meant learning the code and then practicing the sending and receiving of messages, using telescopes to read them at long distances. As a security precaution the enlisted men (or flagmen) were not given access to the code; they simply manipulated the flag or torch at an officer's direction. (Some, no doubt, managed to unravel the mysteries of the talking flags in the process.) The men also

Signal Corps camp of instruction, Red Hill, Georgetown, D.C.

received riding drill, for they were to be mounted and, armed with carbines, able to fight either on horseback or on foot. In the spring of 1862, when the Army of the Potomac embarked upon the Peninsula campaign, the drain on personnel led to the camp's closing. But Myer reopened it early the following year, and it remained in operation for the rest of the war.[29]

For field duty Myer divided his officers and men into sets (as he called them) of two officers and four enlisted men. He planned to have one set serve with each regiment and a signal officer on duty at each divisional headquarters.[30] Each set could be split into a half set as needed. Myer sent signal parties, consisting of several sets, to occupy stations along the Potomac. In October a party accompanied the expedition to Port Royal, South Carolina, led by Brig. Gen. Thomas W. Sherman. Myer recognized two members of this group, Lts. Henry S. Tafft and William S. Cogswell, by citing them for distinguished service at Port Royal Ferry and awarding them special battle flags.[31]

By this action Myer intended to recognize "every signal officer who shall skillfully and bravely carry in action and use his signal flag." The honorary flags displayed a star in the center, and each point of the star would be embroidered with the name of a battle in which the flag had been used. Due to the large number of engagements as the war continued, the Signal Corps determined that the flags would be decorated at the end of the conflict. Today the battle star is depicted on the Signal Corps regimental flag and insignia.[32]

In November 1861 Myer submitted to the secretary of war his first annual report as the Army's signal officer. He recommended that "officers be detailed to organize and instruct signal parties, or corps, with every army or corps of any army that is or may be in the service of the United States." Depending upon the wishes of the commanding general, the detailed officers could serve solely on signal duty as members of signal parties or return to their regiments to perform signaling as an additional duty. Using previously trained signal officers as instructors, Myer believed that every brigade could be provided with signal communication in three months. He again recommended that Congress enact legislation organizing a temporary signal corps for the duration of the war. He also suggested that the U.S. Military Academy at West Point include signaling in its curriculum.[33] Congress approved his requested appropriation of $20,000 plus a contingency fund of $1,000, but despite its endorsement by General McClellan, Myer's second attempt to organize a signal corps fared no better than his first.[34] Although legislation was introduced, the concern that a new body of officers would be created manifested itself once again. Ultimately the bill was amended to delete the organizational portion, rendering it solely an appropriations measure.[35]

Myer remained undaunted and continued his lobbying efforts. In January 1862 the House Committee on Military Affairs asked him to draft a plan for the organization of a signal corps. He also wrote several letters to the new secretary of war, Edwin M. Stanton, requesting his support, but the secretary's replies offered little encouragement. In April the House passed an organizational bill, but once again the Senate proved to be a roadblock. Myer, by then engaged in the Peninsula campaign, had not been able to direct the legislative effort personally. He did achieve a degree of satisfaction, however, when the War Department issued general orders in June directing that officers detached from their regiments for signal duty could not be relieved except by orders from the adjutant general of the Army.[36] When Myer prepared his second annual report in November 1862, he still had not secured the much-needed legislation, and he "earnestly" called the problem to the attention of the secretary of war. This time Stanton responded positively, praising the services of the Signal Corps (as even he referred to it) in his annual report of 1 December 1862 and recommending a separate organization.[37]

Myer now began a determined campaign to win legislative approval. He had resigned his field position as chief signal officer of the Army of the Potomac in October so that he could devote more attention to running the Corps and, no doubt, to his lobbying. He distributed copies of his 1862 annual report to the members of the House and Senate Committees on Military Affairs, the House Committee on Ways and Means, and various other influential congressmen. In late December he submitted to the secretary of war his third draft of an organizational bill. Receiving Stanton's approval, Myer then sent his proposal to both the House and Senate military committees. To promote his cause, Myer appeared before the Senate Committee on Military Affairs and solicited testimonials on the

Secretary Stanton

usefulness of signals from important officers, such as McClellan. Myer also circulated petitions to acting signal officers in the field as a means by which they and the enlisted men on signal duty could demonstrate their support for the legislation.

In February 1863 a bill emerged from the Senate committee that provided for the organization of a Signal Corps during the "present rebellion." It created the position of chief signal officer, with the rank of colonel, who would be assisted by two clerks in the Washington office. Additional officers included a lieutenant colonel, two majors, a captain for each army corps or military department, and as many lieutenants (not more than eight) per corps or department as the president deemed necessary. The bill provided for one sergeant and six privates for each officer. The legislation also required entrance examinations for both officers and enlisted men in order to establish high technical standards for the branch. Furthermore, Regular Army officers appointed to the Signal Corps would be restored to their units after the war without the loss of rank or the right of promotion.

Myer's campaign must have been persuasive, for the bill passed the Senate without debate and then moved to the House, where its provisions were incorporated into the sundry civil appropriations bill. After approval by a conference committee and reconfirmation by both houses, President Abraham Lincoln signed the bill into law, with the signal provisions intact, on 3 March 1863. It was truly a signal victory.[38]

As specified in the legislation, candidates had to appear before an examining board in order to join the Signal Corps. Those already performing signal duties were not exempt from testing; if they failed, they returned to their regiments. One board, known as the central, or principal board, sat in Washington, and others convened in the various military departments. The boards examined potential signal officers in reading, writing, composition, arithmetic, elementary chemistry, natural philosophy, surveying, and topography. They also tested the prospective officers in the use and management of field signals. Current members received additional examination upon the operation of signal parties in the field and the preparation of reports. The boards questioned candidates for warrants on reading, writing, geography, and arithmetic. A separate, or revising, board reviewed the findings of the other boards and then submitted its reports to the secretary of war for approval. Of course, the possibility existed of being reduced in rank as a result of the examination, and the chief signal officer later reported "quite a number" of resignations for this reason. From the beginning the Signal Corps expected its soldiers to be highly qualified.[39]

On 28 April 1863 Myer appeared before the central board, which unanimously recommended him for the position of chief signal officer with the rank of colonel. He received the appointment, signed by Secretary Stanton, the following day, and he immediately accepted it. Since Congress was in recess, however, Myer's appointment could not be immediately confirmed by the Senate.[40]

The Military Academy introduced a course in signaling in July 1863, fulfilling a request repeatedly made by Myer since early in the war. Unfortunately, for reasons that are not clear, West Point discontinued the course the following year. Signal instruction continued at the U.S. Naval Academy where it had been introduced in 1862 when the Navy adopted Myer's signals.[41] In July 1864 Myer issued a General Service Code to facilitate communication between the Army and the Navy. (*Table 1*)

Even more important was the publication in 1864 of the first edition of Myer's *A Manual of Signals: For the Use of Signal Officers in the Field*, which codified signal doctrine for the first time. In it he discussed at length the principles of signaling and included a section on the history of signals, tracing the origins of military communication to the writings of the Greek historian Polybius, who had described a system in which the letters of the alphabet were transmitted by means of lighted torches. This manual, subsequently revised and expanded, remained the basis of signal doctrine for many years.[42]

Signal Equipment and Methods

The regulation signal equipment carried by a signal officer during the Civil War comprised three parts: the kit, the canteen, and the haversack. The canvas kit contained the flags, staffs, torches, a torch case, and a wormer used to extract the wick if it became lodged inside the torch. These were rolled together and bound by straps. The copper canteen carried one half-gallon of turpentine or other flammable fluid to fuel the torches. The haversack housed wicking, matches, pliers, shears, a funnel, two flame shades, and a wind shade. All three pieces had shoulder straps by which the officer could carry them. (*Figure 2*)

The flags came in seven varieties of colors and sizes to provide optimal visibility under prevailing conditions. Light colors were used to signal against dark backgrounds and vice versa. Made of cotton, linen, or another lightweight fabric, the types were:

     6' x 6', white, with red center, 2' x 2'
     6' x 6', black, with white center, 2' x 2'
     4' x 4', white, with red center, 16" x 16"
     4' x 4', black, with white center, 16" x 16"

TABLE 1—GENERAL SERVICE CODE*

A	 22	R	 211
B	 2112	S	 212
C	 121	T	 2
D	 222	U	 112
E	 12	V	 1222
F	 2221	W	 1121
G	 2211	X	 2122
H	 122	Y	 111
I	 1	Z	 2222
J	 1122	&	 1111
K	 2121	ing	 2212
L	 221	tion	 1112
M	 1221		•
N	 11		•
O	 21	3	. . . . end of word
P	 1212	33	. . . . end of sentence
Q	 1211	333	. . . end of message

*The flag movements were the reverse of those in Myer's original code, i.e., a movement to the right indicated "1" and to the left, "2." The movement of the flag to the front of the flagman indicated the numeral "3." The Army continued to use the General Service Code until 1912.

Source: Cir, HQ, Military Division of West Mississippi, 11 Jul 1864.

4' x 4', red, with white center, 16" x 16"
2' x 2', white, with red center, 8" x 8"
2' x 2', red, with white center, 8" x 8"

The flags were tied to a hickory staff constructed in four-foot jointed sections. The Signal Corps most commonly used four-foot flags attached to a twelve-foot staff, with white being the most versatile color. Red flags were generally used at sea. Under exceptional circumstances when a flagman had to seek shelter while signaling, or did not want to attract the enemy's attention, he used the two-foot flag, known as the "action flag."

Signal torches were copper cylinders, eighteen inches long and one and one-half inches in diameter. The torch used cotton wicking, and the flagman attached it to the staff by clamp-rings and screws. The flame shade, a circular piece of copper, prevented the flame from traveling down the side of the torch. The signalman also used a wind shade, consisting of copper strips, when necessary. The foot torch, used as a reference point, was similar in structure but slightly wider. When flags or torches were not appropriate, signalmen could send messages by means of rockets or colored lights.[43]

Officers carried telescopes for reading signals at long distances and used binoculars or field glasses for reading messages at distances of four miles or less. (The latter were also useful on shipboard where the movement interfered with

FIGURE 2—REGULATION SIGNAL EQUIPMENT

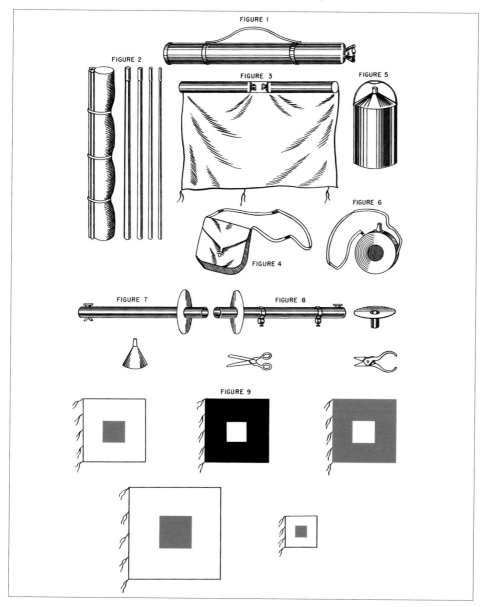

Figure 1: complete signal kit when packed; *figure 2*: contents of signal kit, ready to be placed in the canvas case (the four joints of the staff are bound to the rolled flags); *figure 3*: torch case (made of rubber cloth about three feet long by two and one-half feet wide; the torches were inserted into pouches inside the case); *figure 4*: haversack; *figure 5*: service can (capable of carrying five gallons of fuel); *figure 6*: canteen; *figure 7*: flying torch with flame shade attached; *figure 8*: foot torch with flame shade attached; *figure 9*: signal flags, showing their relative sizes.

Source: Albert J. Myer, *A Manual of Signals: For the Use of Signal Officers in the Field* (Washington, D.C.: Government Printing Office, 1877).

telescopes.) Signal officers' equipment also included pocket compasses for reconnaissance and the locating of signal stations as well as notebooks for keeping a record of the messages sent and received.

Signal security posed a serious problem. The chief of staff of the Army of the Potomac, Maj. Gen. Daniel Butterfield, expressed this concern during the battle of Chancellorsville when he ordered that signals not be used because the enemy could read them. Capt. Benjamin F. Fisher, chief signal officer of the Army of the Potomac, lamented in his report of the battle that "the corps is distrusted, and considered unsafe as a means of transmitting important messages. It is well known that the enemy can read our signals when the regular code is used."[44] To prevent the Confederates from reading Union messages, the Signal Corps developed a cipher disk that consisted of two concentric disks upon which letters and their numerical equivalents, according to the code in use, were inscribed. To encipher a message, the signal officer selected an "adjustment letter" on the inner disk and then made this letter correspond with a preselected numerical code or "key number" on the outer disk. This method proved effective, and the enemy apparently never broke it.[45]

Signal stations consisted of two types—communication and observation—but one station could serve both purposes. A distinguishing call sign, a letter or combination of letters, was assigned to each station. Each signal officer, likewise, had a call or signature by which his messages could be identified.[46] Careful site selection proved especially important to avoid such obstacles as dust or rows of tents. Signal officers often used trees as stations and, according to the signal manual:

The flag-man may then secure himself in the tree with a belt or rope. The officer fixes his own position at some other place in the same tree, and rests his telescope among its branches; or what is better, ascends another tree for this purpose: as the first is apt to be so shaken by the motions of the flag-man, as to disturb the vision through the telescope.[47]

In some cases soldiers constructed special towers as signal platforms. Church steeples and other tall buildings also made good stations. While the Union Army often used balloons for reconnaissance early in the Civil War, they never came under the Signal Corps' auspices during the conflict. The Army employed civilian aeronauts, of whom Thaddeus S. C. Lowe is the best known. Signal officers, however, sometimes made observations from aloft and relayed the information to the ground using flags or the electric telegraph.[48]

Myer was already knowledgeable about electric telegraphy when he became signal officer in 1860 because of his experience as an operator in Buffalo. This background may explain why he interpreted his duties under the 1860 legislation to include electrical signaling. Another factor may have been the formation early in the war of an organization known as the U.S. Military Telegraph. Despite its name, the Military Telegraph employed civilian operators, and its supervisory personnel received military commissions in the Quartermaster Department so that they could disburse funds and property. Anson Stager, an official of the Western Union Telegraph Company, became its general manager. After President Lincoln took control of the nation's commercial telegraph lines in February 1862, they became available for use by Stager's organization.[49]

Although technically under the Quartermaster Department, the Military Telegraph was actually controlled by Secretary Stanton. As a former director of and attorney for the Atlantic and Ohio Telegraph Company, Stanton, like Myer, possessed considerable knowledge about telegraph operations. He placed the telegraph office next to his own in the War Department, and one of his biographers described the operators as Stanton's "little army . . . part of his own personal and confidential staff."[50] Myer saw this organization as a rival and believed that Stanton and the telegraph companies conspired against the Signal Corps. Whether collusion existed or not, Myer took on a formidable adversary when he challenged Stanton, a man whom one historian has described as a "stubby, whiskered, ill-tempered conniver."[51]

The fact that the Military Telegraph functioned independently of the army commanders it was supposed to serve created potential problems of command and control. Only the operators themselves knew the cipher codes used to transmit messages, and even President Lincoln, a frequent visitor to the War Department telegraph office, was denied access to them.[52] The placement of electric telegraphy under the Signal Corps could have alleviated this situation and provided a more closely coordinated communication system. Failing that, a reasonable compromise would have been to place tactical communications under the Signal Corps and leave strategic lines with the Military Telegraph.

In June 1861 Myer first sought to gain control over electric telegraphy in addition to aerial signals. Such a request merited consideration, because Myer's visual signaling system was restricted to use in good weather over relatively open terrain with favorable atmospheric conditions. Message transmission by flag or torch was also slow, averaging about three words per minute with a range of ten to fifteen miles. By contrast, electrical signals were faster and less affected by the weather.[53]

Myer's 1 August 1861 proposal to the secretary of war for the organization of a signal corps had specified that it have control of all telegraphic duty within the Army, both aerial and electrical. On 6 August he again wrote to Cameron, this time requesting a "Telegraphic or Signal Train to accompany the Army on the march." The train would carry all the equipment needed for both aerial and electric signals and would include among its personnel "selected electric telegraphists." Myer's plan received favorable endorsements from Generals Irvin McDowell and George B. McClellan.[54] On 14 August Assistant Secretary of War Thomas A. Scott authorized Myer to purchase a small telegraph train.[55]

When using the term *train*, Myer was not referring to a vehicle that ran along tracks, but to light wagons drawn by horses. The wagons carried the telegraph sets and other necessary items, such as reels of insulated copper wire and iron lances, for stringing temporary field lines—called "flying telegraph lines." Each train was to be equipped with five miles of wire and two wagons, each with a telegraph instrument.[56] In battle, one wagon remained at the starting point as a receiving station, while the other traveled into the field with the sending instrument.

Myer contracted with Henry J. Rogers, a telegraphic engineer from New York City, to construct a model train. Rogers had assisted Samuel F. B. Morse in building the first commercial telegraph line between Washington and Baltimore in 1844, and his arrangement with Myer began a tradition of civilian-military cooperation in the development of signal equipment that continues to this day.

In January 1862 Rogers delivered the model to the Georgetown signal camp. He had adapted the conventional Morse telegraph instrument for field use by replacing the sending key and the sound receiver with a dial indicator. The indicator consisted of a circular index plate bearing the letters of the alphabet and a pointer that was turned to the letter to be transmitted. A similar pointer spelled out the message at the receiving end. This adaptation eliminated the need for skilled operators with a knowledge of Morse code and required only the ability to read and write. To provide power, Rogers had designed a galvanic battery that eliminated the danger of acid spills.[57]

Shortly after the train's arrival in Georgetown a board of three signal officers examined it, and on 25 February they issued a generally favorable report. The examiners tested two miles of wire laid by the train and found that it "transmitted the galvanic current *uninterruptedly*." Even the passage of heavily laden wagons over the wire did not damage it. The officers concluded that the train was satisfactory for experimental purposes but that Rogers needed to make the mechanical portions more durable for field service. Overall, they believed that such a train would be of great use as an auxiliary to the permanent telegraph lines.[58]

The telegraph train received its first field test during the Peninsula campaign. In May 1862 a detachment from the Georgetown signal camp took a modified train to Myer in the field. For this model Rogers had substituted a new type of telegraph instrument, the invention of George W. Beardslee of New York City. The Beardslee magneto-electric telegraph required no heavy, acid-filled batteries; rather, the turning of a crank generated current by revolving a set of magnets. Rogers had retained the dial indicator, however. In its final form the Beardslee telegraph was housed in a wooden chest with handles and weighed about one hundred pounds.[59]

Signal Corpsmen primarily employed visual signals during the Peninsula campaign, but they used the telegraph train on a limited basis to connect general headquarters with the field. Messages received at the field telegraph from visual stations were transmitted to headquarters, providing coordination between the visual and electrical systems. As the French and British had discovered in the Crimea, the novelty of the telegraph line brought some unforeseen problems. Curious soldiers cut off pieces of the wire for examination, and some evidently thought the wire to be an enemy device. To prevent tampering, patrols were stationed along the line.

Beardslee telegraph

In his report covering the operations on the Peninsula, General McClellan spoke highly of the Signal Corps' services, including its field telegraph:

In addition to the flags and torches, Major Myer introduced a portable insulated telegraph wire, which could be readily laid from point to point, and which could be used under the same general system. In front of Washington, and on the Lower Potomac, *at any point within our lines not reached by the military telegraph*, the great usefulness of this system of signals was made manifest.[60]

While McClellan's conception of the Signal Corps as a supplement to the Military Telegraph probably did not entirely please Myer, it is nonetheless clear that the Corps performed satisfactorily in the general's view.

The telegraph train received more extensive use in December 1862 during the battle of Fredericksburg where fog and smoke from the burning town often impeded visual signaling. Telegraph lines connected Maj. Gen. Ambrose E. Burnside, who now commanded the Army of the Potomac, with the headquarters of the commanders of grand divisions (consisting of two or more corps), Maj. Gen. Edwin V. Sumner and Maj. Gen. William B. Franklin, and with the supply base at Belle Plain, seven and one-half miles away. On 13 December, the main day of the battle, Signal Corpsmen, while under fire, extended a line across the Rappahannock River into the town of Fredericksburg in twenty minutes. The successful use of the telegraph during this battle enabled Myer to secure funds for additional trains, and by late 1863 thirty of them were in service throughout the Army.[61]

The Signal Corps' success, however, exacerbated the still unsettled issue of control over electric telegraphy. Both the Signal Corps and the Military Telegraph were operating lines in the field. Congress failed to solve the problem in the legislation organizing the Corps in 1863, because it did not specify the branch's duties. Secretary Stanton, however, sympathized with the civilians and in his 1863 annual report wrote of placing restrictions upon the duties of signal officers. Although he did not elaborate, it is reasonable to assume that he did not consider electric telegraphy to be a Signal Corps function. At the same time, he praised the services of the Military Telegraph. General Manager Stager, meanwhile, reporting on the Military Telegraph's activities, lauded the secretary in print.[62]

Concurrently, the technical limitations of the Beardslee device created serious problems for the Signal Corps. At the battle of Chancellorsville, in the spring of 1863, the Corps had to relinquish some of its lines to the Military Telegraph to operate with its more powerful machines. The Beardslee's revolving magnets could not generate enough electricity to transmit signals more than about five to eight miles. Therefore, it alone could not connect the new commander of the Army of the Potomac, Maj. Gen. Joseph Hooker, situated on the south side of the Rappahannock, with his chief of staff, General Butterfield, at general headquarters over ten miles away on the other side of the river. Using both electrical and visual signals, the Signal Corps took three hours to deliver messages between them. To make matters worse, many of the Corps' operators were new, and the telegraph wire itself was in poor condition, having been in constant use for several months. The system broke down completely when Hooker and Butterfield overloaded it, sending more messages than the officers and equipment could handle, and obliging the Military Telegraph to take over. Even with this change, the inadequacy of the Union's field communications contributed to the failure of the Chancellorsville campaign.[63]

Despite the mitigating circumstances, the Signal Corps could not escape the fact that the Beardslee system had considerable technical shortcomings. The ten-

The signal telegraph train as used at the battle of Fredericksburg.

dency for the sending and receiving index pointers to get out of synchronization and thereby transmit garbled messages posed yet another difficulty, and much time was lost by sending the machines back to New York for repair. Clearly, something drastic had to be done.

By the autumn of 1863 Myer had decided to convert the Beardslee machines to use Morse keys and sounders, but it was a calculated risk. Morse telegraphs required trained operators, and the recruitment process placed Myer in direct competition with the Military Telegraph for personnel. In September 1863 Myer placed a series of advertisements in the *Army and Navy Official Gazette* calling for expert telegraphers to apply for commissions in the Signal Corps. Because he had not cleared these notices with the secretary of war, he incurred Stanton's wrath. On 22 September Assistant Secretary of War W. A. Nichols wrote a letter to Myer informing him that his actions had been "irregular and improper" and reminding him to "bear in mind that the Signal Corps is not an independent organization, but a branch of the Service under the direction of the War Department."[64] Stager, meanwhile, reacted by recommending to Stanton that all field telegraphs be placed under the direction of the Military Telegraph.[65] The crisis culminated in Stanton's removal of Myer as chief signal officer on 10 November 1863. The secretary turned all telegraph apparatus over to Stager and relegated Myer to duty in Memphis, Tennessee.[66]

After his dismissal, Myer met with Stager in an attempt to establish a working relationship between their respective organizations. They reached an agreement, but it was never put into effect; perhaps if Myer had made such an overture two years earlier, he would not have found himself in virtual exile.[67]

Ironically, after all the controversy, the Military Telegraph never used the Beardslee machines it acquired from the Signal Corps. The civilian telegraphers considered them unreliable and an "expensive failure."[68] For the remainder of the

Colonel Nicodemus   *Colonel Fisher*

war the Military Telegraph and its Morse equipment provided telegraphic support for the Union Army. For field service, the Military Telegraph adopted Myer's telegraphic train technique. According to Stager's annual report for 1866, the Military Telegraph constructed a total of 15,389 miles of field, land, and submarine lines.[69] Despite the abandonment of the Beardslee, the Signal Corps deserves credit for developing the first portable, rugged, electrical communication system designed for the battlefield. The machines used in the signal telegraph train were the ancestors of the sophisticated battlefield communication devices used by the Army today.

With Myer's departure, Maj. William J. L. Nicodemus became acting chief signal officer. A native of Maryland and a West Point graduate, class of 1858, Nicodemus' first signaling assignment had come when he assisted Myer during the New Mexico campaign in 1861. He returned to signal duty in February 1863 as commander of the Georgetown training camp, and the following September he was appointed to one of the two majorities in the Signal Corps. Upon becoming chief, he took command of a branch that had grown to include approximately two hundred officers and one thousand enlisted men.[70] Like Myer before him, however, Nicodemus soon ran afoul of Secretary of War Stanton. His transgression consisted of printing copies of his 1864 annual report on the Signal Corps' press and distributing them in pamphlet form without the secretary's approval. Because the report revealed the fact that the Corps could read the enemy's signals, Stanton considered it a breach of security, and he dismissed Nicodemus, now a lieutenant colonel, from the Army in December 1864.[71]

In the wake of Nicodemus' removal, Col. Benjamin F. Fisher took command of the Signal Corps. Fisher had been captured near Aldie, Virginia, in June 1863, while serving as chief signal officer of the Army of the Potomac, and he spent the next eight months in Libby Prison. After a harrowing escape in the middle of winter, he returned to his former duties. As the U.S. Army's chief signal officer, Fisher managed to avoid Stanton's ire and retained his position into the postwar period.[72]

Wartime Operations

Signal Corpsmen served throughout the Union Army, with the largest number of officers assigned to the Army of the Potomac and the Departments of the Cumberland and the Tennessee. When Myer was chief signal officer of the Army of the Potomac, he urged that signal personnel be centralized and that the chief signal officer of the army, after obtaining details of coming operations at headquarters, direct the signal parties to wherever they were needed. Instead, commanding generals usually determined the employment of the signal parties, most often assigning them to army or corps headquarters. When inclement weather or unfavorable terrain made visual signaling impossible, signal officers often served commanders as aides.[73]

As new additions to the Army, signal soldiers did not immediately gain universal acceptance and recognition. Commanders had to become familiar with the Signal Corps' mission and accustomed to calling upon its services. An example of this situation occurred during the battle of Shiloh in April 1862 when Maj. Gen. Ulysses S. Grant unwittingly rode through a signal station belonging to the Army of the Ohio, apparently unaware of its purpose. Not recognizing the intruder (as Grant disdained the badges of his rank), the lieutenant guarding the station called out: "Git out of the way there! Ain't you got no sense?" The general quietly apologized and removed himself from the signal officer's line of vision.[74] Grant was among those who were slow to include signal parties in their commands; his Army of the Tennessee did not have an active signal detachment in the field until March 1863.[75]

In the field, confusion over how best to employ signal personnel had been evident from the start. During the war's first major encounter, the battle of Bull Run, the chief signal officer reached the battlefield, but the Union Signal Corps did not. Myer had intended to command a balloon detachment at Manassas, but a delay in the receipt of his orders left him with little time for preparation. Although he requested signal personnel from Fort Monroe to assist him, there was not enough time for them to reach Washington before the fighting began. Consequently, the eve of the battle found Myer rushing toward Manassas with a balloon and a detachment of twenty men from the 26th Pennsylvania Infantry. In their haste, the balloon became caught in some trees and was badly damaged.

Chief Signal Officer Myer (standing) *during the Peninsula campaign*

Abandoning the sphere, Myer continued to the battlefield where he served as an aide to Brig. Gen. Daniel Tyler. During this engagement at Bull Run, the Union Army relied solely upon the services of the Military Telegraph, which provided administrative support only.[76]

As chief signal officer of the Army of the Potomac, Myer personally directed signal activities during the Peninsula campaign in the spring and summer of 1862. With the conclusion of that campaign and the second Union defeat at Bull Run in August, the North feared a Confederate invasion. Apprehension became reality early in September when a signal officer atop Sugarloaf Mountain, overlooking the Potomac valley, relayed the news that Confederate forces were crossing the river. Southern troops subsequently captured the signal officer, 1st Lt. Brinkerhoff N. Miner, and his flagman.[77] Union signalmen reoccupied the station several days later, and it served as an important link in the chain of communications along the Army of the Potomac's route of march through the mountains. From Point of Rocks, Maryland, a telegraph line ran to Washington, and the Signal Corps transmitted messages between this station and McClellan's headquarters.[78]

On 17 September 1862 the town of Sharpsburg, overlooking Antietam Creek, became the site of the decisive engagement of the Maryland campaign, the battle of Antietam. McClellan ordered that signal stations be established on the right and left of the line to communicate with his headquarters, and other stations to be opened as needed. A signal station on Elk Mountain commanded the battlefield, and from this vantage point a signal officer, 1st Lt. Joseph Gloskoski, relayed information about enemy movements to the Union commanders. In particular, a message to General Burnside—"Look out well on your left; the enemy are moving a strong force in that direction."—warned of Maj. Gen. A. P. Hill's arrival from Harpers Ferry to reinforce Lee. When the message arrived at the signal station near Burnside's headquarters, however, the general was not there and, consequently, he did not receive the information in time for it to be of use.[79] Hill's counterattack forced Burnside to retreat, ending the last federal threat to destroy Lee's army that day. While ostensibly a Union victory, Antietam proved to be the single bloodiest day of the Civil War, with over 23,000 casualties. Lee had been beaten but not destroyed, and withdrew his forces across the Potomac, where they remained under the watchful eyes of Union signalmen.[80]

In June 1863 Lee once again invaded the North, and this time the opposing armies met at Gettysburg, Pennsylvania, on the first three days of July. This decisive engagement presents an excellent example of the effective use of flag signals both for communication and for conveying intelligence. Although Capt. Lemuel B. Norton, chief signal officer of the Army of the Potomac, had field telegraph trains at his disposal, he did not deploy them.[81] During the fighting on the first day a Union signal officer, Lt. Aaron B. Jerome, successively occupied several prominent locations within the town of Gettysburg, such as the cupola of the Lutheran Seminary and the courthouse steeple. From there he observed the enemy's approach and reported their movements to Maj. Gen. Oliver O. Howard, the officer in overall command of the first units of the Army of the Potomac to arrive in the town. He informed Howard that "Over a division of the rebels is making a flank movement on our right; the line extends over a mile, and is advancing, skirmishing. There is nothing but cavalry to oppose them."[82] Unfortunately, Howard was badly outnumbered and could do little with this accurate intelligence. By the end of the day the Confederates had captured the town, and Jerome had to vacate his posts.

The Union forces retreated to a line of hills south of Gettysburg where they were joined by heavy reinforcements and the new commander of the Army of the Potomac, Maj. Gen. George G. Meade. By midmorning on 2 July, Union signal officers had established communication between General Meade and his corps commanders. They had located stations at key positions along the Union line: Cemetery Hill, Culp's Hill, Power's Hill, Little Round Top, and the Leister House, where Meade made his headquarters.

Little Round Top proved a particularly important location because it offered a panoramic view of the battlefield, and signalmen were the first Union troops to occupy the strategic hilltop. Just before noon on 2 July, Lieutenant Jerome (now

General Warren at the signal station on Little Round Top

serving on this rocky promontory) signaled to General Butterfield at army head-quarters: "The rebels are in force, and our skirmishers give way. One mile west of Round Top signal station, the woods are full of them."[83] Later that afternoon Capt. James S. Hall, a signal officer with the II Corps, detected an attempt by Lt. Gen. James Longstreet's corps to outflank the Union left. Longstreet, aware that they could be seen from the station, had ordered his men to countermarch, and it was this movement that Hall observed. Hall signaled to General Butterfield that "A heavy column of enemy's infantry, about 10,000 strong, is moving from opposite our extreme left toward our right."[84] The delay caused by the countermarch gave Meade time to send troops to meet the threat.[85] The Confederate effort that day to seize Little Round Top resulted in failure, but only after a long and bloody strug-gle. During the contest the signal station became a target of such intense fire that it was temporarily abandoned. Another signal detachment later reoccupied the station, and it remained in service throughout the rest of the battle.

The new signal party included Sgt. Luther C. Furst, flagman for Capt. Edward C. Pierce, a signal officer attached to the VI Corps. Like those before him, Furst faced the dangers of the exposed position. Fighting became very heavy on 3 July, with shell, shot, and shrapnel filling the air. The deadly aim of the sharpshooters in Devil's Den at the foot of the hill prevented Furst from using his flag. Furst noted in his diary that seven men had been wounded or killed that day near the sta-tion. Unable to send visual signals, Furst acted as a mounted courier to Meade's headquarters. Warned that he would never make it through, Furst defied the odds and delivered his message. The following morning, Furst reported the situation to be "all quiet," as the Confederates withdrew from the field in defeat.[86]

The station at Little Round Top remained open until 6 July. After that the signalmen accompanied Meade's army as it pursued Lee back across the Potomac.[87]
Brig. Gen. Edward P. Alexander, who acted as Longstreet's corps artillery commander at Gettysburg, later referred to "that wretched little signal station" and
remarked that he "was particularly cautioned, in moving the artillery, to keep it
out of sight of the signal station on Round Top."[88] Today, a Signal Corps monument on the hill commemorates the dedicated men who served there.

In his report of the campaign Captain Norton also cited the services on 3 July
of Capt. Davis E. Castle, who operated from the signal station at the Leister
House. On that day the Confederates launched a massive assault against the
Union center, known as Pickett's charge, in which Alexander commanded the
artillery. After all others had abandoned the signal station during the onslaught,
including his flagman, who left with the signaling equipment, Captain Castle
remained on duty, sending messages with a bedsheet attached to a pole.[89]

During the Gettysburg campaign, some authorities in Washington feared that
the capital might be attacked. Personnel from the Georgetown signal camp, and
even those working in the signal office, were called out to observe and report on
rebel movements. Among the signal stations established was one in the unfin-
ished Capitol dome. A more serious threat to the capital occurred during Lt. Gen.
Jubal Early's raid in 1864. At that time signal stations were set up in most of the
forts surrounding the city. While the Confederates never launched a full-scale
attack, skirmishing did take place at Fort Stevens, where the signal officer narrowly escaped being killed.[90]

Not all signaling occurred on land. During the joint Army-Navy operations in
1863 to open navigation on the Mississippi River, Army signalmen maintained
communication between ship and shore. When Rear Adm. David Farragut ran his
fleet past the defenses of Port Hudson, Louisiana, in March, signal officers high
in the mastheads kept the vessels in contact with each other. They continued on
duty throughout the siege of that city that ended with its fall on 9 July. Signal
officers provided similar service at Vicksburg, Mississippi, where the garrison
surrendered the day after the Union victory at Gettysburg.[91]

Having finally achieved formal existence, the Signal Corps continued to gain
recognition and use by commanders during the final two years of the war. One of
the most famous instances occurred in October 1864 at Allatoona, Georgia, a battle that marked the end of the fighting around Atlanta. Allatoona, about thirty
miles northwest of Atlanta, was the site of a strategic railroad pass through the
mountains, as well as a supply base for Maj. Gen. William T. Sherman's army
group. Moreover, the capture of Allatoona Pass by the Confederates would cut off
Sherman's communications to the north. A small force under the command of Lt.
Col. John E. Tourtellotte, 4th Minnesota Infantry, defended the position. After a
signal officer atop Kennessaw Mountain, about eighteen miles south of
Allatoona, spotted enemy movement toward the latter place, General Sherman
called to Brig. Gen. John B. Corse at Rome, Georgia, north of Allatoona, to reinforce the threatened garrison. Lt. Charles H. Fish, stationed at Kennessaw, relayed

General Alexander   *Major Norris*

the message by flag signals to the station at Allatoona, from which it was transmitted via telegraph and locomotive (the telegraph wires having been cut) to
Rome.[92] Messages sent to the garrison at Allatoona during the ensuing siege
reputedly inspired the song "Hold the Fort," which became famous as a gospel
hymn and later served as an anthem of the labor movement.[93] On 4 October Brig.
Gen. William Vandever signaled to Tourtellotte from Kennessaw that: "Sherman
is moving in force. Hold out." Later that day another message read: "General
Sherman says hold fast. We are coming." The following day Tourtellotte received
a third message from Kennessaw. "Tell Allatoona hold on. General Sherman says
he is working hard for you."[94] Fortunately, Corse arrived in time, and despite
heavy fighting on 5 October, in which members of the Signal Corps participated,
the position held.[95]

Ironically, Sherman did not place a great deal of reliance on the Signal Corps.
In his memoirs he commented that he had "little faith in the signal-service by
flags and torches, though we always used them; because, almost invariably when
they were most needed, the view was cut off by intervening trees, or by mists and
fogs." The one notable exception was at Allatoona "when the signal-flags carried
a message of vital importance over the heads of Hood's army." Sherman placed
his faith in the magnetic telegraph and felt that the commercial lines would
"always supply for war enough skillful operators."[96]

During the war years not all signal parties operated against the
Confederates. In the spring of 1865 signal officers accompanied the Powder

River expedition to Wyoming and Montana, commanded by Brig. Gen. Patrick E. Connor. Seeking out Indians who were attacking travel and communication lines, Connor used signals to communicate between the troop columns.[97]

Because of the nature of its duties, the Signal Corps provided fewer opportunities for heroic acts of bravery on the battlefield of the type for which medals are usually bestowed. While perhaps not glamorous, signal duty proved to be especially hazardous, with a ratio of killed to wounded of 150 percent.[98] The Signal Corps had one Medal of Honor winner, Pvt. Morgan D. Lane, who entered the Signal Corps in 1864 as a second-class private and served with the Army of the Potomac. In the spring of 1865 he was attached to Headquarters, V Corps, as the orderly of Lt. P. H. Niles, a Signal Corps officer. On 6 April 1865, near Jetersville, Virginia, during Lee's retreat from Petersburg, Niles, Lane, and an engineer officer captured several members of the crew of the Confederate gunboat *Nansemond*. In the process, Lane captured the *Nansemond*'s flag, a feat that during the Civil War warranted recognition by the Medal of Honor.[99] Three days after Lane's accomplishment Lee surrendered to Grant at Appomattox, bringing the war to an end.

The Confederate Signal Corps

The Signal Corps of the United States Army and its rival the Military Telegraph did not monopolize the field of Civil War communications. The Confederate Army had a signal corps of its own, thanks to the knowledge possessed by Edward P. Alexander, Myer's able assistant in his early testing of wigwag. Alexander was a native of Georgia and ranked third in his class of 1857 at West Point. When the Civil War broke out, he resigned his commission in the United States Army and accepted one in the Confederate Army as a captain of engineers. Because Jefferson Davis was aware of Alexander's work with Myer, he sent the talented captain to Manassas, Virginia, to set up a system of signals for the forces under the command of Brig. Gen. Pierre G. T. Beauregard.[100]

Alexander selected four locations in the vicinity of Bull Run as signal stations. With men detailed to him for signal instruction and duty, Alexander prepared for the clash that would come when Union forces attempted to dislodge the rebel threat to Washington. Serving as signal officer on Beauregard's staff during the battle on 21 July, Alexander successfully used Myer's system to warn of a federal attempt to turn the Confederate left.[101] In his report of the victory, Beauregard cited the "seasonable and material assistance" rendered by Alexander and his signals.[102] Shortly afterward, however, Alexander was named chief of ordnance of the Army of Northern Virginia. Although he retained his position as signal officer, his other duties took precedence.

In April 1862 the Confederate Congress authorized the establishment of a signal corps—a year before the U.S. Congress passed such legislation. Alexander apparently declined an offer to lead the new organization, and Capt. William Norris, a Yale-educated lawyer from Maryland, took command.[103] Norris had previously served as a volunteer civilian aide on Brig. Gen. John B. Magruder's staff. Norris had impressed Magruder by setting up a signaling system on the Peninsula employing flags and balls set on poles, similar to marine signals. Attached to the Adjutant and Inspector General's Department, the Confederate Signal Corps initially comprised ten officers not exceeding the rank of captain and ten sergeants. A subsequent augmentation elevated Norris to the rank of major and added ten first and ten second lieutenants as well as twenty sergeants, for a total strength of sixty-one officers and men. Additional personnel could be detailed for service as required. A signal officer was authorized for the staff of each corps and division commander.[104] The Confederate Signal Corps remained considerably smaller than that of the Union. All told, approximately 1,500 men served the Confederate Army as signal soldiers.[105]

In general, the Confederate Signal Corps performed communication duties similar to those of its Union counterpart. Its use of electric telegraphy, however, remained confined to strategic communications because the Confederacy lacked both supplies of telegraph wire and a pool of experienced telegraphers.[106] An important distinction between the two organizations was the Confederate Signal Corps' additional role as its government's secret service. While signaling and intelligence are closely connected functions, and the Union Army's Signal Corps can be said to have provided certain intelligence-related services, such as reconnaissance, the Confederate Signal Corps also worked in the realm of espionage. In its capacity as a secret service bureau, the corps administered the covert operations of the Secret Line, an information network that ran between Richmond and the North and extended into Canada. Norris himself may have served as an agent, since he was often absent from Richmond on trips of an undetermined nature.[107]

As for equipment and methods, the Confederate Signal Corps closely paralleled those of the Union. Both organizations used flags that were similar in design and size.[108] Alexander apparently made some minor modifications in Myer's alphabet code, and he may also have reversed the flag motions. Alexander's brother, Capt. James H. Alexander, prepared a classified manual of instruction that preceded Myer's publication by two years. Despite the use of various cipher systems, however, the Confederates could not keep the Union from reading their messages.[109]

Because of its clandestine nature, much of the work of the Confederate Signal Corps is shrouded in secrecy. Moreover, most of the documentary record of its activities has been lost. The Confederate government burned its records upon the fall of Richmond, and a subsequent fire at Norris' home destroyed most of his personal papers.[110]

The Signal Corps Survives Its Baptism of Fire

In its wartime debut, the Signal Corps did not contribute significantly to the Union's victory. Yet its presence on the battlefield was important, because it marked the beginning of a new era in military communications. The Signal Corps' birth in 1860 coincided with technological advances that were drastically altering the nature of warfare and would ultimately make communications an integral part of the combat team. The increased range and accuracy of rifled weapons enlarged the killing zone and made close-order tactics suicidal. With his troops widely dispersed, a commander could no longer control them with his voice alone. Transmitting orders by messenger was slow, and couriers were extremely vulnerable to enemy action. The situation demanded new methods of tactical signaling, and Myer's wigwag system helped to bridge this communication gap. Before the invention of the telephone and the radio, the soldier possessed no tactical communication device that he could carry onto the battlefield. Wigwag, despite its limitations, enabled signalmen to communicate between prominent points on or near the battlefield and the commander's headquarters. The portability of the equipment permitted its use on horseback and on shipboard as well.

While the electric telegraph had received some combat testing by European armies, it had by no means been perfected as a tactical communication device in 1861. With his development of the field telegraph train, Myer attempted to adapt the telegraph to the needs of a mass, mobile army. At the same time, the creation of the Military Telegraph, of which Secretary of War Stanton tightly held the reins, placed a powerful competitor in the field. No doubt Stanton's inability to control the operations of the Signal Corps contributed to his stormy relationship with Myer. Moreover, the Signal Corps could not expect to compete with the established commercial lines for strategic communications, and its Beardslee machines proved no match for the Morse instruments used by the civilian operators. Consequently, the Corps lost both Myer and electrical communications after November 1863. Yet, with the end of the war, the Military Telegraph ceased to exist and the Signal Corps survived.[111]

Albert Myer may have been stubborn and contentious, but he was also resourceful. Through determination and hard work he succeeded in establishing an important branch of the Army. At the outset, the Signal Corps' birth may have seemed premature: Both Congress and the Army resisted the idea. No other army in the world contained such an organization, and the need for a specialized communications branch was not generally recognized. As with many novel endeavors, Myer's efforts met with mixed results, but they were not futile. Although the Signal Corps' military role and mission remained largely undefined when the Civil War ended in 1865, the foundation for its future achievements had been laid. The Civil War experience made possible the expansion of an organization consisting of a signal officer and temporary assistants into a Signal Corps that was part of the permanent military establishment.

Notes

[1]United States Army, *Regulations for the Order and Discipline of the Troops of the United States*, as printed in facsimile in Joseph R. Riling, *Baron von Steuben and His Regulations* (Philadelphia: Ray Riling Arms Books Co., 1966). See also Raoul F. Camus, *Military Music of the American Revolution* (Chapel Hill: University of North Carolina Press, 1976) and Robert K. Wright, Jr., *The Continental Army*, Army Lineage Series (Washington, D.C.: Center of Military History, United States Army, 1983).

[2]Chester L. Kieffer, *Maligned General* (San Rafael, Calif.: Presidio Press, 1979), p. 254; K. Jack Bauer, *The Mexican War: 1846–1848* (New York: Macmillan Publishing Company, Inc., 1974), pp. 237 and 396; Erna Risch, *Quartermaster Support of the Army: A History of the Corps, 1775–1939* (Washington, D.C.: Center of Military History, United States Army, 1989), p. 250.

[3]Duane Koenig, "Telegraphs and Telegrams in Revolutionary France," *Scientific Monthly* 59 (Dec 1944): 431–37; James Dugan, *The Great Mutiny* (New York: G. P. Putnam's Sons, 1965), pp. 22, 81–82; Baron de Jomini, *The Art of War*, trans. G. H. Mendell and W. P. Craighill (Philadelphia: J. B. Lippincott, 1862), ch. 6, art. 42.

[4]R. F. H. Nalder, *The Royal Corps of Signals: A History of Its Antecedents and Development (circa 1800–1955)* (London: Royal Signals Institution, 1958), pp. 9–13.

[5]See "Report of the French Minister of War to the Emperor, on the Administrative Arrangements for the War in the East," in Alfred Mordecai, *Military Commission to Europe in 1855 and 1856*, 36th Cong., 1st sess., 1860, S. Doc. 60, p. 87.

[6]Richard Delafield, *Report on the Art of War in Europe in 1854, 1855, and 1856*, 36th Cong., 1st sess., 1860, S. Doc. 59, p. 110. Two other American Army officers observed the conflict, Maj. Alfred Mordecai and Capt. George B. McClellan.

[7]Dennis Showalter, "Soldiers into Postmasters? The Electric Telegraph as an Instrument of Command in the Prussian Army," *Military Affairs* 37 (Apr 1973): 49.

[8]Myer's daughter later gave the year as 1829, but this is the date accepted by Myer's biographer, Dr. Paul J. Scheips, in "Albert J. Myer, Founder of the Signal Corps: A Biographical Study" (Ph.D. dissertation, American University, 1966), p. 5. The information given here on Myer's early life is taken from this study, hereafter cited as Scheips, "Myer."

[9]This company operated instruments developed by Alexander Bain of Scotland. Unlike the electromagnetic Morse system, the Bain telegraph operated by an electro-chemical process. The codes were similar, with the Bain consisting of dots and lines instead of dots and dashes. Myer may also have been employed at some point by a company that used the Morse system. See Scheips, "Myer," pp. 65–69.

[10]While some authors have attributed Myer's inspiration for his invention to his observation of Southwestern Indians signaling with lances, Dr. Paul J. Scheips, the foremost authority on Myer, has seen no evidence to validate this contention. See Paul J. Scheips, "Albert James Myer, an Army Doctor in Texas, 1854–1857," *Southwestern Historical Quarterly* 82 (Jul 1978): 20.

[11]See Ltr, Myer to Davis, 1 Oct 1856, in the Albert J. Myer Papers. The letter is on roll 1 of the microfilmed papers in the custody of the U.S. Army Center of Military History (hereafter cited as CMH). The papers reproduced are among the collections of the Library of Congress and the U.S. Army Military History Institute, Carlisle Barracks, Pennsylvania (hereafter cited as MHI).

[12]End, Davis, 11 Dec 1856, on Myer to Davis, 1 Oct 1856, on roll 1, Myer Papers microfilm, CMH.

[13]Scheips, "Myer," pp. 177–78.

[14]A copy of the report to Adjutant General Col. Samuel Cooper, 12 Mar 1859, is on roll 1, Myer Papers microfilm, CMH. The original copy of the report that is reproduced on the film is in the custody of the Signal Corps Archives at Fort Gordon, Georgia. See also Scheips, "Myer," pp. 182–87.

[15]For more details on the code and its variations, see J. Willard Brown, *The Signal Corps, U.S.A. in the War of the Rebellion* (Boston: U.S. Veteran Signal Corps Association, 1896), pp. 91–97; Albert J. Myer, *A Manual of Signals: For the Use of Signal Officers in the Field* (Washington, D.C.: Signal Office, 1864), pp. 28–47; *Historical Sketch of the Signal Corps (1860–1941)*, Eastern Signal Corps Schools Pamphlet no. 32 (Fort Monmouth, N.J.: Eastern Signal Corps Schools, U.S. Army, 1942), pp. 15–17.

[16]Scheips, "Myer," pp. 227–29.

[17]U.S. War Department, *Annual Report of the Secretary of War*, 1859, p. 8 (hereafter cited as *ARSW* followed by year). On Floyd's subsequent actions relative to Myer's signals, see Scheips, "Myer," pp. 235–44.

[18]*Congressional Globe*, 36th Cong., 1st sess., 1859–1860, 29, pt. 2: 1430.

[19]This is the date that is officially celebrated as the Signal Corps' birthday. See the Senate debates of 2, 5, and 7 June 1860 in *Congressional Globe*, 36th Cong., 1st sess., 1859–1860, 29, pt. 3: 2558–60, 2636–37, 2727–31. A detailed discussion of the congressional action is given in Scheips, "Myer," ch. 8.

[20]War Department General Orders 17, 2 Jul 1860, p. 4 (hereafter cited as WDGO with date).

[21]E. P. Alexander, *Military Memoirs of a Confederate* (New York: Charles Scribner's Sons, 1907; Bloomington: Indiana University Press, 1962), pp. 1–4. The reprint contains a very useful introduction by T. Harry Williams discussing Alexander's work with Myer.

[22]Among those who expressed an interest was J. E. B. Stuart, then a cavalry lieutenant in Kansas. See Scheips, "Myer," pp. 274–75; on signal operations in New Mexico, see ch. 9.

[23]For a discussion of their views, see Scheips, "Myer," pp. 327–32.

[24]As quoted in Scheips, "Myer," p. 327.

[25]See letter of 1 August 1861 in U.S. War Department, *War of the Rebellion: A Compilation of the Official Records of the Union and Confederate Armies*, 128 vols. (Washington, D.C.: Government Printing Office, 1880–1901), ser. 3, vol. 1, pp. 375–76 (hereafter cited as *OR* with series and volume numbers). An extract appears in Brown, *Rebellion*, pp. 46–47.

[26]For details on Myer's service at Fort Monroe, see Scheips, "Myer," pp. 337–42, and Brown, *Rebellion*, pp. 39–42.

[27]Prentice G. Morgan, "The Forward Observer," *Military Affairs* 23 (Winter 1959–1960): 209–12. Morgan incorrectly places this first performance of fire direction in May 1862 rather than June 1861. See Brown's account in *Rebellion*, pp. 41–43. While Morgan indicates that this was a unique event, signal officers in fact performed this function many times throughout the war.

[28]Diary of Luther Furst, MHI. The quote is from the entry for the period from 28 August to 19 October 1861.

[29]Brown, *Rebellion*, ch. 3; Scheips, "Myer," p. 384.

[30]Scheips, "Myer," p. 423. Myer set forth his plan in a letter to Brig. Gen. Seth Williams, McClellan's assistant adjutant, on 30 October. Brown extracts this letter in *Rebellion*, pp. 63–65.

[31]See Rpt, Brig Gen Isaac I. Stevens, commander of the land forces, to Capt L. H. Pelouze, assistant adjutant general expeditionary corps, 3 Jan 1862, in *OR*, ser. 1, vol. 6, pp. 47–53, in which he praises the services of Tafft and Cogswell. See Tafft's recollection of his service with the expedition in "Reminiscences of the Signal Service in the Civil War" in *Personal Narratives of the War of the Rebellion, Being Papers Read Before the Rhode Island Soldiers and Sailors Historical Society*, Sixth Series, no. 3 (Providence: Published by the Society, 1903).

[32]GO 20, Headquarters, Signal Corps, 19 Mar 1862, and GO 3, Office of the Signal Officer, 7 Feb 1863, Record Group 111, Records of the Chief Signal Officer, National Archives and Records Administration (hereafter cited as RG 111, NARA). There are three bound volumes of orders that cover the years 1861 to 1869. The first volume contains orders from August 1861 to March 1862; the second from March 1862 to November 1863; and the third from January 1864 to December 1869. GO 20 is found on pages 126 to 128 of the first volume and GO 3 on page 51 of the second volume.

[33]U.S. War Department, *Annual Report of the Chief Signal Officer*, 1861 (hereafter cited as *ARSO* with year), in *OR*, ser. 3, vol. 1, pp. 694–97; *ARSO*, 1862, in *OR*, ser. 3, vol. 2, p. 757; *ARSO*, 1863, in *ARSW*, 1863, p. 174. The annual reports of the chief signal officer for the years 1861–1866 are reprinted in volume 1 of Paul J. Scheips, ed., *Military Signal Communications*, 2 vols. (New York: Arno Press, 1980).

[34]The act appropriating funds for the Signal Corps is printed in WDGO 21, 26 Feb 1862. Myer also mentioned the need for "countersign" signals which were to be used to distinguish friendly from hostile troops. Although Congress appropriated nearly $35,000 to equip each regiment with supplies for making these signals, their use never became widespread, and they were eventually abandoned. On countersign signals, see Brown, *Rebellion*, pp. 107–13.

[35]Scheips, "Myer," pp. 410–13; *Congressional Globe*, 37th Cong., 2d sess., 1861–1862, 32, pt. 1: 240, 269–71, 859 and pt. 4, app., p. 337.

[36]Scheips, "Myer," pp. 413–19; WDGO 68, 18 Jun 1862.

[37]*ARSW*, 1862, p. 17.

[38]See Scheips, "Myer," pp. 520–35, for details on Myer's efforts and the resulting legislation. The provisions of the bill pertaining to the Signal Corps are printed in WDGO 73, 24 Mar 1863, pp. 22–23.

[39]*ARSO*, 1864, in *OR*, ser. 3, vol. 4, p. 819.

[40]See the provisions of WDGO 106, 28 Apr 1863, and WDGO 223, 17 Jul 1863. Myer's appointment was announced in WDGO 316, 18 Sep 1863. Scheips, "Myer," pp. 535–44.

[41]See Myer's original request for a course at the Military Academy in *ARSO*, 1861, p. 695. The chief signal officer stated in his 1864 report that "For some cause unknown the course of instruction at West Point was not continued during the past year." *ARSO*, 1864, p. 819. On naval signaling, see Linwood S. Howeth, *History of Communications-Electronics in the United States Navy* (Washington, D.C.: Government Printing Office, 1963), p. 9.

[42]Subsequent editions were published in 1866, 1868, 1871, 1877, and 1879.

[43]For details on signal apparatus and methods, see Brown, *Rebellion*, chs. 5 and 6.

[44]Rpt, Cushing to Myer, 23 May 1863, and Rpt, Fisher to Lt William S. Stryker, Adjutant, Signal Corps, 9 May 1863, both in *OR*, ser. 1, vol. 25, pt. 1, p. 220 and p. 228, respectively.

[45]Brown describes the disk in *Rebellion*, pp. 99–102, 118–19. See also *Historical Sketch*, p. 11.

[46]Myer, *Manual*, 1864, pp. 87–88.

[47]Ibid., p. 61.

[48]Balloon operations never found a niche within the Union Army. They were initially placed under the Bureau of Topographical Engineers where they remained until March 1862 when they were placed under the Quartermaster Department. In April 1863 balloons were transferred to the newly created Corps of Engineers. A few months later, in June 1863, Myer declined an offer to direct the balloon corps, and it was subsequently disbanded. For additional details, see F. Stansbury Haydon, *Aeronautics in the Union and Confederate Armies With a Survey of Military Aeronautics Prior to 1861* (Baltimore, Md.: Johns Hopkins Press, 1941), ch. 8. A brief essay by Lowe, entitled "Balloons in the Army of the Potomac," is included in Francis T. Miller, ed., *The Photographic History of the Civil War*, 10 vols. (New York: Review of Reviews Co., 1911), 8: 369–82. See also Tom D. Crouch, *The Eagle Aloft: Two Centuries of the Balloon in America* (Washington, D.C.: Smithsonian Institution Press, 1983), chs. 12 and 13.

[49]Risch, *Quartermaster Support*, pp. 366–68.

[50]Frank A. Flower, *Edwin McMasters Stanton, The Autocrat of Rebellion, Emancipation, and Reconstruction* (Akron, Ohio: Saalfield Publishing Co., 1905; New York: AMS Press, Inc., 1973), p. 219. Legislation passed in January 1862, drafted by Stanton, gave the president control over the nation's railroad and telegraph lines. Lincoln, in turn, delegated these powers to Stanton. See Benjamin P. Thomas and Harold M. Hyman, *Stanton: The Life and Times of Lincoln's Secretary of War* (New York: Alfred A. Knopf, 1962), pp. 153–55. The authors do not, however, discuss Stanton's relationship with Myer and the Signal Corps.

[51]Myer later expressed this belief in writing after losing the battle with Stanton over control of electric telegraphy in November 1863. At that time, Myer wrote: "For many months a hostile feeling had been provoked by the continued success of this element in war, and though at first provocative of mirth, its importance was now so great that the gigantic arm of monopoly had been stretched out in greed to clutch this condemned instrumentality." He is quoted in Brown, *Rebellion*, p. 423. The description of Stanton is by Robert V. Bruce, *Lincoln and the Tools of War* (1956; reprint, Urbana, Ill.: University of Illinois Press, 1989), p. 153.

[52]See David Homer Bates, *Lincoln in the Telegraph Office: Recollections of the United States Military Telegraph Corps During the Civil War* (New York: Century Co., 1907).

[53]In his 1863 annual report Myer indicated that twenty miles was the longest distance over which a telegraph train had been used. The average distance was five to eight miles. *ARSO*, 1863, p. 176.

[54]See copy and endorsements in Letters Sent, vol. 1, RG 111, NARA.

[55]His letter is printed in Brown, *Rebellion*, p. 50.

[56]Beardslee Magneto-Electric Co., *Beardslee's Military Telegraph: The History of Its Invention, Introduction, and Adoption by the Government of the United States* (New York: John A. Gray & Green, 1863), p. 11.

[57]A good article on the development of the train is that by George R. Thompson, "Development of the Sig C Field Telegraph, 1861–1863," *Signal* 12 (Jul 1958): 28–34.

[58]"Proceedings of a Board of Examination on the Field Telegraphic Train," file number C–28, Letters Received 1861–1862 A-W, RG 111, NARA. One of the board members was 1st Lt. Benjamin F. Fisher, who went on to become chief signal officer.

[59]Beardslee's son, Frederick, joined the Signal Corps as a telegraph operator.

[60]*OR*, ser. 1, vol. 5, p. 31. Author's emphasis added.

[61]For reports of the battle of Fredericksburg, see those by signal officers Samuel Cushing, Benjamin Fisher, Frederick Beardslee, David Wonderly, and others in *OR*, ser. 1, vol. 21, pp. 151–67. For a breakdown of the placement of the thirty telegraph trains, see *ARSO*, 1863.

[62]*ARSW*, 1863, p. 13. Stager's report for fiscal year 1863 is printed in William R. Plum, *The Military Telegraph During the Civil War in the United States, . . . ,* 2 vols. (Chicago: Jansen, McClurg and Company, Pubs., 1882), 2: 368.

[63]Douglas Southall Freeman, *Lee's Lieutenants: A Study in Command,* 3 vols. (New York: Charles Scribner's Sons, 1942–1944), 2: 644–45; Rpt, Cushing to Myer, 23 May 1863, *OR*, ser. 1, vol. 25, pt. 1, pp. 217–23; John Emmet O'Brien, *Telegraphing in Battle: Reminiscences of the Civil War* (Scranton, Pa.: The Raeder Press, 1910), p. 124 (O'Brien served with the Military Telegraph); Plum, *Military Telegraph,* 1: 363; Edward Hagerman, *The American Civil War and the Origins of Modern Warfare* (Bloomington: Indiana University Press, 1988), pp. 82–87. The Signal Corps did operate some telegraph lines during the battle. According to Myer in his 1863 annual report, the shorter lines were successful while the longer lines failed (p. 176). For a detailed study of the Chancellorsville campaign, see John Bigelow, Jr., *The Campaign of Chancellorsville: A Strategic and Tactical Study* (New Haven: Yale University Press, 1910). A more recent analysis is Jay Luvaas and Harold W. Nelson, eds., *The U.S. Army War College Guide to the Battles of Fredericksburg and Chancellorsville* (Carlisle, Pa.: South Mountain Press, 1988).

[64]See copy of letter on roll 1, Myer Papers microfilm, CMH.

[65]His letter of 27 Oct 1863 is printed in Plum, *Military Telegraph,* 2: 100–101.

[66]An extract from War Department Special Orders 499, dated 10 Nov 1863, relieving Myer from his position, is printed in Plum, *Military Telegraph,* 2: 102. An extract is also on roll 1, Myer Papers microfilm, CMH. See also Scheips, "Myer," pp. 564–78.

[67]Scheips, "Myer," pp. 586–87, contains details on their meeting and agreement.

[68]Plum, *Military Telegraph,* 1: 71 and 2: 99.

[69]See extract in Plum, *Military Telegraph,* 2: 346–50.

[70]Biographical information about Nicodemus can be found in George W. Cullum et al., comps., *Biographical Register of the Officers and Graduates of the U.S. Military Academy at West Point, N.Y. . . . ,* 9 vols. (Cambridge, Mass.: Riverside Press and others, 1891–1950), 2: 711–12. Nicodemus was graduate number 1820. Brown, *Rebellion,* gives the Corps' strength in October 1863 as 198 officers and 1,012 men.

[71]Nicodemus was dismissed per WDGO 304, 26 Dec 1864. He was later restored to the rank of lieutenant colonel in the Signal Corps and mustered out in August 1865. He returned to the line as a captain and was honorably discharged on 29 December 1870. He became a professor at the University of Wisconsin where he taught military science and civil and mechanical engineering. Nicodemus died at Madison, Wisconsin, in 1879 at age 45. Cullum, *Biographical Register,* 2: 711–12. Records of the Confederate War Department examined after the war revealed that Nicodemus, while serving in New Mexico in 1861, may have attempted to secure a commission in the Confederate Army. Stanton would not have known about this in 1864, and whether Myer ever knew is uncertain. Scheips, "Myer," pp. 323–24.

[72]Scheips, "Myer," p. 461; Brown, *Rebellion,* pp. 358, 370.

[73]*ARSO*, 1863, p. 166; Rpt, Myer to the Adjutant General, Army of the Potomac, 21 Oct 1862, in *OR*, ser. 1, vol. 11, pt. 1, p. 247.

[74]John D. Billings, *Hardtack and Coffee or the Unwritten Story of Army Life* (1887; reprint, Williamsport, Mass.: Corner House Publishers, 1980), p. 405; Brown, *Rebellion*, pp. 460–61.

[75]Hagerman, *Origins of Modern Warfare*, p. 172; Brown, *Rebellion*, p. 509.

[76]Scheips, "Myer," pp. 343–49. See also the account in Haydon, *Aeronautics in the Union and Confederate Armies*, pp. 68–71, which is not complimentary to Myer. After this disappointing episode, Myer made no further attempts to obtain control of balloon operations.

[77]Brown, *Rebellion*, pp. 241–42. Brown relates that Maj. Gen. J. E. B. Stuart personally captured the signalmen, but this story may be apocryphal.

[78]The Military Telegraph operated this line. Due to the demand for telegraphers on the Peninsula, however, "there was no military operator at Point of Rocks, at the time of Lee's forward movement from Chantilly, and Stuart's approach seems not to have been telegraphed." Plum, *Military Telegraph*, 1: 230.

[79]Stephen W. Sears, *Landscape Turned Red: The Battle of Antietam* (New Haven, Conn.: Ticknor and Fields, 1983), p. 286. Earlier in the day Burnside had requested information from the signal station as to enemy movement in the area. See Rpt, Gloskoski to Lt William S. Stryker, Adjutant, Signal Corps, 29 Nov 1862, in *OR*, ser. 1, vol. 19, pt. 1, pp. 137–39.

[80]On signal operations in Maryland, see Rpt, Myer to Brig Gen S. Williams, Assistant Adjutant General, Army of the Potomac, 6 Oct 1862, in *OR*, ser. 1, vol. 19, pt. 1, pp. 117–25; Rpt, Capt B. F. Fisher to Myer, 30 Sep 1862, in *OR*, ser. 1, vol. 19, pt. 1, pp. 126–30. See also Brown, *Rebellion*, pp. 324–37, and Scheips, "Myer," pp. 481–85. Myer, still serving as McClellan's signal officer, apparently oversaw signal operations from Elk Mountain, as both Fisher and Gloskoski mention his presence there.

[81]Norton became chief signal officer of the Army of the Potomac following Fisher's capture by the Confederates in June 1863. Norton states in his report that "signal telegraph trains were sent to Frizellburg [nineteen miles from Gettysburg], and everything held in readiness to extend the wire at a moment's notice to the points desired by the commanding general." Apparently, Meade never called for their use. Rpt, Norton to Brig Gen S. Williams, 18 Sep 1863, in *OR*, ser. 1, vol. 27, pt. 1, pp. 199–207.

[82]*OR*, ser. 1, vol. 27, pt. 3, p. 488. Although the *Official Records* gives the date of this message as 2 July, Col. Alexander W. Cameron, a student of the use of signals at Gettysburg, believes the correct date is 1 July. See his article, "The Signal Corps at Gettysburg," *Gettysburg* (Jul 1990): 9–15. For a more in-depth study, see A. W. Cameron, *A Communicator's Guide to the Gettysburg Campaign* (Carlisle Barracks, Pa.: U.S. Army War College, 1989).

[83]*OR*, ser. 1, vol. 27, pt. 3, p. 488.

[84]Ibid.

[85]Accounts differ as to who first transmitted the information about enemy movement. Not surprisingly, perhaps, Norton's report and J. Willard Brown in *Rebellion* credit the signalmen with first discovering the flanking activity. Shelby Foote, however, in vol. 2 of *The Civil War: A Narrative* (New York: Random House, 1963), p. 503, states that Maj. Gen. Gouverneur K. Warren, chief engineer of the Army of the Potomac, while reconnoitering the position on Little Round Top, noticed the troops and delivered the information to Meade himself. According to Foote, Warren instructed the signalmen to look busy "whether they had any real messages to transmit or not" so as to confuse the enemy. Brown, on the other hand, contends that it was because of the signaled information that

Warren went to Little Round Top (*Rebellion*, p. 367). Edwin B. Coddington, in *The Gettysburg Campaign: A Study in Command* (New York: Charles Scribner's Sons, 1984), remarks that "romantic tradition has accorded General G. K. Warren the glory of the main role in that drama" (p. 388). He notes that Warren's own account of what happened "puts a strain upon belief" and that Warren probably arrived on Little Round Top about the time that the signal officers reported the flanking movement (see n. 20, p. 740). For Warren's version of events, see the letter printed as part of his biographical sketch in Cullum, *Biographical Register*, 2: 401–09. Warren was graduate number 1451. There is no report from Warren in *OR*, ser. 1, vol. 27, pt. 1, that contains the reports of the Gettysburg campaign, and Meade's report sheds no light on the question. According to Maurice Matloff, gen. ed., *American Military History*, Army Historical Series (Washington, D.C.: Office of the Chief of Military History, United States Army, 1969), pp. 251–52, Warren, upon discovering that no infantry held Little Round Top, persuaded Maj. Gen. George Sykes to send two brigades and some artillery there, and they arrived in time to meet the assault.

[86]Furst diary, entries for 3 and 4 Jul 1863.

[87]The work of the signal stations after the battle is discussed in Bill Cameron, "The Signal Corps at Gettysburg Part II: Support of Meade's Pursuit," *Gettysburg* (Jan 1991): 101–09. The author wishes to thank Colonel Cameron for providing copies of his very useful publications.

[88]As quoted in Brown, *Rebellion*, p. 367.

[89]*OR*, ser. 1, vol. 27, pt. 1, pp. 206–07.

[90]Brown, *Rebellion*, pp. 650 and 661.

[91]On operations at Port Hudson, see Brown, *Rebellion*, pp. 507–17, and Paul J. Scheips, "Signaling at Port Hudson, 1863," *Civil War History* 2 (Dec 1956): 106–13; on Vicksburg, see Brown, *Rebellion*, pp. 571–84.

[92]Paul J. Scheips, The Battle of Allatoona, a preliminary draft [Washington, D.C.: Historical Section, Signal Corps Intelligence Agency, 1956]. Earlier in the fighting the Confederates had operated a signal station on Kennessaw Mountain.

[93]Paul J. Scheips, *Hold the Fort! The Story of a Song from the Sawdust Trail to the Picket Line*, Smithsonian Studies in History and Technology, no. 9 (Washington, D.C.: Smithsonian Institution Press, 1971).

[94]See published copies of messages in *OR*, ser. 1, vol. 39, pt. 3, pp. 78 and 97. For slightly different wording and punctuation, see Brown, *Rebellion*, p. 547. Messages transmitted between Kennessaw and Allatoona are printed on pages 547–52. Sherman remained on Kennessaw during the battle. See Fish's report in *OR*, ser. 1, vol. 39, pt. 3, pp. 111–12.

[95]Although he had no direct involvement in the Allatoona operation, Myer received a brevet brigadier generalcy for the Signal Corps' services there. See citation, dated 3 Dec 1867, on roll 2, Myer Papers microfilm, CMH. Allatoona provides an interesting case study on the uses and effects of visual signals in battle. Shelby Foote writes that Maj. Gen. Samuel G. French, leader of the Confederate attack, intercepted the wigwag messages for help and decided to withdraw (*The Civil War: A Narrative*, vol. 3 [New York: Random House, 1974], p. 612). French, however, in his report of 5 Nov 1864 mentions that Sherman "had been signaled to repeatedly during the battle" but he does not say whether the messages were being read (*OR*, ser. 1, vol. 39, pt. 1, p. 817). On this point, see Scheips, "Allatoona," p. 70, who states that French probably did not know what the messages said until after their publication. Could the psychological effect of all the "mys-

terious" flag-waving have influenced French's decision to withdraw? Conversely, French later contended that Sherman's messages inspired hope in the defenders (Scheips, "Allatoona," pp. 70 and 79). Due to battle conditions, there was considerable difficulty getting a message through to Sherman regarding Corse's arrival and consequent confusion as to the size of the reinforcements. French writes in his 5 November report that he learned from prisoners that Corse had arrived at Allatoona. He explains that he decided to withdraw because he feared that his division was in danger of being cut off by Sherman's advancing army. For a discussion of the battle, see Fred E. Brown, "Battle of Allatoona," *Civil War History* 6 (Sep 1960): 277–97.

[96]William T. Sherman, *Memoirs of General William T. Sherman by Himself*, 2 vols. (New York: D. Appleton and Company, 1875), 2: 398.

[97]J. Willard Brown was one of the signal officers on this expedition, and he devotes considerable space to it. See *Rebellion*, ch. 23. See also Robert M. Utley, *Frontiersmen in Blue: The United States Army and the Indian, 1848–1865* (New York: Macmillan Publishing Company, Inc., 1967), pp. 323–32.

[98]A. W. Greely, "The Signal Service," in Francis T. Miller, ed., *The Photographic History of the Civil War*, 10 vols. (New York: Review of Reviews Co., 1911), 8: 318.

[99]Niles' report of the incident is quoted in Ltr, Capt Charles L. Davis, Chief Signal Officer, Army of the Potomac, to Col George D. Ruggles, Assistant Adjutant General, Army of the Potomac, 20 Apr 1865, *OR*, ser. 1, vol. 46, pt. 3, p. 851. Davis forwarded the *Nansemond*'s flag with his letter. See also Paul J. Scheips, "Private Lane's Gold Medal," *Military Affairs* 24 (Summer 1960): 87–91 and Rebecca Robbins, "For 'gallantry in action and other soldierlike qualities,'" *Army Communicator* 5 (Fall 1980): 59.

[100]See extract of Special Orders 84, Adjutant and Inspector General's Office, 29 Jun 1861, in *OR*, ser. 1, vol. 51, pt. 2, p. 150.

[101]For details of Alexander's service at Bull Run, see his *Military Memoirs*, ch. 2.

[102]*OR*, ser. 1, vol. 2, p. 500.

[103]Alexander, *Military Memoirs*, p. 52. According to Alexander, he was offered the leadership of a "Department of Signals" with the rank of colonel in the fall of 1861. See Brown, *Rebellion*, p. 205, and David W. Gaddy, "William Norris and the Confederate Signal and Secret Service," *Maryland Historical Magazine* 70 (Summer 1975): 170. Alexander may have passed up the chance to be chief signal officer, but he distinguished himself as an artillery commander and was promoted to brigadier general in 1864. After the war he became a successful businessman. Alexander died on 28 April 1910 at age 74 and is buried in Augusta, Georgia. Besides his *Military Memoirs*, Alexander also penned *Fighting for the Confederacy: The Personal Recollections of General Edward Porter Alexander* (Chapel Hill: University of North Carolina Press, 1989). See also Maury Klein, *Edward Porter Alexander* (Athens: University of Georgia Press, 1971).

[104]Special Orders 40, Adjutant and Inspector General's Office, 29 May 1862, printed in *OR*, ser. 4, vol. 1, pp. 1131–33, and Special Orders 93, Adjutant and Inspector General's Office, 22 Nov 1862, in *OR*, ser. 4, vol. 2, p. 199. In another quirk of fate, the adjutant general to whom the Confederate Signal Corps was attached was General Samuel Cooper. Cooper had been the adjutant general of the U.S. Army when Myer first presented his system and had been a supporter of it.

[105]David W. Gaddy, "Confederate States Army Signal Corps Insignia," *Military Collector and Historian* 25 (Summer 1973): 87, based on an estimate by Charles E. Taylor in "The Signal and Secret Service of the Confederate States," *North Carolina Booklet* 2 (Hamlet, N.C.: Capital Printing Co., 1903).

[106]Hagerman, *Origins of Modern Warfare*, p. 146.

[107]Gaddy, "William Norris," pp. 173 and 175. For a full-scale study of the Confederate Signal Corps' involvement with intelligence operations, see William A. Tidwell, James O. Hall, and David W. Gaddy, *Come Retribution: The Confederate Secret Service and the Assassination of Lincoln* (Jackson: University Press of Mississippi, 1988). For the Union, the famous detective Allan Pinkerton directed secret service activities in the Army of the Potomac under McClellan. A Bureau of Military Information was later set up to perform similar functions.

[108]Gaddy, "Confederate Signal Corps Insignia." This article raises the intriguing possibility that the Confederate Signal Corps first used the crossed flags insignia.

[109]Brown states that "The alphabet or code first used by the Confederate Signal Corps was a modification of that introduced by Maj. Myer into the service of the United States" (*Rebellion*, p. 213). Gaddy surmises that Alexander changed the letter values for security reasons and may also have reversed the flag motions. See his correspondence of 23 and 29 July 1974 with Dr. Paul J. Scheips in the possession of Dr. Scheips. See also Gaddy, "William Norris," p. 172.

[110]Other sources of information on the Confederate Signal Corps are Brown, *Rebellion*, ch. 11, and Edmund H. Cummins, "The Signal Corps in the Confederate States Army," *Southern Historical Society Papers* 16 (1888): 93–107.

[111]The Military Telegraph returned the commercial lines to their owners and sold those it had constructed. Plum, *Military Telegraph*, 2: 347–48; Risch, *Quartermaster Support*, pp. 458–59.

CHAPTER II

Weathering the Postwar Years

With the agony of the Civil War over at last, the nation began to rebuild. The demands made upon the Army by Reconstruction duty, Indian uprisings in the West, and French machinations in Mexico caused demobilization to proceed gradually. For the Signal Corps, peacetime meant a return to virtual nonexistence because the legislation creating the Corps in 1863 provided for its organization only "during the present rebellion." From a strength in November 1864 of over 1,500 officers and men, the branch had been reduced by October 1865 to just 160 officers and men.[1] In the absence of definitive congressional authority, its postwar status remained uncertain.

The War Clouds Lift

Chief Signal Officer Benjamin F. Fisher addressed the issue of organizing the peacetime Signal Corps in his 1865 annual report. In reviewing the last year of the war, he lamented the lack of defined duties which had often "crippled the usefulness of the corps by its not being properly understood what it could do or was expected to do." Each departmental commander had used his signal officers in a different way. Ideally, in Fisher's view, the Signal Corps in wartime should not only provide communications but also serve as the military intelligence bureau. Signal officers would collect information from all sources, analyze it, and present it "reduced to logical form" to the commanding general. Only in the Department of the Gulf, Fisher reported, had signal operations been conducted in this manner. During peacetime, however, the chief signal officer envisioned a much more limited role for the Corps. In general he recommended that signal officers be attached to garrisons and posts "liable to be besieged" in order to communicate over the heads of the enemy. These men would also constitute a nucleus of trained officers who could serve in the event of war. Congress could provide this nucleus either by "continuing a small permanent organization with specifically defined duties" or through a detail system. Fisher favored the adoption of the former course and recommended the appointment of a board of officers to define the mission and develop the organization of the Signal Corps.[2]

Congress failed to act on Fisher's recommendation. Instead, when it passed legislation in July 1866 authorizing personnel for the peacetime Signal Corps, it left the branch's duties undefined and also reverted to the objectionable detail system to obtain personnel. Under the provisions of this act the Signal Corps was to consist of one chief signal officer with the rank of colonel. In addition, the secretary of war could detail six officers and up to one hundred noncommissioned officers and privates from the Battalion of Engineers. Before being detailed to signal duty, both officers and enlisted men had to be examined and approved by a military board convened by the secretary of war.[3] By choosing to use engineers as signal soldiers, Congress conformed to the practice of several foreign armies. The British Army, for instance, detailed its military telegraphers from the Royal Engineers and, in fact, did not establish a separate signal corps until after World War I.

At the same time, Fisher had another serious matter on his mind—keeping his job. His appointment as chief signal officer would expire on 28 July 1866 without guarantee of renewal. Meanwhile Myer, who left active duty in the summer of 1864, had been devoting considerable effort to preparing his case for restoration as the Signal Corps' chief. Soon after his relief in November 1863, Myer had requested signal officers in the field to secure testimonials in his behalf and have their subordinate officers sign petitions to be sent to Washington. This tactic prompted Maj. Gen. Philip H. Sheridan to call Myer an "old wire puller," but Sheridan nonetheless prepared a statement.[4] After completing the signal manual in 1864, Myer had become signal officer of the Military Division of West Mississippi under Maj. Gen. Edward R. S. Canby, his old commander in New Mexico before the war. Under Canby, Myer had issued a "General Service Code" to be used for communication between land and sea forces and had participated in combat operations around Mobile, Alabama. Later, Canby served in the War Department as an assistant adjutant general with responsibility for oversight of the Signal Corps.[5]

In January 1865 Myer presented his case to the Senate in the form of a printed memorial consisting of a summary of his involvement with signals and signaling and the reasons why he should be reinstated. He later supplemented it with copies of various pertinent documents. Myer requested that the Senate delay the confirmation of any nomination for chief signal officer until it had examined his claim. Myer also met with President Lincoln, who promised not to appoint someone else as chief signal officer without studying the merits of the case. Myer followed up the meeting with a letter written the day before the president's assassination in April 1865. He also wrote to Secretary of War Stanton but received no reply.[6] Despite these apparent setbacks, Myer did not abandon his efforts.

Fisher, for his part, wished to retain the position in which he had served for over a year. Holding that Myer had waited too long after his dismissal to argue his case, he believed that the former chief "ought not be permitted to come forward now and work injury to an innocent party."[7] Although Fisher had performed adequately, Myer, as the Signal Corps' founder, had a strong claim to the job. General Ulysses S. Grant, now the commanding general of the Army, championed Myer's cause and urged Stanton to reappoint him.[8] Stanton, however, neglected to act upon the recommendation, presumably because of the wartime friction between himself and Myer. Finally, on 25 October 1866, President

Andrew Johnson ordered Stanton to make the appointment, and he did so five days later.

Although Myer accepted the appointment on 3 November and the Senate confirmed it the following February, he did not immediately resume his former duties. Fisher remained chief signal officer until 15 November 1866, despite the expiration of his appointment. After that date Bvt. Capt. Lemuel B. Norton ran the office. He was the only wartime signal officer to serve continuously in the Signal Corps into the postwar period.[9] Most likely Myer hoped that Stanton, at odds with the president over Reconstruction policy and in declining health, would soon resign. As it happened, the tenacious secretary held on to his post until suspended by the president on 12 August 1867, an act that resulted in Johnson's impeachment. When Grant stepped in as acting secretary of war, Myer resumed his duties on 21 August 1867.

General Myer

Myer, vindicated at last, found himself once again at the head of the organization he had created. Not one to waste time, he soon submitted a proposal to Grant to reinstate the course in signaling and telegraphy at West Point. With Grant's approval, instruction began on 1 October 1867.[10] Meanwhile, the Naval Academy continued to teach signaling, and the academy's superintendent, Vice Adm. David D. Porter, enthusiastically supported Myer's signal system. In 1869 the Navy established its own signal office based on the Army's model, but it never organized a distinct naval signal corps.[11]

Late in October 1867 the War Department issued orders authorizing the chief signal officer to furnish two sets of signal equipment and two copies of the signal manual to each company and post. Significantly, these orders allowed the chief signal officer to provide for the equipment and management of field electric telegraphs for active forces in the field. Thus in four years events had come full circle for Myer. By sheer tenacity he had won the Signal Corps' struggle for control of the kind of communications that would dominate the future.[12]

Further advances in signal training came in July 1868 when Secretary of War John M. Schofield directed that one officer from each geographical department be selected to receive signal instruction in Washington. Formal classes began in August at the Signal Office under the supervision of Capt. Henry W. Howgate. A signal school for enlisted men opened in September 1868 at Fort Greble, one of the forts built to protect Washington during the Civil War. The officers and men were detailed under the authority of the act of July 1866, but the War Department never invoked the provision to take them from the engineers. Myer believed that Congress had not intended to limit the details to the engineers alone, and that to do so would "be injurious both to the corps of engineers, by depriving it of officers whose services might be otherwise needed, and to the signal service, by the complications constantly to arise." Secretary of War Schofield accepted his argument and permitted the detail of up to fifty men from the general service for signal instruction at Fort Greble.[13] Several naval officers also attended the school. Among the Army officers reporting for instruction in October 1868 was 2d Lt. Adolphus W. Greely of the 36th Infantry, a man whose subsequent career became inextricably linked with the Signal Corps.

Both officers and men received similar instruction based on Myer's manual in the use of the various types of signal equipment. Officers additionally learned the cipher codes. Field practice comprised an important component of the training; an officer was not considered "well practiced" until he could send and receive visual messages readily, day or night, at a distance of fifteen miles. John C. Van Duzer, formerly of the Military Telegraph, taught electric telegraphy. In the new field trains, machines using batteries and sounders replaced the Beardslee instruments. A properly qualified officer could send and receive ten words per minute, and his men were expected to erect field lines at a rate of three miles per hour. Upon completion of their training, the secretary of war directed that one officer and two men be sent to each department to conduct signal training at the various posts.[14]

Because the United States Army's Signal Corps was the first organization of its kind, it drew the attention of other nations, and Myer received requests for information about signaling from several foreign governments. In February and March 1868, before the official opening of the Signal School, a Danish officer received instruction in the signal office in Washington. After the opening of the school, two Swedish Army officers were among the first students.[15]

Early in 1869 the Signal School moved across the Potomac River to Fort Whipple, Virginia. Of the new location Myer wrote:

> The post is well located . . . on the heights overlooking the valley of the Potomac, whence ranges for near and distant practice may be had, ranging from five to thirty miles. The ground in the vicinity is suited for the drills of telegraphic trains and for experiments with electric lines erected and left standing.[16]

In his annual report for 1869 Myer expressed pride in the Signal Corps' recent accomplishments, but he could not forecast the changes the branch would soon undergo as the result of congressional hearings then underway regarding Army organization.

The Signal Corps Becomes the Weather Service

Despite the successful establishment of the Signal School, the Signal Corps still lacked a clear-cut mission. During hearings before the House Committee on

Military Affairs in 1869, Secretary of War Schofield testified that he felt the
Army did not need a separate Signal Corps. The committee shared his view that
the signal function could be performed by the engineers, but Congress did not act
on this proposal.[17] Nevertheless, when Congress reduced the size of the Army to
save money, Myer knew that the Signal Corps needed a stronger footing in order
to survive further scrutiny. One solution appeared to lie in weather observation
and reporting, a field in which he had some experience from his days as an Army
doctor.

Weather has always regulated daily activities, especially for those whose liveli-
hood is intimately tied to the land. Its study in the United States antedated the
founding of the republic. Benjamin Franklin, who was not only a political leader
but also a noted scientist in colonial America, had theorized about the origin and
movement of storms. Another founding father, Thomas Jefferson, kept a daily journal of weather observations and corresponded widely with others of similar interest. Jefferson envisioned a national meteorological system, but until some means of
rapidly reporting the weather was invented, a nationwide forecasting service was
impossible.[18]

The Army's formal involvement in meteorology had begun in April 1814
when Dr. James Tilton, physician and surgeon general of the Army, directed military surgeons to record weather data. Regulations published for the Medical
Department in December of that year required senior hospital surgeons to keep
weather diaries. The collection of such information was believed to be important
because weather was thought to influence disease.[19]

In addition to the Army, the Smithsonian Institution, founded in 1846, played
an important role in the advancement of meteorology within the United States.
Under the auspices of its first secretary, Joseph Henry, it organized the nation's
first telegraphic system of weather reporting in 1849. Henry was a pioneer in the
development of the electric telegraph, the instrument that made widespread,
simultaneous weather observation and reporting feasible. The Smithsonian made
arrangements with commercial telegraph companies to carry the reports of its
voluntary observers, from which the first current weather maps were compiled.
By 1860 five hundred stations reported to the Smithsonian, but the onset of the
Civil War caused the network to decline and its importance to diminish. A fire at
the institution in 1865 also inflicted considerable damage to meteorological
instruments and records.[20]

After the war, as the nation's commercial and agricultural enterprises expanded, the need for a national weather service became apparent. Because the
Smithsonian lacked the funds to operate such a system, Joseph Henry urged
Congress to create one.[21] A petition submitted in December 1869 to Congressman
Halbert E. Paine by Increase A. Lapham, a Wisconsin meteorologist, provided
further impetus for national legislation. Lapham advocated a warning service on
the Great Lakes to reduce the tremendous losses in lives and property caused by
storms each year. Paine supported this proposition and soon introduced legislation authorizing the secretary of war "to provide for taking meteorological obser-

vations at the military stations in the interior of the continent, and at other points in the States and Territories of the United States, and for giving notice on the northern lakes and on the seacoast, by magnetic telegraph and marine signals, of the approach and force of storms."[22] Paine chose to assign these duties to the War Department because "military discipline would probably secure the greatest promptness, regularity, and accuracy in the required observations."[23] Congress approved Paine's proposal as a joint resolution, and President Ulysses S. Grant signed it into law on 9 February 1870.

Myer recognized that Paine's bill provided the mission the Signal Corps needed. As Paine later recalled: "Immediately after the introduction of the measure, a gentleman called on me and introduced himself as Col. Albert Myer, Chief Signal Officer. He was greatly excited and expressed a most intense desire that the execution of the law might be entrusted to him."[24] Myer's efforts were rewarded when Secretary of War William W. Belknap assigned the weather duties to the chief signal officer on 15 March 1870.[25] Now the Signal Corps embarked upon a new field of endeavor, one that soon overshadowed its responsibility for military communications.

At this time, before the advent of such weapons as long-range artillery and the airplane, weather forecasting had little relevance for Army operational planning. But the Army had long been performing duties not directly related to its military mission. Throughout the nineteenth century the Corps of Engineers, for example, had been carrying out projects such as river and harbor improvements that were not military in the strictest sense. Moreover, Congress had created the Corps of Topographical Engineers in 1838 specifically to conduct surveys and to build roads and canals that promoted national expansion. Thus, the assignment of weather duties to the Signal Corps was only another example of the Army's performance of essentially civil functions for the welfare of the nation.[26]

Having acquired the weather duties, Myer set about establishing a national reporting system. From the outset the Signal Corps directed its services chiefly toward the civilian community, as reflected in the title of the new "Division of Telegrams and Reports for the Benefit of Commerce" within the Office of the Chief Signal Officer. Myer subsequently added the words "and Agriculture" to reflect the additional services authorized by Congress in 1872.[27] To provide weather information to the nation's farmers, the Signal Office published a *Farmers' Bulletin* that included daily weather summaries and predictions. It was telegraphed daily to and distributed from centers in the middle of agricultural areas. The Corps later added such services as frost warnings for tobacco, sugar, and fruit growers and special reports for cotton planters.

During the 1870s American scientific education was in its formative stages. The rudiments of meteorology could be learned at such schools as Harvard and Yale, but no formal training for meteorologists existed. Therefore, the Signal Corps carried out its own program. The Corps conducted meteorological training at Fort Whipple in addition to regular military drills and signal instruction. "Full" training prepared a soldier to perform both field signal duties and those of the weather service, while "field" training excluded weather duties. The Signal Corps selectively recruited personnel for the weather service—only unmarried men between the ages of twenty-one and forty were eligible—and required them to pass both physical and educational examinations. Upon acceptance, the men enlisted as privates and received at least two months of instruction at Fort Whipple. After an additional six months of duty on station as assistants (later extended to one year), followed by further training at Fort Whipple and appearance before two boards of examination, the men qualified for promotion to "observer-sergeant." After one year's service, an observer could again be called before a board for yet another examination.[28]

The work of the observer was often demanding. Three times daily he recorded the following data: temperature; relative humidity; barometric pressure; direction and velocity of the wind; and rain or snow fall. The Corps soon added to this list the daily measurement of river depths at stations along many major rivers. The observer also noted the cloud cover and the general state of the weather. Immediately upon completing his observations, the officer prepared the information for telegraphic transmission to the Signal Office in Washington. In a separate journal he recorded unusual phenomena, such as auroral and meteoric displays. In addition to the three telegraphic reports, he made another set of observations according to local time and mailed them weekly to Washington. The Corps also required a separate midday reading of the instruments, but the observer only forwarded the results if they differed greatly from the earlier readings. At sunset he recorded the appearance of the western sky to be used as an indication of the next day's weather. In case of severe weather, an observer could be on duty around the clock, making hourly reports to Washington.[29]

The extent and the hour of the observations changed over time. Originally the observers took the readings at 0735, 1635, and 2335, Washington time, but the last reading was soon changed to 2300 so that the information could be included in the morning newspapers. Before the introduction of standard time and time zones within the United States, a confusing multiplicity of local times existed. In 1870 there were over 100 such regional times. For the purposes of the meteorological observations, observers used Washington time until 1885. Thereafter the observers took their readings according to eastern time, or that at the 75th meridian west of Greenwich, England. Observers also made local-time readings from 1876 to 1881.[30]

In addition to long hours, the observer's job involved considerable paperwork: he recorded and forwarded all data to the Signal Office weekly and submitted a monthly digest as well. Record keeping was doubly important because the information often served as evidence in court cases in which weather was a factor. The observer was also responsible for the proper care and functioning of his instruments. If he did not have an assistant, the officer could select and train a civilian to perform his duties when necessary. To ensure a high standard of operation, signal officers periodically inspected the stations. Among those who served in this capacity were two future chief signal officers, Adolphus Greely and James Allen.

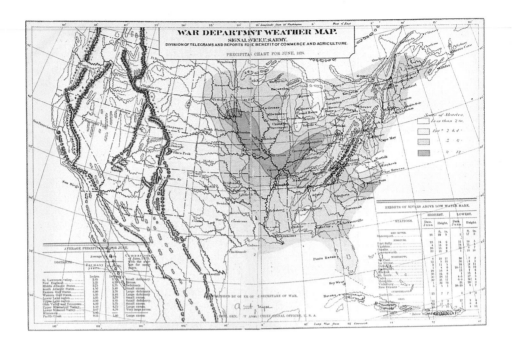

War Department weather map, 1875

Despite the Signal Corps' rigorous training requirements, not all observers upheld its high standards. Human nature being what it is, a few proved to be unscrupulous in their work. After examining past submissions in 1890, records officer 2d Lt. William A. Glassford reported that some of the early weather watchers "were so confident of their ability to successfully counterfeit the laws of nature that they wrote up their observations several hours before or after the schedule time."[31] One of these presumptuous individuals was Sgt. John Timothy O'Keeffe, or O'Keefe, stationed on Pikes Peak, Colorado. O'Keeffe filled out many of his reports without actually making the observations, believing that the authorities in Washington would not know any better.[32]

In addition to the demands of the work itself, some observers faced considerable physical danger. The sergeant at Chicago had his office destroyed during the great fire of October 1871, but luckily escaped with his life. During the nationwide cholera epidemic in 1878, signal observers remained at their posts in disease-ridden cities, and three of them died in the line of duty. The remoteness of frontier stations also posed many hardships, including the constant threat of Indian attacks. The observer atop Mount Washington, New Hampshire, faced winters that averaged over 200 inches of snowfall and temperatures well below zero. In February 1872 Pvt. William Stevens, an assistant at that station, was caught in a blizzard on the mountain and perished.[33]

Once the observers had gathered the weather data, the means of reporting and disseminating it became most important. Like the Smithsonian, the chief signal officer made arrangements with the leading commercial telegraph companies to carry the tri-daily reports. Civilian telegraph experts established special circuits routed to the Signal Office. The initial arrangement with Western Union regarding transmission was only temporary, and at the end of the trial period the company refused to continue service. The House Appropriations Committee held hearings over the dispute and ruled that the company had a mandate to transmit the weather information as government business. The Signal Corps compensated the company, however, at rates determined by the postmaster general.[34]

When making the daily telegraphic reports, the weather observers used special codes to reduce their length to twenty words in the morning and ten in each of the other two reports, thereby saving the government both time and money.[35] Regular transmission of the reports began at 0735 on 1 November 1870 from twenty-four stations stretching from Boston, Massachusetts, south to Key West, Florida, and west to Cheyenne in the Wyoming Territory. In addition to the station atop Mount Washington (opened in December 1870), the Signal Corps soon reached new heights in weather reporting with the station on Pikes Peak that began reporting in November 1873.[36]

To provide a picture of weather conditions across the country, the observers made their reports as nearly simultaneous as possible. The weather service did not initially make forecasts, and the enabling legislation did not specifically call for it to do so. Eventually general forecasts, referred to as probabilities, emanated from the Signal Office in Washington. Locally, the observers posted bulletins and maps in the offices of boards of trade and chambers of commerce to provide weather information to the public. Post offices also displayed daily bulletins, and observers supplied local newspapers with data. Some communities appointed meteorological committees to confer with the chief signal officer and to serve as a check upon the operations of the local weather station. On the national level, the Signal Office in Washington issued daily weather maps compiled from the reports received from all the stations. It also published the *Daily Weather Bulletin*, *Weekly Weather Chronicle*, and the *Monthly Weather Review*. All were available for sale to the public. Myer estimated that through these various means at least one third of American households received the Signal Corps' weather information in some form. A railway bulletin service, initiated in 1879, enabled stations along many major railroads to display weather information.[37]

The *Monthly Weather Review* contained a summary of the meteorological data collected by the Signal Office during the month as well as notes on current developments in the field of meteorology. Until 1884 the chief signal officer published the year's issues in his annual report. The *Review* became a leading meteorological journal, and it continues to be published today by the American Meteorological Society.

To help establish his system, Myer looked to civilian meteorologists for expertise. Among the first he hired was Increase Lapham, who had played an important

Cleveland Abbe

role in getting the weather service started. Lapham worked briefly as supervisor of weather reports on the Great Lakes, and he continued to provide information about shipping disasters to the Signal Office until his death in 1875.[38] In January 1871 the Signal Corps hired Professor Cleveland Abbe of the Cincinnati Observatory as a weather forecaster. Abbe had begun issuing forecasts in Cincinnati in 1869, and the Signal Corps adopted many of his methods and procedures.[39] Although Abbe had originally been skeptical about the quality of a military weather system, he remained with the Signal Corps' weather service throughout its twenty-year history.[40] In addition to forecasting, Abbe founded the *Monthly Weather Review* and was its editor.

Although weather reporting called for a new set of equipment (thermometers, hygrometers, etc.), flags still found a role in the weather-oriented Signal Corps. A red flag with a black square in the center, for example, became known as the "cautionary signal." When flown from observation stations, primarily those on the Great Lakes and the eastern seaboard, it indicated the likelihood of a storm in the vicinity. At night, a red light served as the storm warning. A white flag with a square black center flying above the red flag was known as the "cautionary offshore signal," meaning that winds were blowing from a northerly or westerly direction.[41]

Weather reporting also led the Signal Corps into a new relationship with the electric telegraph. At least one writer has incorrectly attributed the assignment of weather duties to the Signal Corps in 1870 to the fact that the Corps controlled its own telegraph lines.[42] Actually, the Corps did not begin constructing lines until 1873, under authority of legislation approved in March of that year. The act directed the Signal Corps to establish signal stations at lighthouses and to construct telegraph lines between them if none existed. These lines were to work in conjunction with the stations of the United States Life-Saving Service, the forerunner of the Coast Guard. In some cases the Signal Corps located its offices within the life-saving stations.[43] During 1873 and 1874 the Corps built lines between Sandy Hook and Cape May, New Jersey, and from Cape Hatteras, North Carolina, to Norfolk, Virginia, along some of the most perilous stretches of the Atlantic coast. Leased wires connected these lines with the Signal Office in Washington. Further extensions between Wilmington, North Carolina, and the mouth of the Cape Fear River and from the Delaware Breakwater, at the mouth of Philadelphia Harbor, to Chincoteague, Virginia, brought the total length of sea-coast lines to just over 600 miles, a figure that remained about the same through-out the 1880s.[44]

The Signal Corps filled the critical need for a storm warning system along the Atlantic coast to warn vessels of approaching storms and to aid in the rescue of ships wrecked in the treacherous waters. When a wreck occurred, the Corps opened a special station at the scene to call for assistance and to maintain com-munication with those still on board the ship. Knowledge of naval and interna-tional signal codes enabled Army signal officers to establish communication with ships of any registry. Officers could also signal with flags and torches across breaks in the telegraph lines, a frequent occurrence on the stormy coastline. Their services saved many lives and untold tons of cargo.

One of the wrecks to which the Signal Corps gave assistance was that of the *Huron*, a steamer that ran aground off Nags Head, North Carolina, in the early morning hours of 24 November 1877. Two of the survivors on a raft headed for what appeared to be the masts of fishing vessels but turned out to be the Signal Corps' telegraph poles on the shore. The nearest signal station was at Kitty Hawk, eight miles from the site of the wreck. It was housed in the upper story of the life-saving station, then closed for the season, a fact that severely inhibited the rescue effort. At midmorning, two fishermen brought news of the disaster to the signal station, and the observer, Sgt. S. W. Naylor, headed for the scene to assist the victims. He set up a telegraph station on the shore that transmitted over 550 messages through 11 December. Only 34 men out of the crew of 132 survived the wreck of the *Huron*. Five others, including the superintendent of the Sixth Life-Saving District, lost their lives during the rescue operations, making the *Huron* one of the worst shipwrecks of the era.[45]

The following year a signal officer, 1st Lt. James A. Buchanan, on his way to inspect coastal signal stations, was himself a victim of a shipwreck when the schooner *Magnolia* went down in Albemarle Sound, North Carolina, during a hurricane. Buchanan lashed himself to the gunwale and eventually managed to swim ashore.[46]

The Signal Corps' telegraph network soon expanded beyond the eastern seaboard. In 1874 Congress enacted legislation directing the War Department to build lines to connect military posts and protect frontier settlements in Texas against Indians and Mexicans. Other acts authorized lines in Arizona and New Mexico and, somewhat later, the Northwest. These lines were intended to serve sparsely settled areas where commercial lines were not yet available. For the most part, soldiers maintained and operated the lines, but the Corps employed some civilians. As the telegraph extended its reach, the weather system also grew, because the operators doubled as weather observers. The Signal Corps' lines achieved their maximum mileage in 1881, when 5,077 miles were under its control. In succeeding years the mileage steadily dropped as commercial lines followed the railroads westward, and by 1891 only 1,025 miles remained under the Signal Corps' supervision. In total, the Corps was responsible for building 8,000 miles of telegraph lines, to include both seacoast and frontier lines.[47]

First Lieutenant Adolphus W. Greely supervised much of the Signal Corps' telegraph construction. In Texas, where the Army built nearly 1,300 miles of line, one of the major obstacles was the shortage of timber for poles. Greely obtained some from the Rio Grande Valley, about 500 miles from where the lines were being constructed, and even imported juniper poles from the Great Dismal Swamp in Virginia. He later oversaw the construction of 2,000 miles of line from Santa Fe to San Diego, and in 1878 he went to the Dakota Territory to erect a line from Bismarck to Fort Ellis, Montana. The discovery of gold in the Black Hills and the Indian troubles in the area, highlighted by the Custer massacre in 1876, made the need for lines more acute.[48]

Will Croft Barnes was one of the Signal Corps operators assigned to a western station. Enlisting as a second class private in 1879, Barnes trained at Fort Whipple and, after duty constructing seacoast telegraph lines, was sent to Fort Apache, Arizona, "then about as far out of civilization as it was possible to get."[49] Barnes arrived there in February 1880, much to the relief of the previous operator. To Barnes' dismay, the first weather observation had to be made at 0339 for transmission at 0400. Of greater concern to him were the Indian troubles in the area; Indians often cut the telegraph wires, making repairs a risky business. In the summer of 1881 the Army's relations with the Indians became especially tense when a shaman named Nakaidoklini became influential among the Apaches. Anticipating the later Ghost Dance movement of the 1890s, Nakaidoklini preached a doctrine that included the raising of the dead and the elimination of the white man. When the commander of Fort Apache, Col. Eugene A. Carr, was ordered to arrest the medicine man, violence resulted. His followers attacked Carr's party as the soldiers returned to the post following the arrest. Nakaidoklini was killed, along with one officer and three men; four others were mortally wounded and died before reaching Fort Apache. The day after Carr returned to the post, Barnes accompanied the burial party. In the midst of their work, Indians attacked, and soon the fort was under siege. Fortunately, the attackers were driven off, and for his part in the defense Barnes received the Medal of Honor, the second Signal Corpsman so recognized.[50]

The Signal Corps' weather reporting network gained additional strength in 1874 from the absorption of the Smithsonian's nearly 400 volunteer observers, as well as by an agreement made with the surgeon general to turn over to the Signal Corps the monthly reports made by medical officers. These acquisitions brought to over 800 the total number of reports received regularly by the Signal Office. Naval and merchant vessels also began to feed information into the system.[51]

Besides reporting on the weather, Signal Corps observers sometimes relayed other types of information. In 1877 they provided President Rutherford B. Hayes with details about local conditions arising from labor unrest. During the so-called Great Strike—actually a wave of railroad strikes that spread across the nation in

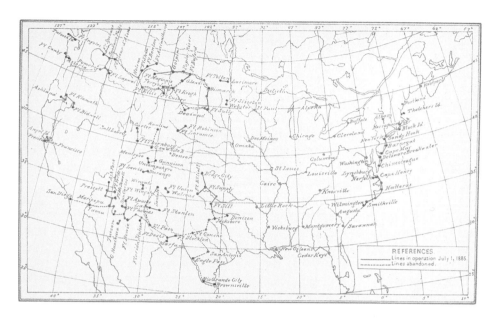

Map of U.S. military telegraph lines, 1885

the summer of 1877—Chief Signal Officer Myer ordered the observers at key points to report every six hours, and more frequently if necessary.[52] Sgt. Leroy E. Sebree, for example, wired from Louisville on 25 July that "The wildest excitement prevails—troops are resting on their arms in City Hall—striking laborers are marching through the city forcing others to join. Every precaution is being taken to prevent serious trouble." Using the information gleaned from his observers, Myer could give the president his own assessment of conditions. On 26 July he cautioned Hayes that the news from Chicago in the afternoon papers seemed to be "purely sensational. The city is reported to be comparatively quiet." Indeed, order returned to most cities within a few days. By 29 July Myer could report to Hayes that "The regular night reports show absolute Quiet everywhere on the Atlantic & Picific [sic] Coast & the interior. The riots seem ended." He also congratulated the president and the secretary of war "on the sucess [sic] and conclusion of this campaign." Some trouble spots remained, and the Signal Corps continued its strike-related reports until 13 August 1877.[53]

From the beginning the weather service contained an international component. In the 1870s the Signal Corps established several stations in Alaska, only recently purchased from Russia. The Alaskan observers were also naturalists who collected specimens for the Smithsonian. One of these men, Pvt. Edward W. Nelson, while stationed at St. Michael, documented the life and culture of the Bering Sea Eskimos.[54] Beginning in 1871, Canadian stations exchanged reports with the Signal Corps, and reports received from the West Indies proved especially valuable during the hurricane season.

Eventually Myer established contact with many foreign weather offices. In 1873 he attended the first International Meteorological Congress in Vienna where the participants agreed to exchange a daily observation, with the United States assuming the expense of publishing the results.[55] By sharing such information, meteorologists could track storms from continent to continent and study weather patterns. In 1875 the Signal Office began publishing the *Daily Bulletin of International Simultaneous Meteorological Observations*, containing the daily observations made on a given date up to a year earlier. A daily International Weather Map followed in 1878 based upon the data appearing in the bulletin of the same date. Through its weather service, the Signal Corps helped the United States become part of the international scientific community.[56]

In order to provide these myriad services, the Signal Office worked around the clock. To facilitate its operation, the chief signal officer divided the office into a dozen sections: general correspondence and records; telegraph room; property room; printing and lithographing room; *International Bulletin*; instrument room; map room; artisan's room; station room; the computation, or fact, room; the study room; and the library. The instrument room, for example, maintained the standard instruments against which all those being sent to the weather stations were compared. The Corps also manufactured new types of equipment, including self-recording instruments to continuously gather data. The Corps' library contained thousands of volumes and pamphlets, many of them gifts from foreign governments and institutions. In addition to maintaining the heavy administrative load of correspondence, the office responded to voluminous numbers of requests for weather information. In 1880 a complement of 110 enlisted men kept the office running.[57]

Indeed, the burgeoning duties of the Signal Corps created a need for additional personnel. Consequently, the secretary of war authorized increases in its detailed enlisted strength, and by 1874 the Corps comprised 150 sergeants, 30 corporals, and 270 privates.[58] The number of detailed officers remained at six as specified in the 1866 legislation. Although Congress in 1874 limited the strength of the Army to 25,000, it did not include the Signal Corps in this total and specified that its strength was not to be diminished.[59] But when Congress reduced the size of the Army two years later, in the midst of the depression that followed the Panic of 1873, it no longer exempted the Signal Corps and cut its enlisted force by fifty. In 1878, however, Congress restored the Corps to its previous strength of 450 enlisted men. The new law also provided that two signal sergeants could be appointed annually to the rank of second lieutenant, thus offering some upward mobility for Corps members. In 1880 Congress added 50 privates, bringing the Signal Corps' total enlisted strength to 500, where it remained until 1886.[60]

By 1880, after a decade of operation under Myer's leadership, the weather service was flourishing. It had grown to comprise 110 regular stations in the United States that reported by telegraph three times daily, and its annual budget totaled $375,000.[61] But on 24 August 1880, the man who had contributed so much to the development of the weather system, not to mention having founded the Signal Corps itself, died of nephritis at the age of 51. Myer had become ill in 1879 while traveling in Europe, and his condition gradually worsened. Brig. Gen. Richard C. Drum, the adjutant general, temporarily took command of the Signal Corps following Myer's death, and his signature appears at the end of the 1880 annual report. In honor of the Army's first signal officer, Fort Whipple was renamed Fort Myer on 4 February 1881.[62]

Death claimed Myer at the peak of his career. He had just received his commission as brigadier general, effective 16 June 1880, putting him on a par with the other bureau chiefs within the War Department. As head of the Signal Corps' weather service, he had become popularly known as Old Probabilities.[63] In addition to the sobriquet, Myer received much professional recognition for his public service. Among the numerous awards conferred upon him were honorary memberships in the Austrian Meteorological Society and the Italian Geographical Society; an honorary Doctor of Laws degree from his alma mater, Hobart College, in 1872; and an honorary Doctor of Philosophy from Union College in 1875. To recognize Signal Corps veterans, Myer had founded the Order of the Signal Corps shortly after the Civil War, but this organization no longer exists.[64]

The Stormy Years

Col. William B. Hazen became the fourth person to hold the position of chief signal officer, taking office on 15 December 1880. A native of Vermont, Hazen had graduated from West Point in 1855 and then served in Oregon and Texas. During the Civil War he distinguished himself at such battles as Stone's River, Chickamauga, and Atlanta, where he commanded a division in the Army of the Tennessee. In 1865 he received a brevet major generalcy in the Regular Army for meritorious service in the field. After the war he returned to duty in the West. Never one to avoid controversy, Hazen created a sensation when he charged the War Department with corrupt management of the post trader system. The resulting congressional investigations led to the resignation and impeachment of Secretary of War William W. Belknap during the Grant administration.[65] Hazen also acted as an observer during the Franco-Prussian War, and in 1872 he published a book about military reform, *The School and the Army in Germany and France.*[66]

Hazen, promoted to the permanent rank of brigadier general in the Regular Army, quickly made some changes upon taking command of the Signal Corps. To begin, he reorganized the Signal Office into ten divisions that roughly corresponded to the various rooms created by Myer. Unlike Myer, who stressed the practical over the scientific, Hazen shifted the emphasis toward basic research.[67] He established, for example, the Scientific and Study Division to prepare special reports and conduct other research projects. Professor Abbe supervised the work of the study room within that division, and he was assisted by three civilians with scientific backgrounds, known initially as "computers" because of the mathematical calculations involved in their work. Topics of inquiry included hurricanes, tornadoes, and thunderstorms. Copies of papers prepared by the study room appeared in many of the chief signal officer's annual reports. To supplement this staff, Hazen called upon several "consulting specialists," among them Alexander Graham Bell and Professor Samuel P. Langley of the Allegheny Observatory in Pennsylvania.[68] A committee of the National Academy of Sciences also acted in an advisory capacity as needed by the chief signal officer. To formally present the results of the studies undertaken by the Corps, Hazen introduced a series of professional papers as well as a set of publications known as "Signal Service Notes." He also initiated the compilation of a general bibliography of meteorology. To further meteorological education, members of the study room delivered lectures to the students at Fort Myer. Hazen also directed Professor William Ferrel, one of the assistants in the office, to compile a textbook of meteorology for classroom use. Thus Hazen sought to combine the practical arts of observation, recording, and prediction with the science of meteorology.[69]

Under Hazen the Signal Corps' work took off in some new directions. To study the upper atmosphere, signal soldiers sometimes accompanied balloonists aloft in order to make observations. A leading aeronaut, Samuel King of Philadelphia, invited Signal Corps personnel to ride in his balloon on several occasions. One such adventurous soldier, Pvt. J. G. Hashagen, accompanied King on a flight from Chicago in October 1881 and ended up eating hedgehog in the wilds of Wisconsin after landing in a cranberry bog. (King had packed no food for the journey.) Hashagen succeeded in making meteorological observations during the flight, but he recommended including condensed soup as part of the equipment for future ascensions.[70] During the weather service years the Signal Corps possessed no balloons of its own, but Abbe stressed the need for aerial investigations into weather, and he was prophetic when he wrote in 1884, "As the use of the balloon for military purposes has received much attention and is highly appreciated in Europe, it is probable that this also may at some time become a duty of the Signal Office."[71]

To raise the standard of personnel, Hazen sought to recruit promising graduates from the nation's colleges. By doing so he hoped "to furnish from the ranks of the Signal Corps, men who may take high standing in the science of meteorology."[72] At the same time, some of the Signal Corps' current members were sent to private schools for further education. Pvts. Austin L. McRae and Alexander McAdie of the Boston weather station attended Harvard University to study atmospheric electricity. Pvt. Park Morrill, on duty in Baltimore, took similar courses at the Johns Hopkins University. These schools provided the courses without cost, and other schools located near signal stations offered similar arrangements.[73]

Hazen encouraged the expansion of weather activities through the establishment of state weather services with which the Signal Corps cooperated. In some cases enlisted men served as assistants to the state directors. These organizations proved especially helpful in distributing weather information to remote agricultural areas. By 1884 fourteen states had their own weather offices, with the six

New England states forming the New England Meteorological Society. Most states had organized weather agencies by 1890.[74]

The paucity of weather information on the West Coast had long concerned both Myer and Hazen, and in 1885 the Corps improved this situation by opening a signal office for the Division of the Pacific, which encompassed California, Oregon, and Washington. The new office at San Francisco issued forecasts twice daily and distributed them by means of the daily newspapers, the Associated Press, and the *Farmers' Bulletin*. When necessary, cautionary signals were displayed at several points along the coast. In addition to providing weather information, the division signal officer was directed to repair the telegraph cable between Alcatraz and

General Hazen

the Presidio of San Francisco. The harbor's powerful currents and the fact that vessels frequently anchored there made repair and maintenance of the cable an expensive job.[75]

The Signal Corps' expanding duties required a great deal of office space. By 1882, the Corps occupied rooms in ten different buildings in Washington. Myer had first requested a new building in 1875, and Hazen took up the cause in his annual report of 1882. The State-War-Navy Building (now known as the Old Executive Office Building) had recently opened, and the chief signal officer, along with the other bureau chiefs, had his office there. But the new building could not house all of the Signal Corps' activities. In the absence of congressional action, Hazen repeatedly asked for a fireproof structure to provide protection for the branch's valuable records and property. Second Lieutenant Frank P. Greene, in charge of the Examiner's Division in 1886, complained of the condition of his division's quarters. Not only were the rooms "small and dark, cold in winter and warm in summer," but there was also an "ever-present stale, ill-smelling odor, rising at frequent times to a pitch that is all but visible." In 1889 the Signal Corps finally moved to new quarters at 2416 M Street, Northwest, that contained a fireproof vault for its records.[76]

In many ways success and growth had marked Hazen's tenure. But troubles, some of a serious nature, had also begun to arise. Ironically, given his role in the post trader hearings, scandal rocked Hazen's own bureau when Capt. Henry W. Howgate abruptly resigned from the Signal Corps in December 1880. To his chagrin, Hazen soon discovered that Howgate had helped himself to a substantial portion of the Corps' funds. The exact amount was never determined, but it could have been as much as $400,000. Howgate, British by birth, had served with distinction in the Signal Corps during the Civil War. Rejoining the Army in 1867 as a member of the 20th Infantry, he subsequently returned to the Signal Corps where he worked in the Signal Office as property and disbursement officer under Myer. Howgate had hoped to succeed Myer as chief signal officer, but Hazen's friendship with then Senator James A. Garfield helped him win the appointment from President Rutherford B. Hayes.

Instead of chief signal officer, Howgate became a fugitive. He fled to Michigan with his mistress and was not tracked down until August 1881. Authorities arrested Howgate and returned him to Washington for trial. Released on bail, he dropped out of sight once more. When found, he was finally placed in jail. But the wily captain was not finished. With the aid of his daughter and his mistress, he escaped again. This time Howgate eluded capture for thirteen years. He was finally seized in New York City in 1894, where he had been posing as a rare book dealer. At his first trial in 1895, the jury found Howgate not guilty, but he was not so lucky when tried on a second indictment and was sentenced to fifteen years in prison at Albany, New York. After five years, he received parole due to good conduct and poor health, and he died shortly afterward in 1901.[77]

Not surprisingly, Hazen assigned an officer to duty as examiner of accounts in the wake of the scandal.[78] Howgate had spent a great deal of the embezzled money on his mistress, but he also used some of it to finance Arctic exploration, an area in which the Signal Corps became involved as part of the First Interpolar Year (1882–1883), the forerunner of what is now known as the International Geophysical Year. Unfortunately, this well-intentioned scientific endeavor became a new source of controversy and even scandal for the Signal Corps.

Participating countries established stations around the North Pole to conduct meteorological, geological, and other scientific observations. In the summer of 1881 the United States sent two parties, both led by Signal Corps officers, one to Point Barrow, Alaska, and the other to Lady Franklin Bay on Ellesmere Island in northern Canada, less than 500 miles from the North Pole. The expedition to Alaska, commanded by 1st Lt. Patrick Henry Ray, spent two relatively uneventful years there. The second party, led by 1st Lt. Adolphus W. Greely, met a far different fate. When the scheduled resupply effort failed in 1882, the twenty-five men were left to fend for themselves in the frozen north. A relief expedition the following year, commanded by 1st Lt. Ernest A. Garlington, also failed to reach Greely's party. Garlington, facing a disaster of his own after his vessel sank and most of his supplies were lost, hastily withdrew south, leaving insufficient rations behind to sustain the stranded soldiers.

Despite their precarious situation, Greely and his men continued their scientific work. They had also succeeded, during the first year of the expedition, in achieving the "farthest north" up to that time. But their subsequent ordeal was harrowing. When the rescue effort commanded by Capt. Winfield Scott Schley

Members of the Greely Arctic Expedition. Greely is fourth from left, front row.

finally found Greely at Cape Sabine in June 1884, where he had retreated south according to plan, only the commander and six others remained alive, one of whom died soon thereafter. Unfortunately, sensational charges of murder and cannibalism initially overshadowed the accomplishments of the expedition. Greely denied knowledge of such acts and was ultimately exonerated. In 1888 the government published his massive two-volume report, containing a wealth of information about the Arctic. Greely received numerous honors for his work, among them the Founder's Medal of the Royal Geographic Society of London. He also became a charter member of the National Geographic Society, serving as a vice president and trustee of that organization.[79]

The outspoken Hazen publicly criticized Secretary of War Robert Todd Lincoln for his handling of the Greely affair. When Garlington's rescue mission failed in the fall of 1883, Lincoln had refused to send further assistance that year, leaving Greely and his men to face a third winter in the Arctic. Unwilling to abandon her husband and his men, Greely's wife, Henrietta, aroused public opinion and forced Lincoln to act. The secretary defended his actions in his 1884 annual report and censured Hazen for his criticisms. Ultimately, court-martial proceedings were instituted against the chief signal officer, resulting in a reprimand from President Chester A. Arthur.[80]

Hazen and Lincoln also disagreed upon another issue, the admission of blacks into the Signal Corps. In April 1884, W. Hallet Greene, a senior at the College of the City of New York, sought to enlist in the Corps. Hazen rejected his application, based on his understanding that black membership in the Army was

Signal station at Point Barrow, Alaska

limited to the two black infantry and two black cavalry regiments. Secretary Lincoln, however, overruled Hazen's action and directed that Greene be accepted. By direct order of the secretary of war, Greene joined the Signal Corps on 26 September 1884.[81]

These controversial incidents did not help the Signal Corps' reputation with Congress. In an era of cost cutting, when the Army's total budget dropped sharply, the Signal Corps' appropriation had continued to rise, topping a million dollars in 1884.[82] This fact alone, in the wake of the Howgate calamity, made the Signal Corps a natural target of congressional scrutiny. Beginning in fiscal years 1883 and 1884 its expenses were separated from those of the Army as a whole, and the categories of its expenditures were itemized for the first time. Hazen appealed this procedure to Secretary of War Lincoln, but received no sympathy. "I deem it prejudicial to the interests of the Army," wrote Lincoln in his 1884 annual report, "that its apparent cost of maintenance should be so largely increased by adding to it the cost of the Weather Bureau service, with which the Army is not concerned."[83]

When Congress appropriated less than the Signal Corps had requested, Hazen was forced to close a number of meteorological stations. Moreover, the budget cuts prevented the Corps from paying Western Union for transmitting reports from the Pacific coast during May and June 1883. Congress also refused to fund the West Indian stations that were of such importance during the hurricane season. As

Hazen complained in his annual report, the elimination of stations reduced the data received for forecasting, thus making predictions less accurate. (The average percentage of correct forecasts for 1883 was 88 percent, an accuracy rate rivaling that of forecasters today.) Other economies included the closing of cautionary signal stations and the dismissal of civilian assistants. Hazen also reduced the size of his annual report by about two-thirds by eliminating many tables and discontinuing the publication of the *Monthly Weather Review* within its pages.[84]

The operation of military telegraph lines was also substantially reduced. The Signal Corps abandoned many miles of line, in part because its services had been superseded by commercial companies, but also because Congress had stipulated that enlisted men from the line of the Army could no longer be used as operators and repairmen. Furthermore, line receipts could no longer be applied toward repair and maintenance.[85]

A new commission to investigate the role of science in the federal government posed an even greater threat to the Signal Corps' operations. Chaired by Senator William B. Allison of Iowa, and hence known as the Allison Commission, it began hearings in 1884. For the Signal Corps, the question was whether its weather duties properly belonged within the military.[86] Few men in the late nineteenth century saw any relation between the study of the weather and military operations. As early as 1874 Commanding General of the Army William T. Sherman had testified before the House Committee on Military Affairs that the men of the Signal Corps were "no more soldiers than the men at the Smithsonian Institution. They are making scientific observations of the weather, of great interest to navigators and the country at large. But what does a soldier care about the weather? Whether good or bad, he must take it as it comes."[87]

Hazen defended his program before Allison's committee and reiterated his arguments in his annual reports. But his superiors, particularly Sherman's successor as commanding general of the Army, Lt. Gen. Philip H. Sheridan, condemned the work of the Signal Corps, even its military signaling function. Sheridan had feuded with Hazen since the battle of Missionary Ridge during the Civil War, and he may have allowed his personal animosity to influence his attitude toward the Signal Corps. Secretary Lincoln, who had his own reasons for disliking Hazen, repeated his negative opinion of the weather duties as too expensive and not related to the Army.[88]

In their report the commission members divided evenly over the question of civilian versus military control of the weather service, and consequently they presented no plan for its separation from the Signal Corps. Thus, for the time being, the Corps retained its weather function but not without some changes being made. One immediate result of the commission's report was the closing of Fort Myer, site of the Signal School for nearly twenty years.[89] Furthermore, as recommended by the commission, the new secretary of war, William C. Endicott, ordered the closure of the study room within the Signal Office.[90]

The Signal Corps' appropriations continued to decrease as Congress placed increasing pressure on the branch in the wake of the Allison hearings. In 1886

General Greely

Congress authorized an investigation into the Corps' disbursements by the Committee on Expenditures in the War Department. While the committee found no evidence of fraud aside from the Howgate matter, it did feel that "proper economy has not always been observed" and recommended that legislation be enacted that more fully defined the scope of the Signal Corps' duties.[91]

In the midst of these troubled times, the chief signal officer's health failed, and in December 1886 Capt. Adolphus W. Greely assumed charge of the Signal Office as senior assistant. The following month General Hazen died of kidney trouble, apparently brought on by old wounds received in action against the Comanches prior to the Civil War.[92]

Captain Greely became the new chief signal officer, receiving a promotion in rank to brigadier general. Although the Signal Corps was beset with difficulties, Greely was a man well qualified to deal with them, having survived much worse situations in his twenty-five years of military service. Educated in the public schools of his native Massachusetts, he graduated from high school in his home town of Newburyport in 1860. The following year, while still only seventeen, he enlisted in the 19th Massachusetts Volunteer Infantry. During the Civil War he participated in several major battles and was seriously wounded at Antietam.[93] When mustered out in 1867, he had attained the rank of captain with a brevet majority. Greely soon joined the Regular Army as a second lieutenant in the 36th Infantry and served in the West before receiving an unexpected detail to the Signal Corps in 1868. As a member of the Corps, he performed numerous duties and achieved world fame as an Arctic explorer.

Greely became chief signal officer at a critical point in the Signal Corps' history. Denounced both within the War Department and in the halls of Congress, the branch saw its future clouded in doubt. For the immediate present at least, it continued to operate primarily as the nation's weather service. While Greely generally carried on the weather duties as inherited from Hazen, he did institute some changes. One of these was the addition of predictions of the force of storms, as called for in the 1870 joint resolution. This service began on 1 September 1887 with the display of flag signals to indicate whether a storm was to be light or severe and whether the center had reached or passed the weather station. Signals also indicated the quarter from which winds could be expected. Greely relied much more heavily than his predecessors on volunteer observers, and their ranks grew substantially under his leadership. Thus, while the number of regular stations declined during this period, the total number of weather-related stations continued to increase due to the expansion of such services as special river stations and rainfall and cotton region stations that were manned by civilian volunteers. (Such volunteers are, in fact, still a vital component of the nation's weather reporting system.)[94]

The availability of trained personnel was another significant issue. The discontinuance of the Signal School at Fort Myer meant that Greely had to send untrained men to operate the regular weather stations, and the observer-sergeants became responsible for teaching their new assistants.[95] Meanwhile, the legislative restriction on the number of officers detailed to the Signal Corps led to the eventual discharge of many of those who were knowledgeable about weather duties. This situation had a negative impact on weather forecasting, a skill which could only be learned by experience and practice. The loss of expert forecasters in the Signal Office resulted in a decline in the accuracy of the weather predictions by about 7 percent. Although part of the decline could also be attributed to the fact that the time period of the forecasts had recently been increased from twenty-four to thirty-two hours, the situation provided the Signal Corps' critics with further ammunition in their quest for change.[96] In 1889 the Corps for the first time allowed some local observers to make forecasts for their area for the next twenty-four hours.[97] Previously, all forecasts had been issued either from the Washington or the San Francisco office. With these increased responsibilities, Greely stressed the need to select well-qualified recruits. To obtain such men, the Signal Corps still required a written examination as well as recommendations of good moral standing and general character.

Beginning on 1 July 1888 Greely established a new system of meteorological observations. He replaced the tri-daily observations with two made at 0800 and 2000, 75th meridian time (or eastern time). River observations would be made at 0800, 75th meridian time. Sunset observations would be replaced by a prediction made at 2000 as to whether rain would fall during the next twenty-four hours, based upon prevailing atmospheric conditions.[98]

Greely also modified the Signal Corps' weather publications in ways that proved to be very popular. In 1887 the Corps began issuing a weather crop bulletin each Sunday morning from March to October. During the off-season it appeared monthly. The bulletin provided a summary of weather conditions for the previous seven days and their effect upon such major crops as corn, cotton, tobacco, and wheat. Farmers were pleased, and many metropolitan newspapers published the information as well.[99]

Other projects were more scientific. The Signal Corps finally completed one of its major long-term enterprises, the publication of a general bibliography of meteorology, containing 65,000 titles, begun under Hazen in 1882.[100] Despite the lack of funds, the Signal Corps also sent a display to the Paris Exhibition of 1889.

The presentation emphasized the Corps' weather duties and featured a small array of instruments as well as sets of the service's publications and charts. The daily weather map drew special attention, and the judges were impressed enough to award the exhibit three grand prizes.[101]

To increase the Corps' efficiency, Greely favored streamlining the force. In 1886 Congress had reduced the branch's enlisted strength to 470 and further cut the number in 1888 to 320. But 101 of the discharged men simply changed their standing from enlisted to civilian and continued to work for the weather service.[102] Greely, however, felt that a further cut in the enlisted ranks would be beneficial, and he recommended bringing the total down to 225. He also favored replacing most enlisted assistants at weather stations with civilians and eliminating the rank of second lieutenant from the Corps' structure. Congress, however, made no further reductions in the Corps' enlisted strength.[103]

Officers continued to be detailed to the Signal Corps from the line, but their numbers did not vary greatly throughout the remainder of the weather service period. In 1883 Congress authorized the detail of up to ten officers, exclusive of the second lieutenants provided for in 1878 and those detailed to Arctic service. Thereafter the number steadily declined, falling to a low of four in 1885 and leveling off at five from 1886 through 1890. Likewise, Congress set a ceiling on the number of second lieutenants within the Corps. The number rose to sixteen in 1886, but fell to fourteen in 1888 and remained there for the rest of the weather service years.[104]

Despite the efforts to restructure and economize, the question of the status of the Signal Corps (or the Signal Service, as it was often called in this period) finally came to a head. In 1887 Secretary of War Endicott stated in his annual report that because of its concentration on weather duties the Signal Corps could no longer be relied upon for military signaling.[105] Further pressure came from Congress in the form of a movement to raise the Department of Agriculture to cabinet rank. Senator Allison, among the leaders of this endeavor, favored placing the weather service within that agency. But the initial efforts to pass legislation that included the transfer of the weather duties were unsuccessful, and in 1888 Congress created the new executive department without them.[106]

Given the prevailing political climate, Chief Signal Officer Greely knew that the Signal Corps must relinquish its civil duties in order to survive. On a practical level, however, separating the work of the soldiers from that of the civilians would be difficult, because their responsibilities were so intertwined. Although the Corps had managed to retain its weather mission for the moment, its ultimate loss appeared inevitable, for the winds of change were blowing briskly.[107]

Military Signals Weather the Storm

While the performance of military signaling faded into the background in the years after 1870, it did not disappear altogether. Until the closing of the school at

Fort Myer in 1885, signal soldiers continued to receive training in field signaling. Upon Hazen's recommendation, the adjutant general issued general orders in October 1885 directing that all post commanders provide signal instruction, a revival of the system practiced for a time without great success under Myer. These orders required commanders to keep not less than one officer and three enlisted men constantly under instruction and practice in signaling at each garrison in the United States.[108]

When Greely became chief signal officer in 1887, he found the system no more successful than before. He noted in his 1888 annual report that one-quarter of the Army's regiments lacked any signal instruction program, while in one-half of the regiments practically no signal training had taken place. This lack of preparation "simply indicates the practical abolishment of this Corps for any future war, since an efficient force for signaling could not be instantly created."[109] Conditions improved in 1889 when the Army revised its regulations in relation to signal training to make department commanders responsible for instruction and practice in military signaling for the line officers and enlisted men in their departments. The commander was to appoint an acting signal officer at each post to conduct instruction and supervise field practice for at least two months each year. "Constant instruction will be maintained until at least one officer and four enlisted men, of each company, are proficient in the exchange of both day and night signals by flag, heliograph, or other device." Furthermore, the department commander was authorized to designate an officer on his staff as the departmental signal officer.[110] The construction of practice telegraph lines at most Army posts provided further incentive and opportunity for soldiers to learn at least the rudiments of signaling. Greely maintained a list of the most capable men in case he needed to call upon their expertise to supplement the Corps during an emergency.[111]

The growing professionalism within the Army during the closing decades of the nineteenth century significantly affected signal training. In 1881 General William T. Sherman, commanding general of the Army, created the School of Application for Cavalry and Infantry at Fort Leavenworth, Kansas. After an uncertain start, the school evolved into a true postgraduate course in the profession of arms, with signaling becoming part of the curriculum in 1888.[112] In 1891 the Cavalry and Light Artillery School at Fort Riley, Kansas, was established, and signal training comprised part of the curriculum from the beginning. Also located at Fort Riley was a school for the instruction of signal sergeants. It offered a six-month course consisting of four months of classroom instruction and two months of practical application covering electricity, military surveying, telegraphy, telephony, and signaling.[113] The signal courses at Riley and Leavenworth at least partially compensated for the loss of the separate signal school.

In the aftermath of the Allison hearings, Hazen established a Division of Military Signaling within the Signal Office in June 1885 and placed it under an officer whose duties included the care and improvement of the field telegraph train and other signal apparatus, the preparation of a signal manual, and the supervision of the theoretical and practical instruction of signal officers and enlisted men. The new division also collected information from American and foreign sources relating to signaling.

After leading the world during the Civil War, the United States Army Signal Corps had fallen behind its European counterparts. The Swedish government, for example, had developed a smaller and lighter field telegraph train, while the U.S. Signal Corps' equipment had improved little since the immediate postwar period.[114] Instruction in its use had continued at Fort Myer until 1883 when the Corps' budget lacked an appropriation for the necessary horses. While signal soldiers still learned telegraphy, the train had been rendered immobile.[115] After six years of neglect, the Signal Corps in 1889 had only enough equipment to outfit two trains. At Washington Barracks, D.C. (now Fort Lesley J. McNair), where some of the equipment was stored, the Potomac River rose so high that lances floated from the truck. First Lieutenant Richard E. Thompson, in charge of the Division of Military Signaling, wrote that "We have the shadow rather than the substance of a field equipment."[116] Because the Corps lacked the money for new equipment, it made some efforts to adopt the Army wagon or ambulance for use in carrying the telegraph apparatus. In 1891 Chief Signal Officer Greely sent a field train to Fort Riley to be used in the signal training being offered there.[117]

In the area of visual signals the Signal Corps had made a few improvements since the Civil War. The signal flags remained unchanged, but the Corps had tried to improve the torch using such new materials as asbestos and brickwood, a mixture of clay and sawdust. Flash lanterns began to replace torches, however, as they gave off a much brighter light that could be seen at greater distances. To facilitate the reading of visual signals, the Corps worked on the development of a binocular telescope that combined the extensive field of the marine glass with the power of the telescope. Although patented in 1880, incandescent lamps had not yet been perfected sufficiently for signaling purposes.[118]

In the Southwest, where the Army spent most of the post–Civil War years engaged in Indian campaigns, the hot, dry climate provided ideal conditions for visual signaling. The heliograph, a device that communicated by using a mirror to direct the sun's rays, was perfectly suited for this environment and had a much greater range than signal flags. Such an instrument had been used successfully by the British in India, and the Signal Corps apparently began studying its possibilities about 1873. Signal soldiers had practiced using the heliograph at Fort Whipple, Virginia, in 1877 and flashed messages a distance of thirty miles.[119] Nearly ten years passed, however, before the Army used the heliograph in a major campaign. In 1886 Brig. Gen. Nelson A. Miles began operations against the Apaches under Geronimo in the Southwest. Miles knew of the British experiences with the heliograph and requested that Hazen send a detachment of men skilled in its use.[120] The chief signal officer sent a detachment of eleven men equipped with 34 heliographs, 10 telescopes, 30 marine glasses, and an aneroid barometer. They set up a heliograph system in Arizona and New Mexico that Miles praised as "the most interesting and valuable . . . that has ever been estab-

U.S. Signal Service heliograph. Clockwise from top, *heliograph with two mirrors, sun in rear; screen mounted on tripod; heliograph with one mirror and sighting rod, sun in front.*

lished."[121] While perhaps not the decisive factor in bringing about Geronimo's surrender, as Miles claims in his memoirs, the heliograph provided the general with an effective communications network.[122]

Field experience indicated that the heliograph needed improvement, and Greely organized a special board to study the problem. The board ordered the construction of a standard heliograph that was easily portable yet strong and with interchangeable parts. The new device, which the Army adopted in 1888, used a square rather than a circular mirror because it provided "about one-fourth more reflecting surface for practically the same packing space."[123] In May 1890 the Army conducted an extensive practice of heliograph signaling in the Department of Arizona. During a two-week period soldiers established two thousand miles of lines and transmitted nearly four thousand messages. One of the officers participating in this test was 2d Lt. John J. Pershing of the 6th Cavalry. Signalmen relayed messages at distances up to 125 miles, a record for that time.[124] Four years later, however, a signal detachment commanded by Capt. William A. Glassford broke this record by flashing a message 183 miles between Mount Ellen, Utah, and Mount Uncompahgre, Colorado.

Again taking a lead from European armies, the Signal Corps investigated the use of pigeons for communicating. These winged messengers had become popular in Europe after their successful employment during the siege of Paris in 1870. In 1878 the Army unsuccessfully experimented with pigeons when Myer sent some to General Miles in Dakota Territory. In many cases hawks attacked the birds before they could return to their lofts. Four years later 1st Lt. William Birkhimer made a detailed report on pigeons in which he concluded that the birds were unreliable and the Army need not develop a comprehensive plan for their use.[125] The Signal Corps did, however, open a pigeon station at Key West, Florida, in 1888, but discontinued the experiment after four years. Although the Army found no need for the birds (it transferred them to the Naval Academy), they proved reliable for carrying messages across long stretches of water, flying from Key West to Havana, Cuba, and thus could be used to communicate between ships and their home stations. The Army did not find a use for pigeons until World War I.[126]

Alongside these relatively simple forms of communication came the inventions of the burgeoning technological age. Chief among these was the telephone, patented in 1876. The Signal Corps began using the telephone soon after its commercial introduction in 1877, placing calls over the ten miles of telegraph line that ran between Fort Whipple and the Signal Office in Washington. Corpsmen practiced on a forty-mile-long line erected at Fort Whipple, and they were soon using telephones on many of the military telegraph lines. By 1892 one-half of all Army posts had been equipped with telephones.[127] Sgt. Adolf Eccard of the Signal Corps developed a portable field telephone that combined the Bell telephone, the Morse key, and a battery and that could be used as either a telephone or a telegraph. However, this device brought the Corps into conflict with the Bell Telephone Company over patent rights.[128] The high cost of the Eccard, $500 per instrument, proved too expensive for the Corps, and it continued to lease and purchase Bell instruments.

The Signal Corps' limited appropriations in the years after 1883 hampered its efforts to develop new equipment. In 1887 and 1888 Congress allotted only $3,000 annually for signal equipment and stores, less than one-third of the average appropriation for the years 1873 to 1883. The branch could not even meet the demand for existing supplies, and its stock was soon exhausted. In allotting items, Greely assigned priority to requests from posts west of the Mississippi due to the higher probability that they would be needed for field service there.[129] In sum, military signaling had suffered during the twenty years that the Army ran the weather service, and the Signal Corps would spend the next decade catching up with European developments.

A Change in the Weather

When President Benjamin Harrison called for the transfer of the weather service from the War Department in his first annual message in December 1889, he sounded the death knell for the Signal Corps' weather service.[130] Congress subsequently enacted legislation in 1890 reassigning the weather duties to the Department of Agriculture, and the change became effective on 1 July 1891.

The transition had a significant impact upon the Signal Corps' personnel. Congress set the Corps' strength at nine officers and fifty sergeants in addition to the chief signal officer. The law provided that the enlisted men who wished to remain on weather duty could be discharged from the Army and appointed to the Agriculture Department. Meanwhile, up to four officers could be assigned to duty with the new Weather Bureau. Among them were Maj. Henry Harrison Chase Dunwoody, who served as chief of the forecast division for several years, and then Lieutenant Glassford. The civilian workers were transferred as a group, and there was no break in their weather duties.[131] Professor Abbe, so long a prominent member of the Signal Corps' weather service, continued to work for the Agriculture Department until his retirement from government service in 1916. A joint board of officers, appointed by the president, divided the weather-related funds and property between the Signal Corps and the Weather Bureau. While the Signal Corps continued its traditional communication duties, it also retained responsibility for military meteorology, although that function did not yet have much significance. The Signal Corps would not again have a meteorological section until World War I.[132]

Bereft of its weather mission, the Signal Corps finally returned to its roots: the provision of military communications. While the Corps had strayed from its origins for two decades, its very real achievement of establishing the first national weather bureau should not be overlooked or underestimated. Despite the criticism the Signal Corps' weather service had received, the Agriculture Department retained much of what the Army had pioneered.[133] With the legislation of 1890 the Signal Corps could once more focus its attention on military signaling in its various forms. The timing was right because the dawn of the electrical age and the nation's emergence as a world power soon propelled the Signal Corps around the world and into a new era of communications.

Notes

[1]*ARSO*, 1865, in *ARSW*, 1865, vol. 2, pp. 999–1000. The report is reprinted in Scheips, ed., *Military Signal Communications*, vol. 1. The "Preliminary List of Officers and Enlisted Men Who Served on Signal Duty During the War of the Rebellion, 1861 to 1866" (Washington, D.C.: Signal Office, 1891) contains the names of 2,922 men. The annual reports of the chief signal officer were published each year as part of the annual report of the secretary of war. For the years 1866 to 1874, they appeared in volume 1 of the secretary's report. From 1875 to 1891, they were published as volume 4.

[2]*ARSO*, 1865, pp. 999–1002.

[3]The provisions of the act of 28 July 1866 are published in WDGO 56, 1 Aug 1866, sec. 22, p. 7.

[4]Scheips, "Myer," pp. 603–04, n. 63.

[5]Scheips, "Myer," pp. 590–92. Myer was still a major because the Senate had failed to confirm his appointment as colonel.

[6]Copies of the memorial and supplement are among the Myer Papers at MHI. See Scheips, "Myer," pp. 610–11.

[7]Fisher made this argument in a list of "Reasons why the Executive should protect Col. B. F. Fisher in place and reputation," an unsigned and undated draft in the Benjamin F. Fisher Papers at MHI.

[8]Ltr, Grant to Stanton, 30 Jul 1866, reel 21, vol. 47, Ulysses S. Grant Papers, Library of Congress, Washington, D.C. See also Scheips, "Myer," pp. 611–13.

[9]Scheips, "Myer," pp. 597–98 and p. 599, n. 57. The expiration of Fisher's appointment by constitutional limitation was announced in WDGO 71, 31 Aug 1866, p. 276.

[10]*ARSO*, 1867, pp. 614–15 and apps. A, B, and C.

[11]See Porter's letter to Myer of 15 Oct 1866 on roll 2 of Myer Papers microfilm, CMH, and the plan for the course at Appendix D, *ARSO*, 1867. See also Howeth, *Communications-Electronics in Navy*, p. 10.

[12]WDGO 92, 31 Oct 1867, also published as Appendix E to *ARSO*, 1867.

[13]WDGO 47, 18 Jul 1868; *ARSO*, 1867, p. 617.

[14]*ARSO*, 1868, pp. 780–81. See also Howgate's report therein, pp. 799–801, and that of Capt. S. C. Plummer, in charge of Fort Greble, pp. 803–04. The telegraphic rate of ten words per minute is given as the standard in [U.S. War Department, Office of the Chief Signal Officer], *Instructions for Acting Signal Officers, 1869* (n.p., 1869) and *ARSO*, 1878, Paper 1, "Course at Fort Whipple," p. 185. See also extract of Special Orders 40, Headquarters of the Army, Adjutant General's Office, 17 Feb 1869, assigning officers and men to the various commands, included as Appendix A to *ARSO*, 1869.

[15]*ARSO*, 1868, pp. 784, 799, and 805.

[16]*ARSO*, 1869, p. 191.

[17]U.S. Congress, House Committee on Military Affairs, *Army Organization*, 40th Cong., 3d sess., 1869, Rpt no. 33, pp. 3 and 127.

[18]See James Rodger Fleming, *Meteorology in America, 1800–1870* (Baltimore, Md.: Johns Hopkins University Press, 1990).

[19]Mary C. Gillett, *The Army Medical Department, 1775–1818*, Army Historical Series (Washington, D.C.: Center of Military History, United States Army, 1981), p. 154 and app. J; Edgar E. Hume, "The Foundations of American Meteorology by the United States Army Medical Department," *Bulletin of the History of Medicine* 8 (Feb 1940): 202; Lewis J. Darter, Jr., "Weather Service Activities of Federal Agencies Prior to 1891,"

introduction to *List of Climatological Records in the National Archives* (Washington, D.C.: National Archives, 1942), p. vii.

[20]Donald R. Whitnah, *A History of the United States Weather Bureau* (Urbana: University of Illinois Press, 1965), pp. 12–13; Darter, "Weather Service Activities," pp. x–xiv; Fleming, *Meteorology in America*, chs. 4–7.

[21]*Annual Report of the Smithsonian Institution*, 1865, p. 57.

[22]*Congressional Globe*, 41st Cong., 2d sess., 1869–1870, 42, pt. 1: 177. The quotation is taken from the resolution as printed in WDGO 29, 15 Mar 1870. Whitnah, *Weather Bureau*, pp. 17–19; Eric R. Miller, "New Light on the Beginnings of the Weather Bureau from the Papers of Increase A. Lapham," *Monthly Weather Review* 59 (Feb 1931): 67–68.

[23]As quoted in Miller, "New Light," p. 68.

[24]As quoted in ibid. Cleveland Abbe, a longtime member of the Weather Bureau, claims that Myer had submitted a plan for weather reporting to the secretary of war in 1869 but was turned down because he lacked legislative authority for such activity. See Cleveland Abbe, "The Meteorological Work of the U.S. Signal Service, 1870 to 1891," *Bulletin no. 11* (Washington, D.C.: Weather Bureau, 1894): 235, one of the *Bulletins of the Weather Bureau* in *Report of the International Meteorological Conference, Chicago, 1893* (U.S. Department of Agriculture); Darter, "Weather Service Activities," p. x.

[25]WDGO 29, 15 Mar 1870.

[26]See, for example, Gaines M. Foster, *The Demands of Humanity: Army Medical Disaster Relief*, Special Studies (Washington, D.C.: Center of Military History, United States Army, 1983).

[27]Legislation approved on 10 June 1872 contained the agricultural provisions. See extract thereof in WDGO 52, 24 Jun 1872.

[28]See *ARSO*, 1871, app., pp. 61–63; *ARSO*, 1872, p. 4; *ARSO*, 1873, pp. 234, 318, and 352. *ARSO*, 1877, p. 6 and Paper 22, p. 328, indicate that a year of service as an assistant was necessary. See also *ARSO*, 1881, p. 6.

[29]Beginning in 1870, many annual reports of the chief signal officer contain detailed instructions for the observer-sergeants.

[30]For a detailed discussion of the records kept at the observation stations, see Darter, "Weather Service Activities." The first federal legislation establishing standard time for the nation was not passed until 1918. See also Carlene Stephens, *Inventing Standard Time* (Washington, D.C.: Smithsonian Institution, 1983).

[31]*ARSO*, 1890, p. 271.

[32]Scheips, "Myer," pp. 625–26.

[33]The reports from the Chicago and Mount Washington stations are published in *ARSO*, 1872, pp. 17–20 and 47–48, respectively.

[34]On this case, see Joseph M. Hawes, "The Signal Corps and Its Weather Service, 1870–1890," *Military Affairs* 30 (Summer 1966): 71–72; opinion by Assistant Adjutant General Reverdy Johnson in *ARSO*, 1874, Paper 53, pp. 798f, upholding the commercial telegraph companies' obligation to transmit the Signal Corps' weather reports and the Army's right to construct telegraph lines of its own. Johnson had been commissioned by the attorney general to handle the disputes between the government and the commercial telegraph companies. See also *ARSO*, 1875, p. 107.

[35]A barometric reading of 18.74, for example, was replaced by the word "April." Rainfall of .94 inches was referred to as "Recess." For tables of the codes, see *ARSO*, 1877, Paper 23, pp. 337–55.

[36]For a history of the Pikes Peak station, see Phyllis Smith, *Weather Pioneers: The Signal Corps Station at Pikes Peak* (Athens: Ohio University Press, 1993). The Signal Corps also maintained a summer station for a time atop Mount Mitchell, North Carolina.

[37]*ARSO*, 1873, pp. 304–05. On the initiation of the railway bulletin service, see *ARSO*, 1879, p. 206. Along some lines weather symbols were displayed on railway cars. By 1888 this system had largely been replaced by the work of the state weather services. See *ARSO*, 1888, p. 15.

[38]Several reasons are given in the literature for Lapham's brief tenure with the Signal Corps. According to Cleveland Abbe, Lapham's poor health caused him to turn down a permanent position with the Corps. See Truman Abbe, *Professor Abbe and the Isobars: The Story of Cleveland Abbe, America's First Weatherman* (New York: Vantage Press, 1955), pp. 123–24, and Cleveland Abbe, "Meteorological Work of the Signal Service," p. 239. Both Whitnah, *Weather Bureau* (p. 22), and Scheips, "Myer" (p. 627), indicate that personal business kept him away from the job. Lapham's biographer in the *Dictionary of American Biography*, 10: 611–12, states that he was offered the leadership of the weather bureau upon its establishment within the War Department, but he refused the position because of his Quaker beliefs. Miller, in "New Light" (p. 70), cites a letter written to Lapham in 1872 by Capt. Henry Howgate informing him that a lack of funds necessitated the termination of his services as assistant to the chief signal officer.

[39]T. Abbe, *Isobars*, chs. 11 and 12.

[40]On his skepticism, see his letter to Lapham, quoted in T. Abbe, *Isobars*, p. 119, and Miller, "New Light," p. 68.

[41]*ARSO*, 1871, p. 9 and Paper 7 therein. See also *ARSO*, 1878, pp. 159–60 and Paper 45, pp. 662f. At stations on the lakes the white flag above the red was known as the "cautionary northwest signal." At night a white light above a red light served as the signal. *ARSO*, 1881, p. 47. Beginning in 1883 a white flag with a black center signified a cold wave warning. See *ARSO*, 1885 (in two parts), pt. 1, app. 54, pp. 509–15. The same flag also served as a frost warning. *ARSO*, 1890, app. 5, p. 69. Other flags were used to indicate weather conditions and their meanings are explained in *ARSO*, 1885, pt. 1, app. 2, p. 54, and *ARSO*, 1886, app. 3.

[42]Whitnah, *Weather Bureau*, p. 22, makes this assertion.

[43]WDGO 40, 21 Mar 1873. On the Life-Saving Service, see Dennis R. Means, "A Heavy Sea Running: The Formation of the U.S. Life-Saving Service, 1846–1878," *Prologue* 19 (Winter 1987): 222–43. Samuel I. Kimball, head of the Life-Saving Service, had recommended that the Signal Corps place observers at the life-saving stations (p. 229). Myer thanks Kimball for his cooperation in *ARSO*, 1873, p. 307.

[44]See *ARSO*, 1882 (in two parts), pt. 1, p. 33, and *ARSO*, 1884, app. 5, p. 87, that give the total as 618 miles. See also *ARSO*, 1885, pt. 1, app. 63, p. 547. In 1884 commercial lines replaced the leased lines to the Signal Office.

[45]The wreck occurred only two and one-half miles from the Nags Head life-saving station, also closed for the season. See report of the Kitty Hawk weather station in *ARSO*, 1878, pp. 47–48, and Myer's comments, pp. 173–75. See also David Stick, *Graveyard of the Atlantic* (Chapel Hill: University of North Carolina Press, 1952), pp. 73–85; Means, "Heavy Sea Running," p. 233.

[46]His account of this experience is contained in the entry for the Kitty Hawk station in *ARSO*, 1879, p. 55.

[47]*ARSO*, 1874, Paper 51, p. 796; *ARSO*, 1876, p. 118; *ARSO*, 1880, p. 220; *ARSO*, 1881, p. 34; *ARSO*, 1888, app. 8, p. 152; *ARSO*, 1891, p. 7. Some of the lines were actu-

ally underwater cables, such as those under San Francisco Harbor and between Wood's Hole and Nantucket, Massachusetts.

[48]L. Tuffly Ellis, "Lieutenant A. W. Greely's Report on the Installation of Military Telegraph Lines in Texas, 1875–1876," *Southwestern Historical Quarterly* 69 (July 1965), reprinted in Scheips, ed., *Military Signal Communications*, vol. 1, and ch. 17 in Greely's *Reminiscences of Adventure and Service* (New York: Charles Scribner's Sons, 1927). Greely was also responsible for building many of the seacoast lines. See *ARSO*, 1874, Paper 53, p. 979. Soldiers stationed at the various posts aided in much of the construction.

[49]Will C. Barnes, *Apaches and Longhorns: The Reminiscences of Will C. Barnes*, ed. by Frank C. Lockwood (Los Angeles: Ward Ritchie Press, 1941; facsimile edition, Tucson: University of Arizona Press, 1982), p. 9.

[50]Barnes, *Apaches and Longhorns*, ch. 6; Robert M. Utley, *Frontier Regulars: The United States Army and the Indian, 1866–1891* (New York: Macmillan Publishing Company, Inc., 1974), pp. 371f; Joseph C. Porter, *Paper Medicine Man: John Gregory Bourke and His American West* (Norman: University of Oklahoma Press, 1986), pp. 144–45.

[51]*ARSO*, 1874, pp. 506–07 and Papers 20–22, pp. 704–05. See also Papers 27a and b in *ARSO*, 1875, p. 362. In 1887 the surgeon general of the Army turned over to the Corps its original meteorological records dating to 1819. The Navy began supplying maritime observations in 1876. *ARSO*, 1877, p. 118; *ARSO*, 1888, app. 14, p. 184.

[52]Robert V. Bruce, *1877: Year of Violence* (Chicago: Quadrangle Books, 1970), p. 213; Jerry M. Cooper, *The Army and Civil Disorder: Federal Military Intervention in Labor Disputes, 1877–1890* (Westport, Conn.: Greenwood Press, 1980), p. 64. The chief signal officer only alludes to this aspect of the observers' duties in *ARSO*, 1877, p. 5. President Hayes and Myer were also personal friends. See Scheips, "Myer," p. 641.

[53]The original telegrams are among the collections of the Rutherford B. Hayes Memorial Library, Fremont, Ohio. References herein are to typescripts thereof compiled into a "Strike File": Zebree [*sic*] to chief signal officer, 25 Jul 1877, 11:45 a.m.; Myer to the president and the secretary of war, telegram no. 39, 26 Jul 1877, 9:47 p.m.; Myer to the president, telegram no. 11, 29 Jul 1877; Myer to the president, 13 Aug 1877.

[54]The Russians had been taking weather observations at Sitka since 1828. Whitnah, *Weather Bureau*, p. 37. On Nelson's ethnographic work, see Michael Olmert, "Spirit World of the Bering Sea Eskimos," *Smithsonian* 13 (May 1982): 50–59. See also Nelson's preliminary reports in *ARSO*, 1881, Appendix 38, and *ARSO*, 1882, pt. 1, pp. 79–86.

[55]According to Whitnah, Myer was one of the major advocates of this idea. See *Weather Bureau*, p. 36, n. 48. The observations were taken at 0735 and later at 0700 Washington time.

[56]The first bulletin is included as Paper 40 in *ARSO*, 1875, and summarizes data collected on 11 April 1875. The Signal Office discontinued the daily publication of the international bulletin and the accompanying map in July 1885. These included observations made through 30 June 1884. Monthly summaries continued to be published until 1889. Publication of the maps resumed for a limited time in 1886–1887. See *ARSO*, 1885, pt. 1, pp. 29–30 and app. 65 and Cleveland Abbe, "Meteorological Work of the Signal Service," pp. 258–59. See also the table in *ARSO*, 1891, p. 18, and Appendix 17 to that report, which is Greely's summary of "International Pressure and Storm Charts," pp. 747f. Darter, "Weather Service Activities," gives a slightly different listing on p. xxiv.

[57]*ARSO*, 1878, Paper 25, p. 429; *ARSO*, 1880, p. 171.

[58]*ARSO*, 1874, p. 424; *ARSO*, 1875, Paper 6, p. 116.

[59]WDGO 58, 18 Jun 1874.

[60]For a discussion of the Corps' status, see *ARSO*, 1882, pt. 1, Appendix 74, pp. 927–50. Extracts of the legislation affecting the Corps' strength are published in WDGO 70, 26 Jul 1876; WDGO 41, 25 Jun 1878; and WDGO 57, 2 Jul 1880. See also Table A, "Organization of the Regular Army of the United States," in vol. 1 of the annual reports of the secretary of war, which includes personnel totals for the Signal Corps. Strength figures are also given in *ARSO*, 1879, p. 6 and *ARSO*, 1880, p. 6.

[61]Congress appropriated $375,000 for the observation and report of storms for the fiscal year ending 30 June 1881. See WDGO 57, 2 Jul 1880, and *ARSO*, 1880, pp. 166 and 175. The Corps classified the regular stations as first, second, or third order. In the very beginning, the regular stations were those that reported their observations three times daily by telegraph. The definitions of the categories changed over time, however, and a first order station came to be defined as one using self-recording instruments. Until 1888 only the Washington office fit this description. By 1890 there were twenty-six such stations. Thirteen of these were among the original twenty-four stations opened in 1870. Seven other original stations remained in operation as second order stations. Other than the use of self-registering equipment, little difference existed between first and second order stations in terms of the service provided, and both were staffed with full-time personnel. Third order stations used few, if any, recording instruments and usually made just one visual observation per day. Some stations made sunset observations only. Other categories included display stations, special river stations, and repair stations along the military telegraph and seacoast telegraph lines. Stations of all types in 1880 totaled 344. For a breakdown of the types of stations from 1870 to 1888, see *ARSO*, 1888, Appendix 10, p. 171. See also *ARSO*, 1890, p. 18. For a list of stations see, *ARSO*, 1891, p. 299. For additional background, see *ARSO*, 1891, p. 344.

[62]WDGO 12, 4 Feb 1881.

[63]Myer could perhaps also be called the Willard Scott of his day. As his son Truman relates, Cleveland Abbe was also referred to by the nickname "Old Probabilities." See T. Abbe, *Isobars*, p. 125.

[64]Scheips, "Myer," pp. 643–45. Another post–Civil War organization, the United States Veteran Signal Corps Association, is a forebear of the present Armed Forces Communications and Electronics Association.

[65]For biographical details, see *Dictionary of American Biography*, s.v. "Hazen, William Babcock," 8: 478–79 and George W. Cullum, *Biographical Register*, 2: 632–35. Hazen was West Point graduate number 1704. Hazen wrote of his Civil War experiences in *A Narrative of Military Service* (1885: reprint, Huntington, W.V.: Blue Acorn Press, 1993). For a study of his early post–Civil War career, see Marvin E. Kroeker, *Great Plains Command: William B. Hazen in the Frontier West* (Norman: University of Oklahoma Press, 1976). See also Paul J. Scheips, "William Babcock Hazen," *Cosmos Club Bulletin* 38 (Oct 1985): 4–7.

[66]Edward M. Coffman, "The Long Shadow of *The Soldier and the State*," *Journal of Military History* 55 (Jan 1991): 69–82. Coffman compares Hazen's little-known work with Emory Upton's *The Armies of Asia and Europe*, published six years later.

[67]*ARSO*, 1881, p. 11; A. Hunter Dupree, *Science in the Federal Government* (Cambridge, Mass.: Belknap Press of the Harvard University Press, 1957; Baltimore, Md.: Johns Hopkins University Press, 1986), p. 189; Robert V. Bruce, *The Launching of Modern American Science, 1846–1876* (New York: Alfred A. Knopf, 1987), p. 319.

[68]*ARSO*, 1881, pp. 61–62. Although the Signal Office had included a study room for several years, its work apparently consisted more of compiling statistical data than preparing original reports. Abbe's assistants were referred to as professors, junior professors, or assistant professors. Langley later became secretary of the Smithsonian Institution and was an early aviation pioneer (see ch. 4).

[69]*ARSO*, 1881, pp. 61–62 and 70–71. The Corps published both series until 1886. Ferrel's textbook is printed as part 2 of the 1885 annual report. See Abbe's comments in *ARSO*, 1883, Appendix 69, p. 665.

[70]*ARSO*, 1882, pt. 1, pp. 75–76 and app. 67, pp. 874–80. For details of King's aeronautical career, see Crouch, *The Eagle Aloft*, pp. 451–63.

[71]*ARSO*, 1884, app. 4, p. 66.

[72]*ARSO*, 1882, pt. 1, pp. 4–5.

[73]*ARSO*, 1883, app. 69, pp. 663 and 665. In January 1886 special stations to observe atmospheric electricity were set up at Yale College, Cornell University, Ohio State University, and the Massachusetts Institute of Technology (to replace that at Harvard). A station was already in operation at Johns Hopkins (*ARSO*, 1886, app. 22, p. 219). McAdie published a number of articles relating to atmospheric electricity and coauthored one with McRae that appeared in the *Periodical of the American Academy of Science*. A list of publications by Corps members appears in *ARSO*, 1891, pp. 406–07. McAdie later became director of the Blue Hill Meteorological Observatory near Boston. During World War I he assisted in the organization of the Navy's weather service. See Charles C. Bates and John F. Fuller, *America's Weather Warriors 1814–1985* (College Station: Texas A&M Press, 1986), pp. 24–25.

[74]Darter, "Weather Service Activities," p. xxvii, reports that all states had such services by 1892. See *ARSO*, 1884, app. 8 and *ARSO*, 1889 (in two parts), pt. 1, app. 5, p. 101. Whitnah discusses earlier attempts at establishing state weather services in *Weather Bureau*, pp. 11–12.

[75]*ARSO*, 1885, pt. 1, app. 3; *ARSO*, 1890, app. 22, pp. 681–82.

[76]*ARSO*, 1886, p. 25 and app. 15, p. 199; *ARSO*, 1889, pt. 1, pp. 103 and 113–14.

[77]Howgate eventually married his mistress, Nettie Burrill, following his wife's death. For an entertaining account of the scandal, see George Walton, "The Fugitive Captain," *Washington Post Potomac* [magazine], 16 Feb 1969. On Hazen's relationship with Garfield, see Scheips, "Hazen," pp. 4–7. Edward M. Coffman in *The Old Army* (New York: Oxford University Press, 1986), p. 267, mentions Hazen's efforts on Garfield's behalf when he ran for president in 1880. Whitnah also recounts the Howgate scandal in *Weather Bureau*, pp. 46–48.

[78]The hiring of an examiner is reported in *ARSO*, 1882, pt. 1, p. 9.

[79]A list of Greely's awards is included in *Dictionary of American Biography*, s.v. "Greely, Adolphus Washington," 21: 352–55. For accounts of the expedition, see Greely's *Three Years of Arctic Service*, 2 vols. (New York: Charles Scribner's Sons, 1886); A. L. Todd, *Abandoned: The Story of the Greely Arctic Expedition, 1881–1884* (New York: McGraw-Hill Book Co., Inc., 1961); (Todd discovered Greely's papers and used them in the preparation of his manuscript. They now reside in the Library of Congress.) Theodore Powell, *The Long Rescue* (Garden City, N.Y.: Doubleday and Co., 1960); Pierre Berton, *The Arctic Grail: The Quest for the North West Passage and the North Pole, 1818–1909* (New York: Viking, 1988), ch. 11. On the ill-fated Garlington rescue attempt, see Lawrence J. Fischer, "Horse Soldiers in the Arctic: The Garlington Expedition of 1883," *American Neptune* 36 (Apr 1976): 108–24. Fischer counters the

negative portrait of Garlington presented by Todd and Powell. Instead, he places most of
the blame for Garlington's failure on Hazen. See also Charles R. Shrader's article on
Greely in Roger J. Spiller, ed., *Dictionary of American Military Biography*, 3 vols.
(Westport, Conn.: Greenwood Press, 1984), 1: 403–08. As a result of the two Arctic
expeditions, Hazen has a bay in Alaska and a strait and a lake in Canada named for him.

[80]*ARSW*, 1884, pp. 22–26. The censure incident is discussed in the Hazen article in
the *Dictionary of American Biography*. See also Todd, *Abandoned*, pp. 306–07.

[81]The correspondence between Hazen and Lincoln is reproduced in Bernard C. Nalty
and Morris J. MacGregor, eds., *Blacks in the Military: Essential Documents*
(Wilmington, Del.: Scholarly Resources, Inc., 1981), pp. 54–58. Greene's case is also
discussed in Jack D. Foner, *The United States Soldier Between Two Wars: Army Life and
Reforms, 1865–1898* (New York: Humanities Press, 1970), p. 141; and Whitnah, *Weather
Bureau*, p. 51.

[82]The amount appropriated for fiscal year 1884 equaled $1,028,241.81. *ARSO*, 1884,
pp. 10 and 58.

[83]*ARSW*, 1884, p. 22.

[84]For Hazen's comments regarding the effects of the budget cuts, see *ARSO*, 1883,
pp. 3–5. See page 17 for a list of the actions taken to save money. A ten-year list of forecasting percentages appears in *ARSO*, 1883, p. 6. According to the table, the best percentage up to that time had been 88.3 in 1876.

[85]*ARSO*, 1883, pp. 12–13 and app. 60; see act of 3 Mar 1883 published in WDGO 17,
20 Mar 1883. Because Hazen complained to the secretary of war about the lack of funds,
the secretary issued WDGO 35 on 23 May 1883 authorizing temporary details to be made
when necessary "to prevent interruption of the public business."

[86]Comprising three members each from the House and Senate, its full title was the
Joint Commission To Consider the Present Organization of the Signal Service,
Geological Survey, Coast and Geodetic Survey, and the Hydrographic Office of the Navy
Department, with a View To Secure Greater Efficiency and Economy of Administration
of the Public Service in said Bureaus. For a more detailed discussion of the commission
and its impact, see Dupree, *Science in Federal Government*, chs. 9 and 11. Dupree char-
acterizes the commission's probe as "one of the fullest congressional investigations of the
nineteenth century" (p. 190). See also Whitnah, *Weather Bureau*, pp. 50–58.

[87]Portions of his testimony are published in the *Army and Navy Journal*, issues of 7
and 14 February 1874.

[88]Dupree, *Science in Federal Government*, p. 191; Paul Andrew Hutton, *Phil
Sheridan and His Army* (Lincoln: University of Nebraska Press, 1985), pp. 43–44.

[89]Dupree, *Science in Federal Government*, p. 192, states that three members favored
transfer to a civilian bureau within the War Department and three wanted no change. He
also mentions (p. 191) that Sheridan had recommended that Fort Myer be closed. *ARSO*,
1886, p. 6, announces the closing of Fort Myer through the action of the Joint
Commission of Congress. See also Hawes, "The Signal Corps and Its Weather Service,"
pp. 74–75.

[90]The Allison Commission's findings are published as House Report 2740, 49th
Cong., 1st sess., 1886. For the recommendations regarding Fort Myer and the study
room, see page 18. For a discussion of the commission's recommendations regarding the
Signal Corps, see Dupree, *Science in Federal Government*, p. 192; Bates and Fuller,
Weather Warriors, p. 13; Cleveland Abbe, "Meteorological Work of the Signal Service,"
p. 242; Darter, "Federal Weather Activities," pp. xxxii–xxxiii.

[91] *ARSO*, 1886, app. 14, pp. 191–92, and Whitnah, *Weather Bureau*, p. 56.

[92] His widow, Mildred McLean Hazen, the daughter of wealthy newspaperman Washington McLean, later married Admiral George Dewey of Manila Bay fame.

[93] Greely was shot in the face, and this injury may account for the splendid beard that he wore for the remainder of his life. He details his Civil War service in his memoirs, *Reminiscences of Adventure and Service.*

[94] *ARSO*, 1887 (in two parts), pt. l, pp. 16, 25–27; *ARSO*, 1888, p. 10. The number of regular stations reached its peak in 1881 at 219. In 1888 the total of all types of stations equaled 509. See *ARSO*, 1888, app. 10, p. 171. By 1890 there were 1,924 volunteers, a gain of 1,577 over the decade. *ARSO*, 1890, p. 261. In his 1891 annual report, Greely boasted of his four years of "earnest, well-directed effort" to produce such astonishing results (p. 24).

[95] *ARSO*, 1887, pt. 1, p. 30; *ARSO*, 1890, app. 7, p. 208.

[96] *ARSO*, 1887, pt. 1, pp. 11–15. Due to the difficulties, the prediction period returned to twenty-four hours. Furthermore, in 1888 the number of daily forecasts was reduced from three to two. *ARSO*, 1888, p. 9, and *ARSO*, 1889, pt. 1, app. 3, p. 59.

[97] Many of the larger newspapers provided local forecasts based on the information received from the Signal Corps. See *ARSO*, 1889, pt. 1, pp. 9 and 27, as well as Appendix 9, "Report of the Officer in Charge of the Stations Division," p. 133.

[98] *ARSO*, 1888, app. 10, pp. 171–72.

[99] *ARSO*, 1887, pt. 1, p. 19; *ARSO*, 1889, pt. 1, p. 129; *ARSO*, 1890, p. 15.

[100] *ARSO*, 1887, pt. 1, p. 39.

[101] *ARSO*, 1889, pt. 1, pp. 39–40; *ARSO*, 1890, app. 7, p. 211 and the report of Sgt. Park Morrill, in charge of the exhibit, at app. 23, pp. 683f. A fourth grand prize was awarded to the War Department for the Lady Franklin Bay Expedition.

[102] In 1887 Greely had recommended that the 125 enlisted men occupying clerical positions in the Washington office be converted to civilian status. This action would save the government the transportation expenses of moving soldiers from other posts to Washington and provide a more stable clerical force. *ARSO*, 1887, pt. 1, pp. 49–50; *ARSO*, 1889, pt. 1, p. 28. On the personnel reductions, see WDGO 59, 12 Aug 1886, and WDGO 79, 12 Oct 1888.

[103] In 1887 he recommended a force consisting of 14 officers (1 chief signal officer, 1 major, 6 captains, 6 first lieutenants) and 225 enlisted men (25 first class observers, 100 second class observers, 50 corporals, and 50 privates). In his plan, the office would also include two professors and two junior professors. In 1888 he altered his recommendation by reducing the officers to twelve, eliminating a captain and a first lieutenant. He increased the office staff by adding a third assistant professor. *ARSO*, 1888, pp. 38–39. In 1889 he added a major to his projected officer corps and further reduced the enlisted strength to 50 first sergeants, 50 sergeants, 50 corporals, and 50 privates—for a total of 200. See *ARSO*, 1889, pt. 1, p. 41.

[104] The authorizations for the Signal Corps' strength are provided in the following orders: WDGO 17, 20 Mar 1883; WDGO 70, 15 Jul 1884; WDGO 32, 20 Mar 1885; WDGO 59, 12 Aug 1886; WDGO 22, 15 Mar 1887; WDGO 79, 12 Oct 1888; WDGO 32, 29 Mar 1889.

[105] *ARSW*, 1887, vol. 1, p. 33.

[106] Whitnah, *Weather Bureau*, p. 58, and Darter, "Weather Service Activities," pp. xxxiii–xxxiv.

[107] Darter, "Weather Service Activities," pp. xxxiv–xxxv.

[108]WDGO 109, 12 Oct 1885.

[109]*ARSO*, 1888, p. 7.

[110]Army Regulations, 1889, secs. 1761 and 1762 (hereafter cited as AR). See also *ARSO*, 1889, pt. 1, app. 1, p. 52.

[111]*ARSO*, 1891, app. 1, p. 37.

[112]Timothy K. Nenninger, *The Leavenworth Schools and the Old Army* (Westport, Conn.: Greenwood Press, 1978): pp. 29–30. See also William H. Carter, "The Infantry and Cavalry School," *Journal of the Military Service Institution of the United States* (hereafter cited as *JMSI*) 15 (Jul 1894): 752.

[113]The report of the school commandant is published *ARSW*, 1892, vol. 1, pp. 137–42. See also *ARSO*, 1892, appendix C, p. 621, in *ARSW*, 1892, vol. 1.

[114]*ARSO*, 1885, pt. 1, pp. 3–4; *ARSO*, 1887, pt. 1, app. 1.

[115]*ARSO*, 1883, p. 1.

[116]*ARSO*, 1889, pt. 1, app. 1, p. 45.

[117]*ARSO*, 1891, app. 1, p. 42.

[118]*ARSO*, 1887, pt. 1, pp. 5–6 and app. 1, p. 59. An electric signal lamp did not become standard equipment until World War I.

[119]Scheips, "Myer," p. 618; *ARSO*, 1877, p. 3.

[120]Miles claims in his *Personal Recollections and Observations* (Chicago: Werner and Co., 1896), p. 481, that he borrowed six heliographs from Chief Signal Officer Myer in 1878 to set up a line between Forts Keogh and Custer, Montana, but Myer never mentions this transaction in his annual reports. Miles also states (p. 402) that in the early 1880s he established heliographic communication between Vancouver Barracks, Washington, and Mount Hood, Oregon. See Roger E. Kelly, "Talking Mirrors at Fort Bowie: Military Heliograph Communication in the Southwest," manuscript prepared for the National Park Service, Chiricahua National Monument in January 1967, copy in author's files. Miles has no report in the *ARSW* for 1878 and he makes no mention of his use of the heliograph in his report the following year in *ARSW*, 1879, vol. 1, pp. 68–75.

[121]Quotation from Miles' report to the Assistant Adjutant General, Division of the Pacific, dated 18 Sep 1886, in *ARSW*, 1886, vol. 1, p. 175. See also *ARSO*, 1886, app. 1, p. 34; report of 2d Lt. A. M. Fuller, acting chief signal officer during the Miles campaign, in Paul J. Scheips, comp., The Military Heliograph and Its Use in Arizona and New Mexico [Washington, D.C.: Signal Corps Historical Division, 1954], copy in CMH library.

[122]Bruno Rolak in an essay, "The Heliograph in the Geronimo Campaign of 1886," in *Military History of the Spanish-American Southwest: A Seminar* (Fort Huachuca, Ariz., 1976), takes issue with Miles' claims for the heliograph and with those writers who accepted his statements. Rolak states that the heliograph did not play a crucial role in bringing about Geronimo's surrender, but it did provide an effective communications network over a vast territory of operations. This essay is a revised and expanded version of his article "General Miles' Mirrors: The Heliograph in the Geronimo Campaign of 1886," which appeared in *The Journal of Arizona History* 16 (Summer 1975): 145–60. According to another source, General Crook, rather than Miles, was the first to use heliographs during the Indian campaigns. See Tom Horn, *Life of Tom Horn, Government Scout and Interpreter . . . ; A Vindication* (Norman: University of Oklahoma Press, 1964), p. 128.

[123]R. E. Thompson, "Instructions for the Use of the Service Heliograph," p. 11, published in WDGO 99, 15 Nov 1888. See also comments in *ARSO*, 1888, app. 1, pp. 43–47.

[124]*ARSO*, 1890, pp. 4–5 and app. 1, pp. 40–41.

[125]*ARSO*, 1882, pt. 1, app. 75, pp. 951–55.

[126]*ARSO*, 1887, pt. 1, app. 1, p. 60; *ARSO*, 1888, p. 6 and app. 1; *ARSO*, 1891, app. 1, p. 42.

[127]*ARSO*, 1878, p. 3. According to Capt. Charles E. Kilbourne, in charge of the Division of Military Signaling, fifty-nine of the ninety-nine garrisoned posts were equipped with telephones. *ARSO*, 1892, app. C, p. 621.

[128]*ARSO*, 1883, p. 14.

[129]See table of appropriations in *ARSO*, 1886 and 1887, pp. 7 and 8, respectively; *ARSO*, 1888, p. 7.

[130]James D. Richardson, ed., *A Compilation of the Messages and Papers of the Presidents*, 20 vols. (New York: Bureau of National Literature, Inc., 1897–1914), 12: 5487. The previous calls for the transfer by Presidents Arthur and Cleveland are published in ibid., 10: 4637 and 11: 4934, respectively.

[131]Among the civilians transferred to the Agriculture Department was Alexander Ashley, who had worked as a clerk in the signal office since the Civil War. Scheips, "Myer," p. 404.

[132]WDGO 124, 17 Oct 1890; Whitnah, *Weather Bureau*, pp. 58–60.

[133]Whitnah, *Weather Bureau*, ch. 4.

CHAPTER III

From the Tropics to the Arctic

Having concentrated on its weather duties for the past twenty years, the Signal Corps had fallen behind in the field of military communications. Although the Army still used flags and torches to convey information, the rapidly developing technology of the late nineteenth century carried communications into the electrical age. The growing sense of professionalism both in society at large and within the Army, along with the concomitant specialization of functions, finally gave the Signal Corps the sense of mission and identification for which it had long been striving. The emergence of the United States as a great power in the wake of the War with Spain found the Signal Corps providing communications around the globe.

Organization, Training, and Operations, 1891–1898

The act transferring the weather service outlined the functions assigned to the Signal Corps in some detail. In addition to performing all military signal duties and retaining charge of the "books, papers, and devices connected therewith," the branch's responsibilities now included:

telegraph and telephone apparatus and the necessary meteorological instruments for use on target ranges, and other military uses; the construction, repair, and operation of military telegraph lines, and the duty of collecting and transmitting information for the Army by telegraph or otherwise, and all other duties usually pertaining to military signaling.[1]

Finally, the legislation specified that the Corps' operations would be "confined to strictly military matters." While Congress thus defined the Corps' mission more explicitly than in previous legislation, it still left a considerable area open to interpretation under the category of "other duties usually pertaining to military signaling." The legislation set the Signal Corps' strength at one brigadier general, one major, four captains, four first lieutenants, and fifty sergeants.

Upon the transfer of the weather duties, the Signal Corps turned its attention to the rather sorry state of its military signaling apparatus. During the twenty years that the branch had operated the weather service, it had lost its technical predominance in the signaling field. Chief Signal Officer Greely described the telegraph train as "antiquated," and the Corps' tiny appropriation of $22,500 (excluding personnel costs) for fiscal year 1892 barely covered regular expenses, let alone extensive research and development of new equipment.[2]

Despite the lack of research funds, the ingenuity of signal officers frequently led to the creation of new items. In 1892, for example, Capt. Charles E. Kilbourne developed the outpost cable cart. A wheeled vehicle weighing slightly over fifty pounds, it included an automatic spooling device that enabled a man to lay two miles of insulated double-conductor telephone cable. Because the existing portable field telephone kit contained only one-third mile of cable, Kilbourne's invention became valuable when longer lines were needed. The versatile cart could also be adapted to other uses—for instance, to carry wounded soldiers from the field. Two years later, Capt. James Allen developed a method of "duplexing" whereby both telegraphic and telephonic messages could be sent simultaneously over the same line, greatly increasing its efficiency.[3]

The United States Army had to catch up with its European counterparts, most of whom had by now successfully employed field telegraphy. The British Army, in particular, made extensive use of field lines while fighting a series of colonial wars in Africa.[4] After the long period of neglect, the telegraph train began to receive some attention. To provide more opportunities for practice, Greely sent trains to Fort Grant, Arizona; Fort Sam Houston, Texas; and the Presidio of San Francisco to supplement those at the Infantry and Cavalry School at Fort Leavenworth and the Cavalry and Light Artillery School at Fort Riley.

In May 1892, "for the first time since the war of the rebellion," the Signal Corps constructed a field telegraph line. At the request of the International Boundary Commission, the Corps ran a line from Separ, New Mexico, to the monument marking the international boundary between Mexico and the United States. Four Signal Corps sergeants, assisted by Company D, 24th Infantry, built the 35-mile line in twenty-five working hours, despite difficult working conditions. The Corps used the line to transmit chronometric signals between the monument and the observatory at El Paso, Texas, 100 miles to the east, for the purpose of determining the monument's exact longitude.[5]

A more urgent need for a field telegraph arose later that year when the possibility of border trouble loomed with Mexico. At the insistence of the Mexican government, the Army was called upon to stop a band of Mexican revolutionaries headed by Catarino Garza that based its operations in southern Texas. In response to rumors of the band's activities, Army units rushed back and forth across the countryside in pursuit of Garza. As might be expected, communications in this part of the country were poor. Because Congress did not appropriate sufficient funds to build permanent lines, the Corps drew on its available stock of field line around the country to build a temporary connection of nearly 75 miles between Fort McIntosh, Texas (at Laredo), and Lopena, Texas.[6]

The signal students from Fort Riley constructed the Texas line, only one of several occasions on which they demonstrated the signal skills they had learned. They provided communications for the dedication ceremonies of the World's Columbian Exposition held in Chicago in October 1892, and then they returned for more serious duty during the violent strike against the Pullman Sleeping Car Company in July 1894. Against the wishes of Illinois Governor John Peter

Atgeld, President Grover Cleveland called out troops to expedite movement of the mail and to protect interstate commerce. Maj. Gen. Nelson A. Miles, commander of the 2,000 federal troops sent to Chicago, requested the services of signal soldiers. Under Capt. James Allen, the signal troops (1st Lt. Joseph E. Maxfield and twelve sergeants) established a system of visual, telegraph, and telephone lines that connected Miles with his subordinate commanders. The signal troops also operated lines in conjunction with the commercial telephone and telegraph companies.[7]

In addition to its temporary field duties, the Signal Corps continued to operate permanent telegraph lines. According to the terms of the agreement to transfer the weather service, the Corps relinquished control over its 600 miles of seacoast telegraph lines, which thereupon became the property of the Department of Agriculture. The Corps retained, however, the lines that connected military posts, totaling just over 1,000 miles in length. Signal Corps sergeants operated the more important lines, such as those at departmental headquarters, and civilian operators worked the rest.[8]

The Corps discontinued its lines where no longer needed, but it also occasionally built new ones. When appropriations became available, the Corps completed, late in 1893, a permanent line between Fort Ringgold and Fort McIntosh in Texas to replace the temporary flying line. Maintenance proved difficult, however, due to a tendency of some of the local inhabitants to damage it "by pistol practice on the insulators and lariat practice on the poles." The chief signal officer reported in 1894 that the situation had improved "through the judicious influence of the more intelligent citizens."[9]

While coping with such circumstances, the Signal Corps constantly sought more efficient methods to perform line repair and maintenance. In keeping with the bicycle craze then rolling across the nation, the Corps found its own uses for the velocipede, as it was then called. Bicycles provided a faster and more economical means for making repairs. In the time it took to secure a horse and wagon, a linesman could jump on his bicycle, repair the line, and return to his station. The Corps also began adapting the bicycle to lay and take up wire. The replacement of wooden with iron poles also lessened the damage caused by deterioration or fire.[10]

In addition to the frontier land lines, the Signal Corps had retained control of the cables in San Francisco Harbor that linked its fortifications to the mainland. Unfortunately, the weather and ships' anchors conspired to render them inoperative much of the time. The Corps lacked the funds to make substantial repairs or to build new cables, and Greely's requests for additional funds went unanswered. Cable connections were also needed in New York and Boston, harbors that were vital to the nation's defense. These difficulties spurred the Signal Corps' development of wireless communication.[11]

The Signal Corps' involvement in coastal defense went beyond its control of electrical cables in major harbors. In addition to improvements in communication methods, the technological achievements of the post–Civil War era revolutionized coast artillery through the introduction of such items as steel guns, more powerful propellants, and high explosive shells. These advances rendered obsolete the existing coastal fortifications, which dated from the Civil War or earlier. Concern over the poor condition of the nation's coastal defenses led to the assembly of the Endicott Board by President Cleveland in 1885. The board conducted an extensive review of coastal fortifications and developed an ambitious improvement program. Congress responded by creating the Board of Ordnance and Fortification in 1888 to supervise projects relating to coast defense. The Signal Corps became involved by installing electrical communication systems for fire direction that made more precise fire control possible. Prior to this time aiming had been done by each individual gun. Now several sighting stations took optical bearings of the moving target and telephoned the information to a central plotting room where targeting positions were determined. The results were then communicated to the gun emplacements to direct their fire. The Signal Corps had only begun the installation program when war broke out with Spain in 1898, but work would resume in the postwar period.[12]

The Board of Ordnance and Fortification did not concern itself solely with matters of coast defense. While the enabling legislation gave it responsibility to "make all needful and proper purchases, investigations, experiments, and tests" of guns and other items of ordnance, it also could investigate "other implements and engines of war." This broad mandate made the board, in effect, a vehicle to support research and development. The board's grant of $25,000 to Samuel P. Langley, secretary of the Smithsonian Institution, in 1898 for building an aerodrome marked an important milestone in the evolution of heavier-than-air flight. Greely had urged the secretary of war to support Langley's efforts, and the board made the chief signal officer responsible for the expenditure of this money and a subsequent grant of equal amount. (Greely later called his work with Langley "the most important peace duty I ever performed.")[13]

Besides its association with Langley, the Signal Corps became directly involved in aeronautical matters as it expanded its communications mission. 1st Lt. Richard E. Thompson, in charge of the Division of Military Signaling, remarked in his report to Greely in 1889 that several European countries were using captive balloons for reconnaissance and had devised balloon trains.[14] The United States Army had not used captive balloons for observation since the work of Thaddeus Lowe and others during the Civil War. Greely, noting the success of the French with the use of captive balloons in maneuvers, included an estimate of $11,000 for the purchase and construction of a balloon train in his budget request to Congress for the fiscal year ending 30 June 1893.[15] The balloon would accompany each telegraph train and be used as a portable observation platform to gather information on topography, the disposition and movement of troops, and the like. Communication between the train and the balloon would be carried through the anchor rope, which contained insulated copper wires and doubled as a telephone cable. (During the Civil War Lowe had communicated with the ground via telegraph.)[16]

The Signal Corps' balloon at the World's Columbian Exposition in Chicago, 1893

When Congress refused to appropriate funds for balloons, Greely sought and received approval from the secretary of war and the commanding general of the Army to use part of the Signal Corps' regular appropriation for this purpose. The secretary of war assigned responsibility for obtaining a balloon to 1st Lt. William A. Glassford and released him from his duties with the Weather Bureau. In the summer of 1892 Glassford traveled to Paris, the center of European ballooning activity, and purchased a balloon from a French manufacturer for $1,970.[17] Christened the *General Myer* in honor of the first chief signal officer, the balloon became part of the Corps' exhibit at the World's Columbian Exposition in Chicago, where it made demonstration ascensions under the supervision of Thompson, now a captain. At a conference on aerial navigation held in conjunction with the fair, the delegates discussed the newly realized possibility of aerial warfare. When the fair closed in the fall of 1893, the chief signal officer sent the balloon to Fort Riley for use by the signal detachment stationed there.[18]

The Signal Corps' balloon was spherical in shape and made of goldbeater's skin, a polite term for a material made from the intestines of cattle. The balloon was inflated with hydrogen that was usually generated from sulfuric acid and iron filings, but this process was a slow one. For service in the field, steel cylinders of compressed hydrogen provided a portable means of gas supply. The *Myer* needed

135 such cylinders per inflation. The balloon train would carry these cylinders in 3 wagons, each loaded with 45 tubes weighing about 70 pounds each. A fourth wagon hauled the balloon and its additional accouterments. During the Civil War Lowe had used portable gas generators for his balloons, but the Signal Corps had difficulty in securing suitable equipment.[19]

The Corps' initial aeronautical attempts proved somewhat disappointing. During the Pullman strike in Chicago, the commander of the Department of Missouri, General Miles, requested the use of the *General Myer*, but improving conditions in the city made its deployment unnecessary.[20] When the signal detachment returned to Fort Riley from duty in Chicago, it found the *Myer* suffering from the lack of maintenance.[21] The men nevertheless resumed their aerial operations, but with limited results. Difficulty with gas generation posed a chronic problem, and erratic weather conditions, especially sudden high winds, aborted many of the ascension attempts. With the encouragement of Captain Glassford, now signal officer of the Department of the Colorado, the balloon detachment transferred in 1894 to Fort Logan, near Denver, Colorado, where conditions were better suited to aeronautics. However, when the *Myer* arrived from Fort Riley, it had deteriorated to the point that it burst while being inflated. Unable to afford a new French balloon, the Signal Corps agreed to purchase a homemade silken sphere from the aeronaut Ivy Baldwin, who had enlisted in the Corps to assist with ballooning. Meanwhile, a balloon shed, a gas generating plant, and a compressor were made ready. By 1897 the balloon detachment was able to resume its operations under somewhat improved conditions, but the Corps' limited funds kept experimentation to a minimum.[22]

Despite his initiatives in several fields, Greely did not meet with complete success in his efforts to obtain new duties for his branch. During 1892 he engaged in a bureaucratic struggle for control of the Military Information Division, which had been created within The Adjutant General's Office in 1885. Greely claimed that this function fell within the Signal Corps' auspices, as outlined in the legislation of 1890. The chief signal officer lost this fight, however, and the military information function remained with the adjutant general.[23]

In 1894 the Signal Corps did acquire another new responsibility: supervision of the War Department library. In addition to books, the library's holdings included the photographs taken by Mathew Brady during the Civil War. The War Department had purchased the pictures in 1875 when financial difficulties had forced Brady to sell them. In order to preserve this precious resource, Greely discontinued loaning out the negatives, a practice that had resulted in considerable loss and damage. He also instituted a cataloging project to correctly identify the remaining photographs.[24]

While Greely solidified the Signal Corps' position within the Regular Army, the state militia also provided a fertile ground for the growth of signaling in the closing decades of the nineteenth century. The labor unrest of the 1870s had stimulated a revival of interest in the organized militia or National Guard, and between 1881 and 1892 every state revised its military code to provide for an organized militia.[25] As early as the autumn of 1882 the state of Massachusetts detailed men to signal duty during the annual brigade encampment. A Regular Army signalman attended the encampment to aid in signal instruction and to take weather observations.[26]

In fact, signal units were organized in the militia before their counterparts existed in the Regular Army. New York became one of the first states to organize signal units in 1885. The 101st Signal Battalion of the New York Army National Guard traces its lineage to those early units. Another signal unit with a long history, the 133d Signal Battalion of the Illinois Army National Guard, was originally organized as a signal company in 1897. In that year nearly a dozen states reported having a signal corps within their militia structure. Several other states reported some form of signal organization at brigade, regimental, or battalion level. In the District of Columbia an engineer company performed signal duties.[27]

In 1892 Andrew Carnegie's attempt to break the iron and steel workers' union at his plant in Homestead, Pennsylvania, resulted in a violent strike, and Governor William Stone called up the militia to restore order. Although the Pennsylvania National Guard had no organized signal corps per se, several of its companies had signaling experience, and Company H, 12th Pennsylvania Infantry, provided communications during the riots. As Assistant Adjutant General Maj. William J. Volkmar reported:

Signal stations were soon established on both sides of the Monongahela River and communication constantly maintained between the separated forces by flag, heliograph, and lantern. It is true there is no regular signal corps in the guard, but various officers have voluntarily taken interest in signaling. . . . When dense smoke rising from the chimneys of the Carnegie works rendered signaling with flags impossible, the penetrating power of the heliograph flash enabled troops on opposite sides of the river to maintain almost constant communication by day. Lanterns were used by night and a telegraph line was built to division headquarters upon the hill, connecting with commercial lines.[28]

One of the projects delayed by the strike was work on the armored battleship *Maine*, then under construction at the Carnegie mills.[29]

While state forces made progress, the federal government hesitated. Throughout the 1890s Greely expressed concern about the Army's shortage of trained signalmen. As in the past, the system of instruction at the various posts had not proved very successful. The departments were not devoting enough time to signal training for the men to become skilled. Moreover, the line soldiers who were detailed for signal training would probably be needed by their own companies in the event of combat. Although the Corps had been able to provide sufficient numbers of signalmen during the Pullman riot in Chicago, Greely worried that, in the event of a more serious emergency, there would not be enough experienced men available. Therefore, in both 1894 and 1895 he recommended to the secretary of war that fifty privates be added to the branch. In 1896 he increased his request to four companies of fifty men each.[30] But his pleas for additional personnel went unanswered. In addition, two of the Corps' allotment of ten officers served on detached duty until the outbreak of the War with Spain. Maj. H. H. C.

Dunwoody (promoted to lieutenant colonel in 1897) remained with the Weather Bureau while Capt. George P. Scriven served as the military attaché to Rome.

Thus, as the United States moved toward its first conflict on foreign soil since the Mexican War, the Signal Corps had available only eight officers and fifty men to provide the necessary communications. A new national commitment would be required to create an army that was ready for war.

The War With Spain

The sinking of the *Maine* in Havana harbor in February 1898 precipitated the crisis. When Spain failed to respond to diplomatic pressure, Congress declared war in April of that year. While it proved to be a "little" war, lasting only a few months, the nation emerged from the conflict as a world power. The war also provided a glimpse of the impact that the technological innovations of the era would have on the nature of warfare. Before the fighting was over, the Signal Corps demonstrated that it could link the Army electrically with its commander in chief thousands of miles away.

In the beginning the United States Army and the Signal Corps in particular found themselves unprepared for war. Since the massive demobilization after the Civil War, Congress had limited the Army's strength to an average of 26,000 officers and men; in April 1898 it stood at slightly over 28,000.[31] The tiny Signal Corps of eight officers and fifty enlisted men comprised a minuscule percentage of this total. Moreover, the Corps counted just $800 in its war chest. Greely had to obtain additional money from Congress, amounting to $609,000 through December 1898.[32]

To provide the needed manpower for wartime operations, Congress authorized the formation of a Volunteer Signal Corps which, as in the Civil War, was authorized only "for service during the existing war." Congress set its strength at 1 colonel, 1 lieutenant colonel, 1 major as disbursing officer, and other officers as required, not to exceed 1 major for each army corps. Each division was allotted 2 captains, 2 first lieutenants, and 2 second lieutenants, as well as an enlisted force of 15 sergeants, 10 corporals, and 30 privates. Significantly, the legislation specified that two-thirds of the officers below the rank of major and the same proportion of enlisted men be skilled electricians or telegraph operators.[33]

The regular signal establishment provided the nucleus around which the wartime corps was formed. Dunwoody, relieved from his weather duties, became the colonel of the Volunteer Signal Corps, and James Allen received the lieutenant colonelcy.[34] The remaining junior officers became field officers in the volunteer organization. Most of the enlisted force also joined the volunteers. To free signal soldiers for field service, civilians replaced the signal sergeants on duty with the military telegraph lines. To quickly obtain skilled men to fill its expanded ranks, the Signal Corps recruited men from private business, particularly the electrical and telegraph industries. The signal units in the National Guard also provided a significant source of experienced personnel as well as a supply of much-needed equipment.[35] Upon enlistment, these men reported to Washington Barracks, D.C., for training in signal techniques and military drill. There they were organized into companies of approximately four officers and fifty-five men each. Despite the wording of the legislation setting up the volunteer corps, the companies were not assigned to divisions, but were consolidated at corps headquarters (generally three to a corps) for distribution as the commanding general saw fit.[36] Due to the short duration of the conflict, most of these companies did not serve overseas but instead performed communication duties at the various mobilization camps.

Upon the declaration of war on 25 April, President William McKinley ordered Chief Signal Officer Greely to take possession of the nation's telegraph system, both cable and land lines. The Signal Corps particularly exercised its jurisdiction over those lines with termini in New York City, Key West, and Tampa. The commercial companies, including those owned by foreign firms, censored themselves under the supervision of a signal officer. The censors prohibited the transmission of information regarding military movements and of any messages between Spain and its colonies except for personal and commercial messages in plain text that were deemed not to contain sensitive information. The Corps also disallowed messages in cipher to foreign nations except those between the diplomatic and consular representatives of neutral governments.[37]

Through its perusal of telegraphic traffic the Signal Corps derived much valuable information. One of the most critical items concerned the arrival in Santiago harbor on 19 May of a Spanish squadron under Admiral Pascual Cervera. Americans feared an attack on the East Coast by Cervera's ships. The Navy had last sighted the squadron on 13 May west of Martinique, and three days later the American consul at Curaçao reported Cervera's arrival there. Then Cervera disappeared from sight once more, his destination unknown. On the morning of the 19th, James Allen, who was monitoring telegraphic traffic at Key West, received news of the squadron's entrance into Santiago from a special agent in the Havana telegraph office. Allen, then a captain, immediately sent the news on to Greely, who relayed it in person to McKinley. The Navy Department, while unable to confirm Cervera's arrival for another ten days, took the Signal Corps' report seriously and initiated action to close the port of Santiago.[38]

Shortly before the declaration of war, the Navy Department had dispatched a squadron under Admiral William T. Sampson to blockade the Cuban coast. On 19 May, the same day the Signal Corps received its report of Cervera's arrival in Santiago, a squadron commanded by Commodore Winfield Scott Schley (Greely's Arctic rescuer) left for Cienfuegos, on the southern coast of Cuba, thought to be Cervera's likely destination. Even after receiving orders from Sampson on 23 May indicating that Cervera was probably at Santiago and directing him to proceed to that port, Schley remained for several days at Cienfuegos in the mistaken belief that Cervera was anchored there. Meanwhile, Sampson's squadron moved to intercept Cervera should he attempt to enter Havana. Schley finally arrived off Santiago on 26 May, but left almost immediately for Key West without reconnoitering the harbor. After more delay and a profusion of orders from Sampson and Secretary of the Navy John D. Long, Schley returned to Santiago on 28 May to blockade the port. The following day one of his ships sighted a Spanish man-of-war near the harbor entrance, putting the speculation about Cervera's location to an end at last. With this confirmation of Allen's report, the Navy Department requested that the Army send troops to Santiago to help destroy the Spanish squadron. The War Department, which had previously focused its attention on Havana, now hastily planned a campaign against Santiago.[39]

Among the Signal Corps' first operations was the outfitting of an expedition to cut the underwater telegraph cables that connected Cuba with Spain and to establish cable communication between American forces arriving in Cuba and the United States. The Corps, however, had no ships in its inventory, and the Navy had purchased all the submarine cable available in the United States. With the help of officials of the Western Union and Mexican Telegraph companies, Greely chartered the Norwegian ship *Adria*, outfitted it, and secured a small amount of cable. The Mexican Telegraph Company provided the necessary cable gear. When ready, the *Adria* sailed from New York to Key West where it came under the command of Allen, by now a lieutenant colonel. A major problem arose, however, when the captain and crew of the private vessel balked at the hazardous nature of the mission. Eventually they agreed to sail, but the experienced cable handlers hired for the job refused. To replace these men, Allen received three Signal Corps sergeants and, at the last minute, ten privates from the 1st Artillery at Key West. Unfortunately, only one of these men had ever been to sea before, and none had ever seen a cable. Nevertheless, the *Adria* set sail on 29 May and arrived off Santiago on 1 June to begin destruction of the three cables believed to connect Cuba with the outside world.

The task proved to be a dangerous one. The crew worked within the range of Spanish guns, to which the unarmed *Adria* could not reply. Moreover, the job proved more difficult than anticipated because of the deep waters and the fact that the cable became caught up on the coral sea bottom. Allen and his men did succeed in twice severing a cable but, as luck would have it, both cuts were made in the same line. After being exposed to repeated shelling, the captain and crew refused to continue working, forcing the abandonment of the operation. The War Department later cited Allen in general orders for his meritorious service in raising and severing the cables, and in 1925 he received the Distinguished Service Cross for his actions off Santiago.[40]

Allen then turned his attention to the second portion of his mission: establishing cable communication with the War Department in Washington. First he made arrangements to repair and use a French cable running from Guantanamo to New York via Haiti, which had been cut by the Navy. On 20 June he reported from shipboard the arrival of Maj. Gen. William R. Shafter and his V Army Corps off Santiago. The next day Allen opened a cable office near Guantanamo. From this point he could communicate with the War Department within five minutes. After Shafter's troops landed signal soldiers constructed land lines to complete the cir-

Field Telephone Station No. 4 near San Juan Hill

cuit between the front and Washington. Somewhat later, in mid-July, the Signal Corps laid its own cable between Guantanamo and Daiquiri to establish a connection independent of the French cable.[41]

If General Shafter had gotten his way, such electrical communication between the front and Washington would have been impossible. When his signal officer, Maj. Frank Greene, tried to persuade him to take signaling equipment to Cuba, Shafter replied that he only wanted soldiers with guns on their shoulders.[42] Shafter's attitude notwithstanding, Greene and his signalmen accompanied the V Corps to Cuba and maintained flag communication between the ships of the fleet during the voyage. Despite the Signal Corps' ability to provide electrical communications, Shafter refused to allow the field telegraph train to be sent to Cuba. Once ashore, the folly of this decision became apparent, because the island's dense vegetation severely inhibited the use of visual signals. They were employed, however, to communicate with Sampson's squadron offshore. The Army thus would have been dependent on messengers to communicate between its commands had not Greely foreseen the difficulties. Before the *Adria* sailed, he had taken steps to obtain electrical equipment, insulated wire in particular, and loaded it aboard for Allen to use in Cuba. Since the Spanish enjoyed the benefits of both telephonic and telegraphic communications, the Americans would have been at a great disadvantage without them.

Thanks to Greely's efforts, the War with Spain became the first conflict fought by the United States in which electrical communications played a predom-

White House communications center during the War with Spain. Captain Montgomery is seated at left.

inant role. For tactical purposes, the Signal Corps established telephone communication within camps and headquarters. For long-distance communication, it installed telegraph lines. While the telephone had the advantage of simpler operation, it did not, like the telegraph, provide a written record of all message traffic. Through the connections with the undersea cable, Shafter could communicate with Washington within twenty minutes even in the midst of battle. Like Secretary of War Stanton during the Civil War, President McKinley set up a war room next to his office in the White House with telegraphic connection to the front in Cuba. In addition, telephone lines linked McKinley with the War and Navy Departments, other key officials in Washington, and the port of embarkation at Tampa. A signal officer, Capt. Benjamin F. Montgomery, operated the White House communications center, known as the Telegraph and Cipher Bureau, a significant departure from Stanton's regime. Moreover, the executive departments also enjoyed telegraphic communication with Army and Navy officers in the field.[43]

Because the Signal Corps could not take its horses to Cuba due to the shortage of transport space, the men had to carry coils of wire into the field themselves or, when possible, use pack mules for that purpose. Even if telegraph wagons had been available, they would have been unable to travel over the rough terrain where unpaved trails often served as the only roads. Moreover, the jungle vegetation yielded few poles on which to string line. This fact made it all the more important that Greely had sent insulated wire that could be laid directly on the ground or atop bushes. The Signal Corps' efforts under these difficult conditions enabled Shafter to communicate by telephone with his subordinate commanders throughout the campaign.[44]

Perhaps the Signal Corps' most famous (or infamous) incident in Cuba involved its use of the captive balloon during the battle of Santiago on 1 July. Because the jungle concealed both troop movements and terrain features, such as trails and streams, aerial reconnaissance could be of great advantage. The balloon saga began with its shipment in early April from Fort Logan to Fort Wadsworth in New York Harbor. There Greely intended it to be used to watch for the anticipated arrival of Cervera's squadron off the coast. The balloon became the responsibility of Lt. Joseph Maxfield, who had been relieved from duty as departmental signal officer in Chicago and transferred to New York. With his main task being the monitoring of international cable traffic into New York City, Maxfield had little time to spare for ballooning. When Greely finally received funds to purchase additional balloons and equipment after the war began, he directed Maxfield to procure them. As the Signal Corps had done in the past, Maxfield turned to French sources and purchased two balloons from the aeronaut A. Varicle. He was not able to complete them, however, in what proved to be the short time available. While Varicle labored, Maxfield shipped the old Fort Logan envelope and associated equipment to Tampa, where the V Corps awaited orders to embark. Maxfield, now a major in the Volunteer Signal Corps, arrived several days later and found his outfit scattered among various unmarked freight cars on sidings outside the city. Hastily locating the balloon and equipment, Maxfield and his recently organized detachment boarded ship just in time to sail with the V Corps. A second balloon detachment remained behind at Tampa.[45]

Once in Cuba, the balloon remained aboard ship for a week waiting to be unloaded. In the steaming hold, the varnished sides of the sphere stuck together. When Shafter finally called for a balloon reconnaissance before attacking the Spanish defenses outside Santiago, he denied Maxfield's request to unload the gas generator. Thus the balloon would have to depend on the gas brought along in storage cylinders—enough for only one inflation.

Maxfield made the first ascent on 30 June, during which he noted terrain features and observed Cervera's ships in Santiago harbor. When the battle opened the next morning, the balloon was ready for action. Maxfield, accompanied by Lt. Col. George F. Derby, Shafter's engineer officer, ascended about a quarter of a mile to the rear of the American position at El Pozo. Derby, however, wished to get closer to the fighting and ordered that the balloon be moved toward the front. Maxfield objected, but he obeyed the command of his superior officer, and the balloon detachment hauled the sphere forward. Maxfield's concerns soon proved justified. The balloon floating overhead not only marked the location of the American troops but also gave the Spaniards an excellent target. Disaster followed. In the hands of an inexperienced crew, the guide ropes became entangled in the brush, completely immobilizing the craft. When the Spanish opened fire at

Signal Corps balloon at San Juan ford

the balloon, shrapnel and bullets rained down upon the troops below, resulting in numerous casualties. Maxfield and Derby escaped injury, but one member of the detachment received a wound in the foot. The balloon, meanwhile, was torn apart. Even if the holes could have been repaired, the signal detachment had no reserve gas available for reinflation.

Despite the damaged balloon, the aerial reconnaissance had not been a total failure. The officers had observed the Spanish entrenchments on San Juan Hill and found them to be heavily defended. They then passed this information to the commanding general, with a recommendation to reopen artillery fire upon them. More important, Derby discovered a previously unknown trail through the woods that helped to speed the deployment of troops toward San Juan Hill.[46]

Although the Americans suffered heavy casualties during the fighting on 1 July, the Spanish had been more seriously harmed. The subsequent destruction of Cervera's squadron on 3 July in a desperate dash for freedom signaled the conclusion of the Santiago campaign. Shafter laid siege to the city and, after threatening to attack, forced the Spanish to surrender on 17 July.

Following the end of the fighting in Cuba, troops under Maj. Gen. Nelson A. Miles undertook the capture of Puerto Rico, Spain's other major colony in the Caribbean. Of the six signal companies participating in this campaign, two bore the distinction of being among the Regular Army's first permanent signal units. They had been among the four companies, designated A through D, authorized by

General Greely on 27 July 1898. Companies A and D saw their first service in Puerto Rico. The other four signal companies that served there belonged to the volunteer corps. These six companies were organized into two provisional battalions, one commanded by Lt. Col. William A. Glassford and the other by Lt. Col. Samuel Reber, who later became Miles' son-in-law.[47] Both Glassford and Reber held volunteer rank during the conflict.

The invasion force landed on Puerto Rico's southern coast on 25 July and encountered only weak Spanish resistance as it moved toward the capital of San Juan. By 28 July Miles had captured Ponce, Puerto Rico's largest city. The Signal Corps promptly took charge of the city's telegraph office, which became the center of the Army's communication system on the island. Moreover, from Ponce two cable lines ran to the United States. Before abandoning the office, however, the Spanish had destroyed nearly all the equipment, and signal officers, short of repair material, had to improvise with the items at hand. Colonel Reber, for example, fashioned a telephone switchboard from a brass sugar kettle. Although the Spanish still held San Juan when the signing of a peace protocol ended the fighting on 12 August, the island, for all intents and purposes, was in American hands. By the time the Spanish evacuated Puerto Rico in mid-October the Signal Corps was operating nearly two hundred miles of lines there.[48]

Concurrent with operations in Cuba and Puerto Rico, the Army launched a third expedition to the Philippines, seeking to take advantage of an overwhelming naval victory. Upon the declaration of war, the Navy Department had ordered Commodore George Dewey, commander of the Asiatic Squadron, to sail from Hong Kong to Manila. With Spanish forces concentrated in the Caribbean, the Philippines lay vulnerable to attack. After winning control of Manila Bay by destroying the relatively weak Spanish squadron on 1 May, Dewey requested troops from the United States to capture the city. Meanwhile, Filipino insurgent forces led by Emilio Aguinaldo surrounded Manila, hoping to win Philippine independence from Spain with the assistance of the United States. The McKinley administration, however, chose not to ally with Aguinaldo's forces.[49]

Communication difficulties hampered Washington's ability to direct operations in the Philippines nearly ten thousand miles away. In fact, news of Dewey's victory did not reach Washington until 7 May. Dewey had cut Manila's cable to Hong Kong after the Spanish authorities refused his request to use it, and it did not return to operation until 22 August. In the interim, dispatches to the outside world traveled by ship to Hong Kong for transmission.[50]

As volunteer troops from western states as well as some Regular Army units gathered at San Francisco to sail for the Philippines, Maj. Gen. Wesley Merritt assumed command of what eventually became known as the VIII Army Corps. Recognizing the necessity of communications, Merritt requested signal soldiers, especially those who could speak Spanish, to accompany his troops. Since, as Greely commented, the Signal Corps was "fortunate in the linguistic acquirements of its officers," he could comply with Merritt's wishes.[51] With little of the confusion and supply problems that plagued the Army at Tampa, the vanguard of

Merritt's force sailed from San Francisco on 25 May, stopped along the way to occupy Guam, and arrived in Manila on 30 June.

The 1st Volunteer Signal Company was the first signal unit to land in the Philippines, arriving at Manila Bay on 31 July. The next day it began the construction of a telegraph line to connect Cavite, the base of supply, with the American troops stationed outside Manila. Working in heavy rains and excessive heat, the task was not an easy one. Difficulties notwithstanding, the company completed the job on 5 August. The 18th Volunteer Signal Company arrived on 24 August to assist with the establishment and maintenance of telegraph and telephone lines.[52]

Although the protocol signed on 12 August called for a cease-fire on all fronts, the troops in the Philippines did not receive the news for several days because of the severed cable. Thus, the armies fought the Battle of Manila on 13 August after peace had been declared. Like the Battle of New Orleans fought and won eighty-five years earlier by Maj. Gen. Andrew Jackson after the formal conclusion of hostilities, the Battle of Manila occurred solely as a result of the slowness of communications. Because the Spanish could not successfully defend Manila, they made arrangements with the Americans to surrender after a token resistance. According to the agreement, the insurgents were not allowed to enter the city. All commanders had not been apprised of the arrangement, however, and hard fighting in several sectors resulted in some casualties. Having salvaged their honor, the Spanish finally surrendered, bringing the war to an end.[53]

During the Battle of Manila signal detachments served with each division and brigade commander, with one held in reserve. Another detachment ran an insulated wire along the beach as the troops advanced. Signalmen maintained communication with the Navy with flags, which they also used to direct naval gunfire against the Spanish positions. Within fifteen minutes after the troops seized the Spanish lines the Signal Corps ran its telegraph wires to the front. As Capt. Elmore A. McKenna, commander of the 1st Volunteer Signal Company, reported, "A red and a white flag of the Signal Corps were the first American emblems shown within the Spanish intrenchments, being there some minutes before the Spanish flag was pulled down and the American flag run up in its place."[54] Among those cited for distinguished service during the battle was Sgt. George S. Gibbs, Jr., later a chief signal officer and father of the last man to bear that title, Maj. Gen. David P. Gibbs.[55]

According to the terms of the peace treaty signed with Spain in December 1898, the United States acquired the islands of Puerto Rico and Guam. Spain further agreed to American occupation of Cuba and the annexation of the Philippines by the United States, for which Spain received $20 million in compensation. With the Hawaiian Islands, also annexed in 1898, the nation now held significant overseas territories.

Despite the war's successful conclusion, the Army received much criticism, especially in regard to the health and diet of the troops in Cuba. The "embalmed beef" scandal is perhaps the best known. While few soldiers died of wounds, scores contracted typhoid, dysentery, yellow fever, and malaria. Many of the victims never

Signal Corps at work during the Battle of Manila, 13 August 1898

left the United States. Despite these problems, the Signal Corps escaped with a relatively low casualty rate, losing one officer in combat and only three officers and
nineteen men to disease, about 2 percent of its total wartime strength of 1,300 officers and men. Four others died in accidents.[56] Not only had the Signal Corps
remained healthy, it had performed its communication functions well. The government's Dodge Commission, which investigated the conduct of the war, concluded
that "the work accomplished by the Signal Corps was of great aid to the army in the
field and very efficient in maintaining communication in all of the camps."[57]

The Signal Corps' aeronautical activities, however, did not fare as well.
Although the Dodge Commission did not address the issue in its report to the
president, the Corps' handling of the balloon received considerable rebuke, especially from members of units exposed to the fire it had drawn. One of these units
was the 10th Cavalry, in which 1st Lt. John J. Pershing served as regimental quartermaster. Caught beneath the balloon, the 10th Cavalry received, in Pershing's
words, "a veritable hail of shot and shell."[58] According to Pershing, no one in the
line knew the balloon's purpose, and the only intelligence furnished by its occupants was "that the Spanish were firing upon us—information which at that particular time was entirely superfluous."[59] The novelist Stephen Crane, reporting on
the war in Cuba, wrote of the balloon's "public death before the eyes of two
armies."[60] Aeronautics was still a largely unexplored area of Army operations,
with no clear-cut doctrine yet developed for its use. Despite the mixed results in
Cuba, the Signal Corps continued to explore the possibilities of airborne observation and reconnaissance in the postwar period.

During the war the Signal Corps also experimented with another device—the
camera. Although not an officially assigned function, photography fell within the

broad definition of communications. Beginning in 1894 photography had been taught as part of the signal course at Fort Riley, and in 1896 the Corps had published a *Manual of Photography* written by then 1st Lt. Samuel Reber. While serving in Puerto Rico, Reber used his skills to draw topographical maps based on photographs.[61] Moreover, signal companies in all three campaigns carried cameras with which to document their operations. Improvements in photographic technology since the Civil War made combat photography an easier task than it had been for Mathew Brady. Smaller cameras using rolled film had replaced cumbersome glass plates; high-speed shutters and shorter exposure time made action photographs possible.[62] Thus began one of the activities with which the Signal Corps is most closely identified—one that has made "Photo by the U.S. Army Signal Corps" a well-known phrase. The Corps displayed a collection of its wartime photos as part of its exhibit at the Pan-American Exposition held in Buffalo, New York, in the fall of 1901, and some of the photographs were reproduced in Greely's annual reports for 1898 and 1899.[63]

With the return to peace, the Signal Corps shrank to its prewar size. As the volunteer companies began to be mustered out, Greely expressed his appreciation for their service in lengthy orders published on 13 September 1898, in which he reviewed the contributions of the Corps in the three theaters of operation. Despite the hardships of the war, signalmen had "filled neither the guardhouse nor the hospital." In his words: "Battles may be fought and epidemics spread, but speedy communications must nevertheless be maintained."[64]

Postwar Operations

The acquisition of foreign territories by the United States carried with it increased duties and responsibilities for the Army. With the end of the war, soldiers could not return to business as usual, because the nation had become a major power. For the Signal Corps, its mission now included the administration of the communication systems in the Caribbean and the Pacific, in addition to its domestic duties.

After the signing of the peace treaty with Spain, the United States sent troops to occupy Cuba until the Cubans established a government of their own. Maj. Gen. John R. Brooke commanded the American forces on the island and also served as military governor. Colonel Dunwoody became chief signal officer of the newly established Division of Cuba. Effective 1 January 1899, the Signal Corps took over the telegraph and telephone lines formerly operated by the Spanish government and assumed supervision of the private telephone and telegraph companies that had been granted licenses by Spain. First of all, Dunwoody arranged for the separation of the postal and telegraphic services, which had been combined in a single bureau. Then he turned his attention to repair and extension of the existing lines. The Spanish had built lines primarily in the western portion of the island, leaving two-thirds of Cuba without telegraph or telephone service. To enable General Brooke to communicate with his various subordinate commands and posts, by April 1899 the Signal Corps had completed a 600-mile telegraph line from Havana to Santiago, or practically from one end of the island to the other. The Corps also built a new telephone system for the city of Havana and laid two cables in Havana Harbor. In addition to filling the Army's communication needs, the Signal Corps transmitted commercial business over its system. To meet the demand, the Corps constructed a second line between Havana and Santiago.

With the mustering out of the Volunteer Signal Corps in April and May 1899, Dunwoody lost most of his men. To compensate for these losses, he hired Cuban workers to supplement his force and ultimately to replace Army personnel. When the Corps turned over operations to the Cuban government in 1902, it transferred nearly 3,500 miles of line that covered the entire island.[65]

In Puerto Rico, Major Glassford, who had reverted to his permanent rank after the war, directed signal operations. After the Spanish evacuated the island, the communication systems that had formerly been the province of the Spanish government or its licensees came under the Signal Corps' control. As in Cuba, the Signal Corps found most of the Spanish lines in a dilapidated state. It reconstructed and extended the system, but disaster struck when a hurricane hit the island in August 1899 and destroyed all the Signal Corps' work. Glassford began the task again, completed it, and in February 1901 the Signal Corps turned over the system to the new civil government of Puerto Rico.[66]

In the Philippines, meanwhile, a new war was brewing. Tensions had steadily increased between the Americans and the Filipino insurgent forces; their leader Aguinaldo had organized a provisional government for which he sought recognition. When it became clear that independence would not be forthcoming and that the United States would replace Spain as the ruler of the archipelago, Aguinaldo began an active resistance. On the night of 4 February 1899 fighting broke out around Manila, the beginning of what became known as the Philippine Insurrection.

The next day a signal officer, 1st Lt. Charles E. Kilbourne, Jr. (son of the inventor of the outpost cable cart), distinguished himself at Paco Bridge, in a suburb of Manila. Under enemy fire he climbed a telegraph pole to repair a broken wire, reestablishing communication with the front. For this feat he became the third Signal Corpsman to win the Medal of Honor.[67]

American commissioners arrived in March primarily to act as a fact-finding body for President McKinley in preparation for the establishment of a civil government. On 4 April they issued a proclamation intended to convince the Filipinos of America's good intentions. It included a pledge to construct a communications network throughout the archipelago.[68] The Signal Corps, under Maj. Richard E. Thompson and his successor Lt. Col. James Allen, became responsible for installing this system, which entailed laying cables between the principal islands. In addition to the permanent lines, the Corps ran temporary lines to accompany the troops in the field. Because the two volunteer signal companies still serving in the Philippines could not handle the expanded duties, a third company was formed out of personnel drawn from the two existing companies as well as from other units. Each company operated with a division, forming detachments as needed for a variety of duties. The 18th Company, serving with Maj. Gen. Arthur MacArthur along the railroad from Manila to Dagupan, became railway dispatchers. As the volunteer signal units were gradually mustered out, Regular Army units replaced them.

As in Cuba, the Signal Corps labored under adverse conditions. Lack of roads hindered the transportation of material and equipment; the terrain was often either jungle or swamp. To facilitate transportation, signalmen used carabao, or water buffalo, as pack animals. When possible, they employed either Filipino laborers who were friendly to the Americans or Chinese coolies as porters and linesmen. Wooden poles required constant repairs because they rotted in the intense heat or were destroyed by ants. The tropical climate, with its alternate wet and dry seasons, caused the soldiers physical discomfort and exposed them to indigenous diseases, such as malaria and amebic dysentery. The insurgents posed the greatest danger, however, incessantly sabotaging the lines and ambushing the soldiers who came to fix them. Armed escorts often accompanied the signal parties to provide protection, as the signalmen carried only revolvers.[69]

Perhaps the most ambitious job undertaken by the Signal Corps was the laying of submarine cables between the major islands. (Although a British firm, under concession from Spain, had already constructed cables between many of the islands, the Army needed its own system.) Other forms of communication were too slow, with mail sometimes taking two to four months to travel from one island to another. In some areas the Signal Corps conducted inter-island communication by heliograph and the newly adopted acetylene lantern. The transport *Hooker*, having been outfitted by the Quartermaster Department, arrived in the Philippines in June 1899 to begin cable-laying operations. While the Corps had received some experience with underwater cables in Cuba, it obtained assistance for the Philippine project from professional cable engineers. Unfortunately, on the way to Hong Kong to obtain coal, the *Hooker* was wrecked on a reef near Corregidor. Luckily, most of the cable and machinery were saved, and in April 1900 a second ship, the *Romulus*, began laying the recovered cable. With the arrival of the *Burnside* in December 1900, the Corps extended its system, laying over 1,300 miles of cable connecting the principal islands of the archipelago by June 1902.[70]

By early 1900 organized Filipino resistance had declined markedly. Despite American control of most of the provinces on Luzon, which was Aguinaldo's home and the center of the independence movement, guerrilla warfare continued and the pacification of the entire archipelago proceeded slowly. It was difficult for the Americans to tell friend from foe: The insurgents posed as civilians by day and took up arms at night. The hundreds of raids and ambushes mounted by the guerrillas cost the Americans dearly in casualties. With the capture of Aguinaldo in March 1901, guerrilla activity subsided but did not cease. Given the improving conditions in the islands, the Army shed its governmental responsibilities, and William Howard Taft became the civil governor in June 1901. Although sporadic

Signal party on the way to Malolos, Philippines, 1899

fighting continued for several years thereafter, the United States declared the insurrection at an end on 4 July 1902.[71]

A gradual transfer of the Signal Corps' communications system to the civil government began in 1902. Initially the Army retained control of the entire cable system as well as those land lines needed for military purposes, but by 1907 the Corps had completed the transfer of over five thousand miles of land lines and cable, retaining only its system of post telephones and about one hundred and twenty-five miles of military land lines and cable.[72] The acquisition of overseas territories made the laying of a Pacific cable a matter of urgent concern to the United States; without it, messages from the Philippines had to travel to the United States via China, India, Egypt, France, and England. President McKinley recommended its construction in his special message of 10 February 1899.[73] Although Greely hoped that the Signal Corps would have a role in the project, the government instead granted permission to the Commercial Pacific Cable Company to construct a cable from San Francisco to China via Honolulu, Midway, Guam, and Luzon. The cable reached the Philippines in July 1903.[74]

America's growing involvement in Asian affairs received added impetus from the Boxer Rebellion of 1900. The United States had already espoused the Open Door policy, proclaiming the principle that all nations should share equally in trade with China. China's exploitation by foreign nations aroused resentment among young Chinese, who formed a secret society called the "Righteous Fists of Harmony" or Boxers. With the connivance of the Dowager Empress, the Boxers launched a bloody campaign to rid the country of foreigners who, fearing for their lives, took refuge in their legations in Peking. The legations, defended by

Signal Corps soldiers in China during the Boxer Rebellion, 1900

small numbers of soldiers and armed civilians, were soon besieged by a much
larger force of Boxers and Chinese imperial troops.

Because it already had substantial forces in the Philippines, the United States
contributed a sizable contingent to an international relief force sent to China. A
signal detachment of four officers and nineteen men under the command of Maj.
George P. Scriven accompanied the American troops on their march to Peking in
August 1900.[75] These men, in conjunction with British signal personnel, constructed a telegraph line to accompany the advance of the allied army from
Tientsin to Peking, a distance of about ninety miles. The allies entered Peking on
14 August and saved the beleaguered legations. For several days the British-
American telegraph line provided the only means of communication between the
city and the outside world. During the period of occupation that followed, additional Signal Corpsmen arrived to construct a permanent telegraph line between
Peking and Taku, on the coast, a distance of 122 miles. The occupation troops
withdrew from China in September 1901, but a small American force remained
to guard the Tientsin-Peking railway in accordance with the Boxer protocol.[76]

During the few years since the sinking of the *Maine*, the United States had
firmly established itself as an active participant in world affairs. In the
Philippines and China, the Army had demonstrated that it could operate success-

fully thousands of miles from home. By providing the necessary communications support, the Signal Corps contributed significantly to the nation's rise as a world power.

Organization and Training, 1899–1903

The Signal Corps' greatly expanded duties required far more personnel than the ten officers and fifty enlisted men it had been authorized when the War with Spain began. The expansion of the Signal Corps by more than twenty times (from 60 to 1,300 officers and men) for wartime purposes seemingly convinced Army and congressional leaders that the Corps needed a larger peacetime force in the new electrical age. To meet the Army's current manpower demands caused by occupation duties and continued fighting in the Philippines, Congress on 2 March 1899 temporarily increased the size of the regular and volunteer forces. For the Signal Corps, Congress provided 720 enlisted men. In separate legislation, Congress authorized the president to retain in service or appoint 31 volunteer Signal Corps officers to supplement its complement of 10 regular officers. For the immediate future, this action helped to alleviate the Corps' critical need for trained officers.[77]

Over the next few years the Signal Corps underwent numerous reorganizations. By July 1899 all of the volunteer signal companies had been mustered out except those in the Philippines. Because the conditions of service were so poor and the length of overseas tours so long (from two to four years), especially in the Philippines, few volunteer signal soldiers chose to transfer to the Regulars. The Corps needed, therefore, a sizable pool of new personnel to provide replacements for these overworked soldiers. In 1900 President McKinley increased the enlisted strength of the Signal Corps to 800 and Congress, by joint resolution, authorized the appointment for one year of ten additional volunteer officers.[78] When Congress legislated a permanent expansion of the Army in February 1901, however, it reduced the Signal Corps' enlisted strength to 760, causing the discharge or reduction in rank of many men who had served with distinction in China and the Philippines.[79] In the next year the lawmakers reversed themselves, boosting the branch's enlisted strength in June 1902 once more to a total of 810, adding 50 sergeants. Subsequent legislation allowed the temporary addition of another 50 sergeants for as long as deemed necessary by the secretary of war or the president.[80]

As for the officer ranks, the February 1901 legislation provided some relief by setting the Signal Corps' permanent commissioned strength at 35 (a brigadier general, a colonel, a lieutenant colonel, 4 majors, 14 captains, and 14 first lieutenants). The law also authorized the retention "only for the period when their services may be absolutely necessary" of 10 volunteer officers: 5 first lieutenants and 5 second lieutenants. Chief Signal Officer Greely, however, wanted more than such stopgap measures. Not only did Signal Corps officers have increasingly complex duties to perform, but the arduous service expected of them in the tropics placed many on the sick and disabled lists.[81] Moreover, the percentage of officers (17.1) in relation to the total strength of the branch ranked far below that of the other staff corps (the proportion of officers in the Medical Department, which had the next lowest percentage, was 24.9).[82] In March 1903 Congress responded to the Signal Corps' needs by authorizing the addition of 11 commissioned officers (1 lieutenant colonel, 2 majors, 4 captains, and 4 first lieutenants), bringing the total to 46.[83]

Meanwhile, signal training also underwent some changes, as Fort Myer once again became the home of the Signal Corps in 1899.[84] The branch returned to centralized training and discontinued the schools at Fort Logan, the Presidio of San Francisco, and San Antonio, Texas. Individual signal instruction at the departmental level, while still mandated by Army regulations, could not be relied upon to produce skilled signal soldiers, as previous experience had demonstrated. In fact, the War Department had made matters worse by amending the regulations in 1899 to require only such instruction as the departmental commanders "deemed necessary for the public service," rather than the previously required two months' worth.[85] Moreover, the Corps had been unable to furnish a signal officer to each department to oversee the instruction.

Recruits sent to Fort Myer received training in telegraphy, telephony, line repair, and visual signaling. While six months of training was preferable, the demand for signal soldiers in the field limited it to as few as four months. Once telegraph operators achieved a competency of twenty words per minute, they served as assistants on the military telegraph lines in preparation for duty overseas. Officer-level instruction was also conducted on a limited basis. In addition to its training function, the post became a depot for supplies being returned from the various Signal Corps posts, domestic and overseas.

With the closing of the signal school at Fort Logan, Fort Myer also became the new home of the Signal Corps' balloon operations. In 1900 Congress appropriated funds to build a balloon house on the post, which was completed early the following year.[86] Congress did not, however, appropriate additional funds to support aeronautical activities. In particular, Fort Myer lacked a gas generating plant, an essential facility for successful ballooning. Despite the continuing shortage of resources, both in personnel and equipment, the Signal Corps formed a balloon detachment at Fort Myer in 1902, and it participated in the Army maneuvers held in Connecticut that year.[87]

Although the Signal Corps remained earthbound for lack of a gas plant, the year 1903 witnessed several significant events in aeronautical history. In October and December, Samuel P. Langley made two unsuccessful attempts to launch his so-called Aerodrome, a machine that resembled a giant dragonfly. A few days after his second failure, the Wright brothers flew successfully at Kitty Hawk, North Carolina, on 17 December. Their achievement remained virtually unknown to the world at large for several years because the Wrights avoided publicity pending the receipt of a patent for their airplane. Nevertheless, above the windswept dunes of the Outer Banks, a new age of flight had begun.

New Frontiers: Alaska and the Dawn of the Electrical Age

While the military potential of aeronautics was yet to be discovered, the value of electricity to Army communications had been clearly demonstrated during the War with Spain. In 1902 the Signal Corps recognized its increasing importance by establishing an Electrical Division, headed by Capt. Edgar Russel, to take responsibility for the field of electrical signaling, exclusive of the military telegraph lines. In the division's laboratory and carpentry shop, the construction and testing of improved telephones and other devices took place. The Corps also undertook the installation of electric lighting at Army posts. Because not enough signal soldiers were available to fully staff the division, the Corps hired civilian electrical engineers.[88]

While the telegraph and the telephone had dramatically improved communications, a new technology began to make its appearance—wireless telegraphy, or radio, as it became known. This new form of communication had been demonstrated in Europe by Guglielmo Marconi, an Italian inventor and entrepreneur. Although others had discovered the principles of radio, Marconi successfully exploited its commercial potential. He brought his system to the United States in 1899, where he used it to report the results of the America's Cup yacht races held that fall.[89] Radio had many advantages over the visual, wire, and cable systems then in use. For example, it was not limited by hindrances to visibility such as darkness or fog. Moreover, with the Army and the world at large becoming more mobile through the introduction of motorized transport, radio had the ability to go where wires and cables could not. Radio had particular application for communication from ship to ship and between ship and shore. Its availability during the War with Spain might have dispelled some of the confusion between Sampson and Schley concerning Santiago. Still, in the early twentieth century, "radio" simply meant the transmission of Morse dots and dashes through the air. The technology for the wireless transmission of the human voice and music had not yet been developed.

The Signal Corps began its investigations into radio even before Marconi's arrival in America. To lead its research efforts, the Corps had its own electrical expert, 1st Lt. George O. Squier. After graduating from West Point in 1887, Squier had attended the Johns Hopkins University and received a doctorate in electrical engineering in 1893, becoming one of the first soldiers to earn this advanced degree. He selected as his dissertation topic "Electro-Chemical Effects Due to Magnetization."[90] Originally commissioned as an artillery officer, Squier served in the Volunteer Signal Corps during the War with Spain and transferred to the Signal Corps of the Regular Army in February 1899. Assisted by Lt. Col. James Allen, a signal officer with considerable experience in electrical communication, Squier developed a wireless system that was first used in April 1899 to communicate between Fire Island and the Fire Island lightship off Long Island, a distance of about twelve miles. With this success, the Signal Corps next established a wireless connection between Governors Island and Fort Hamilton in New

York Harbor, followed by Fort Mason and Alcatraz in San Francisco. In May 1899 Squier traveled to London to study under Marconi.[91] While wireless still had many "bugs" (it could be easily intercepted by the enemy, for example), the Signal Corps had taken the initial steps toward launching this new form of communication.

If wireless had been further along the road to perfection, it would have been ideally suited for the Signal Corps' next major project, the installation of a military communications system for Alaska. The discovery of gold in Alaska along the Yukon River and at Nome in the late 1890s and the consequent rush of fortune seekers created the need for a significant Army presence as a police force in that untamed wilderness. In 1897 rumors of starvation among the miners led Secretary of War Russell A. Alger to prepare a relief expedition to prevent a tragedy. Besides foodstuffs, the War Department purchased 500 Norwegian reindeer to carry the supplies over the frozen terrain. Just before the relief force departed from Portland, Oregon, reports from Alaska indicated that the rumors of famine had been unfounded. When Canadian and American authorities confirmed that no danger existed, Alger canceled the expedition. The whole affair had highlighted, however, the problems to be faced in communicating with the nation's northernmost territory.[92]

In 1899 the War Department created the Department of Alaska, with headquarters at Fort St. Michael on Norton Sound. To establish communication links, Congress in 1900 authorized construction of the Washington-Alaska Military Cable and Telegraph System (WAMCATS) and assigned its supervision to the Signal Corps. The new lines would connect the nation's capital to the military posts and the posts to one another as well as serve the commercial telegraph needs of the territory.[93] The Alaskan system, in fact, became the last in the chain of frontier telegraph lines to be built by the Signal Corps.

After enduring service in the tropical climes of the Caribbean and the Philippines, signal soldiers now faced the opposite extreme. As in the tropics, the environment itself would present one of the most formidable obstacles to progress. In Alaska, featureless tundra and treacherous muskeg swamps replaced jungles as natural obstacles, while the accompanying temperatures plunged as low as -72 degrees Fahrenheit. In the summer when the weather moderated, hordes of mosquitoes plagued the linesmen, and forest fires posed an additional hazard.

Funds from the initial appropriation of $450,550 became available in June 1900, and Greely hurried to secure supplies so that work could begin before winter. The first detachment of men from Company D, Signal Corps, under 1st Lt. George C. Burnell, landed at Port Valdez on 9 July. By August, when most of the equipment had finally arrived from the United States, construction parties had taken the field. Difficulties in finding suitable routes for the line and the onset of winter slowed the rate of progress, and Greely expressed concern that the system would not be completed before Congress cut off the money.

The chief signal officer, who had himself strung thousands of miles of wire early in his career, could apply his considerable experience to the task at hand.

From his Arctic service, Greely knew only too well the rigors under which his men would be laboring. Alaska was virtually unexplored and uninhabited, with a climate to test the mettle of the most sturdy soldier. Luckily the Signal Corps had such a man in 1st Lt. William ("Billy") Mitchell. Mitchell, who later became famous as an outspoken advocate of air power, joined the Volunteer Signal Corps in 1898 and served in Cuba and the Philippines. In the summer of 1901 Greely sent him to investigate the conditions in Alaska. After traveling extensively throughout the territory, Mitchell submitted his report to the chief signal officer. To expedite the construction project, Mitchell suggested that work continue throughout the winter when supplies could be easily transported over the ice and snow and cached for work in the warmer months. In the fall of

Captain Mitchell in Alaska

1901 Mitchell returned to Alaska to help build the lines, later writing an account of his observations and travails that makes fascinating reading.[94]

Greely assigned to Mitchell the job of surveying and laying the telegraph line south from Eagle City (site of Fort Egbert) on the Yukon River to meet the line northward from Valdez (Fort Liscum) being built by Burnell, now a captain. The total length of this line measured approximately four hundred and twenty miles. While surveying the route, Mitchell nearly died when he and his sled broke through the ice of a frozen river with the air temperature at about sixty degrees below zero. Fortunately, his lead dog gained a foothold on the ice and pulled the lieutenant to safety.[95] After completing this job in August 1902, Mitchell constructed the line westward from Eagle toward Fairbanks to connect with the wire run eastward from St. Michael by 1st Lt. George S. Gibbs. When he finished his Alaskan duties in the summer of 1903, Mitchell and his sled dogs had traveled more than 2,000 miles.[96]

Infantry and artillery troops posted to Alaska performed much of the line construction, while signal soldiers handled the technical aspects. Telegraph maintenance stations were established every forty miles and were manned by three soldiers—one signalman with two infantrymen as assistants. Some men found this lonely vigil more than they could take, especially during the long, dark Alaskan winters, and a few desperate souls committed suicide.[97]

As originally planned, the first Alaskan lines made no connections outside of the territory. To establish telegraphic communication with the United States it would be necessary to connect the Alaskan lines with those of Canada. Therefore, Greely arranged a meeting with his personal friend, Canadian Premier Sir Wilfrid Laurier, to request permission for the Army to connect its wires to the Canadian lines terminating at Dawson in the Yukon Territory. Laurier agreed to the proposal, and by the spring of 1901 telegraphic messages from Alaska traveled via Canada to the United States.[98] To provide an "all-American" communication system, the final portion to be constructed consisted of cables connecting southeastern Alaska to the continental United States. The *Burnside*, the Army's only cable ship, was transferred from the Philippines to begin the job in the summer of 1903. Colonel Allen and Captain Russel supervised the installation. During the winter, while operations were suspended for several months, the buoyed sea end of the cable was washed away, and 600 miles of cable had to be recovered and put back in place. By October 1904 Allen and Russel had laid over 2,000 miles of cable from Seattle to Valdez to include a section between Sitka and Skagway.[99]

Because the movement of ice floes prevented a cable from being maintained across the 107 miles of Norton Sound, the Signal Corps established a wireless link across its waters in 1904.[100] This project, successfully carried out by Capt. Leonard D. Wildman after a private contractor had failed, finally made communication possible between St. Michael and Nome. Because radio was still in its infancy and generally reliable only over short distances, the success at Norton Sound was significant; Greely declared it to be "the longest wireless section of any commercial telegraph system in the world."[101]

Upon completion, the Washington-Alaska Military Cable and Telegraph System comprised 2,079 miles of cable, 1,439 miles of land lines, and the wireless system of 107 miles, for a total mileage of 3,625.[102] It had proven to be an enormous undertaking, and an accomplishment of which the Signal Corps could be justifiably proud.[103]

The Roots of Change

The early years of the twentieth century marked an important transitional period for both the nation and the Army. In the War Department, Secretary of War Elihu Root effected a major reorganization in 1903 with the establishment of the General Staff, headed by a chief of staff. Root recognized, as had the Dodge Commission, that the Army, with its global responsibilities, could not afford to repeat the chaos it had experienced during the mobilization for the War with Spain. The General Staff would conduct overall military planning for the Army and coordinate the activities of its bureaus. Consequently, the bureau chiefs lost

Telegraph repair work at Fort Gibbon, Alaska; below, interior of Fort Gibbon telegraph office.

some of their autonomy, and henceforth they would report to the chief of staff, who would serve as intermediary between them and the secretary of war. The chief of staff also replaced the commanding general as the principal military adviser to the secretary of war and the president. This consolidation of power within the Army reflected a trend toward centralization of administration and control then taking place in the business world as well.[104]

In the same year the Dick Act, also supported by Root, reformed the militia system and increased federal support to the National Guard. The act allowed the War Department to furnish signal equipment to Guard units and to detail Regular signal soldiers to state units to conduct signal training. Furthermore, both Regular and Guard officers were to periodically inspect the state units to ensure that they conformed to federal requirements.[105]

The Army that resulted from the Root reforms was better prepared to help the nation administer its growing overseas commitments. The Signal Corps had an important role in this process. Having emerged from the weather service years with a clearer sense of mission and purpose, the branch had finally established a place for itself within the Army's structure. Adapting to the ongoing evolution of communications technology, the Corps rendered diverse and arduous service in far-flung areas of the globe, in the words of Chief Signal Officer Greely, "whether in isolated Alaska, storm-stricken Porto Rico, the yellow fever districts of Cuba, the arid plains of China, or among the Philippine insurgents."[106] Even greater challenges lay ahead.

Notes

[1]WDGO 124, 17 Oct 1890. The act is also printed in *ARSO*, 1891, p. 3, in *ARSW*, 1891, vol. 4.

[2]As specified in WDGO 27, 9 Mar 1891, the Corps' appropriation consisted of: personnel, $64,296; equipment, $7,500; military telegraph lines, $15,000; all totaling $86,796.

[3]On the initial development of the cart, see *ARSO*, 1892, p. 596 and app. C, pp. 622–23, in *ARSW*, 1892, vol. 1. After the separation of the weather service, the chief signal officer's annual report is published in volume 1 of the secretary of war's report unless otherwise stated. The chief signal officer reported Allen's accomplishment in *ARSO*, 1894, p. 492.

[4]David L. Woods, *A History of Tactical Communication Techniques* (Orlando, Fla.: Martin Company, Martin-Marietta Corporation, 1965), pp. 116–20.

[5]*ARSO*, 1892, pp. 597–98 and app. A, pp. 612–18. The U.S. Coast Survey perfected this method of determining longitude during the 1840s and 1850s. See Carlene E. Stephens, "Before Standard Time: Distributing Time in 19th-Century America," *Vistas in Astronomy* 28 (1985): 113–18.

[6]*ARSO*, 1893, pp. 647–48 and Rpt, 1st Lt Joseph E. Maxfield to the Chief Signal Officer, 16 Jul 1893, pp. 661–62. See also Porter, *Paper Medicine Man*, pp. 284–91.

[7]*ARSO*, 1894, pp. 489–91; *ARSO*, 1895, pp. 581–82; Matloff, ed., *American Military History*, p. 286; *Historical Sketch*, p. 31; Cooper, *Army and Civil Disorder*, ch. 6.

[8]*ARSO*, 1893, app. A, p. 657.

[9]*ARSO*, 1894, pp. 483–84.

[10]Ibid., pp. 483–84 and 491; *ARSO*, 1895, pp. 575–77; *ARSO*, 1896, p. 595. Capt. Howard A. Giddings, a Signal Corpsman in the Connecticut National Guard, was the author of a *Manual for Cyclists* (Kansas City, Mo.: Hudson-Kimberly Publishing Co., 1898). On the uses of the bicycle by European armies as well as by the United States, see Henry H. Whitney, "The Adaptation of the Bicycle to Military Uses," *JMSI* 17 (Nov 1895): 542–63.

[11]Greely made this request as early as 1892. In 1897 the Signal Corps installed a cable between Governors Island and Ellis Island in New York Harbor in conjunction with the Bureau of Immigration. See *ARSO*, 1897, p. 667.

[12]The act creating the Board of Ordnance and Fortification is published in WDGO 76, 5 Oct 1888. For a discussion of fire direction and the operation of the board, see Emanuel Raymond Lewis, *Seacoast Fortifications of the United States: An Introductory History* (Washington, D.C.: Smithsonian Institution Press, 1970), pp. 75–95. See also Matloff, ed., *American Military History*, p. 294, and Russell J. Parkinson, "Politics, Patents, and Planes: Military Aeronautics in the United States, 1863–1907" (Ph.D. dissertation, Duke University, 1963), ch. 7.

[13]Greely, *Reminiscences*, pp. 162–63.

[14]See Thompson's report in *ARSO*, 1889, app. 1, p. 48, published in *ARSW*, 1889, vol. 4, pt. 1.

[15]Parkinson, "Politics, Patents, and Planes," p. 46; *ARSO*, 1891, p. 6.

[16]*ARSO*, 1892, p. 9 and app. B.

[17]Parkinson, "Politics, Patents, and Planes," p. 61. Chapter 3 of this dissertation describes the Signal Corps' efforts to obtain the balloon.

[18]Ibid., pp. 20–21 and 62–68. See also Charles deForest Chandler and Frank P. Lahm, *How Our Army Grew Wings* (Chicago: Ronald Press Company, 1943), pp. 42–43.

[19]Parkinson, "Politics, Patents, and Planes," chs. 3 and 4. Thompson's report on ballooning in *ARSO*, 1892, Appendix B, reflects the Signal Corps' plans for the train rather than the realities. Written in October 1892, the Corps had not yet purchased the *Myer*. At that time the Corps intended to purchase a British silk balloon. Hydrogen generation had been a problem since the earliest days of ballooning. For a description of how it was done in the 1780s, see Crouch, *Eagle Aloft*, page 81 and the illustration on page 121.

[20]*ARSO*, 1894, p. 490.

[21]*ARSO*, 1895, p. 581; Parkinson, "Politics, Patents, and Planes," pp. 74–75.

[22]Parkinson, "Politics, Patents, and Planes," pp. 70–97. For information on Ivy Baldwin, whose real name was William Ivy, and his service with the Signal Corps' balloon detachment, see Crouch, *Eagle Aloft*, ch. 16.

[23]Parkinson, "Politics, Patents, and Planes," p. 52. Lt. Thompson in his 1891 report refers to the Corps' assumption of "the functions of a bureau of military information, which have been imposed upon it by law." See his report in *ARSO*, 1891, app. 1, p. 43. See also Elizabeth Bethel, "The Military Information Division: Origin of the Intelligence Division," *Military Affairs* 11 (Spring 1947): 17–24; Marc B. Powe, "The Emergence of the War Department Intelligence Agency: 1885–1918" (M.A. thesis, Kansas State University, 1974), pp. 20–24.

[24]*ARSO*, 1895, p. 588. The cataloging project resulted in the publication of a *List of Photographs and Photographic Negatives Relating to the War for the Union, Now in the War Department Library* (Washington, D.C.: Government Printing Office, 1897).

[25]Matloff, ed., *American Military History*, p. 287; Coffman, *The Old Army*, p. 251.

[26]See Rpt, Pvt Alexander McAdie to the Chief Signal Officer, 26 Sep 1882, in *ARSO*, 1883, app. 67, pp. 650–51.

[27]U.S. War Department, *The Organized Militia of the United States: Statement of the Condition and Efficiency for Service of the Organized Militia from Annual Reports, and Other Sources, Covering the Year 1897* (Washington, D.C.: Government Printing Office, 1898), pp. 381, 430–36 (hereafter cited as *Organized Militia* with year).

[28]Volkmar's report is quoted from in *ARSO*, 1892, p. 605. Volkmar served on special duty during the strike at the request of the governor of Pennsylvania. See Cullum, *Biographical Register*, 4: 182. Volkmar was West Point graduate number 2249. See also *Organized Militia*, 1893, p. 114.

[29]Leon Wolff, *Lockout: The Story of the Homestead Strike of 1892: A Study of Violence, Unionism, and the Carnegie Steel Empire* (New York: Harper and Row, 1965), p. 131.

[30]On Greely's personnel requests, see *ARSO*, 1894, pp. 488 and 490–91; *ARSO*, 1895, pp. 579 and 582; *ARSO*, 1896, p. 601.

[31]Matloff, ed., *American Military History*, pp. 322–23; *Official Army Register*, 1898, pp. 346–47, gives the Army's aggregate strength as 28,267.

[32]*ARSO*, 1898, p. 903, in *ARSW*, 1898, vol. 1. pt. 1. Both this annual report and that for 1899 are published in Scheips, ed., *Military Signal Communications*, vol. 1.

[33]WDGO 52, 24 May 1898.

[34]Congress enacted legislation in July 1898 repealing the provision for the detailing of signal officers to the Weather Bureau. See WDGO 103, 21 Jul 1898.

[35]In particular, the states of New York, Connecticut, New Jersey, Maryland, Indiana, and Iowa. Under the provisions of the acts of 22 and 26 April 1898 outlining the organiza-

tion of the wartime Army, National Guard units entering the volunteer force were required to conform to the organization of Regular Army units. Because the Regular Army did not contain signal units, these specialized state units were not accepted into federal service. See Graham A. Cosmas, *An Army for Empire: The United States in the Spanish-American War* (Columbia, Mo.: University of Missouri Press, 1971), pp. 109–10 and 114–15.

[36]Howard A. Giddings, *Exploits of the Signal Corps in the War with Spain* (Kansas City, Mo.: Hudson-Kimberly Publishing Co., 1900), p. 20. Giddings served as a captain in the Volunteer Signal Corps.

[37]See *ARSO*, 1898, pp. 891–95 and app. 6, pp. 966–68. See also Giddings, *Exploits of the Signal Corps*, pp. 114–16.

[38]See Rpt, Col James Allen to the Chief Signal Officer, 1 Sep 1898 in *ARSO*, 1898, app. 3, pp. 946–49. On the presence of agents supplying information from Cuba he simply states (p. 946): "Arrangements were made by which confidential information could be obtained from Cuba." G. J. A. O'Toole in *The Spanish War: An American Epic—1898* (New York: W.W. Norton and Company, 1984), identifies the Cuban informant as Domingo Villaverde (see pp. 207–15).

[39]After the war, a board of inquiry investigated Schley's activities of 19–29 May and strongly criticized him in its report. For a detailed discussion of the Cuban blockade, see David F. Trask, *The War with Spain in 1898* (New York: Macmillan Publishing Co., Inc., 1981), ch. 6. See also Cosmas, *Army for Empire*, pp. 177–80 and William T. Sampson, "The Atlantic Fleet in the Spanish War," *The Century Magazine* 57 (Apr 1899): 886–913.

[40]See *ARSO*, 1898, pp. 880–882 and Colonel Allen's report at app. 3. Allen is cited in WDGO 15, 13 Feb 1900. See also Allen's obituary in *Annual Report of the Association of Graduates of the United States Military Academy at West Point, New York* (1934), p. 56 (hereafter cited as *USMA Graduates Report*). Giddings, *Exploits of the Signal Corps*, pp. 28–36, contains an account of Allen's cable-cutting mission.

[41]See *ARSO*, 1898, pp. 882–83 and Allen's report at appendix 3 cited above. On naval cable-cutting operations, see Trask, *War with Spain*, p. 110, and Sampson, "Atlantic Fleet."

[42]Greely, *Reminiscences*, p. 185. Woods, *Tactical Signal Communications*, p. 91, relates a similar story and quotes Shafter as saying: "I don't want men with flags! I want men with guns!" See also *ARSO*, 1898, p. 884.

[43]Montgomery had worked as the White House telegraph operator since 1877. List of White House Employees, 1 Dec 1880, Rutherford B. Hayes Presidential Center, Fremont, Ohio (copy in author's files). On presidential communications during the War with Spain, see Richard T. Loomis, "The White House Telephone and Crisis Management," *United States Naval Institute Proceedings* 12 (Dec 1969): 63–73; Trask, *War with Spain*, p. 169; Adolphus W. Greely, "The Signal Corps in War-Time," *The Century Magazine* 66 (Sep 1903): 812–13.

[44]See *ARSO*, 1898, pp. 883–88 and app. 4, pp. 953–59. In addition to his official report, Greely discusses the Santiago campaign in chapter 19 of his *Reminiscences*. See also Howard A. Giddings, "Electric Communication in the Field: Remarks on Equipment," *JMSI* 45 (Jul 1899): 58–64 (reprinted in Scheips, ed., *Military Signal Communications*, vol. 1).

[45]On the prewar preparations of the balloon detachment, see Parkinson, "Politics, Patents, and Planes," ch. 5.

[46]On ballooning at Santiago, see *ARSO*, 1898, pp. 888–91 and Maxfield's report at app. 5, pp. 960–66. Other accounts include Charles Johnson Post, *The Little War of*

Private Post (New York: Signet Books, 1961), pp. 118–24; Parkinson, "Politics, Patents, and Planes," chapter 6, which includes excerpts from Derby's report; John R. Cuneo, "The Balloon at Hell's Corner," *Military Affairs* 7 (Fall 1943): 189–95; Giddings, *Exploits of the Signal Corps*, pp. 47–65; Crouch, *Eagle Aloft*, pp. 524–26.

[47]Companies A and D are perpetuated by the 121st Signal Battalion. Neither Company B nor Company C is perpetuated by an active unit. According to notes in the file of the 121st Signal Battalion, Organizational History Branch, U.S. Army Center of Military History (hereafter cited as DAMH-HSO), the companies were formed per Orders no. 10, War Department, Signal Office, 27 Jul 1898. The volunteer companies serving in Puerto Rico were the 4th, 5th, 7th, and 9th.

[48]*ARSO*, 1898, pp. 895–97 and the reports of Allen, who served as the chief signal officer of the expedition, and Reber at app. 3, pp. 946–53. A photograph of Reber's improvised switchboard faces p. 952. Glassford's report of 7 July 1899, covering his service in Puerto Rico, is published as Appendix 5 to *ARSO*, 1899 in *ARSW*, 1899, vol. 1, pt. 2.

[49]Cosmas, *Army for Empire*, pp. 191–92; Trask, *War with Spain*, chs. 5 and 16.

[50]Trask, *War with Spain*, pp. 105 and 369.

[51]*ARSO*, 1898, p. 877.

[52]Ibid., pp. 877–78 and app. 1; *ARSO*, 1899, p. 798.

[53]For a discussion of the Battle of Manila and the surrender arrangements, see Trask, *War with Spain*, ch. 18.

[54]*ARSO*, 1898, p. 910. For details on the Corps' service in the Philippines, see *ARSO*, 1899, pp. 745–46 and Rpt, Maj Richard E. Thompson to the Chief Signal Officer, 20 Aug 1899, at app. 6; see also Thompson's report to the Adjutant General, Department of the Pacific and Eighth Army Corps, in *ARSW*, 1898, vol. 1, pt. 2, pp. 126–27.

[55]Ltr, Maj R. E. Thompson to the Adjutant General, Department of Pacific and Eighth Army Corps, 14 Aug 1898, printed as inclosure 2 to app. 1, *ARSO*, 1898, p. 918.

[56]For casualty statistics, see *Statistical Exhibit of Strength of Volunteers Called Into Service During the War with Spain; With Losses From All Causes* (Washington, D.C.: Adjutant General's Office, 1899), pp. 2–3.

[57]U.S. Congress, Senate, *Report of the Commission Appointed by the President to Investigate the Conduct of the War Department in the War with Spain*, 56th Cong., 1st sess., 1900, S. Doc. 221, 8 vols., 1: 202.

[58]Donald Smythe, *Guerrilla Warrior: The Early Life of John J. Pershing* (New York: Charles Scribner's Sons, 1973), p. 51.

[59]John J. Pershing, "The Campaign of Santiago," in Hershel V. Cashin et al., *Under Fire with the Tenth U.S. Cavalry* (Chicago: 1902; New York: Arno Press and the New York Times, 1969), p. 206. See also Parkinson, "Politics, Patents, and Planes," pp. 141–53.

[60]From "The Price of the Harness," *Wounds in the Rain* (London: 1900), as quoted in Parkinson, "Politics, Patents, and Planes," p. 142. Crane's comments on the balloon are also quoted in Frank Freidel, *The Splendid Little War* (Boston: Little, Brown and Company, 1958), p. 150.

[61]Reber's map is published as part of Appendix 3, *ARSO*, 1898. See also Greely, "The Signal Corps in War-Time," p. 823.

[62]Rpt, Capt Eugene O. Fechet, Disbursing Officer, to the Chief Signal Officer, 12 Aug 1899 in *ARSO*, 1899, app. 9, p. 818. On photographic techniques, see Beaumont Newhall, *The History of Photography*, revised edition (New York: Museum of Modern Art, 1982), pp. 126f.

[63]The report of the Corps' exhibit, written by Sgt. Harry W. Chadwick, is published as Appendix 20 to *ARSO*, 1901 in *ARSW*, 1901, vol. 1, pt. 2, pp. 1080–81. The Buffalo exposition is, unfortunately, better known as the site of the assassination of President McKinley.

[64]Orders no. 13, War Department, Signal Office, 13 Sep 1898; also published as app. 9, *ARSO*, 1898, pp. 983–85, and in Giddings, *Exploits of the Signal Corps*, pp. 121–26.

[65]On Cuban operations, see *ARSO*, 1899, pp. 931–37 and apps. 1–3; *ARSO*, 1900, pp. 964–71 and app. 3 in *ARSW*, 1900, vol. 1, pt. 2; *ARSO*, 1901, pp. 924–27 and app. 6; *ARSO*, 1902, pp. 671–77. Capt. Otto Nesmith replaced Dunwoody in 1901.

[66]On Puerto Rican operations, see *ARSO*, 1899, pp. 737–39 and app. 5; *ARSO*, 1900, pp. 971–74 and app. 4; *ARSO*, 1901, pp. 927–28 and app. 7.

[67]See Kilbourne's entry in U.S. Congress, Senate Committee on Veterans' Affairs, *Medal of Honor Recipients, 1863–1978*, 96th Cong., 1st sess., 1979, Senate Committee Print no. 3, p. 375. See also *ARSO*, 1899, p. 802. Details of Kilbourne's career are given in Paul D. Hughes, "Charles E. Kilbourne: A Study in Leadership," *Army Communicator* 10 (Summer 1985): 7–9 and "Kilbourne, Charles E.," biographical files, Historical Resources Branch, U.S. Army Center of Military History (hereafter cited as DAMH-HSR). Kilbourne's feat is mentioned in William Thaddeus Sexton, *Soldiers in the Sun: An Adventure in Imperialism* (Freeport, N.Y.: Books for Libraries Press, 1971), p. 96.

[68]On the proclamation, see John M. Gates, *Schoolbooks and Krags: The United States Army in the Philippines, 1898–1902* (Westport, Conn.: Greenwood Press, Inc., 1973), pp. 80–81.

[69]Sexton, *Soldiers in the Sun*, pp. 211–14, describes the rescue of several prisoners to include two members of the Signal Corps, Pvts. Leland S. Smith and Frank Stone. A third signal soldier, Pvt. John G. Desmond, captured along with Smith and Stone, managed to escape from the insurgents. See *ARSO*, 1900, p. 1058. On Philippine operations, see *ARSO*, 1899, pp. 745–46 and app. 6; *ARSO*, 1900, pp. 974–89 and apps. 5–12.

[70]On Philippine cable operations, see *ARSO*, 1899, pp. 739–43 and app. 7; Rpt, Maj Richard E. Thompson to the Chief Signal Officer, 20 Aug 1899, published as app. 6 to *ARSO*, 1899 and app. K to Rpt, Maj Gen E. S. Otis, Commander of the Department of the Pacific and VIII Army Corps, to The Adjutant General, 31 Aug 1899, in *ARSW*, 1899, vol. 1, pt. 4, pp. 254–57; *ARSO*, 1900, p. 986–89 and app. 13; *ARSO*, 1901, pp. 931–32 and apps. 8 and 9; *ARSO*, 1902, pp. 677, 682–84; Paul Wilson Clark, "Major General George O. Squier: Military Scientist" (Ph.D. dissertation, Case Western Reserve University, 1974), pp. 89–95.

[71]On signal operations, see *ARSO*, 1901, pp. 928–33 and apps. 8 and 10; *ARSO*, 1902, pp. 677–96. Maj. William Glassford succeeded Allen in March 1902.

[72]*ARSO*, 1902, pp. 692–93; *ARSO*, 1908, p. 194 in *ARSW*, 1908, vol. 2. According to Heath Twichell, *Allen: The Biography of an Army Officer, 1859–1930* (New Brunswick, N.J.: Rutgers University Press, 1974), p. 143, the Army initially turned over the telephone and telegraph system to the Philippine Constabulary, which operated it until 1906 when the Bureau of Posts assumed control.

[73]*ARSO*, 1899, p. 743. Richardson, ed., *Messages and Papers of the Presidents*, 14: 6354–55.

[74]Clark, "Squier," pp. 89, 95–108.

[75]*ARSO*, 1901, app. 5, p. 959; *Historical Sketch*, p. 49.

[76]For details on the Signal Corps' service in the Boxer Rebellion, see *ARSO*, 1900, pp. 960–64; *ARSO*, 1901, app. 5; *Historical Sketch*, pp. 47–48.

[77]WDGO 37, 9 Mar 1899, announces the increase in enlisted strength; WDGO 36, 4 Mar 1899, contains the provision on volunteer officers.

[78]The personnel increase is announced in WDGO 17, 16 Feb 1900. On the appointment of volunteer officers, see WDGO 86, 16 Jun 1900. The officers were to be first lieutenants whose commissions would expire on 30 June 1901.

[79]WDGO 9, 6 Feb 1901; *ARSO*, 1901, pp. 940–41.

[80]WDGO 63, 1 Jul 1902. On the temporary sergeants, see WDGO 68, 5 Jul 1902, p. 4.

[81]*ARSO*, 1902, pp. 713–14.

[82]*ARSO*, 1901, p. 940.

[83]WDGO 24, 7 Mar 1903.

[84]WDGO 193, 2 Nov 1899.

[85]Under the new Army Regulations of 1895, departmental signal instruction fell under paragraph 1544. This paragraph was amended by WDGO 114, 22 Jun 1899.

[86]WDGO 18, 16 Feb 1900.

[87]On balloon operations, see *ARSO*, 1900, app. 2; *ARSO*, 1901, app. 2. There were no operations to discuss in the reports of 1902 and 1903. See also Parkinson, "Politics, Patents, and Planes," ch. 10; Chandler and Lahm, *How Army Grew Wings*, pp. 50–52; and Crouch, *Eagle Aloft*, pp. 518–29.

[88]*ARSO*, 1902, pp. 717–20; *ARSO*, 1903, pp. 353–54 in *ARSW*, 1903, vol. 2.

[89]For a masterful discussion of the early development of radio technology, see Hugh G. J. Aitken, *Syntony and Spark—The Origins of Radio* (Princeton, N.J.: Princeton University Press, 1985). See also Susan J. Douglas, *Inventing American Broadcasting, 1899–1922* (Baltimore, Md.: Johns Hopkins University Press, 1987), which emphasizes the social and cultural aspects of radio.

[90]Clark, "Squier," pp. 8, 16–17.

[91]A brief report on wireless in San Francisco Harbor is published in *ARSO*, 1901, app. 17, pp. 1073–74. On the Signal Corps' experiments with wireless telegraphy, see Clark, "Squier," pp. 76–78, and *ARSO*, 1900, pp. 992–93.

[92]Rodney Ellis Bell, "A Life of Russell Alexander Alger, 1836–1907" (Ph.D. dissertation, University of Michigan, 1975), pp. 310–11. See also Rpt, Maj Gen H. C. Merriam, Commander of the Department of the Columbia, to The Adjutant General, 1 Oct 1898, in *ARSW*, 1898, vol. 1, pt. 2, pp. 180–81.

[93]WDGO 76, 1 Jun 1900.

[94]William L. Mitchell, *The Opening of Alaska*, ed. Lyman L. Woodman (Anchorage: Cook Inlet Historical Society, 1982).

[95]Ibid., p. 44.

[96]Ibid., p. 87 and p. 88, n. 1. In 1967 Mitchell was posthumously elected to the Mushers' Hall of Fame in Knik, Alaska, for his exploits while working on the telegraph line.

[97]*ARSO*, 1903, p. 329.

[98]See Greely, *Reminiscences*, ch. 20, on his meeting in Canada.

[99]*Historical Sketch*, p. 46.

[100]Some sources, such as the *Historical Sketch*, give the date as 1903. H. L. Chadbourne in his unpublished study "Leonard D. Wildman and the First Alaskan Radio (Safety Harbor-St. Michael)" documents the trials and tribulations of building this system that delayed its successful operation until 1904. The confusion may stem, as Chadbourne believes, from the chief signal officer's annual report of 1904. Although the report is supposed to cover the Corps' operations up to 30 June 1904, it includes the successful open-

ing of the Norton Sound station two months later. This date has apparently been misinterpreted by some writers as August 1903. A copy of Chadbourne's study is in the author's files.

[101]*ARSO*, 1904, p. 368 in *ARSW*, 1904, vol. 2.

[102]Ibid., p. 359.

[103]Details about the construction of the system are contained in the following chief signal officer's annual reports: 1900, pp. 956–60 and app. 18; 1901, pp. 921–24 and apps. 3 and 4; 1902, pp. 663–71; 1903, pp. 327–33; and 1904, pp. 359–69.

[104]James E. Hewes, Jr., *From Root to McNamara: Army Organization and Administration, 1900–1963*, Special Studies (Washington, D.C.: Center of Military History, United States Army, 1975), pp. 2–12; Matloff, ed., *American Military History*, pp. 346–50; Russell F. Weigley, *History of the United States Army* (Bloomington: Indiana University Press, 1984), pp. 313–20. The provisions of the General Staff Act are published in WDGO 15, 18 Feb 1903.

[105]Matloff, ed., *American Military History*, pp. 350–51; Weigley, *History of Army*, pp. 320–22. The Dick Act's provisions are published in WDGO 7, 24 Jan 1903.

[106]*ARSO*, 1900, p. 982. Greely uses the contemporary spelling of Puerto Rico.

CHAPTER IV

The Signal Corps Takes to the Air

Above and beyond the branch's work with balloons, the air took on increased importance for the Signal Corps between 1904 and 1917. During the opening decade of the new century, man realized one of his most ancient dreams—to fly with wings. In addition, the atmosphere assumed new significance as a communications medium. Scientists strove to perfect the broadcast of voice and music by means of wireless telegraphy, better known as radio. Mankind was now "on" the air as well as "in" it. Both technologies possessed great military potential. Although soldiers took some time to fully recognize their value, the Signal Corps, in its search for new and improved forms of communication, introduced both the airplane and the radio into the Army.

International crises accelerated the drive for technical innovation. In Europe, war broke out in August 1914. Closer to home, the United States moved toward confrontation with its southern neighbor. Border clashes became a common occurrence from 1911 onward as Mexico endured bloody revolution and civil war. Tensions culminated with the Mexican Expedition of 1916. While fortunately falling short of a full-scale conflict, the campaign provided the Signal Corps with a laboratory for testing its aerial equipment, and the Army itself garnered valuable experience for the difficult years that lay ahead.

Organization, Training, and Operations, 1904–1907

The years 1904 to 1907 constituted a period of institutional change for the Signal Corps. Like the Army as a whole, the Signal Corps felt the effects of the Root reforms. On a doctrinal level, Army leaders began to consider integrating Signal Corps operations with those of the Army's combat arms in what would later be called combined arms warfare.[1] On a more practical level, new and improved communications devices made their way into the Signal Corps' inventory, even as it supported military operations at home and abroad.

The Signal Corps also continued to cope with its long-standing personnel problem, and its overseas responsibilities placed an enormous strain upon its limited manpower. To provide relief, Congress expanded the Corps' enlisted strength in April 1904 to 1,212 men, an addition of 402 men or nearly 50 percent of its previous strength of 810. This increased complement included thirty-six slots in the new category of master signal electrician. These men, selected through the examination of first-class sergeants, performed a variety of duties to include ballooning, cable splicing and laying, telegraphy, telephony, and working in power plants.[2]

The authorized number of Signal Corps officers remained forty-six. Chief Signal Officer Greely continued to lament the Corps' low percentage of field-grade officers, which allowed only a few men to receive promotions within the branch. Nevertheless, the Corps continued to perform exemplary service and in 1904 received praise for its work in Alaska from the new Secretary of War, William Howard Taft. Taft singled out General Greely for special commendation.[3]

One of the Root reforms, however, exacerbated Greely's personnel difficulties. The Army Reorganization Act, signed into law by President McKinley on 2 February 1901, eliminated permanent appointments to staff departments or corps. Officers would be detailed to the staff for four years and then serve for two years with the line before again becoming eligible for staff duty.[4] In theory, this system provided more officers with the opportunity to gain staff experience, while the alternating tours with line units kept them from becoming too entrenched in the bureaucracy and ignorant of conditions within the line. Unfortunately, few chose to serve their detail with the Signal Corps. Despite efforts to secure volunteers, Greely had to resort to conscription to obtain the needed officers. Of the sixteen men detailed as of 1905, he explained, "fully one-fourth have endeavored to evade service through personal or political influence."[5] As in past attempts, the detailing process, even in its new guise, did not prove very satisfactory for the Signal Corps. The chief signal officer continued to request that Congress increase the Corps' officer strength, but to no avail.

In addition to staff-line rotation, the improvement and standardization of education throughout the Army constituted one of the main objectives of the Root reforms. Beginning with the establishment of the Army War College in 1901, the War Department created a tier of service schools. As part of this system, the Signal School opened at Fort Leavenworth on 1 September 1905, while the school at Fort Myer closed. The inclusion of a separate signal school at Leavenworth explicitly recognized that the Signal Corps constituted a distinct branch of the Army.[6]

The Signal School was only one of several that comprised what became known as the Leavenworth Schools. It shared the post with the Army Staff College, the Infantry and Cavalry School (renamed in 1907 as the School of the Line), and, in 1910, the Field Engineer School. The officers attending the Leavenworth Schools received signal instruction as part of their curriculum, thus becoming familiar with the Signal Corps' role as part of the combined arms team.[7]

Maj. George O. Squier became the first head of the new Signal School, with the title of assistant commandant. (The commandant of the Staff College, Brig. Gen. J. Franklin Bell, also served as commandant of all the schools at the post.) The chief signal officer could recommend up to five Signal Corps officers for attendance each year. Officers from other branches as well as from the National

Guard could also enroll. The course of instruction included visual, acoustical, and electrical signaling; electrical and mechanical engineering; aeronautics; photography; topography; and foreign languages.[8] The officers and men of Company A, Signal Corps, served as school troops, conducting exercises to demonstrate practical applications. The school's graduates would, ostensibly, provide the Signal Corps with the trained officers it needed.

In the field, however, signal training in line units remained problematical. In 1905 the Signal Corps consisted of 11 provisional companies: 6 in the United States, 2 in Alaska, and 3 in the Philippines.[9] Usually less than half of the Army's nine geographical departments within the United States had a full-time signal officer, and Army regulations still contained the requirement that two men in each company, troop, and battery maintain competence in flag signaling.[10] The Corps continued, however, to issue kits containing two-foot flags and field glasses, with over three hundred such kits having been distributed by 1907.[11] Yet the increasingly technical nature of the Corps' operations demanded specialized training and a better distribution of signal personnel.

Consequently, the chief of staff recommended and the secretary of war approved a plan in 1905 to station a signal company in each of the Army's four geographical administrative divisions. (Each division contained two or more departments, and each department comprised several states or territories. The Philippines constituted a fifth division.) The new stations selected were Fort Wood, on Bedloe's Island in New York Harbor, for the Atlantic Division; Omaha Barracks, Nebraska, for the Northern Division; Benicia Barracks, California, for the Pacific Division; and Fort Leavenworth for the Southwest Division. Fort Wood, manned by Company G, Signal Corps, housed the school for fire-control work and submarine cables and became the home of the Corps' East Coast cable ships, the *Joseph Henry* and the *Cyrus W. Field*. Company G's duties included the care and lighting of the island's most famous resident, the Statue of Liberty.[12] Companies B and D, Signal Corps, garrisoned Omaha Barracks where the instruction of enlisted men and the ballooning activities, formerly located at Fort Myer, continued. Benicia Barracks, home of Companies E and H, Signal Corps, served as the rendezvous point for men going to and returning from the Philippines and Alaska. Finally, at Fort Leavenworth Company A handled the departmental duties in addition to its work at the Signal School.

Under the Root reforms, the War Department General Staff became the Army's planning and coordinating agency, and the development of unit organization formed an important aspect of the General Staff's plans for future wars. In 1905 the War Department published the Army's first *Field Service Regulations*, which provided for the formation of provisional brigades and divisions in the event of mobilization. While European armies used the corps as their primary unit, the division became the U.S. Army's basic combined arms unit, containing all the types of smaller units necessary for independent action. Signal troops were included among them.

Although the Signal Corps for many years had grouped its personnel into provisional companies for administrative purposes, the chief signal officer had never received statutory authority to organize permanent tactical units. (The Regular Army signal companies formed during the War with Spain had been established under orders of the chief signal officer.) According to the 1905 *Field Service Regulations*, a division would include a signal company comprising 4 officers and 150 enlisted men. These men would be divided into detachments to provide corps-level communications, visual signaling, and the construction, operation, and repair of telegraph and telephone lines.[13] While the Army never fully implemented these regulations, they represented an attempt to prepare for future conflicts, rather than to rely on hastily organized forces as the nation had done during previous wars.[14]

Although he still lacked legislative authority, the chief signal officer issued a circular in October 1907 that outlined a provisional organization for divisional signal companies. Each division would contain three signal companies of four officers and one hundred men. These companies were differentiated by function into field, base, and telegraph companies: A field company operated tactical lines of communication; a base company provided strategic communications; and a telegraph company served the division's administrative communication needs.[15] The chief signal officer provisionally organized Companies A, D, E, and I as field signal companies, but the shortage of men and officers limited them to only about three officers and seventy-five men each. A fully equipped company could establish forty miles of telegraph lines, thirty miles of electrical buzzer lines, two portable wireless telegraph stations, and six visual stations.[16]

On an operational level, the Signal Corps continued to perform a wide variety of duties at home and abroad. In 1904 it still operated over five hundred miles of military telegraph lines within the United States that handled over forty-one thousand messages during the year. But the total mileage was steadily decreasing, and by 1907 it stood at less than one hundred fifty miles.[17] The discontinuance of the more than two hundred miles of line between Forts Brown and McIntosh, Texas, in 1906 (the War Department having abandoned both posts in that year) contributed significantly to this precipitous drop. While domestic military telegraph duties declined (the Corps still operated sizable systems in Alaska and the Philippines), the installation of post telephone systems kept signalmen busy. These systems were divided into two classes: those for coast artillery fire control and those for administrative purposes. By 1907 the Corps had installed telephone systems at fifty-nine of the seventy-one posts within the continental United States, in addition to those already in operation at coastal fortifications. The demand for telephones led the secretary of war to limit the number that could be installed at each post. While the Signal Corps did not maintain and run these post systems, it did retain the right to inspect them.[18]

On 9 April 1904, Secretary Taft relieved the Signal Corps of one of its duties, the supervision of the War Department library. In the eleven years that the branch had managed the library it had doubled the number of volumes, eliminated the fictional works in the collection by distributing them among Army post libraries, and generally introduced modern library methods. Control of the library passed to the Military Information Division of the General Staff.[19]

As the United States Army sought to modernize, foreign armies served as important sources of information and new ideas. The War Department learned a great deal from the observations of officers sent to witness the Russo-Japanese War of 1904–1905.[20] The Japanese victory stemmed in large part from their superior use of modern battlefield techniques, including efficient means of communication. Like the Americans, the Japanese had studied such recent conflicts as the War with Spain and the Boer War, and they effectively applied the lessons learned. In addition to tactical and strategic telegraphy, they made considerable use of the field telephone,

General Allen

especially to control the indirect fire of field artillery. The United States Army also experimented with this technique and in 1905 adopted indirect fire as the preferred method of employing field artillery. The Signal Corps provided the necessary telephones to field artillery units.[21] The Russians, meanwhile, made greater use of wireless than the Japanese, but their personnel lacked adequate training. Moreover, wireless technology had not yet been perfected.[22]

The Signal Corps ended an era on 10 February 1906 when President Theodore Roosevelt promoted Chief Signal Officer Greely to major general and the War Department assigned him to command the Pacific Division with headquarters at San Francisco. He had guided the Signal Corps through its transition from the controversial weather service period into the modern electrical age. Greely's tenure of nearly nineteen years stands as the longest of any chief signal officer in history. His lifetime of "splendid public service" was recognized nearly thirty years later, on his ninety-first birthday, when Greely received the Medal of Honor.[23]

Greely passed the torch to Col. James Allen, who had been serving as his assistant in Washington. Allen was a West Point graduate, class of 1872, and had joined the Signal Corps in 1890. His accomplishments since then had been many and varied. In recommending Allen for the appointment, Greely referred to him as "one of the ablest and most competent officers I have known in 45 years of active service."[24] Allen's promotion to brigadier general was concurrent with Greely's elevation in rank.

Upheavals at Home and Abroad

Greely had hardly pinned on his second star when he was faced with a major challenge: the San Francisco earthquake during the early morning of 18 April 1906 and the subsequent fire that raged for four days. Learning of the disaster while on his way East for his daughter's wedding, Greely hurried back to the devastated city, arriving on the 22d. In his absence, troops under Brig. Gen. Frederick Funston, commander of the Department of California, had assisted with the firefighting, helped to maintain law and order, and undertaken the administration of emergency relief services.

Amid the chaos, the maintenance of communications posed a difficult problem. The earthquake had knocked out the city's telephone system and destroyed virtually all of its telegraph lines. In the immediate aftermath of the disaster the only remaining communication with the outside world was provided by "one or two insecure wires to the East operated by the Western Union and Postal Telegraph Companies from their shattered main offices."[25] Later in the day flames destroyed even these tenuous connections, and the city's half million residents found themselves isolated from the rest of the country. Fortunately, the Signal Corps could step in during the emergency. By 1000 on the 18th, about five hours after the earthquake occurred, Capt. Leonard D. Wildman, the departmental signal officer, had established a field telegraph line between the Presidio and the outskirts of the fire. With the aid of the Corps' operators, instruments, and material, the commercial telegraph companies gradually restored operations.

Luckily, due to the new stationing plan, the Signal Corps had storehouses and two companies (E and H) located at Benicia Barracks, only thirty-six miles away. Local National Guard units, to include the 2d Company Signal Corps, assisted in the relief efforts. This company laid telegraph lines connecting the city's Guard headquarters with subordinate units.[26] On 1 May, Company A, Signal Corps, commanded by Capt. William Mitchell, arrived from Fort Leavenworth to provide additional men and material. They remained on duty in the city for a month.[27] In the burned areas, military telegraph lines remained in use until 10 May. Citywide, Wildman set up a system of forty-two telegraph offices and seventy-nine telephone offices that connected all the military districts, federal buildings, railroad offices and depots, the offices of the mayor and governor, and other locations as needed.[28] Because the cables in the harbor had been destroyed, the Signal Corps employed visual signals, including flags, heliographs, and acetylene lanterns, to communicate between Angel Island and Alcatraz. To restore the cables, the Corps called upon the *Burnside*, usually on duty in Alaska.

General Funston, in his report, commended Wildman for his proficiency and ability "in establishing and maintaining telegraph and telephone communication under the almost impossible conditions existing during the conflagration and immediately afterwards." Greely echoed Funston's praise.[29]

A modern machine, the automobile, proved especially useful during the emergency, when the streets were full of rubble and the city's famed cable cars

Signal Corps telegraph office, San Francisco, 1906

out of service. The Signal Corps had purchased four commercial automobiles in the previous two years, and at the time of the earthquake one of them was in San Francisco.[30] On the first day alone, this redoubtable vehicle traveled over two hundred miles carrying not only messages but signal equipment, medical supplies, food, the sick and wounded, and just about anything that needed hauling "over broken and piled-up asphalt pavement, through walls of flames, under or through networks of trailing wires and over piles of brick and broken cornices lined with scrap tin, and with sharp splinters of iron and wood everywhere."[31] While the automobile performed well during this crisis and the Signal Corps experimented during this period with an auto-telegraph car, neither the Corps nor the Army made extensive use of motor vehicles until the Mexican Expedition, just prior to America's entrance into World War I.[32]

The year 1906 continued to be an eventful one for the Signal Corps. That fall U.S. troops once again landed on Cuban soil, four years after the end of the military occupation that had followed the War with Spain. The deployment of the "Army of Cuban Pacification" was authorized by the Platt Amendment, embodied in the Cuban Constitution of 1901, which granted to the United States the right to intervene to preserve Cuban independence.[33] The United States invoked the amendment in September 1906 when a revolt by the opposition party caused the Cuban republic to collapse. Secretary of War Taft, already in Cuba as part of a peace mission, established a provisional government with himself as temporary governor. Pending the arrival of the Army, about two thousand marines landed to maintain order and protect property. In October the occupation force of 5,000 Army troops arrived. One thousand marines making up the 1st Provisional Marine Regiment remained under Army command, bringing the total American strength to 6,000.[34]

Army forces in Cuba included Company I, Signal Corps, commanded by Capt. George S. Gibbs. The newly organized unit comprised a total of 4 officers and 153 enlisted men. It also contained the Corps' first field wireless platoon, which soon established communication between Camp Columbia, the Army's headquarters west of Havana, and the fleet in Havana Harbor. With the help of a 100-foot antenna, the platoon also established communication with Key West, ninety miles away. In the field the Corps sometimes used portable wireless sets (weighing over four hundred pounds and carried by mules) instead of temporary telegraph or telephone lines. Signalmen also operated telephone and telegraph lines in Havana, including those belonging to the Cuban government, and connected the American troops at their stations throughout the island.[35] Company I returned to the United States in January 1909 as the American intervention came to an end with the restoration of Cuban self-government.[36]

Simultaneously, in the Philippines, sporadic fighting continued in the ongoing attempt to bring the primitive peoples of the southern islands under American control. On the island of Jolo a band of fierce Moros had taken refuge atop Mount Bud-Dajo, venturing forth on occasion to launch raids in the surrounding countryside. Fearing a worsening of the situation, the Army decided to send troops against them. During this operation, on 7 March 1906, 1st Lt. Gordon Johnston joined the list of Signal Corpsman to have earned the Medal of Honor when he "voluntarily took part in and was dangerously wounded during an assault on the enemy's works."[37] Ironically, Johnston, commissioned in the Cavalry, numbered among those line officers unhappily detailed to the Signal Corps. He had tried to secure relief from his detail, but Chief Signal Officer Greely had denied his request. Following his distinguished service in the Philippines and after recovering from his wounds, Johnston finally found himself back in the Cavalry in 1907.[38]

In both Cuba and the Philippines, the Signal Corps increasingly relied upon buzzer lines which used telephones to transmit Morse code. (The high-pitched hum of the telegraphic signals as heard through the telephone receiver has been likened to the sound of "a giant mosquito singing to its young.")[39] The value of the buzzer lay in its ability to operate successfully over poorly insulated or even bare wires where an ordinary telegraph would fail. Buzzer lines could also be employed as regular telephone lines. A smaller version of the device, known as the cavalry buzzer, could be carried on horseback.[40] Maj. Charles McK. Saltzman, a future chief signal officer, wrote in 1907 that "The day of the mounted orderly has passed, and the most important enlisted man in the fifty-mile battle line of the future will be the man behind the buzzer."[41]

During the early years of the new century, the Signal Corps had undergone modernization in response to the reforms implemented by the General Staff and the advances being made in communications technology. In a world that was becoming increasingly professionalized there remained, however, room for achievement by amateurs. Two brothers from Dayton, Ohio, owners of a bicycle shop, finally solved the long-standing problem of heavier-than-air flight through hard work and ingenuity. Chief Signal Officer Allen and the Signal Corps, along with the rest of the world, would soon become well acquainted with Wilbur and Orville Wright and their flying machine.

The Signal Corps Gets the Wright Stuff

Since 1892 lack of funds and facilities had continually hampered the Signal Corps' aerial operations. Although the Corps had constructed a balloon house at Fort Myer in 1901, Chief Signal Officer Greely never succeeded in getting a gas generating plant built there. With the closing of the school at Myer in 1905, Greely sent the Corps' aerial equipment to Benicia Barracks pending completion of new facilities at Fort Omaha.

Meanwhile, several factors combined to spur a revival of the Army's aeronautical program. In particular, a growing interest in aeronautics among the general public led to the formation of the Aero Club of America in 1905. This organization sponsored many aerial events and administered the licensing of pilots.[42] Its early membership included two Signal Corps officers, Maj. Samuel Reber and Capt. Charles deForest Chandler. Moreover, another soldier, 1st Lt. Frank P. Lahm, then attending the French cavalry school at Saumur, won the first Gordon Bennett international balloon race held in France in 1906.[43]

Under Chief Signal Officer Allen, aviation assumed a more prominent role in the Signal Corps' mission. His assistant, Maj. George O. Squier, was instrumental in bringing about this change. While at Leavenworth Squier had pursued the study of aeronautics in addition to his other scientific interests. He recognized the importance of the work being done by the Wright brothers and closely followed their progress. When he came to Washington in July 1907, Squier brought not only his expertise but his extensive list of contacts within the scientific community at large and the aeronautical community in particular. Shortly after Squier's arrival Allen issued a memorandum on 1 August 1907 creating an Aeronautical Division within the Office of the Chief Signal Officer, which was to have charge "of all matters pertaining to military ballooning, air machines, and all kindred subjects."[44] Captain Chandler became the division's head. In the fall of 1907 the Corps shipped its balloon equipment from Benicia Barracks to Washington so that Chandler and the men assigned to his division could conduct ascensions. During some of these flights they successfully experimented with the reception of wireless messages in the balloon car.[45] Meanwhile, Lieutenant Lahm, who remained in France while recovering from illness, received orders from the War Department to observe the aeronautical sections of the British and German armies. He exceeded his orders and visited the Belgian and French armies as well. On his return to the United States, Lahm reported for duty to the Signal Office.[46] In 1908 the Corps completed its new balloon facilities at Fort Omaha, which included a plant for hydrogen generation. The proximity of this post to the Signal School made it possible for the students at Leavenworth to travel there for aeronautical instruction.

Although their accomplishment remained relatively unknown, the Wright brothers had demonstrated the feasibility of heavier-than-air flight nearly five years earlier, in December 1903.[47] In fact, they had offered to sell their airplane to the United States government through the Board of Ordnance and Fortification on two occasions in 1905. That body, still skeptical about flying machines after supporting Samuel P. Langley's failed project two years earlier, had ignored the Wrights' offers. Rebuffed at home, the Wrights pursued opportunities to sell their plane in Europe. Finally, in 1907, the War Department reopened communication with them. Wilbur Wright appeared before the Board of Ordnance and Fortification in December 1907 and convinced the members and Chief Signal Officer Allen, who also attended, of the legitimacy of their claims. Subsequently, on 23 December 1907, the Signal Corps issued an advertisement and specifications to solicit bids for a heavier-than-air flying machine. The Corps' requirements included that the machine carry two persons, travel at least forty miles per hour, and be capable of sustained flight for at least an hour. The Corps also preferred that the machine be compact enough to be dismantled for transport in an Army wagon and readily reassembled. While the specifications closely followed the capabilities of the Wrights' airplane, the Corps also consulted with other scientists and engineers, to include Alexander Graham Bell, prior to their issuance.[48]

Despite the advent of heavier-than-air flight, the Signal Corps continued its work with lighter-than-air craft. Early in 1908 the Signal Office issued another set of specifications, these calling for a dirigible, that is, a sausage-shaped, engine-powered balloon that could be steered, later known as an airship. Europeans had taken the lead in dirigible development, and the name of the German Count Ferdinand von Zeppelin was most closely associated with this type of flying machine. The Signal Corps required the dirigible to also carry two persons and travel at least twenty miles per hour.[49] Although it had previously lost a considerable sum by backing Langley, the Board of Ordnance and Fortification granted funds to purchase both the heavier-than-air and the lighter-than-air craft because the Signal Corps had no money within its own budget to do so.[50] The flight trials of both the dirigible and the airplane were scheduled to be held at Fort Myer during the summer of 1908.

Not surprisingly, the Wright brothers numbered among the forty-one applicants submitting plans for a flying machine to the Signal Office. The Corps received many unusual proposals, including one from a prisoner in a federal penitentiary who promised to furnish an acceptable plane on the condition that the Army secure his release from prison. Of the three serious bidders who complied with the specifications, only the Wrights delivered a plane to Fort Myer for the flight trials.[51]

Dirigible at Fort Myer, Virginia, 1908

Major Squier headed an Aeronautical Board formed to supervise the trials, which began in August with the testing of the dirigible. Thomas S. Baldwin of Hammondsport, New York (he moved there after his airship factory was destroyed in the San Francisco earthquake), had submitted the winning bid, and his machine successfully met the Corps' requirements. The Army purchased his airship, which became known as Dirigible Number 1. The Corps used the dirigible at Fort Omaha until it became unserviceable, and in 1912 the Army sold the airship rather than invest in a new envelope.[52]

When the airplane trials began on 3 September 1908, crowds of curious spectators flocked to Fort Myer to witness the spectacle. Orville Wright conducted the tests, since Wilbur was then making flight demonstrations in Europe. The first flight lasted only one minute and eleven seconds, but on 9 September he remained aloft for one hour and two minutes. Earlier that day Lieutenant Lahm had accompanied Orville on a flight lasting over six minutes. Three days later Major Squier flew with Orville for over nine minutes. On 17 September Orville's passenger was 1st Lt. Thomas E. Selfridge, also a member of the Aeronautical Board. Selfridge had acquired considerable aeronautical experience, having until recently worked

Orville Wright flies over Fort Myer, 1908.

with Alexander Graham Bell, Glenn Curtiss, and others in a group known as the Aerial Experiment Association.[53] On this day, however, disaster struck when a propeller blade cracked, causing the plane to crash. Selfridge died of his injuries, thus becoming the first American soldier killed in an airplane; Orville spent over six weeks recuperating in the Fort Myer hospital before returning home to Dayton.[54] The Signal Corps postponed the airplane trials for nine months to allow the Wrights to try again. Despite the tragedy, Chief Signal Officer Allen remarked in his 1908 annual report, "The preliminary tests of the aeroplane at Fort Myer, Va., have publicly demonstrated, however, the practicability of mechanical flight."[55]

After rebuilding their plane and making some improvements, both of the Wright brothers returned to Fort Myer in June 1909 to resume the trials. Following a month of practice flights, the official tests began on 27 July with Orville once again at the controls. For the endurance test, Lieutenant Lahm accompanied Orville on a flight lasting 1 hour, 12 minutes, and 40 seconds, thereby exceeding the one hour called for in the specifications. For the speed test on 30 July, Orville and 1st Lt. Benjamin D. Foulois flew a ten-mile cross-country course between Fort Myer and Alexandria, Virginia. A captive balloon marked the halfway point at Shooter's (Shuter's) Hill in Alexandria, now the site of the George Washington Masonic National Memorial. A crowd of approximately seven thousand people, including President Taft, witnessed the historic flight. Completing the course at an average speed of 42.583 miles per hour, Orville again exceeded the contract requirements. With the successful conclusion of the trials, the Army purchased the Wrights' plane for $30,000.[56]

Their contract with the Army stipulated that the Wrights would teach two soldiers how to fly. Because of the limited open area at Fort Myer, the Signal Corps selected a more spacious location for the training in College Park, Maryland, about eight miles from Washington, D.C. Here, in the fall of 1909, Lieutenant Lahm and Lt. Frederic E. Humphreys became the Army's first pilots, with Wilbur Wright as their instructor. Lieutenant Foulois returned from an assignment in Europe in time to receive about three hours of instruction before operations shut down for the winter. (Not only was the fragile plane unable to withstand severe winter weather, especially strong winds, but no one had yet developed warm flight clothing for the pilots, who sat out in the open air.) Wilbur Wright, having fulfilled his contractual obligation, returned to Dayton. Lieutenants Lahm and Humphreys, only on temporary detail with the Signal Corps, went back to their regular units.[57] Their departures left Foulois alone with a plane and no one to teach him how to fly it. In December he received orders to accompany the aircraft to Fort Sam Houston, Texas. As Foulois recalls in his memoirs, Chief Signal Officer Allen called him into his office and ordered him to "take plenty of spare parts, and teach yourself to fly." If the lieutenant had any questions, he could write to the Wright brothers for the answers. Thus, at Fort Sam Houston, Foulois took the first "correspondence course" in flying.[58]

For the next two years Foulois and the Wright plane constituted the Signal Corps' entire air force. As usual, Congress appropriated no funds to support aviation, despite General Allen's repeated requests. As one congressman reputedly remarked: "Why all this fuss about airplanes for the Army—I thought we already had one."[59] Consequently, Foulois footed much of the airplane's maintenance costs out of his own pocket. Despite his straitened circumstances, the novice aviator accomplished a great deal. Most important, he succeeded in learning to fly and lived to tell about it. But his education proved to be a difficult and dangerous one, punctuated by a number of crash landings. On one such occasion, after nearly being thrown from the plane, Foulois installed the first aircraft seat belt.

While in Texas, Foulois' one-man air force received its first field experience early in 1911 in conjunction with Army maneuvers held along the Mexican border. In the process, he gave many soldiers their first glimpse of an airplane in flight. Foulois performed aerial reconnaissance and used a radio to make his report. With this device he could communicate in Morse code with Signal Corps stations on the ground. After February 1911, Foulois did not fly the Army's plane but rather a Wright machine owned by Robert F. Collier, magazine publisher and member of the Aero Club of America. Collier loaned his airplane to the Army pending the appropriation of funds to obtain new equipment. Subsequently, the Army sent its first and only aircraft to Dayton for restoration and eventual display in the Smithsonian.[60]

While Foulois participated in the maneuvers along the border, Congress, faced with the threat of hostilities in Mexico, finally included $125,000 for aviation in the budget for fiscal year 1912. The lawmakers made $25,000 of the sum immediately available, and the Signal Corps used the money to purchase five new planes: three designed by the Wrights (Type B) and two manufactured by their rival, Glenn Curtiss, with whom the Wright brothers were entangled in a bitter patent suit. With new planes and pilots ordered to Fort Sam Houston, a provisional "aero company" was organized there in April 1911. The operations of this unit ceased, however, following the death of one of the pilots, Lt. G. E. M. Kelly, in a crash on 10 May.[61]

In June 1911 the Signal Corps officially opened a flying school at College Park, Maryland.[62] Foulois did not number among the pilots reporting there, having been reassigned to a tour of duty with the Militia Bureau. Two of the new pilots at College Park, 2d Lts. Henry H. ("Hap") Arnold and Thomas DeW. Milling, had previously received training at the Wright Company in Dayton.[63] Training on a Wright machine, however, did not prepare a pilot to fly a Curtiss plane, and vice versa. While the Wrights controlled their planes by means of the wing-warping method, on which they had received a patent in 1906, Curtiss used movable ailerons between rigid wings.[64] In these early years pilots usually knew how to fly either one type of plane or the other. Filling out the roster at College Park, an enlisted detail performed maintenance and guard duty. In addition to taking flying lessons that summer, the pilots experimented with a bombsight.

With the onset of cold weather, aviation operations again moved south. This time the Corps selected Augusta, Georgia, known for its mild winter climate, as its destination. As luck would have it, the winter of 1911–1912 proved to be an exception, with heavy snows falling in Georgia during both January and February. In the spring the melting snow plus excessive rainfall caused flooding. Fortunately, the soldiers had placed the planes on platforms, and they were not damaged. Between the bouts of bad weather the pilots managed to fit in some practice. They also received a visit in January from Wilbur Wright, no doubt a source of much valuable advice. The aviation world lost this pioneer when he died of typhoid fever at age forty-five the following May.[65]

Flying resumed at College Park in April 1912. The next month several new planes arrived. These more powerful "scout" planes (Wright Type C) had been designed to perform reconnaissance and could carry radio and photographic equipment in addition to two men.[66] Experimental activities conducted at College Park during this year included night flying, aerial photography, use of the radio, and the testing of the Lewis machine gun from the air.[67] Despite this experiment and the earlier one with the bombsight, few military experts recognized the offensive value of airplanes. Indeed, the rather flimsy machines themselves gave little indication of their potential for combat.

Yet Army fliers continued to gain experience and knowledge. During the summer of 1912 several pilots from College Park made reconnaissance flights in conjunction with maneuvers held in Connecticut. Later that fall Arnold and others went to Fort Riley, Kansas, to perform aerial observation of field artillery. By 1 November 1912 the number of personnel at the school had grown to twelve officers and thirty-nine men.[68] When operations at College Park ended for the winter, the Curtiss pilots went to San Diego, California, where Curtiss operated a school and experimental station. On 8 December 1912 the Signal Corps established its own flying school on North Island in San Diego Bay.[69] Meanwhile, the Wright pilots returned to Augusta. During the winter training there the Wright Company delivered its new "speed scout" plane (Type D), which carried only the pilot and could travel over sixty-six miles per hour. The Signal Corps intended to use this type of plane for strategic reconnaissance and the rapid delivery of messages.[70]

Aviation was an especially hazardous undertaking for the aerial pioneers, and many brave men lost their lives. To provide professional recognition and incentive for pilots, the War Department established the rank of military aviator in 1912. To achieve this rating a pilot had to be able, for example, to attain an altitude of at least 2,500 feet; to fly in a wind of at least 15 miles per hour for 5 minutes; and to make a reconnaissance flight of at least 20 miles cross-country at an average altitude of 1,500 feet. These requirements exceeded those previously prescribed by the Aero Club of America and reflected the introduction of more powerful planes. Qualified fliers wore the newly authorized military aviator's badge.[71] The following year Congress acknowledged the risks taken by pilots when it authorized flight pay for those assigned to full-time aviation duty. The bonus amounted to a 35 percent increase in salary, but Congress limited to thirty the number of men who could receive the extra payment.[72]

After seven years at the head of the Signal Corps, General Allen relinquished his position on 13 February 1913, having reached the mandatory retirement age of sixty-four. Less than a month later, on 5 March, Brig. Gen. George P. Scriven became the Army's seventh chief signal officer.[73] A member of the West Point class of 1878, Scriven had over twenty years of experience with the Corps. While not an aviator when he became chief, he soon began taking lessons in order to better understand the problems the pilots faced.[74] His views on aviation would set the Signal Corps' policy in the crucial years leading up to World War I.

General Scriven

Increased interest in aviation soon obliged the Signal Corps to defend its dominion over the Army's air force. Early in his tenure Scriven testified before the House Committee on Military Affairs concerning proposed legislation to create a separate Aviation Corps. In his report Scriven argued against the idea.

It is no time now to make experimental changes, whatever the future may develop in regard to the organization of a separate corps. This may come, and may really be the fourth arm of the service; but now we are crossing the stream, and it is not time to swap horses or to make changes which will certainly cost the advance of military aviation many years of delay.[75]

Several Army aviators, including Foulois and Arnold, agreed with Scriven and testified against the proposal.[76] The committee also heard another voice defending the status quo, that of Capt. William Mitchell, then serving a tour on the General Staff and not yet an Army aviator. Mitchell stated that in his opinion aviation's role was that of reconnaissance and, for that reason, part of the Signal Corps' communications mission.[77] The arguments of Scriven and the other opponents convinced the committee to reject the bill as written. While aviation remained something of a stepchild, the hearings did focus attention on its potential importance to the Army. Meanwhile, statistics compiled for the hearings clearly showed the lowly status then held by Army aviation: The United States ranked fourteenth out of twenty-six nations in the amount of its expenditures for aviation over the past five years. Germany ranked first.[78]

While congressmen debated their future, the Signal Corps' pilots were being put to work. Trouble flared again with Mexico in February 1913, and President Taft ordered the War Department to mobilize the 2d Division along the border. The Army aviators at Augusta were called to service, and at Texas City, Texas, the Signal Corps' aviation assets were organized to form the 1st Aero Squadron (Provisional) to support the division. Captain Chandler served as the squadron's first commander. During this period Lieutenant Milling made a cross-country flight from Texas City to San Antonio and back, totaling 480 miles, that set American distance and endurance records. Milling's observer, Lt. William C. Sherman, demonstrated the airplane's value for reconnaissance by making a detailed sketch map of the ground covered during the flight. (When finished, the map measured eighteen feet in length!)

By mid-June it had become apparent that no hostilities would ensue. Most of the squadron then left Texas for San Diego, where the Signal Corps had opened a new flying school. The California location possessed one significant advantage over Maryland: The climate permitted year-round training. On 13 December 1913 the school at San Diego officially became the Signal Corps Aviation School, and the Army did not renew its lease on the land at College Park.[79]

Meanwhile, serious problems with both planes and pilot training were coming to light. In 1913 alone seven officers had died, bringing the total number of aviation fatalities since 1908 to eleven officers and one enlisted man. Half of the deaths had occurred in the Wright Model C. All six of the Model Cs purchased by the Army had crashed, and Lieutenant Lahm could count himself among the lucky few to have survived. While operating a Wright C at Fort Riley in 1912, Lieutenant Arnold had come so close to death that he swore to give up flying forever.[80] The Wright planes in general had a tendency to nose dive: When they crashed, the engine often tore loose and fell upon the pilot or passenger. With its extra power, the Model C proved more hazardous than its predecessors.

The rapidly rising death toll among Army aviators led to an investigation into the situation. In its report, the board of inquiry condemned the Wright C as "dynamically unsuited for flying."[81] But the problems did not lie solely with the planes. The school at North Island received a very unfavorable report early in 1914 from the Inspector General's Department.[82] Consequently, the Signal Corps hired Grover Loening, a former employee of the Wright Company, as the Army's first aeronautical engineer to oversee operations at San Diego. Furthermore, and most important, the Signal Corps outlawed the use of all pusher planes (that is, those with the engine and propellers behind the pilot), whether manufactured by the Wright Company or by Curtiss. The switch to tractor planes, in which the engine and propellers are in front of the wings and the pilot, did not meet with the approval of Loening's former employer: For several years Orville Wright refused to begin to manufacture this type of aircraft. The conversion to tractors did, however, cause an immediate drop in the number of fatalities. Only one pilot died in the next six months, and this mishap occurred when his plane was blown out to sea in a storm.[83]

Having concentrated its aeronautical pursuits on the airplane, the Signal Corps no longer needed a balloon plant. Thus, in October 1913, the Corps abandoned its post at Fort Omaha, and the Army transferred the balloon facilities to the Agriculture Department for use by the Weather Bureau in the making of balloon explorations of the upper atmosphere. Meanwhile, the Corps moved the signal companies stationed at Omaha to Leavenworth.[84]

On 4 December 1913 the War Department finally issued general orders that outlined the provisional organization for a Signal Corps aero squadron, although such a unit had participated in the maneuvers on the border earlier that year. The squadron would consist of twenty officers and ninety enlisted men organized into two aero companies, each with four airplanes and eight aviators. The unit would also have its own ground transportation in the form of sixteen tractors and six motorcycles.[85]

The Signal Corps had gotten the Army off the ground, but it had not yet really soared. After more than six years of existence, the Aeronautical Division remained small and underfunded. By the end of 1913 the Corps had received less than a half million dollars in total appropriations for aviation and had only twenty officers on duty at the San Diego flight school.[86] On the positive side, fifty-two officers had been detailed to aeronautical duty since 1907; the Army had purchased twenty-four planes since 1909 (fifteen of which remained in operation); and the Signal Corps had established an aviation school.[87] Despite its initial lead in military aviation and subsequent accomplishments, the United States had fallen far behind the flourishing aerial operations of the major European powers.

Radio—The Wave of the Future

Next to aviation, radio was considered to be the wonder of the age during the early twentieth century. Initially known as wireless telegraphy, it freed long distance communication from the constraints of wires. Wireless telegraphy meant exactly that—Morse code transmitted by electromagnetic waves instead of wires. The discharge of a spark across a gap caused by the pressing of a telegraph key generated the electromagnetic waves that relayed the message. The years 1900 to 1915 constituted "the golden age of the spark transmitter," with the names of Guglielmo Marconi, Reginald Fessenden, and Lee de Forest the most prominent in the early development of radio.

Spark-gap technology possessed several important drawbacks. From a security standpoint, a spark transmission could not be tuned; it covered a span of frequencies and could be intercepted by anyone with a receiver. Moreover, the signals of all stations within range of each other caused mutual interference. Not only did the noisy spark create a great deal of distortion, the consequent dissipation of energy over the broad band of frequencies lessened the distance over which the signals could travel. Only with advances in continuous wave technology would wireless telegraphy evolve into wireless telephony, or radio broadcasting.[88]

Within the military the Navy, rather than the Army, took the lead in radio development. Wireless telegraphy provided a heretofore unavailable means of communication with and between ships at sea. The Navy installed the first shipboard radios in 1903, and by the following year it had established twenty shore stations and had plans for immediate expansion. Meanwhile, the Army, the Weather Bureau, commercial firms, and private individuals competed with the Navy for the airwaves. Concerns expressed by the Navy about the need for regulation led President Roosevelt in 1904 to appoint a board to study radio activities. The use of wireless by the combatants during the Russo-Japanese War provided the president with an additional incentive to take action.

Chief Signal Officer Greely served as a member of the Inter-Departmental Board on Wireless Telegraphy, generally known as the Roosevelt Board, along

Colonel Squier inspects radio equipment in the laboratory.

with representatives of the Navy, the Agriculture Department, and the Commerce and Labor Department. The board's report, which received the president's approval, established the government's first radio policy. The board recognized the Navy's priority in radio matters, while allowing the Army to operate stations as necessary, provided that they did not interfere with those of the Navy. It additionally recommended that the Weather Bureau turn over its stations to the Navy and urged Congress to enact regulatory legislation. Nevertheless, Congress waited until 1912 to act, after the *Titanic* disaster had tragically demonstrated the need for control over wireless activities. It then passed a law requiring the licensing of private stations and operators by the secretary of commerce and labor and dividing the electromagnetic spectrum between its public and private users.[89]

Still, the lack of international radio regulations created problems, among them the Marconi company's attempt to establish a radio monopoly. Marconi initially leased rather than sold his equipment to his clients and supplied the operators as well. He further stipulated that there must be no intercommunication between Marconi sets and those of other manufacturers, except in emergencies. By this means he hoped to force all those wanting wireless service to use Marconi equipment. At the invitation of the German government, representatives of eight nations, including Chief Signal Officer Greely, gathered at the first international conference on wireless telegraphy, held in Berlin during August 1903. The meeting produced a protocol that remains the cornerstone of international radio agreements. Its provisions contained a statement upholding the policy of intercommunication, thus striking a blow to the Marconi interests.[90] A second conference convened in Berlin in October 1906, with Chief Signal Officer Allen in attendance. The resulting treaty embodied the intercommunication principle of the 1903 protocol and received the endorsement of President Roosevelt. The conference also adopted the signal "SOS" as the international distress call because these letters could be easily sent and deciphered. General Allen and other government officials concerned about radio policy jointly submitted arguments in favor of the treaty before congressional hearings. Due to strenuous opposition by various radio companies, especially the Marconi Wireless Telegraph Company of America, as well as of amateur operators, the Senate did not ratify this treaty until 1912.[91] Majors Squier, Russel, and Saltzman attended the third international conference, held in London in 1912 to revise the 1906 treaty. Convening shortly after the *Titanic* disaster, the conference devoted much of its attention to safety at sea.[92]

While the legal questions were being settled, research to improve radio continued. The Signal Corps worked on the development of both fixed and portable wireless equipment. As already noted, the Corps took its first field sets to Cuba in 1906. During 1907 and 1908 the Corps introduced pack and wagon sets to the Philippines. A pack set had a range of about twenty-five miles, while a wagon set could operate at a range upwards of two hundred miles.[93] Finding commercial sets unsuitable for field conditions, the Corps constructed its own equipment in its laboratory. Once a standard model had been developed, the Corps sought a commercial manufacturer. By mid-1908 forty-five sets had been assembled and sent to the field. Also during that year, the Corps installed a wireless connection in the Philippines between the islands of Zamboanga and Jolo. These stations communicated over a distance similar to that across Norton Sound in Alaska and, as in that case, wireless replaced a cable that had been destroyed by the elements—this time a coral reef. The year 1908, a particularly busy one for the Corps in radio matters, witnessed the completion of a wireless system connecting the principal posts protecting New York Harbor. The Corps subsequently installed wireless equipment at other important coastal fortifications both within the United States and in the Philippines and Hawaii. For training purposes, the Corps also established a permanent station at Fort Omaha in 1908 and sent portable sets to Forts Leavenworth and Riley, subsequently replacing them with permanent stations. The Corps also conducted wireless training for enlisted men at Fort Wood.

In the far northwest, radio began to supplement wire within the Alaska communication system. By 1908 the Signal Corps was operating a series of wireless stations along the Yukon River. The stations cost much less to maintain than wire in the rugged climate that often wreaked havoc with the lines. But radio had not yet become reliable enough to replace wire completely. Under the guidelines established by the Roosevelt Board, the Navy operated the radio stations that connected Alaska with the continental United States. In addition to its stations on land, the Signal Corps supplied wireless sets for Army transports, cable ships, harbor tugs, and mine planters.[94]

In the air, the Signal Corps combined its two incipient technologies by installing wireless equipment in airplanes. In 1911 a message was successfully transmitted from an Army airplane over a distance of two miles; a year later the distance had increased to fifty miles. Improvement came steadily. By 1916 a pilot at the San Diego school was sending signals and messages from an airplane over 140 miles distant, and plane-to-plane communication was achieved for the first time.[95]

Aware of the deficiencies inherent in wireless telegraphy, the Corps turned its attention to the development of wireless telephony. Based on Allen's request for funds, the Army appropriation act of 1909 included $30,000 for the purchase and development of wireless telephone equipment.[96] In order to conduct experiments, the Corps made arrangements for laboratory space at the recently created National Bureau of Standards in Washington, D.C., and Allen placed Major Squier in charge of the research effort there. Just down the hall, the Navy had undertaken its own radio research a year earlier. The bureau subsequently tried to concentrate all governmental radio research under its auspices, and Congress voted $50,000 for a radio laboratory there in 1916.[97]

While at the bureau, Squier conducted experiments with the transmission of radio waves along wires, which he called "wired wireless." By this method radio signals could be multiplexed—that is, many messages could be sent simultaneously along the same wire. He also found that voice signals could be sent by radio along telephone lines. These radio communications could, moreover, travel along the wires without interference with the regular telephone traffic. The "wired wireless" method of transmission provided greater secrecy than broad band radio and made more efficient usage of existing wires. In September 1910 Squier demonstrated his multiplex telephony system for General Allen over a line between the Bureau of Standards and the Signal Corps' lab at 1710 Pennsylvania Avenue. Pleased with the results, Allen initiated proceedings to secure a patent on the invention. Successful application of the technique, however, awaited the development of improved components, especially electronic tubes.[98]

Squier's reassignment as military attaché to London in March 1912 cut short his further experimentation in this area, but it did not curtail his research activities, for he had apparently received the assignment because of his scientific background. With his technical expertise, Squier could observe and report on the latest European developments.[99]

A former member of the Signal Corps, H. H. C. Dunwoody, made a significant contribution to radio technology in 1906 when he discovered that the carborundum crystal (carbon plus silicon) could detect wireless signals. Dunwoody had retired from the Army in 1904 after more than forty years' service and promotion to the rank of brigadier general. His last assignment had been as commander of Fort Myer. The carborundum detector, on which he received a patent, provided an inexpensive and effective receiver of spark transmissions. Because carborundum could also receive voice transmissions, it became a key component in the development of radio telephony. Dunwoody, meanwhile, became a vice president of de Forest's radio company.[100]

About the same time, de Forest invented the audion, a three-element vacuum tube that made radio broadcasting possible. Although de Forest was among the first to envision broadcasting's potential for providing entertainment and information, he did not immediately grasp the significance of his creation. De Forest initially used the audion as a receiver in conjunction with spark transmitters, but his attempts to broadcast operatic performances and lectures met with only minimal success. Several years later a student at Columbia University, Edwin H. Armstrong, made the necessary engineering breakthrough. Recognizing that the audion could both amplify and transmit continuous radio waves capable of carrying voice and music, Armstrong devised the feedback circuit—a discovery that provided the foundation for the subsequent development of radio technology.[101]

Meanwhile, in 1913 the Navy opened its first high-powered radio station at Arlington, Virginia. Using equipment designed by Reginald Fessenden that took spark technology to its limits, the station could transmit signals up to one thousand miles. Arlington served as the first link in a chain of worldwide high-powered stations that connected the Navy Department with its major bases and units of the fleet wherever they might be.[102]

Despite the Navy's leading role in radio development, many naval officers had resisted radio's adoption, especially on shipboard. Historically, the commander, once leaving shore, had total operational control because his superior officers on land had no means of communicating with him. Radio destroyed this autonomy. Older officers, accustomed to flag signaling, also resisted the change. It thus took considerable time and effort to integrate radio into fleet operations.[103]

The Army, on the other hand, with its combined arms philosophy, depended upon the ability to communicate between its various commands. Radio accomplished this more easily than messengers, flags, or even the telegraph. While field commanders lost some autonomy once the commander in chief could communicate directly with the battlefield (as Lincoln's intervention via telegraph during the Civil War had demonstrated), on balance the Army had more to gain than lose from the introduction of radio. The centralization of command and control, fostered on an administrative level by the Root reforms, found technological support in the radio.

Organization, Training, and Operations, 1908–1914

Aside from its involvement with aviation and radio, the basic duties of the Signal Corps remained relatively unchanged between 1908 and 1914, which is not to say that they lacked importance. The branch continued to operate the Alaska communication system; to provide fire control, fire direction, and target range communications; and to establish post telephone systems. Due to advances in telephone technology, the Corps labored to upgrade the systems it had previously installed. By 1911 most post telephones operated by common battery rather than the hand-cranked magneto method, and underground lines replaced aerial wires at many posts. The Corps also operated a 100-mile telephone system in Yellowstone

National Park, which it turned over to the Interior Department in 1914.[104] The opening of the Panama Canal that year, however, gave the Army a new strategic point to defend and a critical site for Signal Corps communications to be installed.

As for the military telegraph lines, once a major function of the Corps, that system had been reduced to "almost nothing."[105] By 1913 but one line remained: between Fort Apache and Holbrook, Arizona, about ninety miles in length. The Corps continued to maintain some additional lines that connected military posts with commercial companies, but between 1913 and 1914 the number of such stations dropped from sixty to twenty-four. To release signal personnel for other duties, civilian operators worked at fourteen of these stations. At most posts telegraphic messages could now be received by telephone from commercial stations.

As had been true for most of its nearly fifty years of existence, the Signal Corps suffered from a chronic shortage of personnel. Like his predecessors, Chief Signal Officer Allen requested that Congress increase the Corps' size, but his pleas went unanswered, and the branch's authorized strength remained at 46 officers and 1,212 enlisted men. As Allen stated in his 1908 annual report, "until Congress takes some action to increase the number of officers and men of the Signal Corps, the mobile Army of the United States must remain vitally weak in a service where it should be strongest."[106]

While the Corps' authorized strength remained static, some changes did occur in the organization of its personnel. On 11 March 1910 the War Department reduced the size of the field signal company to three officers and seventy-five men, more closely approximating what the Corps could actually support. General orders issued on 5 April officially redesignated Companies A, D, E, I, and L (newly organized in 1909) as field signal companies.[107] Company L served at Fort McKinley in the Philippines, while the others occupied stations within the continental United States until 1913, when Company E moved to Hawaii. In 1911 the War Department increased the strength of the field companies to four officers and ninety-six enlisted men. The company was divided into six sections: four to provide wire communications and two equipped with field radio pack sets.[108]

The 1910 edition of the *Field Service Regulations* significantly increased the number of signalmen allotted to a division. They provided each division (either of infantry or cavalry) with a field battalion consisting of two field companies. But because the Signal Corps had only enough resources to organize five field companies, it did not form these battalions. The regulations also called for an "aero-wireless battalion" for each field army (equivalent to a corps) to consist of a wireless and an aero company. But again, as the Corps then possessed only one plane and one pilot, these units represented what the Army hoped to organize upon mobilization, rather than what it expected to field in peacetime.[109]

Telegraph companies, also envisioned by the chief signal officer in 1907, received official sanction via general orders issued by the War Department in 1913.[110] Somewhat larger in size than a field company, with 4 officers and 139 enlisted men, each telegraph company was to be supplied with enough wire to run approximately 125 miles of line and to establish 60 telephone and 10 telegraph stations. Each company comprised 6 sections, 3 for telephone work and 3 for telegraph operations. Not only did the Signal Corps lack the men to fill these organizations, it also lacked the horses and mules needed to transport the men and equipment.[111]

In 1914 the Army published its first Tables of Organization and Equipment (TOEs) based on the *Field Service Regulations* issued that year. Henceforth, changes in unit organization appeared in this form rather than in War Department general orders. The tables outlined the structure of both a peacetime and a wartime army. For the Signal Corps, a radio company was to be paired with a wire company to form a field signal battalion in an infantry division during wartime. In a wartime cavalry division, a headquarters company replaced the wire company found in an infantry division. The headquarters company had, however, both a radio platoon and a wire platoon. In peacetime, a single field company contained the cadres of signalmen from which the wartime battalions would be formed. The separation of the wire units from the radio units in the 1914 TOEs reflected the increasingly specialized nature of signal communications. The tables further provided for a telegraph battalion comprising two telegraph companies. These companies carried heavy-duty line intended for tactical use rather than the lighter and more portable variety used by the wire sections of the field companies. As for the Corps' aerial function, the tables assigned an aero squadron to each division in wartime.[112]

With no increases forthcoming from Congress, the War Department looked for other solutions to the Signal Corps' perennial personnel predicament. In 1913 Secretary of War Lindley M. Garrison requested that the Post Office Department take over the Washington-Alaska Military Cable and Telegraph System, thereby releasing 5 officers and 200 men for other work. Garrison argued that the system's commercial business overshadowed its military usage, thus making it a public utility.[113] Pending a transfer and to satisfy immediate requirements, the Signal Corps withdrew 20 percent of the enlisted men from Alaskan service and placed them with field units. Ultimately, however, the Post Office turned down the secretary's proposal.[114]

Other initiatives proved more successful. The National Guard, as a result of the reforms initiated by the Dick Act of 1903, constituted an important manpower pool for the Signal Corps. Although the 1903 legislation had allowed the states and territories five years for their units to reach conformity in organization, equipment, and training with those of the Regular Army, full compliance had not been reached by 1908. In May of that year Congress extended the time period to 21 January 1910.[115] Chief Signal Officer Allen used this legislation to encourage the formation of signal units within the National Guard as nearly half the states and territories still lacked organized signal troops. Due to the small size of the Regular Army's Signal Corps, the War Department needed the signal units of the National Guard in wartime to supplement the full-time force. Allen wanted the states to organize their units into field companies so that they could train as such in peacetime and thus be prepared for service in the event of mobilization. Moreover, the participation of Regular Army signal units in summer maneuvers with the National Guard provided important practical training.[116]

Despite the introduction of radio, visual signals still played a role in military signaling, and the Signal Corps continued to distribute visual signaling kits as provided for in Army regulations. The expansion in the types of signaling had consequently led to a proliferation of codes in use. In 1908 the Signal School had conducted tests which concluded that Morse code could easily be adapted for signaling with wigwag flags. The chief signal officer in his 1909 annual report cited "a growing aversion" on the part of officers and enlisted men to the use of the Myer code in visual signaling.[117] As it stood, they had to learn three codes: the Myer, the American Morse for ordinary telegraphy, and the Continental or International Morse for wireless and cable service. Finally, in 1912, the Army adopted the International Morse code as its general service code; the American Morse code would continue to be used on telegraph lines, field lines, and short cables. Thus, the Army abandoned the Myer code, which had been employed, although not continuously, since 1860.[118] Furthermore, in 1914 the Army adopted two-arm semaphore signaling for general use. (The Field Artillery had adopted it somewhat earlier.) Semaphore signaling was faster and simpler than wigwag and had been employed by the Navy for some time. The Army continued to use wigwag for long-distance communication, for which it was better suited than semaphore, thus retaining some of Myer's original contributions to military signaling. The Signal Corps, meanwhile, acquired responsibility for distributing the semaphore equipment.[119]

The Army Signal School at Fort Leavenworth continued to train Signal Corps officers for their increasingly complex duties. In its electrical laboratory, students conducted research and sought to make improvements to field equipment. As commandant, Major Squier had instituted semimonthly technical conferences that provided the faculty and students with a forum for the presentation of papers and the exchange of ideas. The school published the best papers on an occasional basis and distributed them to Signal Corps officers, both of the Regular Army and of the National Guard. These papers served as a precursor to a professional journal.[120] With the closing of the Signal Corps post at Fort Omaha in 1913, its school for enlisted instruction moved to Leavenworth along with the two signal companies stationed there.

But the relatively quiet years since the conclusion of the War with Spain were coming to an end. In 1910 revolt broke out in Mexico against the regime of Porfirio Diaz, who had ruled that country for over thirty years. Recurrent incidents led President Taft in March 1911 to order 30,000 troops to the border to conduct maneuvers and enforce neutrality. The bulk of these units were assembled from posts around the nation to form the Maneuver Division, which made its headquarters near San Antonio. (The Army then had no regular TOE divisions.) Meanwhile, Company A, Signal Corps, had traveled in February from Fort Leavenworth to Eagle Pass, Texas, presumably to lay down communication lines in anticipation of the division's deployment. The divisional troops included Field Companies D and I, Signal Corps.[121] The role of Signal Corps aviation has already been discussed. Maj. George O. Squier served as the division's chief signal officer, while a young infantry officer, 1st Lt. George C. Marshall, Jr., acted as his assistant. Although the communication systems provided by the Signal Corps worked well, the maneuvers proved less than a complete success. After ninety days the division still had not been fully organized.[122] When Diaz resigned in May 1911 and the revolutionary leader Francisco Madero assumed power, peace had seemingly been restored to the troubled country. The War Department discontinued the Maneuver Division in August, but some troops remained in Texas, including Company I, Signal Corps, which stayed until November 1911.[123]

The overthrow and assassination of Madero by General Victoriano Huerta in February 1913 launched a protracted and bloody civil war within Mexico that necessitated further American troop concentrations along the border. Just before leaving office, President Taft requested that troops be sent to supplement the border patrols. Consequently, on 21 February, Secretary of War Henry L. Stimson ordered the 2d Division, one of the Army's newly organized tactical divisions, to assemble at Galveston and Texas City.[124] When the new president, Woodrow Wilson, refused to recognize the Huerta regime, he set the stage for possible confrontation. During this mobilization Field Company D, Signal Corps, once again served as a divisional asset.[125] Meanwhile, Field Company I, scattered at several stations along the border and with its headquarters at Fort Bliss, provided communication with units in the field by means of radio, buzzer, and even the heliograph.[126] Companies B and H, reorganized as telegraph companies, also served in Texas. The Signal Corps strung 130 miles of telegraph wire along the border which, in conjunction with commercial lines, made communication possible along most of the border's length.[127] In addition, the Corps' aero squadron provided aerial support.

In April 1914 an international incident erupted at Vera Cruz, Mexico's principal port. The crisis began when Huertista soldiers arrested an officer and several crew members of an American warship at Tampico. Although the Mexicans soon released the prisoners, President Wilson demanded an apology, which the Mexican government refused to give. About the same time, a German ship arrived at Vera Cruz with a cargo of arms and ammunition for Huerta. President Wilson ordered American naval forces at Vera Cruz to prevent the ship from unloading. Later that day, 21 April, marines went ashore and seized the customs house. By the following day, despite Mexican resistance, the Americans controlled the city. Elements of the 2d Division thereupon embarked for Vera Cruz for occupation duty. Field Signal Company D, part of this contingent, arrived on 3 May to establish buzzer lines from the headquarters of the expeditionary force to six points in the city. It also installed radio connections between Army headquarters and a refugee train and maintained communication with the Navy. This campaign probably also marked the last field use of the heliograph by the United States Army.[128]

Brig. Gen. Frederick Funston served as military governor of Vera Cruz for the seven months of its occupation. At first war with Mexico seemed imminent. But Huerta, failing to rally sufficient support to oust the Americans, ultimately resigned and fled to Europe. Nevertheless, the troubles had only subsided temporarily. The subsequent recognition of the new government of Venustiano Carranza by the Wilson administration in October 1915 and Carranza's break with Francisco "Pancho" Villa set off the chain of events that led the United States to intervene in Mexico once again in 1916.[129]

The Signal Corps Spreads Its Wings

On 18 July 1914 Congress passed legislation creating the Aviation Section of the Signal Corps, to consist of up to 60 officers and 260 enlisted men. These men would serve in addition to the Corps' existing authorized strength. For the first time, the Army had soldiers permanently assigned to aviation duties. The act limited aviation officers, however, to unmarried lieutenants no older than thirty. The section's responsibilities included:

operating or supervising the operation of all military air craft, including balloons and aeroplanes, all appliances pertaining to said craft, and signaling apparatus of any kind when installed on said craft; also with the duty of training officers and enlisted men in matters pertaining to military aviation.[130]

Lt. Col. Samuel Reber headed the new section. The Aeronautical Division, meanwhile, continued in existence as the Washington office of the section. As for budget matters, Congress had specified in previous legislation that up to one-half of the Signal Corps' appropriation of $500,000 could be spent on aviation-related items.[131]

The retention of aviation within the Signal Corps indicated that Congress held the prevailing opinion that aviation served a support, rather than a combat, function. The *Field Service Regulations* of 1914 reinforced this view by assigning to aviation a passive reconnaissance mission. Its only direct combat role concerned the use of aircraft to prevent aerial observation by the enemy.[132] As Chief Signal Officer Scriven wrote in his 1914 annual report, "much doubt remains" regarding the offensive value of aviation and "little of importance has been proved" as to the capabilities of planes in the dropping of bombs. "In reality," he stated, "little is known of this power of air craft, though much is guessed and more feared."[133] He went on to remark that

if the future shows that attack from the sky is effective and terrible, as may prove to be the case, it is evident that, like the rain, it must fall upon the just and upon the unjust, and it may be supposed will therefore become taboo to all civilized people; and forbidden at least by paper agreements.[134]

Although Scriven, like most of his contemporaries, could not imagine the havoc that would be wreaked by aerial bombardment during World War II, he did have an insight into its deadly possibilities.

Colonel Reber

Aviation instruction continued at North Island, San Diego, now known as the Signal Corps Aviation School.[135] Earlier in the year the school had sent 5 pilots, 30 enlisted men, and 3 planes to Galveston as part of the border alert. They arrived too late, however, to catch the transport to Vera Cruz and never even unpacked the planes. Captain Foulois, who led the detachment (he had returned to aviation duty late in 1913 and received a promotion the following year), recalled that for six weeks he and his men "sat on the sea wall . . . waiting for whatever the fates decided."[136] With no call for their services, the aviators returned to San Diego where, in September, they became part of the 1st Aero Squadron, now permanently organized at the school with Foulois as commander. The squadron comprised 16 officers, 77 enlisted men, and 8 planes.[137]

Meanwhile, only a few weeks after the establishment of the Aviation Section, the assassination in Sarajevo of Archduke Franz Ferdinand, the heir-apparent to the throne of Austria-Hungary, precipitated the outbreak of war in Europe. Although President Wilson urged Americans to remain neutral in thought and deed, such a stance could not be maintained indefinitely.

Despite the efforts toward modernization made between 1903 and 1914, neither the United States Army nor its Signal Corps was prepared to fight a major war. While the Signal Corps had adopted the latest forms of communication, its inadequate budgets, particularly in relation to aviation, had kept progress to a minimum. The Army remained a relatively small, horsepowered, and earthbound organization—no match for the fighting machines of Europe. Yet in less than three years the United States would be fighting "over there."

Bordering on War

While the major European powers early in the century had raised huge conscript armies numbering in the millions, the United States continued to maintain a volunteer force of less than 100,000 men. The Regular Army's small size meant that the United States could not meet a first-class opponent on land without a prolonged mobilization—which public opinion would not condone and the

Wilson administration, committed to negotiating a peace without victory among the belligerents, would not consider.[138]

Reform-minded individuals, including such influential men as ex-President Theodore Roosevelt and Senator Henry Cabot Lodge, launched a campaign to prepare the nation for war. Among the soldiers themselves, former chief of staff Maj. Gen. Leonard Wood, who became commander of the Eastern Department in July 1914, led the preparedness effort.[139] Within the generally peace-minded Wilson administration, Secretary of War Lindley Garrison sounded the call for preparedness in his 1914 annual report. To meet present defense needs, he recommended that the units of the mobile Army (excluding the Coast Artillery, which occupied fixed positions) be recruited to war strength. He also advocated other measures, such as the creation of a reserve force and a larger "Aviation Corps."[140] While the situation overseas gave urgency to the cause, the majority of Americans remained either unconcerned about or unconvinced of America's military weakness.

The war in Europe finally aroused public outrage within the United States with the sinking of the British liner *Lusitania* by a German submarine on 7 May 1915. Over one hundred Americans on board lost their lives. This hostile act jolted the Wilson administration and the public out of their complacency. While the cry for preparedness rose, the politicians argued over what form it should take. In the private sector, the Aero Club of America numbered among the many organizations calling for a stronger defense.[141] At odds with the president regarding the administration's policy, Secretary of War Garrison resigned in February 1916. Wilson replaced him with the more moderate Newton D. Baker. Then, in the midst of the preparedness controversy, an event in a small southwestern town focused the nation's attention upon the persistent problems along its border with Mexico.

On 9 March 1916 Pancho Villa led a raid against Columbus, New Mexico, killing several Americans, both civilians and members of the 13th Cavalry who were on duty there. In retaliation, President Wilson ordered Brig. Gen. John J. Pershing to lead an expedition into Mexico in pursuit of Villa. Troops began arriving in Columbus the day after the raid, and Pershing opened his headquarters there on 14 March.[142]

The so-called Punitive Expedition spurred the growth of anti-Americanism within Mexico. Although following Villa's raid the two nations had mutually agreed to permit U.S. troops to cross the border in pursuit of bandits, President Venustiano Carranza never authorized Pershing's forces to enter his country. The lack of cooperation by the Mexican government and the hostility of the Mexican people, many of whom helped Villa evade his pursuers, added greatly to the difficulties faced by Pershing and his men. The denial of full use of the Mexican railways, for example, hindered supply efforts. The Americans agreed to avoid Mexican cities and towns, but living off the countryside proved nearly impossible in a region devastated by years of civil war.[143]

The deployment of the 1st Aero Squadron provided some relief. This unit received its orders at Fort Sam Houston on 12 March and immediately began dis-

Signal Corps airplane at Dublán, Mexico

mantling and packing its planes and equipment for the trip by rail to Columbus. As one of the few Army organizations with organic motorized transportation, the squadron took with it ten trucks and one automobile. This equipment represented, however, less than half of that authorized in its tables of organization. Upon arrival at Columbus on 15 March, the squadron turned over its vehicles to the Quartermaster Department to be used for hauling supplies across the border. When new vehicles started arriving at Columbus, the squadron's machine shop made the necessary modifications to render them suitable for the rough job ahead.[144]

In the air, the squadron met with less success. It went to the border with 11 pilots, 82 enlisted men, 1 civilian mechanic, and 8 planes.[145] The number of planes soon dwindled to six, as the squadron wrecked two machines during the first few days of operation. By the end of April only two planes remained intact, and they had been rendered unserviceable. Fortunately, none of the men had received serious injuries. The fragile, underpowered planes could not cope with the high altitudes and strong winds encountered in the Mexican mountains. Foulois ordered new and more powerful aircraft, but when these planes finally arrived, they were also found unsuitable. The Army's aircraft had been manufactured at sea level and were not designed for operation in thin mountain air. Moreover, the dryness of the climate caused the wooden propellers to warp and split. Thus, in late June, technicians from the Curtiss Aeroplane Company came to Columbus and set up a propeller manufacturing plant. Nevertheless, continuing difficulties effectively grounded the Army's air force for the duration of the campaign.[146]

During its brief period of activity, the squadron's most dramatic experience probably occurred at Chihuahua City, Mexico, on 7 April. Two planes, piloted by

Lts. Herbert A. Dargue and Joseph E. Carberry, flew to that city with messages for the American consul. Foulois, suspecting trouble, had arranged for duplicate messages to be delivered. He accompanied Dargue as an observer while Lt. Townsend Dodd flew with Carberry. After landing, Foulois and Dodd set out for the consulate while the pilots remained with the planes, which had landed on opposite sides of town. Before leaving for the consulate, Foulois had instructed Dargue to join Carberry. As Dargue prepared to take off, four riflemen opened fire on him, luckily from a considerable distance. Foulois, hearing the shots, started back in the direction of the shooting. Failing to stop Dargue, the riflemen then turned on Foulois, taking him prisoner and escorting him to the city jail. Fortunately, Foulois succeeded in contacting the Mexican military governor, who secured his release, and went on to complete his mission. (Dodd had delivered his set of messages without incident.)

Meanwhile, the parked aircraft had sustained considerable damage from a local mob. To avoid their complete destruction, Dargue and Carberry decided to take to the sky. Carberry made a clean getaway, but the crowd showered Dargue with stones. He had barely become airborne when the top of his fuselage blew off, forcing him to land. Foulois arrived just in time with a guard provided by the military governor, which kept the mob at bay. Carberry landed at a nearby American-owned ore smelter and refinery and returned to Chihuahua City later that afternoon. With the guard's protection, the four Americans were able to repair the planes. After spending the night at the American consulate, the aviators departed the following day, no doubt feeling fortunate to have escaped relatively unscathed.[147]

Pershing had pinned great hopes on the airplanes' performance, expecting them to be able to find Villa and direct the troops to effect his capture. The Signal Corps had even been instructed to flash a code word, YAXKH, to indicate that the villain had been taken either dead or alive.[148] Expressing his disappointment Pershing remarked: "The aeroplanes have been of no material benefit . . . either in scouting or as a means of communication. They have not at all met my expectations."[149] From the pilots' point of view, they had risked their lives daily in aircraft they considered unfit for service. Once news of the aviators' woes reached the press back home, Congress included $500,000 for aviation, the largest single sum appropriated to date for that purpose, in an act passed in March 1916.[150]

Not all of the squadron's activities resulted in failure or frustration. The pilots successfully performed reconnaissance in a region that was virtually untouched by mapmakers, delivered messages to troops that could not be reached by other means, and took aerial photographs. Between 15 March and 15 August the squadron flew 540 missions covering a total distance of 19,553 miles.[151]

As for communication on the ground, one author has criticized it as "a weak point . . . from first to last."[152] To begin with, Mexico had a poor internal communications network. The country's only telegraphic system ran along the railway lines, which the Carranza government controlled. Thus the Signal Corps had to depend entirely upon its own resources. Problems arose because the radio pack

Radio tractor in Mexico, 1916

sets, with a range of twenty-five miles, could not keep up with the cavalry moving at twice that distance each day. The Corps experimented with radio tractor sets, the term used for wireless sets carried in motor vehicles, with one at Columbus and one at Pershing's headquarters, but these proved no panacea. Atmospheric conditions in the Mexican mountains hampered radio transmissions, and spare parts for the foreign-made sets were scarce.[153] With radio still in the developmental stages, the Army relied mainly on buzzer lines.[154] Unfortunately, the uninsulated telegraph wire did not work particularly well, especially when wet. Moreover, it was frequently severed by the trampling of horses, mules, and wagons. Because the field lines were unreliable, the Signal Corps built a permanent pole line from Columbus to Pershing's base at Colonia Dublán, but it was not completed until after active pursuit of Villa had ceased.[155] Nevertheless, establishing communications along the largely uninhabited border constituted no mean feat, and the Signal Corps could take credit for constructing lines along its entire length. This system ultimately comprised 677 miles of buzzer and telegraph lines; 642 miles of telephone lines; and 19 radio stations.[156] Although not mentioned by the chief signal officer in his annual report, the Army apparently used yet another form of communication, the carrier pigeon, at least to a limited extent.[157]

The threat of war with Mexico and the events in Europe spurred Congress to finally reach a compromise regarding defense policy, resulting in the passage of the National Defense Act. This bill, which Wilson approved on 3 June 1916,

Signal Corps camp telephone office at Dublán

gradually increased the peacetime size of the Regular Army over a five-year period to 175,000. In wartime its authorized strength would rise to nearly three hundred thousand. Meanwhile, Congress quadrupled the size of the National Guard
to over four hundred thousand and made it subject to the call of the president. On
a unit level, it authorized, for the first time, the creation of permanent divisions
and brigades. However, with its incremental increases, the Defense Act looked
toward the Army's involvement in a future war rather than eventual participation
in the conflict already raging in Europe.[158]

In light of the unhappy plight of Army aviation in Mexico and the successful
performance of planes in the European war, the Defense Act effected several
changes to Army aviation. First, it increased the size of the Aviation Section to
148 officers: 1 colonel, 1 lieutenant colonel, 8 majors, 24 captains, and 114 first
lieutenants. The new law also lifted the restriction that had limited those eligible
to become aviators to bachelors under thirty and had thus filled the ranks with
young and inexperienced officers. This revision, which had been recommended
by the chief signal officer, broadened the base from which pilots could be chosen.[159] The law also provided for the enlistment of civilian pilots if an insufficient number of eligible officers existed. Furthermore, Congress backed up
these changes with an appropriation of over $13 million for aviation in August
1916, a vast sum in comparison with its previous outlays.[160] With adequate funds
finally available, the Aviation Section could begin to prepare for whatever lay
ahead.

In regard to the ground troops of the Signal Corps, the legislation fixed the branch's commissioned strength at 127: 1 chief signal officer, 3 colonels, 8 lieutenant colonels, 10 majors, 30 captains, and 75 first lieutenants. Congress gave the president authority to set the Corps' enlisted strength, which he subsequently fixed at 4,000, to be reached by 1 July 1920.[161] Moreover, the law provided for the creation of an Officers' Reserve Corps and its counterpart, the Reserve Officers Training Corps (ROTC). Of particular importance to the Signal Corps, the act created an Enlisted Reserve Corps for the recruitment of technical specialists such as telegraphers and telephone operators.[162]

With the creation of tactical divisions came the need to form organic division-level signal units. Each infantry division included a field signal battalion, while a cavalry division contained a mounted field signal battalion. In addition, an army corps was to have both a telegraph battalion and a field signal battalion. Congress furthermore authorized the president to organize both the Signal Corps' commissioned and enlisted personnel "into such number of companies, battalions, and aero squadrons as the necessities of the service may demand."[163]

While Congress deliberated, relations with Mexico continued to deteriorate. Carranza's government insisted upon Pershing's withdrawal, and Villa's men still raided border towns at will. (Villa himself had been badly wounded on 28 March and spent several months in hiding while recuperating.) President Wilson responded on 9 May by calling up the National Guard of Arizona, New Mexico, and Texas. When Carranza increased the pressure upon Wilson by threatening to attack American troops heading in any direction but north, the president replied by invoking the provisions of the newly minted Defense Act. On 18 June he called up most of the remainder of the National Guard for border service.[164] The subsequent clash with Carranza's troops at Carrizal on 21 June, during which two officers and seven enlisted men of the 10th Cavalry were killed and another officer and nine men wounded, brought the two nations to the brink of war.[165]

Before Pershing could fight a full-fledged war with Mexico, however, he needed reinforcements. Given the small size of the Regular Army, the mobilization of the militia presented the only means available to quickly obtain enough men to protect the border against invasion. By 31 July approximately one hundred eleven thousand guardsmen had reached the border. The National Guard troops called into federal service included 4 signal battalions, 16 signal companies, and 1 aero company.[166] The aero company, organized in New York City, received support from the Aero Club of America and was commanded by Capt. Raynal C. Bolling. It did not see service in Mexico, however, and was mustered out in October 1916.[167] Fortunately, the largely untrained and unequipped units were not severely tested, as tensions between the two nations subsided. Late in 1916 the National Guard troops began to be mustered out, although not all had been sent home by the time war with Germany was declared. While they had acquired no combat experience, the mobilization had provided these men with much useful training.[168]

Meanwhile, the escalating problems with the Mexican government had forced Pershing to abandon his pursuit of Villa, who remained at large. Nevertheless, the Americans had succeeded in dispersing his followers and killing a number of his principal lieutenants. With these accomplishments, the United States began to withdraw Pershing's forces from Mexico in January 1917, and the last of his men recrossed the boundary onto American soil early in February.[169] The United States continued, however, to concentrate a significant force along the border in the event of further flare-ups.

While tensions with Mexico relaxed, those with Germany steadily worsened. In early 1917 neutrality became increasingly untenable, and on 3 February Wilson broke diplomatic ties with Germany following the announcement by the German government that it would resume unrestricted submarine warfare. The subsequent publication of the so-called Zimmermann note, actually an intercepted cable communication supplied by the British, revealed how Germany intended to exploit the ill-feelings held by many Mexicans toward the United States. In a telegram to the German ambassador in Mexico, German Foreign Secretary Arthur Zimmermann proposed that if Mexico joined his country in arms against the United States, Germany would, upon victory, assist Mexico in regaining her lost territories in Arizona, New Mexico, and Texas.[170] As the toll from German submarines rose, President Wilson finally had to take action. On 2 April 1917 he delivered his war message to Congress: The United States must "make the world safe for democracy." Four days later Congress responded by declaring war on Germany.

In the words of historian Walter Millis, the Punitive Expedition provided a "dress rehearsal" for World War I.[171] While the conditions that would be faced in Europe differed greatly from those encountered in Mexico, the Army found itself much better prepared for the contest ahead. First of all, senior officers had received much-needed experience in handling large numbers of troops. General Pershing's skillful command of 11,000 soldiers earned him the position of commander of the American Expeditionary Forces (AEF) soon to be bound for France. In addition, the expedition itself and the preceding series of maneuvers along the border between 1911 and 1916 provided a valuable training ground for such junior officers as George C. Marshall and George S. Patton, Jr. For its part, the Signal Corps gained first-hand experience with its new field units and equipment. The lessons learned regarding the capabilities of motor vehicles and airplanes, for example, would soon be applied on and over the battlefields of Europe.[172] Most important, the expedition created a nucleus of seasoned soldiers around whom the wartime Army would be formed.[173]

Notes

[1]For an overview of this evolution, see Jonathan M. House, *Toward Combined Arms Warfare: A Survey of 20th-Century Tactics, Doctrine, and Organization*, Combat Studies Institute Research Survey no. 2 (Fort Leavenworth, Kans.: U.S. Army Command and General Staff College, 1985). For an in-depth study, see John B. Wilson, Divisions and Separate Brigades, draft Ms, CMH.

[2]This grade should not be confused with that of the electrical sergeant within the artillery. The legislation increasing the Corps' strength is published in WDGO 76, 28 Apr 1904. See also *ARSO*, 1905, p. 229, in *ARSW*, 1905, vol. 2. From 1903 to 1909 the chief signal officer's reports were published in volume two of the secretary of war's report. From 1910 to 1916 they were published in volume one.

[3]*ARSW*, 1904, vol. 1, pp. 21–25.

[4]WDGO 9, 6 Feb 1901, sec. 26.

[5]*ARSO*, 1905, p. 228.

[6]The system of schools was set forth in WDGO 115, 17 Jun 1904. The Army War College stood at the pinnacle, followed by the Infantry and Cavalry School, and then the special service schools, such as the Signal School. At the lowest level were post schools that provided elementary military instruction. See Nenninger, *Leavenworth Schools*, pp. 56–57.

[7]Nenninger, *Leavenworth Schools*, p. 75; Clark, "Squier," p. 111.

[8]Regulations governing the school are published in WDGO 140, 19 Aug 1905; WDGO ·145, 16 Aug 1906; WDGO 211, 15 Oct 1907. See also A. C. Knowles, "The Army Signal School: The Training School of the New Combatant Arm," *JMSI* 43 (Jul–Aug 1908): 31–37. On Squier's service at the school, see Clark, "Squier," ch. 5.

[9]*ARSO*, 1905, pp. 235–36. The stations given are those as of the end of 1905. See table in *ARSO*, 1905, p. 228, and reports of changes of station in the *Report of the Military Secretary* (the term from 1904 to 1907 for the position of The Adjutant General) in *ARSW*, 1906, vol. 1, pp. 568–71.

[10]AR, 1904, par. 1594.

[11]*ARSO*, 1907, p. 183.

[12]For more on this unusual aspect of Signal Corps history, see Rebecca C. Robbins, "Carrying a Torch for Lady Liberty," *Army Communicator* 11 (Fall 1986): 40–43.

[13]*Field Service Regulations, United States Army* (Washington, D.C.: Government Printing Office, 1905), p. 21.

[14]For a detailed discussion of these regulations, see John B. Wilson, "Army Readiness Planning, 1899–1916," *Military Review* 64 (Jul 1984): 60–73.

[15]Cir 7, War Department, Signal Office, 11 Oct 1907.

[16]*ARSO*, 1908, pp. 181–83.

[17]See tables in *ARSO*, 1904, p. 385, and *ARSO*, 1905, p. 179.

[18]*ARSO*, 1907, p. 180; *Historical Sketch*, pp. 50–51. Directives governing the installation of post telephone systems include WDGO 90, 12 Apr 1905; WDGO 110, 11 Jul 1905; WDGO 175, 21 Oct 1905; WDGO 97, 25 May 1906; and WDGO 219, 29 Oct 1907.

[19]*ARSO*, 1904, p. 405; WD Cir 12, 31 Mar 1904.

[20]John T. Greenwood, "The American Military Observers of the Russo-Japanese War (1904–1905)" (Ph.D. dissertation, Kansas State University, 1971), pp. 500–545. No signal officers were sent, but two of the Army's observers later became chief of staff—Peyton C. March and John J. Pershing.

[21]*ARSO*, 1905, pp. 207, 242; *ARSO*, 1906, pp. 197–98; Dulany Terrett, *The Signal Corps: The Emergency*, United States Army in World War II (Washington, D.C.: Office of the Chief of Military History, Department of the Army, 1956), p. 16.

[22]On communications during the Russo-Japanese War, see M. C. Sullivan, "Signal Service in Modern Warfare," *Scientific American* 91 (10 Sep 1904); C. McK. Saltzman, "The Signal Corps in War," *Arms and the Man* 46 (Apr 1909); and E. D. Peek, "The Necessity and Use of Electrical Communications on the Battle-Field," *JMSI* 49 (Dec 1911). All of these articles are reprinted in Scheips, ed., *Military Signal Communications*, vol. 2.

[23]The award came about largely through the efforts of William Mitchell, who later published a biography of the former chief signal officer, *General Greely: The Story of a Great American* (New York: G. P. Putnam's Sons, 1936). See George M. Hall, "Renaissance Warrior," *Army* 38 (Dec 1988): 56. General Greely died quietly at his home in Georgetown, D.C., in 1935.

[24]For a summary of Allen's career, see his obituary in *USMA Graduates Report* (1934), pp. 52–62. Greely's comments are quoted on p. 60. See also Cullum, *Biographical Register*. Allen was West Point graduate number 2438.

[25]Leonard D. Wildman, "The Reconstruction of Communications at San Francisco," *Army and Navy Life and The United Service* 9 (Jul 1906): 1.

[26]Phil Jordan, "The First Great San Francisco Earthquake," *National Guard* 44 (Feb 1990): 30.

[27]According to GO 32, Hq, Pacific Division, 26 May 1906, Company A was not relieved until 1 June. The order is printed in *ARSW*, 1906, vol. 1, p. 161.

[28]See Rpt, Maj Gen Adolphus W. Greely to the Military Secretary, War Department, 30 Jul 1906, published as Appendix A to *ARSW*, 1906, vol. 1, pp. 91–140. He gives these figures on p. 117. Wildman, on page 6 of his article cited in note 25 above, differs slightly in his statistics. He does not give the total number of telephone offices, but states that forty-six telegraph stations had been set up by 10 May.

[29]Funston is quoted by Greely on p. 97 of the report cited above. Greely discussed "lines of information" on pages 116–17 of this report.

[30]Norman M. Cary, Jr., "The Mechanization of the United States Army: 1900–1916" (M.A. thesis, University of Georgia, 1971), p. 24.

[31]Wildman, "Reconstruction of Communications," p. 7.

[32]Waldon Fawcett, "The Auto-Telegraph Car of the U.S. Signal Corps," *The Army and Navy Magazine* 14 (Mar 1906): 7–10.

[33]Congress originally passed the Platt Amendment as part of the Army Appropriation Act of 1901. It was later ratified as a treaty between Cuba and the United States. See Allan R. Millett, *The Politics of Intervention: The Military Occupation of Cuba, 1906–1909* (Columbus: Ohio State University Press, 1968), pp. 39–42.

[34]Millett, *Politics of Intervention*, p. 122.

[35]On the Signal Corps in Cuba, see George A. Wieczorek, "Field Wireless Operations in Cuba," *Journal of the United States Cavalry Association* 17 (Jan 1907): 526–29; William Mitchell, "Report of the Chief Signal Officer, Army of Cuban Pacification," dated 18 Nov 1906, in Serial no. 11, app. 6, Army War College, Monographs, Problem Reports, Army War College Studies, and Committee Reports ("Serial Set"), 1906–1909, RG 165, War Department General and Special Staffs, NARA. (An interesting aspect of this report is Mitchell's recommendations for the organization of signal units. He took issue with the *Field Service Regulations*, which did not provide for separate organizations

to handle permanent and field lines.) *ARSO*, 1907, pp. 170–72; and the report of the Army of Cuban Pacification in *ARSW*, 1907, vol. 3, p. 348.

[36]Company I's change of station from the *Annual Report of The Adjutant General* (hereafter cited as *ARAG*), 1909, in *ARSW*, 1909, vol. 1, p. 228. See also Mitchell, "Report of the Chief Signal Officer, Army of Cuban Pacification."

[37]*Medal of Honor Recipients*, p. 374. For a brief description of the Mount Dajo operation, see the report of the Department of Mindanao in *ARSW*, 1906, vol. 1, pp. 278–79. See also Bowers Davis, "Mount Dajo Expedition," *Infantry Journal* 25 (Sep 1924): 250–56.

[38]The details of Johnston's career were obtained from "Biographical Sketches of Former Signal Corps Personnel," an unpublished manuscript prepared by the Signal Corps Historical Division, Washington, D.C., in 1957. A copy is in the possession of Dr. Paul J. Scheips, who generously lent it to the author.

[39]This unattributed quotation is taken from A. Lincoln Lavine, *Circuits of Victory* (Garden City, N.Y.: Country Life Press, Doubleday, Page, and Company, 1921), p. 107.

[40]Articles on the buzzer include Charles McK. Saltzman, "Signal Troops in Campaign," *National Guard Magazine* 1 (Aug 1907): 399–402; Raymond Sheldon, "Experiments with the Cavalry Buzzer," *Journal of the United States Infantry Association* 4 (Nov 1907): 341–48; A. T. Ovenshine, "Should the Buzzer Be Issued to Troops of the Line?" *Infantry Journal* 6 (Sep 1909): 240–48.

[41]Charles McK. Saltzman, "Signal Troops in Campaign," *National Guard Magazine* 1 (Sep 1907): 454. This is a continuation of his article cited above.

[42]On the club's influence, see Herbert A. Johnson, "The Aero Club of America and Army Aviation, 1907–1916," *New York History* 66 (Oct 1985): 374–95.

[43]Parkinson, "Politics, Patents, and Planes," pp. 259–61; Chandler and Lahm, *How Army Grew Wings*, ch. 4.

[44]Memorandum, Office of the Chief Signal Officer, 1 Aug 1907. The memo is printed in Chandler and Lahm, *How Army Grew Wings*, p. 80, n. 6. The Air Force considers 1 August 1907 to be its official birthday. On Squier's role, see Clark, "Squier," chs. 5 and 6.

[45]Parkinson, "Politics, Patents, and Planes," p. 255; *ARSO*, 1908, p. 210.

[46]Chandler and Lahm, *How Army Grew Wings*, pp. 80–81.

[47]The Wrights maintained a high degree of secrecy about their invention, especially prior to their receipt of a patent in 1906.

[48]Fred Howard, *Wilbur and Orville: A Biography of the Wright Brothers* (New York: Alfred A. Knopf, 1987), p. 230; Chandler and Lahm, *How Army Grew Wings*, pp. 144–46. The specifications are published as Appendix 6. Clark, "Squier," pp. 136–38, discusses Squier's role in preparing the specifications.

[49]Dated 21 January 1908, these specifications are published as Appendix 3 to Chandler and Lahm, *How Army Grew Wings*.

[50]*Report of the Board of Ordnance and Fortification*, 1908, in *ARSW*, 1908, vol. 2, pp. 262, 266–67. See also Chandler and Lahm, *How Army Grew Wings*, pp. 148–50.

[51]Chandler and Lahm, *How Army Grew Wings*, pp. 147–48.

[52]Ibid., ch. 8; Merle C. Olmsted, "Dirigible Balloon #1: A History of the First U.S. Military Powered Aircraft," *Military Collector and Historian* 26 (Fall 1974): 149–52; *ARSO*, 1912, p. 964. Baldwin had worked with but was not related to Ivy Baldwin, who had previously served with the Signal Corps (see ch. 3). For more on Baldwin, see Crouch, *Eagle Aloft*, ch. 16. Howard, *Wilbur and Orville*, also contains considerable information about Thomas Baldwin. During World War I, Thomas Baldwin received a

commission as a major and served as balloon inspector for the Army in Akron, Ohio (Crouch, *Eagle Aloft*, p. 529).

[53]For details of Selfridge's aeronautical work, see Chandler and Lahm, *How Army Grew Wings*, ch. 11; Robert V. Bruce, *Alexander Graham Bell and the Conquest of Solitude* (Boston: Little, Brown, and Company, 1973), ch. 32; Howard, *Wilbur and Orville*, chs. 24 and 26.

[54]Howard discusses the flight trials of both the airplane and the dirigible in chapter 30 of *Wilbur and Orville*. The tragedy of 17 September is discussed separately in chapter 31. See also Clark, "Squier," pp. 139–47, and Chandler and Lahm, *How Army Grew Wings*, pp. 113–16 and 152–54.

[55]*ARSO*, 1908, p. 215.

[56]On the 1909 flight trials, see Chandler and Lahm, *How Army Grew Wings*, pp. 155–62; Howard, *Wilbur and Orville*, ch. 34.

[57]Chandler and Lahm, *How Army Grew Wings*, pp. 162–67; Rebecca Hancock Welch, "The Army Learns To Fly: College Park, Maryland, 1909–1913," The *Maryland Historian* 21 (Fall/Winter 1990): 38–51.

[58]Benjamin D. Foulois and C. V. Glines, *From the Wright Brothers to the Astronauts: The Memoirs of Major General Benjamin D. Foulois* (New York: McGraw-Hill Book Company, 1968), p. 70.

[59]As quoted in Chandler and Lahm, *How Army Grew Wings*, p. 183, n. 6. Their source was a story in a Washington, D.C., newspaper.

[60]Foulois, *Memoirs*, chs. 5 and 6; Chandler and Lahm, *How Army Grew Wings*, pp. 180–84; Clark, "Squier," p. 165, n. 128.

[61]Chandler and Lahm, *How Army Grew Wings*, pp. 184–92; Juliette A. Hennessy, *The United States Army Air Arm, April 1861 to April 1917* (1958; reprint, Washington, D.C.: Office of Air Force History, 1985), pp. 40–47; Foulois, *Memoirs*, pp. 87–94.

[62]William F. Lynd, "The Army Flying School at College Park," *Maryland Historical Magazine* 48 (1953): 227–41.

[63]Arnold relates his early flying experiences in *Global Mission* (New York: Harper and Brothers, 1949).

[64]Howard, *Wilbur and Orville*, p. 314. In chapter 38 Howard explains how the use of ailerons became a part of the dispute between the Wrights and Curtiss. An equally compelling biography that emphasizes the psychological dimension behind the Wright brothers' legal battles is that by Tom Crouch, *The Bishop's Boys: A Life of Wilbur and Orville Wright* (New York: W. W. Norton and Company, 1989). The implications of the suits brought by the Wrights on the development of Army aviation will be discussed below.

[65]On winter operations in Georgia, see Chandler and Lahm, *How Army Grew Wings*, pp. 210–14.

[66]A Curtiss Scout had been delivered to Augusta during the winter. Chandler and Lahm, *How Army Grew Wings*, pp. 209–10, 216, and 220.

[67]*ARSO*, 1912, pp. 966–68; *ARSO*, 1913, pp. 781–82; Chandler and Lahm, *How Army Grew Wings*, pp. 222–27 and photo facing page 248. See also George M. Chinn, *The Machine Gun: History, Evolution, and Development of Manual, Automatic, and Airborne Repeating Weapons*, 3 vols. (Washington, D.C.: Government Printing Office, 1951), 1: 275–78; G. H. Powell, "The Lewis Automatic Gun," *Infantry Journal* 9 (Jul–Aug 1912): 44–48.

[68]*ARSO*, 1913, p. 781; Chandler and Lahm, *How Army Grew Wings*, pp. 229–30, 235–38; Foulois, *Memoirs*, pp. 100–102; Thomas M. Coffey, *Hap: The Story of the U.S.*

Air Force and the Man Who Built It, General Henry "Hap" Arnold (New York: Viking Press, 1982), pp. 54–55.

[69]Hennessy, *Army Air Arm*, p. 86.

[70]Chandler and Lahm, *How Army Grew Wings*, p. 252; Foulois, *Memoirs*, p. 97.

[71]Alfred Goldberg, ed., *A History of the United States Air Force, 1907–1957* (Princeton, N.J.: D. Van Nostrand Company, Inc., 1957), p. 8; Chandler and Lahm, *How Army Grew Wings*, p. 228 and apps. 9 and 10 containing both sets of requirements. The Aero Club used the qualifications drawn up by the Federation Aeronautique Internationale (F.A.I). The new badge is announced in WDGO 39, 27 May 1913.

[72]WD Bull 17, 6 May 1913, p. 14; WD Bull 18, 7 Jun 1913, p. 3.

[73]Scriven is number seven if Myer is counted only once.

[74]Coffey, *Hap*, p. 68.

[75]An extract of his report appears in *ARSO*, 1913, pp. 790–98. The quotation is from p. 791.

[76]Foulois, *Memoirs*, pp. 110–11; Coffey, *Hap*, pp. 72–73.

[77]Alfred E. Hurley, *Billy Mitchell: Crusader for Air Power* (Bloomington: Indiana University Press, 1975), p. 17.

[78]*ARSO*, 1912, pp. 964–71; Chandler and Lahm, *How Army Grew Wings*, pp. 258–59. Capt. Paul Beck, an Army pilot, was the only officer to testify in favor of the bill. For his arguments, see his article, "Military Aviation in America: Its Needs," *Infantry Journal* 8 (May–Jun 1912): 796–817. Extracts from the hearings are published in Maurer Maurer, comp. and ed., *The U.S. Air Service in World War I*, 4 vols. (Washington, D.C.: Office of Air Force History, 1978–1979), 2: 3–17.

[79]On operations at Texas City, see *ARSO*, 1913, pp. 783–85; Chandler and Lahm, *How Army Grew Wings*, pp. 253–58; Hennessy, *Army Air Arm*, pp. 74–79; WDGO 79, 13 Dec 1913.

[80]On Lahm's accident, see Chandler and Lahm, *How Army Grew Wings*, pp. 247–48. Coffey recounts Arnold's brush with death in *Hap*, pp. 62–63.

[81]Howard, *Wilbur and Orville*, p. 392.

[82]Joseph W. A. Whitehorne, The Inspectors General of the United States Army, 1903–1939, draft Ms, CMH, pp. 319–21; Hennessy, *Army Air Arm*, p. 103.

[83]Loening provides insight into Orville Wright's attitude toward tractor planes in his book *Takeoff into Greatness: How American Aviation Grew So Big So Fast* (New York: G. P. Putnam's Sons, 1968), pp. 56–57. On the adoption of tractor planes at San Diego, see pp. 66–69. See also Howard, *Wilbur and Orville*, pp. 390–92; Foulois, *Memoirs*, p. 114; Hennessy, *Army Air Arm*, p. 103. (This is the only source seen by the author that mentions the Inspector General's investigation.) Goldberg, *History of Air Force*, pp. 8–9. The chief signal officer reports the change to tractor planes in *ARSO*, 1914, p. 517.

[84]*ARSO*, 1914, pp. 536–37; Chandler and Lahm, *How Army Grew Wings*, p. 105.

[85]WDGO 75, 4 Dec 1913.

[86]A table of appropriations is published as Appendix 17 to Hennessy, *Army Air Arm*. The twenty officers are listed on pages 99–100 of that volume.

[87]See Chandler and Lahm, *How Army Grew Wings*, Appendix 1, for a list of those officers ordered to aeronautical duty through March 1914. An expanded list, to include enlisted pilots, is published as Appendix 14 to Hennessy, *Army Air Arm*.

[88]Hugh G. J. Aitken, *The Continuous Wave: Technology and American Radio, 1900–1932* (Princeton, N.J.: Princeton University Press, 1985), p. 59. Aitken presents an excellent discussion of early radio technology.

[89]*Wireless Telegraphy: Report of the Inter-Departmental Board Appointed by the President To Consider the Entire Question of Wireless Telegraphy in the Service of the National Government* (Washington, D.C.: Government Printing Office, 1904); Howeth, *Communications-Electronics in Navy*, pp. 62–63, 72–78, and ch. 12. The board's conclusions and recommendations are published as Appendix C. See also Aitken, *Continuous Wave*, p. 253; Douglas, *Inventing Broadcasting*, pp. 123–26 and ch. 7, which discusses the impact of the *Titanic* tragedy on the passage of regulatory legislation.

[90]Howeth, *Communications-Electronics in Navy*, p. 72, n. 20 (The protocol is published as app. B); *ARSO*, 1903, p. 345.

[91]Howeth, *Communications-Electronics in Navy*, pp. 118–30, 159; Douglas, *Inventing Broadcasting*, pp. 137–42, 216; *ARSO*, 1907, p. 183; *ARSO*, 1909, pp. 251–52.

[92]Howeth, *Communications-Electronics in Navy*, pp. 165–66; *ARSO*, 1912, pp. 962–63.

[93]*ARSO*, 1914, p. 511.

[94]*ARSO*, 1906, pp. 181–84; *ARSO*, 1907, pp. 166, 177–78; *ARSO*, 1908, pp. 195–96, 200, 207–10, 215; *ARSO*, 1909, pp. 238 and 248–52; *ARSO*, 1910, pp. 16–17. (The 1910 citations refer to the report as published in a separate volume. Beginning in 1910 the *ARSO* is included in vol. 1 of the *ARSW*.) *ARSO*, 1911, pp. 730–33; *ARSO*, 1912, pp. 960–61; *ARSO*, 1913, pp. 777–80; *ARSO*, 1914, pp. 510–12 and 554–55; Howeth, *Communications-Electronics in Navy*, pp. 180–81.

[95]Benedict Crowell, *America's Munitions, 1917–1918* (Washington, D.C.: Government Printing Office, 1919), pp. 323–24; Hennessy, *Army Air Arm*, p. 158.

[96]WDGO 49, 15 Mar 1909.

[97]*ARSO*, 1910, pp. 21–22; *ARSO*, 1911, pp. 735–36; Howeth, *Communications-Electronics in Navy*, pp. 172–73; Dupree, *Science in Federal Government*, p. 276. The creation of the Bureau of Standards and its laboratory were part of the government's emerging scientific establishment. See chs. 14 and 15 of Dupree.

[98]George R. Thompson and Dixie R. Harris, *The Signal Corps: The Outcome*, United States Army in World War II (Washington, D.C.: Office of the Chief of Military History, United States Army, 1966), p. 582, n. 9.

[99]*ARSO*, 1910, pp. 21–22; *ARSO*, 1911, pp. 735–36. On Squier's work with "wired wireless," see Clark, "Squier," ch. 7. On Squier's reassignment, see pp. 196–98. His reassignment orders were issued in January 1912 (p. 196, n. 1).

[100]Douglas, *Inventing Broadcasting*, pp. 177 and 196; Aitken, *Continuous Wave*, p. 55, n. 46, and p. 192, n. 54. For a summary of Dunwoody's military career, see his obituary in *USMA Graduates Report* (1933), pp. 54–56. While most accounts credit Dunwoody with the carborundum discovery in 1906, Squier in *Telling the World* (New York: The Century Co., 1933), p. 139, claims that Dunwoody made the discovery "at the beginning of the twentieth century" while still a colonel in the Signal Corps and received the patent in December 1906. W. Rupert Maclaurin in *Invention and Innovation in the Radio Industry* (New York: Macmillan Company, 1949) states that Dunwoody made the discovery in 1906 but while a vice president of de Forest's company (p. 118, n. 21). De Forest himself, in his autobiography, *Father of Radio: The Autobiography of Lee de Forest* (Chicago: Wilcox and Follett Co., 1950), does not clarify these points. De Forest was not the best of businessmen and, with a string of failures over the years, a number of companies bore his name. While the inventor spelled his name de Forest, his companies used the capital "D."

[101]As a consequence, Armstrong entered into a protracted lawsuit with de Forest over the invention of the regenerative, or feedback, circuit. The U.S. Supreme Court eventually ruled in de Forest's favor in 1934. Aitken, *Continuous Wave*, ch. 4; Douglas, *Inventing Broadcasting*, pp. 168–77, 245–46. See also Tom Lewis, *Empire of the Air: The Men Who Made Radio* (New York: Edward Burlingame Books, 1991). Lewis focuses on the careers of de Forest, Armstrong, and David Sarnoff.

[102]Howeth, *Communications-Electronics in Navy*, pp. 182–85, 207; Aitken, *Continuous Wave*, ch. 3.

[103]Susan J. Douglas, "Technological Innovation and Organizational Change: The Navy's Adoption of Radio, 1899–1919," in Merritt Roe Smith, ed., *Military Enterprise and Technological Change: Perspectives on the American Experience* (Cambridge, Mass.: MIT Press, 1985), pp. 117–73; Douglas, *Inventing Broadcasting*, chs. 4 and 8.

[104]*ARSO*, 1913, pp. 758–60; *ARSO*, 1914, p. 539.

[105]*ARSO*, 1912, p. 954.

[106]*ARSO*, 1908, p. 182.

[107]WDGO 40, 11 Mar 1910; WDGO 53, 5 Apr 1910.

[108]WDGO 24, 17 Feb 1911; *ARSO*, 1914, p. 542.

[109]*Field Service Regulations, United States Army* (Washington, D.C.: Government Printing Office, 1910). Excerpts are printed in *ARSO*, 1910, pp. 5–7. The regulations call for a field signal company with four officers and one hundred enlisted men. The aero and wireless companies have the same personnel strength. See also John B. Wilson, "Army Readiness Planning," p. 64.

[110]WDGO 55, 15 Sep 1913.

[111]*ARSO*, 1913, p. 762.

[112]*Tables of Organization, United States Army*, 1914 (Washington, D.C.: Government Printing Office, 1914); *ARSO*, 1914, pp. 542–43.

[113]*ARSW*, 1913, p. 29; *ARSO*, 1913, p. 748.

[114]*ARSO*, 1913, p. 767; *ARSO*, 1914, p. 513.

[115]This and other amendments to the Dick Act are published in WDGO 99, 11 Jun 1908.

[116]See, for example, Allen's comments in *ARSO*, 1909, pp. 240–41. In 1913 there were twenty-two signal companies in the National Guard (*ARSO*, 1913, p. 775). See the discussion of the impact of the Dick Act on the National Guard in Jim Dan Hill, *The Minute Man in Peace and War: A History of the National Guard* (Harrisburg, Pa.: Stackpole Company, 1964), ch. 8.

[117] *ARSO*, 1909, p. 244. Benjamin D. Foulois, "The Elimination of the Myer Code in Visual Signaling," *National Guard Magazine* 2 (Jul 1908): 320–21.

[118]*ARSO*, 1912, p. 956; AR, 1913, par. 1561, secs. 7 and 8.

[119]*Signal Book United States Army, 1914* (Washington, D.C.: Government Printing Office, 1914), par. 3; WDGO 61, 19 Aug 1914; *ARSO*, 1914, p. 512. See also Paul D. Bunker, "The Two-Arm Semaphore Code," *JMSI* 24, extra no. 105 (1880), reprinted in Scheips, ed., *Military Signal Communications*, vol. 2.

[120]*ARSO*, 1910, p. 14. The regulations governing the school, published in WDGOs, first mention such conferences in WDGO 145, 16 Aug 1906. They were then called journal meetings, but later became known as the Leavenworth Technical Conferences. Clark, "Squier," pp. 117–18, indicates that Squier based these meetings on his experiences at Johns Hopkins. For some insight into the operations of the school, see Knowles, "The Army Signal School," pp. 31–37; George A. Wieczorek, "Technical Training for Line

Officers in the Use and Construction of Military Lines of Information," *Journal of the United States Infantry Association* 4 (Mar 1908): 739–43; and Marvin E. Malloy, "The Army Signal School," *Infantry Journal* 9 (May-Jun 1913): 826–35.

[121]The chief signal officer does not mention Company A's movements in his annual report, but they are given in *ARAG*, 1911, in *ARSW*, 1911, vol. 1, p. 241. This report on page 239 also shows Company D, Signal Corps, with the Maneuver Division but does not list Company I. The chief signal officer, while briefly discussing signal operations with the Maneuver Division in his 1911 annual report (p. 721), does not cite the specific units involved. However, he states in his 1912 report (p. 960) that both Companies D and I served with the Maneuver Division. The Department of Texas reports for 1911 and 1912 (in vol. 3 of the *ARSW* for each year) list only Company A. The adjutant general does not include the movements of units along the border in his 1912 and 1913 reports. The *Historical Sketch* states (p. 59) that Companies D and I served on border duty in 1912, but it is possible that this is a reference to their subsequent service (see below).

[122]Forrest C. Pogue, *George C. Marshall*, 4 vols. (New York: Viking Press, 1963–1987), 1: 113–14.

[123]*ARSO*, 1912, p. 960.

[124]*ARSW*, 1913, vol. 1, p. 10; Weigley, *History of Army*, p. 335; Thomas F. Burdett, "Mobilizations of 1911 and 1913," *Military Review* 54 (Jul 1974): 72. The 2d Division was demobilized on 18 October 1915. It is not perpetuated by the current 2d Infantry Division.

[125]*ARSO*, 1913, p. 757; Rpt, Maj Gen William H. Carter, Commander, 2d Division, 30 Jun 1913 in *ARSW*, 1913, vol. 3, pp. 111–20.

[126]*ARSO*, 1913, p. 761; *ARSO*, 1914, p. 536; Rpt, Brig Gen Tasker H. Bliss, Commander, Southern Department, to The Adjutant General, 30 Jun 1913, in *ARSW*, 1913, vol. 3, p. 39. The details of Company I's service given on pages 50–51 indicate that the company began this tour of border duty in September 1912.

[127]*ARSO*, 1914, pp. 536–37, 540, and 543.

[128]*ARSO*, 1914, p. 535; *ARSO*, 1915, p. 767. The 1915 annual report refers only to Company D's use of visual signaling; it does not specify the heliograph. The use of the heliograph at Vera Cruz is mentioned, however, in Scheips, comp., "The Military Heliograph and Its Use in Arizona and New Mexico," p. 8, and Kelly, "Talking Mirrors at Fort Bowie," p. 3. Although rarely used, the heliograph remained in the Signal Corps' inventory for several years. The British and French continued to use the talking mirrors into the post–World War I period.

[129]For details on the Vera Cruz expedition, see Clarence C. Clendenen, *Blood on the Border: The United States Army and the Mexican Irregulars* (New York: Macmillan Company, 1969), ch. 8.

[130]The act is published in WD Bull 35, 4 Aug 1914, as well as in *ARSO*, 1914, pp. 514–16; see also Chandler and Lahm, *How Army Grew Wings*, app. 16. The legislation actually represented a rewritten version of the bill proposed in 1913 to remove aviation from the Signal Corps. Capt. William Mitchell, one of those testifying against the original proposal, claimed to have drafted the revision. Hurley, *Billy Mitchell*, p. 17.

[131]WD Bull 18, 11 May 1914, p. 3.

[132]*Field Service Regulations, United States Army* (Washington, D.C.: Government Printing Office, 1914). Extracts from the regulations are published in Maurer, comp. and ed., *Air Service in World War I*, 2: 22–25.

[133]*ARSO*, 1914, p. 507.

[134]Ibid., p. 508.

[135]WDGO 79, 13 Dec 1913.

[136]Foulois, *Memoirs*, p. 115. See also *ARSO*, 1914, p. 517; Goldberg, *History of Air Force*, p. 9; Chandler and Lahm, *How Army Grew Wings*, p. 276. Chandler and Lahm end their narrative at this point.

[137]*ARSO*, 1914, p. 522.

[138]Weigley, *History of Army*, app., p. 599, gives the Regular Army's strength in 1914 as 98,544.

[139]For an excellent discussion of the preparedness movement, see John Patrick Finnegan, *Against the Specter of a Dragon: The Campaign for American Military Preparedness, 1914–1917* (Westport, Conn.: Greenwood Press, 1974). See also Weigley, *History of Army*, ch. 15. Secretary of War Henry Stimson had rearranged the departmental system in 1913. The rationale behind this change is discussed in John B. Wilson, "Army Readiness Planning," pp. 60–73.

[140]*ARSW*, 1914, vol. 1, pp. 1–14; Finnegan, *Specter of Dragon*, p. 29.

[141]Johnson, "The Aero Club of America and Army Aviation," pp. 390–95; Finnegan, *Specter of Dragon*, p. 100.

[142]Clendenen, *Blood on Border*, p. 216. He discusses the raid in ch. 10.

[143]Smythe, *Guerrilla Warrior*, p. 224; Clendenen, *Blood on Border*, pp. 215, 221–24.

[144]Benjamin D. Foulois, "Report of the Operations of the First Aero Squadron, Signal Corps, with the Mexican Punitive Expedition, for Period March 15 to August 15, 1916," (hereafter cited as Foulois report), published as Appendix B, pp. 236–45, in Frank Tompkins, *Chasing Villa* (Harrisburg, Pa.: Military Service Publishing Co., 1934). See also Clendenen, *Blood on Border*, pp. 223–25.

[145]*ARSO*, 1916, p. 882; Foulois report, p. 236. The squadron also contained two enlisted men from the Hospital Corps. At El Paso the squadron acquired a medical officer and another enlisted man from the Hospital Corps. Foulois, *Memoirs*, p. 126. Weigley, *History of Army*, p. 351, gives the number of planes as six, but this is contradicted by Foulois' report and the *ARSO*, which both say eight. Weigley may be discounting, however, the two planes that were soon put out of commission.

[146]*ARSO*, 1916, pp. 882–83; Foulois report, pp. 242–43; Clendenen, *Blood on Border*, pp. 226 and 321. Foulois, *Memoirs*, ch. 8, discusses aerial operations in Mexico, as does Hennessy, *Army Air Arm*, ch. 9.

[147]Foulois' account of the incident given in his report, pp. 240–41, differs in some details from that in his *Memoirs*, pp. 129–32. This summary follows most closely the account given in his report. See also Clendenen, *Blood on Border*, pp. 319–20, and Smythe, *Guerrilla Warrior*, p. 233.

[148]Haldeen Braddy, *Pershing's Mission in Mexico* (El Paso: Texas Western Press, 1966), p. 37.

[149]As quoted in Smythe, *Guerrilla Warrior*, p. 232.

[150]The *New York World* published an article concerning aviation's woes in which several pilots, including Dargue, were quoted. See discussion in Smythe, *Guerrilla Warrior*, pp. 232–33; Foulois report, p. 243; Foulois, *Memoirs*, ch. 10. On the appropriation, see *ARSO*, 1916, p. 882.

[151]Foulois report, p. 243. Foulois left Mexico in September for duty in Washington, D.C., and Dodd assumed command of the squadron.

[152]Clendenen, *Blood on Border*, p. 333. He also remarks on page 251 that "The distances in northern Mexico were too great for the relatively primitive signal communications of the time."

[153]Extract from Pershing's Report of Operations, in Robert S. Thomas and Inez V. Allen, The Mexican Punitive Expedition under Brigadier General John J. Pershing, United States Army, 1916–1917 [Washington, D.C.: Office of the Chief of Military History, 1 May 1954], app. D, pp. A–18 and –19.

[154]The chief signal officer refers to the successful operation of two-kilowatt tractor sets along the Mexican border (*ARSO*, 1916, p. 879). See also Squier, *Telling the World*, pp. 143–44; *Historical Sketch*, p. 59.

[155]Pershing established his headquarters at Colonia Dublán in June 1918, after active operations ended. Clendenen, *Blood on Border*, pp. 333–34; Smythe, *Guerrilla Warrior*, pp. 239–40, 256; Pershing Rpt, p. A–18.

[156]*ARSO*, 1916, p. 873.

[157]Clendenen, *Blood on Border*, p. 334.

[158]The bill is published as WD Bull 16, 22 June 1916. See the discussion of the Defense Act in Matloff, ed., *American Military History*, pp. 366–68; Daniel R. Beaver, *Newton D. Baker and the American War Effort, 1917–1919* (Lincoln: University of Nebraska Press, 1966), pp. 12–14; Finnegan, *Specter of Dragon*, ch. 9; James L. Abrahamson, *America Arms for a New Century* (New York: Free Press, 1981), pp. 164–65; John B. Wilson, Divisions and Separate Brigades, draft Ms, pp. 2:32 to 2:39.

[159]See Scriven's comments in *ARSO*, 1915, pp. 743–44.

[160]Section 13 of the Defense Act contains the provisions relating to the Signal Corps. For the Signal Corps' appropriation for fiscal year 1917, see WD Bull 33, 9 Sep 1916, p. 4.

[161]*ARSO*, 1916, p. 816.

[162]*ARSW*, 1916, vol. 1, pp. 26–29. The Enlisted Reserve Corps is provided for by Section 55 of the Defense Act.

[163]WD Bull 16, 1916, sec. 3, p. 2, and sec. 13, p. 17.

[164]General Trevino, head of Carranza's forces, made this demand on 16 June. See copy of his telegram in Tompkins, *Chasing Villa*, p. 208. See also Clendenen, *Blood on Border*, p. 275; Hill, *Minute Man in Peace and War*, pp. 229–43.

[165]Casualty statistics from *ARSW*, 1916, vol. 1, p. 9. As with most statistics, they vary with the source consulted. Smythe, *Guerrilla Warrior*, page 259, gives nine killed and twelve wounded. Clendenen, *Blood on Border*, chapter 16, discusses the fight at Carrizal and the events that led to it. His statistics indicate that two officers and ten men were killed and one officer and ten men wounded. In addition, a noncommissioned officer was missing and presumed dead (pp. 310–11).

[166]*Annual Report of the Chief of the Militia Bureau* (hereafter cited as *ARMB*), 1916, in *ARSW*, 1916, vol. 1, p. 896. 1 The number of signal units includes those called up on 9 May. See also *ARSW*, 1916, vol. 1, pp. 10–17.

[167]Bolling was President Wilson's brother-in-law. During World War I he headed the Bolling Commission (discussed below). Bolling was killed during World War I, and Bolling Airfield in Washington, D.C., is named for him. See *ARMB*, 1916, p. 917. On the aero company, see Bruce Jacobs, "Pioneer Aviation and the 'Football Special,'" *National Guard* 37 (Nov 1983): 40.

[168]*ARSW*, 1917, vol. 1, pp. 9–10; *ARMB*, 1917, in *ARSW*, 1917, vol. 1, p. 854. The final demobilization was announced in February 1917. Finnegan, *Specter of Dragon*, pp. 171, 185.

[169]Clendenen, *Blood on Border*, p. 338; Smythe, *Guerrilla Warrior*, pp. 268–69.

[170]Barbara W. Tuchman, *The Zimmermann Telegram* (New York: Dell Publishing Company, Inc., 1958), p. 12. The full text is printed in English on p. 136 and the code text of the telegram is included in the back of the volume.

[171]Walter Millis, *Arms and Men: A Study of American Military History* (New York: New American Library, 1956), p. 205.

[172]Motor transportation on the border is discussed in the *Annual Report of the Quartermaster General* (hereafter cited as *ARQM*), 1916, in *ARSW*, 1916, vol. 1, pp. 382–85. No mention is made, however, of the contributions of the 1st Aero Squadron. See also Norman M. Cary, Jr., "The Use of the Motor Vehicle in the United States Army, 1899–1939" (Ph.D. dissertation, University of Georgia, 1980), pp. 96–105.

[173]Clendenen, *Blood on Border*, p. 341; strength figure from Smythe, *Guerrilla Warrior*, p. 274.

CHAPTER V

World War I

The United States managed to remain neutral in the European conflict from August 1914 to April 1917. The nation had traditionally been isolated and protected from Old World contests by its ocean moat, but such geographic security could no longer be taken for granted when Germany's indiscriminate use of submarine warfare violated the traditional rights of neutrals. Americans' belief in an Allied victory had initially made the necessity of preparations for war seem remote. But as the war in the west developed into a bloody stalemate, the Allies' best efforts appeared able to guarantee only more of the same. On the other hand, the dire prospect of a German victory and the consequent disruption of the European balance of power jeopardized U.S. national interests and spurred the call to arms.

Despite the clamor of the preparedness movement and the loss of American lives at sea, President Woodrow Wilson moved cautiously from a policy of strict neutrality to the adoption of a moralistic crusade "to make the world safe for democracy." His insistence on neutrality until nearly the eve of war, however, severely hampered preparedness efforts by the War and Navy Departments. In his view, such activities would not be "neutral." The Signal Corps, meanwhile, faced the same difficulties as the rest of the Army in preparing its communicators for duty overseas. But the Corps' problems were complicated by dissension within its own ranks, the outcome of which would have a significant impact on the branch's future.

Trouble in the Air

As the experiences in Mexico had clearly illustrated, all was not well with the Signal Corps' Aviation Section. In fact, problems had been brewing for several years. A series of investigations into the section's activities from 1915 to 1917 revealed the growing tension between those Corps members who flew and those who did not.[1]

When Col. David C. Shanks of the Inspector General's Department visited the aviation school in San Diego to conduct the annual inspection in January 1915, he made the unsettling discovery that, besides the hiring of an aeronautical engineer, very little had been done in response to the previous year's recommendations. In fact, a subsequent probe revealed that Lt. Col. Samuel Reber, head of the Aviation Section, had suppressed the critical report.[2] Consequently, the

Army's chief of staff, Maj. Gen. Hugh L. Scott, appointed an investigating board headed by the inspector general, Brig. Gen. Ernest A. Garlington, to examine the administration of the Aviation Section. (Garlington had commanded the unsuccessful attempt to rescue Lieutenant Greely and his men from the Arctic in 1883.) About the same time, Senator Joseph T. Robinson of Arkansas called for an investigation of the air service. While the Senate passed his resolution on 16 March, the day after the 1st Aero Squadron arrived in Columbus, the House did not concur, and the congressional initiative ended.[3]

As part of its investigation, the Garlington board inquired into allegations made by Lt. Col. Lewis E. Goodier that improper disbursements of flight pay had been made to Capt. Arthur S. Cowan, commanding officer of the San Diego school, and some of his staff. These men were not, Goodier alleged, qualified pilots.[4] The board, after a month of taking testimony, determined that Goodier's allegations were true. In the meantime, however, a subsequent investigation by the Office of the Judge Advocate General had ruled that Cowan could retain his aviator rating and the extra pay.[5] The Garlington board also found that the officers assigned to monitor contracts with private airplane manufacturers had been accepting substandard machines. The board held Chief Signal Officer Scriven and Colonel Reber responsible for allowing unsafe aircraft to be used and further criticized Scriven for not adequately supervising the Aviation Section. Secretary of War Newton D. Baker concurred with the board's findings and censured Scriven and Reber for failing to enforce and maintain discipline and neglecting to observe military regulations. Baker also announced his intention to reorganize the Aviation Section.[6] Scriven, for his part, accused aviation officers of insubordination and disloyalty.[7]

In April 1916, at Baker's request, the General Staff began its own investigation into the organization and administration of the Aviation Section. Lt. Herbert A. Dargue, the officer in charge of training at San Diego, aired his grievances before the committee and added his voice to those calling for the removal of aviation from the Signal Corps. He complained that the Signal Corps had no unit fully equipped for field service and no radio set for airplanes. Speaking on behalf of most of the aviation officers, Dargue stated their belief that the Signal Corps lacked an officer capable of commanding the Aviation Section. The General Staff's report, completed at the end of June, recommended that the Aviation Section be completely separated from the Signal Corps.[8]

Secretary Baker reacted with caution to the increasingly bitter controversy. Although he did not detach aviation from the Signal Corps, he did remove Reber as chief of the Aviation Section on 5 May 1916 and temporarily replaced him with Capt. William Mitchell. Reber's dismissal ended his official aviation duties and also effectively finished his career as a Signal Corps officer. He went overseas during World War I, but he did not receive any Signal Corps–related assignments. After returning from France, he retired in 1919 with thirty-seven years of military service. As a private citizen, he embarked upon a successful second career with the Radio Corporation of America where his Signal Corps experience served him well.[9]

Baker selected Lt. Col. George O. Squier to succeed Reber as the head of the Aviation Section upon the completion of Squier's tour as attaché to London. As attaché, Squier had been able to observe European aviation and had even conducted several secret missions to the front. His contacts within the industrial and scientific communities as well as his long association with Army aviation made him a good choice for the job. Upon Squier's arrival in Washington, Captain Mitchell became his assistant.[10] In his new position, Squier contended with pressure from outside as well as inside the Army. The Aero Club of America, for example, criticized the Signal Corps for failing to adequately promote aviation within the National Guard, while the press, reacting to the misadventures in Mexico, sharply castigated the entire program.[11]

Captain Arnold

Meanwhile, at San Diego Captain Cowan was relieved as commander of the aviation school and replaced by Col. William A. Glassford, a signal officer who had served in the Corps since 1874.[12] Many of the staff and faculty also lost their jobs. Two pioneer aviators, returning to aeronautical duty after completing other assignments, served under Glassford: Capts. Frank P. Lahm and Henry H. Arnold. (While serving as the school's supply officer, Arnold eventually overcame his fear of flying that stemmed from his harrowing experience at Fort Riley several years earlier.) But despite the change in administration, the troubles at the school had not ended. Glassford, too, came under fire in January 1917 regarding his lack of vigor in searching for two pilots from the school who had crashed in the Mexican desert. Fortunately they were found by a civilian search party, alive but somewhat the worse for wear after more than a week of wandering in the desert. Consequently, the Inspector General's Department launched yet another inquiry, which recommended that Glassford and several of his staff members be relieved. Glassford retired on 11 April 1917, only five days after the declaration of war with Germany.[13]

With Scriven's retirement in February 1917, Squier became the new chief signal officer, and Lt. Col. John B. Bennet took over the duties of the Aviation Section. In his last annual report as chief signal officer Scriven remarked: "The plan of the General Staff, approved by the Secretary of War, contemplates, and as I think very properly, the eventual separation of the aviation service from the

Signal Corps. The separation of this service from any technical corps should take place when the Air Service is capable of standing alone. This time has not yet come."[14] After all the squabbles of the past few years, the Signal Corps and its Aviation Section headed toward war still tethered uneasily to each other.

"Over Here": Mobilization and Training

Germany's resumption of unrestricted submarine warfare forced President Wilson to request a declaration of war in April 1917. Following this action came the daunting task of mobilizing the nation's resources, both men and materiel, with which to fight. Even after war was declared the Wilson administration found it difficult to define America's role in the contest. The War Department initially felt no sense of urgency regarding mobilization and foresaw no massive commitment of troops to Europe. Military planners estimated that it would take about two years to raise and train an army large enough to achieve victory in Europe.[15] In the meantime, the administration could only provide moral support to the Allied cause by responding to the French government's request to immediately deploy one division. In May 1917 Secretary Baker authorized the organization of the 1st Expeditionary Division (later redesignated as the 1st Division), and its elements began arriving in France late the following month. But these units needed extensive training before they would be ready to enter the line.

The type of total war being waged in Europe required military forces far greater than those the nation then had in uniform. Shortly after the declaration of war Congress passed the Selective Service Act, which President Wilson signed on 18 May 1917. Unlike the unsuccessful attempt to draft recruits during the Civil War, this bill eliminated such unfair practices as bounties, purchased exemptions, and substitutes. Moreover, local civilian draft boards rather than a federal agency administered the process. The law aroused little opposition, and about twenty-four million men registered. Nearly three million of them entered the armed forces between May 1917 and November 1918. Approximately forty-one thousand men, or slightly over 17 percent of those inducted, joined the Signal Corps.[16] The selective service legislation also authorized the president to raise the Regular Army and National Guard to war strength and to mobilize the National Guard for federal service. It further created a third segment of the defense structure, known as the National Army, a force to be raised in two increments of 500,000 men each.[17]

For the Signal Corps, mobilization meant a rapid and vast expansion. In April 1917 the ground troops of the Signal Corps consisted of 55 officers and 1,570 enlisted men. These soldiers were divided into 4 field signal battalions, 4 field telegraph battalions, and 6 depot companies (administrative units with no fixed strength assigned to each territorial department).[18] Shortly after arriving in France, Pershing called for approximately one million men to be sent over by the end of 1918. As Allied fortunes declined, Pershing increased his request to one hundred divisions to arrive by July 1919. These divisions would be organized in

accordance with new tables of organization calling for a "square" structure—that is, a division comprising
two infantry brigades, each with two
infantry regiments. The square divisions, based upon study of the British
and French armies, were to be larger
than their predecessors and include
the necessary support troops to withstand sustained combat. Pershing's
request, meanwhile, would require the
Signal Corps to supply at least one
hundred field signal battalions, or
roughly twenty-five thousand officers
and men as organized in the spring of
1917. While President Wilson ultimately approved a projected force of
only eighty divisions, the Signal
Corps still faced a tremendous task.[19]

The training of the mass of men
called to the colors for signal duty
overwhelmed the capacity of the

General Squier

Signal School at Fort Leavenworth. Thus, in May 1917 the Corps established
additional mobilization and training camps at Little Silver, New Jersey (Camp
Alfred Vail); Leon Springs, Texas (Camp Samuel F. B. Morse); and the Presidio
of Monterey, California. In 1918 the Signal Corps transferred its activities at
Camp Morse and Fort Leavenworth to Camp Meade, Maryland, where it had earlier opened a radio school in December 1917. In addition, many of the nation's
colleges and universities offered technical training for prospective Signal Corps
personnel.[20]

To fight a total war such as that in Europe, the nation, and the Signal Corps
in particular, had to mobilize its technological, scientific, and economic resources
as never before. Consequently a huge bureaucracy emerged, familiar to us today
as the military-industrial complex but unparalleled at that time, to coordinate the
many war-related activities. Not only did the War Department balloon in size, but
the civilian side of government likewise underwent tremendous expansion.[21]

To obtain needed technical expertise in communications, the Army called
upon the private sector. While the United States lagged behind Europe in some
major technological areas such as aviation, it led the world in the field of telephone technology, thanks largely to the achievements of the Bell System. Unlike
its European allies, the U.S. government did not control the national telegraph
and telephone systems in peacetime. As a preparedness measure, the War
Department in 1916 had begun issuing commissions in the Signal Corps
Officers' Reserve Corps to executives of leading commercial telephone and tele-

graph companies. John J. Carty, chief engineer of the American Telephone and Telegraph Company (AT&T), figured prominently in this group. Commissioned as a major in the Signal Reserve, Carty undertook the recruitment of men from the Bell System and other communications companies.[22] The Army needed a variety of specialists: telephone and telegraph operators, linemen, and cable splicers, to name a few. (As previously noted, the prewar Signal Corps had only four telegraph battalions.) The recruitment of men already possessing the requisite skills obviously lightened the Signal Corps' training load. Ultimately the Bell System provided twelve telegraph battalions to the war effort (numbered 401 to 412) that served at the army and corps levels. Each unit comprised men drawn from a regional company. The 406th Telegraph Battalion, for example, contained employees from Pennsylvania Bell, while the 411th came from Pacific Bell. The Signal Corps obtained another four battalions from railway telegraph organizations.[23] Western Electric, the manufacturing arm of the Bell System, additionally furnished two radio companies: Company A, 314th Field Signal Battalion, and Company A, 319th Field Signal Battalion.[24]

In order to release men for the front lines, the Army employed approximately two hundred women telephone operators to serve overseas. These women, who retained their civilian status, became members of the Signal Corps Female Telephone Operators Unit.[25] They are perhaps better known as the "Hello Girls." In order to operate switchboards in France and England, they needed to be fluent in both French and English. Moreover, because the Army contained few French-speaking operators, these women no doubt made inter-Allied communications proceed much more smoothly. Beginning in November 1917, the Signal Corps recruited women from the commercial telephone companies; to obtain enough bilingual operators, the Corps also accepted untrained volunteers who met the language requirement. After a training period, the first detachment of women, in the charge of chief operator Grace Banker, departed from New York City early in March 1918. Soon members of the unit were operating telephone exchanges of the American Expeditionary Forces in Paris, Chaumont, and seventy-five other cities and towns in France as well as in London, Southampton, and Winchester, England.[26]

The Navy had taken the lead in mobilizing science by establishing the Naval Consulting Board in 1915. Composed of representatives of the nation's leading engineering societies and chaired by Thomas A. Edison, its major activity became the screening of inventions submitted by private citizens.[27] The following year the National Academy of Sciences created the National Research Council and offered its services to the government to coordinate military-related research. The council's membership embraced governmental, educational, and industrial organizations. Chief Signal Officer Squier served on the council's Military Committee along with the heads of the other technical bureaus of the Army and Navy. With his scientific background, Squier actively promoted the council's efforts and exerted considerable control over its activities in general. First of all, Robert A. Millikan, professor of physics at the University of Chicago and the council's exec-

"Hello Girls" operate a switchboard at Chaumont, France.

utive officer, became a major in the Signal Corps Officers' Reserve Corps and
served as head of the Signal Corps' new Science and Research Division, established in October 1917. The division's offices were located in the building housing
the National Research Council, and many of the council's scientists donned uni-
forms and served under Millikan. Through the Officers' Reserve program, the
Signal Corps recruited additional scientists and engineers from the private sector.[28]

In the past the Signal Corps' Engineering Division had performed what is
now called research and development in its laboratories on Pennsylvania Avenue
and at the Bureau of Standards.[29] But the wartime demand for new and improved
communication methods fostered a greater specialization of functions. In July
1917 the chief signal officer established a separate Radio Division with electrical
engineering becoming a section of the new Equipment Division. After several
reorganizations within the Signal Office, electrical and radio engineering were
reunited as sections of the Research and Engineering Division in July 1918.[30]
Radio research activities soon outgrew the Signal Corps' existing laboratory
space. Thus, in the spring of 1918, the Corps transferred this work to new facilities at Little Silver, New Jersey, where a training camp had already been established. At Camp Vail, located on the site of a former racetrack, laboratory buildings and several airplane hangars soon appeared. Later the post would become
known as Fort Monmouth.[31]

The primary mission of the Signal Corps' laboratories was the development
of new types of radios, both air and ground. The Army needed radios for many

different purposes—air-to-ground and plane-to-plane communication, aerial fire-control, direction-finding, and, of course, for ground tactical communication. Not only did radios have to be made in large numbers for the first time, they needed to be constructed sturdily enough to withstand the rigors of combat. In other words, they had to be rugged, reliable, and portable. To achieve these goals, the Radio Division devoted considerable effort to the improvement of vacuum tubes. While these devices had been used prior to the war, in particular as telephone signal repeaters or amplifiers, they had never been mass-produced. Western Electric and General Electric manufactured thousands for the Army. The engineering facilities of these and many other companies provided significant assistance to the Signal Corps in developing radio apparatus. The Army also benefited from advances in radio design made by the Navy. The profusion of new equipment prompted the Signal Corps to adopt standard nomenclature for its items, and the now familiar letters SCR began to appear. This designation originally stood for "set, complete, radio" but has come to signify "Signal Corps radio."[32]

Despite the conscientious efforts by government and industry, the limited duration of America's involvement in the war left little time for the development and application of new technology, and the United States relied chiefly on Allied radio equipment. Nevertheless, the Signal Corps made some breakthroughs, especially in airborne radiotelephony, an achievement on which General Squier placed great emphasis. Not only would radio allow the pilot and his observer to communicate more easily between themselves (instead of using hand signals) as well as with the ground, it would also make voice-commanded squadrons possible. An aero squadron based at Camp Vail made nearly one hundred flights per week to test new equipment. In a public demonstration held in early 1918, President and Mrs. Wilson talked with a pilot flying over the White House. While some aerial radiotelephone apparatus arrived in France by the fall of 1918, it did not see use in combat. The Signal Corps also experimented with land-based radiotelephone equipment, but it did not attain notable success prior to the Armistice. Although most of the new devices failed to reach fruition before the war ended, they had a profound effect on communications in the post-war period, for out of these wartime efforts grew the American radio broadcasting industry in the 1920s.[33]

The electrical engineering section's work was initially hampered by the transfer of both of the Signal Corps' laboratories to the Radio Division. With the relocation of the radio facilities to Camp Vail, electrical engineering returned to the laboratory on Pennsylvania Avenue. The section's responsibilities included the preparation of drawings and specifications for all Signal Corps equipment to be produced, except for radios. It also investigated inventions submitted to the Signal Corps by private citizens.[34] The section's developmental efforts concentrated on designing and adapting equipment suitable to conditions on the battlefields of France. While the Signal Corps based its field telephone on a model manufactured by Western Electric for the Forest Service, the Corps also developed a special type of phone for use when wearing a gas mask.[35] Among their other projects, the section's electrical engineers made improvements in the design of animal-drawn wire carts, making them relatively light in weight yet strong enough to carry heavy-duty wire. They also worked on the manufacture of a new type of wire for field lines known as twisted pair, which the Signal Corps had initially tested in Mexico. This wire derived its name from its composition of two wires twisted about each other and covered with insulation. Each wire, in turn, was composed of seven fine wires, four bronze and three steel. By using twisted pair, also known as outpost wire, circuits could be made secure because they did not utilize a ground return that the enemy could easily tap. The wire was manufactured in various colors in order to readily identify connections in the field: for example, red for lines to the artillery and yellow to regimental headquarters. To enable a man on foot to lay and pick up this wire, the section designed a breast reel that held about a half-mile of wire. Unfortunately, twisted pair's original light rubber insulation led to poor performance when wet and caused at least one unit to refer to it as "please don't rain wire." The wire was subsequently improved with heavier insulation.[36]

In the late summer of 1916 Congress created the Council of National Defense to facilitate national economic and industrial mobilization. Despite its name, this body did not set policy but rather acted as a central planning office to coordinate military needs with the nation's industrial capabilities. The council included the secretaries of war, navy, interior, agriculture, commerce, and labor, with Secretary of War Baker serving as chairman. Congress also established an advisory commission to the council comprising seven prominent specialists from the private sector. The commission, in turn, divided its work among several committees, each headed by the member with expertise in that area. Daniel Willard, president of the Baltimore and Ohio Railroad, chaired the Transportation and Communication Committee on which Chief Signal Officer Squier served. Both the National Research Council and the Naval Consulting Board worked in conjunction with the Council of National Defense.[37]

Within the War Department, decentralization hindered mobilization efforts because the various bureaus continued to act independently. The resulting chaos crippled the Army's supply system while the nation's entrance into the war necessitated better coordination. The Signal Corps competed with all the other branches for its supplies, and the War Department waited until January 1918 to establish a centralized Purchasing Service within the Office of the Chief of Staff.[38] Meanwhile, in July 1917 the Council of National Defense had created the War Industries Board which, under the chairmanship of Bernard Baruch, ultimately wielded considerable influence over the setting of priorities and the fixing of prices for items purchased by both the United States government and the Allies. Although military representatives sat on the board's various commodities sections, the Army successfully resisted civilian control of its purchasing.[39]

American business faced the challenge of creating several new industries to replace products supplied by belligerent nations, particularly Germany. In connection with the Signal Corps' operations, most high-quality optical lenses for field glasses and cameras had formerly been imported from Germany or

Belgium, now occupied by German forces. Such companies as Bausch & Lomb of Rochester, New York, stepped in to fill the void. Meanwhile, citizens were urged to lend their binoculars to the military services. Germany had also produced most photographic chemicals and materials which American firms, such as the Eastman Kodak Company, now began to manufacture.[40]

While the majority of Signal Corpsmen served overseas, there remained important communication duties to handle on the home front. Prior to the war the Corps had installed, maintained, and operated the telephone systems at most Army posts. The tremendous growth of wartime facilities, however, overwhelmed the branch's resources, and the Army turned to the local telephone companies for assistance. The Army contracted with the Bell System to provide the central office plants and to tie the post systems into the commercial wire network. Moreover, the Army hired civilian operators to handle the increased message traffic. The Signal Corps continued to operate the Alaska communication system, and signal units performed construction, maintenance, and operations in the Canal Zone, Hawaii, and the Philippines. Meanwhile, the chronic troubles along the Mexican border kept the 7th Field Signal Battalion busy during the war years.[41]

The Signal Corps did not become involved, however, in the types of intelligence-gathering operations it had conducted during the War with Spain, such as the monitoring of cable traffic. Although a Military Information Division had been created as part of the General Staff in 1903 (superseding the Military Information Division within The Adjutant General's Office), it had subsequently diminished in importance, becoming a committee in the 2d (War College) Section of the General Staff. In 1917 the Army established a military intelligence section on the staff, which by the end of the war had achieved division status. During World War I the director of military intelligence, rather than the chief signal officer, acted as the chief military censor, while overseas the chief of the Intelligence Section, AEF, handled similar responsibilities.[42]

Likewise, the Signal Corps did not control the national civilian communication systems during World War I. The president did not take over the commercial telephone and telegraph systems until July 1918, and then he placed them under the postmaster general.[43] As with other aspects of the war, however, the government created a sizable and overlapping bureaucracy to control the flow of information both within the country and with the outside world. In October 1917 the president established the Censorship Board to censor communications by mail, cable, radio, telegraph, and telephone between the United States and foreign nations. But the chief signal officer was not a member; again, the postmaster general administered those operations. In addition, the Transportation and Communication Committee of the Council of National Defense, on which the chief signal officer did serve, dealt with the adaptation of the telephone and telegraph lines to defense needs. In the case of cable communications, the Navy exercised censorship. The director of naval communications became the chief cable censor, and his authority extended to include the War Department cable to Alaska. The Navy also regulated radio transmissions beginning as early as 1914. Stations owned by foreign firms caused particular concern lest they might be conveying military information. With the nation's entry into the war, the Navy assumed control over all radio stations, taking over those needed for naval communications and closing the rest.[44]

Once mobilized, the Signal Corps stood ready to provide communications at home in support of its operations overseas. In October 1917 the chief signal officer's rank was raised to that of a major general. To better handle his multifarious duties, Squier reorganized his office on several occasions as the war progressed. By April 1918 its principal divisions included Administration, Air, Civilian Personnel, Equipment, Land, Medical, Science and Research, and Supply. The Land Division had responsibility for organization and training (exclusive of aviation), telegraph and telephone service, radio station maintenance, and coast artillery fire control. Because of their significance, the activities of the Air Division will be discussed in detail below. With the wartime expansion, the Signal Office scrambled to find enough space for its personnel in sixteen different buildings scattered throughout the nation's capital.[45]

"Over There": Organization and Training

When General Pershing set sail for Europe on 28 May 1917 aboard the British steamship *Baltic*, his key staff officers accompanied him. Among them was Col. Edgar Russel, whom Pershing had designated as chief signal officer of the American Expeditionary Forces. (Russel was promoted to brigadier general in the National Army on 5 August 1917.) A contemporary of Squier from the West Point class of 1887, Russel had begun his service with the Signal Corps during the War with Spain and for several years had headed the Corps' Electrical Division. Most recently he had served as chief signal officer of the Southern Department under Pershing's command. After stopping in England, where Russel observed British signal practices, Pershing and his staff arrived in France on 13 June and set up their headquarters in Paris.[46]

Within AEF headquarters, Pershing placed the Signal Corps under the Line of Communications, later redesignated as the Services of Supply, which included the AEF's technical services.[47] Russel, in turn, divided his own office into several divisions, the major ones being Engineering, Telegraph and Telephone, Supplies, Radio, Photographic, Pigeons, and Research and Inspection.[48]

The Research and Inspection Division, modeled after similar organizations in the British and French armies, operated in conjunction with the scientific efforts being conducted in the United States. The Signal Corps maintained a laboratory in Paris, and among the civilian scientists recruited to work there was Edwin H. Armstrong, the young electrical engineer from Columbia University who had discovered the capabilities of de Forest's audion. Commissioned as a captain, Armstrong began developing the superheterodyne radio receiver, which greatly amplified weak signals and enabled precise tuning. Unfortunately, he could not perfect it prior to the Armistice. After the war Armstrong became known as the father of FM (frequency-modulated) radio.[49] Another primary project of the divi-

General Russel

sion was designing radios for tanks. Moreover, inspection detachments from this division, located at supply depots and factories, checked all Signal Corps apparatus received from the United States or purchased from the Allies before distributing them to the troops.[50]

For the first few months Russel and his staff undertook the planning and organization of signal operations for the AEF. The chief signal officer's responsibilities included:

all that pertains to the technical handling and maintenance of the U.S. military telegraph and telephone lines and radio stations of the American Army in France. He will exercise supervision over the duties of the Signal Corps in connection with the construction, operation and maintenance of all telegraph, telephone and radio installations of the system.[51]

His duties did not include aviation, which was managed by a separate Air Service created by Pershing.

Russel initially leased telephone and telegraph service from the French, but they had few lines and little equipment to spare. Moreover, their equipment was antiquated by American standards, and the French did not "multiplex" their lines to allow them to carry simultaneously both telephone and telegraph traffic. Such a system required far less wire and fewer poles, an important consideration given wartime shortages of material and transport.[52] Consequently, planning soon began for the construction of an all-American wire network to serve the strategic communication needs of the AEF. This system as initially conceived would run 400 miles across France to connect the initial base port of St. Nazaire with the rear of the American sector of operations at Gondrecourt.[53] In September 1917 two Bell battalions, the 406th and 407th Telegraph Battalions, began construction. In keeping with modern American methods, the system ultimately incorporated repeaters, the latest in telephone technology, which had recently made coast-to-coast service possible in the United States.[54] As AEF operations expanded, so did the extent of the wire network. By the end of the war, the Signal Corps built over 1,700 miles of permanent pole lines and strung nearly 23,000 miles of wire. The entire strategic network, to include wires leased from and maintained by the French, totaled approximately 38,000 miles.[55]

Transatlantic communication also ranked high on Russel's list of priorities, and the experience he had acquired with underwater cables in Alaska proved

Telegraph operating room at Chaumont

invaluable. Due to the limitations of existing radio technology, cables remained the most reliable means of long-distance communication. Early in the war the British had severed Germany's cable connections with the United States, and the British and French governments had appropriated and rerouted these cables for their own use. German submarines posed a constant threat, however, and the presence of this underwater menace kept repairs from being made. To ensure transatlantic communication in the event that cable connection was lost, the Navy expanded its series of high-powered radio stations along the Atlantic coast and constructed a station at Bordeaux, France, which became known as Radio Lafayette. The Navy cooperated with the Signal Corps in the use of this system. The British, meanwhile, laid a cable across the English Channel for the Corps' use.[56]

While the U.S. Army established itself in France, Pershing dealt with the complexities of Allied command relationships. From the outset, in accordance with Secretary Baker's instructions, Pershing remained adamant on one point: that the Americans would fight independently and not be amalgamated with other Allied troops. He had to resist the intense pressure applied by Allied leaders who were desperate for manpower after three years of brutal combat and horrific losses. During the spring of 1917 the French Army had been further weakened by mutiny, while the British suffered enormous casualties in Flanders. Moreover, the outbreak of the Bolshevik revolution in Russia in November 1917 led to the collapse of the Eastern Front the following spring, thus freeing large numbers of German troops for fighting in the west. Despite these circumstances, Pershing held his ground.

In September 1917 Pershing transferred his headquarters to Chaumont, located on the Marne River about 150 miles southeast of Paris in Lorraine province. Russel moved along with him. Some Signal Corps operations remained based in Paris, such as photography, research and inspection, meteorology, and procurement of supplies.[57] Because the sector of the front around Chaumont had been quiet for some time, Pershing considered it a good place for American forces to eventually enter the line. Meanwhile, at Gondrecourt elements of the 1st Division, including its 2d Field Signal Battalion, awaited the start of combat training.[58]

With the arrival of American troops, tactical communication in the forward areas came under the control of the Zone of Advance. Col. George S. Gibbs, who had served with the Volunteer Signal Corps during the War with Spain and the Philippine Insurrection, became chief signal officer, Zone of Advance, as well as assistant chief signal officer of the AEF. He described his job as follows:

The day's work in the zone of the advance division was quite like that in the lost and found department of a big railroad. There were hurried trips to inspect equipment and correct requisitions. Lost shipments were traced by telephone and sometimes by automobile. Material for training was needed at once, and the normal means of delivery was neither fast enough nor sure enough. The personal service from the office Chief Signal Officer gave assistance right where it was needed, and no signal outfit was allowed to remain in doubt or in need.[59]

Moreover, each army, corps, and division had a chief signal officer who coordinated the signal operations of his unit and carried out the orders of the chief signal officer, AEF. In March 1918 Russel moved his office to Tours, the headquarters of the Services of Supply, while Gibbs remained at Chaumont.[60]

Organizationally, signal units needed to adapt to conditions on the Western Front. Trench warfare demanded changes in the structure of the field signal battalion, specifically in the size of the outpost signal company. As originally organized with five officers and seventy-five men, the outpost company could not meet the communications requirements of a square division. Working at the front lines to connect brigade and regimental headquarters, these men had an extremely dangerous job. Consequently, upon Pershing's recommendation, the War Department expanded the company's enlisted strength to 280 men. As reorganized, the company was divided into a headquarters section and four regimental sections. These regimental sections, each containing an officer and sixty-five men, would remain attached to infantry signal platoons (part of the headquarters company of an infantry regiment) for the duration of trench warfare. In open warfare the sections would be withdrawn to form a division reserve.[61] Moreover, a new unit came into existence, the depot battalion, comprising 15 officers and 400 men, which became a source of replacement personnel overseas. Finally, all Signal Corps personnel not assigned to tactical organizations became members of service companies that were located at the base ports, supply depots, and headquarters.[62]

Because of the scarcity of experienced soldiers in the AEF, considerable training took place in France. To this end, Pershing established a series of Army

schools at Langres that included those for technical training. This system included three schools for signal instruction: one for the training of personnel from
field units; one for officer candidate training; and a third for radio operators. Due
to the demand for signal officers, the candidates' school took precedence at
Langres while corps-level schools trained commissioned and noncommissioned
officers from field units. A three-month course for candidates was eventually
developed at Langres which provided instruction in all types of signal equipment
as well as in administration, discipline, and field service regulations. Besides
Signal Corps personnel, the Langres schools trained communicators from the
Infantry, Artillery, Engineers, and Air Service.[63]

Additional education took place at the divisional level in accordance with a
three-phase training plan devised by Pershing. Beginning with the 1st Division,
soldiers learned the techniques of trench warfare as well as the handling of such
weapons as the hand grenade and the machine gun. French units conducted the
preliminary training, which included the digging of practice trenches to familiar-
ize the men with the conditions they would be facing. Members of the 2d Field
Signal Battalion, the first signal unit to undergo this process, received instruction
in both French and British signaling methods and went to the front to observe signal equipment in action.[64] Soon they would be putting their newly acquired skills
to the test.

"Over the Top": Signalmen in Battle

On 21 October 1917 the units of the 1st Division began spending trial periods
in the trenches. For a month one battalion at a time from each regiment spent ten
days with a French division. A detachment from the 2d Field Signal Battalion
supported each infantry battalion. Although stationed in a quiet area, the division
experienced its first combat on the night of 2–3 November when the Germans
bombarded and raided a portion of the sector, killing several Americans. During
the attack signalmen received their initiation in repairing lines under fire.[65] At the
end of November the 1st Division pulled back for a final month of instruction in
open warfare tactics, training upon which Pershing had insisted despite French
objections. In January 1918, six months after its arrival in France, the division
began defending its own portion of the line, a sector northwest of Toul.[66]

Pershing continued to follow a similar training sequence with subsequent
units as they arrived. Meanwhile, many American officers and Secretary Baker,
not to mention the British and French, grew impatient with the slow progress.
Costly campaigns like that at Caporetto, Italy, in October 1917 continued to bleed
the Allies white. Without substantial infusions of American troops, the Allies
could lose the war.[67] Fortunately, with the arrival in France of the 2d Division
(half Army and half Marine), as well as two National Guard divisions, the 26th
and the 42d, the Americans slowly but surely began to build their strength.[68]

Hoping to win a final victory before the Americans could save the Allies, the
Germans launched a massive offensive in the spring of 1918. They began in

March by attacking the British lines along the Somme River, with the objective of splitting the British and French armies. Ironically, what they finally achieved was the speedier entry of American troops into the fighting. The Allies increased their pressure upon Pershing to amalgamate American servicemen with their units, but he remained firm about the eventual formation of an independent American army. After prolonged negotiations, Pershing agreed to allow the British to transport six American divisions to France, where they would train with British units. He further agreed that during May and June shipment of combat elements of these divisions (infantrymen and machine gunners) would receive priority, with artillery, signal, and other support units to follow. Ten divisions ultimately went to France under this program.[69] While this arrangement delayed Pershing's plans for the formation of an American army, it bolstered Allied morale in the face of the German onslaught. Furthermore, during the spring crisis the Allies formed a unified command, headed by General (later Marshal) Ferdinand Foch of France, to better coordinate operations.

Meanwhile, on 28 May 1918 the 1st Division launched the first American offensive at Cantigny, in the Picardy region of northern France. This village, located on high ground in the center of a German salient in the French lines, had already seen considerable fighting. Prior to the attack the division carefully outlined and rehearsed the details of its combat debut.[70]

Signal planning constituted an important part of the process. In front of Cantigny the 2d Field Signal Battalion established a communications network adapted to the conditions of trench warfare. In general, from division headquarters forward, telephone lines ran to each infantry battalion as well as between adjoining battalions. But the traditional lance poles did not prove suitable for use in the trenches. Instead, the wires were strung on short (four-foot) stakes or run along the trench walls. The major trunk lines were placed in special shallow trenches (known as *carniveaux*) or buried several feet underground to provide protection from enemy shelling and from foot and vehicle traffic.[71] At division headquarters the telephone switchboards were installed in underground dugouts where they could withstand artillery bombardment. Liaison with the artillery was maintained by telephone, and from the division to the rear, pole, or aerial, lines ran back to the corps with which it served. Forward from the battalions to the frontline companies the Signal Corps employed earth telegraphy, which worked by driving iron poles into the ground to pick up electrical currents by means of electrical induction. This system was also referred to as T.P.S., from the French *telegraphie par sol.*[72] Earth telegraphy did not provide a very secure form of communication because the Germans could just as easily pick up the messages. Since it did not depend upon wires, however, it was less vulnerable to artillery. Due to its limited range, this technique was used primarily at the front. Wireless sets provided another means of communication, but not yet a reliable one. When necessary, visual signals supplemented these other methods.[73]

The thorough preparation paid off, for the 1st Division initially took Cantigny fairly easily. During the battle the signal troops went "over the top" close behind

Signal communications at the front

the advancing infantry "and maintained remarkably satisfactory liaison through-out."[74] The repair teams sustained many casualties, however, due to heavy concentrations of poison gas. While the enemy repeatedly knocked the division's telephones and radios out of action, the earth telegraphy stations remained in operation. But holding on to the town proved more difficult. The Germans launched several counterattacks, and fighting continued for three days. When the battle finally ended on 31 May, the 1st Division had suffered substantial losses but remained in possession of its prize. Moreover, it had demonstrated that the doughboys could fight.[75]

With this successful introduction to combat, American units began to shoulder more of the burden of warfare. The 2d Division, fighting in such costly battles as Belleau Wood and Vaux, helped the French to stop the German advance toward Paris in the area of Château-Thierry. By mid-July the German offensive had ground to a halt. For its part in the defense, the 3d Division earned the nickname "Rock of the Marne." With the influx of American troops, the Allies launched a counteroffensive, known as the Aisne-Marne campaign. The deadlock on the Western Front was finally broken, and the tide of battle began to turn.

As a result of these events, Pershing's plan for an independent American army at last was realized. In August 1918 Pershing assumed command of the newly created U.S. First Army. Lt. Col. Parker Hitt served as the army's chief signal officer.[76] Comprising two corps and nineteen divisions, its initial objective was the reduction of the St. Mihiel salient that had jutted into the Allied lines for four years. The salient spread across the plain between the Meuse and the Moselle rivers in eastern France. The First Army, supported by French units and a huge Allied aerial force controlled by Col. William Mitchell, launched its attack on 12 September.[77]

As always, the Signal Corps played a vital role in the operation. For example, members of the 55th Telegraph and 317th Field Signal Battalions, assigned to the V Corps, had to dig a cable trench six feet deep and one kilometer long to establish connection with the 26th Division. The trench ran through a hill of nearly solid rock, and the men had no explosives available. "For three days and two nights the signal men had one piece of bread and one cup of coffee a meal each. There was no rest. When a man fainted from exhaustion his comrades worked the harder, and even the officers in charge wielded picks and shovels with them."[78] To handle communications with the French units, six of the women telephone operators served at First Army headquarters, less than fifteen miles from the front.[79]

The Americans carefully planned the attack on St. Mihiel and maintained its secrecy. Though the Germans expected such an assault, they did not know when it would occur. Caught unaware before they had fully carried out an intended withdrawal, they offered minimal opposition. Advancing rapidly through what for four years had been no man's land, the first American units entered St. Mihiel on 13 September. By 16 September the campaign had come to a successful conclusion; the salient had been eliminated and an all-American army had won its first victory.[80]

Before the fighting at St. Mihiel had ended, the Allies began preparations for a final offensive. The American contribution would be known as the Meuse-Argonne campaign. In addition to the First Army, American units participating in the Allied effort included the 2d and 36th Divisions, which served with the French, and the II Corps, which fought with the British. Beginning on 26 September, American and French divisions attempted to surround the German forces in the Argonne Forest of eastern France. Along with the British and Belgian armies fighting to the north, the Allies planned to drive the Germans out of France before winter. The Allies would then push north toward Sedan (a city that France had lost to Germany in 1870) to cut the vital railroad line that supplied the German Army. All told, more than a million Americans, most of them with little or no combat training or experience, took part in this campaign. Meanwhile the newly created U.S. Second Army (organized 20 September 1918) occupied the old St. Mihiel sector.

Although the troops initially made substantial progress, they eventually bogged down as the Germans increased their resistance. The defenders occupied a series of well-fortified positions, known collectively as the Hindenburg Line, against which the Americans made costly frontal assaults. From the Argonne foothills on the left and the Heights of the Meuse on the right, German batteries delivered devastating artillery fire upon the attackers. In addition to the enemy, the inexperienced soldiers faced difficulties of transportation and command and control. The formidable ter-

Testing a telephone line left behind by the Germans at St. Mihiel

rain, heavily forested and cut by ravines, hindered movement of any type, and the existing roadways were usually jammed with men and vehicles. Man-made obstacles, especially barbed wire, presented additional impediments.

The transportation problem exacerbated the already severe supply shortages suffered by the Signal Corps in particular and the AEF in general.[81] The Signal Corps further lacked sufficient numbers of vehicles to haul its equipment. In May 1918 control of all motor vehicles had been placed under the Motor Transport Corps, and "the officers handling Motor Transport never understood that Signal Corps combat motor vehicles used for laying wires and maintaining lines were technical instruments of that business, not just so much truck tonnage."[82] Consequently, signalmen sometimes had to carry poles on their backs for several miles. Despite the exertions of the Signal Corps, communication between divisions and corps often broke down, particularly in units experiencing their first combat. As Pershing remarked regarding the 317th Field Signal Battalion, assigned to the V Corps, this unit "joined on the eve of battle and had to learn its duties under fire."[83]

In this last ditch defense, the Germans hurled some of their best battle-hardened units against the Allies. Nevertheless, despite slow progress and mounting casualties, the French and American forces inexorably pushed the Germans back. By 10 October, with the addition of more seasoned soldiers from the St. Mihiel area, the Americans controlled the Argonne Forest. But much bitter fighting remained between the Argonne and the Meuse River before the Americans completely penetrated the Hindenburg Line. Exhausted and demoralized after four years of combat, the Germans had no fresh troops to throw into the fray, and the unrelenting pressure applied by the Allies led the German government to sue for peace.

While diplomatic negotiations proceeded, Pershing prepared for the final thrust by reorganizing his forces. Maj. Gen. Robert L. Bullard became commander of the Second Army on 12 October, with Col. Hanson B. Black as his chief signal officer. Four days later Maj. Gen. Hunter Liggett assumed command of the First Army. Pershing, meanwhile, took control of the new army group.[84] After restoring his battered troops to combat readiness, Liggett resumed the offensive on 1 November. Forcing the Germans to withdraw behind the Meuse, the Americans pursued them in the direction of Sedan. During this rapid advance, the Signal Corps succeeded in maintaining communications by using the German permanent lines.[85] American units had reached the outskirts of Sedan when the signing of the Armistice ended the campaign and the war on 11 November 1918.[86]

Each signal unit participating in this campaign made its own unique contribution to victory. One that merits specific mention is the 325th Field Signal Battalion of the 92d Division, the only black signal unit to serve in World War I. Arriving in France in June 1918, the 325th had first undergone training and then served in the trenches of the St. Die sector for four weeks before heading for the Argonne. A platoon of the 325th, supporting the 368th Infantry, saw action during the battle. In addition to their signal duties, several platoon members volunteered to take a German machine gun nest encountered while scouting a location for a new command post. One of these signalmen, Cpl. Charles S. Boykin, was killed during this engagement, which ultimately succeeded in capturing the enemy position.[87]

Throughout the Meuse-Argonne campaign, members of the Female Telephone Operators Unit continued to work at First Army headquarters, now located near Verdun, with the initial complement of six supplemented by seven additional women. On 13 October a fire broke out in the barracks housing the main switch-

Members of the 325th Field Signal Battalion string wire in no man's land.

board. The women remained on duty until they were finally forced to evacuate, but they returned to their posts within an hour. Their devotion to duty won them a commendation from the chief signal officer of the First Army.[88] A detachment of women also served at Second Army headquarters, but not during active operations. Grace Banker, who was chief operator at First Army headquarters, received a Distinguished Service Medal for her wartime efforts.[89]

While most signalmen served in France, some saw action in other locations. In September 1918, Company D, 53d Telegraph Battalion, arrived in Vladivostok to provide communications for American troops in Siberia. The following month the 112th and 316th Field Signal Battalions, belonging to the 37th and 91st Divisions, respectively, went to Belgium to participate in the fighting in the Ypres district. The Army also sent a detachment of signal soldiers to Italy to serve with the signal platoon of the 332d Infantry.[90]

As for signaling methods, wire communications, in particular the field telephone, proved to be the chief means of signaling used by the United States Army during World War I. A field telephone could operate over a range of from fifteen to twenty-five miles, and a field telegraph, which required less current, could relay messages up to hundreds of miles.[91] The Signal Corps soon found, however, that it had to make some adjustments to its equipment. It learned early that the buzzer, which had operated well on the Mexican border and was best suited to use on improvised field lines, could be easily intercepted by the enemy. Later in the war improved buzzerphones came into use.[92] Furthermore, the inadequate insulation of outpost wire enabled the Germans to intercept messages by means of leaks through the ground. The introduction of heavier insulation alleviated the problem. Since the signalers left most of this wire where it lay, the Army used tremendous quantities. By the summer of 1918 the United States manufactured twenty thousand miles of outpost wire per month.[93] To increase mobility, the Signal Corps developed portable telegraph and telephone stations, mounted on truck chassis. Because the truck's engine supplied power to the storage batteries, each station could operate independently. Myer's telegraph train had entered the age of the automobile.[94]

The Germans, influenced by the successful use of the telephone by the Japanese in the Russo-Japanese War, had discarded the telegraph as obsolete in 1910. They entered World War I entrusting their communications to the telephone and the radiotelegraph. The shortcomings of these methods, especially for long-distance communications, soon caused the German Army to reinstate wire telegraphy as part of its signaling system.[95]

Although radio held great promise for military communications, the instruments available during World War I proved unsuitable for extensive frontline use. The prewar radios used by the Signal Corps had been relatively high-powered sets designed for a large operating area; they were not meant to be used in the restricted conditions of trench warfare where their inability to be finely tuned caused them to interfere with the sets used by the Allies. Moreover, the spark-gap equipment weighed too much—up to 500 pounds—to be easily moved and often broke down. With the assistance of European radio experts, the Signal Corps developed its own models and had approximately twenty-five different types in production when the war ended. In the meantime, American forces used French radios. Despite some improvements, particularly in the production of vacuum tubes, "radio carried little of the war's communications load," a fact that had a direct impact on the battlefield.[96]

The high combat casualty rates of World War I can partly be attributed to the lack of a reliable wireless communications system. Once soldiers went "over the top," they found themselves isolated. During deafening artillery barrages a commander could not control his men with his voice, and vision became limited amid the fog of battle. In order to maintain contact, troops tended to move in groups that made them easy targets for enemy machine gunners. Although wire lines were portable, they could not last long under constant and withering artillery bombardment that chewed them to bits; what the shellfire spared often fell victim to the treads of tanks or other vehicles. With their communications cut off, attackers found it difficult if not impossible to call for reinforcements or artillery support.

The situation did not improve significantly under defensive conditions. Shelling continued to destroy wire lines, and standard radio antennas proved a popular enemy target. To solve the latter problem, the Signal Corps developed a loop set with a receiving antenna that lay on the ground and a small loop connected with the spark gap that served as the transmitting antenna.[97]

Radio's chief role was for intelligence purposes. While aviators handled reconnaissance and intelligence gathering from the air, the signalmen on the ground used their radios to obtain information about the enemy. The Radio Division of the chief signal officer, AEF, had responsibility for both air and ground radio operation, including radio intelligence, and a radio section served with each field army.[98] At intercept stations, Signal Corpsmen copied coded messages sent from German ground radio stations and forwarded them to the radio sections for decoding. In addition to those in the field, the Signal Corps operated an intercept station at general headquarters. (At listening stations located in no man's land, the Signal Corps similarly monitored enemy telephone and telegraph messages.)[99] Using goniometry, or direction finding by means of measuring angles, Signal Corpsmen also obtained bearings on enemy radio transmitters so that the location of the stations could be identified.[100] Goniometric stations could also detect incoming airplanes from their radio signals. Furthermore, from the amount of radio traffic, the strength of enemy troops could be determined. Radios could also be used to divert the Germans away from where attacks were being planned by broadcasting false radio traffic. The Signal Corps successfully exercised this ploy prior to the resumption of the offensive along the Meuse on 1 November 1918. The radio section of the Signal Corps worked closely with the radio intelligence section of the General Staff, passing along the information it collected for transcription and analysis regarding enemy operations and intentions.[101]

Although cryptography, the enciphering and deciphering of messages according to specified codes, had been included in the curriculum of the Signal School since 1912, the Signal Corps had not strictly practiced communications security prior to the war. The new War Department Telegraph Code of 1915 had chiefly served as an economy measure to reduce the length of transmissions, rather than as a means to assure their secrecy.[102] In the AEF, however, the office of the chief signal officer included a Code Compilation Section where officers devised the so-called River and Lake Codes, which were distributed to the First and Second Armies, respectively, for use in both wire and wireless communications. Maj. Joseph O. Mauborgne, future chief signal officer and head of the Research and Engineering Division, developed an improved field cipher device which replaced the cipher disk. Mauborgne's apparatus, a cylinder with twenty-six rotating disks, bore a striking similarity to one invented by Thomas Jefferson when he was secretary of state to protect diplomatic correspondence. However, the existence of the earlier device remained unknown until 1922, when a researcher found its description among Jefferson's papers.[103] To enforce security, listening stations monitored friendly traffic for lapses in procedure.[104] While signal officers performed cryptography, military intelligence officers conducted cryptanalysis, or the breaking of unknown codes.[105]

Despite advances in speed, electrical communications could not always be relied upon to get the message through. Wire communications, in particular, were extremely vulnerable to artillery fire and the ravages of wheeled and tracked vehicles, not to mention enemy wire cutters. Thus, the Signal Corps built a measure of redundancy into its communications system as insurance. Traditional communication methods, such as runners and mounted messengers, continued to perform their services, with the use of motorcycle dispatch riders constituting a modern variation. Signal repair parties also used motorcycles, when they were available, to travel to the scene of a problem.[106]

Visual signaling had likewise not entirely disappeared from the Signal Corps' arsenal. The familiar red and white wigwag flags remained in use to a limited extent, but the flagstaff underwent some changes. Since the wooden staffs broke rather easily, the Corps contracted with a fishing rod company to manufacture steel staffs.[107] Other visual signaling methods included pyrotechnics (rockets, flares); battery-powered electric lamps, based on a French model, to replace the previously used acetylene type; and projector lamps. The heliograph remained in the Army's inventory but received little if any use. To communicate with airplanes, ground troops placed panels in various prearranged patterns upon the ground.[108]

Carrier pigeons contributed another "low-tech" but effective means of communication. In July 1917, impressed with the French and British pigeon services, Pershing requested that pigeon specialists be commissioned into the U.S. Army. The Signal Corps had used the birds rather unsuccessfully in Mexico, but without properly trained handlers. In November 1917, the Signal Corps' Pigeon Service received official authorization, and a table of organization for a pigeon company to serve at army level was published the following June. The company comprised 9 officers and 324 soldiers and provided a pigeon group to each corps and division.[109] By the war's end the Signal Corps had sent more than fifteen thousand trained pigeons to the AEF.[110]

Probably the most famous use of pigeons occurred during the fighting in the Argonne Forest in October 1918 when elements of the 77th Division, commanded by Maj. Charles W. Whittlesey, became separated and trapped behind the German lines. These units became known as the "Lost Battalion." When runners could no longer get through, Whittlesey employed pigeons to carry messages back to division headquarters requesting supplies and support. After several days without relief, with hope for survival fading and friendly artillery fire raining down, the men pinned their lives on their last bird, Cher Ami, to get word back to silence the guns. With one eye gone, his breast bone shattered, and a leg missing, Cher Ami completed his mission. In recognition of his remarkable accomplishment, Cher Ami received a medal and a pension.[111]

Although the Signal Corps had been taking pictures since the 1880s, World War I marked the first time that photography had been assigned to the branch as an official function. In July 1917 the Corps established a Photographic Section responsible for both ground and aerial photography at home and abroad.[112] A

Signal Corps photographer operates a camouflaged camera in France.

school for land photography opened at Columbia University in January 1918, followed six weeks later by an aerial photography school at the Eastman Kodak Company in Rochester, New York.

Signalmen began documenting the war aboard the *Baltic*, taking still and motion pictures of Pershing and his staff. The Army controlled all combat photography, and civilian photographers were not permitted to operate within the zone of the AEF. A photographic unit served with each division and consisted of one motion-picture operator, one still photographer, and their assistants. Each army and corps headquarters had a photo detachment of one officer and six men.[113] Photographic units also served with such private agencies as the American Red Cross and the Young Men's Christian Association (YMCA) to document their activities. Photographic technology had progressed considerably since the days of Mathew Brady, and a combat photographer in World War I could develop a picture in fifteen minutes using a portable darkroom. By 1 November 1918 the Signal Corps had taken approximately 30,000 still pictures and 750,000 feet of motion pictures that were used for training, propaganda, and historical purposes. Wartime censorship kept the public from seeing the most graphic images, however. The Signal Corps' invaluable photographic collection resides today in the National Archives.[114]

Aerial photography included pictures taken from planes and balloons. As a new discipline, it required the development of suitable equipment and techniques. The Signal Corps' aerial photographers performed photo reconnaissance and aerial mapping that provided valuable intelligence about enemy forces and their disposition. Edward J. Steichen, who later became one of the world's most famous photographers, served as an officer in the Photographic Section of the Air Service, AEF.[115]

Another Signal Corps function, dormant for many years, gained new prominence: meteorology. Before the United States entered the war, the British, French, and German armies had created meteorological sections. Commanders needed meteorological information for many purposes: to support antiaircraft and long-range artillery; aviation; sound ranging to detect enemy artillery; and general operational planning. The use of gas warfare also required knowledge of wind currents and velocity. Russel soon discovered that he, too, needed weather warriors and requested that trained observers be sent overseas. Consequently, in June 1917, the Signal Corps established the Meteorological Section, and Lt. Col. Robert A. Millikan of the Science and Research Division drew up plans for the meteorological service both at home and in Europe.[116] Because the Signal Corps no longer contained trained meteorologists, Squier sought the assistance of the National Research Council and other outside agencies to obtain qualified men. Ironically, many of the Corps' wartime meteorological personnel came from the ranks of the Weather Bureau.[117] One such individual, William R. Blair, received a commission as a major in the Signal Corps' Officers Reserve Corps and became chief of the Meteorological Service in the AEF.[118] Beginning in May 1918 the section established stations at aviation and artillery training centers. Stations in the combat zone were normally linked to corps headquarters by telephone but transmitted information to tactical units by radio. The meteorological section of the AEF eventually numbered 49 officers and 404 men divided among 33 forecasting and observation stations.[119] Meanwhile, within the United States the Signal Corps set up its first weather station in November 1917 at a familiar location, Fort Omaha, Nebraska. Eventually the Corps had stations at most Army posts and flying fields.[120]

Through a variety of means, the Signal Corps successfully supplied communications to the front lines, and its casualty figures reflected that fact. Its total of 2,840 casualties ranked second only to the Infantry. This figure is particularly impressive because the Signal Corps (less its Aviation Section) comprised only about 4 percent of the total AEF.[121] Over three hundred decorations, both American and foreign, were awarded to Signal Corps personnel, but none of them received the Medal of Honor.[122] Following the Armistice, Pershing had warm words of praise for his signal soldiers who "in spite of serious losses in battle, accomplished their work, and it is not too much to say that without their faithful and brilliant efforts and the communications which they installed, operated, and maintained, the successes of our Armies would not have been achieved."[123]

The Signal Corps Loses Its Wings

The European powers, utilizing the aviation establishments they had developed in the preceding years, made World War I the first air war. Germany entered the conflict with nearly one thousand planes; France with about three hundred; and England approximately two hundred fifty.[124] Despite being the first country to give its army wings, the United States was not prepared for participation in aerial combat. In April 1917 the Signal Corps' Aviation Section comprised just 52 officers and 1,100 men plus 210 civilian employees. Its inventory contained just 55 planes, all of which were training models.[125] The Signal Corps had no combat aircraft because it continued to stress aviation's reconnaissance mission. The War Department reinforced this view by retaining aviation within the Signal Corps instead of making it a separate service. Although Congress had finally appropriated substantial sums for the aviation program, "the sudden availability of funds," as Maj. Benjamin D. Foulois observed, "does not buy an instant air force."[126] This lesson, unfortunately, would be learned the hard way.

As with other aspects of the war, the Army had done little planning for aviation, and the small scale on which aerial activities had previously been conducted provided few lessons upon which the Aviation Section could draw. Furthermore, while the United States remained a neutral power, the Allies had been reluctant to allow American observers to study air operations. When asked by Congress in 1914 whether we were keeping up with foreign developments, Colonel Reber had replied, "As far as it is possible to say, we are keeping abreast of conditions that we do not know anything about."[127] There had been a few exceptions, however. In addition to Squier's secret visits to the front while an attaché in England, another signal officer, Maj. William Mitchell, had gone abroad in March 1917.[128] Yet the United States had gained very little current information on which to base its aerial program.

Once the United States entered the war, the Allies expected it to contribute significantly to the aviation effort. After three years of fighting, their air as well as ground forces were nearing exhaustion. In a telegram to President Wilson dated 24 May 1917, French Premier Alexandre Ribot requested that the United States provide 4,500 planes, 5,000 pilots, and 50,000 mechanics by the spring of 1918. He further asked that the Americans build 2,000 airplanes and 4,000 engines each month. Unfortunately, the cable did not specify the types of planes or the proportions in which they should be produced. Ribot's request nonetheless became the basis for the War Department's aviation program.[129]

Fulfilling the order would be quite an accomplishment for a nation that had no aviation industry to speak of: only about one thousand planes, both military and civilian, had been built in the United States from 1903 to 1916.[130] In fact, the nation had only about a dozen aircraft manufacturing companies, the Curtiss Aeroplane and Motor Corporation being the largest.[131] Nevertheless, various government officials, including the members of the Council of National Defense and the Aircraft Production Board, optimistically assumed that the automotive industry could quick-

Generals Foulois and Pershing

ly convert its mass production techniques to the building of aircraft.[132] They believed America would rise to the challenge. As Howard Coffin, former president of the Hudson Motor Car Company and now head of the Aircraft Production Board, remarked in a speech in New York on 8 June, "The road to Berlin lies through the air. The eagle must end this war."[133] In the press, headlines heralded that American planes would soon "darken the skies of Europe." Even Chief Signal Officer Squier remained undaunted by the job ahead and spoke of our "winged cavalry" that would "sweep the Germans from the sky."[134]

The onerous task of turning Ribot's cable into a concrete program fell to Major Foulois. Sharing the prevailing optimism but with a sense of urgency, he came up with a total figure of nearly 17,000 planes (12,000 for combat and 4,900 for training) and 24,000 engines to be manufactured during the next year. He estimated the cost of such a program at nearly two-thirds of a billion dollars.[135] In keeping with the Signal Corps' emphasis on reconnaissance, observation and pursuit planes (to protect the former) predominated in Foulois' plan over the offensive aircraft that had become so important as the war progressed. Foulois, having recently been promoted to brigadier general, became the chief of the Aeronautical Division in the Office of the Chief Signal Officer on 30 July 1917, and he served in that capacity until November 1917 when he went overseas to direct aviation at the front. Hap Arnold, having been promoted to full colonel in August 1917, became the division's executive officer.[136]

Despite its ambitious goals, the aviation program suffered from a fatal flaw—decentralization of control. In addition to the Signal Corps, a large number of agencies and individuals, both military and civilian, had a voice in its development: Coordination between them proved difficult if not impossible.[137] In 1915, Congress had created the National Advisory Committee for Aeronautics (NACA) "to supervise and direct the scientific study of the problems of flight" and also "to direct and conduct research and experiment in aeronautics."[138] The committee consisted of up to 12 members appointed by the president: 2 from the Army; 2

from the Navy; 1 each from the Smithsonian, the Weather Bureau, and the Bureau of Standards; and up to 5 other qualified individuals, either civilian or military. Initially Scriven and Reber were the Army's representatives, with Scriven serving as chairman in 1915 and 1916.[139] The Aircraft Production Board, created by the Council of National Defense in May 1917, supervised the manufacturing activities of both the Army and the Navy. Both General Squier and his naval counterpart, Admiral David W. Taylor, sat on this board along with various prominent businessmen. It became a separate entity in November 1917.[140] A third body, the Joint Army and Navy Technical Aircraft Board, also formed in May 1917, attempted to standardize the types of aircraft built by each service.[141]

Pershing further complicated matters when he created the Air Service, AEF, in June 1917. In his words, "as aviation was in no sense a logical branch of the Signal Corps, the two were separated in the A. E. F. as soon as practicable and an air corps was organized and maintained as a distinct force."[142] Although this separation worked well on the battlefield, it created complications at home. Once the leaders in Washington put the aviation program into place, they had to respond to orders received from Pershing and his staff that often conflicted with the advice given by officers in Europe reporting directly to the Signal Office. Members of Allied missions to Washington also added their advice. The constantly changing requirements for airplanes resulted in frequent revisions to the production program, thus creating more delays than planes. The lack of a clear direction to the aviation program, coupled with its decentralized control, led to serious problems.[143]

The Joint Army and Navy Technical Aircraft Board was the first to consider Foulois' proposal, approving it on 29 May. Having leaped this hurdle, Squier decided to save time by bypassing the chain of command and sent the plan directly to Secretary Baker. Baker, for his part, endorsed the proposal and forwarded it directly to Congress without consulting the General Staff. Responding to widespread public enthusiasm for aviation, Congress appropriated $640 million, the largest sum appropriated for a single purpose to that time, and President Wilson approved the sum on 24 July.[144]

From the start, manufacturers faced a serious obstacle that hampered production: the maze of patents controlling the manufacture of airplane components. The automobile industry had earlier solved a similar situation with a cross-licensing agreement through which the manufacturers pooled their patents. The NACA, with Squier as a key participant in the negotiations, played a critical role in working out a comparable arrangement for the aircraft industry. In this case, the Manufacturers Aircraft Association was formed to administer the agreement.[145] It charged a flat fee for the use of each patent within the pool and, in turn, reimbursed the patent holders. This consensus finally brought an end to the patent fight between the Wright and Curtiss interests.[146]

Through Squier, the NACA became involved in the selection of a site for an aviation proving ground for the Signal Corps. The location chosen, what is now known as Langley Air Force Base in Newport News, Virginia, also became the site of the NACA's Langley Aeronautical Laboratory.[147] As an active committee member, Squier also helped develop nomenclature for the emerging aircraft industry. For example, he urged the adoption of the word "airplane" to replace the previously used term, "aeroplane."[148]

Even with the patent licensing agreements, the United States still faced serious aircraft production problems. The assumption that the nation's automobile industry could be easily converted to the manufacture of airplanes did not prove valid. American airplanes were still chiefly custom-built and could not readily be adapted to mass production. To secure the necessary technical expertise, the government requested that France, England, and Italy send to this country experienced aircraft pilots, engineers, and designers to assist in developing both manufacturing and training methods. To obtain up-to-date information from the front, the chief signal officer dispatched a fact-finding mission to Europe. Headed by Maj. Raynal C. Bolling, and hence known as the Bolling Commission, the group left in mid-June to discuss aviation matters with the Allies and to determine which types of aircraft the United States should build.[149] At the end of July the group issued its report recommending four major types of planes: the British De Haviland DH–4 for observation and daylight bombing; the French SPAD and British Bristol for fighters; and the Italian Caproni for night bombing.[150] They even sent home models of these planes for the manufacturers to follow. For training purposes, the Army adopted the Curtiss JN–4 (nicknamed the Jenny). With these guidelines, the American production effort began.[151]

In addition to administrative obstacles, there remained many other hurdles to clear before the aviation program got off the ground, especially the procurement of the necessary raw materials. World War I planes remained relatively fragile structures fashioned mainly of wood, preferably spruce, which is lightweight yet strong and less prone to splintering than other softwoods. The Allies, however, could not supply enough aircraft quality timber to meet their wartime needs. Although the forests of the Pacific Northwest contained bountiful supplies of the needed spruce, labor strife prevented the mills from meeting the demand. Therefore, the Army stepped in. In November 1917 the Signal Corps created the Spruce Production Division with headquarters at Portland, Oregon. Its operation represents one of the more unusual aspects of the Signal Corps' aviation-related activities during World War I. Under the command of Col. Brice P. Disque, the division eventually employed nearly thirty thousand "spruce soldiers" in the forests and lumber mills of the Northwest. In a successful effort to ease the labor unrest, the Army organized civilian forestry workers into a new union, the Loyal Legion of Loggers and Lumbermen.[152]

Planes also required fabric, usually linen, for covering their outer surfaces. Before the war Belgium, Russia, and Ireland had been the principal suppliers of flax. With Ireland remaining as the sole source following Belgium's occupation by the Germans and the Russian revolution, another material had to be found. Scientists at the Bureau of Standards developed a suitable substitute made of mercerized cotton. With the change in fabric, a new formula also had to be creat-

De Haviland airplanes with Liberty engines being manufactured at the Dayton-Wright Company.

ed for the "dope," a varnish-like substance used to coat the fabric to protect, tighten, and waterproof it. Consequently, the government oversaw the establishment of factories to produce the required chemicals.[153] The Signal Corps became involved in yet another new endeavor when it became necessary to obtain castor beans from India and cultivate over 100,000 acres of them to yield the oil used to lubricate aircraft engines.[154]

Other impediments to production included the need to translate the metric measurements used in European aircraft designs into inches and feet. Besides the planes themselves, the Army also had to supervise the manufacture of numerous auxiliary items, such as instrumentation; machine guns, bombs, and other armament; radios; cameras; and special clothing for the pilots.[155] American pilots did not carry parachutes until the postwar period.[156] Finally, shipping delays, with priority given to the movement of ground troops, slowed the delivery of the planes and engines once they had been built.

While the United States depended heavily on European aircraft technology, it did contribute something new and noteworthy to military aviation: the Liberty engine. Designed by two automotive engineers, Jesse G. Vincent and Elbert J. Hall, the initial eight-cylinder model generated two hundred horsepower and was produced in less than six weeks. The twelve-cylinder version achieved over three hundred horsepower, and further modification increased its output to more than four hundred. The twelve-cylinder Liberty went into mass production and became the standard American aircraft engine both during and after the war.[157]

The Liberty finally solved the dilemma faced by the Wright brothers and their successors since 1903 of finding an engine that was relatively light yet could generate sufficient horsepower for sustained flight.[158] While the Liberty engine itself met with success, efforts to adapt the selected European-designed planes to accommodate it did not. Only the De Havilands underwent successful conversion and mass production by American manufacturers. De Haviland planes fitted with the twelve-cylinder Liberty engine were called Liberty planes.[159] Unfortunately, the De Havilands became better known as "flaming coffins" because of their vulnerability to explosion upon being hit.[160] American factories had produced over 15,000 Liberty engines by the end of the war, but only a fraction of these reached the front.[161]

Although Congress made generous wartime appropriations for aviation (Squier requested a billion dollars for fiscal year 1919 and received $800 million), the United States did not succeed in putting many planes into the air. Fewer than one thousand American-built planes saw action, despite the promises of darkened skies. Throughout the war American pilots relied mainly upon French machines.[162]

While the Army struggled with its production plight, it had no trouble attracting aviation personnel. Thousands volunteered, lured by the romance of the Air Service and the possibility of becoming an "ace." To screen these candidates, the Signal Corps pioneered in the use of psychological testing.[163] It lacked, however, the training facilities to turn these men into pilots. At the outbreak of the war, the Army had just two permanent flight schools, one at San Diego and another at Mineola, Long Island, which had been established in 1916 for training National Guard and Reserve personnel. A third field, a temporary facility at Essington, Pennsylvania (near Philadelphia), had opened just five days before the United States entered the conflict. As part of his planning function, Foulois had selected sites for new installations, and eventually the War Department was operating twenty-seven training fields within the United States. These included Wilbur Wright Field, located on Huffman Prairie not far from Dayton, Ohio, where the brothers had conducted many of their early experimental flights and which is now part of Wright-Patterson Air Force Base.[164]

During the summer of 1917, while the new fields were being built, the Canadian government provided flying facilities in exchange for the use of American fields during the winter. Moreover, many cadets, especially in these early months of American involvement, received their training in England, France, and Italy. In addition to the training fields at home, the United States eventually constructed sixteen flying fields in Europe, the largest being the aviation center at Issoudun, France, that covered an area of thirty-six square miles.[165]

As the problems at San Diego had indicated, however, pilot training was not a simple process. While it took three to four months to train a ground soldier, the time required to adequately train a pilot could be anywhere between six and nine months.[166] First, prospective pilots underwent two to three months of ground, or pre-flight, training at several leading universities where they studied the theory and principles of flight.[167] The students next moved on for six to eight weeks of preliminary flight training at the Signal Corps aviation schools, which culminated in a solo 60-mile cross-country flight.[168] They then graduated to advanced training where they specialized in reconnaissance, pursuit, or bomber flying. Once overseas, the pilots underwent combat training behind the lines.[169] In addition to flying, all pilots were instructed in aerial gunnery. Specialized radio and photographic personnel also had to be trained, as well as mechanics to keep the planes in the air.[170]

The Air Service, AEF, could not make its presence felt at the front until the last months of the war, and a detailed discussion of its combat operations will not be given here. When the United States entered the war, only the 1st Aero Squadron had been immediately available to serve overseas, and it had arrived in Europe on 1 September 1917. The unit received training in France as an observation squadron and became part of the I Corps Observation Group under French tactical control.[171] Although their service was relatively brief, American aviators gave a good account of themselves.[172]

As part of its aviation program, the Signal Corps renewed its interest in lighter-than-air craft. In Europe captive balloons were being used for artillery observation, and the observers communicated with the ground via telephone. Shortly after the declaration of war the Signal Corps reopened its Balloon School at Fort Omaha.[173] The Army also established balloon schools at Camp John Wise, Texas (near San Antonio); Arcadia, California (later known as Ross Field); and Lee Hall, Virginia. Veteran Army aeronaut Col. Charles deF. Chandler was in charge of the Balloon Service, AEF, and seventeen balloon companies eventually saw action.[174] In addition, Millikan's Science and Research Division conducted a variety of experiments with balloons, among them attempts to use them to distribute propaganda.[175]

The beginning of the end for the Signal Corps' Aviation Section came in November 1917 when Gutzon Borglum (later the sculptor of the presidents at Mount Rushmore, South Dakota), a member of the Aero Club of America, accused the War Department of plotting to give control of the aircraft industry to the automobile manufacturers. With President Wilson's permission, Borglum launched his own investigation of the aircraft industry.[176] Hoping to reassure the public, Secretary of War Baker announced on 21 February 1918, just before leaving for France, that the first American planes with Liberty engines were on their way to the front, giving the impression that production was ahead of schedule. Rather than ease tensions, he had added fuel to the fire. In actuality, only one DH–4 had been shipped from Dayton, and it was destroyed when the Germans torpedoed the ship carrying it to Europe. Not until May 1918 did the first

Colonel Deeds

American-built DH–4 fly in France.[177] The press, meanwhile, had been printing exaggerated stories about the thousands of American planes in France. Pershing, in response, sent a cable to Baker on 28 February in which he urgently recommended that the publication of such articles be stopped.[178] As the public became aware of the shortcomings in the aviation program, the backlash began.

Borglum, in his report to the president, claimed that the Aircraft Production Board had squandered the hundreds of millions of dollars appropriated by Congress. Singling out Edward A. Deeds, head of the Signal Corps' Equipment Division and thereby in charge of aircraft procurement, as the culprit, Borglum caused a sensation. Before the war Deeds had gained prominence as a businessman in Dayton, having served as an executive of the National Cash Register Company and as a founder of the Dayton Engineering Laboratories Company (Delco). He was also one of the organizers of the Dayton-Wright Airplane Company.[179] To conduct his wartime work with the Signal Corps, Deeds had received a commission as a colonel. Although Wilson ultimately repudiated Borglum, the wheels of change had been set in motion as Congress and other agencies began probing into aviation matters.[180]

Acting Secretary of War Benedict Crowell, in Baker's absence, had ordered an investigation, as did Chief Signal Officer Squier and Howard Coffin, chairman of the Aircraft Production Board.[181] The Crowell committee's preliminary report, issued on 12 April, pointed out that few soldiers had possessed any knowledge of aviation when the program began, and a tremendous burden had fallen upon a relatively small division of the Signal Corps. It recommended that military aviation be immediately removed from the Signal Corps and that aviation eventually become a separate department.[182] During its own investigation, the Senate Committee on Military Affairs questioned Deeds and found his answers to be satisfactory. Its final report, however, labeled the aircraft program a "substantial failure."[183]

Amid the controversy, Squier did receive some support. Charles D. Walcott, secretary of the Smithsonian and a member of the NACA, wrote to the president on 15 April urging him to withdraw only aircraft production from the Signal Corps' control.[184] The public and press, however, feeling betrayed by the promises of a vast aerial fleet, came down hard on the chief signal officer. The *New York Times* was especially critical of Squier, judging him a "lamentable failure."[185]

On 24 April 1918 Secretary Baker initiated the actions that led to the Signal Corps' loss of its aviation duties. On that date he created two new entities within the Office of the Chief Signal Officer: the Division of Aircraft Production and the Division of Military Aeronautics. The latter had charge of the operation and maintenance of aircraft and the training of personnel. John D. Ryan, former president of the Anaconda Copper Company, became head of the Division of Aircraft Production, while Brig. Gen. William L. Kenly became the director of the Division of Military Aeronautics. Kenly had served as chief of the Air Service, AEF, from August to November 1917.[186] Chief Signal Officer Squier would henceforth devote his full attention to the Signal Corps proper.[187] The final separation came on 20 May 1918 when the president issued an executive order completely detaching aviation duties from the Signal Corps and placing them under the direct control of the secretary of war. The Division of Military Aeronautics and the Bureau of Aircraft Production thereupon became independent agencies within the War Department. The Signal Corps continued to retain, however, responsibility for airborne radio.[188]

But the scrutiny of the air service had not yet ended. Beginning in May 1918 the Justice Department, at President Wilson's behest, launched a thorough inquiry into the aeronautical program. Charles Evans Hughes, former presidential candidate and future secretary of state and chief justice of the Supreme Court, headed this probe.[189] After five months of work, in which almost three hundred witnesses testified, the attorney general turned over Hughes' findings to the president. Aviation's problems, the report concluded, stemmed largely from disorganization and incompetence rather that rampant corruption. Hughes had found evidence of wrongdoing, however, on the part of Edward A. Deeds, against whom Borglum had leveled serious charges.[190] While Hughes cleared Deeds of Borglum's more sensational accusations of major corruption and pro-Germanism, he found that Deeds had used his position within the Signal Corps to benefit the Dayton-Wright Company. Hughes also held him responsible for grossly misleading the public in regard to the progress of the aircraft production program. His report therefore recommended that Deeds be court-martialed, since he still held his military commission.[191] As for the chief signal officer, the investigation had found no "imputation of any kind upon Gen. Squier's loyalty or integrity."[192] With the imminent end of the war, however, the public outcry over aviation abated, and an Army board of review subsequently exonerated Deeds of any wrongdoing.[193]

As in any dispute, it is easy to cast blame, and Squier received his share. Grover Loening, who became an aircraft manufacturer after leaving the Army's employ in 1915, accused the chief signal officer of being a dupe of the automobile manufacturers.[194] Robert A. Millikan, who had directed the Signal Corps' Science and Research Division, described Squier as a "strange character" who "considered himself a scientist." Millikan further referred to Squier as "in no sense an organizer nor a man of balanced judgment." While Millikan credited Squier with "a willingness to assume responsibility and go ahead," he nonetheless disparaged his "quick, impulsive decisions."[195] Deeds, on the other hand, who had also worked closely with the chief signal officer, thought highly of his abilities.[196]

Whatever his strengths or weaknesses, Squier cannot be held solely responsible for the Signal Corps' loss of aviation. The separation of this function from the Corps had been impending for some time and was probably inevitable. The pilots had always chafed under the control of non-flyers. Aviation was fast becoming an armed service in its own right, although it would not achieve independent status until after World War II. Despite the controversy surrounding his wartime program, Squier's significant contributions to aviation should not be overlooked. He had played a central role in the development of Army aviation from its inception, having urged the Army to investigate the Wrights' invention and drafted the Army's initial airplane specifications.[197] Moreover, he had overseen the greatest expansion of the aerial arm to date while concurrently running the Signal Corps' ground operations. That one man would have difficulty managing all these activities should not be surprising.

Less than ten years had passed from the time the Army purchased its first airplane until the United States entered World War I and, on balance, the Signal Corps' Aviation Section had achieved a great deal by May 1918. Despite shortcomings and failures, which were not restricted to the Signal Corps' operations alone, the Corps had laid the foundation for the air program that the Army followed for the duration of the war. From a one man/one plane air force in 1907, the Army's Air Service had grown by November 1918 to nearly two hundred thousand officers, men, and civilian workers. During the course of the war the Army had received nearly seventeen thousand planes from both domestic and foreign manufacturers.[198] With the removal of the aviation function, the Signal Corps also lost some prominent names from its rolls, among them Mitchell, Foulois, and Arnold. While passing from the pages of Signal Corps history, these men continued their notable careers with the Army's Air Service.[199]

The Signal Corps Comes of Age

The aviation story constituted yet another episode in the evolution of the Signal Corps' mission as changes in technology constantly redefined the nature of military communications. Once before the Signal Corps had experienced the wrenching away of a major function, weather reporting, only to see military meteorology achieve new importance under its auspices during World War I.

In the case of the weather service, the cost of what was perceived as a mostly civilian duty had grown too much for the military to justifiably maintain. With aviation, the case was somewhat different. Clearly, aviation performed a military mission, and its relationship to communication was recognized and accepted. But aviation had outgrown its early beginnings when reconnaissance was seen as its only military purpose. Now its combat value was beginning to overshadow its other roles. Although Chief Signal Officers Scriven and Squier had recognized that aviation would eventually strike out on its own, they had not been ready to let it go. As with the weather service, it took the touch of scandal to precipitate events. But the Signal Corps' child, aviation, had grown and matured much faster than its parent had anticipated. Like any offspring, it was rebellious and agitated for independence, not only from the Signal Corps but in the postwar period from the Army as a whole.

Aviation aside, the Signal Corps as a branch was negotiating an institutional rite of passage of its own. During the war it had multiplied its strength by a factor of nearly thirty-five. Comprising just 55 officers and 1,570 men when Congress declared war, the Corps had grown to 2,712 officers and 53,277 men when the war ended. These men were organized into 56 field signal battalions, 33 telegraph battalions, 12 depot battalions, 6 training battalions, and 40 service companies.[200] Besides the huge increase in size, the Signal Corps that emerged from World War I differed significantly in other ways from the organization that had entered the conflict. The Corps had become a technical leader with its own laboratories: It could no longer confine its scientific work to the basement of the Signal Office in Washington. Along with the unprecedented scale of Signal Corps operations came closer ties with the nation's industrial leaders. While the Corps gained much in strength and efficiency, it also lost something: the force of personality. Figures such as Myer, Greely, and Squier would no longer loom as prominently over and direct so closely the workings of what had become a complex bureaucracy. Although powerful and important individuals would continue to appear in subsequent chapters of the Signal Corps' history, the branch no longer functioned as the sole province of one man: the chief signal officer. In a sense, the Signal Corps had lost its innocence; as an organization, it had reached maturity.[201]

Notes

[1]The term Aviation Section refers to the portion of the Signal Corps to which all aviation personnel were assigned. Within the Office of the Chief Signal Officer, the subdivision that dealt with aviation matters was known as the Aeronautical Division. In 1917 that entity became the Air Division; in 1918 it was redesignated as the Air Service Division.

[2]There is no single source that fully discusses all the investigations into the Air Service during this period. The Shanks investigation is discussed at some length in Whitehorne, The Inspectors General of the United States Army, 1903–1939, draft Ms, pp. 319–23. Hennessy, *Army Air Arm*, pp. 137–38, discusses this inspection but makes no mention of the controversy that it stirred.

[3]Hennessy, *Army Air Arm*, p. 153, indicates that the Signal Corps initiated Shanks' investigation in response to Robinson's resolution, but Whitehorne, Inspectors General, pp. 321–22, explains that it resulted from Shanks' annual inspection in 1915 and his discovery of Reber's suppression of the previous report.

[4]Goodier was the father of a pilot at San Diego who had been badly injured in a crash in November 1914 (Hennessy, *Army Air Arm*, pp. 123 and 144). Clark, "Squier," discusses the Goodier case (p. 254). He does not, however, refer to the Garlington board by name.

[5]Hennessy, *Army Air Arm*, p. 144. The Judge Advocate General's ruling is not mentioned by Whitehorne. Goodier was court-martialed for his role in filing the charges and received a reprimand from President Wilson.

[6]Clark, "Squier," p. 254, states that Baker added a personal censure of Scriven to the board's report. Whitehorne, Inspectors General, p. 323, indicates, however, that the board itself criticized the chief signal officer. Baker makes no mention of this case in his 1916 annual report. See extract of Baker's remarks to Congress in Frederick Palmer, *Newton D. Baker: America at War*, 2 vols. (New York: Dodd, Mead and Company, 1931), 1: 283–85.

[7]Maurer, comp. and ed., *Air Service in World War I*, 2: 91.

[8]Clark, "Squier," pp. 252–53; Hennessy, *Army Air Arm*, p. 157.

[9]While Hennessy, *Army Air Arm*, states on page 144 that nothing was done to correct the situation at the school, Whitehorne, Inspectors General, p. 323, explains that some steps were taken to improve the functioning of the school.

[10]Clark, "Squier," ch. 9; Hennessy, *Army Air Arm*, p. 165; ARSW, 1916, pp. 40–42; Arthur Sweetser, *The American Air Service: A Record of Its Problems, Its Difficulties, Its Failures, and Its Final Achievements* (New York: D. Appleton and Company, 1919), p. 39.

[11]Hennessy, *Army Air Arm*, pp. 136–54.

[12]Ibid., pp. 153–55.

[13]Whitehorne, Inspectors General, pp. 324–28; Hennessy, *Army Air Arm*, pp. 188–91; Coffey, *Hap*, pp. 86–89; Arnold, *Global Mission*, pp. 45–46. Arnold and Dargue are involved in this imbroglio versus Lahm and Glassford, and both testify to the Army investigators. As a result, Arnold is transferred to Panama and Dargue is returned to the Coast Artillery.

[14]ARSO, 1916, p. 891.

[15]On America's attitude toward and preparedness for intervention in Europe in the spring of 1917, see Beaver, *Baker and War Effort*, ch. 2; Finnegan, *Specter of Dragon*,

chs. 12–13; Abrahamson, *America Arms*, ch. 8; Edward M. Coffman, *The War To End All Wars: The American Military Experience in World War I* (New York: Oxford University Press, 1968), ch. 1; Robert H. Ferrell, *Woodrow Wilson and World War I, 1917–1921* (New York: Harper and Row, Publishers, 1985), ch. 1; Ronald Spector, "'You're Not Going To Send Soldiers Over There Are You!': The American Search for an Alternative to the Western Front 1916–1917," *Military Affairs* 36 (Feb 1972): 1–4; Allan R. Millett, "Cantigny, 28–31 May 1918," in Charles E. Heller and William A. Stofft, eds., *America's First Battles, 1776–1965* (Lawrence: University Press of Kansas, 1986), p. 156.

[16]Marvin A. Kreidberg and Merton G. Henry, *History of Military Mobilization in the United States Army, 1775–1945* (Washington, D.C.: Government Printing Office, 1955), pp. 263, 277, and table 40, p. 309.

[17]See provisions of the act published in WD Bulls 31 and 32, 23 and 24 May 1917. For discussion of the Selective Service, see Kreidberg and Henry, *Military Mobilization*, pp. 253–81; Weigley, *History of Army*, pp. 354–57; Matloff, ed., *American Military History*, pp. 373–74; Beaver, *Baker and War Effort*, pp. 25–39; Coffman, *War To End All Wars*, p. 29; Ferrell, *Wilson and World War I*, pp. 16–18; Hill, *Minute Man in Peace and War*, ch. 11.

[18]*ARSO*, 1919, pp. 6 and 23. The citations for this report refer to a separately published volume. The chief signal officer's annual report for 1919 is also included in *ARSW*, 1919, vol. 1.; WDGO 81, 3 Jul 1917. According to GO 61, 11 Nov 1916, the six companies were stationed at Valdez, Alaska; Fort Gibbon, Alaska; Fort Wood, New York; Fort Leavenworth, Kansas; Fort Sam Houston, Texas; and Fort Mason, California. See also Historical Section, Army War College, *The Signal Corps and Air Service: A Study of Their Expansion in the United States, 1917–1918*, Monograph no. 16 (Washington, D.C.: Government Printing Office, 1922), p. 4 and table A, p. 116.

[19]*Tables of Organization, United States Army, 1917* (Washington, D.C.: Government Printing Office, May 1917), table 20, "Field Signal Battalion"; Matloff, ed., *American Military History*, p. 374; Kreidberg and Henry, *Military Mobilization*, p. 304. It should also be noted that the size of an American division, totaling about 28,000 men, was about twice that of a British, French, or German division. See John B. Wilson, Divisions and Separate Brigades, draft Ms, ch. 3.

[20]*ARSO*, 1918, pp. 1085–86 in *ARSW*, 1918, vol. 1; *ARSO*, 1919, pp. 66–73; *Signal Corps and Air Service*, pp. 9–14; Historical Section, Army War College, *Order of Battle of the United States Land Forces in the World War*, 5 vols. (Washington, D.C.: Government Printing Office, 1931–1949; reprint, Washington, D.C.: Center of Military History, United States Army, 1988), vol. 3, pt. 1, pp. 478–80 and descriptions of posts in vol. 3, pt. 2 (hereafter cited as *OB*); *Historical Sketch*, pp. 62–63.

[21]Paul A. C. Koistinen, "The 'Industrial-Military Complex' in Historical Perspective: World War I," *Business History Review* 41 (Winter 1967): 378–403.

[22]Carty eventually achieved the rank of brigadier general. See *Dictionary of American Biography*, s.v. "Carty, John Joseph," 21: 155–56. His role in establishing a research laboratory at Bell and in the achievement of transcontinental telephone service is discussed in Leonard Reich, *The Making of American Industrial Research* (Cambridge, England: Cambridge University Press, 1985), ch. 7. During World War II a similar program would be known as the Affiliated Plan.

[23]Two telegraph battalions were assigned to each army and one to each corps. Rpt, Services of Supply, AEF, 23 Jun 1919, sub: Signal Corps Activities in *United States*

Army in the World War, 1917–1919, 17 vols. (1948; reprint, Washington, D.C.: Center of Military History, United States Army, 1988–1992), 15: 104; Lavine, *Circuits of Victory*, chs. 10 and 11; *ARSO*, 1919, p. 35.

[24]The Bell System also supplied personnel for a portion of an outpost company of the 301st Field Signal Battalion, and many of its employees joined nonsignal units. According to Lavine, *Circuits of Victory*, 21,000 Bell System employees "served in the war emergency" and about one-fifth of them served in the Signal Corps (see pp. 88 and 108). The Bell System's contributions to military telephone and radio technology are discussed in M. D. Fagen, ed., *A History of Engineering and Science in the Bell System: The Early Years (1875–1925)* (Bell Telephone Laboratories, Inc., 1975).

[25]Pershing had requested that women be employed in this capacity. See John J. Pershing, *My Experiences in the World War*, 2 vols. (New York: Stokes, 1931), 1: 175. These women did not become entitled to veterans' benefits until 1979 as a result of a review board study. See Roderick M. Engert, comp., Signal Corps Female Telegraph Operators in World War I (report compiled for the Advisory Panel, Civilian/Military Service Review Board, Mar 1979). According to this report, the operators' unit had no official title but was given its name by Chief Signal Officer Squier.

[26]*ARSO*, 1919, pp. 539; Lavine, *Circuits of Victory*, p. 277. For details on the service of these women, see also Karen L. Hillerich, "Black Jack's Girls," *Army* 32 (Dec 82): 44–48; Engert, Signal Corps Operators; Michelle A. Christides, "Women Veterans of the Great War: Oral Histories Collected by Michelle A. Christides," *Minerva* 3 (Summer 1985): 103–27.

[27]On the Naval Consulting Board, see David K. Allison, *New Eye for the Navy: The Origin of Radar at the Naval Research Laboratory*, NRL Report 8466 (Washington, D.C.: Naval Research Laboratory, 1981), ch. 3; Dupree, *Science in Federal Government*, pp. 306–07; Howeth, *Communications-Electronics in Navy*, pp. 302, 326; Robert D. Cuff, *The War Industries Board: Business-Government Relations During World War I* (Baltimore, Md.: Johns Hopkins University Press, 1973), ch. 1. The Naval Research Laboratory, which opened in 1923, evolved from proposals made by Edison and the board during the war.

[28]*ARSO*, 1919, p. 225. See also George Ellery Hale, "War Services of the National Research Council," in Robert M. Yerkes, ed., *The New World of Science: Its Development During the War* (1920; reprint, Freeport, N.Y.: Books for Libraries Press, 1969), pp. 13–30, and Robert A. Millikan, "Contributions of Physical Science," pp. 33–48, in same volume; Robert A. Millikan, *The Autobiography of Robert A. Millikan* (New York: Prentice-Hall, Inc., 1950), pp. 149–50; Irving B. Holley, Jr., *Ideas and Weapons: Exploitation of the Aerial Weapon by the United States During World War I* (New Haven, Conn.: Yale University Press, 1953), p. 112; Dupree, *Science in Federal Government*, pp. 308–15; Clark, "Squier," pp. 321–23; Nathan Reingold, Science and the United States Army, pp. 105–07, undated typescript in CMH library.

[29]See Rexmond C. Cochrane, *Measures for Progress: A History of the National Bureau of Standards* (Washington, D.C.: U.S. Department of Commerce, 1966).

[30]Engineering and research in the United States by the Signal Corps during World War I is discussed in *ARSO*, 1919, ch. 11. See also *OB*, vol. 3, pt. 1, pp. 474–75. Maj. Joseph O. Mauborgne headed the radio section of the Research and Engineering Division.

[31]Camp Vail was named for Alfred E. Vail, an early associate of Samuel F. B. Morse. Sources on the early history of Camp Vail include "The Mission and Early History of the Signal Corps Engineering Laboratories" and "History Camp Alfred Vail, New Jersey

1918." Both are typescripts provided to the author by the Historical Office of the U.S. Army Communications-Electronics Command (CECOM), Fort Monmouth, New Jersey. See also A History of Fort Monmouth, New Jersey, 1917–1945, a typescript available in the CMH library, and A Concise History of Fort Monmouth, New Jersey (Fort Monmouth, N.J.: Historical Office, U.S. Army Communications-Electronics Command, 1985).

[32]Dulany Terrett, The Signal Corps: The Emergency, United States Army in World War II (Washington, D.C.: Office of the Chief of Military History, Department of the Army, 1956), p. 28, n. 30. During the war the Signal Corps published and distributed the pamphlet "Equipment List and Standard Nomenclature of the Signal Corps."

[33]On radio developments, see ARSO, 1919, pp. 244–69; Signal Corps and Air Service, pp. 99–101; Crowell, America's Munitions, ch. 6. Vacuum tube production during World War I is discussed by Reich, Industrial Research, pp. 93 and 180–81. See also Howeth, Communications-Electronics in Navy, chs. 23 and 24; George R. Thompson, "Radio Comes of Age in World War I," in Max L. Marshall, ed., The Story of the U.S. Army Signal Corps (New York: Franklin Watts, Inc., 1965), pp. 157–66; Douglas, Inventing Broadcasting, ch. 8.

[34]The developmental work of the electrical engineering section is specifically discussed in ARSO, 1919, pp. 230–44.

[35]See Gary Craven Gray, "Radio on the Fireline: A History of Electronic Communication in the Forest Service 1905–1975" (Washington, D.C.: U.S. Department of Agriculture, Forest Service, 1982).

[36]ARSO, 1919, pp. 115–16, 231–32; Crowell, America's Munitions, p. 569; Signal Corps and Air Service, pp. 17–19; Lavine, Circuits of Victory, pp. 400–402; A Record of the Activities of the Second Field Signal Battalion, First Division (Cologne: J. P. Bachem, 1919), p. 55.

[37]The Council of National Defense is provided for in an appropriations bill approved 29 August 1916. See WD Bull 33, 9 Sep 1916, p. 44. See also Cuff, War Industries Board, pp. 34–42, 46; David M. Kennedy, Over Here: The First World War and American Society (New York: Oxford University Press, 1980), pp. 114–17; Lavine, Circuits of Victory, ch. 7; Beaver, Baker and War Effort, ch. 3; Dupree, Science in Federal Government, p. 312.

[38]Hewes, Root to McNamara, p. 33, and WDGO 5, 11 Jan 1918. In February 1918 Baker reorganized the General Staff to include a Supply and Purchase Division. See WDGO 14, 9 Feb 1918 and Edward M. Coffman, "The Battle Against Red Tape: Business Methods of the War Department General Staff 1917–1918," Military Affairs 26 (Spring 1962): 3. See also Beaver, Baker and War Effort, pp. 94–96; Risch, Quartermaster Support, ch. 14; Kreidberg and Henry, Military Mobilization, pp. 318–23.

[39]The War Industries Board became an independent body in May 1918 and was dissolved in January 1919. For a detailed study of the board, see Cuff, War Industries Board. See also the entry "War Industries Board" in Handbook of Federal World War Agencies and Their Records, 1917–1921 (Washington, D.C.: Government Printing Office, 1943).

[40]Cochrane, Measures for Progress, pp. 186–91; Crowell, America's Munitions, pp. 567–83; ARSO, 1919, pp. 110, 114; Dupree, Science in Federal Government, p. 322; Reese V. Jenkins, Images and Enterprise: Technology and the American Photographic Industry, 1839 to 1925 (Baltimore, Md.: Johns Hopkins University Press, 1975), pp. 313, 323; Harrison E. Howe, "Optical Glass for War Needs," in Yerkes, ed., New World of Science, pp. 103–20.

[41]*ARSO*, 1918, p. 1084; *ARSO*, 1919, pp. 227–30; *Historical Sketch*, pp. 67–68.

[42]For a brief survey of military intelligence history, see John Patrick Finnegan, *Military Intelligence: A Picture History* (Arlington, Va.: History Office, Deputy Chief of Staff, Operations, U.S. Army Intelligence and Security Command, 1985). See also Powe, "Emergence of War Department Intelligence Agency"; Kreidberg and Henry, *Military Mobilization*, pp. 352–55.

[43]*OB*, vol. 3, pt. 1, pp. 11–12; John Brooks, *Telephone: The First Hundred Years* (New York: Harper and Row, 1976), pp. 148–53.

[44]*Handbook of Federal Agencies*, p. 96; Aitken, *Continuous Wave*, pp. 284–88; Douglas, *Inventing Broadcasting*, ch. 8; Howeth, *Communications-Electronics in Navy*, chs. 19 and 20; Kreidberg and Henry, *Military Mobilization*, ch. 10.

[45]"Major General George Owen Squier," *Signal Corps Bulletin* 79 (Jul–Aug 1934): 1; *OB*, vol. 3, pt. 1, p. 475; *Handbook of Federal Agencies*, p. 309.

[46]See Donald Smythe, *Pershing: General of the Armies* (Bloomington: Indiana University Press, 1986), p. 11, on Pershing's criteria for choosing his staff. For details of his military career, see Cullum, *Biographical Register* and *USMA Graduates Report* (1929), pp. 302–08. Russel was graduate number 3184.

[47]In addition to the Signal Corps, the Services of Supply comprised the Quartermaster Corps, Medical Corps, Corps of Engineers, Ordnance Department, Air Service, Gas Service, Transportation Service, Provost Marshal Service, and General Purchasing Board. See GO 8, Hq, AEF, 5 Jul 1917 and GO 31, Hq, AEF, 16 Feb 1918. See also Paul J. Scheips, The Line and the Staff (Some Notes on the Signal Corps as a Combatant Arm and a Technical Service), typescript [Washington, D.C.: Signal Corps Historical Division, 1960], pp. 22–26, copy in author's files. See also *OB*, vol. 1, pp. 31–80.

[48]There were, of course, reorganizations during the course of the war. See *ARSO*, 1919, pp. 366–68.

[49]Lawrence Lessing, *Man of High Fidelity: Edwin Howard Armstrong* (Philadelphia: J. B. Lippincott Company, 1956), ch. 7.

[50]The work of this division is discussed in *ARSO*, 1919, ch. 12; C. F. Martin, Signal Communications in World War I, typescript [Washington, D.C.: Historical Section, Army War College, Aug 1942], pp. 23–25 (copy in author's files); Lavine, *Circuits of Victory*, ch. 16.

[51]GO 25, Hq, AEF, 23 Aug 1917. The functions of the Signal Corps, AEF, are specified in GOs 8 and 25, AEF, 1917, and GOs 30, 31, 48, and 152, GHQ, AEF, 1918.

[52]*ARSO*, 1919, pp. 185–86; Lavine, *Circuits of Victory*, pp. 116–19; A. E. Kennelly, "Advances in Signalling Contributed During the War," in Yerkes, ed., *New World of Science*, pp. 221–46.

[53]Lavine, *Circuits of Victory*, p. 112, refers to "the famous '400-Mile Line'" and its 265-mile extension. See also *ARSO*, 1919, pp. 119–20, 195–96.

[54]AT&T developed repeaters based on de Forest's audion (he had sold the patent rights to the company in 1913) to achieve coast-to-coast telephone service. The first transcontinental call between New York and San Francisco was made on 25 January 1915. See Reich, *Industrial Research*, pp. 160–70 and 207–11. Douglas, *Inventing Broadcasting*, p. 243, explains the repeater process. See also Brooks, *Telephone*, pp. 137–41; *ARSO*, 1919, p. 203. In conjunction with the Navy, AT&T also achieved transatlantic wireless telephony in 1915.

[55]An exact figure is difficult to determine. These mileage totals are based on statistics given in *ARSO*, 1919, p. 162, and Historical Branch, War Plans Division, General Staff,

Organization of the Services of Supply, American Expeditionary Forces, Monograph no. 7 (Washington, D.C.: Government Printing Office, 1921), p. 84. The total mileage of lines leased from the French is in question due to an inconsistency in the chief signal officer's report. Apparently the total should be either 15,252 (*ARSO*) or 15,352 (Monograph 7). If all the figures listed in the *ARSO* were added, the total mileage of the wire network would be approximately 50,000, yet the report states that the total is 37,944. On the basis of the monograph, it appears that only about 3,000 miles of leased French lines were both maintained and operated by the Signal Corps. Lavine, *Circuits of Victory*, discusses the background to and the building of this network in chapters 12–14. Its extension is covered in subsequent chapters. See also Frank H. Fay, "A.E.F. Telephone and Telegraph System," *Military Engineer* (Jan-Feb 1926), reprinted in Scheips, ed., *Military Signal Communications*, vol. 1.

[56]Before the war, seventeen cables had crossed the Atlantic, two of which had belonged to Germany. Eventually, with the help of the Japanese, all cables connecting the Central Powers with the Americas, Africa, and the Far East were severed. See *ARSO*, 1919, ch. 8 and p. 202; Rpt, Services of Supply, AEF, 23 Jun 1919, sub: Signal Corps Activities, p. 115; Lavine, *Circuits of Victory*, pp. 290–91 and ch. 36; Aitken, *Continuous Wave*, pp. 256–57; Douglas, *Inventing Broadcasting*, ch. 8; Tuchman, *Zimmermann Telegram*, p. 15. Before the United States entered the war, we had allowed the German government to use our cables for diplomatic communications. Consequently, the Germans sent the Zimmermann telegram to Mexico in code over our own wires! On the Navy's high-powered stations, see Howeth, *Communications-Electronics in Navy*, chs. 18 and 20. It does not appear that the Signal Corps laid any cables of its own. The Signal Corps also operated a telephone system in England. See Lavine, *Circuits of Victory*, pp. 394–95.

[57]Rpt, Services of Supply, AEF, 23 Jun 1919, sub: Signal Corps Activities, p. 102, and *ARSO*, 1919, p. 129.

[58]Company C, 2d Field Signal Battalion, was included in the first contingent of troops that arrived in France in late June. See *ARSO*, 1919, pp. 27 and 368; Pogue, *Marshall*, 1: chs. 9 and 10. Marshall served on the 1st Division staff until July 1918.

[59]As quoted in *ARSO*, 1919, p. 365.

[60]Martin, Signal Communications in World War I, p. 3; Rpt, Services of Supply, AEF, 23 Jun 1919, sub: Signal Corps Activities, pp. 102–03.

[61]Both the 1917 and 1918 tables of organization are published in volume 1 of *United States Army in the World War, 1917–1919*. The 1917 table for the field signal battalion is table 20, p. 180, while the revised 1918 tables for the outpost company and the battalion are found on pp. 362–63. See also *ARSO*, 1919, pp. 358–60; *Historical Sketch*, p. 62; Martin, Signal Communications in World War I, pp. 38, 41–42; and Thompson and Harris, *Outcome*, p. 14.

[62]*ARSO*, 1918, p. 1086; *ARSO*, 1919, p. 30; Rpt, Services of Supply, AEF, 23 Jun 1919, sub: Signal Corps Activities, pp. 104, 107.

[63]*ARSO*, 1919, ch. 5; *Historical Sketch*, pp. 89–91; Charles E. Kirkpatrick, Pershing Builds an Army: The School System of the American Expeditionary Forces, unpublished study [Washington, D.C.: Center of Military History, United States Army, Dec 1988].

[64]Society of the First Division, *History of the First Division During the World War, 1917–1919* (Philadelphia: John C. Winston Co., 1922), p. 24; *Record of Second Field Signal Battalion*, ch. 2.

[65]*History of First Division*, p. 28; *ARSO*, 1919, p. 371; *Record of Second Field Signal Battalion*, p. 12.

[66]*History of First Division*, ch. 2; Weigley, *History of Army*, p. 375; Coffman, *War To End All Wars*, pp. 135f; Pershing, *My Experiences*, 1: 200–202.

[67]On the recognition of the need for U.S. intervention, see Abrahamson, *America Arms*, p. 175; Beaver, *Baker and War Effort*, p. 111; Weigley, *History of Army*, p. 376.

[68]For their arrival dates, see the divisional entries in *OB*, vol. 2. Hill, *Minute Man in Peace and War*, has an interesting section on General Clarence Edwards' machinations to get his 26th Division to France.

[69]These extended (and confusing) negotiations resulted in the controversial London and Abbeville agreements. See Smythe, *Pershing*, chs. 13 and 14; Coffman, *War To End All Wars*, pp. 168–73; Beaver, *Baker and War Effort*, ch. 5; Matloff, ed., *American Military History*, p. 383; Weigley, *History of Army*, pp. 383–84.

[70]Millett, "Cantigny," in Heller and Stofft, eds., *First Battles*; *Record of Second Field Signal Battalion*, ch. 6; *History of First Division*, ch. 4.

[71]"Report of Signal School" with appended lectures—lecture 35, "Trench Wiring I and II," copy in Special Collections, USMA library.

[72]Kennelly, "Advances in Signalling," in Yerkes, ed., *New World of Science*, p. 243.

[73]Millett, "Cantigny," in Heller and Stofft, eds., *First Battles*, pp. 160–61; John Keegan, *The Face of Battle: A Study of Agincourt, Waterloo and the Somme* (New York: Vintage Books, 1977), pp. 259–60.

[74]*History of First Division*, p. 84.

[75]*Record of Second Field Signal Battalion*, ch. 6; *ARSO*, 1919, ch. 19; Millett, "Cantigny," in Heller and Stofft, eds., *First Battles*.

[76]Hitt was also known for his cryptological abilities. Although he had written the *Manual for the Solution of Military Ciphers,* published in 1916, he did not participate directly in intelligence activities during the war.

[77]The First Army was organized on 10 August 1918. John B. Wilson, comp., *Armies, Corps, Divisions, and Separate Brigades* (Washington, D.C.: Center of Military History, United States Army, 1987), p. 10; Matloff, ed., *American Military History*, p. 395. For the description of the salient, see American Battle Monuments Commission, *A Guide to the American Battle Fields in Europe* (Washington, D.C.: Government Printing Office, 1927), p. 68.

[78]*ARSO*, 1919, p. 445. The 55th Telegraph Battalion was redesignated in 1921 as the 51st Signal Battalion.

[79]Lavine, *Circuits of Victory*, pp. 490–94; Engert, Signal Corps Operators, p. 6.

[80]The official St. Mihiel campaign dates are 12 to 16 September 1918 according to AR 672–5–1, *Military Awards*, 1 October 1990. For summaries of the battle, see, for example, Matloff, ed., *American Military History*, pp. 396–98; Pogue, *Marshall*, 1: ch. 11.

[81]According to Pershing, *My Experiences*, 2: 222, in August 1918, "The Signal Corps reported lack of many essentials of unit equipment for battle." The entire AEF suffered from shortages, as priority was given to infantry units and machine gunners. In June, July, and August 1918, shipments of Signal Corps materiel fell 52 percent short of estimated allotments. Comparably, shortages in other branches equaled: Medical Corps, 23 percent; Ordnance, 33 percent; Chemical, 51 percent; Motor Transport, 81 percent. Pershing, *My Experiences*, 2: 310. Smythe writes in *Pershing*, p. 230, "Only the armistice saved the AEF from a logistical disaster."

[82]Martin, Signal Communications in World War I, p. 35.

[83]Pershing, *My Experiences*, 2: 302.

[84]Ibid., 2: 335.

[85]*ARSO*, 1919, p. 491. Fortunately, the Germans did not always dismantle their lines when they fell back, thus leaving behind valuable equipment. Lavine, *Circuits of Victory*, p. 470.

[86]On communications during the Meuse-Argonne campaign, see *ARSO*, 1919, ch. 27; Lavine, *Circuits of Victory*, ch. 45. For general discussions of the campaign, see Matloff, ed., *American Military History*, pp. 398–403; Coffman, *War To End All Wars*, ch. 10; Smythe, *Pershing*, chs. 23–26.

[87]The 368th Infantry had been detached from the division and placed at the disposal of the French XXXVIII Corps where it acted as combat liaison. Historical Section, Army War College, *The Ninety-Second Division, 1917–1918* (Washington, D.C.: 1923), p. 24. On the wartime service of the 325th Field Signal Battalion, see Samuel A. Barnes, "Signaling Souls on the Western Front," *Army Communicator* 5 (Winter 1980): 30–35. Barnes explains very well the various means of signaling employed. See also *ARSO*, 1919, pp. 485–86. The Army's other black division, the 93d, which contained infantry only, served entirely under French command. See Ferrell's comments on the 92d and 93d Divisions, *Wilson and World War I*, pp. 214–15. On the experiences of black troops in general during World War I, see Arthur E. Barbeau and Florette Henri, *The Unknown Soldiers: Black American Troops in World War I* (Philadelphia: Temple University Press, 1974).

[88]The text of the commendation is printed in Lavine, *Circuits of Victory*, pp. 576–77.

[89]Lavine, *Circuits of Victory*, pp. 564–66, 575–79; Hillerich, "Black Jack's Girls," pp. 44–48; *ARSO*, 1919, pp. 466–67. Grace Banker's award is announced in WDGO 70, 26 May 1919.

[90]*ARSO*, 1919, p. 522–23, 454–55; *OB*, vol. 1, pp. 385–89; Terry M. Mays, "The Signal Corps in Siberia," *Army Communicator* 14 (Winter 1989): 26–28.

[91]Paul W. Evans, "Strategic Signal Communications—A Study of Signal Communication as Applied to Large Field Forces, Based Upon the Operations of the German Signal Corps During the March on Paris in 1914," *Signal Corps Bulletin* 82 (Jan–Feb 1935): 33, reprinted in Scheips, ed., *Military Signal Communications*, vol. 2.

[92]*ARSO*, 1919, pp. 233, 236. The British first devised an improved version of the buzzerphone, known as the Fullerphone. See also Lavine, *Circuits of Victory*, p. 116; *Signal Corps and Air Service*, p. 17.

[93]Crowell, *America's Munitions*, p. 575; David J. Marshall, "The Signal Corps in World War I," in Marshall, ed., *Story of Signal Corps*, p. 146.

[94]*ARSO*, 1919, pp. 238–39; Lavine, *Circuits of Victory*, pp. 470–73; Crowell, *America's Munitions*, p. 569. According to Martin, Signal Communications in World War I, p. 58, the telegraph unit contained equipment for six operators and a clerk and up to nine operators could be accommodated.

[95]Evans, "Strategic Signal Communications," p. 34.

[96]Quote from Terrett, *Emergency*, p. 18. See also *ARSO*, 1919, p. 128–29; *Signal Corps and Air Service*, pp. 20–22; Crowell, *America's Munitions*, pp. 572–74; Sweetser, *American Air Service*, p. 135.

[97]Terrett, *Emergency*, p. 19; Millett, "Cantigny," in Heller and Stofft, eds., *First Battles*, pp. 160–61, 182. Keegan, *Face of Battle*, pp. 260–61, refers to the "cloud of unknowing" that descended upon a World War I battlefield.

[98]*ARSO*, 1919, pp. 308–09. It was originally intended to have a radio section of three officers and seventy-five enlisted men assigned to each army headquarters. Because the armies varied in size, the Signal Corps eventually organized one radio section and assigned officers and men therefrom to each army.

[99]An account of work at a listening post is given in Peter Lambert Schauble, *The First Battalion: The Story of the 406th Telegraph Battalion, Signal Corps, U.S. Army* (Philadelphia: Redfield-Kendrick-Odell Company, Inc., 1921), ch. 15.

[100]Goniometric stations obtained "fixes" on enemy transmitters and determined their location by the intersection of the angles. Terrett, *Emergency*, p. 18.

[101]On the activities of the Radio Division, see *ARSO*, 1919, ch. 13, pp. 304–37. See also Kennelly, "Advances in Signalling," in Yerkes, ed., *New World of Science*, pp. 233, 238–42; Lavine, *Circuits of Victory*, ch. 44.

[102]On the 1915 code, see Finnegan, *Military Intelligence*, p. 32; *Historical Sketch*, p. 53; Wayne G. Barker, ed., *The History of Codes and Ciphers in the United States Prior to World War I* (Laguna Hills, Calif.: Aegean Park Press, 1978), p. 134; lecture by Dr. Thomas R. Johnson, "American Cryptologic History, 1912–1952," delivered to CMH, 29 Dec 1986, notes in author's files.

[103]*ARSO*, 1919, p. 240. In 1922 the Army adopted the device as model M–94. Ronald Clark, *The Man Who Broke Purple: The Life of Colonel William F. Friedman, Who Deciphered the Japanese Code During World War II* (Boston: Little, Brown and Company, 1977), pp. 72–73; David Kahn, *The Codebreakers: The Story of Secret Writing* (New York: The New American Library, Inc., 1973), pp. 114–16. Kahn calls Mauborgne "an extraordinary cryptanalyst" (p. 198). Silvio A. Bedini, *Thomas Jefferson: Statesman of Science* (New York: MacMillan Publishing Co., 1990), pp. 237–43; Thompson and Harris, *Outcome*, p. 335.

[104]For a brief survey of military intelligence during World War I, see Finnegan, *Military Intelligence*, pp. 18–41. See also *ARSO*, 1919, ch. 23.

[105]Johnson lecture, "American Cryptologic History."

[106]*ARSO*, 1919, pp. 471 and 1090; Millett, "Cantigny," in Heller and Stofft, eds., *First Battles*, pp. 160–61.

[107]*ARSO*, 1919, pp. 113, 225.

[108]*ARSO*, 1918, p. 1090; *ARSO*, 1919, pp. 93, 113, 239.

[109]The company was organized under Table 348, "Pigeon Company—Army Troops—Signal Corps," 18 June 1918. This table is printed in *United States Army in the World War, 1917–1919*, 1: 268.

[110]On the Pigeon Service, see *ARSO*, 1919, ch. 14; Rpt, Services of Supply, AEF, 23 Jun 1919, sub: Signal Corps Activities, p. 104; *OB*, vol. 3, pt. 1, p. 486; Crowell, *America's Munitions*, pp. 581–82; Terry M. Mays, "A Signal Company for the Birds," *Army Communicator* 12 (Summer 1987): 26–30. Besides winged messengers, the Army, in a few instances, also used dogs. References to the use of dogs in *ARSO*, 1919, include the photograph on p. 396 and mention of their use by the 77th Division on p. 413.

[111]Thomas M. Johnson and Fletcher Pratt, *The Lost Battalion* (Indianapolis: Bobbs-Merrill Company, 1938), pp. 135–37, 140–41; Coffman, *War To End All Wars*, pp. 323–25; *History of the 77th Division, 1917–1918* (New York: Wynkoop, Hallenbeck, Crawford Company, 1919), pp. 199–206. The exploits of another notable bird, John Silver, are described by C. V. Glines in "John Silver: Signal Corps Airman Extraordinary," in Marshall, ed., *Story of Signal Corps*, pp. 153–56.

[112]*ARSO*, 1919, ch. 15; Terrett, *Emergency*, p. 21, n. 46.

[113]*ARSO*, 1919, p. 345; Rpt, Services of Supply, AEF, 23 Jun 1919, sub: Signal Corps Activities, p. 104.

[114]This total is taken from *Signal Corps and Air Service*, p. 23. See Herbert E. Ives, "War-Time Photography," in Yerkes, ed., *New World of Science*, pp. 89–102. (He chiefly discusses aerial photographic techniques.) *ARSO*, 1919, ch. 15; Peter Maslowski, *Armed with Cameras: The American Military Photographers of World War II* (New York: Free Press, 1993), pp. 5–6; K. Jack Bauer, comp., *List of World War I Signal Corps Films*, Special Lists no. 14 (Washington, D.C.: National Archives and Records Service, 1957).

[115]Edward Steichen, *A Life in Photography* (New York: Doubleday and Company, Inc., 1963); Patrick D. McLaughlin, "Aerial Recon," *Army* 23 (Jun 1973): 39–44.

[116]Bates and Fuller, *Weather Warriors*, pp. 17–18; Millikan, *Autobiography*, p. 156.

[117]Whitnah, *Weather Bureau*, pp. 132–33, states that about 25 percent of the Weather Bureau's personnel entered military service. He does not indicate whether all or only part of this number joined the Army.

[118]Blair later became head of the Fort Monmouth laboratories and a key figure in the development of radar (see chapter 6).

[119]*ARSO*, 1919, pp. 347–53; Rpt, Services of Supply, AEF, 23 Jun 1919, sub: Signal Corps Activities, p. 104; Robert A. Millikan, "Some Scientific Aspects of the Meteorological Work of the United States Army," in Yerkes, ed., *New World of Science*, pp. 49–62; Philip M. Flammer, "Meteorology in the United States Army, 1917–1935" (M.A. thesis, George Washington University, 1958), ch. 2.

[120]Bates and Fuller, *Weather Warriors*, p. 20.

[121]Terrett, *Emergency*, p. 21.

[122]*ARSO*, 1919, pp. 524–25. Although the chief signal officer reports that Col. William Adair received the Medal of Honor, in fact he did not.

[123]*ARSO*, 1919, p. 524.

[124]Crowell, *America's Munitions*, p. 240; Foulois, *Memoirs*, pp. 147–48.

[125]*ARSO*, 1918, p. 1075; Arnold, *Global Mission*, p. 50, remarks that of the 55 planes, "51 of them [were] obsolete, 4 obsolescent, and not one of them a combat type"; Weigley, *History of Army*, pp. 362–63.

[126]Foulois, *Memoirs*, p. 142.

[127]As quoted in Palmer, *Baker*, 1: 282.

[128]Hurley, *Billy Mitchell*, p. 21; Clark, "Squier," ch. 9. Clark remarks, p. 220, that Squier's "three trips in the course of the war before American entry were unique among attaches." Goldberg, *History of Air Force*, p. 13; *Signal Corps and Air Service*, p. 40; Crowell, *America's Munitions*, p. 259, gives February 1917 for Mitchell's trip; Arnold, *Global Mission*, p. 49.

[129]Major Mitchell apparently had some role in the formulation of these figures. See Hurley, *Billy Mitchell*, p. 27. For a detailed discussion of the Ribot cable and its doctrinal implications, see Holley, *Ideas and Weapons*, ch. 3.

[130]Goldberg, *History of Air Force*, p. 14.

[131]Orville Wright had sold his airplane company in 1915. The following year it merged with a California company owned by Glenn Martin to form the Wright-Martin Aircraft Corporation. During World War I, Orville received a commission as a major in the Signal Corps Reserve but did not serve in uniform. Howard, *Wilbur and Orville*, pp. 404–05, 410–11. Crowell, *America's Munitions*, p. 251, lists five companies that had produced more than ten machines.

[132]*Signal Corps and Air Service*, p. 43.

[133]As quoted in Palmer, *Baker*, 1: 289.

[134]As quoted in Palmer, *Baker*, 1: 293.

[135]Foulois, *Memoirs*, pp. 143–45; Maurer, comp. and ed., *Air Service in World War I*, 2: 105; Holley, *Ideas and Weapons*, p. 45.

[136]Coffey, *Hap*, p. 90; Foulois, *Memoirs*, pp. 149–58; Holley, *Ideas and Weapons*, pp. 134–35; *OB*, vol. 3, pt. 1, p. 94.

[137]Coffman, *War To End All Wars*, p. 193.

[138]Created by an act of 3 Mar 1915. See George W. Gray, *Frontiers of Flight: The Story of NACA Research* (New York: Alfred A. Knopf, 1948), p. 13.

[139]Hennessy, *Army Air Arm*, pp. 130–31; Clark, "Squier," pp. 258–69; Dupree, *Science in Federal Government*, pp. 283–87. This body had conducted the survey that found only a dozen capable aircraft manufacturers. On its role early in the war, see Coffman, *War To End All Wars*, p. 190.

[140]Beaver, *Baker and War Effort*, pp. 57–59.

[141]Holley, *Ideas and Weapons*, p. 40; *Signal Corps and Air Service*, p. 36.

[142]Pershing, *My Experiences*, 1: 161.

[143]Palmer, *Baker*, 2: 176–79; Holley, *Ideas and Weapons*, ch. 4; Coffman, *War To End All Wars*, ch. 7.

[144]Foulois, *Memoirs*, pp. 146–47, 150; Holley, *Ideas and Weapons*, p. 45; Arnold, *Global Mission*, p. 50; Goldberg, *History of Air Force*, p. 14; Clark, "Squier," pp. 281–82.

[145]Not to be confused with the Aircraft Manufacturers Association. See Clark, "Squier," p. 274, n. 53.

[146]Hennessy, *Army Air Arm*, p. 156; Clark, "Squier," pp. 272–80; Howard, *Wilbur and Orville*, p. 405; Loening, *Takeoff into Greatness*, pp. 114–15. Loening indicates that the fee was $200 for each plane built.

[147]Clark, "Squier," pp. 328–39; Frank W. Anderson, Jr., *Orders of Magnitude: A History of NACA and NASA, 1915–1980* (Washington, D.C.: National Aeronautics and Space Administration, 1981). These facilities are named for Samuel P. Langley, former secretary of the Smithsonian and aviation pioneer. The laboratory is today used for research by the National Aeronautics and Space Administration (NASA), the successor to the NACA.

[148]Clark, "Squier," pp. 268, n. 41 and p. 269.

[149]Holley in chapter 3 of *Ideas and Weapons* discusses the Bolling mission at length and its implications (or the lack thereof) on the doctrine of American air power. An extract from the Bolling report is contained in Maurer, comp. and ed., *Air Service in World War I*, 2: 131–33.

[150]In many sources De Haviland is spelled De Havilland.

[151]Details of the production of the various types of planes will not be given here. For more on the country's aircraft production program during World War I, see Crowell, *America's Munitions*.

[152]Gail E. H. Evans and Gerald W. Williams, "Over Here, Over Here: The Army's Spruce Production Division During 'The War To End All Wars.'" Revised version of a paper presented at the Washington State Military History Conference at Camp Murray, Washington, 29–31 March 1984. Copy in author's files. Squier discusses this program very briefly in *ARSO*, 1918, p. 1078. See also Crowell, *America's Munitions*, pp. 243–50; Foulois, *Memoirs*, pp. 154–55; Sweetser, *American Air Service*, ch. 9; Kennedy, *Over Here*, pp. 265–66.

[153]The scientists also developed a linen substitute made from paper, but too late for wartime use. The bureau also became involved in finding new formulas for airplane

dope. These two projects reflect only a small portion of the bureau's aviation-related work. See Cochrane, *Measures for Progress*, pp. 176, 179–86; Sweetser, *American Air Service*, ch. 9; Foulois, *Memoirs*, pp. 154–55; Crowell, *America's Munitions*, pp. 247–50.

[154]*ARSO*, 1918, p. 1078; Crowell, *America's Munitions*, pp. 242, 248–50; Weigley, *History of Army*, p. 363; Sweetser, *American Air Service*, ch. 9.

[155]On production of these and other items, see Crowell, *America's Munitions*, pp. 294–30.

[156]Only the aerial observers in captive balloons used parachutes during the war. Although German pilots used parachutes, the Allied armies did not adopt them during World War I. See Lois Walker and Shelby E. Wickham, *From Huffman Prairie to the Moon: The History of Wright-Patterson Air Force Base* (Wright-Patterson Air Force Base, Ohio: Office of History, 2750th Air Base Wing, 1986), p. 194; Maurer Maurer, *Aviation in the U.S. Army, 1919–1939* (Washington, D.C.: Office of Air Force History, 1987), pp. 161–64.

[157]The chief signal officer briefly discusses the Liberty engine in *ARSO*, 1918, pp. 1076–77. For more detailed coverage, see Crowell, *America's Munitions*, pp. 265–80; Walker and Wickham, *Huffman Prairie to Moon*, pp. 181–83; Loening, *Takeoff into Greatness*, pp. 133–38; Isaac F. Marcosson, *Colonel Deeds: Industrial Builder* (New York: Dodd, Mead and Company, 1947), ch. 11.

[158]The Wrights built their own motor for the original flyer, a four-cylinder, twelve-horsepower affair. Orville Wright, *How We Invented the Airplane: An Illustrated History*, ed. Fred C. Kelly (1953; reprint with additional text, New York: Dover Publications, Inc., 1988), p. 20.

[159]Walker and Wickham, *Huffman Prairie to Moon*, pp. 182–83.

[160]The first American-built De Haviland with a Liberty motor took to the air over France on 17 May 1918 (Sweetser, *American Air Service*, p. 198). See comments by Edgar S. Gorrell, *The Measure of America's World War Aeronautical Effort*, James Jackson Cabot Professorship of Air Traffic Regulation and Air Transportation, Publication no. 6 (Burlington, Vt.: Lane Press, Inc., 1940), pp. 65–68, where he disputes the assertions about the DH–4. See also Howard, *Wilbur and Orville*, p. 415.

[161]Crowell, *America's Munitions*, p. 278; Walker and Wickham, *Huffman Prairie to Moon*, p. 181.

[162]Pogue, *Marshall*, 1: 203.

[163]John B. Watson, the founder of behaviorism, was among the psychologists who served in the Signal Corps during World War I. Clark, "Squier," pp. 319–21; Goldberg, *History of Air Force*, p. 18, states that 38,000 men volunteered between July 1917 and June 1918.

[164]Mineola became known as Hazelhurst Field and was the location from which Charles Lindbergh took off on his cross-Atlantic flight in 1927. See Jacobs, "Pioneer Aviation," p. 40; Hennessy, *Army Air Arm*, pp. 177–81. On Wilbur Wright Field, see Walker and Wickham, *Huffman Prairie to Moon*, ch. 2; Howard, *Wilbur and Orville*, pp. 506–07. See also the list of fields in Maurer, *Aviation in U.S. Army*, app. 1.

[165]For details about flight training, see Goldberg, *History of Air Force*, pp. 18–21; Sweetser, *American Air Service*, ch. 7; Maurer, *Aviation in U.S. Army*, pp. xxi–xxii; Coffman, *War To End All Wars*, pp. 197–200.

[166]Arnold, *Global Mission*, p. 51; Weigley, *History of Army*, p. 374; Gorrell, *America's Aeronautical Effort*, p. 5; Clark, "Squier," p. 293.

[167]This phase of the training initially lasted eight weeks and was later increased to twelve. The participating schools were Massachusetts Institute of Technology, Cornell, Ohio State, Princeton, Georgia Institute of Technology, and the Universities of Illinois, Texas, and California. Goldberg, *History of Air Force*, p. 19.

[168]Goldberg, *History of Air Force*, p. 19; Sweetser, *American Air Service*, p. 113.

[169]*Signal Corps and Air Service*, p. 54; Goldberg, *History of Air Force*, pp. xx; Sweetser, *American Air Service*, pp. 114–23.

[170]Sweetser, *American Air Service*, especially chs. 7 and 8 and the "Chart of Air Service Training and Channels of Transfer," p. 260.

[171]Hennessy, *Army Air Arm*, p. 176; Gorrell, *America's Aeronautical Effort*, p. 55; Goldberg, *History of Air Force*, pp. 23–25.

[172]For details on the air war, see *Signal Corps and Air Service*, pp. 52f; Goldberg, *History of Air Force*, pp. 23–27; Coffman, *War To End All Wars*, pp. 200–211.

[173]Inez Whitehead, "Fort Omaha Balloon School: Its Role in World War I," *Nebraska History* 69 (Spring 1988): 2–10.

[174]Sweetser, *American Air Service*, p. 289 and ch. 14; Crowell, *America's Munitions*, pp. 331–44; Whitehead, "Fort Omaha Balloon School," p. 9.

[175]Charles A. Ziegler, "Technology and the Process of Scientific Discovery: The Case of Cosmic Rays," *Technology and Culture* 30 (Oct 1989): 939–63. In 1923 Millikan received the Nobel Prize in physics for his work with electrons and the photoelectric effect. R. H. Kargon, *The Rise of Robert Millikan* (Ithaca, N.Y.: Cornell University Press, 1982), p. 87; Millikan, *Autobiography*, pp. 176–77.

[176]Beaver, *Baker and War Effort*, pp. 161–65; *Dictionary of American Biography*, s.v. "Borglum, John Gutzon de la Mothe," supplement 3, pp. 87–90; Johnson, "Aero Club and Army Aviation," p. 378, mentions Borglum's membership. Sweetser, *American Air Service*, p. 215. Howard discusses Borglum at some length, especially regarding his ill-will towards Deeds, in *Wilbur and Orville*, pp. 413–14.

[177]Beaver, *Baker and War Effort*, p. 163; Goldberg, *History of Air Force*, p. 17. Baker left for France on 27 February 1918 and returned in mid-April.

[178]This cable is quoted from in Pershing, *My Experiences*, 1: 334 and in Palmer, *Baker*, 2: 189–90.

[179]Orville Wright served as a director and consulting engineer for the Dayton-Wright Company. See Marcosson, *Colonel Deeds*, p. 216; Howard, *Wilbur and Orville*, pp. 410–11; Merlo J. Pusey, *Charles Evans Hughes*, 2 vols. (New York: Columbia University Press, 1963), 1: 377.

[180]Pusey, *Hughes*, 1: 375; Palmer, *Baker*, 2: ch. 27.

[181]Palmer, *Baker*, 2: 190.

[182]Beaver, *Baker and War Effort*, p. 164; Sweetser, *American Air Service*, pp. 213f; Clark, "Squier," pp. 287–89; Palmer, *Baker*, 2: 190–93.

[183]The minority report, however, said that Americans should be proud of its achievements. See Pusey, *Hughes*, 1: 375; Palmer, *Baker*, 2: 187 and 191; Sweetser, *American Air Service*, pp. 216–17; Holley, *Ideas and Weapons*, pp. 119f; Beaver, *Baker and War Effort*, p. 165.

[184]The letter is quoted from in Clark, "Squier," p. 288.

[185]Ibid., pp. 289–90.

[186]*OB*, vol. 3, pt. 1, p. 93. On Kenly, see Maurer, comp. and ed., *Air Service in World War I*, 2: 138.

[187]Palmer, *Baker*, 2: 193; Clark, "Squier," p. 289.

[188]Wilson acted in accordance with the Overman Act, which authorized him to reorganize governmental departments as he saw fit. The order to separate aviation from the Signal Corps is published in WDGO 51, 24 May 1918. See also Clark, "Squier," p. 289; *OB*, vol. 3, pt. 1, pp. 96–97; *ARSO*, 1918, p. 1073; Coffman, *War To End All Wars*, p. 196.

[189]Beaver, *Baker and War Effort*, pp. 165–70.

[190]As a civilian employee, Deeds had served as acting chief of the Equipment Division. After receiving his commission on 24 August 1917, he became its chief. Marcosson, *Colonel Deeds*, p. 221.

[191]Marcosson, *Colonel Deeds*, pp. 272–83; Sweetser, *American Air Service*, pp. 93–94. The original Hughes report, consisting of folders on the persons who testified, is located in RG 60 (General Records of the Department of Justice), NARA.

[192]Chief of Staff to Squier, 16 Nov 1918, as quoted in Clark, "Squier," pp. 289–90, n. 96.

[193]Pusey, *Hughes*, 1: 375–82; Marcosson, *Colonel Deeds*, ch. 13; Martha E. Layman and Chase C. Mooney, "Organization of Military Aeronautics, 1907–1935: Congressional and War Department Action," Army Air Forces Historical Studies no. 25 (Washington, D.C.: Assistant Chief of Air Staff, Intelligence, Historical Division, Dec 1944), ch. 2.

[194]Clark, "Squier," p. 280; Loening, *Takeoff into Greatness*, pp. 100–103.

[195]Millikan, *Autobiography*, pp. 148–49 and 156.

[196]On Deeds' views, see Marcosson, *Colonel Deeds*, pp. 219–20; Clark, "Squier," p. 283, n. 76. Foulois speaks well of Squier in his *Memoirs*. See also the favorable comment about Squier by Theodore Roosevelt cited by Clark, "Squier," p. 283, n. 75.

[197]Charles J. Gross, "George Owen Squier and the Origins of American Military Aviation," *Journal of Military History* 54 (Jul 1990): 281–305.

[198]Crowell, *America's Munitions*, p. 243.

[199]Of these officers, only Mitchell had received a commission in the Signal Corps; the others had been detailed. The Air Service became a separate branch under the National Defense Act of 1920.

[200]*ARSO*, 1919, pp. 11 and 543. Service companies replaced depot companies within the Signal Corps' organizational structure per WDGO 18, 14 Feb 1918.

[201]This theme is touched on by Marshall, "Signal Corps in World War I," in Marshall, ed., *Story of Signal Corps*, p. 145.

CHAPTER VI

Between the World Wars

World War I abruptly ended on the eleventh hour of the eleventh day of the eleventh month in 1918. At that time the United States Army had nearly four million men in uniform, half of them overseas. President Wilson negotiated the peace treaty in Paris with other world leaders against a backdrop of immense if short-lived American power. As in the aftermath of the nation's earlier wars, a massive demobilization began which soon reduced the Army to about 224,000 men, a force far smaller than that of the other major powers.[1] Limited budgets as well as reduced manpower became the order of the day.

Despite Wilson's efforts, the Senate rejected the Treaty of Versailles, and the nation hastened to return to its traditional isolation. The League of Nations, centerpiece of the president's peace plan, was formed without U.S. participation. Yet the years that followed, often viewed as an era of withdrawal for the United States and of stagnation for the Army, brought new developments to the field of military communications. Technical advances in several areas, especially voice radio and radar, had major consequences for the Signal Corps. When events abroad made it clear that the Wilsonian dream of a lasting peace was only that, such innovations helped to shape the nation's military response to the new and more terrible conflict that lay ahead.

Organization, Training, and Operations, 1919–1928

The silencing of the guns in November 1918 did not complete the U.S. Army's work in Europe. In spite of pressures for rapid demobilization, shipping shortages delayed the departure of most units from European shores until the spring and summer of 1919. Although Pershing embarked for home on 1 September 1919, American troops remained in France through the end of the year. For its part, the Signal Corps gradually turned over its communication lines, both those it had built and those it had leased, to the French. In addition, the Corps had to dispose of vast quantities of surplus war materiel and equipment.[2]

According to the terms of the Armistice, the Third Army (organized in November 1918) moved up to the Rhine River, and American soldiers continued to occupy a zone in the Rhineland until 1923.[3] The 1st Field Signal Battalion comprised part of these forces and operated the German military and civilian telephone and telegraph lines, which had been turned over to the Americans. The unit returned home in October 1921.[4]

In addition to these activities, the Signal Corps provided communications for the Paris Peace Conference, which began in January 1919. Brig. Gen. Edgar Russel placed John J. Carty of AT&T, who had not yet doffed his uniform, in charge of setting up this system. The Signal Corps installed a telephone central switchboard at the conference site in the Crillon Hotel and provided communications for President Wilson at his residence. Several of the women operators from the front operated these lines. The Signal Corps could also connect the president with the American forces in Germany.[5]

Despite the importance of its work in Europe, the main story of the Signal Corps, as of the Army, was one of rapid demobilization. From a total at the Armistice of 2,712 officers and 53,277 enlisted men, the Corps had dropped by June 1919 to 1,216 officers and 10,372 men. A year later its strength stood at less than one-tenth its wartime total, with 241 officers and 4,662 enlisted men on the rolls.[6]

As the soldiers came home, the government lifted the economic restrictions imposed during the war, restored control over the civilian communications systems to the commercial companies, and dismantled most of the wartime boards and commissions.[7] These changes were aspects of the return to normalcy, reflective of the nation's resurgent isolationism and its desire to escape from the international arena it had entered during the war.

Meanwhile, Congress debated the future military policy of the United States. The War Department favored the maintenance of a large standing Army numbering some 500,000 officers and men, but its proposal failed to win the support of the war-weary public or their representatives in Congress. As part of the usual postwar review of lessons learned, Congress held lengthy hearings on Army reorganization, but twenty months passed before it enacted new defense legislation.[8]

On 4 June 1920 President Wilson signed into law the National Defense Act of 1920. Written as a series of amendments to the 1916 defense act, the new legislation enacted sweeping changes and remained in effect until 1950.[9] It established the Army of the United States, comprised of three components: the Regular Army, the Organized Reserves, and the National Guard. It set the Regular Army's strength at approximately 300,000 (17,700 officers and 280,000 men), with 300 officers and 5,000 men allotted to the Signal Corps.[10] The act also abolished the detail system for Signal Corps officers above the rank of captain. In the future, they would receive permanent commissions in the Corps. Congress also abandoned the system of territorial departments within the continental United States and replaced them with nine corps areas. These were intended to serve as tactical commands rather than simply as administrative headquarters. Each corps area would support one Regular Army division.[11] Hawaii, the Philippines, and Panama continued to constitute separate departments. Other significant provisions included the creation of the Air Service as a new branch along with the Chemical Warfare Service and the Finance Department.[12]

Ironically, while the Signal Corps received recognition in the new defense act as a combat arm, changes in doctrine concurrently took away its tactical communications function.[13] In April 1919 Pershing had convened a committee of high-ranking officials, called the Superior Board, to examine the organizational and tactical experiences of the war. Col. Parker Hitt, who had served as chief signal officer of the First Army, represented the Signal Corps' interests. Drawing upon the proceedings of boards previously held at the branch level, the board concentrated on the structure of the infantry division and recommended that the division be increased in size to achieve greater firepower even at the expense of mobility. Because Pershing disagreed with the panel's advice, favoring a smaller, more mobile organization, he withheld its report from the War Department for a year.[14]

For the Signal Corps, the Superior Board's recommendations resulted in a dramatic change in its role within the Army. In their postwar reviews, both the infantry and artillery boards had expressed a desire to retain their own communication troops. The Superior Board agreed and, with the approval of the secretary of war, this modification made its way into policy. Henceforth, the Signal Corps' responsibility for communications would extend only down to division level. Below that echelon the individual arms became responsible for their own internal communications as well as for connecting themselves with the command lines of communication established by the Signal Corps.[15] Although the Signal Corps retained overall technical supervision, it no longer controlled communications from the front lines to Washington as it had done successfully during World War I. Understandably, Chief Signal Officer Squier protested the change, arguing that it would result in confusion:

This office is more than ever of the opinion that the present system of dividing signaling duties and signaling personnel, in units smaller than divisions, among the various branches of the service, is not wise and a return to the former system which provided Signal Corps personnel for practically all signaling duties is recommended.[16]

But his protest fell on deaf ears. The Army's revised *Field Service Regulations*, approved in 1923, reflected the doctrinal changes.[17]

In a further departure from the past, Congress had given the War Department discretion to determine the Army's force structure at all levels.[18] Col. William Lassiter, head of the War Plans Division of the General Staff and a member of the Superior Board, presided over a panel to study the Army's organization. Unlike the Superior Board, this body, designated the Special Committee (but more commonly known as the Lassiter Committee), favored a reduction in the infantry division's size, while retaining its "square" configuration of two brigades and four infantry regiments. Much of the reduction resulted from proposed cuts in the number of support troops. Under its plan, divisional signal assets were reduced to a single company, reflecting their reduced mission under the postwar doctrine. Approved by the Army chief of staff, General Peyton C. March, and written into the tables of organization, the new policy placed the infantry division's signal company (comprising 6 officers and 150 men) in the category of special troops, along with a military police, a light tank, and an ordnance maintenance

Code class at Camp Alfred Vail, New Jersey

company.[19] For the cavalry division, a new unit, the signal troop, was specified. At the corps and army levels signal battalions replaced the telegraph and field signal battalions.[20]

Yet few of these units were actually organized. For most of the interwar years the Army had just three active infantry divisions in the continental United States (the 1st, 2d, and 3d) and the 1st Cavalry Division. Thus the Signal Corps contained very few tactical units. Signal service companies, meanwhile, served in each of the nine corps areas as well as at Camp Vail, New Jersey, and in Alaska, Hawaii, the Canal Zone, and the Philippines. A shrunken organization carried out a more limited mission in a nation that seemingly wanted to forget about military matters.

Despite a booming national economy, the Army did not prosper during the "Roaring Twenties." Budget-minded Congresses never appropriated funds to bring it up to its authorized strength. In 1922 Congress limited the Regular Army to 12,000 commissioned officers and 125,000 enlisted men, only slightly more than had been in uniform when the United States entered World War I.[21] Eventually Congress reduced enlisted strength to 118,000, where it remained until the late 1930s. Army appropriations, meanwhile, stabilized at around $300 million, about half the projected cost of the defense act if fully implemented. The Army remained composed of skeleton organizations with most of its divisions little more than "paper tigers."[22]

Under these circumstances, the fate of the Signal Corps was not exceptional. But it did suffer to an unusual degree because its operations were far-flung and its need for costly materiel was great. The Corps' actual strength never reached the

Signal students take a break from their classes.

figures authorized in the defense act; in 1921 Congress cut its enlisted personnel to 3,000, and by 1926 this figure had dropped to less than 2,200. At the same time, officer strength remained well below 300.[23] Moreover, the Signal Corps lost a significant percentage of its skilled enlisted personnel each year to private industry, which could offer them significantly higher salaries.[24] The branch's annual appropriation plummeted from nearly $73 million for fiscal year 1919 to less than $2 million for fiscal year 1923, and by 1928 it had risen only slightly.[25] The War Department's financial straits dictated that surplus war equipment be used up, even if obsolete, and only limited funds were available to purchase or develop new items.

Signal training suffered as well. During demobilization, most of the wartime camps had been shut down. The Signal School at Fort Leavenworth, which had been closed during the war, opened briefly to conduct courses for officers from September 1919 to June 1920 before shutting its doors permanently. But there was an important exception to the general picture of decline: Camp Vail, New Jersey, became the new location of the Signal School, officially opening in October 1919. The school offered training for both officers and enlisted men of the Signal Corps as well as those from other branches.[26] In 1920 the school began instructing members of the Reserve Officers Training Corps, and the following year added courses for National Guard and Reserve officers. Students from foreign armies, such as Cuba, Peru, and Chile, also received training at Camp Vail. Here the Corps prepared its field manuals, regulations, and other technical publications as well as its correspondence courses and testing materials.[27] The post also had the advantage of being close to New York City, where the students traveled to view the latest in commercial communication systems. They gained practical field experience by participating in the annual Army War College maneuvers. Signal officers could further enhance their education by attending communication engineering courses at such institutions as Yale University and the Massachusetts Institute of Technology.[28] In 1925 Camp Vail became a permanent post known as Fort Monmouth.[29] Here the 51st Signal Battalion (which had fought during World War I as the 55th Telegraph Battalion), the Signal Corps' only active battalion-size unit, made its home during the interwar years, along with the 15th Signal Service Company and the 1st Signal Company.[30]

Fort Monmouth also became the home of the Signal Corps' Pigeon Breeding and Training Center. Although the Army had sold most of its birds at the end of the war, the Signal Corps retained a few lofts along the Mexican border, in the Panama Canal Zone, and at several camps and flying stations. At Monmouth, the Corps' pigeon experts devoted much effort to training birds to fly at night. Some may also have wished that they could breed the pigeons with parrots so the birds could speak their messages.[31]

Each year the Corps entered its pigeons in exhibitions and races, winning numerous prizes. In April 1922 the Signal Corps' pigeons participated in a contest that, however ludicrous to a later age, was taken seriously at the time. Responding to an argument raised by the San Francisco press, Maj. Henry H. Arnold of the Army Air Service challenged the pigeons to a race from Portland, Oregon, to San Francisco, to determine whether a pigeon or a plane could deliver a message faster. As the race began, the pigeons disappeared from view while Arnold struggled for forty-five minutes to start his airplane's cold engine. Then he had to make several stops for fuel. Meanwhile, in San Francisco, citizens received telegraphic bulletins of the race's progress, with the pigeons apparently holding their early lead. Bookies did a brisk business as bettors began backing the birds. When Arnold finally landed in San Francisco after a seven-and-a-half-hour journey, he expected to be the loser. But surprisingly, no pigeons had yet arrived, and none did so for two more days. Perhaps aviation was not just for the birds after all.[32] Despite the outcome, the Signal Corps did not abandon its use of pigeons, and in 1927 was maintaining about one thousand birds in sixteen lofts in the United States, the Canal Zone, Hawaii, and the Philippines.[33]

Although the Signal Corps had lost much of its wartime mission, it still performed an important peacetime function by providing the Army's administrative communications. As it had for many years, the Corps continued to operate the telephone and telegraph systems at Army installations and to maintain coast artillery fire control systems. In addition, the Signal Corps received authorization in 1921 to set up a nationwide radio net. Stations were located at the headquarters of each corps area and department, as well as in certain major cities. Each corps area in turn established its own internal system connecting posts, camps, and stations. The 17th Service Company (redesignated in 1925 as the 17th Signal Service Company) operated the net's headquarters in Washington, D.C., which bore the call letters WVA (later changed, appropriately enough, to WAR).[34]

Signal Corps soldier demonstrates the employment of pigeons at Camp Alfred Vail; below, *mobile pigeon loft.*

Stations at Fort Leavenworth, Kansas, and Fort Douglas, Utah, relayed messages to the West Coast. Due to atmospheric disturbances and other forms of interference, good service meant that a message filed in Washington reached the West Coast by the following day.[35] Although established to serve as an emergency communications system in the event of the destruction or failure of the commercial wire network, on a day-to-day basis the radio net handled much of the War Department's message traffic formerly carried by commercial telegraph, saving the government a considerable expense. By 1925, 164 stations, including those on Army ships and in Alaska, came under the net's technical supervision, and the chief signal officer described it as "the largest and most comprehensive radio net of its kind in the world today."[36]

The success of the radio net led to the establishment of the War Department Message Center on 1 March 1923, through the merger of the War Department's telegraph office with the Signal Corps' own telegraph office and radio station. The chief signal officer became the director of the center, which coordinated departmental communications in Washington and dispatched them by the most appropriate means, whether telegraph, radio, or cable. Although originally intended for War Department traffic only, the center eventually handled messages for over fifty federal agencies.[37]

In an attempt to supplement its limited regular force, the Signal Corps formed the Army Amateur Radio System in 1925, with the net control station located at Fort Monmouth. The system operated every Monday night except during the summer months, when static interfered too greatly. The volunteer operators constituted a sizable pool of skilled personnel upon whom the Army could call in case of emergency. Each corps area signal officer appointed an amateur operator, known as the radio aide, to represent the operators in his area.[38]

Among President Wilson's concerns during the 1919 peace negotiations in Paris had been the future of postwar communications. In the past British companies had controlled global communications through their ownership of most of the world's submarine cables. During the war the British government had exercised its jurisdiction by intercepting cable traffic. Wilson sought to prevent such a monopoly in the future, and debate at the conference revolved around how the captured German cables would be allocated.[39]

Radio did not appear as an issue on the agenda at Paris, even though it constituted a new force in international communications that would greatly change the balance of the equation. Indications of its potential importance had appeared during the war when the Navy used its station at New Brunswick, New Jersey, to broadcast news to Europe—in particular, the Fourteen Points enunciated by President Wilson. The Germans in turn had used radio to transmit to the United States their willingness to negotiate an armistice with the Allies. When Wilson crossed the Atlantic to attend the peace conference, he had maintained communication with Washington via radiotelephone. (Due to technological limitations, there would be no transatlantic voice telephone cables until after World War II.)

Despite these early achievements, radio remained in its infancy. Lacking a nation-wide radio broadcasting network, Wilson was compelled to fight for the peace treaty by embarking upon a strenuous barnstorming tour that destroyed his health.[40]

After the war the new medium soon fulfilled its promise. Radio technology rapidly moved away from the spark-gap method to the continuous waves generated by vacuum tubes, which were capable of carrying voice and music. Radio's ability to be broadcast made it more difficult for any one party or nation to control the dissemination of information. Instead of the point-to-point communications of the telegraph and telephone, radio could reach all who wanted to listen and who possessed a simple receiver. The era of mass communications had arrived.

Within the United States, the Navy endorsed the retention of governmental control over radio as a means to prevent foreign domination of the airwaves. Congress did not act accordingly, however, and the government returned the stations to their owners.[41] To counter foreign competition, particularly that of the British-controlled Marconi Company, a solution was soon found. In 1919 an all-American firm, the Radio Corporation of America (RCA), was formed through the merger of General Electric and the American Marconi company. By means of cross-licensing agreements with the industry's leaders (AT&T, Westinghouse, and the United Fruit Company), RCA obtained the use of their radio patents, thus securing a virtual monopoly over the latest technology.[42] Under the leadership of its general manager, David Sarnoff, a former Marconi employee, RCA helped to create the nation's first broadcasting network, the National Broadcasting Company (NBC), in 1926.[43]

With the wartime restrictions lifted, an extraordinary radio boom swept over the United States. It began in November 1920 when the nation's first commercial radio station went on the air, KDKA in Pittsburgh, owned and operated by the Westinghouse Company.[44] In 1922, when more than five hundred new stations went on the air, Chief Signal Officer Squier referred to the radio phenomenon as "the outstanding feature of the year in signal communications."[45] The thousands of veterans who had received wireless training during the war plus legions of amateur "hams" with their homemade crystal sets fueled the movement. The spectacular growth of private and commercial radio users necessitated, however, more stringent regulation of licenses and frequencies. A power struggle ensued over who should control the medium, the federal government or private enterprise. Since the Commerce Department had been granted certain regulatory powers under the radio act of 1912, Secretary of Commerce Herbert Hoover attempted to bring order out of the chaos by convening a series of conferences among radio officials in Washington. Ultimately, in 1927, Congress enacted a new Radio Act that created an independent agency to oversee the broadcasting industry, the Federal Radio Commission, forerunner of the present Federal Communications Commission (FCC). Radio thus remained a commercially dominated medium, but subject to governmental regulation.[46]

The Signal Corps played a role in the industry's growth. The Fourth International Radio Conference was to have met in Washington in 1917, but the war forced its postponement. In 1921 Chief Signal Officer Squier headed an American delegation to Paris to help plan the rescheduled meeting. The rapid technological changes of the next several years, however, caused a further delay. When the conference finally convened in Washington in October 1927, a decade after its initial date, one of the chief items on its agenda was the international allocation of radio frequencies.[47]

Radio technology was beginning to link the entire world together, including remote and inaccessible regions such as Alaska. Radio had a considerable impact upon the Washington-Alaska Military Cable and Telegraph System, which continued to serve as an important component of the Signal Corps' chain of communications. By 1923 over 40 percent of the Alaskan stations employed radio.[48] Meanwhile, the deteriorating condition of the underwater cable, nearly twenty years old, mandated its replacement as soon as possible. Despite the Army's restricted budget, the Signal Corps succeeded in securing an appropriation of $1.5 million for the project. First, the Corps acquired a new cable ship, the *Dellwood*, to replace the *Burnside*, which had been in service in Alaska since 1903. Under the supervision of Col. George S. Gibbs, who had helped string the original Alaskan telegraph line as a lieutenant, the Corps completed the laying of the new cable in 1924. With five times the capacity of the earlier cable, it more than met the system's existing and anticipated needs. On land, the total mileage of wire lines steadily dwindled as radio links expanded. Radio cost less to maintain both in monetary and in human terms. No longer would teams of men have to endure the hardships of repairing wires in the harsh climate. In 1928 the Signal Corps discontinued the last of its land lines, bringing a colorful era of WAMCATS history to an end.[49]

Weather reporting continued as an important Signal Corps function, even though the branch had lost most of its experienced observers upon demobilization. New personnel were trained at Fort Monmouth, and officers could receive meteorological instruction at the Massachusetts and California Institutes of Technology. By July 1920 the Corps had fifteen stations providing meteorological information to the Field and Coast Artillery, Ordnance, and Chemical Warfare branches as well as to the Air Service. As in the past, the Signal Corps' weather watchers made their observations three times daily.[50] The Corps refrained from duplicating the work of the Weather Bureau, however, and passed its information along for incorporation into the bureau's forecasts. In 1921 the Corps began exchanging data between some of its stations by radio.[51]

The Air Service, soon to become the Army Air Corps, placed the heaviest demands upon the Signal Corps' meteorological services. In 1921 the Air Service established a model airway between Washington, D.C., and Dayton, Ohio. Although the Signal Corps provided weather information to the Army pilots, it did not initially have enough weather stations to provide the level of assistance needed. In the meantime, the Air Service depended upon the Weather Bureau, only to find that it too had difficulty meeting the airmen's requirements.

Consequently, by 1925 the Signal Corps had expanded its meteorological services to include a weather detachment at each Air Service flying field.[52] As planes became more sophisticated and powerful, Army pilots attempted more ambitious undertakings. In 1924 they made their first flight around the world, assisted by weather information from the Signal Corps. At its peak the Signal Corps maintained forty-one weather stations across the country.[53]

The Corps also retained its photographic mission, even though it had lost responsibility for aerial photography in 1918. The branch maintained two photographic laboratories in Washington, D.C.; one for motion pictures at Washington Barracks (now Fort Lesley J. McNair), and the other at 1800 Virginia Avenue, Northwest. Among its services, the Signal Corps sold photos to the public. Its collection of still photographs included its own pictures, as well as those taken by other branches. The Corps also operated a fifty-seat motion-picture theater where films could be viewed for official purposes or the public could view films for prospective purchase.[54] In 1925 the Signal Corps acquired responsibility for the Army's pictorial publicity. In this capacity it supervised and coordinated the commercial and news photographers who covered Army activities.[55]

Following their successful use during World War I, the Army increasingly relied upon motion pictures for training purposes. With the advent of sound films in the late 1920s, film production entered a new era. In 1928 the War Department made the Signal Corps responsible for the production of new training films but neglected to allocate any funds. To obtain needed expertise, the Signal Corps called upon the commercial film industry for assistance, and in 1930 the Signal Corps sent its first officer to Hollywood for training sponsored by the Academy of Motion Picture Arts and Sciences.[56] While photography played a relatively minor role in the Corps' overall operations, it nonetheless provided valuable documentation of the Army's activities during the interwar period.

The Signal Corps underwent its first change of leadership in half a dozen years when General Squier retired on 31 December 1923. In retirement Squier continued to pursue his scientific interests. One of his better known inventions, particularly to those who frequently ride in elevators, was Muzak. Based on his patents for "wired wireless," a system for transmitting radio signals over wires, Squier founded Muzak's parent company, Wired Radio, Inc., in 1922. He did not coin the catchy name, however, until 1934, when he combined the word music with the name of another popular item, the Kodak camera. In that year the Muzak Corporation became an entity and sold its first recordings to customers in Cleveland.[57] In addition to his commercial ventures, Squier received considerable professional recognition for his contributions to science, among them the Elliott Cresson Gold Medal and the Franklin Medal, both awarded by the Franklin Institute in Philadelphia. In 1919 he had become a member of the National Academy of Sciences, and he also received honors from the governments of Great Britain, France, and Italy.[58]

The new chief signal officer, Charles McKinley Saltzman, was a native of Iowa and an 1896 graduate of the U.S. Military Academy. As a cavalry officer, he had served in Cuba during the War with Spain. After transferring to the Signal

General Saltzman   *General Gibbs*

Corps in 1901, Saltzman embarked upon a new career that included serving on the board that examined the Wrights' airplane during its trials at Fort Myer in 1908 and 1909. During World War I he remained in Washington as the executive officer for the Office of the Chief Signal Officer. Saltzman possessed considerable knowledge about radio and had attended the national and international radio conferences since 1912. With this background he seemed extremely well qualified for the job when, as the Signal Corps' senior colonel, he received the promotion to chief signal officer upon Squier's retirement.

The four-year limitation placed on the tenure of branch chiefs in the 1920 defense act obliged General Saltzman to step down in January 1928.[59] But retirement did not end his involvement with communications. In 1929 President Hoover appointed him to the Federal Radio Commission, and he served as its chairman from 1930 to 1932. He also played an important role in the formation of the Federal Communications Commission.[60]

Saltzman's successor, Maj. Gen. George S. Gibbs, also hailed from Iowa but had not attended West Point. He received both the bachelor's and master's degrees of science from the University of Iowa. During the War with Spain he enlisted in the 51st Iowa Volunteer Infantry and sailed for the Philippines. There he transferred to the Volunteer Signal Corps and distinguished himself during the Battle of Manila. In 1901 he obtained a commission in the Signal Corps of the Regular Army, and several highlights of his subsequent career have already been mentioned. Immediately prior to becoming head of the branch in 1928 he was serving as signal officer of the Second Corps Area. Under his leadership the Signal Corps entered the difficult decade of the 1930s.[61]

Research and Development

World War I had witnessed the growth and strengthening of ties between government and business, the beginnings of what President Dwight D. Eisenhower later called the military-industrial complex. But the drastic military cutbacks following victory endangered this relationship. While research became institutionalized in the commercial sector with the rise of the industrial labs, such as those of AT&T and General Electric, the Army lagged behind.[62]

The Signal Corps' research and development program survived the Armistice, but in reduced form. The scientists recruited for the war effort returned to their own laboratories, although some, like Robert A. Millikan, retained their reserve commissions. While the Signal Corps lacked the money to conduct large-scale research, it did continue what it considered to be the most important projects. However, as Chief Signal Officer Saltzman remarked in his 1924 annual report, "The rapid strides being made in commercial communication makes the military development of a few years ago obsolete and if the Signal Corps is to be found by the next emergency ready for production of modern communication equipment, a materially larger sum must be expended on development before the emergency arises."[63]

Because radio had not yet proved itself on the battlefield, wire remained the dominant mode of communication. The 1923 version of the *Field Service Regulations* reiterated the traditional view: "Telegraph and telephone lines constitute the basic means of signal communication. Other means of communication supplement and extend the service of the telegraph and telephone lines."[64] Hence the Signal Corps devoted considerable energy to improving such familiar equipment as field wire, wire carts, the field telephone, and the storage battery. Until 1921 the Signal Corps conducted nonradio research in its electrical engineering laboratory at 1710 Pennsylvania Avenue. In that year the laboratory moved to 1800 Virginia Avenue, Northwest. The Corps also continued to support a laboratory at the Bureau of Standards, where Lt. Col. Joseph O. Mauborgne was in charge from 1923 to 1927.[65]

One significant advance made in wire communications during the interwar period was the teletypewriter. Although printing telegraphs had been used during World War I, they had not achieved the sophistication of the teletypewriter, which was more rapid and accurate than Morse equipment yet relatively simple to operate. Like the Beardslee telegraph of the Civil War, the teletype did not require operators trained in Morse code. On the other hand, teletype machines were heavier, used more power, and were more expensive to maintain than Morse equipment. Teletypewriters came in two general versions: page-type, resembling an ordinary typewriter, and tape-type, which printed messages on paper tape similar to ticker tape that could be torn off and pasted on sheets. By

the late 1930s the Signal Corps had converted most of its administrative telegraph system from Morse to teletype. Teletype's adaptation to tactical signaling
awaited, however, the development of new equipment that was portable and
rugged. After making a good showing during the Army's interwar maneuvers,
such teletype machines were on their way to the field by the time the United
States entered World War II.[66]

Although wire remained important, military and civilian scientists attained
advances in radio technology that launched Army communications into the electronics age. The Signal Corps conducted radio research in its laboratories at Fort
Monmouth. Here in 1924 the Signal Corps Board was organized to study questions of organization, equipment, and tactical and technical procedures. The commandant and assistant commandant of the school served as its top officers.[67] A
second consultative body, the Signal Corps Technical Committee, had the chief
and assistant chief of the Research and Development Division as its chairman and
vice chairman, respectively.

Transmission by shortwaves, or higher frequency waves, enabled broadcasts
to be made over greater distances using less power and at lower cost.
Consequently, the Corps gradually converted most of its stations, especially those
belonging to the War Department Radio Net, to shortwave operation. By 1929
direct radio communication with San Francisco had been achieved.[68] Meanwhile,
work continued on the loop radiotelegraph set, first devised during World War I,
which became known as model SCR–77. Other ground radio sets included the
SCR–131 and 132, the latter with both telegraph and telephone capabilities.

Signal Corps engineers made other significant discoveries, among them a new
tactical communications device, the walkie-talkie, or SCR–194 and 195. This AM
(amplitude-modulated) radiotelephone transceiver (a combination transmitter and
receiver) had a range of up to five miles. Weighing about twenty-five pounds, it
could be used on the ground or in a vehicle or carried on a soldier's back. The
Signal Corps field tested the first models in 1934, and improved versions passed
the infantry and field artillery service tests in 1935 and 1936. Lack of funds prevented production until 1939, when the new devices were used successfully during
the Plattsburg maneuvers. Walkie-talkies provided a portable means of battlefield
communication that increased the ability of infantry to maneuver and enabled
commanders to reach units that had outrun field telephone lines.[69]

As the Army slowly moved toward motorization and mechanization during
the 1920s and 1930s, the Signal Corps also addressed the issue of mobile communications. Without radios, early tankers communicated by means of flags and
hand signals. As in airplanes, a tank's internal combustion engine interfered with
radio reception. The friction of a tank's treads could also generate bothersome
static. With the development of FM radio by Edwin H. Armstrong, vehicular
radio finally became feasible, but the Signal Corps was hesitant to adopt this revolutionary technology.[70]

FM eliminated noise and static interference and could transmit a wider range
of sound than AM radios. When coupled with crystal control, permitting a radio

to be tuned automatically and precisely with just the push of a button, rather than by the intricate twirling of dials, FM radios could easily be used in moving vehicles. Although demonstrations at Fort Knox, Kentucky, in 1939 did not conclusively prove FM's superiority over AM, the chiefs of infantry and field artillery recognized FM's potential and pushed for its adoption. The mechanized cavalry also called for the new type of sets. Nevertheless, the Signal Corps remained skeptical. The Corps' preference for wire over radio, the shortage of developmental funds, and the resistance to FM within the communications industry (where it would render existing AM equipment obsolete) delayed FM's widespread introduction into military communications. Meanwhile, with the Army far from being completely motorized, the Signal Corps continued working on a pack radio set for the Cavalry. Only in late 1940 did the Signal Corps begin to respond to the demands from the field for FM radios.[71]

When the War Department reduced the Signal Corps' communication duties in 1920, it gave the Air Service responsibility for installing, maintaining, and operating radio apparatus for its units and stations. The Signal Corps retained control, however, over aviation-related radio development. The rapid improvements being made in aircraft design necessitated equal progress in aerial radio. In its Aircraft Radio Laboratory at McCook Field, Ohio, the Signal Corps conducted both the development and testing of radios designed for the Air Corps.[72]

Expanding on its work during World War I, the Signal Corps made significant strides in airborne radio during the postwar period. Improvements took place in the models of the SCR–130 series. Sets were designed for each type of aircraft: observation, pursuit, and bombardment. The pursuit set (SCR–133) provided voice communication between planes at a distance of 5 miles; the observation and bombardment sets (SCRs 134 and 135) had ranges of 30 and 100 miles, respectively. The SCR–136 model provided communication between ground stations and aircraft at distances of 100 miles using radio and 30 miles using telephony. Many technical problems had to be solved in developing these radios, including the interference caused by the plane's ignition system. With the installation of proper shielding, this difficulty could be overcome.[73] But despite advances in aerial radio, pilots in the 1930s still relied to some extent on hand signals to direct their squadrons.[74]

The Signal Corps also developed radios for navigational purposes, basing its technology on work done during the war in direction finding.[75] One of the most important navigational aids was the radio beacon, which enabled a plane to follow a signal to its destination. When equipped with radio compasses, which they tuned to the beacons on the ground, pilots no longer had to rely on their senses alone; they could fly "blind," guided by their instruments. This system proved itself in June 1927 when it guided two Army pilots, 1st Lts. Lester J. Maitland and Albert F. Hegenberger, on the first nonstop flight from California to Hawaii. This milestone occurred just a few weeks before Charles Lindbergh made his historic flight across the Atlantic.[76] Lieutenant Hegenberger later became head of the Air Corps' Navigational Instrument Section at Wright Field, which was located in the same building as the Signal Corps' Aircraft Radio Laboratory. (McCook Field was incorporated into Wright Field in 1927.)

However, the Signal Corps did not always enjoy a cordial relationship with the Air Corps regarding radio development. In fact, Hegenberger, in an attempt to take over the Signal Corps' navigational projects, went so far as to lock the Signal Corps personnel out of his portion of the building they shared. When the Air Corps failed in its attempt to carry the mail in 1934, suffering twelve fatalities and sixty-six crashes in four months, some senior Air Corps officers tried to blame the high casualty rate on the Signal Corps for neglecting to develop the appropriate navigational aids. In fact, inexperienced pilots and inadequate training had accounted for many of the accidents. The chief signal officer at that time, Maj. Gen. James B. Allison, and Maj. Gen. Benjamin D. Foulois, chief of the Air Corps, finally agreed in 1935 to discontinue Hegenberger's laboratory.[77]

In August 1929 the Signal Corps consolidated its research facilities in Washington with those at Fort Monmouth, establishing the Signal Corps Laboratories at Fort Monmouth. In 1935 a modern, permanent laboratory opened there to replace the World War I–vintage buildings previously in use. The new structure was named, most fittingly, Squier Laboratory, in honor of the former chief signal officer and eminent scientist, who had passed away the previous year at the age of sixty-nine.[78] Meanwhile, the Signal Corps' Aircraft Radio Laboratory remained at Wright Field because the equipment produced there required continuous flight testing.[79]

Probably the most significant research undertaken by the Signal Corps between the wars was that pertaining to radar, an offshoot of radio. The word radar is an acronym for radio detection and ranging.[80] In brief, radar depends on the reflection of radio waves from solid objects. By sending out a focused radio pulse, which travels at a known rate (the speed of light), and timing the interval between the transmission of the wave and the reception of its reflection or echo, the distance, or range, to an object can be determined. The resultant signals are displayed visually on the screen of a cathode-ray oscilloscope. During the interwar years many other nations, including Germany, Great Britain, and Japan, conducted radar experiments, but secrecy increased along with heightening world tensions. In the United States credit for the initial development of radar belonged to the Navy, which conducted its seminal experimentation at the Naval Research Laboratory in Washington during the 1920s and 1930s. While the Signal Corps did not invent radar, its subsequent efforts played an important role in furthering its evolution.[81]

The origins of the Army's radar research dated back to World War I, when Maj. William R. Blair, who then headed the Signal Corps' Meteorological Section in the American Expeditionary Forces, conducted experiments in sound ranging for the purpose of locating approaching enemy aircraft by the noise of their engines. After the war Blair served as chief of the meteorological section in Washington and in 1926 became head of the Research and Engineering Division. In 1930 he was named director of the laboratories at Fort Monmouth. In February

1931 Blair began research on radio detection using both heat and high-frequency, or infrared, waves. Known as Project 88, this undertaking had been transferred to the Signal Corps from the Ordnance Department. When these methods proved disappointing, Blair began investigating the pulse-echo method of detection.[82]

Contrary to its usual procedure, the Signal Corps conducted all of its developmental work on radar in its own laboratories, rather than contracting components out to private industry. Chief Signal Officer Allison did not believe that commercial firms could yet "offer useful results in practical form."[83] Although Allison requested additional money for radar research, the War Department provided none, and the Signal Corps obtained the necessary funds from cutbacks in other projects. In December 1936 Signal Corps engineers conducted the first field test of their radar equipment at the Newark, New Jersey, airport where it detected an airplane at a distance of seven miles. In May 1937 the Signal Corps demonstrated its still crude radar, the future SCR–268, for Secretary of War Harry H. Woodring; Brig. Gen. Henry H. Arnold, assistant chief of the Air Corps; and other government officials at Fort Monmouth.[84] Impressed by its potential, Woodring later wrote to Allison: "It gave tangible evidence of the amazing scientific advances made by the Signal Corps in the development of technical equipment."[85] Arnold, also responding favorably, urged the Signal Corps to develop a long-range version for use as an early warning device. With this high-level support, the Signal Corps received the funds it needed to continue its development program.[86]

The Corps' application of radar to coast defense was an extension of its long-standing work in the development of electrical systems for that purpose, which had begun in the 1890s. Because national policy remained one of isolationism, American military planners envisioned any future war as defensive. Consequently, the Army placed great reliance upon warning systems to protect against surprise attack by sea and especially by air. Hence the Signal Corps developed the SCR–268, a short-range radar set designed to control searchlights and antiaircraft guns, and subsequently designed for the Air Corps two sets for long-range aircraft detection: SCR–270, a mobile set with a range of 120 miles, and SCR–271, a fixed radar with similar capabilities.[87]

In an interesting historical parallel, the Signal Corps carried out its radar testing at the same locations—Sandy Hook and the Highlands at Navesink, New Jersey—where Assistant Surgeon Albert J. Myer had tested his wigwag signals with 2d Lt. Edward P. Alexander prior to the Civil War. While Myer had favored these sites for their proximity to New York Harbor, the later generation of experimenters found them convenient to Fort Monmouth. Here and elsewhere the Signal Corps was bringing the Army into the electronics age.[88]

Organization, Training, and Operations, 1929–1939

While the cost of technology steadily rose, the amount of money the nation was willing to spend on its Army tended to decline during the early 1930s, as the

Clockwise from top, *SCR–268; SCR–270-B; SCR–271 radar station in Panama, 1940.*

nation plunged into the Great Depression that followed the stock market crash of October 1929. Two veteran Signal Corps officers led the branch during this difficult period: General Gibbs and his successor, Maj. Gen. Irving J. Carr. Gibbs, who remained at the helm until 30 June 1931, counted among his major achievements the consolidation of the Corps' laboratories and a reorganization and restructuring of the Signal Office that endured until World War II.[89] Upon retirement he became an executive with several communications firms, an indication of the increasingly close relationship between the military and industry, based in part on the growing similarity of military and civilian technology.[90]

General Carr, who received a degree in civil engineering from the Pennsylvania Military College in 1897, had served as an infantry lieutenant during the Philippine Insurrection. Graduating from the Army Signal School in 1908, he was detailed to the Signal Corps during World War I. Carr served in France successively as chief signal officer of the 2d Division, the IV Army Corps, and the Third Army. In addition to attending the General Staff School and the Army War College after the war, he served as signal officer of the Western Department and as chief of staff of the Hawaiian Division. At the time of his appointment as chief signal officer, Carr held the position of executive officer in the Office of the Assistant Secretary of War.[91]

General Carr faced a situation that had been transformed by the economic crisis. While Americans stood in breadlines, the Army, already experiencing hard times because of national pacifism and war-weariness, felt the added impact of the Great Depression. In the midst of this national tragedy, military preparedness took a backseat to social and economic concerns. Chief of Staff General Douglas MacArthur did nothing to improve the Army's image by dispersing with unnecessary brutality the so-called Bonus Army of World War I veterans who marched on Washington in the summer of 1932. This violent incident may also have contributed to President Herbert Hoover's defeat by Franklin D. Roosevelt in the presidential election that fall.

Despite its lack of funds, the Army sought new roles to assist the nation through its time of economic distress. Its contribution to the organization of the Civilian Conservation Corps (CCC), established as part of President Roosevelt's New Deal in April 1933, proved popular but a drain on its limited resources. The CCC's activities included reforestation, soil conservation, fire prevention, and similar projects. The Army set up and ran the camps and supplied food, clothing, shelter, medical care, and recreation. For its part, the Signal Corps provided radio communication and linked radio stations at CCC district headquarters with the War Department Radio Net. Members of the Army Amateur Radio System participated in this effort. The Signal Corps also helped to advertise this least partisan of New Deal ventures, completing a three-reel historical film about the CCC in 1935.[92]

The Second International Polar Year was held from 1932 to 1934, fifty years after the original event. Financial support from the Rockefeller Foundation helped make this effort possible in the midst of the worldwide depression. While

Arctic studies remained the focus, more countries participated and more branches of science were included than before. Although the Signal Corps did not play as prominent a role as in the 1880s, it nonetheless lent its expertise to the scientists involved in polar research. The Corps established communication facilities for the Army's station near the Arctic Circle and supplied equipment for studying problems of radio transmission.[93]

With General Carr's retirement, Maj. Gen. James B. Allison became chief signal officer on 1 January 1935. Allison had received extensive experience in signal training during the years 1917–1919 when he commanded Signal Corps training camps at Monterey, California; Fort Leavenworth; and Camp Meade, Maryland. From September 1925 to June 1926 he served as commandant of the Signal School. Prior to becoming chief, he had been signal officer of the Second Corps Area at Governors Island, New York. Allison was fortunate to assume his new duties during the same year that the Army acquired a new chief of staff, General Malin Craig, who recognized the value of communications. Craig, concerned about the threatening world situation in both the Far East and Europe, pressed for a limited rearmament. He also supported increases in the Signal Corps' budget that finally ended its years of impoverishment.[94]

The growing danger of war, the demands for improved technology, and even the Great Depression itself improved the Signal Corps' prospects. The turnover rate of its enlisted personnel dropped as joblessness increased in civilian life. When Congress enlarged the size of the Army in 1935, the Signal Corps received an additional 953 enlisted men, enabling the Corps to handle the growing demands on its services caused by the public works programs of the New Deal and the expanding activities of the Air Corps.[95]

The Corps also held onto one of its traditional activities, WAMCATS, in the face of renewed demands that the government sell the Alaska system because of its predominantly commercial nature. It was also argued that the release of the more than two hundred enlisted men assigned to duty in Alaska would help ease the Corps' overall personnel shortage. But Chief Signal Officer Gibbs had opposed the sale, and Congress did not act upon the War Department's enabling legislation. While the long-standing debate continued as to whether to transfer the system to another agency or turn it over to commercial interests, WAMCATS remained in the Signal Corps' hands.[96]

Under the Corps' stewardship the system continued to develop. By 1931 radio had overtaken the use of cables, but the underwater lines were kept in operable condition in case of emergencies. In 1933 the Army transferred the *Dellwood*, now left with little to do, to the U.S. Shipping Board, which in turn sold it to a commercial cannery.[97] To reflect its new image, the WAMCATS underwent a name change in 1936, becoming the Alaska Communication System (ACS).[98]

WAMCATS continued to render important service to Alaskans, proving itself to be a "lifeline to the north." In 1934, when much of Nome went up in flames, the city's WAMCATS station stayed on the air to coordinate relief and rescue

General Carr

General Allison

work. WAMCATS also played a key role in the drama surrounding the plane crash that killed humorist Will Rogers and aviator Wiley Post near Point Barrow in August 1935. Sgt. Stanley R. Morgan, the Signal Corps radio operator there, learned of the accident from a native runner. After summoning help, Morgan traveled to the crash site to do what he could. Unfortunately, both men had died instantly. Returning to his station, Morgan signaled news of the tragedy to the world.[99]

The Signal Corps' photographic mission continued to expand during the 1930s. Photographic training was briefly transferred to the Army War College, but soon returned to Fort Monmouth. In 1933 the Corps produced its first feature-length sound movie, depicting infantry maneuvers at Fort Benning, Georgia. The Corps also released several new training films, including such action-packed features as "Cavalry Crossing Unfordable Stream" and "Elementary Principles of the Recoil Mechanism." The shortage of funds, however, prevented the Signal Corps from making many films prior to World War II. The Corps did work diligently to index and reedit its World War I films, making master copies and providing better storage facilities for these priceless records.[100]

Despite many difficulties, the Signal Corps' operations increased overall during the 1930s. But it lost one function, military meteorology. As the decade progressed, the branch simply could not keep up with the demands made on its weather service by the Air Corps. Following the airmail fiasco, the Air Corps sought to upgrade operations at some stations to provide weather service around the clock

General Mauborgne

and throughout the year. With its limited manpower and varied missions, the task was beyond the Signal Corps' capability. In his 1936 annual report Chief Signal Officer Allison recommended that "if the required additional personnel could not be given [to] the Signal Corps, all meteorological duties . . . be transferred to the Air Corps which is the principal user of the meteorological service."[101] The secretary of war agreed, and returned weather reporting and forecasting to the using arms effective 1 July 1937. As a result, many of the Signal Corps' meteorologists transferred to the Air Corps. Although the Signal Corps retained responsibility for the development, procurement, supply, and maintenance of meteorological equipment, the sun had set once more on its weather service.[102]

Upon General Allison's retirement at the end of September 1937, Col. Joseph O. Mauborgne was designated to become the new chief signal officer, effective on 1 October. Originally commissioned as a second lieutenant of infantry in 1903, he had served with the Signal Corps since 1916 and transferred to the branch in 1920. A well-known expert in radio and cryptanalysis, Mauborgne had been chief of the Corps' Research and Engineering Division during World War I. His postwar assignments included heading the Signal Corps Laboratory at the Bureau of Standards and commanding, for a second time, the Research and Engineering Division in the Signal Office. He also served as a technical adviser at several international communications conferences, including the radio conference held in Washington in 1927. After becoming a colonel in 1934, he was the director of the Aircraft Radio Laboratory from 1936 to 1937. In addition to his scientific expertise, Mauborgne possessed considerable artistic talent as a portrait painter, etcher, and maker of prize-winning violins.[103]

Among its many duties, the Signal Corps held responsibility for revising and compiling all codes and ciphers used by the War Department and the Army. Under General Mauborgne, himself a gifted cryptologist, activities in this area expanded. In 1929 General Gibbs had established the Signal Intelligence Service to control all Army cryptology. In addition to code and cipher work, the Signal Intelligence Service absorbed the covert intelligence-gathering activities formerly conducted by the so-called Black Chamber within the Military Intelligence Division of the War Department General Staff.

William F. Friedman, center back, *and the staff of the Signal Intelligence Service in the 1930s*

William F. Friedman became the Signal Intelligence Service's first chief. After serving in the intelligence section of the General Staff, AEF, during World War I, Friedman had joined the Signal Corps in 1921 to develop new codes and ciphers. In 1922 he became chief cryptanalyst in the code and cipher compilation section of the Research and Development Division where he became known for his remarkable code-breaking abilities. In addition to cryptographic skills, Friedman shared Mauborgne's interest in the violin and formed a musical group that included the chief signal officer and several friends.[104]

In 1935 the Army reinstituted its program of large-scale maneuvers, which it had not held since before World War I. The 51st Signal Battalion, the only unit of its type, provided the communications for these exercises. In 1937 the Army tested its new "triangular"—three regiment—division at San Antonio, Texas. This streamlined unit, reduced from four regiments and without any brigade headquarters, had been favored by Pershing in 1919. Providing more mobility and flexibility than the square division of World War I, the triangular division would become the standard division of the next war. While the divisional signal company was somewhat larger (7 officers and 182 men) than that provided for in the 1920 tables of organization, the signal complement of the combat arms was cut in half.[105]

Thus, helped by a variety of factors, the Signal Corps weathered the years of political isolationism and economic depression. As a technical service, it benefit-

ed from the rapid development in communications technology pioneered by civilian industry and from the growing realization among military and civilian leaders
alike that science would be a crucial factor in any future conflict. Unfortunately,
that future was closer than many Americans liked to think.

The Road to War

Throughout the 1930s the world situation had grown increasingly ominous.
Adolph Hitler came to power in Germany in 1933 and, denouncing the
Versailles treaty, undertook a program of rearmament. Italy's dictator, Benito
Mussolini, began a course of aggression by attacking Ethiopia in 1935. In 1939
Hitler signed a treaty with the Soviet dictator, Joseph Stalin, and invaded
Poland, precipitating a general war in Europe. Across the Pacific, Japan
unleashed its power, seizing Manchuria in 1931 and invading China in 1937.
Finally, the formation of the Rome-Berlin-Tokyo Axis in September 1940
appeared to unite three heavily armed and aggressive nations against the ill-
armed democracies.

After years of stagnation, the United States began a gradual military buildup
in the late 1930s. President Roosevelt, who had once served as assistant secretary
of the Navy, at first championed only a naval rebuilding program, but the Army
eventually began to receive greater attention. In his annual message of January
1938, Roosevelt requested an Army budget of $17 million, a substantial sum but
considerably less than the Navy's allotment of $28 million.[106]

Having learned some hard lessons from its unpreparedness for World War I,
the War Department devoted considerable attention during the interwar period to
planning for future wars. Responsibility for strategic planning rested with the
War Plans Division of the General Staff, while the 1920 defense act assigned
supervision of procurement and industrial mobilization planning to the assistant
secretary of war.[107]

Despite the power wielded by the General Staff, considerable administrative
control still existed at the branch level. For its part, the Signal Corps contained a
procurement planning section which prepared estimates of requirements, conducted surveys of manufacturers, and identified scarce raw materials, such as the
Brazilian quartz used in radios.[108]

The Army's Industrial Mobilization Plan of 1930 established procedures for
harnessing the nation's economic might, while the Protective Mobilization Plan
of 1937 set forth the steps for manpower mobilization, beginning with the induction of the National Guard. These plans failed, however, to envision a conflict on
a scale larger than World War I. For instance, estimates placed the Signal Corps'
monthly requirement for batteries during wartime at five million; the actual number later proved to be more than four times that amount.[109]

With the outbreak of war in Europe, the United States undertook a limited
preparedness effort with the emphasis on hemispheric defense. President
Roosevelt declared a "limited national emergency" on 8 September 1939 and

authorized an increase in the Regular Army's enlisted strength to 227,000.[110] Public opinion, however, remained committed to staying out of war and protecting "America First."

The blitzkrieg tactics of the Nazis in Poland suggested that this war would be a mobile one, unlike the stalemate of the Western Front during World War I. By 1939 the United States Army had undergone extensive motorization, although mechanization remained in its early stages. For the Signal Corps, motorization meant developing light automobiles equipped with radios as reconnaissance vehicles and adapting motor vehicles to lay wire.[111] But little had been done to integrate communications into larger, combined arms mobile formations.

During the spring of 1940 the Army held its first genuine corps and army training maneuvers. The exercises, conducted in May 1940 along the Texas and Louisiana border, "tested tactical communications more thoroughly than anything else had since World War I."[112] Unfortunately, much Signal Corps equipment proved deficient. The W–110 field wire, for instance, worked poorly when wet and suffered considerable damage from motor vehicles. (Local cattle also liked to chew contentedly upon it.) Moreover, the SCR–197, designed to serve as a long-range mobile radio, could not function while in motion. Intended for operation from the back of a truck, the radio could only send or receive messages after the vehicle had stopped. First, however, the crew had to dismount to deploy the antenna and start the gasoline generator. The allocation of frequencies also became a problem with the proliferation of radios throughout the Army's new triangular divisions. In part, the frequency issue arose because the radios in use were obsolescent. They did not reflect the most recent innovations—crystal control and FM—that would both increase the range of available frequencies and enable operators to make precise adjustments to particular frequencies with just the push of a button. Until the Army adopted improved radios, it could not fight a modern war successfully. Moreover, in addition to highlighting the general inadequacy of tactical communications, the 1940 maneuvers demonstrated that the Signal Corps needed additional men and units to carry out its mission.[113]

Although technically a neutral nation, the United States gradually began to prepare for the possibility of entering the war and increased its support to the Allies. On 10 May 1940 Germany invaded France and the Low Countries. The subsequent defeat of the Allied armies, followed by the narrow escape of the British expeditionary force from Dunkirk and the fall of France in June 1940, brought Allied fortunes to the brink of disaster. At the end of August Congress authorized the president to induct the National Guard into service for a year and to call up the Organized Reserves. Furthermore, the Selective Service and Training Act, signed into law on 16 September 1940, initiated the first peacetime draft in the nation's history. While the United States was not yet ready to become a direct participant, the signing of the Lend-Lease Act in March 1941 officially made it the world's "arsenal of democracy."[114]

While the nation moved toward war, the Signal Corps underwent some changes of its own. The pressure of the impending conflict resulted in enormous

General Olmstead

demands for new communications equipment. The Air Corps, in particular, grew increasingly impatient with the slow pace of progress, especially in relation to radar. Under intense criticism from the airmen, Chief Signal Officer Mauborgne was suddenly relieved of his duties by Chief of Staff General George C. Marshall, Jr., in August 1941. Pending Mauborgne's official retirement the following month, Brig. Gen. Dawson Olmstead stepped in as acting chief.[115]

On 24 October 1941, Olmstead officially became chief signal officer with the rank of major general, the fifteenth individual to hold that post. A graduate of West Point, class of 1906, Olmstead had received his commission in the Cavalry. During 1908 and 1909 he had attended the Signal School at Fort Leavenworth. After World War I, during which he had served in the Inspector General's Office of the AEF, he held a number of Signal Corps–related assignments. These included signal officer of the Hawaiian Department from 1925 to 1927, officer in charge of the Alaska communication system from 1931 to 1933, and commandant of the Signal School at Fort Monmouth from 1938 to 1941.[116]

For the new chief signal officer, as for the nation, war was now close at hand. Despite outstanding work by the Signal Intelligence Service, now comprising almost three hundred soldiers and civilians, the exact point of danger eluded American leaders. In August 1940 William Friedman and his staff had broken PURPLE, the Japanese diplomatic code, and the intelligence received as a consequence became known as MAGIC.[117] While MAGIC yielded critical information regarding Japanese diplomatic strategy, the intercepted messages did not explicitly reveal Japanese war plans.[118] American officials knew that war was imminent, but considered a Japanese attack on Hawaii no more than a remote possibility.

During 1940 President Roosevelt had transferred the Pacific Fleet from bases on the West Coast of the United States to Pearl Harbor on the Hawaiian island of Oahu, hoping that its presence might act as a deterrent upon Japanese ambitions. Yet the move also made the fleet more vulnerable. Despite Oahu's strategic importance, the air warning system on the island had not become fully operational by December 1941. The Signal Corps had provided SCR–270 and 271 radar sets earlier in the year, but the construction of fixed sites had been delayed, and radar protection was limited to six mobile stations operating on a part-time

David Sarnoff of RCA (left) *and Captain Stoner, in charge of the War Department Message Center, inspect radio transmitters at Station WAR, Fort Myer, Virginia.*

basis to test the equipment and train the crews. Though aware of the dangers of war, the Army and Navy commanders on Oahu, Lt. Gen. Walter C. Short and Admiral Husband E. Kimmel, did not anticipate that Pearl Harbor would be the target; a Japanese strike against American bases in the Philippines appeared more probable. In Hawaii, sabotage and subversive acts by Japanese inhabitants seemed to pose more immediate threats, and precautions were taken. The Japanese-American population of Hawaii proved, however, to be overwhelmingly loyal to the United States.[119]

Because the Signal Corps' plans to modernize its strategic communications during the previous decade had been stymied, the Army had only a limited ability to communicate with the garrison in Hawaii. In 1930 the Corps had moved WAR's transmitter to Fort Myer, Virginia, and had constructed a building to house its new, high-frequency equipment. Four years later it added a new diamond antenna, which enabled faster transmission.[120] But in 1939, when the Corps wished to further expand its facilities at Fort Myer to include a rhombic antenna for point-to-point communication with Seattle, it ran into difficulty. The post commander, Col. George S. Patton, Jr., objected to the Signal Corps' plans. The new antenna would encroach upon the turf he used as a polo field and the radio towers would obstruct the view. Patton held his ground and prevented the Signal Corps from installing the new equipment. At the same time, the Navy was about to abandon its Arlington radio station located adjacent to Fort Myer and offered it to the Army. Patton, wishing instead to use the Navy's buildings to house his enlisted personnel, opposed the station's transfer. As a result of the controversy, the Navy withdrew its offer and the Signal Corps lost the opportunity to improve its facilities.[121]

Though a seemingly minor bureaucratic battle, the situation had serious consequences two years later. Early in the afternoon of 6 December 1941, the Signal Intelligence Service began receiving a long dispatch in fourteen parts from Tokyo addressed to the Japanese embassy in Washington. The Japanese deliberately delayed sending the final portion of the message until the next day, in which they announced that the Japanese government would sever diplomatic relations with the United States effective at one o'clock that afternoon. At that hour, it would be early morning in Pearl Harbor.

Upon receiving the decoded message on the morning of 7 December, Chief of Staff Marshall recognized its importance. Although he could have called Short directly, Marshall did not do so because the scrambler telephone was not considered secure. Instead, he decided to send a written message through the War Department Message Center. Unfortunately, the center's radio encountered heavy static and could not get through to Honolulu. Expanded facilities at Fort Myer could perhaps have eliminated this problem. The signal officer on duty, Lt. Col. Edward F. French, therefore sent the message via commercial telegraph to San Francisco, where it was relayed by radio to the RCA office in Honolulu. That office had installed a teletype connection with Fort Shafter, but the teletypewriter was not yet functional. An RCA messenger was carrying the news to Fort Shafter by motorcycle when Japanese bombs began falling; a huge traffic jam developed because of the attack, and General Short did not receive the message until that afternoon.

Earlier that day, as the sun rose over Opana on the northern tip of Oahu, two Signal Corpsmen, Pvts. George A. Elliott and Joseph L. Lockard, continued to operate their radar station, although their watch had ended at 0700. At 0702 a large echo appeared on their scope, indicating a sizable formation of incoming planes about 130 miles away. They telephoned their unusual sighting to the radar information center at Fort Shafter, but the young Air Corps lieutenant on duty told them to "Forget it." An attack was not expected, and the planes were assumed to be American bombers scheduled to arrive that morning from California. Nevertheless, Elliott and Lockard tracked the planes until they became lost on their scope. Just minutes before the attack began at 0755, the two men left their station for breakfast.[122] Despite the breaking of PURPLE, the surprise at Pearl Harbor was "complete and shattering."[123]

The following day President Roosevelt went before Congress to ask for a declaration of war against Japan. In an eloquent speech, he called 7 December "a date which will live in infamy," and the House and Senate voted for war with only one dissenter.[124] On 11 December, Germany and Italy declared war on the United States, and Congress replied in kind. Despite Woodrow Wilson's lofty intentions, World War I had not made the world safe for democracy; with Hitler's armies supreme in Europe and Japanese forces sweeping through the Far East, freedom appeared to be in greater peril than in 1917. In just twenty years the hopes for a lasting peace had vanished, and once again the United States prepared to throw its might on the side of the Allies.

Angered by the bombing of Pearl Harbor, the American people entered World War II with a strong sense of mission and purpose. At the same time that Japanese war planes shattered the Pacific Fleet, they also destroyed the American sense of invulnerability—the nation's ocean bulwark had been breached. Nevertheless, displaying his characteristic optimism, President Roosevelt proclaimed on 9 December: "With confidence in our armed forces, with unbounded determination of our people, we will gain the inevitable triumph."[125] In this triumph, the Signal Corps would play a pivotal role.

Notes

[1]The U.S. Army's strength in November 1918 was 3,703,273 according to Coffman, *War To End All Wars*, p. 357. The strength of the active Army by the end of 1919 had been reduced to just 19,000 officers and 205,000 enlisted men (Matloff, ed., *American Military History*, p. 406).

[2]Ferrell, *Wilson and World War I*, p. 179; *OB*, vol. 1, pp. 390–94; *ARSO*, 1920, in *ARSW*, vol. 1, p. 1251; Smythe, *Pershing*, p. 259.

[3]Coffman, *War To End All Wars*, pp. 357–59.

[4]Crowell, *America's Munitions*, p. 574; Lavine, *Circuits of Victory*, p. 615. The 1st Field Signal Battalion was detached from the 2d Division, which returned to the United States in the summer of 1919. See *OB*, vol. 2, pp. 23, 57. There was also a Signal Corps detachment in Silesia; see *ARSO*, 1920, p. 1243; *Historical Sketch*, p. 95.

[5]*ARSO*, 1919, p. 180; Lavine, *Circuits of Victory*, ch. 50. Ill health forced Russel to resign from the Army in December 1922 with the rank of major general. He died in 1925.

[6]*ARSO*, 1919, pp. 543–44; *OB*, vol. 3, pt. 1, pp. 490–91.

[7]Civilian control of communications was restored in July 1919. Gleason L. Archer, *History of Radio to 1926* (New York: American Historical Society, Inc., 1938), p. 172.

[8]Edward M. Coffman, *The Hilt of the Sword: The Career of Peyton C. March* (Madison: University of Wisconsin Press, 1966), chs. 14 and 15; Matloff, ed., *American Military History*, p. 405; John B. Wilson, Divisions and Separate Brigades, draft Ms, ch. 4; Kreidberg and Henry, *Military Mobilization*, p. 377.

[9]The 1920 defense act is published in WD Bulletin 25, 9 June 1920.

[10]The chief signal officer brought the total number of officers to 301. *ARSO*, 1921, p. 1, AGO 319.12 (10–5–21), RG 407, NARA. Beginning in 1921 the War Department ceased to publish most of the annual bureau reports in order to save money. Only an extract of the chief signal officer's report is included in the *ARSW*. The manuscript copies prepared by the chief signal officer and his counterparts are located in the National Archives in RG 407 (Adjutant General's Office [AGO]), Central File, file no. 319.12. Unless otherwise stated, references are to the manuscript copies of the *ARSO*. After 1937 the preparation of these reports was no longer required. Perhaps to fill the resulting information gap, the Signal Corps in 1920 began publishing the *Signal Corps Information Bulletin* (later the *Signal Corps Bulletin*).

[11]Each corps area also supported two National Guard divisions and (theoretically, at least) three reserve divisions. The territory included within each corps area is defined per WDGO 50, 20 Aug 1920.

[12]Weigley, *History of Army*, pp. 399–400; Matloff, ed., *American Military History*, pp. 407–09; Hill, *Minute Man in Peace and War*, ch. 13; Coffman, *Hilt of Sword*, chs. 14 and 15; Hewes, *Root to McNamara*, pp. 50–56; Abrahamson, *America Arms*, ch. 9.

[13]The Signal Corps is declared one of the combat arms in Section 2 of the 1920 defense act. Terrett, *Emergency*, pp. 22–23.

[14]John B. Wilson, "Mobility Versus Firepower: The Post-World War I Infantry Division," *Parameters* 13 (Sep 1983): 47–52; Millett, "Cantigny," in Heller and Stofft, eds., *First Battles*, pp. 182–85.

[15]"Extracts from Report of Superior Board, A.E.F., on Organization and Tactics," p. 78, RG 407, NARA. The change in doctrine is announced in WDGO 29, 18 May 1920, sec. 3. See also Scheips, "The Line and the Staff," pp. 25–26; Terrett, *Emergency*, p. 23.

[16]*ARSO*, 1922, p. 5, AGO file 319.12 (10–1–22), RG 407, NARA.

[17]*Field Service Regulations, United States Army* (Washington, D.C.: Government Printing Office, 1924), pars. 88–95.

[18]John B. Wilson, "Mobility vs. Firepower," p. 49.

[19]Table 8P and W (peace and war strength), "Signal Company, Infantry Division," 31 Dec 1920 in *Tables of Organization: Infantry and Cavalry Divisions* (Fort Leavenworth, Kans.: General Service Schools Press, 1922).

[20]The divisional signal companies took on the numbers of their respective divisions: e.g., the 2d Field Signal Battalion of the 1st Division became the 1st Signal Company; the 1st Field Signal Battalion of the 2d Division became the 2d Signal Company, and so on. See WDGO 5, 22 Jan 1921, and WD Cir 59, 8 Mar 1921.

[21]Weigley, *History of Army*, p. 357, gives Regular Army strength on 1 April 1917 as 127,588.

[22]John B. Wilson, Divisions and Separate Brigades, draft Ms, pp. 4:40, 5:1; Robert A. Miller, "The United States Army During the 1930s" (Ph.D. dissertation, Princeton University, 1973), p. 55; Matloff, ed., *American Military History*, p. 409; Ferrell, *Wilson and World War I*, p. 187.

[23]*ARSO*, 1926, app. 1, p. 3, AGO 319.12 (10–4–26), RG 407, NARA; WD Cir 24, 20 Apr 1926; Terrett, *Emergency*, p. 74.

[24]See, for example, comments in *ARSO*, 1920, p. 1240; *ARSO*, 1926, p. 9. The turnover rate of the Signal Corps' enlisted personnel in 1924, for example, was 33 percent (*ARSO*, 1924, p. 10, AGO 319.12 [9–10–24], RG 407, NARA).

[25]*ARSO*, 1919, pp. 545–47; *ARSO*, 1923, p. 80, AGO 319.12 (9–10–23), RG 407, NARA; *ARSO*, 1928, p. 12, AGO 319.12 (10–1–28), RG 407, NARA. These figures cover only the appropriation for the "Signal Service of the Army." The Corps received additional funds to cover items not included under "Signal Service," such as the Alaska communication system.

[26]Terrett, *Emergency*, pp. 22–23; see extract of letter from Col F. R. Curtis, acting chief signal officer, dated 23 Aug 1919, to The Adjutant General, printed in Helen C. Phillips, *History of the U.S. Army Signal Center and School 1919–1967* (Fort Monmouth, N.J.: U.S. Army Signal Center and School, 1967), p. 17.

[27]*Historical Sketch*, pp. 113–16; "History of Fort Monmouth," pp. 25, 41–44; *ARSO*, 1920, pp. 1245–48. The school's curriculum is outlined in Phillips, *Signal Center and School*, ch. 4.

[28]The 1920 defense act provided that 2 percent of the commissioned strength of each arm could be detailed as students to technical institutions each year. *ARSO*, 1920, pp. 1248–49.

[29]The camp's redesignation is announced in WDGO 19, 6 Aug 1925.

[30]Unit jacket, 51st Signal Battalion, DAMH-HSO; "History of Fort Monmouth," pp. 33–35, 54–57.

[31]According to a World War I–era joke, the Signal Corps bred pigeons with parrots so that they could speak, with angels so they could sing, and with Western Union boys so that they could both sing and salute. Terrett, *Emergency*, p. 222.

[32]Coffey, *Hap*, p. 107.

[33]*ARSO*, 1919, p. 339; *ARSO*, 1927, p. 22, AGO 319.12 (10–5–27), RG 407, NARA; *ARSO*, 1928, p. 48; "History of Fort Monmouth," pp. 45–48.

[34]The station was located in the Munitions Building, 19th and B Streets, NW, in downtown Washington. B Street was later renamed Constitution Avenue.

[35]Pauline M. Oakes, The Army Command and Administrative Communications System, Part 1: War Department Radio Net Thru Fiscal Years 1920–1940, typescript [Washington, D.C.: Signal Corps Historical Section, Oct 1945], p. 80, copy in CMH files.

[36]*ARSO*, 1925, supplement, p. 14, AGO 319.12 (9–8–25), RG 407, NARA. For details on the net, see discussion in the *ARSO* beginning in 1922. See also *Historical Sketch*, pp. 106–07; Edward F. French, "War Department Radio Net," in Scheips, ed., *Military Signal Communications*, vol. 1. The system later became known as the Army Command and Administrative Network (ACAN).

[37]*Historical Sketch*, pp. 106–07; Terrett, *Emergency*, pp. 49–50; Oakes, Army Command and Administrative Communications System, pt. 1, ch. 1.

[38]*Historical Sketch*, pp. 108–10; Terrett, *Emergency*, pp. 54–55; Oakes, Army Command and Administrative Communications System, pt. 1, pp. 69–73; D. M. Crawford, "The Army Amateur Radio System," *Signal Corps Bulletin* 47 (Mar 1929), reprinted in Scheips, ed., *Military Signal Communications*, vol. 2; *ARSO*, 1926, pp. 7–8; "History of Fort Monmouth," pp. 39–40. Amateur operators had already formed their own organization, known as the American Radio Relay League. The net control station moved to Washington in 1930. *ARSO*, 1930, p. 13, AGO 319.12 (10–10–30), RG 407, NARA.

[39]Aitken, *Continuous Wave*, pp. 256–78.

[40]Howeth, *Communications-Electronics in Navy*, pp. 295–96; Aitken, *Continuous Wave*, pp. 262–67; Erik Barnouw, *A History of Broadcasting in the United States*, 3 vols. (New York: Oxford University Press, 1966–1970), 1: 50–58.

[41]Secretary of the Navy Josephus Daniels urged Congress to give the Navy exclusive control over radio. See Howeth, *Communications-Electronics in Navy*, ch. 27.

[42]The Navy played a central role in the formation of RCA. President Wilson's role in encouraging its creation is less clear. For background about RCA's establishment and the terms of the agreements, see Aitken, *Continuous Wave*, chs. 6–10; Archer, *History of Radio*, chs. 9–11; and Howeth, *Communications-Electronics in Navy*, ch. 30. Douglas, *Inventing Broadcasting*, and Barnouw, *History of Broadcasting*, volume 1, provide briefer treatments. Edward J. Nally, chief executive of American Marconi, became RCA's first president. He was succeeded in 1923 by Maj. Gen. James G. Harbord, formerly chief of staff of the AEF. In 1930 the Department of Justice indicted RCA under the antitrust statutes. Consequently, the corporation was restructured and its exclusive licensing agreements terminated.

[43]The network was formed in conjunction with General Electric and Westinghouse. RCA owned 50 percent, General Electric 30 percent, and Westinghouse 20 percent. Aitken, *Continuous Wave*, p. 486, n. 12. The acquisition of RCA by General Electric in 1985 brought events full circle.

[44]During World War I Westinghouse developed the SCR–69 and SCR–70 radiotelephone transmitters for the Signal Corps. Aitken, *Continuous Wave*, p. 458, n. 55. Westinghouse joined the RCA group in 1921.

[45]*ARSO*, 1922, p. 1; Barnouw, *History of Broadcasting*, 1: 4.

[46]In the interim, an Interdepartmental Radio Advisory Committee (IRAC) had been formed in 1923. The 1927 act is discussed by Barnouw, *History of Broadcasting*, 1: 195–201, and the legislation itself is included in an appendix. Under the Communications Act of 1934 the FCC assumed regulatory control over radio, telephone, telegraph, and cables. A member of the FCC sat on the IRAC, which continued in existence and recommended to the president which frequencies should be assigned to

government agencies. See *ARSO*, 1936, p. 15, AGO 319.12 (8–20–36), RG 407, NARA; Philip T. Rosen, *The Modern Stentors: Radio Broadcasters and the Federal Government, 1920–1934* (Westport, Conn.: Greenwood Press, 1980), chs. 10 and 11; Howeth, *Communications-Electronics in Navy*, ch. 42, which covers the radio conferences up to World War II.

[47]Clark, "Squier," p. 387; Rosen, *Modern Stentors*, pp. 108, 121–23.

[48]*ARSO*, 1923, pp. 22 and 39. Of the forty-three stations, eighteen employed radio.

[49]U.S. Army, Alaska, *The Army's Role in the Building of Alaska* (Pamphlet 360–5, 1 Apr 1969), pp. 56–61; Terrett, *Emergency*, pp. 57–58; *Historical Sketch*, p. 104; *ARSO*, 1927, p. 7; U.S. Army Signal Corps, "The Alaska Cable System," in Scheips, ed., *Military Signal Communications*, vol. 1.

[50]These observations were made at 0800, 1200, and 1700, 75th meridian time. See chapter 2 for information on the Corps' earlier weather activities.

[51]*ARSO*, 1921, p. 69; Flammer, "Meteorology in U.S. Army," ch. 3.

[52]*ARSO*, 1926, p. 14; Maurer, *Aviation in U.S. Army*, pp. 160 and 396–97; Whitnah, *Weather Bureau*, pp. 178–79; Bates and Fuller, *Weather Warriors*, ch. 3.

[53]*ARSO*, 1924, p. 25; *ARSO*, 1925, supplement, p. 16. For more on the flight, see Ernest A. McKay, *A World To Conquer: The Epic Story of the First Around-the-World Flight* (New York: Arco Publishing Inc., 1981); Maurer, *Aviation in U.S. Army*, pp. 186–88; Walker and Wickham, *Huffman Prairie to Moon*, pp. 63–71.

[54]*ARSO*, 1920, pp. 1293–96; *ARSO*, 1922, pp. 38–39. The Virginia Avenue location was known as Tempo Building Number 6.

[55]Per WDGO 26, 30 Dec 1925, which rescinded WDGO 17, 9 Jul 1925; *ARSO*, 1925, supplement, p. 48; Terrett, *Emergency*, p. 80.

[56]Terrett, *Emergency*, pp. 78–82; *ARSO*, 1931, partial report, p. 18, AGO 319.12 (8–12–31), RG 407, NARA.

[57]Otto Friedrich, "Trapped in a Musical Elevator," *Time*, 10 Dec 1984, pp. 110–12; Jeanne McDermott, "If it's to be heard but not listened to, it must be Muzak," *Smithsonian* 20 (Jan 1990): 70–82.

[58]Clark, "Squier," pp. 388–90, discusses many of his honors and awards.

[59]Section 4c of the National Defense Act contains this provision.

[60]See Saltzman's entries in Cullum, *Biographical Register*. He was West Point graduate number 3697. See also his obituary in *Assembly* 2 (Apr 1943): 5–8. In 1942 the West Point association of graduates began a quarterly publication, *Assembly*, and obituaries of former cadets thereafter appear therein.; see also "Saltzman, Charles M.," biographical files, DAMH-HSR.

[61]"Gibbs, George S.," biographical files, DAMH-HSR; *Historical Sketch*, p. 97; Francis B. Heitman, *Historical Register and Dictionary of the United States Army From Its Organization, September 29, 1789, to March 2, 1903*, 2 vols. (Washington, D.C.: Government Printing Office, 1903), 1: 453.

[62]Koistinen, "The 'Industrial-Military Complex,'" pp. 819–39.

[63]*ARSO*, 1924, p. 41.

[64]*Field Service Regulations*, 1923, par. 89.

[65]*ARSO*, 1921, p. 32; Cochrane, *Measures for Progress*, p. 431.

[66]H. P. Browning, "The Application of Teletypewriters to Military Signaling," *Signal Corps Bulletin* 78 (May–Jun 1934): 28–40 (reprinted in Scheips, ed., *Military Signal Communications*, vol. 2); Paul J. Scheips, "Introduction," in Scheips, ed., *Military Signal Communications*, vol. 1; Terrett, *Emergency*, pp. 178, 232–33.

[67]*ARSO*, 1924, p. 28; "History of Fort Monmouth," pp. 31–32; Terrett, *Emergency*, pp. 77–78 (who describes the Signal Corps Board as the most important of the boards and committees at the disposal of the chief signal officer.); *Historical Sketch*, p. 116.

[68]Oakes, Army Command and Administrative Communications System, pt. 1, p. 85. During 1926 and 1927 the War Department Radio Net switched to high-frequency transmitters. See *ARSO*, 1926, app., p. 29.

[69]Terrett, *Emergency*, pp. 139–41.

[70]During the war Armstrong allowed the government the free use of his FM patents for military purposes. Lessing, *Man of High Fidelity*, p. 250.

[71]Miller, "Army During the 1930s," p. 126; Terrett, *Emergency*, pp. 141–47, 178–85; Cary, "Use of the Motor Vehicle in the U.S. Army," chs. 5 and 6.

[72]Maurer, *Aviation in U.S. Army*, p. 158; Terrett, *Emergency*, p. 28. See AR, par. 1556, amended 10 May 1920, that reflects the change in radio responsibilities.

[73]Maurer, *Aviation in U.S. Army*, p. 159; *ARSO*, 1926, app. 1, p. 41; Terrett, *Emergency*, p. 29. Progress on each type of radio set is discussed in each *ARSO*. Beginning in 1932, research and development is included as a classified supplement to the report.

[74]Maurer, *Aviation in U.S. Army*, pp. 231–38.

[75]Terrett, *Emergency*, p. 120.

[76]Ibid., p. 30; *ARSO*, 1928, pp. 30–31; Maurer, *Aviation in U.S. Army*, pp. 256–60; Walker and Wickham, *Huffman Prairie to Moon*, pp. 207–09. Although James D. Dole of the Hawaiian Pineapple Company offered $25,000 in August 1927 to whomever could make the first nonstop flight from the United States to Hawaii, the feat had already been accomplished by Maitland and Hegenberger. For more on their accomplishment, see Robert H. Scheppler, *Pacific Air Race* (Washington, D.C.: Smithsonian Institution Press, 1988).

[77]Terrett, *Emergency*, pp. 88–94. The Air Corps flew the mail from February to June 1934. For details, see Maurer, *Aviation in U.S. Army*, ch. 17; Flammer, "Meteorology in U.S. Army," ch. 4; Coffey, *Hap*, pp. 156–58; Foulois, *Memoirs*, ch. 14.

[78]See Squier's obituary in *USMA Graduates Report* (1934), pp. 157–62.

[79]*ARSO*, 1929, p. 29, AGO 319.12 (9–26–29), RG 407, NARA; Terrett, *Emergency*, p. 27, n. 23.

[80]The term "radar" was coined by the Navy in 1940 and accepted by the Army in 1942. Allison, *New Eye for the Navy*, p. 1, n. 2; Harry M. Davis, "History of the Signal Corps Development of U.S. Army Radar Equipment," in three parts (New York: Office of the Chief Signal Officer, Historical Section Field Office, 1944), pt. 1, p. 2, copy in CMH files; Terrett, *Emergency*, p. 41.

[81]Allison, *New Eye*, pp. 137–41; Howeth, *Communications-Electronics in Navy*, ch. 38. Although the Army exchanged information with the Navy regarding radar, each service conducted its studies independently.

[82]Henry E. Guerlac, *Radar in World War II*, 2 vols. (Los Angeles: Tomash Publishers, 1987), 1: ch. 5; Terrett, *Emergency*, pp. 35–48.

[83]Ltr, Maj Gen James B. Allison to The Adjutant General, 23 Oct 1936, sub: Airplane Detection Device (24 Sep 1936), 2d Ind, quoted by Davis, "Development of Radar Equipment," pt. 1, p. 43.

[84]*Dictionary of American Biography*, s.v. "Blair, William Richards," Supplement 7, p. 58; "Retirement of Col. William R. Blair," *Signal Corps Bulletin* 103 (Jan–Mar 1939): 86–88; "History of Fort Monmouth," pp. 64, 96–102; Davis, "Development of Radar Equipment," pt. 1, chs. 3–6; Terrett, *Emergency*, pp. 35–48. Blair received patent rights for his invention of SCR–268 in 1957. Thompson and Harris, *Outcome*, p. 7, n. 20. Blair

also patented the radiosonde, which used radio signals from unmanned balloons to transmit weather information from the upper atmosphere (Davis, "Development of Radar Equipment," pt.1, p. 19).

[85]Ltr, Harry H. Woodring to Maj Gen James B. Allison, 2 Jun 1937, quoted by Davis, "Development of Radar Equipment," pt. 1, pp. 53–54.

[86]Wesley Frank Craven and James Lea Cate, eds., *The Army Air Forces in World War II*, 7 vols. (Chicago: University of Chicago Press, 1948–1958), 6: 83; Guerlac, *Radar in World War II*, 1: 103.

[87]Terrett, *Emergency*, pp. 46–47; Davis, "Development of Radar Equipment," pt. 1, p. 4.

[88]Scheips, "Introduction," in Scheips, ed., *Military Signal Communications*, vol. 1; Davis, "Development of Radar Equipment," pt. 1, p. 25.

[89]Gibbs increased the number of divisions within his office from four to seven: Meteorological, Personnel, Photographic, Plant and Traffic, Research and Development, Supply, and War Plans and Training. The Signal Office retained this organization until 1941. Terrett, *Emergency*, p. 71.

[90]His positions included vice president of the International Telephone and Telegraph Company, president of the Postal Telegraph Company, and vice chairman of the board and director of the Federal Telephone and Radio Corporation. See Terrett, *Emergency*, pp. 77 and 98.

[91]*Historical Sketch*, pp. 98–99; "Carr, Irving J.," biographical files, DAMH-HSR.

[92]Maurer, *Aviation in U.S. Army*, p. 348; Oakes, Army Command and Administrative Communications System, pt. 1, p. 38; Arch L. Madsen, "CCC Amateur Radio Operators Lauded," *Signal Corps Regimental Association Notes* 6 (Winter 1993): 6–7; Kreidberg and Henry, *Military Mobilization*, pp. 461–63; *ARSO*, 1934, pp. 5–6, AGO 319.12 (9–27–34), RG 407, NARA; *ARSO*, 1935, p. 12, AGO 319.12 (8–19–35), RG 407, NARA; John W. Killigrew, "The Impact of the Great Depression on the Army, 1929–1936" (Ph.D. dissertation, Indiana University, 1960), chs. 12 and 13.

[93]*ARSO*, 1933, p. 6, AGO 319.12 (10–19–33), RG 407, NARA; Leonard S. Wilson, "Army Role in IGY Research," *Army Information Digest* 12 (Oct 1957): 34; Cochrane, *Measures for Progress*, pp. 354–55; J. Tuzo Wilson, *I.G.Y: The Year of the New Moons* (New York: Knopf, 1961), p. 8.

[94]Terrett, *Emergency*, p. 72, n. 7. For information on Allison's career, see *Historical Sketch*, p. 100; "Allison, James Beardner," biographical files, DAMH-HSR; "History of Fort Monmouth," pp. 36–38.

[95]*ARSO*, 1935, p. 2.

[96]Terrett, *Emergency*, p. 70; *ARSO*, 1931, p. 1.

[97]*ARSO*, 1933, pp. 5–6; *Historical Sketch*, p. 104. The *Dellwood* was called back to service as a cableship during World War II. She sank off Attu in the Aleutians in July 1943. See History of Alaska Communication System, typescript in custody of the U.S. Army Signal Museum, Fort Gordon, Georgia. There are two volumes that discuss the cableships during World War II. Volume one contains a chapter about the *Dellwood*. See also U.S. Army, Alaska, *The Army's Role in Building Alaska*, p. 98.

[98]The name was changed per WD Cir 31, 27 May 1936.

[99]Joseph E. Alexander, "Accuracy First," *Recruiting News* 17 (15 Sep 1935): 6–7; Edwin C. Nichols, "Lifeline to the North," *Army Information Digest* 9 (Nov 1954): 32–45.

[100]Bauer, comp., *List of World War I Signal Corps Films*; *ARSO*, 1936, p. 13; Terrett, *Emergency*, pp. 81–82.

[101]*ARSO*, 1936, p. 14.

[102]*ARSO*, 1937, pp. 12–13, AGO 319–12 (8–31–37), RG 407, NARA; *Historical Sketch*, p. 110; Flammer, "Meteorology in U.S. Army," ch. 4; Bates and Fuller, *Weather Warriors*, pp. 46–47. See also AR 95–150, 1 Jul 1937, sub: Air Corps Weather Service.

[103]On becoming chief signal officer, Mauborgne was promoted from colonel to the rank of major general. See "Mauborgne, Joseph Oswald," in *Who Was Who in America* (Chicago: Marquis Who's Who, Inc., 1975); *Historical Sketch*, p. 101; biographical files, DAMH-HSR.

[104]Kahn, *Codebreakers*, p. 7; Finnegan, *Military Intelligence*, pp. 54–55; Clark, *Man Who Broke Purple*, p. 84; Bruce W. Bidwell, *History of the Military Intelligence Division, Department of the Army General Staff: 1775–1941* (Frederick, Md.: University Publications of America, Inc., 1986), pt. 3, ch. 7. After its formation in 1945, Friedman joined the Army Security Agency, which later became the National Security Agency.

[105]The triangular division had a strength of about 13,500, compared to 28,000 for the square division. See T/O 11–7P (Triangular Div), "Signal Company, Division," in *Tables of Organization and Reference Data for the Infantry Division (Triangular)* (Fort Leavenworth, Kans.: Command and General Staff School Press, 1939); Jean R. Moenk, *A History of Large-Scale Army Maneuvers in the United States, 1935–1964* (Fort Monroe, Va.: U.S. Continental Army Command, 1969), pp. 21–22; Terrett, *Emergency*, pp. 84–86, 152; "History of Fort Monmouth," pp. 70–79; John B. Wilson, Divisions and Separate Brigades, draft Ms, ch. 5.

[106]Weigley, *History of the Army*, p. 417.

[107]Kreidberg and Henry, *Military Mobilization*, pp. 380–81; Reingold, Science and Army, pp. 119–31; R. Elberton Smith, *The Army and Economic Mobilization*, United States Army in World War II (Washington, D.C.: Office of the Chief of Military History, Department of the Army, 1959), ch. 2.

[108]Smith, *Army and Economic Mobilization*, p. 45.

[109]Matloff, ed., *American Military History*, pp. 416–17; Terrett, *Emergency*, p. 104.

[110]Matloff, ed., *American Military History*, pp. 417–18; Kreidberg and Henry, *Military Mobilization*, pp. 561–63.

[111]Cary, "Use of the Motor Vehicle in the U.S. Army," p. 193 and table 3, p. 234.

[112]Terrett, *Emergency*, p. 152.

[113]Later that year the Army also conducted maneuvers in New York State, the Carolinas, and Wisconsin. Terrett, *Emergency*, pp. 152–65.

[114]Weigley, *History of Army*, p. 427–33; Matloff, ed., *American Military History*, pp. 419–20.

[115]Terrett, *Emergency*, p. 272. When questioned about his action during congressional hearings four years later, Marshall could not recall why he had relieved Mauborgne.

[116]"Olmstead, Dawson," biographical files, DAMH-HSR; *Historical Sketch*, pp. 118–19.

[117]Roberta Wohlstetter, *Pearl Harbor: Warning and Decision* (Stanford, Calif.: Stanford University Press, 1962), p. 75, n. 5; Finnegan, *Military Intelligence*, pp. 54–55.

[118]PURPLE came into use in 1937. It is a cipher and not a code. See Clark, *Man Who Broke Purple*, ch. 7, and Wohlstetter, *Pearl Harbor*, p. 170, n. 1.

[119]The most comprehensive account of the events leading up to the Pearl Harbor attack is Gordon W. Prange, *At Dawn We Slept: The Untold Story of Pearl Harbor* (New York: McGraw-Hill Book Company, 1981).

[120]Oakes, *Army Command and Administrative Communications System*, pt. 1, pp. 31, 35, 102.

[121]Ibid., pt. 1, pp. 103–07; Terrett, *Emergency*, p. 96.

[122]Davis, "Development of Radar Equipment," pt. 3, ch. 8.

[123]Clark, *Man Who Broke Purple*, p. 169. For details on the role of MAGIC and the Pearl Harbor attack, see Kahn, *Codebreakers*, pp. 1–68; Wohlstetter, *Pearl Harbor*, ch. 3; Bidwell, *Military Intelligence Division*, pt. 4. On the attack itself, see also Terrett, *Emergency*, pp. 299–306; George R. Thompson, Dixie R. Harris, Pauline M. Oakes, and Dulany Terrett, *The Signal Corps: The Test*, United States Army in World War II (Washington, D.C.: Government Printing Office, 1957), pp. 3–10. On Marshall's role, see Pogue, *Marshall*, 2: ch. 10 and app. 1; Mark S. Watson, *Chief of Staff: Prewar Plans and Preparations*, United States Army in World War II (Washington, D.C.: Historical Division, Department of the Army, 1950), pp. 512–18. In the aftermath of the attack, both Kimmel and Short were relieved from their commands.

[124]Henry Steele Commager, ed., *Documents of American History*, 2 vols. (Englewood Cliffs, N.J.: Prentice-Hall, Inc., 1973), 2: 451; Robert Dallek, *Franklin D. Roosevelt and American Foreign Policy, 1932–1945* (New York: Oxford University Press, 1979), p. 312.

[125]As quoted in Charles Hurd, comp., *A Treasury of Great American Quotations* (New York: Hawthorn Books, Inc., 1964), p. 283.

CHAPTER VII

World War II: Establishing the Circuits of Victory

The shock of the Japanese attack on Pearl Harbor galvanized the American people into action. When Congress declared war on the Axis powers in December 1941, a truly global conflict began, with fighting on four of the seven continents and across the seas. By that time the Signal Corps had already undergone a great expansion. Yet its strength of 3,000 officers and 47,000 men represented but a fraction of the manpower needed to support a total war.[1]

The Search for Manpower and Brainpower

On 7 December 1941 Chief Signal Officer Dawson Olmstead had been conducting an inspection of radar sites in Panama. Upon learning of the attack, he hurriedly returned to Washington to oversee the Corps' wartime operations. He faced an extraordinary challenge. The 1941 Troop Basis, the formal War Department authorization for units, envisioned the activation of four field armies and allowed the Signal Corps 1 signal service regiment, 5 air warning regiments, 19 battalions, 32 division signal companies, 2 troops (1 for each cavalry division), 29 platoons, and a variety of specialized companies to meet the needs of radio intelligence, operations, photographic duties, repair, depot storage, construction, and so forth.[2]

Now faced with the problem of finding men to fill these units, the Signal Corps, as in World War I, endeavored to tap the large pool of trained civilian communicators. It did so through a program known as the Affiliated Plan, established in 1940, which enabled the Corps to draw personnel from civilian groups which varied widely, from the telephone and motion picture industries to groups of pigeon fanciers. Rather than organizing an entire unit from the personnel of a particular company, such as the Bell battalions during World War I, the Affiliated Plan used smaller groups of civilian specialists as cadres around which units were created. The Affiliated Plan allowed the Signal Corps to form the nuclei of 404 units. Ironically, radio experts were not among the new recruits, because the Army Amateur Radio System, organized to supplement the Signal Corps during peacetime emergencies such as floods and tornadoes, had no provision for supplying personnel to the Corps in wartime. As a result, many experienced communicators were lost to other branches.[3]

Training men to operate the Signal Corps' increasingly sophisticated equipment presented another challenge. The Corps needed individuals of high aptitude and intelligence for its technical training, but had difficulty securing them. Proficiency in some specialties, such as automatic equipment installation, came only after many months of instruction.[4] The electronics industry could supply skilled personnel, but at the same time the Corps needed to keep those men at their jobs producing communications equipment.[5]

One solution was to seek high-quality recruits. During World War II the Army evaluated its inductees according to the Army General Classification Test (AGCT), which measured both intelligence and aptitude. A score of 100 represented the expected median. Based on the results, the men were divided into five classes, from highest to lowest. Although all arms and services were supposed to receive the same proportion of men from each category, those with needs for high technical proficiency were quick to put in claims for high scorers. The Signal Corps fared well, with 39 percent of the men assigned to its training centers from March to August 1942 coming from Classes I and II; by 1943, 58 percent of its inductees came from these classes.[6]

Even before the war the Signal Corps had opened an enlisted replacement training center at Fort Monmouth in January 1941. The center provided recruits with basic training, after which they enrolled in courses at the center or received advanced specialist training at the Signal School. By December 1941 it had already turned out 13,000 enlisted specialists.[7]

Once war began the Signal Corps quickly outgrew the existing facilities at Monmouth, and Chief Signal Officer Olmstead made arrangements to expand operations to other locations in the vicinity. Consequently, in January 1942 the Signal Corps leased the New Jersey State National Guard Encampment at Sea Girt, a few miles from Monmouth, which became known as Camp Edison. In July 1942 the Corps also established a new post at Eatontown, named Camp Charles Wood, and eventually the headquarters of the replacement center moved there. In October 1942 the training facilities in the Monmouth area became known as the Eastern Signal Corps Training Center. The Signal School, meanwhile, became the Eastern Signal Corps School and included enlisted, officer, officer candidate, and training literature departments.[8]

To handle the wartime flood of personnel, the Signal Corps opened a second replacement training center in February 1942 at Camp Crowder, Missouri, near the town of Neosho in the southwestern corner of the state. Camp Crowder now received most of the Army's signal recruits, including those entering through the Affiliated Plan, who traveled there to receive basic training. Recruits spent three weeks learning the basics of soldiering: drill; equipment, clothing, and tent pitching; first aid; defense against chemical attack; articles of war; basic signal communication; interior guard duty; military discipline; and rifle marksmanship. In July 1942 the Midwestern Signal Corps School opened its doors at Camp Crowder, with a capacity of 6,000 students, and the following month the Corps' first unit training center also opened there. The headquarters established in

Officer candidates at Fort Monmouth march to class.

October 1942 to administer this group of schools was designated the Central Signal Corps Training Center.[9]

But the Army's requirements for technically trained manpower were endless. Camp Crowder soon exceeded its capacity, and a third training facility opened in September 1942 at Camp Kohler, California, near Sacramento. Originally intended to provide basic training only, the Western Signal Corps Training Center eventually became the Corps' third replacement training center as well as its second unit training center. The Western Signal Corps School, part of the center, opened at Davis, California, in January 1943. Using the facilities of the University of California's College of Agriculture, the lucky students learned about radio, wire, and radar in a comfortable academic environment.[10] Meanwhile, the Signal Corps transferred all aircraft warning training to the Southern Signal Corps School at Camp Murphy, Florida, where classes began in June 1942.[11] Thus a nationwide system for preparing signal soldiers took form.

Yet the Signal Corps, like the Army in general, suffered growing pains. The demands of the war mounted faster than the output of the schools, and some men had to be sent to the field before they had learned their jobs. The combat theaters became the finishing schools. Americans invaded North Africa in November 1942, and in early 1943 the Signal Corps instituted a theater training program to produce the signal specialists urgently needed for the fight against German General Erwin Rommel's *Afrika Korps*.[12]

The Signal Corps also suffered from a shortage of adequately trained officers. In some respects, military communications technology had outstripped the civilian variety; the commercial economy had no equivalent for several of the systems being used by the Army, notably radar. Skilled supervisors were hard to find. Although the War Department authorized an additional 500 signal officers shortly after Pearl Harbor, the Corps had difficulty filling the positions. It could draw upon only 10 percent of Reserve Officers Training Corps graduates and, though the output from the officer training schools gradually increased, so too did the demand for qualified men.[13]

Initiated before the nation entered the war, the Electronics Training Group provided another source of officers. The Signal Corps required candidates selected for this program to hold degrees in electrical engineering or physics. They received commissions as second lieutenants in the Reserve. After three weeks of training at the Signal School they went to England to work as student observers at radar stations. They spent three months training at British air warning schools, then five months at defense stations in the British Isles. In the aftermath of Pearl Harbor, the demand for officers caused the British to accelerate and shorten the courses, but the training, though sharply curtailed, proved highly valuable to the United States Army.[14]

Growth was continuous. By mid-1942 the Signal Corps' strength rose to 7,694 officers, 121,727 enlisted men, and 54,000 civilians.[15] Approximately fifty thousand technicians entered the Signal Corps through the Enlisted Reserve Corps and its training program before the president ordered its cessation in December 1942.[16] There were qualitative changes as well, reflecting new outlooks brought by combat experience. In Signal Corps training, the emphasis shifted increasingly from individuals to teams, who received functional on-the-job training in addition to classroom instruction. Radioteletype teams, for example, practiced on the transatlantic systems in the War Department Message Center (later redesignated as the War Department Signal Center), while base depot companies trained at the various Signal Corps depots. The men worked on the same equipment they would find in the field and received instruction geared to their future service in overseas theaters. Thus the 989th Signal Service Company, scheduled for duty in the Pacific, learned pidgin English in addition to its technical specialties.[17] Training continued overseas as well. In sum, approximately 387,000 officers and men completed courses conducted by the Signal Corps.[18]

The Corps also found that it needed more flexible organizations to fit the widely varying conditions encountered in the theaters of war. New "cellular" Tables of Organization and Equipment allowed units to be constructed out of "building blocks" of sections and teams that could be adapted to the situation at hand. Eventually the Signal Corps adopted a master table, TOE 11–500, "Signal Service Organization," dated 1 July 1943, that provided for fifty-four types of teams that could be assembled in any combination and tailored to specific needs. Each team bore a two-letter designation: EF, for example, denoted a sixteen-man radio link team, while EA denoted a four-man crystal grinding section which cut quartz to receive precise radio frequencies. The cellular concept proved so successful that the Army's other technical services adopted it.[19]

By mid-1943 military mobilization was virtually complete, and the Army had nearly reached its authorized strength of 7.7 million men. The Signal Corps, in fact, had a surplus of officers by the summer of 1943, though this situation proved to be short-lived. As of June 1943 the Corps' strength had reached approximately 27,000 officers and 287,000 enlisted men.[20] Beginning in January 1943 the Signal Corps had also begun to receive female soldiers, members of the Women's Army Auxiliary Corps

WACs operate a radio-telephoto transmitter in England.

(WAAC), later designated the Women's Army Corps (WAC). All told, the Signal Corps received at least 5,000 of these women, known as WACs. Both within the United States and overseas, WACs replaced men in such jobs as message center clerks and switchboard operators, releasing the male personnel for other duties. WACs also worked in film libraries and laboratories and performed signal intelligence duties such as cryptography.[21]

Black soldiers played a significant role in the wartime Signal Corps. The Army organized a number of black signal units, many of them to perform construction duties. The first of these units to be deployed outside the continental United States was the 275th Signal Construction Company, which went to Panama in December 1941 to build a pole line. It later participated in four campaigns in Europe. The 42d Signal Construction Battalion, activated in August 1943 at Camp Atterbury, Indiana, served in both the European and the Asiatic-Pacific theaters. Despite the notable accomplishments of these and other units, the Signal Corps remained below its proportionate share of black troops throughout the war.[22]

Under the demands of history's greatest war, the Signal Corps struggled to meet the Army's communications requirements. But even as it reached its greatest expansion in history to that time, an organizational crisis developed at its headquarters that spelled the end of the chief signal officer's career.

Marshall Reshapes the War Department

In order to streamline the operation of the War Department, Chief of Staff George C. Marshall, Jr., initiated a major reorganization that resulted in the most sweeping changes since the early years of the century. Effective 9 March 1942, the Army was divided into three commands: the Army Ground Forces; the Services of Supply, later renamed the Army Service Forces; and the Army Air Forces. General Marshall placed the Signal Corps and the other technical services under the Services of Supply, commanded by Lt. Gen. Brehon B. Somervell, an engineer known for his energy and administrative ability as well as for his prickly personality.[23]

For the Signal Corps, the new setup emphasized its logistics responsibilities over its command and control and its research and development functions. In effect, the Marshall reorganization lowered the Signal Corps' status and allowed it less freedom of action. Chief Signal Officer Olmstead now reported through Somervell rather than directly to the chief of staff, and thus lost much of his former control over the Corps' operations.[24] Yet the Signal Corps retained its designation as a combat arm, and it continued to provide the doctrine and equipment used by every Army communicator.[25]

As the war progressed, General Olmstead found it very difficult to reconcile the many facets of the Corps' mission. He was supposed to guide Army-wide communications, although the Signal Corps controlled communications only to division level, below which the using arms took over. At and above his own level, a number of boards shared his work: the Joint Communications Board (Army-Navy) served the Joint Chiefs of Staff and was the highest coordinating agency in military signals; the Army Communications Board served the General Staff, with the chief signal officer as president.[26] A Signal Corps Advisory Council, with such members as David Sarnoff of RCA, provided him counsel.[27] Such arrangements implied that the chief signal officer was only one player in the complex game of wartime communications, though an important one.

But the Army Service Forces structure, in Olmstead's view, buried him under numerous layers of bureaucracy and hampered operations. As a remedy, he wished to place the chief signal officer on the General Staff and to create a Communications Division with himself at the head and subordinate signal officers in the Ground, Air, and Service Forces. Former Chief Signal Officer Gibbs supported Olmstead's position in a letter to Chief of Staff Marshall. When Marshall in May 1943 appointed a board to investigate Army communications, Olmstead hoped this would provide the opportunity to win the powers he sought. As events unfolded, however, the results differed dramatically from his intent.

The Board to Investigate Communications took testimony from 11 May to 8 June 1943 from officers representing all branches of the Army and from Admiral Joseph R. Redman, Director of Naval Communications. General Somervell, in his appearance before the committee, spoke harshly of the chief signal officer, blaming all of the Corps' problems on him. But the board proved more independent than Somervell may have anticipated. In its report of 21 June, the board asserted that "control and coordination of signal communications within the Army are inadequate, unsatisfactory and confused," and recommended that a Communications and Electronics Division be established on the General

General Ingles

Staff. Despite Somervell's opinion, the board members unanimously agreed that the Army's communication problems could not be solved by personnel changes alone.[28] But this was unsatisfactory to the chief of staff. General Marshall disapproved the board's recommendation, opting instead to remove Olmstead as chief signal officer.[29]

Olmstead stepped down on 30 June 1943. His successor, Maj. Gen. Harry C. Ingles, had been a classmate of Somervell's in the West Point class of 1914. During World War I, Ingles was an instructor at the Signal Corps training camps at Leon Springs, Texas, and Camp Meade, Maryland. Throughout the 1920s and 1930s he held a variety of Signal Corps and staff assignments. When World War II broke out, Ingles was in Panama serving as signal officer of the Caribbean Defense Command. Following his promotion to major general in December 1942, he became deputy commander, United States Forces in Europe, early in 1943. Upon assuming the post of chief signal officer a few months later, Ingles inherited the problems faced by Olmstead as he guided the Signal Corps throughout the remainder of the war.[30]

Maj. Gen. James A. Code, Jr., served both Olmstead and Ingles as assistant chief signal officer and in particular handled supply matters. As the only high-ranking signal officer to serve throughout the war in the same position, he provided continuity to the Signal Corps' policy and administration.[31] One thing had clearly been settled by the changes: the Marshall reorganization stuck, and technical service officers had to adapt to it as best they could.

The Worldwide Network

In contrast to headquarters politics, the Signal Corps had many successes in its practical work for the war effort. Few of its endeavors were more important then providing worldwide communications for America's civilian and military leaders.

In order to tie together the nation's far-flung defense system, the War Department Radio Net expanded its services to become the Army Command and Administrative Network (ACAN), connecting the command headquarters in Washington with all the major field commands at home and overseas. It also maintained connections with the Navy's circuits and the civil communication systems of Allied and neutral nations.[32] By replacing radio circuits with radiotele-type, which operated automatically, transmission speed improved dramatically.[33] The 17th Signal Service Company continued to operate station WAR at the War Department Signal Center, which served as the hub of the network. In January 1943 the center moved from the Munitions Building in downtown Washington, where it had been located since its creation in 1923, to the newly built Pentagon across the Potomac River in Virginia.

Through the ACAN's facilities the Signal Corps provided communications for the conferences held by the Allied leaders, beginning with Casablanca in January 1943 and ending with Potsdam in mid-1945. Arrangements for the Yalta Conference in February 1945 were probably the most difficult and elaborate because the meeting was held on short notice in a remote location on the Crimean Peninsula. A floating radio relay station aboard the USS *Catoctin*, outfitted with one of the first long-range radioteletypewriter transmitters installed on a ship, enabled President Roosevelt to communicate with Washington and with his commanders in the field. The president was so impressed with the facilities that he referred to the "modern miracle of communications" in his report to Congress.[34] In addition to these conferences, the three officers and forty enlisted men of the White House signal detachment, created in the spring of 1942, provided communications for the president and his staff wherever they traveled. Even Roosevelt's private railroad car had its own radio station, with call letters WTE.[35]

To enable the ACAN to provide worldwide service, the Signal Corps designed an equatorial belt of communication circuits that avoided the polar regions where magnetic absorption of radio waves inhibited operation.[36] Maj. Gen. Frank E. Stoner, chief of the Army Communications Service (the division in the Office of the Chief Signal Officer which administered the ACAN), estimated that the Army sent eight words overseas for every bullet fired by Allied troops. An average of 50 million words a day traveled over its circuits by 1945. In May 1944 the Signal Corps, using the ACAN's facilities, sent a nine-word test message around the world in just three and one-half minutes. A similar test a year later accomplished the feat in just nine and a half seconds.[37] The independent Army Airways Communications System also depended in part upon the Signal Corps, which installed its equipment and often operated its stations.[38]

While circling the globe, the Signal Corps encountered a variety of problems. In Iran its men labored under summertime temperatures high enough to kill mosquitoes and sand flies. Equipment likewise suffered under such extreme conditions. The few signal units stationed in the China-Burma-India Theater faced a scarcity of supplies and transport. They utilized whatever means of motive power were available, including donkeys, camels, and elephants. The pachyderms also proved useful both for handling poles and as elevated platforms from which to string wire (giving new meaning to the term "trunk lines").[39] To withstand the torrid climate of the Pacific islands, where field wire deteriorated in just a few weeks, signal equipment required "tropicalization," such as spraying it with shellac, to provide protection from heat, moisture, rust, and fungus. Other tropical hazards included the ants of New Guinea, which attacked the insulation on telephone wires and radio connections.[40]

Signal Security and Intelligence

During World War II the adversaries engaged in spectacular battles on the ground, in the air, and across the seas. They also waged a less visible, yet vitally important, type of combat over the airwaves: electronic warfare. On the Western Front during World War I, listening to and jamming enemy signals had become routine. But advances in communications technology since 1918 had resulted in sophisticated cryptological equipment that produced codes too complex for the human mind alone to solve. Moreover, the immense volume of radio traffic presented an enormous burden of work for intelligence experts. Equally sophisticated solutions had to be found. The success of the Allies in breaking the Japanese and German cipher systems played a crucial role in the outcome of the war. Only since the 1970s, however, has the full story begun to emerge from records long withheld from public view.

For most of World War II the Signal Corps retained responsibility for the Army's signal security and intelligence activity, passing on its results to the Military Intelligence Division of the General Staff for evaluation. The Signal Intelligence Service (redesignated in 1942 as the Signal Security Service and in 1943 as the Signal Security Agency) mushroomed from approximately three hundred employees on 7 December 1941 to over ten thousand by V–J Day.[41] In August 1942 the Signal Intelligence Service moved its headquarters from downtown Washington to Arlington Hall, a former private girls' school in the Virginia suburbs, where it gained the space and security its burgeoning activities demanded. Soon thereafter, Vint Hill Farms near Warrenton, Virginia, became one of the agency's primary monitoring stations. In October 1942 Vint Hill also became the site of the cryptographic school.

The 2d Signal Service Company performed the Signal Intelligence Service's intelligence-gathering duties. Activated at Fort Monmouth in 1939 under the command of 1st Lt. Earle F. Cook, the unit expanded to battalion size in April 1942. In the field its personnel formed detachments that operated the monitoring stations within the United States and around the world. During the war the battalion's strength grew to a maximum of 5,000, including WACs. Despite its size, the Army Service Forces denied the Signal Corps' request to enlarge the unit to a regiment.[42]

The 1942 Marshall reorganization making the Signal Corps a subordinate element of the Army Service Forces created almost insurmountable bureaucratic barriers to the smooth coordination of the collection of communications intelligence by the Signal Corps and its analysis by the Military Intelligence Division. As a result of these strains, operational control of the Signal Security Agency passed in December 1944 to the Military Intelligence Division, and in September 1945 the newly established Army Security Agency took over its functions. By that time the Signal Corps had built a sophisticated intelligence collection system, resting ultimately on new technology.

Several new devices enhanced communications security. For the rapid enciphering and deciphering of written messages, the Signal Corps developed an automatic machine called the Sigaba. William F. Friedman, the Army's foremost cryptologist, had played a primary role in its design.[43] While the enemy never broke the Sigaba's security during the war, the Army did have a close call when a truck carrying one of the machines disappeared near Colmar, France, in February 1945. After six weeks of frantic searching, soldiers found the lost Sigaba in a nearby river. Fortunately, Nazis had not stolen the truck. Instead, a French soldier, unaware of the vehicle's secret cargo, had apparently "borrowed" the vehicle, abandoning its trailer and dumping the contents, encased in three safes, into the water.[44]

Encoding and deciphering were only part of the problem. Early in the war Roosevelt and Churchill had used a scrambler telephone to communicate, but the Germans could intercept its signals. By the spring of 1944 a more secure means was available—a radiotelephone system known as SIGSALY.[45] High-level commanders also used SIGSALY to direct troops and equipment. Designed by Bell Telephone Laboratories and manufactured by Western Electric, a single SIGSALY terminal weighed about ninety tons, occupied a large room, and required air conditioning. Its massive size obviously prevented its use in the field. Members of the 805th Signal Service Company, made up largely of Bell System employees, operated the equipment. Users spoke into a handset, and their speech patterns were encoded electronically and transmitted by shortwave radio. On both the sending and receiving ends, Signal Corps technicians played special phonograph records, destroyed after each use, which contained the secret key that masked the voices of the speakers with white noise. Pushing communications technology into new frontiers, SIGSALY pioneered such innovations as digital transmissions and pulse code modulation. While the Germans monitored the system, they never succeeded in breaking it. The details of SIGSALY's technical features remained classified until 1976.[46]

A third security system, known as SIGTOT, permitted two-way teletype conferences between widely separated parties. The equipment provided a written record of the matters discussed and, in some locations, displayed communications received on a screen. SIG-TOT could be operated over any reliable landline or radioteletype channel, and installations were available at nineteen overseas stations by V–J Day.[47]

While safeguarding the Army's own communications, the Signal Corps actively attempted to breach the security of enemy signals. In the field, radio intelligence units located enemy stations and intercepted them. For example, the 138th Signal Radio Intelligence Company, serving in the Pacific, contained about twenty Japanese-American soldiers, known as Nisei, who could read Japanese cleartext messages.[48] To monitor friendly radio traffic, the Signal Corps created a new type of unit known as SIAM (signal

German troops use the Enigma in the field.

information and monitoring). In addition to detecting breaches of security, these units were intended to inform commanders of the state of operations in forward units.[49]

Certainly one of the greatest signal intelligence feats of the war involved the breaking of the German cipher machine Enigma. While Friedman and his colleagues concentrated on cracking the Japanese codes, the British devoted their efforts to the German encryption systems. Although the Enigma resembled a standard typewriter, it operated by means of complex electrical circuitry. A system of rotors, the number of which could be varied, enciphered messages automatically and in such an infinitely complicated manner that the Germans believed it impregnable.

The Signal Corps, in fact, had purchased an early commercial version of the Enigma in 1928. Additionally, a signal officer, Maj. Paul W. Evans, while serving as assistant military attaché in Berlin in 1931, had been given a demonstration of Enigma's abilities by the German War Department. Friedman attempted to solve the machine's mysteries, but failed to do so as his attention became increasingly focused on Japan and the ultimately successful attempt to break the PURPLE code.[50]

Fortunately, the Polish secret service succeeded during the 1930s in breaking the Enigma enciphering process and in reproducing a copy of the machine. When Poland fell in 1939, the Poles shared their knowledge with the French and British. By that time the Germans had switched to a more complicated Enigma system which the Poles had not yet broken. That task fell to British analysts at Bletchley Park, who eventually solved the puzzle. Once accomplished, they called the intelligence thereby produced ULTRA. As the British became more adept at using the knowledge gained from ULTRA, it began to have a significant effect on the conduct of the war.[51]

The British shared their intelligence with the Americans, but they did not immediately divulge their collection methods. When Eisenhower arrived in London in June 1942 to begin preparations for Operation TORCH, the Allied invasion of North Africa, he received a briefing on ULTRA directly from Prime Minister Churchill.[52] Meanwhile, Friedman and his staff had been able to use PURPLE intercepts to gain information about German war plans via reports to Tokyo from the Japanese embassy in Berlin.[53] Finally, in mid-1943, Friedman and others were given access to the British Enigma machine known as "the bombe." Thereafter American Army officers participated in the intelligence-gathering activities at Bletchley Park.[54]

Radio deception played an important role in the success of the D-day invasion, and much of the information that made that achievement possible came from ULTRA. ULTRA also proved a significant factor during the Allied drive across France. With their communications system disintegrating, the Germans increasingly relied upon radio and thereby unwittingly allowed ULTRA to reveal more and more of their plans. As the Germans fell back on their homeland, however, they could once again employ wire networks that were less susceptible to interception than radio. Before the Ardennes counteroffensive, the Germans imposed radio silence, which rendered ULTRA impotent. Although ULTRA remained important as a source of information until the end of the war, its role after November 1944 was much reduced.[55]

Perhaps the most unusual signal security procedure practiced during the war was the use of American Indians as "code-talkers." Because few non-Indians knew the difficult native languages, which in many cases had no written form, they provided ideal codes for relaying secret operational orders. In the European Theater several members of the Comanche tribe served as voice radio operators with the 4th Signal Company of the 4th Infantry Division. While the Army recruited only about fifty Native Americans for such special communication assignments, the Marines recruited several hundred Navajos for duty in the Pacific.[56]

On the home front the United States government, as it had done during World War I, placed some restrictions upon broadcasting, including the closure of all amateur radio stations on 8 December 1941.[57] The president created the Office of Censorship a few days later. It contained a cable division operated by Navy personnel to censor cable and radio communications, and a postal division operated

Comanche code-talkers of the 4th Signal Company

by Army personnel to censor mail. The domestic press and radio operated under voluntary censorship guidelines, and on several occasions the press leaked the fact that the United States could read the enemy's codes. (Fortunately, the enemy was not paying attention.)[58] Domestic commercial broadcasting, meanwhile, continued with minimal disruption.[59] Unlike during the nation's two preceding wars, the international undersea cables were never cut. Despite fears that the enemy was using them to gain information, investigations after the war found no evidence that this had been the case.[60]

During World War II signal intelligence and security assumed critical importance, and the efforts of the Army's intelligence specialists undoubtedly contributed to bringing the war to a speedier conclusion than would have otherwise been possible. Improvements in the handling and dissemination of signal intelligence had, by 1945, helped remedy the deficiencies evident at the time of Pearl Harbor.

Photography: Shooting the War

While photography had long been part of the Signal Corps' mission, either officially or unofficially, its value and versatility had never been fully appreciated or exploited. For the first half of the war the Signal Corps' photographic activities garnered mostly criticism. For one thing, the duties of Army photographers had not been spelled out clearly either for themselves or for the commanders under whom they served. By the end of the war, however, improvements in training and organization had overcome most of the initial difficulties. As for the significance of the Signal Corps' effort, the photographic record of World War II speaks for itself.[61]

Reflecting the expanded scope of its work during wartime, the Photographic Division of the Office of the Chief Signal Officer became the Army Pictorial Service on 17 June 1942.[62] Photographic training initially took place at Fort Monmouth. In February 1942, however, the Signal Corps had purchased from Paramount Studios its studio at Astoria, Long Island, which became the Signal Corps Photographic Center.[63] After undergoing renovation, the center opened in May 1942. It included the Signal Corps Photographic School, which absorbed the training function from Monmouth and taught both still- and motion-picture techniques. Professional photographers from the New York press assisted with the instruction. Since Army photographers were also soldiers, they first received basic training at a replacement center to learn to aim and shoot with more than just a camera.[64]

The Signal Corps retained its photographic facilities at the Army War College in Washington and augmented them by opening a still-picture sublaboratory in the Pentagon in early 1943. In 1944 the Corps consolidated all of its still-picture laboratory operations there. The Pentagon also housed the Corps' Still Picture Library with its motion-picture counterpart located at Astoria. The Signal Corps also acquired a 300-seat auditorium and four projection rooms at the Pentagon for official screenings.[65]

The Army had conducted little prewar planning regarding the procurement of photographic equipment and supplies. Consequently, the Signal Corps used standard commercial photographic products almost exclusively. Due to the limited supply of those items, the Signal Corps early in the war urged private citizens to sell their cameras to the Army. Film became officially classified as a scarce commodity and came under the control of the War Production Board. In April 1943 the Signal Corps established the Pictorial Engineering and Research Laboratory at Astoria to conduct tests and experiments of photographic material and equipment. Among its projects the laboratory adapted a radio shelter for use as a portable photographic laboratory and darkroom and developed a lightweight combat camera.[66]

The Signal Corps provided photographic support to the Army Air Forces at the training film production laboratory at Wright Field, Ohio. Due to friction between the two branches over the division of responsibilities, however, the Signal Corps withdrew its personnel from the laboratory at the end of 1942 and left it wholly an Air Forces operation. Until the opening of the Astoria center, a training film laboratory had also been housed at Monmouth.[67]

Meanwhile, the Signal Corps continued and expanded its relationship with the commercial film industry. Under the Affiliated Plan, the Research Council of the Academy of Motion Picture Arts and Sciences sponsored the organization of

The Signal Corps Photographic Center at Astoria, Long Island

five photographic companies.[68] Moreover, although the Army had previously used films to teach soldiers how to fight, it needed help explaining why the war was necessary. At General Marshall's instigation, Frank Capra, maker of such classic motion pictures as *It Happened One Night* (1934) and *Mr. Smith Goes to Washington* (1939), received a commission as a major in the Signal Corps in February 1942. As commander of the 834th Signal Service Photographic Detachment, a unit activated especially for the purpose, Capra created a series of orientation films to help the men in uniform understand the war. This series of seven films, titled *Why We Fight*, proved highly successful at informing both soldiers and civilians about the issues at stake.[69] By 1945 Capra had turned out a total of seventeen films for the Army and received the Distinguished Service Medal for his work. One of the members of Capra's documentary film crew was Theodor Seuss Geisel, who later became famous as the children's author, Dr. Seuss.[70] In addition to Capra, several other Hollywood figures contributed their talents to the war effort. Producer Darryl F. Zanuck, a colonel in the Signal Corps, supervised Signal Corps photographic activities during the fighting in North Africa and Italy. Critics have long considered Capt. John Huston's *San Pietro*, depicting operations during the Italian campaign, a masterpiece of documentary filmmaking.[71] Recently, however, historian Peter Maslowski carefully scrutinized the authenticity of Huston's film. The term documentary is misleading because Huston staged much of *San Pietro*'s action after the battle took place.

Making a Signal Corps training film at Astoria

While Huston's film is dramatically effective, it and others of its genre are not necessarily objective accounts of events as they actually happened.[72]

Photography found a variety of uses. Training films provided an effective means for teaching and indoctrinating the masses of inductees. Studies showed that films cut training time by at least 30 percent.[73] The Signal Corps rescored many of these films into foreign languages for use by our non-English–speaking Allies. In the field, the Signal Corps distributed entertainment films that provided an important means of recreation for the soldiers. On the home front, still and motion pictures marked the progress of the struggle. Newsreels, shown in the nation's theaters, brought the war home to millions of Americans in the days before television. Signal Corps footage comprised 30 to 50 percent of each newsreel.[74] Meanwhile, the still pictures taken by Army photographers illustrated the nation's books, newspapers, and magazines. Although the government placed some restrictions upon the kinds of images that could be shown, the public received a more realistic look at warfare than ever before.[75]

Black and white photography remained the norm for combat coverage, but Army cameramen used color film to a limited extent. In addition to being more costly, color film required more careful handling than black and white. A significant innovation occurred with the development of telephoto techniques, or the electronic transmission of photographs, which meant that pictures could reach Washington from the front in minutes. That technology anticipated the "fax" machines of a later era.[76]

For planning purposes General Marshall ordered the compilation of shots illustrating the tactical employment of troops and equipment for presentation weekly to selected staff officers and commanding generals in Washington and all the overseas theaters. Each week the Signal Corps reviewed more than 200,000 feet of combat film to compile the *Staff Film Report.* Declassified versions became combat bulletins that were issued to the troops.[77]

V-Mail represented a new variation in photography. To save precious cargo space in ships and airplanes, the bulk of personal correspondence could be reduced by microfilming it. While the Army Postal Service had overall responsibility for V-Mail operations, the Signal Corps managed its technical aspects. The Signal Corps operated V-Mail stations in active theaters while commercial firms, such as Eastman Kodak, took over where conditions permitted. At the receiving end, the film was developed, enlarged, and printed into 4½ by 5 inch reproductions. V-Mail service began in the summer of 1942 and grew rapidly. From June 1942, when 53,000 letters were handled, usage skyrocketed to reach a peak volume of over 63 million letters processed in April 1944.[78] Although the processing was a laborious and mind-numbing procedure, it paid off in soldiers' morale and the peace of mind of their loved ones at home. Official Photo Mail provided similar service for official documents with the Signal Corps, for security reasons, doing all the processing.[79] In addition to mail, unofficial photos taken by the soldiers themselves had to be developed by the Signal Corps and censored. By April 1944 this amounted to 7,000 rolls in an average week in the European Theater alone.[80]

But some believed there was more to be exposed than just film. In August 1942 the Senate Special Committee Investigating the National Defense Program, chaired by Senator Harry S. Truman, began initial inquiries into the Army's photographic activities. The committee's questions focused on the training film program and its relationship with Hollywood. Critics had alleged that the Research Council of the Academy of Motion Picture Arts and Sciences, which had handled all of the Signal Corps' contracts, exerted too much influence over the program. In particular, they had focused on the role of Colonel Zanuck: he concurrently served as chairman of the Research Council, executive of a film studio (Twentieth Century-Fox), and an officer of the Signal Corps.

The impending congressional inquiry spurred General Somervell to initiate his own series of investigations. As a result, Somervell directed Chief Signal Officer Olmstead to decentralize the operations of the Army Pictorial Service and give more authority to the Signal Corps Pictorial Center. In the future, a western branch of the center would oversee all new production projects in Hollywood, with the Research Council retained in an advisory capacity only.

Early in 1943 the Truman Committee began hearings on the Army Pictorial Service. Although Olmstead had already begun to make the recommended

Signal Corps photographic techni-
cian in full regalia

administrative changes, Somervell removed the Army Pictorial Service from the Signal Corps' control and placed it directly under his own supervision. Meanwhile, the Truman Committee found no fault with the films produced in Hollywood by the Research Council and exonerated Zanuck. After the hearings had concluded, Somervell in July 1943 returned the Army Pictorial Service to the Signal Corps, now headed by General Ingles. Truman, whose work on the committee had made him well known, went on to become Roosevelt's presidential running mate in 1944. When Roosevelt died in office in April 1945, Truman became the nation's thirty-third president.[81]

Somervell remained worried about the Signal Corps' "picture business" as he received complaints about the confusion surrounding photographic operations in the field. Although Army photographers took millions of pictures, too many merely showed high-ranking officers engaged in such activities as eating lunch, reviewing parades, or receiving awards. The new chief signal officer continued to make improvements in the Pictorial Service, and Somervell's concerns gradually disappeared.[82]

The Army Ground Forces' tables of organization assigned one photo company to each field army. Each company contained four general assignment units: Type A units took still and silent motion pictures, while Type B units shot newsreels. The company also included two laboratory units. In the field, the company's personnel actually operated in small teams and detachments wherever needed. Detachments of the same company might be scattered throughout more than one theater. Subsequent revisions to the tables of organization provided for more flexible units using the cellular concept. Special photographic teams from the Signal Corps Pictorial Center supplemented the field units and covered all headquarters installations as well as the Army Service Forces. The assignment of photographic officers to the staffs of theater commanders, which the War Department directed in May 1943, resulted in improved supervision of photographic activities.[83]

As the war began to wind down, Capra, now a colonel, directed two films to explain what happened next and to keep morale up. The first, *Two Down and One to Go*, dealt with the defeat of Germany and the Army's plans for redeployment

Signal Corps cameramen wade through a stream during the invasion of New Guinea, April 1944.

to the Pacific. In particular, it explained the Army discharge system, a topic on everyone's mind. The film was released simultaneously to military and civilian audiences on 10 May 1945. Two weeks later the Army released the second film, *On to Tokyo*.[84] In July 1945 a Signal Corps photograph of the "Big Three" world leaders at Potsdam (President Truman, Prime Minister Atlee, and Marshal Stalin) became one of the first published news pictures transmitted by radio for reproduction in color.[85]

In retrospect, the Signal Corps cameramen performed a remarkable service for historians and for the understanding of World War II by future generations. Many of their pictures, as critics complained, were banal or merely intended to compliment the local brass. Yet they also took memorable pictures, which have helped to define the image of the war for those who never saw it. Overall, they bequeathed a unique, epic, visual record without a parallel for drama, amplitude, and detail.

Equipment: Research, Development, and Supply

Maj. Gen. Roger B. Colton headed the Signal Supply Services, which bore the responsibility for research and development as well. A graduate of Yale University and the Massachusetts Institute of Technology, Colton had worked at the Monmouth laboratories with William Blair on the development of radar. After Blair's retirement in 1938, Colton had succeeded him as director of the Signal

Corps Laboratories.[86] Thus he approached the problems of wartime research and development with an admirable technical background.

As with training, the wartime expansion of research and development activities at Fort Monmouth soon overwhelmed the available facilities. Consequently, the Corps rapidly set up new laboratories nearby. Early in 1942 the Signal Corps Radar Laboratory, later known as the Camp Evans Signal Laboratory, opened at Belmar, New Jersey.[87] Other new research facilities included the Eatontown Signal Laboratory for work on wire, meteorology, and direction-finding and the Coles Signal Laboratory at Camp Coles in Red Bank, New Jersey, which developed radio equipment. The number of laboratory personnel working under Colton increased to 358 officers and over 14,000 civilians within six months after Pearl Harbor.[88] While greatly expanding its own facilities, the Signal Corps also depended heavily upon commercial firms such as Westinghouse and General Electric for research and development.[89]

Problems began with supply. To control the nation's economic mobilization, the federal government created a variety of agencies. In January 1942 President Roosevelt formed the War Production Board, which played a role similar to that of the War Industries Board during World War I. By suspending the manufacture of many consumer goods, such as cars and light trucks and commercial radios and phonographs, the board forced companies to devote full production to military items.[90] But for industry in general, and the electronics industry in particular, prewar estimates fell far below actual requirements, and shortages of essential materials held up production.

In the case of rubber, vital to the manufacture of field wire, the Japanese had cut off much of the supply from the Far East. Although the search began for synthetic materials, technical problems in their production and labor shortages slowed their introduction. Quartz needed for radio crystals remained scarce, and efforts to produce an artificial substitute met with only limited success.[91] To obtain enough copper, "the metal of communications systems," in the summer of 1942 the Army furloughed 4,000 soldiers who had formerly been copper miners. Copper pennies became rare, replaced by zinc versions. Silver, an excellent electrical conductor and not on the government's list of critical materials, became a copper substitute in electrical equipment, and half a billion dollars' worth of silver coins and bullion were borrowed from the United States Treasury for conversion to transformer windings and other items.[92]

The Signal Corps had received its first billion-dollar budget appropriation in March 1942. To meet the need for trained supply officers, the Signal Corps opened a school for supply training at Camp Holabird, Maryland, late in 1943. But long before that the Corps was accepting every two weeks as much equipment as it had acquired throughout the entire course of World War I.[93] The "big five" electronics manufacturers (Western Electric, General Electric, Bendix, Westinghouse, and RCA) received the bulk of the contracts, although the government required that a certain percentage of the work be subcontracted to smaller firms. Radio and radar equipment accounted for over 90 percent of the Corps' procurement budget.[94]

The burgeoning size of the Signal Corps' equipment catalogue gives an idea of the increased specialization of its activities. While the Corps had used some 2,500 different items of equipment during World War I, it needed more than 70,000 by June 1943. By the war's end the number of separate items had risen to over 100,000.[95] The sheer magnitude of the supply effort created problems of production, inspection, storage, and distribution that dwarfed anything the Corps had ever faced and could scarcely have been imagined by prewar planners. The provision of spare parts, in particular, plagued the Corps throughout the war.[96]

Radar equipment remained in short supply. Since there had been no radar industry prior to the war, one had to be built from scratch.[97] The Signal Corps continued to maintain its Aircraft Radio Laboratory at Wright Field, which established a separate radar division in 1942. Through the Joint Communications Board, the Army and Navy worked together on radar development.[98]

In solving the radar problem, the Signal Corps benefited greatly from the contributions of civilian scientists working for the National Defense Research Committee (NDRC), a government agency established in June 1940 through the efforts of Dr. Vannevar Bush, a renowned electrical engineer who served as president of the Carnegie Institution of Washington and chairman of the National Advisory Committee for Aeronautics. Modeled after the NACA, the committee included military representatives and cooperated closely with the technical services of the Army, particularly the Signal Corps, on matters of applied research.[99]

One of the most important accomplishments of the NDRC was the establishment of the Radiation Laboratory at the Massachusetts Institute of Technology where physicists worked on the development of microwave radar. Progress was greatly facilitated by the exchange of technical information with the British, whose discovery of the resonant-cavity magnetron, an electronic vacuum tube that could produce strong, high-frequency pulses, proved especially valuable. Details of this breakthrough had been brought to the United States by the Tizard Mission, a group of scientific experts who arrived in August 1940, led by Sir Henry Tizard, rector of the Imperial College of Science and Technology.[100]

In 1941 the NDRC became part of the new Office of Scientific Research and Development (OSRD), also administered by Dr. Bush. The OSRD focused its efforts on weapons development, notably radar, as well as on radio and other forms of communication. The proximity fuze numbered among the projects with which it became involved. In general, the OSRD negotiated contracts with research institutions, both universities and private firms, as well as with government agencies such as the Bureau of Standards. Under its auspices the government undertook the Manhattan Project to develop the atomic bomb, an endeavor that was subsequently transferred to the Army.[101]

Thanks to the work of both military and civilian scientists, radar technology improved dramatically during the course of the war. Microwave devices, such as the SCR–582 introduced in North Africa, proved especially valuable. Their shorter wavelengths and narrower beams of radiation made them less susceptible to enemy jamming.[102] Even the British, who had earlier severely criticized American radar, praised the new versions.[103] Another model, the SCR–584, was "the answer to the antiaircraft artilleryman's prayer" and the "best ground radar airplane killer of the war."[104] With a longer range, it replaced the SCR–268.[105] Beginning at the Anzio beachhead in February 1944, the SCR–584 proved to be an excellent gun-laying radar. The British, who had chosen not to develop radar for antiaircraft purposes, used the 584 to defeat German "buzz bomb" (V–1) attacks that began in the summer of 1944. The 584 further demonstrated its versatility through addi-tional uses as an aid in bombing and for meteorological purposes to detect storms. Both the SCR–582 and the 584 were the products of the Radiation Laboratory.[106]

Radio relay equipment, the marriage of wire and radio, first used in North Africa, proved to be one of the war's most significant innovations in communica-tions, combining the best features of both systems. Given the nomenclature AN/TRC, for Army-Navy Transportable Radio Communications, it became known as antrac. The multichannel equipment provided several speech and tele-type circuits and connected directly into the telephone and teletype switchboards at either end. It could be installed much faster than conventional wire lines and with fewer personnel. During fast-moving operations, the equipment could be carried forward in a truck and trailer. It differed from standard field radios in that it offered duplex connections and could not be intercepted as easily. Antrac could also transmit pictures, drawings, and typewritten text by facsimile. For operations in the Pacific, antrac (or VHF, as it was commonly called in this theater) solved the problem of communicating over water and hostile jungle terrain. It was also used for ship-to-shore communications and to link beachheads to bases.[107]

At the Signal Corps' request, Bell Laboratories developed the first microwave multichannel radiotelephone system, known as AN/TRC–6. Designed to provide trunk lines for a field army, it was capable of high-grade two-way communications over thousands of miles. AN/TRC–6 arrived in Europe in time for use at the end of the war and became a major communication link in the Rhine Valley. In the Pacific Theater, the equipment moved no farther west than Hawaii before the war ended.[108]

Other advances in communications equipment included the development of spiral-four cable, an improvement over W–110, which had proven of limited use during maneuvers. Originally developed by the Germans, spiral-four received its name from the spiral arrangement of its four wire conductors around a fiber core. Encased in an insulating rubber jacket, the wire provided "long-range carrying power with minimum electrical loss and cross talk."[109] Spiral-four had a greater carrying capacity than multiple open wire lines and did not require tedious instal-lation procedures: setting poles, stringing wire, and attaching crossarms. It could be laid on the ground or through water (fresh or salt) or buried underground. The new wire made long-range, heavy-duty communications possible, and the Signal Corps accepted spiral-four as standard in February 1942. In addition to its other fine qualities, natives in the Southwest Pacific found that the wire made "the best belts they ever had," reminiscent of how curious Civil War soldiers had once used then-novel field telegraph wire for various purposes unrelated to communication.[110] The Signal Corps continued to use W–110 for forward communications as well as the lighter-weight assault wire, W–130.[111]

Despite new developments, the Signal Corps still relied upon older electrical items such as the field telegraph set TG–5 (buzzer, battery, and key), the field telephone EE–8 (battery powered), and a sound-powered phone TP–3 requiring no battery.[112] The original walkie-talkie, designed to be carried on a soldier's back, underwent significant changes to become the SCR–300, an FM set with a range of two miles and which weighed about thirty-five pounds.[113] British Prime Minister Winston Churchill, attending military demonstrations at Fort Jackson, South Carolina, in June 1942, took particular delight in carrying and operating this device.[114] The first models reached the field, where they found ready acceptance, in 1943. Another short-range, portable telephone, the SCR–536, became the infantry frontline set. Operating on AM and weighing just five pounds, it could be used with one hand. Hence this device received the name "handie-talkie."[115]

Armored forces adopted FM radios in the 500 series, and those of the 600 series belonged to the Field Artillery. The clarity of the static-free FM signals allowed soldiers to communicate over the din of artillery firing and tank noise. One infantry battalion radio operator wrote: "FM saved lives and won battles because it speeded our communications and enabled us to move more quickly than the Germans, who had to depend on AM."[116]

The rush to produce new equipment resulted in problems with systems integration. For instance, the FM walkie-talkie could not communicate with the AM handie-talkie. Moreover, because the frequency range of FM tank radios did not overlap that of the walkie-talkie, tank-infantry teams could not talk to each other.[117] Though various attempts were made to solve the problem, the war ended without a satisfactory answer.

The growing demand for electronic communications and the multiplicity of new devices demanded innovations to maximize usage of the finite number of available frequencies. The development of single sideband radio contributed to the conservation of frequencies in the crowded shortwave sector of the electromagnetic spectrum. This technique provided circuits using only one-half of the frequencies that extend on either side of a radio's central frequency, saving the other half for use by others.[118]

During World War II radio's usage expanded beyond simply a means of communication to more deadly pursuits. To improve artillery fire control, the Signal Corps became involved in the development of the proximity, or variable time, fuze. This device consisted of a tiny radar (or doppler radio) set built into the nose of an artillery shell that sensed a target within a hundred feet and automatically detonated when directly over it, rather than upon impact. The fuzes proved considerably more effective than conventional types.[119]

After General Ingles became chief signal officer in 1943, he streamlined the Corps' organization, separating staff and operating functions. In a move that

The SCR–300, better known as the walkie-talkie; below, *radioman with handie-talkie (SCR–536) on Okinawa.*

reflected sound organizational sense plus the growing complexity and size of both operations, he also split General Colton's Signal Supply Services into two elements, divorcing procurement and distribution from research and development.[120] But during the buildup for the Normandy invasion, the Signal Corps was obliged to commandeer trained personnel from wherever it could, including its own laboratories. Consequently, Camp Evans, Eatontown, and Monmouth all took significant cuts during 1943. Yet the restriction on research touched only about 17 percent of the total projects, chiefly in the areas of optics, acoustics, and meteorology.[121]

Nevertheless, the Signal Corps' cutbacks assisted the Army Air Forces in its attempts at expansion.[122] Ever since the inception of the air service, the Signal Corps had struggled with it for authority. Growing ever more powerful as the war progressed, the air arm proceeded with its drive for autonomy. Under the Army's 1942 reorganization the Air Forces had received responsibility for the procurement, research, and development of all items "peculiar" to it.[123] At that time the airmen had tried to capture air electronics, but General Somervell had prevented the transfer of the function.

While the Signal Corps won this opening round, it ultimately lost the battle. Its chronic shortage of scientists, exacerbated by the 1943 personnel reductions, became a decisive factor in the struggle between the two branches. The greatest difficulties stemmed from the Corps' shortcomings in supplying spare parts for radar equipment. The situation came to a head in June 1944 when Maj. Gen. Barney M. Giles, chief of the air staff, completed a study for the chief of staff listing all the reasons why aircraft electronics should be transferred to the Air Forces. Upon reviewing the study, General Marshall agreed with Giles' position, though Somervell lodged his objections to the separation and Chief Signal Officer Ingles argued that it would split "the essential oneness" of all Army communications. Marshall directed that the change be made effective on 26 August 1944.

The details of deciding which items were in fact "peculiar to the AAF" took somewhat longer to determine. The SCR–584, for example, was used by both the air and ground forces. After considerable negotiation, the transfer was completed in the spring of 1945. As a result, the Signal Corps relinquished control over approximately 700 items of electronic equipment along with several of its facilities, including the Aircraft Radio Laboratory at Wright Field. In addition, it lost 600 officers, 380 enlisted men, and over 8,000 civilians from its roster. Among the officers transferred to the Air Forces was General Colton, head of research and development.[124]

Yet there was more to the story than the parochial view of bureaucratic gains and losses. The scientific research effort that accompanied World War II far surpassed anything the nation had ever seen. It was an integrated endeavor that extended beyond the capabilities of the military's technical services to embrace nearly the entire civilian research establishment of the United States. World War II, moreover, witnessed a fundamental shift whereby the federal government, rather than private industry, became the primary source of funds for research and development.[125] Despite the dismantlement of the OSRD after the war, military research and development had become institutionalized both within the Army and throughout industry. Furthermore, the growth of the nation's scientific effort meant that the United States no longer needed to look to Europe for technological leadership.[126]

The Signal Corps' Contribution

At its peak strength, in the fall of 1944, the Signal Corps comprised over 350,000 officers and men, more than six times as many as it had needed to fight World War I. By May 1945 its numbers had declined somewhat to 322,000 and represented about 3.9 percent of the Army's total strength of well over eight million.[127] This percentage corresponded closely to the Signal Corps' proportion of the AEF in 1918. Despite the vast increase in the numbers of men engaged, however, the Signal Corps' battle casualties did not increase substantially over those for the earlier war, totaling just under four thousand officers and men. This relatively low casualty rate clearly reflects the fact that the Signal Corps no longer provided frontline communications.[128]

In other respects, however, the Corps' contribution to the struggle grew enormously. Both strategically and tactically, World War II differed immensely from World War I. New tactics based on mechanization and motorization freed armies from the deadlock of trench warfare. Commanders using field radios could maintain continuous contact with their troops during rapid advances. The increased flexibility of communications helped make mobile warfare possible. Moreover, by means of the ACAN system, worldwide strategic communications became commonplace and required only minutes instead of hours.[129]

More than ever before, success in combat depended upon good communications. General Omar N. Bradley, who finished the war as commander of the 12th Army Group, testified to this reality in his memoirs. Referring to his telephone system as "the most valued accessory of all," he went on to say:

From my desk in Luxembourg I was never more than 30 seconds by phone from any of the Armies. If necessary, I could have called every division on the line. Signal Corps officers like to remind us that "although Congress can make a general, it takes communications to make him a commander."[130]

Never had the maxim been so true as when fast-moving struggles swept over most of the surface of the earth. At home and in all the combat theaters, the Signal Corps provided the Army with rapid and reliable communications that often made the difference between defeat and victory.

Notes

[1] Thompson, Harris, et al., *Test*, p. 23.

[2] Ibid., pp. 36–37. Some signal personnel were assigned to the Army Air Forces. See Craven and Cate, *Army Air Forces in World War II*, 6: 648 and 663–66.

[3] Ruth F. Sadler, History of the Signal Corps Affiliated Plan, typescript [Washington, D.C.: Office of the Chief Signal Officer, Aug 1944], p. 70, copy in CMH files; Thompson, Harris, et al., *Test*, p. 39.

[4] Thompson and Harris, *Outcome*, p. 508.

[5] Thompson, Harris, et al., *Test*, p. 494.

[6] Robert R. Palmer, Bell I. Wiley, and William R. Keast, *The Procurement and Training of Ground Combat Troops*, United States Army in World War II (Washington, D.C.: Historical Division, Department of the Army, 1948), table 2, p. 17, and table 3, p. 18.

[7] Phillips, *Signal Center and School*, pp. 106–09; "History of Fort Monmouth," p. 104; *Historical Sketch*, pp. 126–27; Weigley, *History of Army*, pp. 429–30.

[8] Phillips, *Signal Center and School*, pp. 106–09, 136–49, 153; "History of Fort Monmouth," pp. 103–43; Thompson, Harris, et al., *Test*, pp. 51–52, 319. The replacement training center at Fort Monmouth closed on 10 August 1943, and a unit training center was activated there and remained in operation until November 1943. Phillips, *Signal Center and School*, p. 149.

[9] Thompson, Harris, et al., *Test*, pp. 53–54, 189–96, 319.

[10] Ibid., pp. 196–97, 319.

[11] Prior to completion of the post, classes were held in a warehouse in nearby Riviera, Florida, beginning in April 1942. Camp Murphy closed its doors in October 1944 and air warning training returned to Fort Monmouth. Thompson, Harris, et al., *Test*, pp. 54–55, 212–17, 318; Thompson and Harris, *Outcome*, pp. 537–38.

[12] Thompson and Harris, *Outcome*, p. 29.

[13] Thompson, Harris, et al., *Test*, pp. 44–48.

[14] Terrett, *Emergency*, pp. 288–91; Thompson, Harris, et al., *Test*, pp. 56–57. Besides signal officers, air and antiaircraft officers were also included in the group. For a detailed account, see Ruth F. Sadler, History of the Electronics Training Group in the United Kingdom, typescript [Washington, D.C.: Office of the Chief Signal Officer, Mar 1944], copy in CMH files.

[15] Thompson, Harris, et al., *Test*, p. 315. By the end of 1942 the Signal Corps' percentage of the total Army had risen to 4.5, up from 3 (*Test*, p. 206).

[16] Thompson, Harris, et al., *Test*, p. 318.

[17] Thompson and Harris, *Outcome*, pp. 520–24.

[18] Ibid., p. 539.

[19] Ibid., pp. 22–26.

[20] Ibid., pp. 507, 510–11.

[21] The exact number of WACs serving with the Signal Corps is not known. See Mattie E. Treadwell, *The Women's Army Corps*, United States Army in World War II (Washington, D.C.: Office of the Chief of Military History, Department of the Army, 1954), pp. 307–21; Thompson, Harris, et al., *Test*, p. 316.

[22] Terrett, *Emergency*, p. 284; Thompson, Harris, et al., *Test*, p. 317; Ulysses Lee, *The Employment of Negro Troops*, United States Army in World War II (Washington, D.C.: Office of the Chief of Military History, United States Army, 1966), pp. 132–33; Samuel

A. Barnes, "We, Too, Serve Proudly," *Army Communicator* 2 (Summer 1977): 41–45; unit jackets, 275th Signal Company and 42d Signal Heavy Construction Battalion, DAMH-HSO.

[23]For a brief sketch of Somervell and his previous career, see John D. Millett, *The Organization and Role of the Army Service Forces*, United States Army in World War II (Washington, D.C.: Office of the Chief of Military History, Department of the Army, 1954), "Introduction." For a full-length study of Somervell, see John Kennedy Ohl, *Supplying the Troops: General Somervell and American Logistics in WWII* (DeKalb: Northern Illinois University Press, 1994).

[24]WD Cir 59, 2 Mar 1942; Millett, *Army Service Forces*, ch. 2; Pogue, *Marshall*, 2: ch. 13; Weigley, *History of Army*, pp. 442–43.

[25]Thompson and Harris, *Outcome*, p. 15.

[26]WD Cir 23, 18 Jan 1943.

[27]Thompson, Harris, et al., *Test*, ch. 16. For details on Sarnoff's military service during World War II, for which he received promotion to the rank of brigadier general in the Signal Corps Reserve, see Kenneth Bilby, *The General: David Sarnoff and the Rise of the Communications Industry* (New York: Harper & Row Publishers, 1986), ch. 7.

[28]Thompson, Harris, et al., *Test*, pp. 559–62.

[29]Olmstead was not popular. Although devoted to the Signal Corps and the Army, "he was gruff and careless of human relations and the social amenities" (Thompson, Harris, et al., *Test*, p. 560).

[30]"Ingles, Harry C.," biographical files, DAMH-HSR.

[31]Terrett, *Emergency*, p. 297; Thompson, Harris, et al., *Test*, p. 543; Thompson and Harris, *Outcome*, p. 4; "Code, James Arthur, Jr.," biographical files, DAMH-HSR.

[32]"The ACAN network consisted of the net control station in Washington, a network in the United States, and major trunk routes to overseas theater headquarters, where messages were relayed over the local networks of the individual theaters to their destination." (Thompson and Harris, *Outcome*, p. 142.)

[33]Thompson and Harris, *Outcome*, ch. 18.

[34]Ibid., pp. 588–91; Mary-louise Melia, Signal Corps Fixed Communications in World War II: Special Assignments and Techniques, typescript [Washington, D.C.: Signal Corps Historical Section, Dec 1945], ch. 3, copy in CMH files.

[35]Thompson and Harris, *Outcome*, pp. 603–04; Thompson, Harris, et al., *Test*, pp. 431f; George J. McNally, "The White House Signal Team," *Army Information Digest* 2 (Aug 1947): 24–32.

[36]Thompson, Harris, et al., *Test*, pp. 310–12, 433. On work performed by the Bureau of Standards in this area during the war, see Cochrane, *Measures for Progress*, pp. 403–10.

[37]Thompson and Harris, *Outcome*, pp. 580–82. The complex structure of the Office of the Chief Signal Officer is not discussed in this chapter. For an outline of its organization as of 1 July 1943, see the chart facing page 72 in Terrett, *Emergency*.

[38]Thompson, Harris, et al., *Test*, pp. 427, 448.

[39]Ibid., pp. 460–63.

[40]Ibid., pp. 524–25.

[41]Thompson and Harris, *Outcome*, p. 331.

[42]Thompson, Harris, et al., *Test*, p. 319; Thompson and Harris, *Outcome*, pp. 333–34, 337, 340–42; Kahn, *Codebreakers*, p. 319.

[43]Thompson and Harris, *Outcome*, pp. 336–37, 344; Clark, *Man Who Broke Purple*, pp. 134, 195.

[44]Thomas M. Johnson, "Search for the Stolen Sigaba," *Army* 12 (Feb 1962): 50–55.

[45]Kahn, *Codebreakers*, pp. 294–98.

[46]"SIGSALY Declassified," *Army Communicator* 14 (Spring 1989): 27; David Kahn, "Cryptology and the Origins of Spread Spectrum," *IEEE Spectrum* 21 (Sep 1984): 70–80; Melia, Signal Corps Fixed Communications, pp. 30–33; The Achievements of the Signal Security Agency in World War II, Special Research History 349 [Washington, D.C.: Army Security Agency, 1946], pp. 45–46, copy in author's files. An excerpt from this document is included in James L. Gilbert and John P. Finnegan, eds., *U.S. Army Signals Intelligence in World War II: A Documentary History* (Washington, D.C.: Center of Military History, United States Army, 1993), pp. 88–92. Other names for SIGSALY included the X-System and "Green Hornet," the latter because the system's control tones sounded somewhat like the theme of the popular radio program. For background and technical details of the project, see Fagen, ed., *Bell System, 1925–1975*, pp. 291–317.

[47]Melia, Signal Corps Fixed Communications, pp. 28–30; Thompson and Harris, *Outcome*, pp. 587–88.

[48]Thompson and Harris, *Outcome*, p. 347; Kahn, *Codebreakers*, p. 321.

[49]Thompson and Harris, *Outcome*, pp. 37–38, 65–67, 346–48. The units were organized under TOE 11–875.

[50]Ronald Lewin, *Ultra Goes to War* (New York: McGraw-Hill Book Company, 1978), pp. 27–28, 33–34.

[51]Ibid., pp. 58–60, 69–70. The term ULTRA was also applied to intelligence derived from Japanese sources.

[52]Ibid., p. 239.

[53]Ronald Lewin, *The American Magic: Codes, Ciphers, and the Defeat of Japan* (New York: Farrar Straus Giroux, 1982), ch. 11; Clark, *Man Who Broke Purple*, pp. 161–63; Kahn, *Codebreakers*, p. 273.

[54]Gilbert and Finnegan, eds., *Army Signals Intelligence in World War II*, pp. 8–9.

[55]Lewin, *Ultra Goes to War*, chs. 11 and 12; Charles B. MacDonald, *A Time for Trumpets: The Untold Story of the Battle of the Bulge* (New York: William Morrow, 1985), chs. 1–3.

[56]Alison R. Bernstein, *American Indians and World War II: Toward a New Era in Indian Affairs* (Norman: University of Oklahoma Press, 1991) pp. 46–49; Michael W. Rodgers, "Indian Code-Talkers of WWII" (Fort Gordon, Ga.: U.S. Army Signal Museum, n.d.); Kahn, *Codebreakers*, pp. 289–90; Thompson and Harris, *Outcome*, p. 218. During World War I several Choctaw Indians had briefly been used as code-talkers during the Meuse-Argonne campaign. See material in file 291.2, "Indians," DAMH-HSR.

[57]Thompson, Harris, et al., *Test*, p. 39. Also on 8 December, the War Department authorized the censorship of all communications to and from personnel under military control outside the United States. Stetson Conn, Rose C. Engelman, and Byron Fairchild, *Guarding the United States and Its Outposts*, United States Army in World War II (Washington, D.C.: Office of the Chief of Military History, Department of the Army, 1964), p. 202.

[58]Lewin, *American Magic*, ch. 5.

[59]Kreidberg and Henry, *Military Mobilization*, pp. 614–15; Barnouw, *History of Broadcasting*, 2: 156.

[60]Thompson, Harris, et al., *Test*, p. 447.

[61]Thompson and Harris, *Outcome*, p. 403. For a detailed discussion of the Army Pictorial Service, see James V. Clarke, Signal Corps Army Pictorial Service in World

War II (1 September 1939–16 August 1945), typescript [Washington, D.C.: Signal Corps Historical Section, Dec 1945], copy in CMH files. See also Barbara Burger et al., comps., *Audiovisual Records in the National Archives of the United States Relating to World War II,* Reference Information Paper 70 (revised) (Washington, D.C.: National Archives and Records Administration, 1992).

[62]Thompson, Harris, et al., *Test,* p. 390.

[63]Richard Koszarski, *The Astoria Studios and Its Fabulous Films* (New York: Dover Publications, Inc., 1983); Thompson, Harris, et al., *Test,* p. 390.

[64]Thompson, Harris, et al., *Test,* pp. 394–96; Thompson and Harris, *Outcome,* p. 574; Maslowski, *Armed With Cameras,* pp. 241–43.

[65]Thompson, Harris, et al., *Test,* p. 392; Thompson and Harris, *Outcome,* p. 563.

[66]Thompson, Harris, et al., *Test,* pp. 408–11; Thompson and Harris, *Outcome,* pp. 565–69; Clarke, Army Pictorial Service, ch. 4.

[67]Thompson, Harris, et al., *Test,* pp. 392–94; Clarke, Army Pictorial Service, pp. 25–30.

[68]Sadler, Affiliated Plan, pp. 99–100 and Exhibit F; Maslowski, *Armed With Cameras,* pp. 118–22. In this study of the military cameramen of World War II, Maslowski focuses on the Army's 163d and 166th Signal Photographic Companies and the 832d Signal Service Battalion. He also discusses the work of photographic units of the Army Air Forces, the Navy, and the Marines.

[69]Capra was initially assigned to the Morale Branch of the War Department as chief of its film production section. In September 1943 he and his unit were transferred to the control of the chief signal officer. Thompson, Harris, et al., *Test,* p. 415; Clarke, Army Pictorial Service, p. 176. Capra describes his World War II experiences in his autobiography, *The Name Above the Title* (New York: Vintage Books, 1985).

[70]Thompson, Harris, et al., *Test,* pp. 415–16; Thompson and Harris, *Outcome,* pp. 555–56; "Whimsical Dr. Seuss Dies at 87," *Washington Post,* 26 Sep 91.

[71]Thompson, Harris, et al., *Test,* p. 358; Thompson and Harris, *Outcome,* pp. 54–55. Zanuck chronicled his wartime service in North Africa in *Tunis Expedition* (New York: Random House, 1943).

[72]Maslowski, *Armed With Cameras,* ch. 3; Burger et al., *Audiovisual Records in National Archives,* pp. 6–7.

[73]Thompson and Harris, *Outcome,* p. 548.

[74]Ibid., p. 544.

[75]Signal Corps photographers shot half of the still pictures published in American newspapers, magazines, and books in 1944 (Thompson and Harris, *Outcome,* p. 565).

[76]Thompson and Harris, *Outcome,* pp. 564–66, 605–07; Maslowski, *Armed With Cameras,* pp. 55–61.

[77]Thompson and Harris, *Outcome,* pp. 551–52. This service began in early 1944. See also Maslowski, *Armed With Cameras,* pp. 292–94.

[78]Thompson, Harris, et al., *Test,* pp. 407–08.

[79]For photo regulations, see AR 105–5, 1 Dec 1942, and AR 105–255, 7 May 1942; Thompson and Harris, *Outcome,* pp. 576–79; Judy Barrett Litoff and David C. Smith, "'Will He Get My Letter?': Popular Portrayals of Mail and Morale During World War II," *Journal of Popular Culture* 23 (Spring 1990): 21–43.

[80]Thompson and Harris, *Outcome,* p. 84.

[81]The Inspector General's Department also investigated the Army's photographic program. See Thompson, Harris, et al., *Test,* pp. 418–25; Maslowski, *Armed With Cameras,* pp. 282–83.

[82]Thompson, Harris, et al., *Test*, pp. 404, 418–24; Millett, *Army Service Forces*, pp. 97–98.

[83]Thompson, Harris, et al., *Test*, pp. 396–97, 400–405; Thompson and Harris, *Outcome*, pp. 570–76. The signal photo company was organized under TOE 11–37.

[84]Thompson and Harris, *Outcome*, pp. 556–58.

[85]*ARSO*, 1946, p. 597, typescript in CMH library. A copy of the print faces page 597.

[86]Terrett, *Emergency*, p. 33; Thompson and Harris, *Outcome*, p. 7, n. 20; Guerlac, *Radar in World War II*, 1: 104.

[87]Camp Evans was named for Lt. Col. Paul W. Evans, the signal officer who had seen the early version of Enigma in 1931. He had died in the Canal Zone in April 1936 while serving as signal officer of the Panama Canal Department.

[88]Thompson, Harris, et al., *Test*, pp. 62–63; Guerlac, *Radar in World War II*, 1: 104.

[89]Thompson and Harris, *Outcome*, p. 625; Millett, *Army Service Forces*, p. 272.

[90]Thompson, Harris, et al., *Test*, pp. 150–51. Millett, *Army Service Forces*, contains three chapters on the board and its relationship with the Army Service Forces.

[91]Cochrane, *Measures for Progress*, pp. 375, 408–26; Thompson, Harris, et al., *Test*, pp. 154–73.

[92]Thompson and Harris, *Outcome*, pp. 378f; Cochrane, *Measures for Progress*, p. 416.

[93]Thompson, Harris, et al., *Test*, pp. 184–85.

[94]Ibid., pp. 328–31. See Table 6, "Signal Corps Procurement of Selected Major Items, 1 Jan 40–31 Dec 45," in Smith, *Army and Economic Mobilization*, pp. 18–20.

[95]Thompson, Harris, et al., *Test*, p. 492; *ARSO*, 1946, p. 6.

[96]Thompson and Harris, *Outcome*, pp. 411–17, 530–31.

[97]Thompson, Harris, et al., *Test*, p. 325f.

[98]Thompson and Harris, *Outcome*, p. 431.

[99]Vannevar Bush, *Pieces of the Action* (New York: Morrow, 1970), ch. 2; Millett, *Army Service Forces*, p. 238; Allison, *New Eye*, pp. 155–59.

[100]Terrett, *Emergency*, pp. 191–202; James Phinney Baxter, III, *Scientists Against Time* (Boston: Little, Brown, and Co., 1947), pp. 119–21f.

[101]For a discussion of the NDRC/OSRD's work, see Baxter, *Scientists Against Time*, and Irvin Stewart, *Organizing Scientific Research for War: The Administrative History of the OSRD* (Boston: Little, Brown, and Co., 1948). For its work on radar, see Guerlac, *Radar in World War II*.

[102]Guerlac, *Radar in World War II*, 1: 430–34; Thompson and Harris, *Outcome*, p. 477.

[103]Thompson, Harris, et al., *Test*, pp. 377f.

[104]Thompson and Harris, *Outcome*, pp. 472, 474.

[105]Ibid., p. 470.

[106]Ibid., pp. 468–82; Baxter, *Scientists Against Time*, pp. 234–36; Guerlac, *Radar in World War II*, 1: 282–83, 325–28; 2: 853–57, 891–93.

[107]W. S. Rumbough, "Radio Relay, the War's Great Development in Signal Communications," *Military Review* 26 (May 1946): 3–12; Thompson and Harris, *Outcome*, pp. 92, 224, 259–65.

[108]Fagen, ed., *Bell System, 1925–1975*, pp. 335–38; Thompson and Harris, *Outcome*, p. 224.

[109]Thompson, Harris, et al., *Test*, p. 66.

[110]Thompson and Harris, *Outcome*, p. 250.

[111]Thompson, Harris, et al., *Test*, p. 66; Thompson and Harris, *Outcome*, pp. 223–24; Fagen, ed., *Bell System, 1925–1975*, pp. 265–70.

[112]Thompson, Harris, et al., *Test*, p. 69.

[113]Ibid., p. 73.

[114]Terrett, *Emergency*, p. 5; Pogue, *Marshall*, 2: 335; Thomas Parrish, *Roosevelt and Marshall: Partners in Politics and War* (New York: William Morrow and Co., Inc., 1989), p. 288.

[115]Thompson, Harris, et al., *Test*, p. 75.

[116]Thompson and Harris, *Outcome*, p. 492. Details of the development of these radios by Bell Laboratories is given in Fagen, ed., *Bell System, 1925–1975*, pp. 319–27.

[117]Thompson and Harris, *Outcome*, pp. 503–04.

[118]Ibid., p. 583.

[119]Baxter, *Scientists Against Time*, ch. 15; Cochrane, *Measures for Progress*, pp. 388–99; Thompson and Harris, *Outcome*, p. 463.

[120]Thompson and Harris, *Outcome*, pp. 5–6. Colton's position then became chief of the engineering and technical service.

[121]Ibid., pp. 429–30.

[122]Ibid., pp. 435, 437–40.

[123]WD Cir 59, 2 May 42, par. 6; Thompson and Harris, *Outcome*, p. 438.

[124]For details, see Thompson and Harris, *Outcome*, ch. 14. The personnel losses are as of April 1945. For a list of the categories of equipment transferred to the AAF, see *Outcome*, p. 457, n. 86. The transfer is also discussed in Millett, *Army Service Forces*, pp. 127–29; Craven and Cate, *Army Air Forces*, 6: 374.

[125]Dupree, *Science in Federal Government*, ch. 19; Allison, *New Eye*, pp. 184–85.

[126]Dupree, *Science in Federal Government*, ch. 19; Cochrane, *Measures for Progress*, p. 363; Millett, *Army Service Forces*, pp. 236–39.

[127]Total Signal Corps strength in 1918 stood at about 56,000. *Strength of the Army* (1 Oct 1944), p. 16, gives the Signal Corps' aggregate strength as 352,309. On its strength at the end of the war, see *Strength of the Army* (1 May 1945), p. 22, and Thompson and Harris, *Outcome*, p. 512. Figures on the Army's total strength are given in Smith, *Army and Economic Mobilization*, table 16, p. 122, and Weigley, *History of Army*, p. 435 and appendix. The Signal Corps' peak civilian strength was 61,628 according to Smith, *Army and Economic Mobilization*, p. 114. The date at which this strength was achieved is not given.

[128]The Signal Corps sustained 2,840 casualties during World War I compared to 3,993 in World War II. For World War II casualty figures, see U.S. War Department, *Army Battle Casualties and Nonbattle Deaths in World War II, Final Report (7 December 1941–31 December 1946)* (Washington, D.C.: Office of The Adjutant General, Jun 1953), p. 47.

[129]Thompson and Harris, *Outcome*, pp. 581–82.

[130]Omar N. Bradley, *A Soldier's Story* (New York: Henry Holt and Company, 1951), p. 474.

CHAPTER VIII

World War II: Theaters of War

Signal units served in every theater, from the zone of interior to the most isolated outposts. Courage and technical expertise were needed, as well as a vast amount of sheer hard work; signalmen shed both sweat and blood in order to play their part in the worldwide drama that ended with Allied victory. The brief survey of signal operations that follows can only suggest the magnitude of the task and the effort.

Defending the Hemisphere, December 1941–June 1943

The first need was to provide for hemisphere defense. Army planners defined the Western Hemisphere to include all of the land masses of North and South America, plus Greenland, Bermuda, and the Falklands (but not Iceland or the Azores) in the Atlantic area and, in the Pacific, all of the islands east of the 180th meridian as well as the Aleutian chain.[1]

Along with Oahu, the Panama Canal constituted the major outpost of continental defense. Because of the potential danger from attack or sabotage, the Army had already placed a sizable force in Panama prior to the Pearl Harbor attack. About one-third of the Signal Corps' units and most of its radar equipment had been installed there before December 1941. Afterward, with a Pearl Harbor–like strike upon the canal seemingly imminent, the need for radar in Panama assumed even greater urgency. To guard the Atlantic approaches to the canal, the Signal Corps installed radar throughout the Caribbean.[2]

In addition to reinforcing its continental defenses, the United States needed to obtain bases on foreign soil in Latin America and the Caribbean.[3] The island of Puerto Rico (which was also important for the protection of the canal) lay along the principal air route to Brazil. Consequently, the United States built a major air base on the island. Signal units provided aircraft warning and communications support here and along the string of island airfields making up the airway.[4]

Meanwhile, Germany's occupation of Denmark in the spring of 1940 threatened possible enemy intrusion into the Danish colonies of Greenland and Iceland. In fact, during the summer of 1940 the Germans established radio and weather stations in Greenland, which the British later eliminated. Following the signing of an agreement with the Danish government on 9 April 1941, Army engineer units departed in June to begin construction of military airfields on the island, and signal personnel installed aircraft warning radar.[5] While Iceland did not fall within the usual definition of the Western Hemisphere, it did lie astride the vital sea lanes between the United States and Great Britain. To protect their lifeline, the British had occupied the island in early May 1940, and during the summer of 1941 British forces there were gradually replaced with American troops. In August, advance elements of the 50th Signal Battalion traveled to the remote island to install radar to cover the convoy route through the dangerous North Atlantic waters. The rest of the unit arrived in January 1942 to install wire, poles, and cables and faced a forbidding task amid lava fields in the dark of winter.[6]

Equally cold and just as vulnerable was the vast territory of Alaska. Only weakly defended prior to the war, Alaska witnessed an extensive military buildup during 1942. On Kodiak Island, site of the Navy's main base in Alaska, the Army constructed Fort Greely, named for the former chief signal officer in recognition both of his national fame as an Arctic explorer and as builder of the Alaska Communication System.[7] This was fitting, for the ACS provided the backbone around which the Signal Corps carried out its wartime expansion in the territory. Prewar improvements to the system had included the reconditioning and restoration of the cable to Seattle, whose return to operation on 3 December 1941 reestablished secure communications with the mainland.[8] Anchorage, headquarters of the Alaska Defense Command, also served as the hub of the wartime ACS network. Initial expansion plans called for ten new stations and for improvements to existing facilities. In addition to the administrative network, the Signal Corps engineered and built post telephone systems, harbor defense control systems, and radar sites.

The improvements were welcome for the enemy was close. On 3–4 June 1942, nearly six months to the day after they had bombed Pearl Harbor, the Japanese as part of their Midway campaign struck the naval base at Dutch Harbor in the Aleutians and followed up with the occupation of Attu and Kiska Islands at the western end of the chain. From these outposts the Japanese could harass American lend-lease shipments to Russia and threaten the continental United States. There they remained until ousted by force from Attu in the spring of 1943, after which they abandoned Kiska voluntarily.[9]

The enemy presence on American soil for almost a year stimulated work that was already under way to make Alaska more defensible. In collaboration with Canada, the United States Army in March 1942 began building the Alaska (Alcan) Highway, stretching over 1,400 miles from Dawson Creek, British Columbia, Canada, to Big Delta, Alaska, where it connected with the Richardson Highway to Fairbanks. This roadway provided a land route to Alaska and a means of supplying a number of military airfields stretching across northwestern Canada.[10]

The Signal Corps furnished communications for the engineer troops building the Alaska Highway. While radio provided the necessary mobility, it was unreliable in the far north due to atmospheric and magnetic interference. It also posed a security problem. Better communications were necessary. Consequently, in the summer of 1942 the Signal Corps took on the task of installing an open wire (bare wire) telephone line parallel to the road, using civilian construction crews and uni-

A typical problem along the Alaska Highway telephone line.

formed operating personnel. Because the Signal Corps had few construction units available, civilian crews performed much of the work. Commercial companies, particularly Western Electric, supplied technical specialists and equipment. The 843d Signal Service Battalion furnished the operating personnel. With a capacity of six voice and thirteen teletype circuits, the line required the setting of 95,000 poles in frozen, snow-covered ground and the stringing of 14,000 miles of wire.[11] Completed in just fifteen months, it represented a spectacular construction feat as well as an excellent example of military/civilian teamwork.[12]

By the summer of 1943 the Japanese foothold in North America had been pried loose, greatly reducing concern over Alaska's security. Consequently the Army began to transfer many of the troops stationed there to more active theaters outside the hemisphere. In fact, the Army's focus had shifted from Axis attack to Allied counterattack—a change that had already taken thousands of American soldiers overseas to fight in the South and Southwest Pacific, Asia, and Africa. Signalmen went with them.

Signal Support for the Pacific Theater, 1941–1943

The first units to face the enemy in the field were located in the Pacific. In December 1941 the Japanese coupled their attack on Pearl Harbor with assaults on American air bases in the Philippines. After destructive air strikes, the main

Japanese invasion of the islands began on 22 December 1941, forcing the American and Filipino forces on Luzon, commanded by General Douglas MacArthur, to retreat to the Bataan Peninsula, across the bay from Manila. The Japanese entered that city on 2 January 1942. MacArthur, meanwhile, had removed his headquarters from Manila to Corregidor, the island fortress at the entrance to Manila Bay. Japan's blockade of the islands and its superiority in the air made reinforcement of the beleaguered defenders impossible.

As the situation deteriorated, President Roosevelt ordered MacArthur in mid-March to proceed to Australia to take command of Allied forces in the Southwest Pacific.[13] Lt. Gen. Jonathan M. Wainwright then assumed command of the doomed garrison. Brig. Gen. Spencer B. Akin, MacArthur's signal officer, accompanied MacArthur to Australia, while his assistant, Col. Theodore T. Teague, remained with Wainwright. Akin continued to serve on MacArthur's staff throughout the war and became a member of the group of MacArthur's close associates known as the Bataan Gang. As such, he enjoyed a freedom of decision and action unknown to other theater chief signal officers.[14] Teague was less fortunate. Bataan fell in early April, and the remaining Americans held out on Corregidor, where they endured several weeks of intense aerial-artillery bombardment that turned the once luxuriant island into a no man's land. Under the hail of bombs and shells, maintenance of wire lines became futile. Wainwright's headquarters took refuge in Malinta Tunnel, an extensive underground system originally built to move supplies from one end of the island to the other.[15] The tunnel complex also housed a hospital, machine shops, and storehouse. From this subterranean location, the Army's last radio station in the Philippines continued to operate. By the end of April, however, much of the command was suffering from malnutrition and disease. Having virtually destroyed its defenses, the Japanese landed on Corregidor during the night of 5 May 1942. With defeat inevitable and supplies of water and ammunition nearly gone, Wainwright was forced to surrender the next day. After broadcasting their final messages, signal personnel gutted their equipment and destroyed as much of it as possible. Fifty signal officers, including Teague, and 662 enlisted men became prisoners of the Japanese.[16]

Communication between the Philippines and the Allied forces in Australia was maintained surreptitiously by soldiers who had escaped into the hills and by Filipino guerrillas. Through a network of coast watchers using radios secretly landed by American submarines, MacArthur received valuable information about Japanese troop movements and naval activity. In addition, the Signal Corps organized a unit, the 978th Signal Service Company, to infiltrate the islands and cooperate with the guerrillas. Comprised largely of Filipino-American volunteers, the members received training in the building, operation, and maintenance of radio stations; weather forecasting and aircraft warning; the use of cameras and cryptographic systems; and jungle living and guerrilla fighting. The heroism of these men, some of whom were captured by the Japanese and tortured to death, helped pave the way for the eventual Allied liberation of the Philippines.[17]

Inside the Malinta Tunnel

In the Pacific, the Signal Corps' first experience of ground combat as attackers rather than defenders occurred during the battle for Guadalcanal, part of the Solomon Islands group. Operations in the South Pacific Area were controlled by the Navy, first under Vice Adm. Robert L. Ghormley and, after November 1942, under the command of Admiral William F. Halsey. The Allies invaded the southern Solomons in the summer of 1942 to prevent the Japanese from cutting the line of communications between the United States and Australia. The offensive began on 7 August 1942 when the 1st Marine Division landed on Guadalcanal where the Japanese were constructing a large airfield. The Japanese, taken by surprise, did not oppose the landing, but they soon struck back violently. For six months the combatants waged battles on the ground, in the air, and on the sea for control of the island. For the Americans, the marines handled all of the ground combat until October, when Army reinforcements began to arrive, just in time to help thwart a major Japanese counteroffensive.

The Army eventually committed two infantry divisions to Guadalcanal: the 25th and the Americal. The divisional signal units, the 25th and 26th Signal Companies, respectively, arrived in December 1942 and participated in large-scale offensive operations launched in early January 1943. These units soon became familiar with the vagaries of communications in the tropics. Because radios did not always work well in the jungle, wire lines remained important. Stringing the lines proved a herculean task, however, as the signalmen, without bolos or machetes, "pulled the wire by hand through the mysterious and malevolent jungle, moist and stifling with its stench of vegetable decay."[18] Other signal units on Guadalcanal included the 69th Signal Service Company, complete with a pigeon detachment, and the 162d Signal Photographic Company. The struggle for Guadalcanal finally ended in early February 1943 with a decisive victory for the Allies, and the hard-won island became a base for further offensive operations in the South Pacific.[19]

Passing the Test in North Africa and Italy

While these bitter but small-scale battles raged in the Pacific, the Signal Corps became involved in combat on a far greater scale in North Africa. Here the United States Army undertook its first extended offensive operations in the combined invasion of Morocco, Algeria, and Tunisia, French colonies then under the control of the collaborationist government that had been set up after France surrendered to the Germans in 1940. American units made up the bulk of the invasion force, and an American, General Dwight D. Eisenhower, acted as the overall Allied commander. Eisenhower's staff consisted of British as well as American officers, but the chief signal officer was an American, Brig. Gen. Jerry V. Matejka. Matejka headed the Signal Section of Eisenhower's Allied Force Headquarters (AFHQ), advising him and coordinating signal policy throughout the theater. At the start of the campaign both AFHQ and the signal communications center were located deep within the British fortress on the Rock of Gibraltar.[20]

On 8 November 1942, British and American forces launched Operation TORCH, presenting the Signal Corps with its first major test of the war.[21] A special company had been organized to handle shore party communications.[22] Yet every aspect of the operation, including the signal problems, showed the inexperience of the Allies in conducting amphibious warfare. Until the troops landed, the message centers remained on shipboard, but the shock of naval gunfire knocked out many shipboard radios. Meanwhile, companies of the 829th Signal Service Battalion, one per task force, attempted to set up the administrative communications net for which the Signal Corps had responsibility.[23] These units had intended to use SCR–299 truck and trailer radio sets immediately upon landing to connect the widely separated landing areas and to communicate with Gibraltar. Unfortunately, the weighty sets had been stowed deep in the holds of the convoy ships and only one could be unloaded in time for use during the initial assault. Luckily, the British had outfitted two communications ships; they filled the gap.

Despite efforts to waterproof using canvas bags, salt water damaged much signal apparatus. Even vehicular radio sets could not withstand being drenched. To add to the difficulties, units often became separated from their equipment, and a scarcity of vehicles slowed operations in general.[24] Yet once communications onshore became stabilized, the 299s provided the chief means of long-distance signals until permanent ACAN stations could be installed. Originally designed as radiotelephones with a range of 100 miles when in motion, they proved capable of communicating up to 2,300 miles when operated as radiotelegraphs.

Even when the equipment worked well, however, inadequate training prevented many signal personnel from using it competently. Technical problems were great: Signalmen had to communicate in nets that included the British Army and Navy, the Royal Air Force, and the Army Air Forces; conflicting codes and ciphers caused confusion that was compounded by last-minute changes in the radio procedure plan. The signalmen had to adapt to the chaotic situation as best they could.[25]

After the assault phase ended, wire lines carried more of the communications load. With the cooperation of local French authorities, signal units assumed control over the existing commercial telephone system. The lines, however, were in poor condition and unable to handle the large volume of message traffic. The Signal Corps then found itself facing a problem in the North African desert that it had not seen since the days of the frontier telegraph lines: lack of local timber for poles. For such situations the Corps had developed the rapid pole line (RPL) method of construction, which substituted two 20-foot building studs nailed together for the standard 40-foot pole. The studs were easier to handle and transport, but proved to have problems of their own. They were, for example, unable to carry the weight of crossarms, insulators, and hardware. Furthermore, the studs were subject to twisting and warping in the sun and rain. Consequently, RPL proved only a limited success.[26]

The North African campaign was a learning experience for the whole Army, the place where amateurs became veterans. The theater witnessed a significant innovation in communications—the integration of radio and wire into a system known as radio relay. By this means messages could travel from a radio transmitter over the air, into a receiver and onto wire, to a switchboard, and then to an individual's telephone set, or vice versa. This development stemmed from Eisenhower's wish for a personal radiotelephone in his car with which he could call his headquarters, whatever the distance. Due to security considerations, Eisenhower received a mobile radioteletype, which allowed his messages to be enciphered, rather than a radiotelephone that would broadcast conversations in the clear. Nevertheless, the system worked much like cellular telephones, with radio signals beamed between line-of-sight relay stations placed on high elevations about 100 miles apart. Besides General Eisenhower, II Corps used radio relay to transmit large numbers of messages and press reports between Algiers and Tunis.[27]

Signal Corps ground radar also found its first extensive combat use in an air defense role. In particular the SCR–582, the first American microwave radar, debuted in North Africa. Intended for coast defense, it proved successful in detecting low-flying aircraft and was quickly converted to a truck mount for mobility. The 582 could also be used for detecting surface vessels and providing navigational assistance to ships. Even the British, who heretofore had judged American radar to be poor, found this model superior.[28]

Repairing telephone lines in Tunisia

In addition to these modern methods of communication, some less sophisticated techniques, including signal lamps and messengers, were used when other means were unavailable. Even pigeons flew many missions in North Africa, particularly during periods of radio silence or when wire lines had not yet been installed or had been destroyed.[29]

Despite its initial problems, the Signal Corps passed its first test in North Africa and contributed to the successful campaign, which ended in mid-May 1943 with a sweeping victory in Tunisia. The Corps' central role in coordinating the air-ground-sea operations of the Allied forces received increasing recognition from line units. As General Matejka declared, "This is a signals war," and the communication facilities in North Africa continued to be important as the area became the staging base for the subsequent invasions of Sicily, the Italian mainland, and southern France.[30]

The invasion of Sicily (Operation HUSKY) had several goals: making the Mediterranean safe for Allied shipping, forcing Italy out of the war, and diverting the Germans from the Russian front. General Eisenhower once again was the theater commander, but a British officer, Maj. Gen. Leslie B. Nicholls, replaced General Matejka, who had returned to Washington to serve in the Office of the Chief Signal Officer.

During the predawn hours of 10 July 1943, amid heavy seas, the Allies began landing on the southeastern coast of Sicily against light opposition. This amphibious operation, larger than TORCH, involved more than nine thousand signal troops, including those that belonged to the Army Air Forces. In planning the assault the Signal Corps applied lessons learned in North Africa, with particular emphasis on making certain that its equipment was adequately waterproofed. This time the Signal Corps installed SCR–299s in special moistureproof houses aboard amphibious trucks (DUKWs), which enabled the sets to be operated either offshore or on land. Despite some problems, communications for HUSKY were much improved over those for TORCH.[31]

After five weeks of fighting the Allies drove the Germans out of Sicily. During this period signal troops rehabilitated 4,916 miles of telephone wire; laid almost 1,800 miles of spiral-four cable; and handled over 8,000 radio messages.[32] The Germans had sabotaged many of the existing lines and mined the pole line route from Palermo to Messina. Thanks to the SCR–625 magnetic mine detector, most mines were found and removed harmlessly.[33] Col. Terence J. Tully, the American officer who served as Nicholls' deputy, reported to General Ingles: "We mounted the Sicilian campaign very successfully, and it was said that this particular group of signal units was the best-equipped that ever went into combat."[34]

The fall of Sicily in late August proved significant, leading to the ouster of Italian dictator Benito Mussolini and shortly afterward Italy's decision to quit the war.[35] Germany, however, remained determined to resist the Allies, using its former Axis partner as a battleground. On 9 September the U.S. Fifth Army launched Operation AVALANCHE to seize the port of Naples. After landing at Salerno, it fought its way to Naples, while the British Eighth Army conquered the heel and toe of the Italian boot. Then the Allies combined to advance on Rome.[36]

Yet the campaign that had begun so well quickly bogged down amid mud, mountains, and winter weather. Not only did the Germans fight with determination and skill, they took full advantage of Italy's forbidding topography. Its rugged interior heavily favored the defenders and presented particular problems for communicators. Mountain peaks interfered with radio transmissions and the irregular terrain made laying wire difficult and dangerous. Telephone lines in forward areas were frequently broken by enemy shelling or by vehicles. When possible, the lines were strung overhead. Where standard military vehicles could not go, linemen used mules, carts, jeeps, and sometimes bicycles to carry the spools of wire. If all else failed, the men had to unroll the huge spools by hand, a backbreaking task. Pigeons also flew many missions, at some headquarters conveying up to three hundred messages a week. At Colvi Vecchia in October 1943, the Signal Corps' pigeon, G.I. Joe, saved a British brigade by flying twenty miles in twenty minutes to deliver an order to cancel the bombing of the city which the troops had entered ahead of schedule. (The bird later received a medal for gallantry from the Lord Mayor of London.)[37]

As winter descended, signalmen found themselves wading and swimming across icy mountain streams, now swollen by the autumn rains, to establish communication lines.[38] German defenses known as the Winter Line were domi-

SCR–584 in Italy

nated by the stronghold of Monte Cassino. In an attempt to break the stalemate, the U.S. VI Corps staged an amphibious landing on 22 January 1944 in the rear of the enemy lines at Anzio, a coastal resort about thirty miles south of Rome. Here the Signal Corps benefited from the experience gained during its previous amphibious operations. In addition, the SCR–300, better known as the walkie-talkie, received its first use in combat. Lt. Col. Jesse F. Thomas, signal officer of the 3d Infantry Division, declared it the "most successful instrument yet devised for amphibious communication."[39]

Although the landing was unopposed, a fierce German counterattack halted the advance and drove communications underground. Luckily, the Signal Corps could employ a new and highly accurate gun-laying radar, SCR–584, that proved lethal to German bombers and resistant to the enemy's jamming techniques. Although they failed to wipe out the beachhead, the Germans kept the Allies pinned down and unable to achieve a breakout for several months.[40]

Finally, in May, the main body of the Fifth Army along with the British Eighth Army breached the Winter Line and joined forces with the Anzio beachhead. The Allies then continued their push toward Rome as German resistance began to weaken. The Signal Corps, hampered by a dearth of personnel, especially wire construction men, strove to keep up with the rapidly advancing armies. Rome fell on 4 June 1944, but much of Italy remained in enemy hands and the Allies continued to fight their way north toward the Arno River. By late summer they stood facing the formidable Gothic Line across the northern Apennines. Weary signalmen faced what the 34th Signal Company's historian later called "another Mud, Mountain, and Mule affair."[41]

He was right. Throughout the fall signalmen again endured the rigors of providing communications in trackless mountain terrain where sometimes only pigeons could get the message through. Although fighting slackened during the winter months, the need for communications continued. When the offensive resumed in the spring, signal units participated in what soon turned into an

Operating the SCR–584

enemy rout as the Allies pursued the Germans across the Po Valley to the Alps. With their escape routes into the mountains blocked off, the Germans were trapped. The prolonged struggle that had lasted nearly twenty months came to an end when the German forces in Italy surrendered on 2 May 1945.[42]

Signal Soldiers in Europe: D-Day and After

Meanwhile, planning had proceeded for the long-awaited cross-Channel attack. Since early 1942 the Allies had sought to open a second front against Germany to divert its forces from their drive to Russia and hasten its final defeat. In preparation, the United States slowly began building a huge logistical base in the United Kingdom, an effort that received the code name Operation BOLERO. By the eve of the invasion more than a million and a half American soldiers were stationed there.[43]

Communications planning was a key aspect of the buildup. Before he was assigned to Africa, the future General Matejka had worked in England, making arrangements for the Electronics Training Group and later becoming chief signal officer of the United States Army Forces in the British Isles (USAFBI). After the 827th Signal Service Company arrived in March 1942, the men installed a signal center at 20 Grosvenor Square in London;[44] in mid-July a direct ACAN link was established to Washington; and shortly afterward the overcrowded signal center moved to the annex of Selfridge's department store in London, "a sizeable steel and concrete structure blessed with deep basements running 45 feet down."[45]

The organization of the U.S. forces in the United Kingdom paralleled that of the War Department in Washington with separate commands for ground, air, and support services. Hence the Signal Corps became part of the Services of Supply. In June 1942 the European Theater of Operations, United States Army (ETOUSA), was organized to replace the USAFBI, and General Dwight D. Eisenhower assumed command. Brig. Gen. William S. Rumbough became the theater's chief signal officer as well as the chief signal officer of the Services of Supply. While Rumbough reported to Cheltenham, ninety miles northwest of London, where the headquarters of the Services of Supply had been established, Matejka remained at Grosvenor Square as the Signal Corps' representative at theater headquarters until being tapped to serve under Eisenhower in North Africa.[46]

As the European theater's chief signal officer, Rumbough faced a tremendous task. The invasion of Normandy, the largest Allied military operation of the war, presented the Signal Corps with the biggest challenge thus far in its history: The scale of communications would be roughly twenty-five times greater than that for TORCH.[47] In October 1943 Rumbough became a member of the Allies' Combined Signal Board, set up to conduct high-level coordination between the combined air, naval, and ground elements. It handled such matters as establishing a system of priorities for telephone traffic and allocating radio frequencies for the 90,000 transmitters expected to be in operation.[48]

In January 1944 Eisenhower received the appointment as the European theater commander with the title of Supreme Commander, Allied Expeditionary Force. In tactical matters the new Supreme Headquarters, Allied Expeditionary Force (SHAEF), supplanted ETOUSA. Although General Rumbough continued his job as chief signal officer on the ETOUSA staff, his duties were now confined primarily to the administration and supply of American signal units in the theater.[49] Tactical and strategic signal matters would be handled by the signal division of the supreme headquarters where a British officer, Maj. Gen. C. H. H. Vulliamy, held the position of chief signal officer, SHAEF. Brig. Gen. Francis H. Lanahan, Jr., of the U.S. Army Signal Corps, served as Vulliamy's deputy. While the signal division conducted detailed planning and coordination, the Combined Signal Board determined policy.[50]

On 6 June, through rough seas and under cloudy skies, American forces landed on the Normandy beaches designated as UTAH (VII Corps) and OMAHA (V Corps).[51] To support this vast undertaking, the First Army (the major U.S. ground component, under the command of Lt. Gen. Omar N. Bradley) had assembled 13,420 signalers.[52] Col. Grant A. Williams served as First Army's signal officer. The signal troops included three units of a new type, the Joint Assault Signal Company, or JASCO, originally created in the Pacific in late 1943 specifically to furnish communications during joint (Army-Navy) amphibious operations.[53]

The organization of JASCOs demonstrated one of the ways in which the Army's amphibious assault doctrine and techniques had matured since the North

African campaign. JASCOs operated as part of engineer special brigades, units designed to organize invasion beaches for supply.[54] The joint companies provided the critical communications link between the ships offshore and the assaulting units on the beach as well as among the assault teams themselves. JASCOs also coordinated both naval and aerial fire. Much larger than the standard signal company and commanded by a major, the joint company contained as many as five to six hundred communication specialists from the Army (Signal Corps and Field Artillery), Army Air Forces, and Navy. The JASCO was divided into a battalion shore and beach party communication section, a shore fire control section, and an air liaison section, with each section further subdivided into teams.[55]

The Signal Corps also contributed significantly to the execution of the assault through the use of radio countermeasures (RCM). These included jamming the enemy's radar electronically and such deceptive practices as dropping strips of aluminum foil from planes to blind hostile sensors by producing false echoes.[56] In southeast England the 3103d Signal Service Battalion set up a simulated radio net to mislead the Germans into believing that the Pas de Calais area would be the actual invasion point—a successful ruse that undoubtedly saved the Allies thousands of casualties.[57]

Members of the Signal Corps participated in airborne assaults by the 82d and 101st Airborne Divisions that preceded the landings. Twenty-eight men from the 101st Airborne Signal Company became the first signalmen to land in France. Fighting as infantry, they assisted in the capture of Pouppeville at the southern end of UTAH Beach. Other members of the company arrived in France by glider, bringing with them a long-range SCR–499 radio set, the air-transportable version of the SCR–299. On D-day and for several days thereafter, this set linked the two airborne divisions to England. Meanwhile, members of the 82d Airborne Signal Company either dropped with the division near Ste. Mère-Eglise or came in by glider, losing many men and much equipment. Although scattered during the jump, these airborne forces secured vital roadways and other strongpoints that eased the way for the oncoming ground troops. The landing on UTAH itself met with only light opposition, and the 286th JASCO came ashore quickly to set up wire communications. Both the 82d and the 101st Airborne Signal Companies received the Presidential Unit Citation (Army) for their contributions to the Normandy invasion.[58]

Meanwhile, on OMAHA Beach the invasion forces met with heavy enemy resistance. During the opening hour of the assault, members of the 2d Platoon, 294th JASCO, had to hand-carry much of their equipment ashore after their landing vehicles stalled in deep water and were struck by enemy fire. Nevertheless, they managed to set up the only communications system on the beach until noon of D-day when additional platoons arrived. A detachment of the 293d JASCO, which followed the 294th ashore, lost one-third of its vehicles and one-half of its radio equipment when a shell hit its landing craft. These losses did not, however, prevent the unit from carrying out its mission of providing communications for the 6th Engineer Special Brigade.

Photograph taken by Captain Wall during the D-day invasion on OMAHA Beach.

The First Army's photographic unit, the 165th Signal Photographic Company, covered the action with detachments serving on both beaches. The company commander, Capt. Herman V. Wall, documented operations on OMAHA. Wall also became an early casualty of the Normandy invasion. Despite suffering serious wounds, one of which resulted in the amputation of his left leg, he made sure that his film was delivered to the proper authorities in England for processing. Wall's pictures were the first received of the actual landings on 6 June.[59]

Due to the initial confusion on UTAH and OMAHA, the JASCOs were unable to run wire lines out to the headquarters ships as planned. Thus radio provided the vital links between commanders and troops. During the early phase of the operation, these ships played an important role. The radio nets aboard them furnished communications between the echelons of the First Army afloat and ashore, as well as with the army rear back in England. By mid-June newly laid cables across the English Channel handled large-scale communications with England. Radio was also used to connect UTAH and OMAHA until wires could be laid. Even pigeons found a job on the busy beaches, carrying ammunition status reports, undeveloped film, and emergency messages.[60]

Multichannel radio, or antrac, received its baptism of fire during the Normandy landings. Perched atop an ancient signal tower on the Isle of Wight off the southern coast of England, where observers once had watched for the arrival of the Spanish Armada, twentieth century signalers operating an antrac station anxiously awaited word from the invasion beaches, which they finally received at D plus 2. With its facsimile capability, the antrac could send reconnaissance photos back to the beaches in seven minutes, where they were put to good use by gun control officers.[61]

After six weeks of bitter fighting, the First Army finally broke out of Normandy's hedgerow country in late July. Having pierced the German lines, the Allies then advanced with astonishing speed. The spectacular success of the breakout, however, placed strains upon the logistical system. Such critical items as gasoline and ammunition began to run low, and resupply was often agonizingly slow. The rapidly moving forces consumed enormous quantities of signal materiel and soon depleted the Signal Corps' stockpiles on the Continent. For some items, such as small radio sets, replacements could be shipped by air from the United Kingdom; in other cases, signalmen were able to supplement their supplies with captured enemy equipment.[62]

During this period of highly mobile warfare, events frequently outran communications. First Army, containing some of the best trained and most experienced signal units, devised mobile communication centers mounted in vans that enabled command post moves to be made fairly smoothly. The more rapidly advancing forces of Lt. Gen. George S. Patton's Third Army encountered greater difficulties. Organized in September 1944, the new field army suffered from shortages of both signal units and equipment. Wire lines, which carried the bulk of communications, both tactical and administrative, became particularly strained as the armies used up nearly three thousand miles of wire each day. Even at that rate, line construction could not keep up with the needs of higher headquarters. Moreover, the existing French lines had been so badly damaged by the Germans that they could not be readily repaired. Although radio and messenger service could sometimes take up the slack, serious problems of command and control arose.[63]

Communication between corps and divisions proved especially troublesome. The commander of Patton's VIII Corps, Maj. Gen. Troy H. Middleton, found that he could not maintain contact with his 6th Armored Division as it sped through Brittany. Neither high-powered SCR–399 radios nor radioteletype could satisfactorily bridge the distances between headquarters. Messengers, when they could get through at all, often arrived with orders that had become irrelevant. Thus, the division commander frequently had to act without authority from higher headquarters and could sometimes exert little control over the division's subordinate units.[64]

Fortunately, the new technology of radio relay came to the rescue. The equipment could be made operational very rapidly and needed little maintenance. A single terminal could furnish several telephone and several tele-

graph circuits, each of which became part of the whole communications network, quickly connected with any telephone or any teletypewriter in the
system.[65] While not as secure as wire communications, it could be duplexed as
radio could not. A further advantage resulted from the fact that fewer men were
needed to install radio relay than to run a wire line. To help introduce the
equipment and report on its performance, the Signal Corps sent two of its civilian engineers, Amory H. Waite and Victor J. Colaguori, to Europe. These men
pioneered a novel concept, the new equipment introductory detachment
(NEID), which became a necessity with the rapid appearance of highly
sophisticated items in the combat theaters. Waite and Colaguori later received
Bronze Stars for their efforts.[66]

Sometimes distance was not the primary problem, as in the case of close-sup-
port communications between infantry and tanks. Here the communications gap
resulted from the fact that an infantryman's walkie-talkie did not operate on the
same frequency as a tanker's radio. Climbing onto a tank to communicate with
the occupants was a difficult and dangerous undertaking in the midst of battle.
Although the Signal Corps attempted various solutions, such as putting telephones on the rear of tanks, none proved completely satisfactory and the dilemma
remained.[67]

Yet many of these problems reflected the Allies' overwhelming success. In
late August they liberated Paris, and in just six weeks the Allied armies advanced
from the Normandy beaches to the German frontier. Meanwhile Paris became the
theater communications center, second only in size to station WAR in
Washington, and also a part of the ACAN system. Like the "Hello Girls" before
them, WACs shortly arrived to operate the center's switchboards. The Eiffel
Tower served as a radio relay terminal.[68]

But lengthening supply lines and the severe shortages that resulted stalled the
Allied march to an early victory. The delay allowed the Germans to regroup and
make a last-ditch stand to defend their homeland. As winter approached, the
lightning drives of summer gave way to vicious battles in such places as the
Huertgen Forest and the Vosges Mountains, where the Germans made the Allies
pay dearly for the ground they won. Then, hoping to regain the initiative in the
west and secure a negotiated peace, Hitler ordered an ambitious counteroffensive.
On 16 December 1944 the Germans attacked in the Ardennes region of Belgium
and Luxembourg, used by the Americans as a rest and refitting area. The resulting confrontation became known as the Battle of the Bulge for the salient created
in the Allied lines.

Though taken by surprise, the Americans continued to fight in small and isolated units. Thanks to a flexible wire system, communications likewise withstood
the onslaught. At no time did General Bradley, now commanding the 12th Army
Group, lose contact with his armies. Bradley's signal officer, Col. Garland C.
Black, had made certain that alternate routes existed for important circuits. The
Americans made extensive use of French underground cables backed up by open
wire lines.[69]

Message Center, 101st Airborne Division *by Olin Dows, 1945*

As the Germans advanced the group's radio relay stations had to be frequently relocated. Crewmen manning a relay site near Jamelle, Belgium—a critical link in the 12th Army Group's communications network—stayed on the job even after the Germans overran the area on 24 December. During the day the sounds of battle and troop movements veiled the noise from the station's power unit. At night the men shut down the station to avoid detection. Finally, after three days of surreptitious operation, they were forced to abandon their position. Three of the signalmen failed to reach Allied lines, but their efforts had not been in vain. They had bought enough time for other Signal Corps crews to establish an alternate route.[70]

Despite the confusion communications were maintained with minimal disruption at army and corps level. At the division level, however, signalmen had more difficulty keeping lines open. Germans jammed the radios, and enemy artillery and infantry fire continually destroyed wire facilities. When the wires were down radio relay came to the rescue.

At the vital road center of Bastogne, the 101st Airborne Signal Company labored feverishly to assemble a radio relay set before the Germans encircled the town. Capt. William J. Johnson, the company commander, called it "a necessity in the situation, when we found ourselves surrounded with no other possible ground contact to higher headquarters."[71] From an underground shelter the 101st kept communications open throughout the siege. For its efforts at Bastogne the company received its second Presidential Unit Citation.[72]

The tide of battle turned in the Americans' favor on 26 December when elements of Patton's Third Army broke through the German encirclement and relieved Bastogne. Although much hard fighting remained, the breakthrough signaled the ultimate failure of the Ardennes attack. By the end of January the Allies had destroyed the salient and pushed the Germans back behind the Siegfried Line and within their own borders. The Allied drive across Europe had regained its momentum.

The Allies then began their final assault across the Rhine into the German heartland, crossing the river at Remagen on 7 March. On 25 April American and Russian forces met at the Elbe River at Torgau, an event recorded by the 165th Signal Photographic Company.[73] The formal linkup occurred the next day. Faced with the certainty of defeat, Hitler committed suicide a few days later, and the German government surrendered on 7 May at Eisenhower's headquarters in Reims, France. The next day, 8 May, President Truman proclaimed V–E Day, the official date of the end of the war in Europe.

But peace did not bring a holiday for Army communicators. Some began the task of setting up lines for the occupation troops; others made preparations for the postwar conference at Potsdam; and still others quickly found themselves on their way to the Pacific to take part in the final showdown with Japan.

The Asiatic and Pacific Theaters, 1943–1945

During the struggle to defeat Germany, operations in the Pacific and in China, Burma, and India had received a lower priority in manpower and equipment allocations. At the Casablanca Conference in January 1943 Admiral Ernest J. King estimated that the Allies were allotting only 15 percent of their resources to those theaters.[74]

In numbers of men and units, signal soldiers committed to the war against Japan were much fewer than those in the war against Germany. Despite the lack of communications personnel, the War Department initially denied the Signal Corps' request for WAC units in the Southwest Pacific Area. Army planners questioned the assignment of large numbers of women to a theater where they would face physical conditions considerably worse than those in Europe— extreme heat, primitive housing, and tropical diseases. However, with the men needed for combat, WACs finally began arriving in Australia in mid-1944. Although 5,500 women ultimately served in the Southwest Pacific Area, relatively few handled communications duties—only about 3 percent of the total as compared to roughly 25 percent in the European theater. Though few in number, they performed well under difficult circumstances.[75]

The war against the Japanese was bitter and hard-fought, and it brought the Signal Corps unique problems to solve. Instead of operating in a concentrated area with established communications and extensive road systems, the Signal Corps had to provide communications over enormous distances where tiny dots of land were separated by vast stretches of ocean. The remote islands contained few if any wire lines, and roads had to be hacked out of the dense vegetation. Leafy jungle walls absorbed electromagnetic radiation, inhibiting radio communications and particularly affecting the relatively weak early walkie-talkies (SCRs 194 and 195). The arrival of the new model, SCR–300, registered a marked improvement. The familiar problems of jungle heat, humidity, and fungus growths on equipment and insulation plagued subsequent operations in the Southwest and Central Pacific as they had at Guadalcanal.

Fixed island communications required inordinate amounts of wire. The system established on Okinawa, for example, used enough wire to establish one hundred circuits between Maine and California. The amount of telephone equipment installed there rivaled that of a city the size of South Bend, Indiana.[76] Once established, the island communication systems did not move forward as the troops advanced, but stayed in place. Each island remained a self-contained entity connected to others only by long-range radio, and antrac proved ideal for this purpose.[77]

Because joint operations were the rule in the Pacific, cooperation and coordination between the Army and Navy in communications was more necessary than ever. Only in the Army-run Southwest Pacific Area did the Signal Corps operate independently. In the Navy-run South and Central Pacific Areas joint communications procedures were followed, and Army signalmen provided support that sometimes proved of decisive importance. Because the Navy's radios had proven unsuitable for amphibious operations, naval and Marine forces used Signal Corps equipment. In the Central Pacific the Joint Assault Signal Company (JASCO) was created in late 1943, providing a model for other combat theaters. Moreover, in the South and Central Pacific joint communication centers were set up on each island to serve all the armed forces in the area.[78]

In addition to the Navy and Marine Corps, the Signal Corps worked closely with the Army Air Forces, especially in the South Pacific, to provide the navigational and communications facilities for the heavily traveled airways that served the islands. The Signal Corps was also responsible for the Army's Aircraft Warning Service in the South Pacific until the Army Air Forces took over that function in early 1944. After that the Signal Corps continued to handle the Air Forces' administrative communications there.[79]

The China-Burma-India Theater was unique, a vast inland battleground of jungles and mountains. Few Americans fought there because the British, with their colonial ties to the region, had primary responsibility for this theater. But Lt. Gen. Joseph W. Stilwell commanded both large Chinese armies and the small U.S. contingent. After an Allied defeat in Burma in 1942 cut China off, the United States took charge of reopening a road to supply the embattled republic. Meanwhile, American pilots based in India flew arms and supplies "over the Hump," the high passes through the Himalaya Mountains. In 1943 American engineer units began building the Ledo (later renamed the Stilwell) Road, and the Signal Corps undertook the construction of a pole line running nearly two thousand miles from Calcutta, India, to Ledo near the India-Burma border, and across northern Burma to Kunming, China. Within Burma the line ran alongside the Ledo Road. Comparable in length to the Alcan line, this project faced different but equally daunting problems: monsoons replaced blizzards, and signalmen sloshed through flooded rice paddies instead of sinking into custard-like muskeg.

Overcoming these obstacles as it had those before them, the Corps completed the line in June 1945.[80]

The construction of the Ledo Road through northern Burma had been made possible by the operations of Chinese armies in Burma, aided by the 5307th Composite Unit (Provisional). This unusual organization, commanded by Brig. Gen. Frank D. Merrill, became known as Merrill's Marauders. It customarily operated behind enemy lines, out of contact with General Stilwell's headquarters except by radio. After training in India, the Marauders entered Burma during February 1944. Always on the move, their lives depended upon the services of the long-range set, AN/PRC–1, and shorter-range SCRs 177, 284, and 300. The last set was often used to communicate with aircraft to arrange the vital airdrop of supplies.[81] In addition to supporting the Marauders, teams from the 988th Signal Operation Company (Special) and the 96th Signal Battalion provided communications for the Chinese.[82] As the Chinese advanced, the Marauders blocked the Japanese routes of withdrawal and cut their supply lines.

In performing their unique and dangerous mission, the Marauders faced many communications problems. One stemmed from the inexorable fact that while daytime offered the best propagation conditions for radio transmissions, the unit's operations generally forced the radiomen to wait until nightfall to send their messages, when atmospherics often blocked the signals. Moreover, in keeping with Army policy that confined signal support to division level and above, few Signal Corps radio experts served in such a combat unit, though their proficiency would have been invaluable. On the other hand, while infantry communicators received less specialized training, they were more hardened to the rigors of campaigning. One, 2d Lt. Charlton Ogburn, Jr., commander of the communications platoon of the 1st Battalion, did hold a Signal commission, but he had no experience with radio. Ogburn had, in fact, joined the Signal Corps to be a photographer.[83] Nevertheless, essential communications were maintained, and Maj. Milton A. Pilcher, Merrill's signal officer, commended his men in his after-action report:

> However routine their jobs may be, the work of a communications man is as important and is as arduous as that of any man in the organization. Without communications, no unit can fight well, and without communications a long range penetration unit cannot fight. A communication man's work is never done. He walks all day with his unit and at night he "pulls his shift." If traffic is heavy or radio conditions poor, he works all night. In a fight he stands by his set clearing traffic until relieved.[84]

Merrill's men played a decisive part in driving the Japanese from northern Burma during 1944. Although the combat in Asia was overshadowed by events in the Pacific, it nonetheless contributed to the overall Allied effort to defeat Japan.

After their initial victories on Guadalcanal and Papua (the southern tail of New Guinea), the Allies in early 1943 prepared to mount a two-pronged offensive: one in the Southwest Pacific Area under General MacArthur along the north coast of New Guinea; the other in the Central Pacific Area with Admiral Chester W. Nimitz as commander in chief via the island chains of the Gilberts, Marshalls,

Members of the 43d Signal Company carry wire reels into the jungle of New Georgia, July 1943.

Marianas, Carolines, and Palaus. Each island stronghold seized provided a base for the next advance, and during succeeding months such names as Tarawa, Eniwetok, and Saipan became household words in the United States as anxious citizens followed Allied progress through distant archipelagos and atolls.

On New Guinea, Allied forces pushed slowly up the northeast coast. In planning his strategy for this campaign, MacArthur received valuable assistance from Akin's signal intelligence organization, known as the Central Bureau. This group included American, Australian, British, and Canadian personnel, and by the end of the war it contained over 4,000 men and women.[85] Thanks to ULTRA, MacArthur learned much from decrypted enemy messages about Japanese intentions and capabilities. But such information alone could not win battles.[86] The Japanese, despite the debilitating effects of supply shortages and malnutrition, fought ferociously. Communicators, meanwhile, struggled with the problems endemic to jungle warfare and amphibious operations. ULTRA enabled the Allies to make successful surprise landings at Aitape and Hollandia during the spring of 1944, and the huge base built at Hollandia supported the next objective: the advance to the Philippines.

During 1944 the combat situation in the Pacific improved dramatically as the Allies gained control of both the sea and the air. As a result, they hastened their plans to invade the Philippines. At a conference in September 1944 in Quebec, Canada, where the Allied leaders reached this decision, the Signal Corps connected the Combined Chiefs of Staff by radioteletype with General MacArthur's headquarters in Brisbane, Australia.[87]

GI checks dials in the power room aboard the Apache.

As he had promised when he left the Philippines two years earlier, MacArthur returned to the islands. He fulfilled his pledge on 20 October 1944 when the U.S. Sixth Army, commanded by Lt. Gen. Walter Krueger, assaulted Leyte in the largest amphibious operation yet conducted in the Pacific. A significant feature of the landing was the appearance of the Signal Corps' own communications ships (which became known as the Signal Corps' Grand Fleet) that had been specially designed for this purpose. Outfitted with VHF radio relay sets, the ships furnished multiple circuits for telephone, telegraph, or teletypewriter and maintained these critical connections until fixed stations could be installed ashore. One of these vessels, the *Apache*, was specifically intended for public relations work; communicators aboard that ship recorded MacArthur's famous "I Have Returned" speech and retransmitted it to the United States. Aware of the fleet's importance, Japanese bombers struck the vessels, and signalmen experienced a new form of combat, shipboard fighting.[88] During the crucial Battle of Leyte Gulf (23–26 October 1944), the U.S. Navy destroyed much of the Japanese fleet and opened the way for the liberation of the rest of the Philippines.

Although the ground campaign initially went well, it proved more difficult than MacArthur had anticipated. The Japanese, determined to make Leyte the decisive battle for the Philippines, continued to pour reinforcements onto the island. Moreover, heavy rains (23.5 inches in November alone) hampered Allied operations, particularly the construction of roads and airfields.[89] Despite the commitment of much of its remaining air and naval power, Japan could not match the Allies' strength, and by December the Sixth Army had retaken most of the island.

Naval fire control party of the 293d Joint Assault Signal Company on Luzon

MacArthur's forces then moved on to Luzon, which they invaded on 9 January 1945. Having lost Leyte, the Japanese fought an extended delaying action on Luzon to stall Allied progress toward their homeland, and the ground campaign there became the largest of the Pacific war. MacArthur committed ten divisions, five regimental combat teams, and other supporting elements. General Akin and his signal troops numbered among them. A mobile communications unit accompanied MacArthur's advance toward Manila, containing entire message centers with the necessary radios and other equipment mounted on 100 vehicles. Using antrac, spiral-four cable, and open wire lines, signalmen maintained the theater-level support MacArthur required. The unit moved so rapidly, in fact, that General Krueger complained that signal vehicles were clogging the highway and obstructing the movement of combat units and tanks. MacArthur, however, eager to enter the capital, did not find fault.[90] After a month of bloody street fighting, Manila fell in early March. While the Japanese offered only scattered resistance on Bataan, the recapture of Corregidor proved more costly. By late June 1945 organized Japanese resistance in the Philippines had largely ended, although some forces held out in the mountains of north central Luzon until the end of the war.[91]

While mopping-up operations continued in the Philippines, the Americans proceeded to Iwo Jima and Okinawa, the last major stepping-stones on the way to their ultimate destination, the home islands of Japan. The capture of these and other islands in the Ryukyus chain would provide both air and naval bases within range of the final target. The Army played a supporting role in the month-long battle for Iwo Jima, probably the most heavily defended Japanese position in the Pacific. The marines used a considerable amount of Signal Corps equipment, including antrac.[92] For the assault on Okinawa, half a million men from the Army, Navy, and Marines participated in the invasion launched by the Tenth Army on 1 April 1945.[93] Lt. Gen. Simon B. Buckner, Jr., commanded the Tenth Army with Col. Arthur Pulsifer as his signal officer. The army included a variety of signal units to provide tactical and base communications.

Signal operations on Okinawa proved to be the culmination of the joint practices and procedures developed during the war. A Signal Corps officer, Col. Charles W. Baer, commanded the joint communications activities on the island. Signal units under his command included the 75th and 593d JASCOs. The Signal Corps' fleet did not participate in this campaign, but Army signal personnel served aboard the Navy's communications ships. On shore, the Okinawa joint communication center became "the largest, most completely joint center in the Pacific."[94] It suffered, however, from a shortage of skilled personnel to handle upwards of 475,000 words of record traffic per week by 2 June. Meanwhile the Japanese, who had not opposed the amphibious landing, mounted a tenacious defense from cave and tunnel positions, while from the air kamikaze pilots inflicted extensive destruction on Allied naval forces. Casualties on Okinawa were high; over 12,000 men lost their lives. Despite the fanatical resistance, the Allies prevailed and by midsummer stood poised on Japan's doorstep.[95]

As the Signal Corps prepared its communications plan for the proposed invasion of Japan, known as Operation OLYMPIC, the dropping of the atomic bombs on Hiroshima and Nagasaki brought the war to a sudden and cataclysmic conclusion.[96] On 14 August 1945 Japan accepted the Allies' surrender terms. Offensive action against the Japanese ended the next day. The Signal Corps played a central role in reestablishing radio contact with Japan so that the surrender arrangements could be completed.[97] On 2 September 1945, known as V–J Day, hostilities with Japan officially ceased and the Signal Corps performed its last wartime mission by flashing the formal surrender proceedings aboard the USS *Missouri* in Tokyo Bay around the world.[98]

Notes

[1] Stetson Conn and Byron Fairchild, *The Framework of Hemisphere Defense*, United States Army in World War II (Washington, D.C.: Office of the Chief of Military History, Department of the Army, 1960), p. 410.

[2] Conn et al., *Guarding the United States*, chs. 12, 13, 16; Terrett, *Emergency*, pp. 281–86; Thompson, Harris, et al., *Test*, pp. 93–102.

[3] For a discussion of preparations for continental defense, see Conn et al., *Guarding the United States*, ch. 3. In March 1941 the War Department directed that the continental United States be divided into four strategic areas to be known as defense commands: Northeast, Southern, Central, and Western (to include the Alaska Defense Command, created in February 1941). In 1942 the corps areas were redesignated as service commands. (Conn et al., *Guarding the United States*, pp. 28, 39). See map in Kreidberg and Henry, *Military Mobilization*, p. 585. The Caribbean Defense Command was officially activated on 10 February 1941. (Conn et al., *Guarding the United States*, p. 330.)

[4] Thompson, Harris, et al., *Test*, pp. 106–08; Conn and Fairchild, *Hemisphere Defense*, pp. 249f; Conn et al., *Guarding the United States*, pp. 322–26.

[5] Terrett, *Emergency*, p. 280.

[6] Thompson, Harris, et al., *Test*, pp. 103–04; Conn and Fairchild, *Hemisphere Defense*, p. 129; Conn et al., *Guarding the United States*, chs. 18 and 19. A former member of the 50th Signal Battalion later published his memoirs, which include a section about his service in Iceland. See John Brawley, *Anyway, We Won* (Marcelline, Mo.: Walsworth Publishing Co., 1988).

[7] Thompson, Harris, et al., *Test*, pp. 126–27; U.S. Army, Alaska, *Army's Role in Building Alaska*, p. 96. Construction of Fort Greely began on 1 February 1941. Conn et al., *Guarding the United States*, p. 235; "Fort Greely" in Robert B. Roberts, *Encyclopedia of Historic Forts* (New York: Macmillan Publishing Company, 1988). This installation was closed in 1944; the present Fort Greely is located on the site of a World War II airfield near Delta Junction, Alaska.

[8] Terrett, *Emergency*, pp. 277–78; Thompson, Harris, et al., *Test*, p. 125.

[9] On the war in Alaska, see Conn et al., *Guarding the United States*, chs. 10 and 11.

[10] Stanley W. Dziuban, *Military Relations Between the United States and Canada, 1939–1945*, United States Army in World War II (Washington, D.C.: Office of the Chief of Military History, Department of the Army, 1959), p. 222. See also Conn and Fairchild, *Hemisphere Defense*, ch. 15, and Karl C. Dod, *The Corps of Engineers: The War Against Japan*, United States Army in World War II (Washington, D.C.: Office of the Chief of Military History, United States Army, 1966), pp. 299–318, 334. The literature on the Alaska Highway is fairly extensive and growing. Two of the more recent studies are those by Heath Twichell, *Northwest Epic: The Building of the Alaska Highway* (New York: St. Martin's Press, 1992) and K. S. Coates and W. R. Morrison, *The Alaska Highway in World War II: The U.S. Army of Occupation in Canada's Northwest* (Norman: University of Oklahoma Press, 1992).

[11] Dziuban, *United States and Canada*, p. 237. The telephone line ran from Edmonton, Alberta, Canada, to Fairbanks, Alaska, a distance of just over two thousand miles.

[12] Stanley L. Jackson, Stringing Wire Toward Tokyo: A Brief History of the Alaska Military Highway Telephone Line, typescript [Washington, D.C.: Signal Corps Historical Section, Jan 1944], copy in CMH files; Thompson, Harris, et al., *Test*, pp. 136–41,

482–86. The Signal Corps also provided communications in conjunction with the Canadian Oil (Canol) project by which the United States developed the oil resources along the Mackenzie River in Canada and constructed several pipelines from the wells to Alaska.

[13]This theater encompassed the area from eastern Borneo to western Australia. Pogue, *Marshall*, 2: 376.

[14]D. Clayton James, *The Years of MacArthur*, 3 vols. (Boston: Houghton Mifflin Co., 1970–1985), 2: 80; Thompson and Harris, *Outcome*, pp. 239–43.

[15]Construction of the tunnel had begun under Brig. Gen. Charles E. Kilbourne, Jr., who commanded the harbor defenses of Manila and Subic Bays during the early 1930s. Kilbourne was one of the Signal Corps' Medal of Honor winners (see chapter 3). See Jonathan M. Wainwright, *General Wainwright's Story* (Garden City, N.Y.: Doubleday and Co., Inc., 1946), p. 95, and Kilbourne's biographical file in DAMH-HSR.

[16]Thompson, Harris, et al., *Test*, pp. 116–22. For detailed accounts of these events, see Louis Morton, *The Fall of the Philippines*, United States Army in World War II (Washington, D.C.: Office of the Chief of Military History, Department of the Army, 1953) and Wainwright, *General Wainwright's Story*.

[17]Thompson and Harris, *Outcome*, pp. 271–75.

[18]Thompson, Harris, et al., *Test*, p. 478.

[19]For a complete account of the campaign, see John Miller, Jr., *Guadalcanal: The First Offensive*, United States Army in World War II (Washington, D.C.: Historical Division, Department of the Army, 1949). A recent comprehensive study is Richard B. Frank, *Guadalcanal* (New York: Random House, 1990). Briefer summaries are contained in Matloff, ed., *American Military History*, pp. 503–04; and Ronald H. Spector, *Eagle Against the Sun* (New York: Free Press, 1985), pp. 190–201, 205–14. The Signal Corps' role is outlined in Thompson, Harris, et al., *Test*, pp. 476–81.

[20]Both AFHQ and the Signal Center later moved to Algiers. George F. Howe, *Northwest Africa: Seizing the Initiative in the West*, United States Army in World War II (Washington, D.C.: Office of the Chief of Military History, Department of the Army, 1957), pp. 84, 309. For a list of the duties of the Signal Section, AFHQ, see Thompson and Harris, *Outcome*, p. 28.

[21]For a detailed discussion of the Signal Corps in the North African campaign, see Thompson, Harris, et al., *Test*, ch. 12, on which this section is based.

[22]Such units were organized under T/O 11–517S, 9 Sep 1942. See the discussion of Joint Assault Signal Companies in the section on the Normandy invasion below.

[23]Sidney L. Jackson, Tactical Communication in World War II, Part 1: Signal Communication in the North African Campaigns, typescript [New York: Signal Corps Historical Section, Apr 1945], pp. 14–16, copy in CMH files; Ray S. Cline, *Washington Command Post: The Operations Division*, United States Army in World War II (Washington, D.C.: Office of the Chief of Military History, Department of the Army, 1951), pp. 183–87, discusses the confusion surrounding the unit's activation.

[24]Thompson, Harris, et al., *Test*, pp. 353–64; Theodore F. Wise, "The SCR 299" (Fort Gordon, Ga.: U.S. Army Signal Museum, n.d.).

[25]Thompson, Harris, et al., *Test*, p. 364; Jackson, Tactical Communication, pt. 1, ch. 3, discusses the problems and lessons learned from Operation Torch.

[26]Thompson, Harris, et al., *Test*, pp. 368–69, 457; Jackson, Tactical Communication, pt. 1, p. 154.

[27]Thompson, Harris, et al., *Test*, pp. 371–73; Rumbough, "Radio Relay," pp. 3–12.

[28]Thompson, Harris, et al., *Test*, pp. 377–79.

[29]Ibid., p. 382.

[30]As quoted in Thompson, Harris, et al., *Test*, p. 380.

[31]Thompson and Harris, *Outcome*, pp. 30–35. For additional details, see Sidney L. Jackson, Tactical Communication in World War II, Part 2: Signal Communication in the Sicilian Campaign, typescript [New York: Signal Corps Historical Section, Jul 1945], copy in CMH files.

[32]Thompson and Harris, *Outcome*, p. 43; Albert N. Garland and Howard McGaw Smyth, *Sicily and the Surrender of Italy*, United States Army in World War II (Washington, D.C.: Office of the Chief of Military History, Department of the Army, 1965), p. 419.

[33]Though mine detectors bore Signal Corps designations, the Corps of Engineers had responsibility for their development. The Signal Corps, however, procured, stored, and issued them. The SCR–625 was developed for the Army by the National Defense Research Committee.

[34]As quoted in Thompson and Harris, *Outcome*, p. 36. The Sicilian campaign is detailed in Garland and Smyth, *Sicily and the Surrender of Italy*. See also Matloff, ed., *American Military History*, pp. 478–80.

[35]Mussolini was killed by anti-Fascist partisans in April 1945.

[36]For a detailed account of the Fifth Army's operations in Italy, see Chester G. Starr, ed., *From Salerno to the Alps: A History of the Fifth Army* (Washington, D.C.: Infantry Journal Press, 1948). It is based on the nine-volume official Fifth Army history.

[37]Department of Defense, Office of Public Information, News Release no. 1255–56 (4 Dec 1956), "Pigeon Training Activity to be Closed at Army Signal Corps Post Soon," copy in author's files; "Pigeon that Saved a Brigade," *Parade* (28 Jun 1981), p. 16; Phillips, *Signal Center and School*, p. 310.

[38]*Fifth Army History*, 9 vols. (Florence, Italy: L'Impronta Press, 1945 [vols. 1–4]) 3: 60; W. W. Keen Butcher, 34th Signal Company chronicle, typescript in unit files, DAMH-HSO; Thompson and Harris, *Outcome*, pp. 49–55.

[39]Thompson and Harris, *Outcome*, p. 57.

[40]Starr, ed., *Salerno to Alps*, ch. 5; Thompson and Harris, *Outcome*, pp. 55–60.

[41]Butcher, 34th Signal Company chronicle, p. 55.

[42]Starr, ed., *Salerno to Alps*, chs. 9–11.

[43]The strength figure in the United Kingdom includes both air and ground forces. Roland G. Ruppenthal, *Logistical Support of the Armies*, 2 vols., United States Army in World War II (Washington, D.C.: (Office of the Chief of Military History, Department of the Army, 1953–1959), 1: 231–32. This volume contains a detailed discussion of the buildup. See also Pogue, *Marshall*, 2: ch. 14.

[44]Thompson, Harris, et al., *Test*, p. 105; Thompson and Harris, *Outcome*, pp. 75–76.

[45]Thompson, Harris, et al., *Test*, p. 313; Thompson and Harris, *Outcome*, p. 79.

[46]Until February 1943, when he became commander of the new North African Theater of Operations, Eisenhower continued to serve as commander of ETOUSA in addition to leading the Allied forces in North Africa. Lt. Gen. Frank M. Andrews replaced Eisenhower as commander of the European theater. After Andrews' death in a plane crash in May 1943, Lt. Gen. Jacob L. Devers assumed command. Ruppenthal, *Logistical Support*, 1: 36–37, 43, 113, 123, 162; Thompson, Harris, et al., *Test*, p. 339; Thompson and Harris, *Outcome*, pp. 75–77. Matejka was promoted to colonel on 24 December 1941 and to brigadier general on 2 August 1942 ("Matejka, Jerry V.," biographical files, DAMH-HSR).

[47]Thompson and Harris, *Outcome*, p. 88.

[48]Signal Division, SHAEF, *Report of Signal Division, Supreme Headquarters Allied Expeditionary Force*, 7 vols. (n.p.: n.d.) 1 and 2 [bound together]: 6–7, 66; Thompson and Harris, *Outcome*, pp. 86, 88–89. The combined board included representatives from the Allied navies, Allied air forces, ETOUSA, 21st Army Group (British), and the 1st Army Group (American). The board dated from the ARCADIA conference held in Washington, D.C., during December 1941 and January 1942.

[49]Upon the launching of the invasion the Services of Supply was redesignated as the Communications Zone, and Rumbough then became chief signal officer, Communications Zone. To avoid possible confusion, the Communications Zone is defined as "all the territory in the theater outside of the combat zone." Compare to the term "Line of Communications" used during World War I (see chapter 5). Ruppenthal, *Logistical Support*, 1: 204, n. 22, and p. 206.

[50]With the formation of SHAEF, the ETOUSA and SOS staffs were consolidated. On the somewhat complicated command relationships, see Ruppenthal, *Logistical Support*, 1: ch. 5. Lanahan became chief signal officer, SHAEF, in March 1945.

[51]Bates and Fuller, *Weather Warriors*, pp. 88–95; Ruppenthal, *Logistical Support*, 1: 374–75. GOLD, JUNO, and SWORD were the code names for the beaches on which the British and Canadians landed.

[52]For a list of the types of units, see Thompson and Harris, *Outcome*, pp. 94–95.

[53]Ibid., pp. 231–33.

[54]In addition to engineer and signal units, the special brigades also contained transportation, quartermaster, ordnance, medical, military police, and chemical troops. A flexible organization, the engineer special brigade additionally comprised other components as needed. Ruppenthal, *Logistical Support*, 1: 284.

[55]For the organization of the JASCO, see TOE 11–147S (21 October 1943). See also Thompson and Harris, *Outcome*, pp. 231–33; Vincent W. Fox, The Role of the JASCO [1947], typescript in file of 592d Signal Company, DAMH-HSO; Ruppenthal, *Logistical Support*, 1: 282–85 and ch. 8.

[56]The foil was called British Window or American Chaff. The length of the strips depended on the frequency of the radar to be jammed. Thompson and Harris, *Outcome*, p. 297, n. 63. For an illustration of how it works, see *Outcome*, p. 304. On countermeasures in general, see *Outcome*, ch. 10.

[57]Thompson and Harris, *Outcome*, pp. 115, 318.

[58]Ibid., pp. 97–98, 101. The award citations were published in WDGO 83 and 89, 1944, dated 27 October and 28 November, respectively.

[59]Thompson and Harris, *Outcome*, pp. 100–101, 112–13; Clarke, Army Pictorial Service, pp. 36–37; Interv, Rebecca Raines with Herman Wall, 3 Jul 95. After the war, Wall enjoyed a highly successful career as a commercial photographer.

[60]Thompson and Harris, *Outcome*, pp. 101–04, 107.

[61]Ibid., pp. 104–07.

[62]Ruppenthal, *Logistical Support*, 1: 442, 520; Thompson and Harris, *Outcome*, pp. 144–45.

[63]Thompson and Harris, *Outcome*, pp. 115–21, 124–26, 131–38.

[64]Martin Blumenson, *Breakout and Pursuit*, United States Army in World War II (Washington, D.C.: Office of the Chief of Military History, Department of the Army, 1961), pp. 351–54.

[65]Thompson and Harris, *Outcome*, p. 126.

[66]Ibid., pp. 93; 106, n. 135; 126–27; Brawley, *Anyway, We Won*, p. 197.

[67]Thompson and Harris, *Outcome*, pp. 118–19; Charles B. MacDonald, *The Mighty Endeavor: American Armed Forces in the European Theater in World War II* (New York: Oxford University Press, 1969), p. 293; Blumenson, *Breakout and Pursuit*, pp. 43–44; Richard S. Faulkner, "Learning the Hard Way: The Coordination Between Infantry Divisions and Separate Tank Battalions During the Breakout from Normandy," *Armor* 99 (Jul–Aug 1990): 26–27.

[68]Treadwell, *Women's Army Corps*, p. 318; Thompson and Harris, *Outcome*, pp. 138–43.

[69]Thompson and Harris, *Outcome*, p. 156.

[70]Ibid., pp. 157–58.

[71]As quoted in Thompson and Harris, *Outcome*, p. 163.

[72]Ibid., pp. 162–63. For the award citation, see WDGO 89, 28 Nov 1944.

[73]Thompson and Harris, *Outcome*, p. 171.

[74]Maurice Matloff, *Strategic Planning for Coalition Warfare: 1943–1944*, United States Army in World War II (Washington, D.C.: Office of the Chief of Military History, Department of the Army, 1959), p. 32.

[75]Treadwell, *Women's Army Corps*, pp. 318, 410, 478; Thompson and Harris, *Outcome*, p. 218.

[76]Carroll A. Powell, "Communications in Pacific Ocean Areas," *Military Review* 25 (Jan 1946): 34. Colonel Powell served as the chief signal officer for the Central Pacific Area. According to the 1940 census, South Bend's population was 101,268. For the South Bend metropolitan area, the census counted 147,022 residents. See *The World Almanac and Book of Facts for 1944* (New York: World-Telegram, 1944), p. 448.

[77]Thompson and Harris, *Outcome*, pp. 205, 236.

[78]Ibid., pp. 219–25, 231–33, 261.

[79]Ibid., pp. 206–09.

[80]Thompson, Harris, et al., *Test*, p. 138; Thompson and Harris, *Outcome*, pp. 185–92.

[81]The AN/PRC–1 was a lightweight, high-powered set with a range of 200 to 2,000 miles. Instead of batteries, it required power generation by laborious hand cranking. The SCR–177, weighing 700 pounds, had to be carried by mule. Its range was 30 to 100 miles. The SCR–284, also adapted for pack transport, weighed about 100 pounds and had a range of from 5 to 20 miles. The SCR–300, the improved walkie-talkie, had a range of about 5 miles. Historical Division, U.S. War Department, *Merrill's Marauders (February-May 1944)*, American Forces in Action (Washington, D.C.: 1945), pp. 29–30; Thompson and Harris, *Outcome*, p. 193.

[82]Thompson and Harris, *Outcome*, p. 192; comments on draft manuscript, 21 Feb 1992, by Lt. Gen. Thomas M. Rienzi. As a captain, Rienzi commanded Headquarters Company, 96th Signal Battalion, in Burma. The 988th Signal Operation Company was redesignated in 1945 as the 988th Signal Service Battalion. In 1948 the 96th Signal Battalion became the 320th Signal Battalion.

[83]Charlton Ogburn, Jr., *The Marauders* (New York: Harper & Brothers, Publishers, 1959), p. 33.

[84]As quoted in Thompson and Harris, *Outcome*, p. 198.

[85]Spector, *Eagle Against the Sun*, pp. 455–57; Thompson and Harris, *Outcome*, p. 241.

[86]Edward J. Drea, *Defending the Driniumor: Covering Force Operations in New Guinea, 1944*, Leavenworth Papers no. 9 (Fort Leavenworth, Kans.: Combat Studies

Institute, 1984), pp. 9–11 and ch. 3. See also Edward J. Drea, *MacArthur's ULTRA: Codebreaking and the War Against Japan, 1942–1945* (Manhattan: University Press of Kansas, 1992).

[87]James, *Years of MacArthur*, 2: 538–39; Thompson and Harris, *Outcome*, p. 270.

[88]The Signal Corps had earlier used makeshift communications ships during the fighting in New Guinea, but had had to return them to the Transportation Corps. Rumbough, "Radio Relay," pp. 11–12; Thompson and Harris, *Outcome*, pp. 259–65, 275–80, 283–84.

[89]M. Hamlin Cannon, *Leyte: The Return to the Philippines*, United States Army in World War II (Washington, D.C.: Office of the Chief of Military History, Department of the Army, 1954), p. 185.

[90]Walter Krueger, *From Down Under to Nippon* (Washington, D.C.: Combat Forces Press, 1953), p. 244; Thompson and Harris, *Outcome*, p. 285.

[91]On signal operations, see Sixth United States Army, *Report of the Luzon Campaign, 9 January 1945–30 June 1945*, 4 vols. (1945), vol. 3, "Reports of the General and Special Staff Sections," pp. 133–54. On the campaign in general, see Robert Ross Smith, *Triumph in the Philippines*, United States Army in World War II (Washington, D.C.: Office of the Chief of Military History, Department of the Army, 1963); Matloff, ed., *American Military History*, pp. 516–21; Spector, *Eagle Against the Sun*, ch. 22.

[92]Thompson and Harris, *Outcome*, p. 289, n. 44.

[93]The Tenth Army comprised four Army and three Marine divisions.

[94]Thompson and Harris, *Outcome*, p. 292.

[95]The casualty total is for Army, Navy, and Marine personnel. Roy E. Appleman et al., *Okinawa: The Last Battle*, United States Army in World War II (Washington, D.C.: Historical Division, Department of the Army, 1948), table no. 2, p. 489. For signal operations on Okinawa, see *Tenth Army Action Report Ryukyus, 26 March to 30 June 1945*, 3 vols. (3020th Engineer Topographic Company, 1945), 1: ch. 11, sec. 12; Thompson and Harris, *Outcome*, pp. 288–98.

[96]Matloff, ed., *American Military History*, pp. 521–22, 525–26.

[97]Thompson and Harris, *Outcome*, pp. 600–601; "Surrender on the Air, An Official Signal Corps History of Message Traffic on the Japanese Capitulation," *Military Review* 26 (May 1946): 31–39; ARSO, 1946, pp. 3–4, 472–73.

[98]Thompson and Harris, *Outcome*, p. 300.

CHAPTER IX

The Cold War, Korea, and the Cosmos

The United States emerged from World War II as the most powerful nation in the world. There would be no return to isolationism and withdrawal from world affairs as after World War I. The four-power agreements among the Allies henceforth required the continuous presence of American troops in Europe. Moreover, the Army assumed the tremendous task of administering the military governments of Germany, Austria, Japan, and Korea. Having learned from its failure to support the League of Nations, the United States spearheaded the effort to form the United Nations. Through such programs as the Marshall Plan, the United States also helped to rebuild the world that the war had shattered.

Despite its prominence in international affairs, the nation soon began to dismantle its global military communications system. To many signal officers, particularly Maj. Gen. Frank E. Stoner, wartime administrator of the Army Command and Administrative Network, the policy was shortsighted.[1] Yet while the Army's ability to communicate around the world was disconnected, the technological revolution sparked by the war heralded amazing changes for the future. During the next fifteen years the Signal Corps' domain would come to include the heavens as well as the earth.

Organization, Training, and Operations, 1946–1950

With the return of peace, the Army underwent the typical postwar period of demobilization and reorganization. Discussion revolved around revamping the internal organization of the War Department and creating a unified Department of Defense. On 30 August 1945 General Marshall appointed a board of officers, headed first by Lt. Gen. Alexander M. Patch and later, after Patch's sudden death, by Lt. Gen. William H. Simpson, to study the first of these questions. Chief Signal Officer Ingles served as one of the members. The board, after holding extensive hearings, recommended the functional decentralization of the War Department, in particular the abolition of the Army Service Forces. With the approval of General Eisenhower, who had succeeded Marshall as chief of staff in November 1945, as well as that of President Truman, the reorganization became effective on 11 June 1946. Consequently, the Signal Corps and the other technical services returned to their prewar, independent status. Once again the chief signal officer and his counterparts reported directly to the chief of staff.[2]

But the scope of reorganization soon broadened to include not just the Army but the armed forces as a whole. Here the larger trend proved to be toward unification as espoused by both Marshall and Eisenhower. After much debate, Congress in 1947 passed the National Security Act, which created a unified National Military Establishment headed by a civilian secretary of defense. The new agency comprised the Departments of the Army, the Navy, and the newly independent Air Force. The secretary of war henceforth became known as the secretary of the army. Under this legislation, however, the service secretaries retained their cabinet ranks, and the defense secretary had little authority over their activities.[3] This compromise approach proved unsuccessful, and in 1949 Congress amended the legislation. As a result the National Military Establishment became an executive department, the Department of Defense, with the secretary of defense acquiring a measure of control over the services. While the service secretaries lost their cabinet status, they retained authority to administer the affairs of their own departments.[4]

In the midst of these changes, General Ingles oversaw the Signal Corps' transition from a wartime to a peacetime basis. By 30 June 1946 the Corps' strength had dwindled to just over 56,000 officers and men, only about one-sixth of the total a year earlier.[5] Due to postwar curtailment and consolidation of the Corps' activities, many of its field agencies and training facilities were discontinued, including the Central Signal Corps School at Camp Crowder.[6] The Corps consolidated all of its training at Fort Monmouth, except for the small supply school at Fort Holabird, Maryland.[7] In addition, the Signal Corps lost both personnel and functions to the Air Force and the Army Security Agency.

The Signal Corps suffered another severe blow with the dismantling of much of the ACAN system. General Ingles had proposed that the Army turn over the ACAN to a consortium of commercial companies to be operated as a diplomatic and governmental network during peacetime. Only during wartime, he believed, should the military resume control. Chief of Staff Eisenhower held the opinion, however, that the Army had no reason to maintain such a system at all, and in 1946 he directed the Army to divest itself of its strategic network. The Signal Corps complied, leaving stations only at major overseas headquarters. East and Southeast Asia, including Korea and Vietnam, retained no ACAN links.[8] The Army's global network still included, however, the Alaska Communication System. This network acquired responsibility after the war for the portion of the Alcan telephone line running from Fairbanks to the Canadian border, and demands upon its services grew with the steady rise of population in the Alaska territory.[9]

The Army Pictorial Service also underwent cutbacks. V-Mail services, for example, were discontinued with the end of the war. Although Signal Corps cameramen documented war crimes trials, atomic bomb testing on Bikini atoll, and occupation activities in Germany and Japan, the Army War College photographic laboratory was closed, along with the Pictorial Service's Western Division. On the other hand, the Signal Corps resumed the sale of its photographs, suspended during the war, and requests for them multiplied.[10]

Signal Corps linemen string wire in postwar Japan.

Despite signs of decline, the Army's expanded worldwide commitments soon increased the demand for trained signal personnel and exceeded the capacity of Fort Monmouth's facilities to supply them. Therefore, in November 1948 the Signal Corps opened a new training center at Camp Gordon, Georgia, near the city of Augusta. Almost four decades had passed since the Corps had used this area as a winter flying school (see chapter 4). The post was named for Lt. Gen. John Brown Gordon, a Confederate officer who later served as governor of Georgia and as a United States senator. Established during World War II as a training camp, the site now became the home of the Southeastern Signal School.[11]

With the addition of Camp Gordon to the Signal Corps system, the Army on 23 August 1949 designated Fort Monmouth as the Signal Corps Center. In addition to the school and laboratories, the center included the Signal Corps Board, the Signal Patent Agency, the Signal Corps Publications Agency, the Signal Corps Intelligence Unit, and the Pigeon Breeding and Training Center.[12]

On the tactical level, divisional signal units underwent few major organizational changes in the period of upheaval following World War II. New tables of organization approved in 1948 continued to provide signal companies for infantry, airborne, and armored divisions. The 1st Cavalry Division, reorganized as infantry yet retaining its historic designation, now contained a signal company instead of a troop.[13] One of the more controversial changes in the divisional tables reflected the increasing role of light aircraft. Divisional field artillery had been

General Akin

assigned planes since 1942; the 1948 tables assigned them to both the artillery and the division headquarters company.[14] In 1952 further revisions assigned light aircraft to infantry regiments, while authorizing helicopters for the signal company and other divisional elements.[15]

The Signal Corps had regained its wings. During World War II the Signal Corps had used planes belonging to the Field Artillery to lay wire and deliver messages. Although the Signal Corps, as well as other branches, had lobbied to have planes allotted to it, no decision was made until the war had nearly ended. With the postwar cutbacks, aircraft did not appear in Signal Corps tables of organization and equipment for several years. Field army signal battalions were authorized liaison planes beginning in 1949, and helicopters were added in 1952.[16]

In June 1950 the Army Reorganization Act superseded the Defense Acts of 1916 and 1920 that provided the statutory basis for the technical services. The new law gave the secretary of the army authority to determine the number and strength of the Army's combat arms and technical services. Three branches—Infantry, Armor, and Artillery—received statutory recognition as combat arms. The Signal Corps, having thus officially lost the combat status conferred in 1920, numbered among the Army's fourteen service branches. While the technical services had survived another round in their continuing battle for existence, the act left the door open for further change by authorizing the secretary of the army to reassign the duties of any technical service, except the Corps of Engineers, along functional lines.[17] At the same time, the advent of the atomic bomb seemed to have rendered conventional war and the need for large armies obsolete. By June 1950 the U.S. Army's size had contracted to less than 600,000.[18]

Having guided the Signal Corps through the immediate postwar period, General Ingles retired from the Army on 31 March 1947. Thanks to his wartime association with David Sarnoff of RCA, Ingles began a new career as a director of RCA and president of RCA Global Communications, Inc.[19] The new chief signal officer, Maj. Gen. Spencer B. Akin, had served with distinction on General MacArthur's staff during World War II and accompanied him to Japan after the war. Within a few years his knowledge of the Far East proved particularly valuable for the branch he now headed.

The Korean War

Unfortunately, the tranquil peace hoped for after World War II did not materialize. New international tensions arose as the Cold War brought down an Iron Curtain between Eastern and Western Europe. The United States committed itself to the defense of Western Europe through membership in the North Atlantic Treaty Organization (NATO), whose forces stood aligned against those of the Warsaw Pact formed between Russia and its satellites. Crises such as the Berlin blockade (1948–1949) and the victory of the Communist forces led by Mao Tsetung (Mao Zedong) in the Chinese civil war (1949) cast an ominous pall over world affairs. In that same year, Russia detonated its first atomic bomb, ending the U.S. monopoly over nuclear weapons. The arms race had begun, and the threat of nuclear war thereafter became a constant concern. Meanwhile, the foreign policy of the United States focused on the containment of communism. Although the United States had anticipated and prepared for an outbreak of overt hostilities in Europe, the first armed confrontation involving the Army came thousands of miles away, in Korea.

For forty years, since the Russo-Japanese War of 1904–1905, Korea had suffered under Japanese rule. After World War II the United States and the Soviet Union jointly occupied Korea, with the 38th Parallel separating their jurisdictions. Although the Allies agreed to eventually grant a unified Korea full independence, the temporary boundary, as in Germany, hardened into a lasting division. To the north, the Soviets installed a Communist government, while to the south, a republic with an elected president took form. In 1948 the United States and Russia began removing their occupation troops. Completing its withdrawal in mid-1949, the United States left behind an advisory group to help train South Korea's armed forces.[20] But civil unrest within the divided nation soon disrupted the fragile peace.[21]

On 25 June 1950 North Korean forces invaded South Korea, and the resulting conflict remains one of America's least known wars. Yet it was a bitter one. Initially, the United States did not intend to become engaged in ground combat in Korea or to fight an extended war there. The United Nations, meeting on the afternoon of 25 June, adopted a resolution calling for a cease-fire and withdrawal of the North Koreans to the 38th Parallel. However, it soon became clear that South Korea's lightly armed forces could not stop the North Koreans. The South Korean capital of Seoul fell within a few days, and the Communist forces continued to push southward. On 30 June, to prevent the nation's downfall, President Truman decided to commit American ground forces.

The United States had to draw these troops from the occupation forces in Japan, elements of the Eighth Army under the command of Lt. Gen. Walton H. Walker. Four divisions were serving on occupation duty: the 1st Cavalry Division and the 7th, 24th, and 25th Infantry Divisions. They had lost, however, most of their World War II veterans and were not ready for combat. In addition to being seriously understrength, their World War II–vintage vehicles and equipment had seen better days. Many critical items, such as ammunition and radios, were in short supply. Moreover, unit training opportunities had been limited by the scarcity of open space in Japan. These soldiers, accustomed to the somewhat leisurely pace of occupation duty, were about to meet a tough, disciplined, and well-equipped foe.[22]

The United States Army ultimately sent eight divisions to Korea (six Regular Army and two National Guard), and the Marines provided one.[23] In all, twenty members of the United Nations contributed ground, air, and/or naval forces. General Douglas MacArthur, in charge of the American forces in the theater, also served as commander in chief of the United Nations Command (UNC).[24]

The Signal Corps faced many challenges in preparing to fight another war. By June 1950 its strength stood at only 48,500.[25] To meet wartime manpower demands, Reserve signal officers and units were called up. The Signal Corps also expanded its training facilities at Forts Holabird and Monmouth and at Camp Gordon and established a new training center at San Luis Obispo, California, in December 1951.[26] Moreover, the nation's sudden entrance into the war caught both the Army and industry unprepared: There had been no interim mobilization period. Unlike the two world wars, the Korean War found the Signal Corps responsible for conducting its own industrial expansion program. Shortages of various critical components arose, including polyethylene insulation and nylon covering material for wires, synthetic manganese dioxide used in high-performance dry batteries, and quartz crystals for radios. In time the Signal Corps, working with the manufacturers, found solutions to these and other production bottlenecks.[27]

Meanwhile the Eighth Army, which did most of the fighting in Korea, suffered from a scarcity of signal units. Its two corps-level signal battalions were unavailable, having been inactivated in Japan as part of the postwar troop reductions.[28] Until the reestablishment of the I and IX Corps in the fall of 1950, the Eighth Army's headquarters signal section provided communications support directly to the subordinate divisions, placing a great strain on its limited resources.[29] To meet the immediate need, three of the divisional signal companies, the 13th, 24th, and 25th, were rushed to Korea, while the 7th Infantry Division and its signal company temporarily remained behind in Japan to be "cannibalized" to provide personnel for the other divisions. Other Eighth Army signal units to see action early in the war included the 304th Signal Operation Battalion and the 522d and 532d Signal Construction Battalions.[30] (*Map 1*)

During the first months of combat the city of Taegu became the Eighth Army's headquarters in Korea. This location had been chosen in part because it possessed good communication facilities in the form of a relay station of the Tokyo-Mukden cable.[31] The Mukden cable served as Korea's main telephone-telegraph system and proved an invaluable asset during the war. In the words of Capt. Wayne A. Striley of the 71st Signal Service Battalion, "The Mukden cable advanced and withdrew with our forces. It was a great artery of communication— and a godsend to the Signal Corps. I don't know what we'd have done without it."[32]

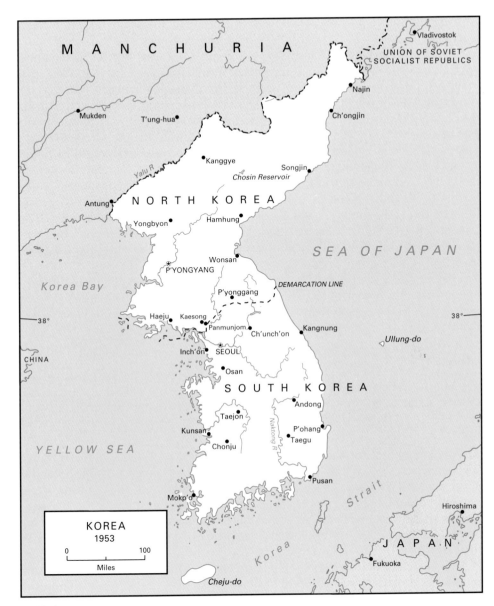

MAP 1

Initial operations went badly for the greatly outnumbered and ill-prepared American forces. The fighting began on 5 July at Osan where Task Force Smith of the 24th Infantry Division met defeat at the hands of the North Koreans. Although they put up a spirited defense, the Americans could not stop the advance of enemy tanks and infantry. To avoid encirclement, the task force made a disorderly withdrawal south to Taejon. Subsequent attempts by reinforcing elements of the 24th Division likewise failed to halt the North Koreans.[33]

Poor communications contributed to the early setbacks. Korea's mountainous terrain and its lack of good roads presented formidable obstacles to the establishment of effective command and control. The distances between headquarters were often too great for radios to net. Moreover, deteriorating batteries in the aging sets lasted only an hour or so if they worked at all, and new batteries proved nearly impossible to obtain. Wire communications proved equally tenuous. Signalmen struggled to string wire through a tortured topography of ridges, ravines, and rice paddies. Wire teams also made attractive targets for enemy ambushes, and many signalmen became casualties from such encounters. Where telephone lines could be installed, they proved difficult to maintain. Enemy artillery and tanks broke the wires, and sabotage inflicted further damage. Even fleeing refugees sometimes cut the wire, using portions as harnesses to secure their possessions. Thus, messengers frequently provided the vital links between units.[34]

For long-distance tactical communication, the troops depended heavily upon very high frequency (VHF), or microwave, radio. Col. Thomas A. Pitcher, who served as the Eighth Army's signal officer until September 1950, remarked that:

the VHF radio companies provided the backbone of our communications system. This method of transmission was so flexible that it could keep up with the infantry in the rapid moves that characterized the fighting in 1950–51. VHF provided communication over mountains, across rivers, and even from ship to shore. It carried teletype. It gave clear reception at all times—even when it was used at twice its rated range. After a headquarters was hooked up by wire, VHF remained as a secondary method of communication.[35]

The principal problem with VHF, which depends upon line-of-sight transmission, was the necessity of establishing stations in high and isolated locations. Since an entire station's equipment weighed two tons, with some individual pieces weighing over three hundred pounds, hand carriage of the equipment up the steep Korean slopes was extremely arduous.[36] The exposed stations also made excellent targets and signal soldiers often found themselves fighting as infantry to defend their positions.[37]

The climate made matters even worse. Although Korea, which extends roughly from the latitude of Boston to that of Atlanta, lies within the temperate zone, it experiences extreme weather variations. During the winter Siberian winds plunged temperatures to well below zero, causing radio batteries to freeze and making it extremely difficult to lay or maintain wire.[38] Radios and telephones became difficult to operate for men wearing heavy gloves. Summertime temperatures climbed as high as 100 degrees Fahrenheit, which combined with oppressive humidity to wreak havoc upon both men and equipment. The soldiers also had to contend with an annual monsoon season that generally lasted from June to September.[39]

Although much of its equipment resembled that used in World War II, the Signal Corps did introduce some new devices in Korea, such as tactical radio teletype. The AN/GRC–26 mobile radioteletype station (known variously as the "Angry 26" or the "Jerk 26") became one of the Signal Corps' most useful pieces of equipment and proved rugged enough to withstand travel over the rough Korean roads.[40] The Corps also employed improved ground radar to locate enemy mortar emplacements. These sets had been engineered on a crash basis with the Sperry Gyroscope Company, and they began to arrive in the field late in 1952.[41] The Corps also benefited from lighter field wire with better audio characteristics than its World War II counterpart.[42]

Above the battlefield, the Signal Corps put its restored wings to work. The aviation section of the 304th Signal Operation Battalion, for exam-

Signalmen in Korea use a water buffalo to stretch wire between poles.

ple, used five L–5 "mosquito" planes to carry as much as 34,000 pounds of messages a month between the Eighth Army and its corps headquarters. Aerial delivery worked especially well for maps, charts, and other bulky documents that could not be transmitted readily by radio or wire. Planes could do the job in a few hours when delivery by jeep might take several days.[43] The Signal Corps also employed planes to lay wire in areas where the terrain proved too rough for signalmen to do it on the ground.[44] In addition, the Signal Corps used wings of another variety, those belonging to its carrier pigeons, which flew many important messages over the fighting front.[45]

As in the past, signal units provided photographic coverage of the war for tactical, historical, and publicity purposes. Instead of separate photo companies, as in World War II, signal battalions at army and corps level were responsible for combat photography. In addition, divisional signal companies now included photo sections. Each section contained seven still photographers and two motion picture cameramen who performed ground as well as aerial photography. The section's six laboratory technicians could process still photos in the field, despite the difficulties of temperature control and limited supplies of fresh water. When necessary, cellular photographic units could also be called upon for special missions.[46]

Securing field wire dropped from a helicopter near the Naktong River

The enemy, meanwhile, generally employed less sophisticated signaling techniques. The North Korean Army used radios and other communications equipment supplied by the Soviet Union.[47] When China entered the war in November 1950, its forces operated without radios, communicating with whistles, bugles, and horns. Often these same devices also served as weapons of psychological warfare. During the night, for example, UN soldiers sometimes heard the eerie sound of an enemy bugler playing taps. Although these methods were primitive, they proved surprisingly effective.[48]

During August and September 1950 the Eighth Army successfully defended the "Pusan Perimeter"—actually a rectangle about 100 miles long and 50 miles wide bounded by the Naktong River on the west and the Sea of Japan on the east. The city of Pusan, the best port in Korea, sat on its southeastern edge.[49] Taegu lay dangerously close to the threatened western edge, and North Korean advances toward the city early in September forced the evacuation of the Eighth Army's headquarters to Pusan. General Walker ordered the move largely to protect the army's signal equipment, especially its large teletype unit, the only one of its kind in the country. Despite a determined North Korean effort to break through the defenses and drive the Americans into the sea, the Eighth Army held on.[50]

On 15 September 1950 the independent X Corps (comprising the 7th Infantry Division and the 1st Marine Division) carried out a successful landing behind enemy lines at Inch'on, and by the end of the month American and South Korean forces had recaptured Seoul.[51] In coordination with the Inch'on landing, the Eighth Army initiated a breakout from its defensive perimeter on 16 September. As North Korean resistance deteriorated in the wake of the reverses at Inch'on and Seoul, the Eighth Army rapidly swept northward to link up with the X Corps. Disorganized, defeated, and demoralized, the North Koreans retreated behind their borders. Victory appeared to be at hand as UN forces crossed the 38th Parallel into North Korea early in October, entering the capital of P'yongyang on the 19th. In order to completely destroy the North Korean armed forces and reunify Korea, UN troops continued to advance toward the Yalu River on the Manchurian border. MacArthur announced that the war would be over by Christmas, but his optimism proved tragically premature.

The war suddenly took on a new dimension when China intervened, as it had threatened to do if UN forces invaded North Korea. South Korean troops heading for the Yalu first encountered Chinese soldiers on 25 October.[52] Battle-hardened veterans of the recent civil war, the Chinese Communist Forces (CCF) soon attacked the UN units in large numbers. Despite the lack of air support and tanks, and with very little artillery, the Chinese defeated the Eighth Army in western Korea and the X Corps at the Chosin Reservoir in late November. They then pursued MacArthur's forces back across the 38th Parallel and by early January had regained control of Seoul. Instead of celebrating the holidays and victory at home, the UN troops fought on throughout the harsh Korean winter.

Throughout these tumultuous months the 7th Signal Company performed exemplary service. It received the first of four Meritorious Unit Commendations it earned in Korea for its support of the 7th Infantry Division from September 1950 to March 1951. The company provided communications during the landing at Inch'on and accompanied the division to the Yalu. At Chosin the signalmen fought alongside the infantry, often dismounting radio equipment so their trucks could be used as ambulances. Throughout the withdrawal, the company maintained a complete communications network until all friendly troops had departed, and then safely evacuated over 400 tons of signal equipment.[53]

After the retreat from North Korea, the X Corps consolidated with the Eighth Army under the leadership of Lt. Gen. Matthew B. Ridgway, who assumed command in December 1950 after General Walker's death in a traffic accident.[54] The new commander intended to resume offensive operations as soon as possible. In his planning, Ridgway emphasized communications, stating that he "wanted no more units reported 'out of communication' for any extended period."[55] When telephones and radios failed, he urged the use of runners and even smoke signals if necessary. By the end of March 1951 the Eighth Army under Ridgway had retaken Seoul and largely cleared South Korea of Chinese and North Korean troops.[56]

A member of the 40th Signal Company washes negatives in an icy Korean mountain stream.

Shortly afterward, General Akin's retirement brought a change of leadership to the Signal Corps. On 1 May 1951, Maj. Gen. George I. Back, a veteran of both World Wars I and II, became the new chief signal officer. From September 1944 to November 1945 he had been chief signal officer of the Mediterranean theater. Having served as signal officer of the Far East Command since 1947 and as signal officer, UNC, since 1950, General Back brought to the job an extensive background of knowledge about Korea. He called upon this experience to guide the Signal Corps through the remainder of the war.[57]

Despite Eighth Army's recent successes, the conflict became increasingly unpopular at home. MacArthur supplied additional controversy with his criticism of Truman's war policy, which led to MacArthur's relief as the theater commander and replacement by Ridgway.[58]

Direct Soviet involvement remained a dire possibility that could lead to World War III, but fortunately did not occur. With neither side able to secure a decisive military advantage, truce negotiations began in July 1951 and continued for two years. In the interim, fighting persisted on a limited scale. Many lives were lost in such bitter engagements as Heartbreak Ridge and Pork Chop Hill, but the battle lines remained virtually unchanged.

In the end, diplomacy halted the Korean War, with victory for neither side. Early in 1953 newly elected President Dwight D. Eisenhower traveled to the battlefront to fulfill a campaign pledge. Following his visit and a veiled threat to use atomic weapons, the belligerents finally signed an armistice agreement on 27 July 1953 at the village of Panmunjom. According to its terms, Korea remained divided by a demilitarized zone roughly following the 38th Parallel.

What has been called the "forgotten war" cost the United States Army nearly 110,000 casualties, 334 of them belonging to the Signal Corps.[59] Throughout the fighting, signal soldiers won recognition both as individuals and as units. While none received the Medal of Honor, two members of the 205th Signal Repair Company, Capt. Walt W. Bundy and 2d Lt. George E. Mannan, were posthumously awarded the Distinguished Service Cross for heroic action at Wonju during the night of 1–2 October 1950 when they covered the escape of seventeen enlisted men from their overrun position at the cost of their own lives.[60] A notable honor was won by the 272d Signal Construction Company, one of several black signal units that served in Korea. The 272d participated in six campaigns and earned the Meritorious Unit Commendation for operations during 1950 and 1951.[61]

General Back

After preserving the independence of South Korea, the Eighth Army remained to enforce the peace. Its signal units continue to provide the U.S. forces stationed in that country with a sophisticated communications system.

Signals in Space

Based upon wartime efforts, the post–World War II era witnessed revolutionary advances in science and technology. The Signal Corps, having already proven that it could send messages anywhere in the world, now looked to the heavens for new frontiers in communications.

The first breakthrough came on 10 January 1946 when scientists at the Evans Signal Laboratory succeeded in bouncing a radar signal off the moon. This project, named Diana for the Roman goddess of the moon, proved that humans could communicate electronically through the ionosphere into outer space. To accomplish this feat, the Signal Corps adapted a standard SCR–271 radar to transmit the signal. At almost 240,000 miles, this was certainly a long-distance communication; a new space-age era in signaling had begun.[62]

In spite of this promising start, postwar austerity stunted the initial growth of the space program. To many, including the prominent scientist Vannevar Bush, satellites and space travel still belonged to the realm of science fiction. The Korean War, however, brought increased defense spending, and space-related research benefited.[63]

The Army hoped to put the United States' first satellite into orbit during the International Geophysical Year (IGY) to be held from July 1957 to December 1958. The IGY was the latest in the series of international scientific undertakings, in which the Signal Corps had participated, that had begun with the International Polar Years of the 1880s and the 1930s. The interval between events had now been reduced from fifty to twenty-five years, largely due to the accelerated pace of technological progress during and after World War II. The new name reflected the wider scope of activities. In 1954 the Special Committee for the International Geophysical Year, meeting in Rome, recommended that the launching of earth satellites be a major goal of the IGY's research effort. The Army's plan, known as Project Orbiter, had to compete with proposals made by the Navy and the Air Force. Ultimately, a special Department of Defense advisory committee selected the Navy's Vanguard program. The Signal Corps, however, operated the primary tracking and observation stations, one in the United States and five in South America.[64]

But the Soviet Union took command of the heavens first. Its successful launching of *Sputnik* on 4 October 1957 shocked the nation. Senator Lyndon B. Johnson of Texas, who soon began an inquiry into satellite and missile programs, called the event a "technological Pearl Harbor."[65] If the Russians could send satellites into space, some argued, then they probably could launch long-range missiles capable of destroying the United States. Many Americans reacted strongly to this perceived threat and wanted to match the Soviets as quickly as possible. As the "space race" began in earnest, the Cold War acquired cosmic complications.

The Soviet achievement did not occur as abruptly as it might have seemed, for the Russians had devoted considerable resources to rocketry since the 1930s.[66] The success of the German V–1 and V–2 ballistic missiles during World War II spurred both the United States and the Soviet Union to undertake similar programs. (Although with less spectacular results than the Germans, American scientist Robert H. Goddard had conducted important experiments with liquid-fuel rockets during the 1920s and 1930s. During World War I his early research had received financing from the Signal Corps.)[67] The surrender of leading German rocket scientists, in particular Wernher von Braun, to the U.S. Army in 1945 brought invaluable expertise to this country via "Project Paperclip." The Russians, meanwhile, captured many of the German laboratory facilities. While the United States' missile program lagged after the war, the Soviet Union's forged ahead.[68]

The Russians quickly followed up their initial triumph with the launching of *Sputnik II* in November 1957. This time a canine passenger went along for the ride. Having suffered a second psychological blow, the United States moved quickly to close the technological gap and recover its lost national prestige. On 31 January 1958 the United States launched its first satellite, *Explorer I*. The Army could take credit for this accomplishment through the work of von Braun and his team of rocket experts at Redstone Arsenal in Huntsville, Alabama, working in conjunction with the Jet Propulsion Laboratory of the California Institute of Technology. Had the Army's plan originally been accepted for the IGY, the United States very likely could have been the first into space. In addition to salvaging the nation's pride, *Explorer*, loaded with sophisticated electronic equipment—components of which had been developed by the Signal Corps—contributed greatly to the scientific knowledge obtained during the IGY by discovering the Van Allen radiation belt encircling the earth.[69]

After many frustrating delays and the spectacular failure of its first launch attempt (which earned the project the nickname "Flopnik"), the Navy successfully launched *Vanguard I* on 17 March 1958. As part of its payload the satellite carried solar cells developed by the Signal Corps that helped to meet the sustained power requirements of space travel. *Vanguard II* followed in February 1959, carrying an electronics package created by the Signal Corps. The payload

The SCR–271 radar set used to bounce signals off the moon during Project Diana.

included infrared scanning devices to map the earth's cloud cover and a tape recorder to store the information. Unfortunately, technical problems with the satellite's rotation limited the usefulness of the images obtained.[70]

Military dominance of the space program proved to be short-lived. In July 1958 President Eisenhower signed into law an act establishing the National Aeronautics and Space Administration (NASA). The new agency, which came into being on 1 October 1958, absorbed the existing National Advisory Committee for Aeronautics, which dated from World War I. To provide future scientists, the government subsidized an expanded science curriculum in the public schools to train the technicians needed to win the space race.[71]

Yet military participation in the field continued. On 18 December 1958 the Signal Corps, with the help of the Air Force, launched the world's first communications satellite. Designated Project SCORE (Signal Communications via Orbiting Relay Equipment), this venture demonstrated that voice and coded signals could be received, stored, and relayed by an orbiting satellite. Its system

The Signal Corps Engineering Laboratory's astrophysics observatory at Camp Evans, New Jersey, 1959. The parabolic antennas tracked the earliest U.S. and Soviet satellites.

could carry one voice channel or seven teletype channels at sixty words per minute. Among its notable feats, SCORE broadcast tape-recorded Christmas greetings from President Eisenhower to the peoples of the world. This pioneering signal station, unfortunately, had a life expectancy of only a few weeks.[72]

The Signal Corps also became involved with the Courier program, a joint military-industrial endeavor to create the first satellite using ultra–high frequency (UHF) communications. This portion of the electromagnetic spectrum had remained relatively unused and generally free from man-made and atmospheric interference. The *Courier* satellite could simultaneously transmit and receive approximately 68,000 words per minute while moving through space at 16,000 miles per hour, and could send and receive facsimile photographs. *Courier* went aloft in October 1960 but inexplicably stopped communicating after seventeen days. Nevertheless, it represented another step forward in space-age signals.[73]

Despite such achievements and the Army's early lead in space technology, its role in the space race became a supporting one. The creation of NASA had institutionalized civilian control of the space program and emphasized America's peaceful purposes. As for the development of the military uses of outer space, the Department of Defense assigned this responsibility to the Air Force in September

1959.[74] Although the Army and the Signal Corps continued to make important contributions to the overall effort, the formation of the Army's Satellite Communications Agency in 1962 ended the Signal Corps' direct role in developing satellite payloads.[75]

During this period the Signal Corps also cooperated with the Weather Bureau, RCA, and several other organizations in developing the world's first weather satellite, *TIROS* (Television and Infra-Red Observation Satellite), launched by NASA in April 1960. Meteorology now soared to heights undreamed of by Myer, Hazen, Greely, or Squier. From its orbit about 450 miles above the earth, *TIROS* used two television cameras to photograph the clouds. Ground stations at Fort Monmouth and in Hawaii instantaneously received the photographic data. A second *TIROS* satellite, launched in November 1960, provided additional atmospheric data, and eight more followed over the next five years.[76]

Other satellites ushered in a communications revolution, connecting the world in a way wire and cables never could. In July 1962 NASA and AT&T jointly launched *Telstar*, the first active communications satellite, which picked up, amplified, and rebroadcast signals from one point on the earth to another. (A passive satellite only reflects the signals received.)[77] Weighing just thirty-five pounds and only three feet in diameter, *Telstar* broadcast the first live television pictures between continents and illustrated the tremendous potential of space-age signals. Later that year Congress passed the Communications Satellite Act of 1962 setting up the quasi-governmental Communications Satellite Corporation (COMSAT). It, in turn, managed an international consortium (INTELSAT), whose member nations shared access to the global telecommunications satellite system. Among their benefits, INTELSAT satellites increased the number of transoceanic telephone circuits and made real-time television coverage possible anywhere in the world.[78] Meanwhile the military, in conjunction with NASA, launched a series of communications satellites, known as SYNCOM, into synchronous orbit with the earth. Because these satellites remained at a fixed point in relation to the earth, they did not require tracking stations.[79]

Soviet propaganda and American panic to the contrary, *Sputnik* had not placed the Soviet Union light years ahead of the United States in the space race. Since 1957 Americans had attempted and accomplished more difficult missions than the Russians and in fact held the lead in satellite technology both for scientific and military purposes. Thanks in part to the work of the Signal Corps, beginning with Diana's echoes just twenty-three years earlier, the United States capped its achievements in space in 1969 by landing the first men on the moon.[80]

From Signals to Communications-Electronics

By the end of 1953 the Signal Corps' strength had grown to approximately seventy-five hundred officers and eighty-three thousand enlisted men as a result of the Korean War. But these numbers soon began to dwindle as the inevitable postwar reductions took effect. With the drawdown the Corps closed its schools at Fort Holabird and Camp San Luis Obispo.[81] The Korean War stimulated, however, a long-term expansion of the Signal Corps' research and development program, whose budget nearly doubled between 1955 and 1959.[82] The introduction of increasingly sophisticated electronic devices seemed to change the nature of communications almost overnight. Moreover, the proliferation of these devices throughout the Army engaged the Signal Corps in several new areas of operation.

For years the Corps had carried out its scientific experimentation in the three laboratories at or near Fort Monmouth: Coles, Evans, and Squier, known collectively as the Signal Corps Engineering Laboratories. To centralize their operations, they began moving into a new, specially designed building at Fort Monmouth in 1954, known as the Hexagon.[83] In 1958 the Army redesignated this facility as the U.S. Army Signal Research and Development Laboratory.[84] There the Corps pursued a long-range program that emphasized advances in the areas of miniaturization and systems integration.

The trend toward miniaturization had begun prior to World War II with the walkie-talkie. The latest version of the device, introduced early in the 1950s, was only about one-half the size and weight of the World War II model and represented the upper limit of miniaturization possible with vacuum tube technology. The redesigned handie-talkie, meanwhile, operated on FM, finally making it compatible with the walkie-talkie. At the same time, the Signal Corps introduced a new series of FM vehicular radios whose components could be arranged in different combinations and easily replaced. The radios also worked in conjunction with the walkie-talkie and the handie-talkie. A new, portable teletypewriter weighed just forty-five pounds, only one-fifth as much as the older equipment, and could be carried by a paratrooper on a drop. Not only did it transmit and receive messages more than twice as fast as previous models, it also was waterproof and therefore suitable for amphibious operations. Field switchboards weighing just twenty-two pounds also began coming off the production lines. Field telephones likewise underwent a weight reduction program, losing some three pounds and slimming down by one-third in size. Several of these streamlined items had begun to appear on Korean battlefields before the war ended.[85]

The key to further improvement was the development of the transistor. The Signal Corps, in conjunction with the electronics industry, in particular Bell Laboratories, facilitated the creation of this revolutionary device that helped to change the shape of communications after World War II. During the 1950s the Signal Corps subsidized much of the research and production costs and became, in fact, the military's center of expertise in this field.[86] The transistor held many implications for military communications: Its small size and low power requirements meshed perfectly with the trend toward miniaturized equipment. A transistor, made of a solid material such as silicon that acts as an electrical semiconductor, operated much more quickly than a vacuum tube and proved less susceptible to damage and such environmental factors as heat, cold, moisture, and fun-

The Hexagon research and development center at Fort Monmouth, New Jersey

gus.[87] Composed of several layers of material, it can be thought of as an electronic sandwich. Rugged, reliable, and portable, the transistor met the demands of battlefield communications.

The subsequent invention in 1958 of the integrated circuit, or electronic microchip, helped usher in the Information Age. Messages to be communicated became information to be processed. An integrated circuit contains all the components that form a complete circuit, to include transistors arrayed on a tiny silicon slice. The necessary interconnections, or wires, are printed onto the chip during manufacture. This type of circuitry is known as solid-state because it has no moving parts, hence its enhanced durability. A single microchip can handle many times the communications load of a traditionally wired circuit while taking up much less space. This innovation, which allowed increasingly powerful yet smaller machines to be built, eventually led to the ubiquitous desktop personal computers of the 1980s and 1990s.[88]

Like Myer's original wigwag code, most computers operate according to a two-element or binary system. Instead of the left and right movements of a signal flag, a computer reads electrical signals in the form of the digits 1 and 0. Digital signals are not continuous like radio waves but rather a series of discrete on and off impulses like those of a telegraph. According to a computer's binary code, the digit 1 represents on and 0 represents off. In early computers, mechanical switches opened and closed to control the current. Later, vacuum tubes and then transistors provided electronic gateways. Through this simple process of on and off signals the complex circuitry of a computer performs complicated tasks very rapidly.[89]

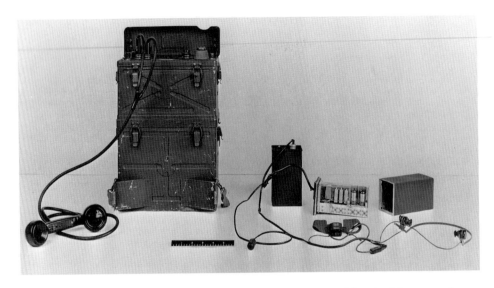

The results of the Army's miniaturization program are evident in this comparison of the SCR–300 and AN/PRC–6 radios.

Electromechanical computers had been built prior to World War II. Vannevar Bush and associates at the Massachusetts Institute of Technology had constructed the differential analyzer in the 1920s to solve complex mathematical equations related to electrical engineering. During the war the Army used this machine to compute artillery-firing tables.[90] The Signal Corps, meanwhile, used IBM punch card machines to analyze large amounts of data, a technique that proved especially useful in code and cipher work. In Britain a computer called Colossus helped crack the Enigma code.[91] Between 1943 and 1946 two scientists at the University of Pennsylvania, John W. Mauchly and J. Presper Eckert, Jr., developed an electronic digital computer for the Army to speed up the calculation of firing tables. Known as ENIAC (Electronic Numerical Integrator and Computer), it employed 18,000 vacuum tubes and weighed nearly thirty tons. Other early computers were similarly mammoth machines.[92]

During the 1950s the Signal Corps studied the feasibility of using computers for tactical application, and subsequently undertook the development of a farsighted program known as Fieldata that envisioned the coupling of computers and communications systems into worldwide networks. In December 1959 Sylvania delivered to the Signal Corps for testing the first model of a family of machines with the designation MOBIDIC (with some humor intended, no doubt, alluding to its large size). The acronym actually stood for mobile digital computer. These transistorized machines, designed to fit into a thirty-foot trailer van, would process information on such battlefield conditions as intelligence, logistics, firepower, and troop strength. Philco and IBM received contracts to build smaller computers, known as Basicpac and Informer. Although

Fieldata anticipated such developments as compatible computers and standard codes, budget constraints led to the premature termination of the program during the 1960s. By the 1980s technological advances finally made such an integrated system possible.[93]

The advent of the electronics age brought about the demise of one of the Signal Corps' oldest forms of communications, pigeons. The Army's birds, like horses and mules before them, had fallen victim to progress. Consequently, the Signal Corps closed the Pigeon Breeding and Training Branch (formerly Center) at Fort Monmouth on 1 May 1957. The Corps sold its birds to the public except for the remaining war heroes, such as G.I. Joe, which it presented to zoos around the country. Although the U.S. Army considered them obsolete, some nations, such as France, retained their feathered messengers for use in the event that more modern forms of communication failed.[94]

Progress brought other changes to Fort Monmouth where, until the early 1950s, the Signal Corps conducted the extensive experimentation associated with electronic warfare. The urban location of the post became a liability, however, due to interference from neighboring radio and TV stations, airports, and other sources ranging from power generators to electric toothbrushes. Consequently, in 1954 the Army established the Electronic Proving Ground at Fort Huachuca, Arizona, an isolated spot in mountainous, desert country about seventy miles south of Tucson. There the Signal Corps could test the latest equipment on thousands of acres relatively free from human or electronic interference. The fort also held historical significance for the Signal Corps, having been the site of a heliograph station during the Geronimo campaign in 1886 and again during the 1890 departmental tests. Now it would host investigations into such areas as battlefield surveillance, avionics, and meteorology.[95]

In 1957 the Signal Corps established the U.S. Army Combat Surveillance Agency to carry out its missions of combat surveillance and target acquisition. The agency also coordinated the Signal Corps' efforts with those of the other armed services, government agencies, and industry. The Signal Corps' work in this field included the development of such devices as drone aircraft, ground and airborne radar, and infrared sensors.[96]

Under the 1947 defense act the Army acquired responsibility for tactical missiles while the Air Force controlled strategic weapons. The Army conducted its guided missile research at the White Sands Proving Ground in New Mexico. Von Braun and his team of experts had initially worked there before moving to Redstone Arsenal. The Signal Corps, meanwhile, established a field agency at White Sands to provide missile range instrumentation.[97] Among its important contributions to air defense, the Corps worked with private industry to develop the Missile Master, an electronic fire control system for Nike air defense missiles.[98]

The Army's increased use of aviation called for a type of expanded communications support which became known as avionics. In addition to radio communication, this term included electronic aids to navigation, instrumentation, stabilization, and aircraft identification and recognition. Lightweight electronic equipment developed by the Signal Corps met the stringent weight requirements of the Army's relatively small aircraft.[99] To control Army air traffic in the battle zone, the Signal Corps developed a mobile flight operations center mounted in vans and trailers.[100] In 1954 the Signal Corps became responsible for the Army Flight Information Program to furnish Army aviators with current flight data such as charts, maps, and technical assistance.[101]

On and off again like the weather itself, the Signal Corps' meteorological activities resurged in the post–Korean War period, in part to support the expanded Army aviation program. Although the Air Force provided operational weather support for the Army, the Signal Corps supplied the associated communications. As it had since 1937, when it lost control of most of its weather-related activities, the Signal Corps remained the primary agent for Army meteorological research and development.[102] The Corps conducted much of this work in the Meteorological Division of the laboratories at Fort Monmouth, with some aspects assigned to the proving ground at Fort Huachuca. Since weather affects even the most sophisticated communications—causing distortion or disruption—the Signal Corps needed to learn more about such phenomena, and the curriculum at Fort Monmouth included courses in meteorological observation. In 1957 the U.S. Army Signal Corps Meteorological Company, the only unit of its kind, was formed at Fort Huachuca. Its nine teams were scattered around the globe to supply meteorological support for special testing exercises.[103] The Signal Corps even explored ways to control the weather, joining with the Navy and General Electric in cloud-seeding experiments.[104] Besides weather prediction, information about winds and conditions in the upper atmosphere proved crucial to missile guidance and control. The influence of weather upon radioactive fallout also warranted serious study.

Modern technology provided weather watchers with many new tools. In addition to the weather satellites already discussed, the Signal Corps pioneered many other techniques. In 1948 Signal Corps scientists at Fort Monmouth used radar to detect storms nearly 200 miles away and track their progress. New high-altitude balloons carried radiosondes (miniature radio transmitters) more than twenty miles aloft to transmit measurements of humidity, temperature, and pressure. To conduct atmospheric studies beyond that range, the Signal Corps used rockets. The Corps developed an electronic computer that could determine high-altitude weather conditions faster and more accurately than any other type of equipment. Using the wealth of data available, computers could also perform the many calculations needed to produce a forecast.[105]

In connection with the IGY, Signal Corps scientists conducted climatological studies around the world. Amory H. Waite, who had traveled extensively introducing new equipment during World War II, directed Signal Corps research teams in Antarctica, an area about which little was then known. In addition to making meteorological observations, these men gathered electromagnetic propagation data through the ice and tested various types of equipment. The Signal Corps conducted similar studies at the North Pole and made weather observations with rockets at Fort Churchill, Manitoba, Canada. The Corps also explored the upper atmosphere to learn more about its effects on communications.[106]

While satellites orbited above, the changing nature of communications had a significant impact at ground level as well. The Army needed satellite and missile tracking stations around the globe, making modernization of the ACAN imperative. To meet its short-term needs, the Signal Corps could call upon the commercial communication companies for assistance. For the long-term, the Corps began planning an entirely new system—UNICOM, the Universal Integrated Communications System. With computers making rapid automatic switching possible, UNICOM would provide greater speed and security in a variety of modes: voice, teletype, digital, facsimile, and video. Implementation of the system began in 1959, with completion slated for as late as 1970, depending upon available resources.[107]

Meanwhile, the immediate future of one portion of the ACAN remained in doubt as the Signal Corps once again contemplated the disposition of the Alaska Communication System. In 1955 the Signal Corps drafted legislation to authorize its sale but with no results.[108] In June 1957, however, the ACS underwent a significant change in mission: It was separated from the ACAN and relieved of primary responsibility for providing strategic military communication facilities at Seattle and within Alaska. Henceforth the system became essentially a public utility, while continuing to serve military and other government agencies in Alaska. Subsequent improvements to the system included the installation of a new cable in 1955 between Ketchikan and Skagway by the Army's cable ship, *Albert J. Myer.* This cable, in conjunction with one laid by AT&T from Ketchikan to Port Angeles, Washington, more than doubled the existing capacity of radio and land-line telephone circuits between Alaska and the United States.[109]

While the service provided by the ACS had been significantly improved, disaster loomed ahead. Earthquakes in 1957 and 1958 damaged equipment and disrupted communications, but they merely served as preludes to the major earthquake of March 1964, which devastated the region. As in San Francisco nearly sixty years earlier, Army units stationed in the area contributed greatly to the relief effort. The 33d Signal Battalion, with headquarters at Fort Richardson, provided vital communications to civilian agencies and communities during the emergency.[110] Although Alaska entered the Union in 1959 as the forty-ninth state, the Army continued to operate the ACS until 1962. At that time it finally divested itself of the system it had maintained since 1900 by transferring it to the Air Force. In 1971 the Air Force sold the ACS to RCA, bringing nearly a century of military communications in Alaska to an end.[111]

The post-Korea era also witnessed the invasion of a new and powerful communications medium into American homes. The economic restrictions imposed by World War II and Korea and the consequent diversion of raw materials to war production had delayed television's widespread commercial introduction. With peacetime, television boomed. Glowing cathode-ray tubes increasingly became a fixture in America's living rooms, and mass communication took on a new face.

Cameras and transmitting van of the Signal Corps mobile television section; below, *students receive television instruction.*

The Army, too, began to explore the applications of this electronic messenger. For combat purposes, the Signal Corps built a mobile television unit employing both ground-based and airborne cameras. Tested during maneuvers, this system promised to allow a commander to observe the battlefield and to control his units personally and more effectively. In August 1954 the Army held the first public demonstration of tactical television at Fort Meade, Maryland.[112]

Television also held much promise for training and educational purposes. During the 1950s the Signal Corps introduced its use at Forts Monmouth and Gordon. Tests demonstrated that television adapted particularly well to the teaching of motor skills—such as the assembly of electronic components. For some subjects it even proved superior to conventional teaching methods. By means of television, one instructor could teach a large number of students, while retaining the sense of individual instruction. The use of film and later videotape eliminated the need for the instructor even to be actually present in the class-room. Television also reduced training time and saved money. Having proven television's utility, the Signal Corps soon began assisting other branches with the development of televised training programs.[113]

In 1951 the Signal Corps began production at its Astoria studios of a public service television program, "The Big Picture." Initially focusing on the war in Korea, this award-winning documentary series used Signal Corps footage to bring news of the Army's activities into millions of homes each week. Its scope later expanded to include all aspects of the Army's role and mission around the world. By 1957 more than 350 stations carried the program. "The Big Picture" remained on the air for nearly twenty years, until the Army ceased production in 1970.[114]

Along with its achievements in space during the 1950s and early 1960s, the Signal Corps pioneered in the field of electronics and its military applications. The Corps' role in the development of the transistor and the use of computers for information processing produced fundamental changes in the nature of communications technology, the effects of which are still being felt.

Force Reductions, Readiness, and the Red Scare

As the space race had made manifest, the communications revolution of the 1950s took place in a political atmosphere of suspicion and hostility between the United States and the Soviet Union. The persistent Soviet threat required the maintenance of a strong defensive posture, despite the pressures to cut the military budget in the aftermath of the Korean War. President Eisenhower's defense policy, known as the New Look, placed reliance on nuclear deterrence rather than on the strength of the ground forces. Consequently, the Army experienced sub-stantial manpower cuts during the 1950s. Meanwhile the United States, closely followed by the Soviet Union, developed tactical nuclear weapons. By 1956 both nations also possessed hydrogen (thermonuclear) bombs a thousand times more powerful than those dropped on Japan.[115]

To meet the contingency of either nuclear or conventional war while keeping within its reduced budget, the Army reorganized its World War II triangular divisions. The new formations, known as pentomic divisions, consisted of five battle groups that could operate independently or concentrate for a major attack. The Regular Army finished reorganizing its divisions by the end of 1957, while the Army Reserve and National Guard completed their divisional restructuring in 1959. These leaner divisions were intended to meet the demands for personnel reductions while providing the capability to engage in modern warfare on a dispersed and fragmented atomic battlefield. Under such conditions, however, communications gained greater importance for command and control. Hence, divisional signal companies were expanded into battalions.[116]

To achieve operational flexibility, the Signal Corps devised the area communications system, a multiaxis, multichannel network. The system sought to satisfy the requirements of atomic warfare: mobility, invulnerability to attack, increased capacity, faster service, and greater range. Unlike the single axis system of the past, a multichannel network could withstand a breakdown in one area, such as that caused by a nuclear attack, and reroute communications along an alternate path. Such built-in redundancy had not been available in Korea, and its absence resulted in frequent communication shutdowns. Radio relay and multichannel cable formed the backbone of the system, with messengers, wire, and radioteletype also available.[117] Later advances in electronics technology helped to make the system work as the Signal Corps adopted transistorized equipment that operated automatically without the inherent delay caused by operators. By 1958, for example, the Signal Corps possessed a family of teletypewriters that handled messages at a rate of 750 words per minute. Smaller and lighter radios, meanwhile, covered a greater range of frequencies than their predecessors.[118]

Modern weaponry and equipment enabled the Army to fight more effectively despite its shrinking size. Active strength dropped below 900,000 in 1958.[119] At the same time, greater reliance on high technology increased the demand for skilled communications-electronics specialists. The Signal Corps revised its training curriculum accordingly, adding such courses as atomic weapons electronics, electronic warfare equipment repair, and automatic data processing. During the four years from 1955 to 1959 the Signal Corps trained 9,000 officers and 99,000 enlisted men at its schools.[120] Yet a shortage of skilled communicators became a chronic problem as the Signal Corps competed for personnel with the higher-paying civilian electronics industry.

Along with rising international tensions, the Cold War intensified domestic paranoia, and the Signal Corps became caught up in the host of Communist spy investigations and trials that pervaded the period. During the late 1940s Congressman Richard M. Nixon of California gained national prominence as a member of the House Un-American Activities Committee (HUAC), particularly for his role in the case of Alger Hiss, a State Department official who had spied for the Russians. With Hiss and others as evidence of widespread subversion, fear

General Lawton greets Secretary of the Army Stevens. Senator McCarthy is on General Lawton's right. Chief Signal Officer Back is second from left.

of communism became a national obsession. The trial and conviction of Julius and Ethel Rosenberg in 1951 for passing atomic secrets to the Soviet Union, played out against the backdrop of the Korean War, heightened the nation's fears. Even the couple's execution in 1953 did little to reassure the American public that the Communist menace was not omnipresent.

During the early 1950s Senator Joseph R. McCarthy of Wisconsin attained notoriety for his investigations into alleged Communist infiltration into American government, particularly the State Department. Loyalty and conformity became paramount, and the word "McCarthyism" entered the American lexicon. Eventually the senator's attention turned to the armed forces and to the Signal Corps in particular. During World War II Julius Rosenberg had worked for the Signal Corps as an electrical engineer, though he had lost his job in 1945 due to charges that he belonged to the Communist Party.[121]

The Signal Corps had scrutinized its security procedures in 1952 after a defecting East German scientist reported that he had seen microfilmed copies of documents from Fort Monmouth. The resulting investigation uncovered neither missing documents nor evidence of espionage. In addition, both the FBI and the HUAC conducted probes at Fort Monmouth to no avail. In late 1953, however, McCarthy picked up the scent, and even cut short his honeymoon in the West Indies to rush to Washington to begin hearings into subversion within the Signal

General O'Connell   *General Nelson*

Corps. The source of the latest accusations was Maj. Gen. Kirke B. Lawton, commander of Fort Monmouth, who had secretly warned the senator of possible subversion at the post. McCarthy used his committee's hearings to fan fears that a spy ring started by Rosenberg continued in operation at the Evans Signal Laboratory. During the probe the Army suspended many civilians from their jobs, but no indictments ever resulted.[122] McCarthy tried again to implicate the Signal Corps the following year when he accused a civilian employee, Mrs. Annie Lee Moss, of being a member of the Communist Party and having access to top secret messages as an Army code clerk. These allegations were also never proven.[123]

The most immediate result of these investigations into the Signal Corps was their effect on McCarthy himself, for they contributed greatly to his political downfall. Televised proceedings of his subcommittee, known as the Army-McCarthy hearings, began in April 1954 and created a national sensation. The senator's virulent attacks on the Army helped to turn public opinion against him. In December 1954 the Senate condemned McCarthy, who thereafter retreated from the public spotlight and died in 1957.[124]

During this period of turmoil Maj. Gen. James D. O'Connell succeeded General Back as chief signal officer in May 1955. Commissioned in the Infantry after graduating from West Point in 1922, O'Connell joined the Signal Corps in 1928. The next year he entered the Sheffield Scientific School of Yale University where he received a Master of Science degree in communication engineering in 1930. During World War II he served in Europe with the signal section of Headquarters, 12th Army Group. After the war he became director of the Fort Monmouth laboratories, followed by a tour as signal officer of the Eighth Army in Japan. Before becoming chief signal officer, O'Connell served as Back's deputy. With his promotion to lieutenant general in 1958, O'Connell became the first chief signal officer to hold that rank. His tenure as chief included the exciting achievements made during the IGY, and he helped launch the Signal Corps into the computer age through his support of the Fieldata program.[125]

When O'Connell retired in April 1959, his deputy, Maj. Gen. Ralph T. Nelson, replaced him effective on 1 May. Nelson, a member of the West Point class of 1928, had served in both World War II and Korea. He subsequently commanded the Signal Corps training center at Fort Gordon and the Electronic Proving Ground at Fort Huachuca. Like O'Connell, Nelson possessed the technical background necessary to steer the Corps through the revolutionary changes taking place in communications.[126]

Organization, Training, and Operations, 1960–1964

In 1960 the Signal Corps celebrated its centennial: A century had passed since Congress had authorized the addition of a signal officer to the Army Staff on 21 June 1860 and Albert J. Myer had received the appointment six days later. The year-long observance (21 June 1960 to 21 June 1961) included: a traveling exhibit that visited all major Signal Corps installations, the Pentagon, and the Smithsonian; the publication of numerous articles in newspapers and magazines about the Signal Corps; a special broadcast of "The Big Picture"; and the burial of a centennial time capsule at Fort Monmouth. The Signal Corps could indeed look back with pride on one hundred years of growth and accomplishment. Having become the Army's third largest branch, comprising about 7 percent of its strength, it had taken military communications from waving flags to speeding electrons and orbiting satellites.[127]

The Signal Corps began its second century, however, with some drastic changes. The centralization of authority that had resulted in the creation of the Department of Defense increasingly insinuated itself into the operations of the Army and resulted in the erosion of power traditionally held by the technical services. In 1955, for instance, the position of chief of research and development had been added to the Army Staff to supervise this functional area, cutting across the traditional authority of each of the technical bureaus.[128] Later, in 1960, the Defense Communications Agency was created to operate and manage the new Defense Communications System. This worldwide, long-haul system provided secure communications for the president, the secretary of defense, the Joint Chiefs of Staff, government agencies, and the military services.[129] The system incorporated the facilities of the ACAN—renamed the Strategic Army Communications Network (STARCOM)—which the Signal Corps continued to operate.[130] In another significant shift, the Signal Corps regained its status as a combat arm, which it had lost ten years before. In 1961 Army regulations designated the Signal Corps (along with the Corps of Engineers) as both a combat arm and a technical service.[131]

In that same year the new president, John F. Kennedy, and his secretary of defense, Robert S. McNamara, set out to reorganize and strengthen the armed forces to allow for a more flexible response to international crises. Concurrently, McNamara initiated far-reaching managerial reforms within the Defense Department that shifted power from the military services to the civilian bureaucracy. In conjunction with these changes at the higher levels, McNamara directed a thorough reorganization of the Army Staff. On 16 January 1962 President Kennedy submitted a plan to Congress that abolished the technical services, with the exception of the Medical Department. Congress raised no objections, and the reorganization became effective on 17 February. Although the positions of the chief chemical officer, the chief of ordnance, and the quartermaster general all disappeared, the chief signal officer and the chief of transportation were retained as special staff officers rather than as chiefs of services. The chief of engineers retained his civil functions only, while the chief signal officer now reported to the deputy chief of staff for military operations (DCSOPS).[132] By eliminating the technical services as independent agencies, McNamara succeeded where Somervell and others had failed.

For the Signal Corps, the McNamara reforms wrought a fundamental transformation. Functional commands took over most of the chief signal officer's duties: the Combat Developments Command became responsible for doctrine; the Continental Army Command (CONARC) took over schools and training; and the Army Materiel Command (AMC) acquired authority for research and development, procurement, supply, and maintenance. While signal soldiers continued to receive assignments within the branch and to wear the crossed flags and torch insignia, personnel assignment and career management became the province of the Office of Personnel Operations. The Signal Corps even lost control of its home, as Fort Monmouth became the headquarters of the Electronics Command, an element of the AMC. Despite the changes in the chain of command at Monmouth, the U.S. Army Signal Center and School remained there, for a time, to maintain the history and traditions of the Corps. Having surrendered much of his domain, the chief signal officer nevertheless retained control over strategic communications, largely because there was no functional command to which to assign them.[133]

Chief Signal Officer Nelson, who had favored the reorganization, left the Army at the end of June 1962 before the reforms had been fully implemented.[134] His successor, Maj. Gen. Earle F. Cook, retired in frustration in June 1963. Before relinquishing his post, he spoke frankly to the chief of staff, General Earle G. Wheeler, telling him that he had found "after one year's functioning under the 1962 Army reorganization that there is lacking in elements of the Army Staff a proper understanding of Army communications and electronics and the role of the Chief Signal Officer."[135] Having been apprised of the problems, Wheeler directed that a board be assembled to study signal activities. Made up of general

General Cook   *General Gibbs*

officers from all the major staff elements in the Department of the Army, the so-called Powell Board (for General Herbert B. Powell, commander of CONARC) made recommendations that resulted in further modifications to the organization and operations of the Signal Corps.

As proposed by the board, the Army established on 1 March 1964 the Office of the Chief of Communications-Electronics, a subordinate agency of the Office of the Deputy Chief of Staff for Military Operations, to replace the Office of the Chief Signal Officer. The incumbent, Maj. Gen. David P. Gibbs (son of Maj. Gen. George S. Gibbs, who had held the post from 1928 to 1931), thus became the last to bear the title of chief signal officer and the first to be chief of communications-electronics. Ironically, his father had advocated the creation of such a staff position twenty years earlier. While the new title perhaps more accurately described the broad nature and scope of the chief's work, it severed the historic connection with the branch's past. After 104 years, the long chain of chief signal officers, stretching back to the Corps' founder, Albert J. Myer, had been broken.[136]

Concurrently, the staff and command responsibilities of the chief signal officer were separated. Gibbs turned over control of strategic communications to the newly established Strategic Communications Command (STRATCOM), with headquarters in Washington, D.C.[137] This major command became responsible for the management of all long-distance Army communications and for engineering, installing, operating, and maintaining the Army portions of the Defense Communications System. Henceforth, Gibbs and his successors became advisers to the Army Staff on communications-electronics issues. Other principal responsibilities included radio-frequency and call-sign management and use, communications security, and Army representation on boards and committees dealing with communications-electronics matters. Gibbs retained control of the Army Photographic Agency in the Pentagon, while the Army Pictorial Center at Astoria became part of the AMC.[138]

Despite the radical realignment, Gibbs declared himself pleased with the new arrangement:

I firmly believe these changes in the management of Communications and Electronics in the Army to be a step in the proper direction. It has clarified many of those gray areas surrounding our previous organization involving the responsibilities of the Chief Signal Officer, and the alignment of the Army long-haul communications functions.[139]

Relieved of his Signal Corps operational duties, the chief of communications-electronics could adopt an Army-wide perspective.

Concurrent with the reorganization of the Army Staff, the Army's tactical divisions underwent restructuring. Early in 1962 the Army began implementing the Reorganization Objective Army Divisions (ROAD) plan. The battle groups of the pentomic divisions had proven too weak for conventional war, and the Kennedy administration's strategy of flexible response emphasized the waging of atomic wars only as a last resort. Hence the Army formed four new types of divisions: infantry, armor, airborne, and mechanized, each with a common base and three brigade headquarters. The division base contained the support units, including a signal battalion comprised of three companies, one to support each brigade.[140] The Army was still in the throes of these changes when a new series of crises threatened the world with war.

From Cold War to Hot

The administration of John F. Kennedy faced several serious international incidents during its brief tenure. One of the earliest occurred during August 1961 when the Soviet Union attempted to expel the Western powers from their occupation zones in the former German capital of Berlin. The showdown that resulted led to the building of the Berlin Wall by the Soviets to separate the eastern and western sectors of the city and thereby halt the flight of East Germans to freedom. In response, the Army deployed additional forces to Europe that included two signal battalions and eight signal companies.[141] Troubles also arose closer to home, in the Caribbean. Tensions between the United States and Cuba had been rising since Fidel Castro seized power in 1959, transforming the island into a Communist state. Castro's increasing ties to the Soviet Union threatened American security interests in the hemisphere, and the Eisenhower administration had severed diplomatic ties on the eve of Kennedy's inauguration. Relations soured further in April 1961 when the United States supported an unsuccessful invasion by Cuban exiles at the Bay of Pigs. The following year the regional dispute threatened to explode into global war. In October 1962 American intelligence sources detected the presence in Cuba of Soviet medium-range missiles, capable of reaching American cities. President Kennedy demanded their removal and ordered the Navy to prevent the further delivery to Cuba of all offensive equipment. For thirteen anxious days the United States and the Soviet Union stood on the brink of nuclear war. Fortunately, Soviet Premier Nikita Khrushchev backed down and ordered the missiles removed. The Cold War had reached its apogee.[142]

Signal support during the Cuban crisis had been hampered by the "fog of reorganization." Confusion resulting from the recent realignment of the Army Staff had excluded the chief signal officer from the initial operational planning.[143] Furthermore, throughout the tense period communications between the United States and the Soviet Union had been plagued by frequent delays. As a consequence, the two superpowers established the "hot line" between Washington and Moscow, and the operation of this vital link became a STRATCOM responsibility.[144]

With tensions in Europe and the Caribbean abating somewhat, the focus of the Cold War once again shifted to Asia. If Korea had seemed remote to most Americans in 1950, then Indochina—Vietnam, Laos, and Cambodia—evoked a similar reaction in the early 1960s. In just a few years, however, there would be few Americans who remained unaware of its existence. As U.S. involvement expanded in Southeast Asia, Army communicators became an integral part of the process—applying the latest technology in a conflict that pitted the world's most sophisticated power against a seemingly backward, primitive foe.

Notes

[1]Thompson and Harris, *Outcome*, pp. 620–23.

[2]The dissolution of the ASF is announced in WD Circular 138, 14 May 1946. The Army Ground Forces and the Army Air Forces were retained for the time being. See also Millett, *Army Service Forces*, epilogue; Smith, *Army and Economic Mobilization*, p. 115; Hewes, *Root to McNamara*, ch. 4.

[3]Edgar F. Raines, Jr., and David R. Campbell, *The Army and the Joint Chiefs of Staff: Evolution of Army Ideas on the Command, Control, and Coordination of the U.S. Armed Forces, 1942–1985* (Washington, D.C.: Analysis Branch, U.S. Army Center of Military History, 1986), chs. 3 and 4; Hewes, *Root to McNamara*, pp. 163–66.

[4]Hewes, *Root to McNamara*, pp. 271–72; Matloff, ed., *American Military History*, pp. 532–33; Weigley, *History of Army*, pp. 490–95.

[5]*ARSO*, 1946, p. 349.

[6]Ibid., pp. 45, 47, 376, 384–86.

[7]*ARSO*, quadrennial report 1951–1955, p. 81. The Office of the Chief Signal Officer published two of these quadrennial reports, one covering its operations from May 1951 to April 1955 and the other from May 1955 to April 1959. Copies of these reports are in the CMH library.

[8]Thompson and Harris, *Outcome*, pp. 620–23; John D. Bergen, *Military Communications: A Test for Technology*, United States Army in Vietnam (Washington, D.C.: Center of Military History, United States Army, 1986), pp. 168–69.

[9]*ARSO*, 1946, p. 560; *ARSO*, quadrennial report 1951–1955, p. 47.

[10]*ARSO*, 1946, devotes chapter 9 to the Army Pictorial Service.

[11]A sketch of Gordon's career is included in Ezra J. Warner, *Generals in Gray* (Baton Rouge: Louisiana State University Press, 1959). During World War I a cantonment near Atlanta had borne the designation Camp Gordon. Carol E. Rios, "The Home of the Signal Corps," *Army Communicator* 11 (Summer 1986): 50–51; Smith, *Army and Economic Mobilization*, p. 449; *ARSO*, quadrennial report 1951–1955, pp. 81–82. Camp Gordon became Fort Gordon on 21 March 1956.

[12]DAGO 35, 3 Aug 49; Phillips, *Signal Center and School*, p. 206.

[13]John B. Wilson, Divisions and Separate Brigades, draft Ms, ch. 8. The 1st Cavalry Division was reorganized on 25 March 1949 and the 1st Signal Troop was redesignated as the 13th Signal Company. See "1st Cavalry Division" in John B. Wilson, *Armies, Corps, Divisions, and Separate Brigades*, pp. 127–28; Lineage and Honors Certificate, 13th Signal Battalion, copy in unit jacket, DAMH-HSO.

[14]John B. Wilson, Divisions and Separate Brigades, draft Ms, pp. 7:7, 8:49; Kent Roberts Greenfield, *Army Ground Forces and the Air-Ground Battle Team Including Organic Light Aviation*, Study no. 35 (Washington, D.C.: Historical Section, Army Ground Forces, 1948).

[15]John B. Wilson, Divisions and Separate Brigades, draft Ms, p. 9:16. In addition to the signal company, the tables assigned helicopters to the headquarters company, division artillery, the infantry regiments, and the engineer battalion. See TOE 7–7 (15 May 1952). Aircraft assets for airborne divisions followed those for the infantry division, while those for the armored division differed only slightly.

[16]On the types of aircraft allotted to the field army signal operation battalion, see TOE 11–95 (13 June 1949), and 11–95A (11 February 1952).

[17]The act is published as DA Bulletin 9, 6 July 1950. See also Matloff, ed., *American Military History*, p. 541; Weigley, *History of Army*, pp. 495–96; Hewes, *Root to McNamara*, pp. 208–12. Paul J. Scheips in his study, The Line and the Staff, pp. 37–38, points out that the term combat arm is not specifically used in the legislation. Because Infantry, Armor, and Artillery are not listed under services, they are thereby imbued with a special status, which is understood to be that of combat arms.

[18]Its actual strength was 593,526. *Strength of the Army* (1 Jun 1950), p. 3; Weigley, *History of Army*, p. 502.

[19]"Gen. Harry C. Ingles, Chief Signal Officer Dies," *Washington Post*, 16 Aug 1976; Bilby, *The General*, p. 153. According to Bilby, Sarnoff actively recruited Ingles for the position.

[20]Matloff, ed., *American Military History*, pp. 535–37; Clay Blair, *The Forgotten War: America in Korea, 1950–1953* (New York: Times Books, 1988), ch. 2.

[21]On this subject, see Bruce Cumings, *The Origins of the Korean War*, 2 vols. (Princeton, N.J.: Princeton University Press, 1981, 1990).

[22]Blair, *Forgotten War*, pp. 28, 48–50; Roy E. Appleman, *South to the Naktong, North to the Yalu*, United States Army in the Korean War (Washington, D.C.: Office of the Chief of Military History, United States Army, 1961), pp. 49–50, 113–14; Roy K. Flint, "Task Force Smith and the 24th Infantry Division," in Heller and Stofft, eds., *America's First Battles*, pp. 271–74.

[23]The six Regular Army divisions were 1st Cavalry, 2d Infantry, 3d Infantry, 7th Infantry, 24th Infantry, and 25th Infantry. The two National Guard units were the 40th Infantry Division from California and the 45th Infantry Division from Oklahoma.

[24]The twenty UN members included the United States, Great Britain, Greece, and Thailand. For a complete list, see Matloff, ed., *American Military History*, p. 550. Because the Republic of Korea (South Korea) did not belong to the United Nations, its army was considered an allied force. Appleman, *South to the Naktong*, p. 382.

[25]*ARSO*, quadrennial report 1951–1955, p. 2.

[26]Ibid., pp. 79, 82, 88.

[27]Ibid., pp. 70–72.

[28]Ibid., p. 2. General Matthew B. Ridgway comments on the lack of corps-level troops in *The Korean War* (Garden City, N.Y.: Doubleday and Company, Inc., 1967), p. 34.

[29]George Lieberberg, "Developing a Signal Organization," in John G. Westover, ed., *Combat Support in Korea* (Washington, D.C.: Combat Forces Press, 1955), p. 88. Although the corps headquarters were activated in August 1950 (I Corps on 2 August 1950 at Fort Bragg, North Carolina, and IX Corps on 10 August 1950 at Fort Sheridan, Illinois), they did not become fully operational in Korea for some time. Appleman, *South to the Naktong*, pp. 544–55.

[30]The divisional companies arrived in Korea as follows: 13th Signal Company, 18 July; 24th Signal Company, 5 July; 25th Signal Company, 14 July. See unit jackets and unit data cards in DAMH-HSO. The earliest *Directory and Station List of the United States Army* in which they appear in Korea is that for 1 September 1950. By that time other signal units had also arrived in Korea from Japan and elsewhere.

[31]Appleman, *South to the Naktong*, pp. 110–11.

[32]Wayne A. Striley, "The Mukden Cable," in Westover, ed., *Combat Support in Korea*, p. 96.

[33]Flint, "Task Force Smith," in Heller and Stofft, eds., *America's First Battles*, pp. 278–82, 298.

[34]Appleman, *South to the Naktong*, pp. 70, 81, 123, 179–80.

[35]Pitcher, "Signal Operations in Korea," in Westover, ed., *Combat Support in Korea*, p. 97.

[36]John W. Pierce, "Answers Not in Textbooks," in Westover, ed., *Combat Support in Korea*, p. 89.

[37]Kenneth E. Shiflet, "'Communications Hill' in Korea," in Marshall, ed., *Story of Signal Corps*, pp. 188–91.

[38]Blair, *Forgotten War*, p. 431.

[39]Ibid., p. 42; Appleman, *South to the Naktong*, p. 2.

[40]*ARSO*, quadrennial report 1951–1955, p. 23; Anon., "News of the Services," *United States Army Combat Forces Journal* 2 (Oct 1951): 45; *The Army Almanac* (Harrisburg, Pa.: Stackpole Co., 1959), p. 38.

[41]The radar set became designated as AN/MPQ–10. *ARSO*, quadrennial report 1951–1955, pp. 22–24, 58, 85; "127th Signal Company," in Paul C. Waring, *History of the 7th Infantry (Bayonet) Division* (Tokyo: Dai Nippon Printing Co., 1967).

[42]Anon., "News of the Services," *United States Army Combat Forces Journal* 2 (Sep 1951): 45.

[43]The aircraft belonged to the battalion's message center operation company. See TOE 11–99A (13 Jun 1949). The pilots, members of the Signal Corps, received their flight instruction at the Division of Air Training of the Field Artillery School. For details on the Signal Corps' use of planes in Korea, see "The World's Biggest Little Airline," reprinted in Westover, ed., *Combat Support in Korea*, pp. 100–102 (originally published in *Signal*, Nov-Dec 1951); Anon., "News of the Services," *United States Army Combat Forces Journal* 2 (Oct 1951): 45; "History, Organization, and Equipment of Aviation Sections" (Fort Sill, Okla.: Army Aviation School, Dec 1953).

[44]"Laying Telephone Wire by Air," from Command Report, 23d Infantry (Oct 1951), in Westover, ed., *Combat Support in Korea*, p. 242.

[45]Phillips, *Signal Center and School*, p. 306.

[46]Cass J. Joswiak, "Division Aerial Photography," in Westover, ed., *Combat Support in Korea*, pp. 102–04; "25th Signal Company," in Richard T. Pullen, Robert E. Christensen, and James C. Totten, eds., *25th Infantry Division, Tropic Lightning in Korea* (Atlanta, Ga.: Albert Love Enterprises, 1954); Charles F. Vale, "Combat Through the Camera's Eye," *Army Information Digest* 8 (Mar 1953): 54–59. See Field Manual 11–40, "Signal Photography," editions of January 1951 and April 1954. See also TOE 11–7N (3 May 1948), and its replacement, TOE 11–7 (15 May 1952). By the end of September 1951 Signal Corps cameramen had shot over 780,000 feet of motion picture film and sent it for processing to the Astoria Photographic Center. See Anon., "News of the Services," *United States Army Combat Forces Journal* 2 (Dec 1951): 43.

[47]Appleman, *South to the Naktong*, p. 12.

[48]Ibid., p. 704. Blair, *Forgotten War*, p. 382.

[49]Appleman, *South to the Naktong*, pp. 252–53; Blair, *Forgotten War*, p. 170.

[50]Army headquarters returned to Taegu on 23 September. Appleman, *South to the Naktong*, pp. 416, 574.

[51]Ibid., chs. 25 and 26.

[52]Ibid., p. 673.

[53]"127th Signal Battalion," in Waring, *History of 7th Infantry Division*; DAGO 33, 31 Mar 1952.

[54]Blair, *Forgotten War*, p. 552.

[55]Ridgway, *Korean War*, p. 119.

[56]Blair, *Forgotten War*, p. 775.

[57]*ARSO*, quadrennial report 1951–1955, p. 3 and app.; "Back, George," biographical files, DAMH-HSR.

[58]Lt. Gen. James A. Van Fleet replaced Ridgway as commander of the Eighth Army in April 1951.

[59]The total casualty figure is that given in Matloff, ed., *American Military History*, p. 569. The Signal Corps casualty figure appears in Scheips, The Line and the Staff, n. 59. The Signal Corps ranked third among the technical services, with the Army Medical Service and the Corps of Engineers sustaining about 3,000 casualties each. See Office of The Adjutant General, *Battle Casualties of the Army, 30 September 1954* (Washington, D.C.: Department of the Army, n.d.).

[60]Appleman, *South to the Naktong*, p. 599, n. 59, and Eighth Army GO 35, 21 Jan 51.

[61]For a discussion of the integration of the Army, see Morris J. MacGregor, Jr., *Integration of the Armed Forces, 1940–1965*, Defense Studies (Washington, D.C.: Center of Military History, United States Army, 1981), ch. 17. For the award to the 272d Signal Construction Company, see DAGO 79, 11 September 1951; Barnes, "We, Too, Serve Proudly," pp. 41–45. In 1952 black soldiers comprised between 8 and 9 percent of the Signal Corps' overall strength. MacGregor, *Integration of Armed Forces*, table 10, p. 458.

[62]Thompson and Harris, *Outcome*, p. 629; *ARSO*, 1946, pp. 13–15; R. T. Nelson, "Signals in Space," *Army Information Digest* 16 (May 1961): 11–21. This article is reprinted in Marshall, ed., *Story of Signal Corps*, pp. 267–75.

[63]Walter A. McDougall, . . . *The Heavens and the Earth: A Political History of the Space Age* (New York: Basic Books, Inc., 1985), ch. 4.

[64]Leonard S. Wilson, "Army Role in IGY Research," pp. 33–40; Clarence T. Smith, "Pioneering in IGY Research," *Army Information Digest* 15 (Mar 1960): 32–50; J. Tuzo Wilson, *Year of the New Moons*, discusses the IGY programs in depth. See also McDougall, *Heavens and Earth*, pp. 118–23; *ARSO*, quadrennial report 1955–1959, pp. 11–12; Hans K. Ziegler, "A Signal Corps Space Odyssey: Part I—Prelude to SCORE," *Army Communicator* 6 (Fall 1981): 19–21.

[65]McDougall, *Heavens and Earth*, p. 152.

[66]Ibid., ch. 1.

[67]Clark, "Squier," pp. 307–13.

[68]McDougall, *Heavens and Earth*, pp. 44–45.

[69]Ibid., pp. 118–23, 168; Anon., "Army Explorer in Orbit," *Army Information Digest* 13 (Apr 1958): 5; J. B. Medaris, "The Explorer Satellites and How We Launched Them," *Army Information Digest* 13 (Oct 1958): 4–16; Dan Cragg, "The Day Army Made U.S. Space History," *Army* 33 (Oct 1983): 260–61; Ziegler, "Space Odyssey: Part I," p. 22; Roger E. Bilstein, *Orders of Magnitude: A History of the NACA and NASA, 1915–1990* (Washington, D.C.: National Aeronautics and Space Administration, 1989), pp. 44–47.

[70]McDougall, *Heavens and Earth*, pp. 129–31, 154; *ARSO*, quadrennial report 1955–1959, p. 25; Ziegler, "Space Odyssey: Part I," p. 23; H. McD. Brown, "A Signal Corps Space Odyssey: Part II—SCORE and Beyond," *Army Communicator* 7 (Winter 1982): 19; *Concise History of Fort Monmouth*, p. 41; Karl Larew, Meteorology in the U.S. Army Signal Corps, 1870–1960, typescript [Washington, D.C.: Signal Corps Historical Division, 1960], pp. 74–75, copy in author's files; John P. Hagen, "The Viking and the Vanguard," *Technology and Culture* 4 (Fall 1963): 435–51; "John Peter Hagen Dies at 82; Headed Satellite Program," *Washington Post*, 1 Sep 1990.

[71]McDougall, *Heavens and Earth*, chs. 6 and 7; Bilstein, *Orders of Magnitude*, pp. 47–48.

[72]Brown, "Space Odyssey: Part II," pp. 12–22; McDougall, *Heavens and Earth*, p. 190.

[73]Brown, "Space Odyssey: Part II," pp. 20–21; "Courier Satellite Widens Communications Horizon," *Army Information Digest* 15 (Dec 1960): 17; Nelson, "Signals in Space," pp. 18–20; Bilstein, *Orders of Magnitude*, p. 56; David J. Marshall, "Modern Signal Research," in Marshall, ed., *Story of Signal Corps*, p. 198.

[74]McDougall, *Heavens and Earth*, p. 198.

[75]Brown, "Space Odyssey: Part II," p. 22.

[76]McDougall, *Heavens and Earth*, p. 221; Brown, "Space Odyssey: Part II," pp. 19–20; *Historical Sketch of the United States Army Signal Corps, 1860–1966* (Washington, D.C.: Historical Division, Office of the Chief Signal Officer, n.d.), p. 36; Whitnah, *Weather Bureau*, pp. 238–40; Bates and Fuller, *Weather Warriors*, pp. 174–76; Larew, Meteorology in Signal Corps, p. 75; "TV Eyes on the World's Weather," *Army Information Digest* 15 (Jun 1960): 65; Morris Tepper, "TIROS Payload and Ground System," *Signal* 14 (Aug 1960): 25.

[77]McDougall, *Heavens and Earth*, p. 358; Bilstein, *Orders of Magnitude*, p. 56; Ziegler, "Space Odyssey: Part I," p. 20.

[78]McDougall, *Heavens and Earth*, pp. 353–60; Bilstein, *Orders of Magnitude*, pp. 64–66, 83. The International Telecommunications Convention of 1973 regulated the use of comsats and radio frequencies. McDougall, *Heavens and Earth*, p. 431.

[79]Bergen, *Test for Technology*, p. 111.

[80]McDougall, *Heavens and Earth*, p. 259.

[81]*ARSO*, quadrennial report 1951–1955, pp. 76–77, 82.

[82]*ARSO*, quadrennial report 1955–1959, p. 2.

[83]George J. Eltz, "New Home for Electronic Wizards," *Army Information Digest* 10 (Aug 1955): 40–42; *ARSO*, quadrennial report 1951–1955, p. 22; *Concise History of Fort Monmouth*, p. 35.

[84]*Concise History of Fort Monmouth*, p. 40; DAGO 12, 28 Mar 1958.

[85]Anon., "News of the Services," *United States Army Combat Forces Journal* 2 (Sep 1951): 45; Harold A. Zahl, "Toward Lighter Signal Equipment," *Army Information Digest* 8 (Jun 1953): 31–35.

[86]Thomas J. Misa, "Military Needs, Commercial Realities, and the Development of the Transistor, 1948–1958," in Merritt Roe Smith, ed., *Military Enterprise and Technological Change: Perspectives on the American Experience* (Cambridge, Mass.: MIT Press, 1985), p. 266.

[87]Misa, "Development of the Transistor," pp. 262–63.

[88]Two scientists independently arrived at the idea of the integrated circuit: Jack Kilby in 1958 and Robert Noyce in 1959. Noyce eventually received the patent. See the detailed account in T. R. Reid, *The Chip: How Two Americans Invented the Microchip and Launched a Revolution* (New York: Simon and Schuster, 1984). See also Michael S. Malone, *The Big Score: The Billion Dollar Story of Silicon Valley* (Garden City, N.Y.: Doubleday and Company, Inc., 1985), pp. 199–220.

[89]Paul J. Scheips, "Introduction," in Scheips, ed., *Military Signal Communications*, vol. 1; Reid, *The Chip*, ch. 6.

[90]Bush, *Pieces of the Action*, pp. 181–85; Larry Owens, "Vannevar Bush and the Differential Analyzer: The Text and Context of an Early Computer," *Technology and Culture* 27 (Jan 1986): 63–95; Cochrane, *Measures for Progress*, pp. 453–54.

[91]Lewin, *Ultra Goes to War*, pp. 129–33; "Alan Turing: Can a Machine Be Made to Think?" in Robert Slater, *Portraits in Silicon* (Cambridge, Mass.: MIT Press, 1987), pp. 12–20. The British government did not begin declassifying information about Colossus until the 1970s.

[92]"John V. Mauchly and J. Presper Eckert: The Men Who Built ENIAC," in Slater, *Portraits in Silicon*, pp. 62–79; Nancy Stern, "The Eckert-Mauchly Computers: Conceptual Triumphs, Commercial Tribulations," *Technology and Culture* 23 (Oct 1982): 569–82.

[93]Marshall, "Modern Signal Research," in Marshall, ed., *Story of Signal Corps*, p. 197; *ARSO*, quadrennial report 1955–1959, pp. 20–22, 41–42; Watts S. Humphrey, "MOBIDIC and Fieldata," *Annals of the History of Computing* 9 (1987): 137–82; "Fieldata Aids for the Command Post of the Future," *Army Information Digest* 17 (Feb 1962): 14–19.

[94]Phillips, *Signal Center and School*, pp. 306–11; Department of Defense, Office of Public Information, News Release no. 1255–56 (4 Dec 1956), "Pigeon Training Activity to be Closed at Army Signal Corps Post Soon," copy in author's files; Tom R. Kovach, "History's Most Useful Warbird," *Military History* 4 (Aug 1987): 52–56; Ron Frain, "The Signal Corps Was for the Birds," *Army Communicator* 1 (Winter 1976): 52–53.

[95]*ARSO*, quadrennial report 1951–1955, pp. 14–16, 89; DAGO 2, 14 Jan 54; John B. Spore, "Quiet Please! Electronics Being Tested," in Marshall, ed., *Story of Signal Corps*, pp. 238–47; F. W. Moorman, "Better Command Control," *Army Information Digest* 14 (Jun 1959): 52–61; Cornelius C. Smith, Jr., *Fort Huachuca, the Story of a Frontier Post* (Fort Huachuca, Ariz.: 1978), pp. 317–20.

[96]*ARSO*, quadrennial report 1955–1959, pp. ix, 8–9, 35–38, 98–100; William M. Thames, "Combat Surveillance Looks to the Future," *Army Information Digest* 15 (Mar 1960): 52–59.

[97]This agency was known as the U.S. Army Signal Missile Support Agency. Von Braun and his team moved to Redstone Arsenal, Alabama, in November 1950. McDougall, *Heavens and Earth*, pp. 89–91, 99; *ARSO*, quadrennial report 1955–1959, pp. 60–63.

[98]*ARSO*, quadrennial report 1955–1959, pp. 11, 83; "Air Defense by Missile Master," *Army* 6 (Apr 1956): 18–19; Public Affairs Office, Hq, U.S. Army Communications Command, "A History of the Signal Corps, 1860–1975," p. 14; Marshall, "Modern Signal Research," in Marshall, ed., *Story of Signal Corps*, p. 195.

[99]Anon., "Signal Corps: Communications, Combat Surveillance, Avionics Spell Command Control," *United States Army Aviation Digest* (hereafter cited as *Aviation Digest*) 7 (Jun 1961): 30–32.

[100]*ARSO*, quadrennial report 1955–1959, pp. 12–16, 39–40.

[101]U.S. Army Aviation Flight Information Office, "The Army's Flight Information Program," *Aviation Digest* 8 (Apr 1962): 41–42; Richard Albright, "Flight Information and Navaids Office," *Aviation Digest* 10 (Jul 1964): 18–20; *ARSO*, quadrennial report 1955–1959, pp. 15, 41, 80; Larew, Meteorology in Signal Corps, p. 65.

[102]Larew, Meteorology in Signal Corps, p. 63; Bates and Fuller, *Weather Warriors*, pp. 163, 171.

[103]Anthony D. Kurtz, "School for Military Meteorologists," *Army Information Digest* 15 (Dec 1960): 40–45; Phillips, *Signal Center and School*, pp. 231, 236; Marshall, "Modern Signal Research," in Marshall, ed., *Story of Signal Corps*, p. 193; Larew, Meteorology in Signal Corps, p. 66; Bates and Fuller, *Weather Warriors*, p. 171; Smith, *Fort Huachuca*, p. 320.

[104]Larew, Meteorology in Signal Corps, pp. 66–67.

[105]*ARSO*, quadrennial report 1955–1959, pp. 16–20, 41; Larew, Meteorology in Signal Corps, p. 68–70; Marshall, "Modern Signal Research," in Marshall, ed., *Story of Signal Corps*, p. 193.

[106]*ARSO*, quadrennial report 1955–1959, p. 17; Marshall, "Modern Signal Research," in Marshall, ed., *Story of Signal Corps*, p. 196; Larew, Meteorology in Signal Corps, pp. 69–70; J. Tuzo Wilson, *Year of the New Moons*; Smith, "Pioneering in IGY Research"; Leonard S. Wilson, "Army Role in IGY Research"; John T. Lorenz, "Far Northern Research Outpost," *Army Information Digest* 13 (May 1958): 24–29.

[107]*ARSO*, quadrennial report 1955–1959, pp. vii, 52–56.

[108]Ibid., p. 127.

[109]Anon., "New Cable Link to Alaska," *Army Information Digest* 12 (Mar 1957): 40–41.

[110]*ARSO*, quadrennial report 1955–1959, pp. 64–65; U.S. Army, Alaska, *Army's Role in Building Alaska*, pp. 109–13; Headquarters, U.S. Army, Alaska, GO 224, 9 Nov 1965, copy in unit jacket, 33d Signal Battalion, DAMH-HSO.

[111]*ARSO*, quadrennial report 1955–1959, pp. 64–65; Mitchell, *Opening of Alaska*, p. x. RCA later sold the network and, as of 1990, Alaskan communications were being provided by Alascom, Incorporated.

[112]*ARSO*, quadrennial report 1951–1955, pp. 95–101; Bilby, *The General*, p. 166.

[113]*ARSO*, quadrennial report 1955–1959, pp. 91–94; Joseph H. Kanner and Richard P. Runyon, "Training by TV," *Army* 6 (May 1956): 25–26; Joseph H. Kanner, "Teaching Through TV," in Marshall, ed., *Story of Signal Corps*, pp. 231–34; Phillips, *Signal Center and School*, pp. 243–46.

[114]*ARSO*, quadrennial report 1951–1955, p. 24; Koszarski, *Astoria and Its Fabulous Films*, p. 116; Stuart Queen, "'The Big Picture,'" *Army Information Digest* 10 (Feb 1955): 34–38; Alex McNeil, *Total Television: A Comprehensive Guide to Programming from 1948 to 1980* (New York: Penguin, 1980), p. 90.

[115]McDougall, *Heavens and Earth*, pp. 55, 105–06.

[116]John B. Wilson, Divisions and Separate Brigades, draft Ms, pp. 10:15 to 10:42; Matloff, ed., *American Military History*, p. 584; Weigley, *History of Army*, p. 537. The 7th Signal Company became, for example, the 127th Signal Battalion.

[117]*ARSO*, quadrennial report 1955–1959, p. 31; G. D. Gray, "Getting the Message Through," in Marshall, ed., *Story of Signal Corps*, pp. 215–18.

[118]*ARSO*, quadrennial report 1955–1959, pp. 7, 32; Earle F. Cook, "U.S. Army Objectives in Field Communications," in Marshall, ed., *Story of Signal Corps*, p. 257; Anon., "Super-Speed Teletypewriter," *Army Information Digest* 13 (Sep 1958): 65.

[119]Strength figure from Weigley, *History of Army*, p. 600.

[120]*ARSO*, quadrennial report 1955–1959, pp. 46–49; Phillips, *Signal Center and School*, pp. 223–40.

[121]Louis Nizer, *The Implosion Conspiracy* (Garden City, N.Y.: Doubleday & Company, Inc., 1973), pp. 23, 227.

[122]Thomas C. Reeves, *The Life and Times of Joe McCarthy: A Biography* (New York: Stein and Day, 1982), pp. 513–25. The hearings are briefly mentioned in *ARSO*, quadrennial report 1951–1955, p. 115. Chief Signal Officer Back attended the hearings, but he was not called upon to testify. Although the FBI has never been able to prove its existence, there may indeed have been a spy ring at Fort Monmouth. Following Rosenberg's arrest, two of his coworkers, Joel Barr and Al Sarant, fled the country. Using their techni-

cal knowledge, they subsequently worked on defense-related projects for the Soviet Union, among them the development of a radar-controlled antiaircraft gun. Eventually they set up a microelectronics laboratory in Leningrad. The 15 June 1992 broadcast of ABC News, "Nightline," was devoted to the careers of Barr and Sarant.

[123]Reeves, *Life and Times of McCarthy*, pp. 548–50, 567–68.

[124]Ibid., chs. 22, 23, and 24; Richard Gid Powers, *Secrecy and Power: The Life of J. Edgar Hoover* (New York: Free Press, 1987), pp. 322–23.

[125]*ARSO*, quadrennial report 1955–1959, pp. 133–34. During Lyndon Johnson's administration O'Connell served as special assistant to the president for telecommunications. See also O'Connell's biographical file in DAMH-HSR and his entries in Cullum, *Biographical Register*. O'Connell was West Point graduate number 6898.

[126]"Nelson, Ralph T.," biographical files, DAMH-HSR. See also Cullum, *Biographical Register*. Nelson was West Point graduate number 8462.

[127]Paul J. Scheips, The Signal Corps Centennial of 1960, typescript [Washington, D.C.: U.S. Army Signal Historical Office, 1961], copy in CMH files. The strength percentage is from the appendix thereto, "100 Years of Signal Corps Manpower, Education and Training." Bergen, *Test for Technology*, p. 171, indicates that it was the third largest branch in 1960.

[128]Hewes, *Root to McNamara*, pp. 253–58.

[129]Ibid., p. 311; John W. Nolan, "The Defense Communications System: Bringing Defense and Readiness Together," *Army Communicator* 1 (Spring 1976): 45–48.

[130]Wallace M. Lauterbach, "STRATCOM—The Army's Global Communications," in Marshall, ed., *Story of Signal Corps*, p. 209.

[131]AR 10–5, 5 May 1961.

[132]Hewes, *Root to McNamara*, chs. 8–10 and chart 31; DAGO 8, 15 Feb 1962.

[133]Hewes, *Root to McNamara*, ch. 10; Bergen, *Test for Technology*, pp. 171–73; Phillips, *Signal Center and School*, pp. 313–18; *Concise History of Fort Monmouth*, pp. 44–47.

[134]Hewes, *Root to McNamara*, p. 350.

[135]Quoted in Bergen, *Test for Technology*, pp. 174–75. Upon his retirement from the Army, General Cook, who had directed the Signal Corps' participation in Project SCORE, joined the Washington staff of the Radio Engineering Laboratories, a private firm. On Cook's career, see his obituary, "Retired Chief Signal Officer Earle F. Cook Dies at 81," *Washington Post*, 21 Feb 89, copy in author's files; "Cook, Earle F.," biographical files, DAMH-HSR.

[136]The change in designation was made effective by DAGO 6, 28 Feb 1964. See Bergen, *Test for Technology*, p. 175; Hewes, *Root to McNamara*, p. 364; Matloff, ed., *American Military History*, p. 605.

[137]The command headquarters moved to Fort Huachuca, Arizona, in 1967.

[138]David Parker Gibbs, "The Army's New Communications-Electronics Organization," in Marshall, ed., *Story of Signal Corps*, pp. 201–07; David P. Gibbs, "C-E Strives for Faster Responses," *Army* 15 (Nov 1964): 87–88, 160. The Army Pictorial Center was discontinued as an Army installation effective 6 October 1972, per DAGO 4, 30 January 1973. It is now the home of the American Museum of the Moving Image.

[139]Gibbs, "New Organization," in Marshall, ed., *Story of Signal Corps*, p. 207.

[140]The Regular Army divisions had completed their reorganizations under ROAD by 30 June 1964. John B. Wilson, Divisions and Separate Brigades, draft Ms, pp. 10:42 to 10:66; Matloff, ed., *American Military History*, p. 607; Weigley, *History of Army*, pp.

540–42. See TOE 11–35E (15 Jul 1963), 11–205T (22 Jun 1965), and 11–35G (31 Mar 1966).

[141]Bergen, *Test for Technology*, p. 38.

[142]Matloff, ed., *American Military History*, pp. 592–96.

[143]Office of the Chief Signal Officer, The Signal Corps Role in the Cuban Crisis, 1962, unpublished manuscript, CMH; Bergen, *Test for Technology*, p. 174.

[144]Smith, *Fort Huachuca*, p. 327.

CHAPTER X

The Vietnam Conflict

The Signal Corps that fought the war in Vietnam differed in significant ways from the Signal Corps that had fought in conflicts from the Civil War through Korea. The chief signal officer had disappeared from the organizational chart and had been replaced by a chief of communications-electronics with no operational responsibilities. The traditional Signal Corps functions continued to be performed, however, by Signal Corps units in the field. Though its form may have changed, the spirit of the Signal Corps lived on in the soldiers who wore the crossed flags and torch insignia. While Army communicators put their technology to the test in Vietnam, the technology on trial represented the culmination of a century of effort in the field of military communications.

The Origins of American Involvement

French colonization of Indochina began in the 1850s, but American military involvement in the region dated from World War II when Indochina was occupied by the Japanese. After the war, with the threat of Communist domination looming over Asia, the United States offered to help France resist a Communist rebellion in Vietnam led by Ho Chi Minh. By assisting France in Asia, the United States sought to ensure French support for the North Atlantic Treaty Organization (NATO). Some American strategists also warned that if Indochina fell to the Communists, the rest of Southeast Asia would follow—the concept that became known as the domino theory. As part of its assistance, the United States sent Signal Corps advisers to Vietnam to monitor the distribution and use of communications equipment and to establish an Army Command and Administrative Network (ACAN) station in Saigon. President Eisenhower, wishing to avoid another Korean-style conflict, refused either to intervene directly in the fighting or to authorize the use of atomic weapons. Defeated by Ho's forces at Dien Bien Phu in May 1954, the French agreed to a cease-fire. The truce agreement, known as the Geneva Agreements, divided Vietnam at the 17th Parallel with a Demilitarized Zone (DMZ) marking the border. As in Korea, a Communist government led by Ho Chi Minh ruled in the north, with its capital at Hanoi, while a nominal republic under President Ngo Dinh Diem governed in the south, with its capital at Saigon.[1]

Following the French withdrawal from Indochina, a U.S. advisory group remained behind to assist the South Vietnamese Army which, like its American counterpart, contained a signal corps. Because the French had handled both civil and military communications, however, the Vietnamese had acquired little technical expertise. American signal advisers were assigned down to divisional level and to each of the country's military regions to provide training, operational, and logistical support. Since the advisory group had no staff signal officer, the signal staff of the Pacific Command, based in Hawaii, conducted most of the operational planning for South Vietnam. The U.S. Army Signal Corps sent training teams to Southeast Asia, and many South Vietnamese officers received instruction at Forts Monmouth and Gordon. Logistical signal support proved particularly difficult due to the language barrier and the lack of familiarity on the part of the South Vietnamese with modern electronic equipment and proper inventory methods. Moreover, the French had removed much of the American-supplied signal equipment, leaving South Vietnamese field units in dire straits. In addition, the commercial communications networks built by the French lay in disrepair after years of war. To provide a permanent communications system to serve the civil, military, and commercial needs of Southeast Asia, the United States hired contractors to construct a regional telecommunications network to link South Vietnam, Laos, Cambodia, and Thailand. Unfortunately, the project encountered a host of problems and took years to complete.

Meanwhile the Viet Cong, the Communist organization that remained in the south after the truce, stepped up its guerrilla movement against President Diem. In July 1959 an insurgent attack on a U.S. advisory detachment at Bien Hoa killed two Americans and wounded another. In rural areas, where local security forces often lacked the communications to alert the army to the presence of Viet Cong military movements, Communist domination spread rapidly. Despite the guidance received from the American advisers, the South Vietnamese Army proved incapable of coping with the situation. By 1960 Saigon's ability to control the countryside was heavily contested.

As the crisis in Southeast Asia deepened, communication methods between the United States and South Vietnam remained extremely vulnerable. A single undersea cable linked the Pacific Command in Hawaii with Guam, but this connection did not extend to Southeast Asia. Thus the Army depended upon high-frequency radio, a medium that could be easily jammed. To improve matters, the Army called upon a new technique, known as scatter communications. This method worked by bouncing high-frequency radio beams off the layers of the atmosphere, which reflected them back to earth. One type, tropospheric scatter, bounced signals off water vapor in the troposphere, the lowest atmospheric layer. A second method, ionospheric scatter, bounced the signals off clouds of ionized particles in the ionosphere, the region that begins about thirty miles above the earth's surface.[2] Using special antennas, both methods provided high-quality signals that were less susceptible to jamming than ordinary radio. Unlike microwave relays, scatter communications did not require a line of sight between stations. Tropospheric relay stations could be as much as 400 miles apart, compared to about 40 miles for microwave stations, a decided advantage when operating in hostile territory.[3]

Billboard antennas of the BACKPORCH system at Phu Lam in 1962

In May 1960 a private firm, Page Communications Engineers, began building the 7,800-mile Pacific Scatter System for the Army along the island chain from Hawaii to the Philippines. From there, the Strategic Army Communications Network system made the final jump to Indochina.[4] Unfortunately, STARCOM's radio circuits proved highly unreliable in the tropical environment. Consequently, in 1962 the Joint Chiefs of Staff approved plans to build a military submarine cable system, known as WETWASH, from the Philippines to South Vietnam. In the meantime, the Army installed radio links westward from Bangkok to Pakistan and eastward from Saigon to Okinawa.

Secretary of Defense Robert S. McNamara approved, in January 1962, the installation of troposcatter equipment within South Vietnam to provide the backbone of a strategic network known as BACKPORCH, which would connect five major cities in South Vietnam with Thailand. Because the Army had little experience with tropospheric equipment, Page Engineers installed BACKPORCH at a cost of $12 million, and the company agreed to operate and maintain the system for a year. Huge "billboard" relay antennas began to appear on mountaintops. Spurs of the system would reach into the field where tactical units used standard Army multichannel radios. At the tails, or extensions, of the system, the advisory detachments at remote sites in the interior were to be equipped with the newly designed and untested troposcatter radios.

In February 1962 the United States established a unified headquarters, the U.S. Military Assistance Command, Vietnam (MACV), to coordinate the expanding American military effort in South Vietnam. Meanwhile, the U.S. Army, Pacific, created a subordinate command to MACV, the U.S. Army Support Group, Vietnam, to control the Army's logistical support elements, including signal units. The 39th Signal Battalion received the mission of providing communications support to MACV, including the operation of the BACKPORCH stations. With headquarters at Fort Gordon, the battalion comprised the 178th, 232d, and 362d Signal Companies. An advance party soon departed for South Vietnam to operate a switchboard for MACV headquarters. Members of the 362d Signal Company, the unit assigned to run the tropo equipment, underwent several months of training at Fort Monmouth, supplemented with practical experience at factories and testing grounds, before joining the rest of the battalion overseas. As communications responsibilities increased throughout South Vietnam during 1962, Lt. Col. Lotus B. Blackwell, the battalion commander, became the first signal officer for the support group. The Page engineers, meanwhile, finished the installation of BACKPORCH in September 1962 and turned it over to the 39th Signal Battalion in early 1963.

Through its pacification program the South Vietnamese government attempted to reduce the Viet Cong's influence among its citizens. Communist political cadres controlled many communities, levying taxes and drafting men into the military. In order to suppress the insurgency, the South Vietnamese had to eradicate this shadow government. Consequently, during the spring of 1962 Diem instituted the Strategic Hamlet Program through which he endeavored to relocate the rural population into fortified camps or hamlets. As part of this effort the 72d Signal Detachment, which arrived in Vietnam in October 1962, established radio communication from more than two thousand villages and hamlets to district and provincial capitals by early 1963. While the Viet Cong continued to exploit the Ho Chi Minh Trail running through Laos and Cambodia as a courier route to the north, the improved local communications helped the South Vietnamese government regain much of the countryside—or so it seemed. By the summer of 1963, with the Diem regime appearing to be winning its counterinsurgency campaign, the United States began planning a gradual withdrawal of its communications support.

American optimism proved premature. The political picture suddenly darkened with the overthrow and assassination of President Diem in early November 1963, just three weeks before the assassination of President Kennedy. With the South Vietnamese military in control in Saigon, a series of rapidly changing governments followed, providing a perfect climate for the resurgence of the Viet Cong. The new American president, Lyndon B. Johnson, reaffirmed the nation's support to South Vietnam but also declared that the scheduled withdrawal would continue.

At the same time, many factors converged to adversely affect signal operations in South Vietnam. The restructuring of the Signal Corps in 1964 and the resulting organizational turmoil diverted attention in Washington away from overseas operations. Chief Signal Officer David P. Gibbs was preoccupied with reorganizing his own staff, while the new signal staff in the Pentagon had yet to learn the ropes. Moreover, technical difficulties developed with BACKPORCH, especially where its circuits connected with tactical equipment. Because this contingency had not been explicitly covered in the contract with Page, the 39th Signal

Battalion had to rely on its own resources to solve the problems. Further troubles resulted from the premature aging of the equipment in the harsh tropical environment. In addition, the absence of any redundancy built into the system left BACKPORCH extremely vulnerable to enemy action. To furnish a measure of security, the 39th Signal Battalion undertook the installation of a supplementary system, also using troposcatter, known as CROSSBOW. By the spring of 1964, however, reductions in the battalion's strength and the reassignment of its original personnel had left operations in the hands of young and inexperienced soldiers.

The increasingly critical situation prompted President Johnson to announce a buildup of forces in Southeast Asia. In March 1964 the 39th Signal Battalion received more personnel, but the training available to these men had not kept up with the technology. Because all available tropo equipment had been sent overseas, none had been left behind for training purposes. Thus the reinforcements arrived in Vietnam inadequately prepared for their duties. The civilian contractors tried to train the men on site, but often lacked the time. With signal personnel rotating every year, too short a period for them to become proficient, it became necessary to retain the Page employees indefinitely.

In August 1964 American and North Vietnamese forces engaged in overt combat for the first time when North Vietnamese patrol boats attacked United States Navy ships in the Gulf of Tonkin. In retaliation, President Johnson ordered air strikes against the boats and their bases in North Vietnam. Congress hurriedly passed what became known as the Tonkin Gulf Resolution, which authorized the president to take the necessary measures to repel attack against U.S. forces and to prevent further aggression in Southeast Asia.[5] On the basis of this broadly worded authority, the Johnson administration justified the escalation of its involvement in Vietnam. Early in 1965 American ground troops began entering the conflict.

Signal Operations in an Expanding Conflict, 1965–1967

Between the years 1963 and 1965, the role of the United States in Vietnam had shifted from the provision of advice and support to active participation in the fighting. Political instability within the South Vietnamese government, institutional corruption, and a lack of the will to fight on the part of the South Vietnamese armed forces prompted the transition. South Vietnam seemed to possess little chance for survival in the face of the Viet Cong insurgency at home and North Vietnam's increasingly active role in the conflict. By 1965, with South Vietnam obviously on the verge of collapse, the United States decided that it had little choice but to commit major military units to the war to salvage the situation.

Unlike Korea several thousand miles to the north, South Vietnam lies entirely within the tropics. Geographically, it consists of three major regions: the Mekong Delta in the south, the nation's rice bowl and most populous area; the remote Central Highlands in the interior; and the Central Lowlands, a narrow coastal plain along the South China Sea. For command purposes, the South Vietnamese Army (known as the ARVN for Army of the Republic of South Vietnam) divided

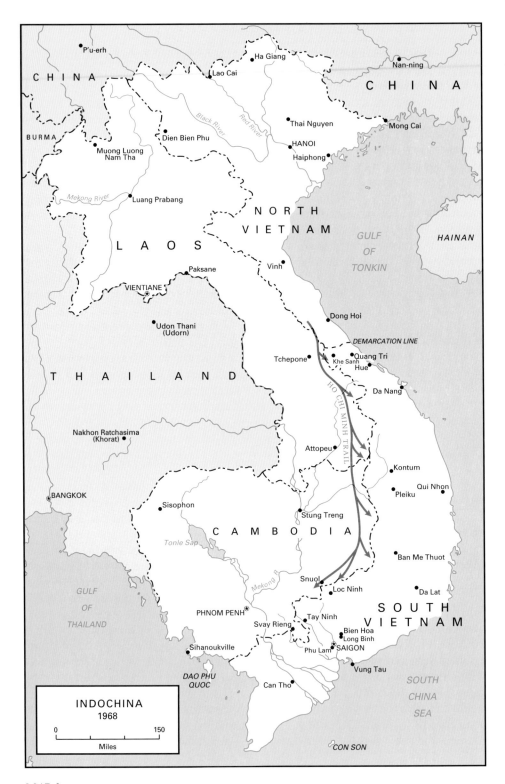

INDOCHINA
1968

0 ————————— 150
Miles

MAP 2

the 700-mile-long country into four corps tactical zones from north to south. To the north and west lay Cambodia, Laos, and Thailand.[6] (*Map 2*)

The United States Army's deployment started in May 1965 with the 173d Airborne Brigade. Other units soon followed, among them the 1st Cavalry Division, which reached Vietnam in September. This unit, the Army's first air-mobile division, had been designed to maneuver rapidly by using aircraft, specifically helicopters. The airmobile concept adapted well to Vietnam, which lacked adequate road networks for land transport.[7] The division's organic signal battalion, the 13th, possessed lighter equipment than standard divisional signal battalions and was smaller in size.[8] By the end of the year, with the arrival of the 1st Infantry Division and other supporting units, the U.S. troop commitment exceeded 180,000.[9]

Advance elements of the 2d Signal Group arrived in South Vietnam during June 1965, and this unit became the Signal Corps' major headquarters there for the next year. The group assumed control over the 39th and 41st Signal Battalions, the latter having recently arrived.[10] The 41st relieved the overextended 39th of some of its workload by taking over operations in the northern portion of South Vietnam (the I and II Corps Tactical Zones), with the 39th retaining control in the southern zones (III and IV).[11] By the end of 1965 the 2d Signal Group's strength had reached nearly 6,000. Despite its substantial growth, the group had difficulty keeping pace with the Army's burgeoning communications requirements.[12]

The expansion of signal activities created organizational problems, since the abolition of the chief signal officer's position in 1964 had left the signal chain of command in disarray. In July 1965 General William C. Westmoreland, the U.S. commander in Vietnam, disbanded the U.S. Army Support Command, Vietnam (formerly the U.S. Army Support Group, Vietnam), and created the U.S. Army, Vietnam (USARV), to command all Army troops in South Vietnam except for the advisers. The signal officer on its staff became responsible for the Army's tactical signal operations, while long-haul communications came under the purview of the Strategic Communications Command.[13]

For tactical signals, the introduction of a new combat radio, the transistorized FM model AN/PRC–25, gave the soldier increased communications capability. More powerful than previous sets, it provided voice communications on 920 channels and covered longer distances (about three to five miles) across a wider span of frequencies. In fact, the ubiquitous "Prick 25" made "the greatest impact on communications of any item of equipment in the war."[14] A later version, the AN/PRC–77, worked even better. The corresponding vehicular and aircraft-mounted series of FM sets, the AN/VRC–12 and AN/ARC–54, respectively, also met with success. Together, their overlapping frequencies enabled the Infantry, Armor, and Artillery to communicate with one another.[15]

Because the walkie-talkie proved too bulky for use in South Vietnam, the Signal Corps attempted to replace it with a new FM squad-level radio consisting of a hand-held transmitter (AN/PRT–4) and a helmet-mounted receiver

AN/PRC–25 radio

(AN/PRR–9). While the new device improved communications between squad leaders and their men, it failed to achieve widespread acceptance by the troops. Squad members were issued only the receivers and could not acknowledge messages. The speaker was often too loud for patrol duty, and the earphones were uncomfortable. Eventually, soldiers stowed the sets in footlockers and forgot them. The PRC–25 proved to be the radio of choice at all echelons.[16]

Special Forces units operating in remote areas without the benefit of conventional signal support depended upon portable single sideband radios, such as AN/PRC–74 and AN/FRC–93.[17] In response to a requirement from General Westmoreland for direct tactical links between the operations center at MACV headquarters in Saigon and all major combat units, the 69th Signal Battalion, which arrived in November 1965, established a theater-wide radioteletype net using AN/GRC–26s, machines that had proven their usefulness in Korea. The mobile command communications they provided enabled the Army to pursue the wide-ranging "search and destroy" tactics that Westmoreland advocated.[18]

For the first time in combat, the Signal Corps also employed an area communications system. Developed during the 1950s, this system linked the chain of command into a grid that allowed it to communicate directly with each subordinate unit. Multichannel and radio relay equipment made the intricate interconnec-

Heliborne command post

tions possible. Unit mobility improved because it was no longer necessary to string new communications wire each time a unit changed position: The unit merely connected with the nearest nodal point of the communications grid at its new location. Consequently, field wire, a staple of military signaling technology since the Civil War, saw relatively little use in South Vietnam. Overall, the area system provided more flexible communications that covered greater distances.[19]

Signal units received their initiation into combat during the fall of 1965, at the battle of the Ia Drang Valley in the Central Highlands near the Cambodian border. Beginning in late October, in what would become the first major ground combat between U.S. Army and North Vietnamese units, the 1st Cavalry Division engaged in fierce fighting.[20] Thanks to superior mobility and firepower, American forces emerged victorious, if bloodied.

Communications played a significant role in the battle, especially the use of FM airborne relay. The 13th Signal Battalion of the 1st Cavalry Division mounted radios in fixed-wing aircraft that circled at 10,000 feet and used them to retransmit voice messages between the widely dispersed combat units on the ground. This approach overcame the limitations of line-of-sight ground-based FM radio by increasing the range of PRC–25 signals from five to sixty miles and by nullifying the effects of the triple canopy jungle growth that absorbed electromagnetic transmissions. Meanwhile, brigade and battalion commanders controlled their units by using innovative heliborne command posts equipped with radio consoles. Only the absence of a significant enemy antiaircraft threat made this technique feasible.[21]

The combat situation in Vietnam did not conform to what Army planners in the post–Korean War period had expected to confront in the next conflict—a nuclear battlefield. According to the rationale for the pentomic and ROAD configurations, the Army had organized and equipped its units to fight in a highly mobile environment, most likely defending against a Soviet attack in Western Europe. Instead, the troops in Vietnam faced guerrilla warfare in jungles and rice paddies. Rather than maneuvering along a rapidly moving front, units mounted expeditions from fixed bases against an elusive enemy.[22]

Signal doctrine, likewise, had not anticipated this situation. In addition to lightweight, portable communications, the Signal Corps in South Vietnam needed to provide fixed-base communications with large antennas and heavy equipment. Divisional signal battalions had to cover operating areas of 3,000 to 5,000 square miles, compared to 200 to 300 miles in a conventional war.[23] Hence signal units had to scramble for assets and divert tactical equipment to the support of base operations. Training also had to be updated, but formal instruction for fixed-station controllers did not begin at the signal schools until 1965.[24]

The Tonkin Gulf crisis had already highlighted weak points in the Army's strategic communications network. During this episode severe sunspot activity and occasional equipment breakdown blocked the high-frequency radio circuits between Washington and Saigon, interrupting the flow of messages traveling between the two capitals. To bolster the system's capabilities, the Army rushed an experimental satellite (SYNCOM) ground terminal to Southeast Asia. By August 1964 a satellite link to Hawaii provided one telephone and one teletype circuit and marked the first use of satellite communications in a combat zone. Improvements expanded the system's capacity to one telephone and sixteen message circuits by October 1964.[25]

Other technical difficulties also surfaced, especially with the BACKPORCH system. In January 1965 the network began to experience severe fading of its signals that prevented the transmission of teletype pulses, and the operators were unable to overcome the problem. Although the Page engineers shut down the terminals for maintenance—the first time BACKPORCH had been off the air—they could not correct the problem. A team of experts from the Defense Communications Agency (DCA) concluded that the phenomenon resulted from a temperature inversion, which occurs when the upper layers of the atmosphere are uncharacteristically warmer than the lower layers.[26]

Already concerned about the vulnerability of his communications, General Westmoreland also worried that the Viet Cong would begin targeting signal sites. The complex at Phu Lam, a suburb of Saigon, then housed the only Defense Communications System message relay facility in the country. (It had replaced the STARCOM station in Saigon.) This communications gateway to Vietnam handled

Aerial view of the communications complex at Phu Lam

250,000 messages per month by early 1965, and a backlog was beginning to develop.[27] Plans were drawn, therefore, to create a base theater network with a diversity of routing and transmission methods that would bring modern communications to the battlefield. Known as the Integrated Wideband Communications System (IWCS), it was to combine coastal undersea cables with automatic telephone, teletype, and data systems. Incorporating the BACKPORCH and WETWASH facilities, the IWCS would become part of the global Defense Communications System.[28] The installation of this fixed network would also free the units' mobile equipment for tactical purposes. Once again, Page Communications Engineers received the construction contract for the Vietnam portion of the system, while Philco-Ford built the terminals in Thailand. Meanwhile, the completion of the WETWASH project in December 1964 made high-quality overseas circuits available between the United States and South Vietnam.[29]

A shortage of personnel to operate troposcatter terminals posed an additional dilemma. The signal schools could not initially produce qualified graduates fast enough. Since few records had been kept of previously trained soldiers, the Army had little way to locate experienced operators still on active duty. Moreover, regulations prohibited the involuntary reassignment of military personnel overseas for two years, a period later reduced to nine months for those with certain critical skills. As a result, the Department of Defense offered increased pay and reenlistment bonuses to recruit and retain soldiers with such skills, many of them in the field of communications-electronics and liable to be lured away by private industry. Westmoreland also worried whether the civilian contractors could be counted on as hostilities intensified, but in this case his concerns proved unjustified.[30]

Despite their dependence on high technology, Army communicators also operated some less-than-modern equipment, such as World War II–vintage teletypewriters and switchboards. Problems developed, however, when these antiquated machines had to interface with modern digital devices. The older equipment was also more susceptible to dust and overheating.[31] Occasionally, communicators reached even further into the past: In the 1st Cavalry Division, pigeons experienced a brief revival, but the experiment proved unsuccessful. When radios went out or were otherwise unavailable, soldiers used colored smoke signals to direct artillery or to call for air strikes and medical evacuation. At night, they used flares, flashlights, and light panels.[32] Although messengers sometimes carried information, they faced the constant threat of ambush. In contrast, the insurgents made extensive use of couriers, since they were able to blend into the general populace much more readily than Americans.

The proliferation of radios, while providing more mobile and flexible communications, nonetheless also created serious problems. Because the electromagnetic spectrum contained too few frequencies to carry the existing traffic, frequency management became a necessity to control the crowded airwaves. In 1965 a division had fifteen frequencies dedicated to the use of each of its brigades. By mid-1967, only seven were available for all three brigades. The remainder of its 200 allotted frequencies had to be shared with other units. Furthermore, the extension of signals beyond their assigned area by means of airborne relay caused them to interfere with radio nets in other areas, including those of the enemy, who was using the same frequencies. Although a solution was reached through the assignment of certain frequencies for the sole use of airborne relay sets, this procedure limited the number of frequencies generally available.[33]

Communications security presented another major concern. The enemy conducted highly successful surveillance of U.S. radio nets, and American units made interception easier by practicing poor radio discipline, such as transmitting large numbers of messages in the clear and neglecting to change call signs periodically. Thus the enemy received advance warning of many U.S. air strikes and gathered other types of intelligence. The situation improved after mid-1967 when the Defense Communications Agency began installing the Automatic Secure Voice Communications (AUTOSEVOCOM) System at major headquarters and command posts. The system scrambled voice impulses prior to transmission.[34]

In the field, standard security measures, such as the manual encryption and decryption of messages, made communications slower and more complicated, a distinct disadvantage in the heat of battle. To make things easier, voice security equipment for stationary and vehicular radios, known as KY–8, began reaching tactical units in 1965. Unfortunately, this device not only reduced transmission range but also generated a great deal of heat.[35] Security equipment for aircraft radios, designated KY–28, and for manpack or mobile use, KY–38, became available in 1967. The latter, in combination with the PRC–77 radio, weighed fifty pounds, a significant burden for the foot soldier. The reliance on voice radio also resulted in an erosion of the operators' ability to communicate in Morse code, a skill that could become necessary when jamming or other forms of interference occurred.[36]

Power generation also posed a problem. Since South Vietnam lacked sufficient supplies of commercially generated electricity, the Army had to supply the power needed to run electrical machinery even at its fixed bases.[37] Communications equipment thus received power either from fixed-plant generators, portable generators, or batteries. Exposed to the elements, batteries soon perished. The development of magnesium batteries helped, for they lasted longer than the zinc and carbon oxide variety and did not need to be kept cool. Fortunately, the enemy rarely exploited the vulnerability of the generators.[38]

Because Signal Corps doctrine had anticipated dependence upon radio relay for long-distance communications on a fluid battlefield, the Corps in 1961 had ceased training its personnel in cable installation and splicing. In fact, the Department of Defense had assigned training in cable splicing to the Air Force, and the Army depended upon contractors for most of this work. When the Signal Corps unexpectedly found itself tasked with upgrading the telephone system throughout South Vietnam, it had only one cable construction battalion, the 40th Signal Battalion, on its rolls. Beginning in the fall of 1966, this unit installed several million feet of cable throughout the theater. The work performed by the men of the 40th enabled the Signal Corps to provide dial telephone service for the first time throughout a combat zone. By 1969 automatic dial exchanges had been installed, giving South Vietnam access to the worldwide Automatic Voice Network (AUTOVON), the principal long-haul voice communications network within the Defense Communications System.[39]

By early 1966 Westmoreland had created the I and II Field Forces as corps-size headquarters to oversee operations in the II and III Corps Tactical Zones, respectively, the areas of heaviest fighting. Each field force had a signal officer and an assigned signal battalion.[40] To improve command and control of signal operations, the Army created the 1st Signal Brigade during the spring of 1966. The brigade consolidated signal units above field force level into one command and merged tactical and strategic communications within the combat zone.

The 1st Signal Brigade was activated on 1 April 1966 with its headquarters initially at Saigon and later at Long Binh. Brig. Gen. Robert D. Terry became the brigade's first commander. In this position, Terry served two functions, operating not only in his normal role, but also as the staff signal officer (J–6) for USARV. The new command, the first TOE brigade in the Signal Corps' history, comprised all signal units in Vietnam except those organic to tactical units.[41] The new arrangement limited the 2d Signal Group, now subordinate to the brigade, to operations in the III and IV Corps zones. The 21st Signal Group took charge of communications in the I and II Corps zones.[42] In May 1967 the 160th Signal Group joined these units to provide headquarters support in the Saigon and Long Binh areas, duties previously performed by the 2d Signal Group.[43] The 1st Signal Brigade also included the 29th Signal Group in Thailand.[44]

Laying cable on Vung Chua Mountain. Clockwise from left, *helicopter delivers 300-pair cable to Company D, 40th Signal Battalion; unreeling the cable; hauling cable down the mountain with the city of Qui Nhon in the background.*

During 1966 the war continued to escalate as the United States increased its bombing of North Vietnam, and American troops continued to pour into South Vietnam. By mid-year U.S. forces were shouldering the burden of combat, relegating the South Vietnamese to a largely subordinate, defensive role. Throughout the next two years, as U.S. forces took the offensive to the most remote corners of the country, communications became the backbone of the Army's tactical doctrine combining mobility and firepower.

In the midst of the intensifying conflict, the Signal Corps had not forgotten its pictorial mission. Division-level signal battalions continued to have organic audiovisual capabilities, and brigade- and field force–level signal battalions also contained photographic sections. The 160th Signal Group received responsibility for countrywide photographic support, providing backup services for the signal battalions. The Southeast Asia Photographic Center at Long Binh, operated by the 221st Signal Company, became the most extensive photographic facility ever operated in a combat zone, capable of color processing and printing.[45] In addition, recently organized special photographic detachments provided quick-reaction documentation of the Army's activities, not only in South Vietnam but around the world. This footage was used for staff briefings and other Army information purposes.[46]

Meanwhile, the Military Affiliate Radio System (MARS) carried on the Signal Corps' long-standing relationship with amateur radio operators. In addition to its primary purpose of providing a backup for Department of Defense communications, the MARS network in South Vietnam connected servicemen with their families back home. When a soldier wanted to call home, a MARS operator would call a "ham" in the United States who would in turn dial the soldier's family on the telephone and then patch the radio transmission into the telephone system.[47]

After overcoming a series of bureaucratic delays and other obstacles, the first links in the Integrated Wideband Communications System became operational by the end of 1966.[48] The 1st Signal Brigade, in conjunction with the Defense Communications Agency, managed the installation of the network, a mammoth job. Site construction alone posed a host of difficulties. Some hilltop locations were so remote that men and equipment had to be brought in by helicopter. In many cases the communicators shared the hills with the enemy, who occupied the slopes. In Thailand, elephants had been used to carry equipment up the mountains, but they had refused to climb above 6,000 feet. Bad weather, combat, and other unanticipated problems also retarded progress. The entire IWCS, comprising sixty-seven links in South Vietnam and thirty-three in Thailand, finally reached completion early in 1969. The system, which totaled 470,000 circuit miles, allowed American commanders to control U.S. air power throughout Southeast Asia, to manage widely separated logistical and administrative bases, and to link major commands throughout South Vietnam. It cost more than $300 million to build.[49]

The completion of the IWCS, with its high-quality circuits, enabled the introduction of digital communications to the combat zone. By mid-1968 South Vietnam had become part of the Automatic Digital Network (AUTODIN), a

Technician from Page Communications Engineers checks equipment at the Long Binh IWCS site.

worldwide all-electronic, computer-controlled traffic directing and routing system. Digital communications replaced the old teletype torn-tape relays and the manual punch cards, which had been both cumbersome and slow. The Army used computers for administrative and logistical communications, and AUTODIN helped reduce the backlog that had developed. The sensitive equipment, however, had to be kept at a constant 73 degrees Fahrenheit and 54 percent humidity, and operators had to wear special shoes to retard dust and dirt.[50]

Satellite communications, meanwhile, proved disappointing. In 1967 the Defense Communications Satellite System began to replace the SYNCOM links, originally designed only for research and experimentation. Using satellites in nonsynchronous orbits, the fourteen ground stations (two of them in South Vietnam) communicated through twenty-seven satellites, using whatever satellites were mutually visible as relays. Due to the poor quality of the signals, the system handled only voice, teletype, and low-speed data transmissions instead of the digital and secure voice circuits for which it had been intended. The Defense Communications Agency also leased channels from the commercial Communications Satellite Corporation.[51]

Back on the ground, the vagaries of combat continued to provide challenges for communications. During Operation CEDAR FALLS, launched on 8 January 1967, General Westmoreland sought to destroy an enemy stronghold known as the Iron Triangle that threatened Saigon. Few enemy soldiers were captured, but the attackers discovered extensive tunnel complexes that served as headquarters and storage depots. During the operation the "tunnel rats"—soldiers who ventured underground to ferret out the enemy—found communications to be a major difficulty. Although they carried hand telephones or microphones strapped to their heads ("skull mikes"), the devices often became inoperable after a short period, as mouthpieces became clogged with dirt or cracked from constant jarring. At least the communications wire trailed by these brave men often aided their rescue or withdrawal through the dark labyrinths.[52]

Riverine operations in the Mekong Delta presented yet another set of problems, as the 9th Signal Battalion of the 9th Infantry Division discovered. Here swamps and heavy jungle made ground combat virtually impossible, and the Viet Cong controlled the few roads in the region. Hence tactical units conducted operations afloat. In this heavily populated region, unoccupied solid ground for signal sites was a scarce commodity. Moreover, the moist soil made a poor electrical ground. To remedy this situation, the battalion buried scrap metal deep below the water table and welded it to large rods that served as grounding points. The battalion also tried to use captive gas-filled balloons to elevate radio transmitters. Although this method greatly extended the transmission range of the sets, heavy monsoon winds rendered the experiment a failure. While supporting the Mobile Riverine Force, a joint Army-Navy endeavor, the 9th Signal Battalion additionally faced the challenges posed by communicating from shipboard. While in motion, operators had to constantly rotate their directional antennas to maintain a strong signal with divisional headquarters on land. When the boats anchored, field wire strung between the vessels carried telephone communications.[53]

By the end of 1967 the United States had committed nearly five hundred thousand troops to South Vietnam. The Army, contributing about two-thirds of the total, had sent seven divisions and two separate brigades.[54] Besides the signal units organic to these combat forces, the 1st Signal Brigade, now commanded by Brig. Gen. William M. Van Harlingen, Jr., comprised twenty-one battalions organized into five groups. Its strength totaled about twenty thousand men who occupied over two hundred signal sites throughout South Vietnam.[55] In addition to American forces, South Korea, Australia, New Zealand, and Thailand all contributed units, as of course did South Vietnam, bringing the total manpower engaged to well over a million. Unlike the situation during the Korean War, however, the American commander had no command authority over the South Vietnamese or other friendly troops.

As the war progressed, the sophisticated level of communications available to the allies proved both a blessing and a curse. Rapidly changing technology caused training to lag behind operations. Despite triple shifts of classes running around the clock, both the Signal Center and School at Fort Monmouth (which had overall doctrinal responsibility for the Signal Corps) and the Southeastern Signal Corps School at Fort Gordon (where most enlisted Signal Corpsmen received their training) had trouble keeping up with their burgeoning student populations. Much of the new equipment was so expensive and in such limited supply that the signal schools had difficulty obtaining prototypes for instructional purposes. Thus, much on-the-job training occurred. To provide the requisite instruction, new equipment training teams from the Electronics Command at Fort Monmouth, successors to the new equipment introductory teams of World War II, accompanied hardware into the field. In the case of commercially designed equipment, the manufacturers sent their own representatives. By the time the operators became proficient, however, their year of duty had come to an end, and the learning process began all over again. The establishment of the

Southeast Asia Signal School at Long Binh by the 1st Signal Brigade in 1968 helped somewhat to alleviate the training dilemma.[56]

Despite these myriad problems, the Vietnam conflict marked a milestone in military signaling. For the first time, high-quality commercial communications became available to the soldier in the field. But there were trade-offs. Although providing the commander with a greater range of command and control, they also limited his freedom of action. The traditional distinction between tactical and strategic communications became blurred when the president and the Joint Chiefs of Staff could use strategic links to direct operations from Washington. As early as 1965 President Johnson had spoken directly to a Marine regimental commander under fire outside Da Nang. Such technical wizardry did not automatically confer upon the users, however, the wisdom about how best to apply the new technology.[57]

The Tet Offensive and the Quest for Peace

The year 1968 proved a crucial one for the future direction of the war. Beginning on 29–30 January, during the celebration of the Vietnamese lunar new year, known as Tet, traditionally a cease-fire period, the North Vietnamese and the Viet Cong launched a general offensive throughout South Vietnam.[58] They hoped to generate a popular uprising against the government and to inflict a military disaster upon the United States similar to that experienced fourteen years earlier by the French at Dien Bien Phu. Although the American high command had received intelligence indicating that the enemy planned a major offensive, Westmoreland and his staff had not anticipated the scale of the attack.[59]

During the course of the Tet offensive, many signal sites came under attack, including ten in the wideband system. From 31 January to 18 February, the period of heaviest fighting, signal troops suffered hundreds of casualties. In the defense of their positions, signalmen proved once again that they could both communicate and shoot. Damage to signal equipment and facilities totaled several million dollars, with exposed cables particularly hard hit. Although communications experienced few serious disruptions, signal support became tenuous as battle fatigue and dwindling supplies took their toll. By the end of February, with most of the 1st Signal Brigade's organic aircraft no longer in good enough condition to ferry repairmen and equipment between sites, only an air courier service established with the assistance of the Air Force kept communications from breaking down.[60]

The northern city of Hue, once the imperial capital of the Nguyen dynasty, became the scene of the most prolonged and bloody engagement of the offensive. Viet Cong and North Vietnamese forces seized and held the city for three weeks before American and South Vietnamese troops regained control. During the initial hours of the battle the U.S. advisers' compound and the 37th Signal Battalion's tropospheric scatter site were the only positions within the confines of the city to remain under American control. At this important signal position, which provided the main link with the Marine base at Khe Sanh, forty-one signal-men repelled repeated assaults and even captured the commander of the attacking unit. After thirty-six hours of fighting, two companies of marines relieved the beleaguered communicators.[61] During the occupation the Communists slaugh-tered thousands of Hue's residents and much of the beautiful historic city was destroyed in the fighting. American and South Vietnamese forces finally recap-tured the city on 25 February.

Located on the outskirts of Saigon, Tan Son Nhut Air Base, which housed both MACV headquarters and the South Vietnamese military, came under attack from three directions during the night of 31 January. With the opening barrage, the 69th Signal Battalion moved quickly to defend its signal facilities in the vicin-ity. The battalion provided communications not only to MACV headquarters but also to various military and civilian agencies in the Saigon area. In addition to its signal positions, the battalion was responsible for manning a sector of the air base's outer perimeter. During the first hour of fighting two of its members were killed while defending a main gate. Elements of the 69th also helped rescue Americans trapped by the attack throughout the city.[62]

While causing considerable disruption within South Vietnam, the Tet offen-sive failed to achieve the decisive military and political victories the Communists had anticipated. Back in the United States, however, the enemy offensive acceler-ated disillusionment with the Southeast Asian conflict. Although U.S. and South Vietnamese forces had inflicted severe casualties upon the Viet Cong and defeat-ed them on the ground, dramatic television footage of burning cities and fleeing refugees demonstrated to many Americans that the war was not going as well as their government and military officials had proclaimed.[63] A "credibility gap" began to grow, along with political pressure for the Johnson administration to bring the conflict to a speedy conclusion.

The Marines' protracted battle for Khe Sanh, beginning in early February, further eroded popular support for the war. It appeared initially that the surround-ed garrison in the mountains near the South Vietnam–Laos border faced annihila-tion. The enemy may have planned to seize this isolated post and use it to claim control of South Vietnam's two northernmost provinces. Westmoreland, who wanted to hold the position as a base for a possible drive into Laos, even consid-ered the employment of tactical nuclear weapons.[64] Meanwhile, the troposcatter system between Khe Sanh and Hue, operated by the 544th Signal Detachment, remained the base's primary link to the outside world. President Johnson, under-standably concerned about the outcome of the battle, arranged for reports to be sent directly to the White House via the troposcatter network. On 2 February this link was disrupted when an enemy rocket struck the signal team's bunker, killing the officer in charge and three radio operators. Assisted by two Marine communi-cators, the team's lone survivor, Sp4c. William Hawkinson, reestablished commu-nications and held out for three days until help arrived. Although the 1st Cavalry Division succeeded in relieving Khe Sanh by early April, some critics compared the costly defense to the French debacle at Dien Bien Phu. Despite the sacrifices made to hold Khe Sanh, the United States decided to abandon the base less than three months later.[65]

Other events around the world exacerbated the public's sense of crisis. Immediately prior to Tet, the North Koreans had seized the intelligence ship USS *Pueblo* on 23 January 1968, an ominous occurrence with ambiguous connections to developments in Vietnam. Fortunately, after extended negotiations the North Koreans released the captain and crew. Of more direct import was the visit in late February of the chairman of the Joint Chiefs of Staff, General Earle G. Wheeler, to the war zone to assess the impact of the Tet offensive. He returned to Washington with a gloomy report that included a request for an additional 200,000 American troops. To achieve this goal, however, the president would have to mobilize the National Guard and other reserve forces.[66]

In setting his policy toward Vietnam, President Johnson had refrained from asking Congress to declare war for fear that the Soviet Union and China would intervene. He had also declined to call up the reserves, relying instead upon the draft to provide the necessary personnel. Johnson had hoped to conduct a limited war in Southeast Asia that would not jeopardize his "Great Society" domestic programs. Nonetheless, he had sought to pursue a course that would eventually achieve a military victory. In the wake of the Tet offensive, the president was forced to reassess his Vietnam strategy. Although he had authorized an additional 10,500 combat troops immediately after Tet, the president faced strong political opposition to any further major troop buildup. Furthermore, Hanoi had indicated a possible interest in peace talks. For several weeks during February and March the president weighed the various options for the future course of the war presented to him by his senior advisers.[67]

With political support for the war crumbling and his health deteriorating, President Johnson surprised the nation by announcing on 31 March 1968 that he would not run for reelection. He also took this opportunity to make public his decisions about the war. There would be no massive infusion of forces. Rather, in an effort to deescalate the conflict and move toward peace, Johnson informed the nation that he had ordered a halt to the bombing of North Vietnam except just above the DMZ. The government's bombing policy had proved increasingly unpopular and, as the Tet offensive clearly demonstrated, had not prevented North Vietnam from moving sufficient forces into South Vietnam to launch a general offensive. Johnson further indicated that the South Vietnamese would henceforth shoulder a greater share of the combat.[68] With the announcement of the bombing halt, the North Vietnamese agreed to begin peace talks. Despite expectations of initial progress, these negotiations, like those during the Korean War, proved to be long and frustrating. For many months the negotiators in Paris could not even agree on the shape of the conference table.

The president's continuing delay in mobilizing the reserves had already adversely affected the Signal Corps by preventing it from drawing upon the trained personnel working in the communications industry upon whom it had relied so heavily in both world wars and Korea. In addition to providing the Army

Signal site on Black Virgin Mountain. Aerial view; below, *antennas.*

with skilled personnel, the signal schools had hoped to use reservists to augment their teaching staffs.[69] A call-up would also have restored the strategic reserve, those forces that remained in the continental United States available for deployment. The resources of the Signal Corps' strategic reserve, the 11th Signal Group at Fort Huachuca, had been seriously depleted to bolster the communications buildup in Southeast Asia. Finally, after the Tet offensive, President Johnson authorized a limited call-up of the reserves in the spring of 1968 to provide support troops for the war effort. As a result, the 107th Signal Company of the Rhode Island Army National Guard soon found itself in South Vietnam assisting the 1st Signal Brigade.[70]

Although the Viet Cong and North Vietnamese generally avoided large-scale offensive operations following Tet, attacks on signal installations increased. One of the worst occurred on 13 May 1968 atop Nui Ba Den, or Black Virgin Mountain, a remote site near Tay Ninh. During the night the Viet Cong killed twenty-three communicators and destroyed most of their equipment. Pfc. Thomas M. Torma of the 86th Signal Battalion won a Silver Star for his heroism while defending the site. In August the enemy again attacked this position and once more put it off the air temporarily. By the summer of 1968 enemy attacks on signal positions numbered eighty per month.[71]

In July 1968 General Westmoreland left Vietnam for a new assignment in Washington as Army chief of staff. His successor, General Creighton W. Abrams, Jr., had previously served as Westmoreland's deputy. For the next four years General Abrams presided over America's changing role in Vietnam in the wake of the Tet offensive.[72] As for the ongoing signal effort, the 1st Signal Brigade reached its peak strength of 23,000 late in 1968. At that time it comprised six signal groups containing twenty-two signal battalions.[73]

Signal Operations in a Contracting Conflict, 1969–1975

With the inauguration of Richard M. Nixon in January 1969, the nation's war policy changed dramatically. Nixon had narrowly defeated Vice President Hubert H. Humphrey in a tumultuous campaign for the presidency in which Vietnam had been the chief political issue. Nixon had pledged to end the war, and he announced plans to begin a gradual disengagement of American forces early in his administration. The number of American servicemen in Vietnam peaked at 543,000 during the spring of 1969.[74] In July the United States began phased troop withdrawals. While the American ground combat role steadily declined, U.S. air support remained significant.

As the United States curtailed its involvement, the war entered a new stage, known as Vietnamization. According to this policy, first proposed by President Johnson in his March 1968 speech, the burden of combat gradually shifted to the South Vietnamese. This process, in conjunction with pacification, would, it was believed, make the South Vietnamese self-reliant and able to carry on the war alone. To achieve this objective, the United States undertook an intensive pro-

Vietnamization—American soldier listens in to a class in radio code at the South Vietnamese Armed Forces Signal School, Vung Tau.

gram to improve the training and to modernize the equipment of the ARVN in preparation for its assumption of expanded responsibilities.

Within the 1st Signal Brigade, Vietnamization had been under way for some time through the "Buddies Together" (Cung Than Thien) program, which matched American signal units with their South Vietnamese counterparts. They trained together, celebrated each other's holidays, and jointly participated in civic action projects. Brig. Gen. Thomas M. Rienzi, who became brigade commander in February 1969, strongly supported the program and was a popular visitor to South Vietnamese signal units.[75] The 39th Signal Battalion, for example, sponsored the South Vietnamese signal school at Vung Tau. Signal units also built schools, dug wells, entertained orphaned children, and distributed food and clothing to local hamlets. By the end of 1969 twenty-five brigade units were actively participating in the program.[76]

Through the Buddies program the 1st Signal Brigade helped prepare the South Vietnamese signal corps to eventually run the fixed-communications system. The Vietnamese communicators were already capable of operating and maintaining tactical communications equipment, but they lacked the skills to handle the more complex strategic facilities. Signalmen received instruction from American technicians at Vung Tau as well as on-the-job training at signal sites throughout the country. As the pace of U.S. troop withdrawal increased, civilian contractors assumed the training mission from the brigade and operated and maintained the sites scheduled for transfer until the South Vietnamese were ready to take them over.[77]

As the United States disengaged from Vietnam and sought a negotiated settlement of the conflict, the fighting continued, especially around Saigon and in the northern provinces. The Communists launched another Tet offensive in 1969, but the attacks were much weaker than the year before. Still, hundreds of American casualties resulted. Although the intensity of the war generally abated, fierce battles remained to be fought, such as that for Hamburger Hill in May 1969. During this battle the din became so loud that it was impossible to use radios.[78]

During the spring of 1970 President Nixon authorized a limited invasion of Cambodia, long used as a sanctuary and logistical base by the North Vietnamese. The U.S. government had not previously allowed its ground forces to operate outside the borders of South Vietnam. By destroying the enemy's bases in Cambodia, the United States hoped to buy time for Vietnamization and to assist the new pro-Western regime of General Lon Nol.

The attack on Cambodia, made on short notice, provided yet another test for Army communicators. The 13th Signal Battalion found that its lightweight equipment served well, allowing the men to move out quickly and provide reliable communications throughout the campaign. The 125th Signal Battalion, however, more dependent upon fixed equipment, could not adapt as quickly. The 1st Signal Brigade, meanwhile, activated circuits in its area network to keep the top commanders in South Vietnam in touch with their force commanders in Cambodia. It also provided units in Cambodia with access to the Defense Communications System, and messages transmitted from field command posts in Cambodia went directly to the White House.[79]

At home, critics viewed the invasion of Cambodia (euphemistically referred to by the administration as an "incursion") as a widening of the war, and vehement protests rapidly spread across the nation, especially on college campuses. On 4 May one such demonstration resulted in tragedy when Ohio National Guard troops opened fire on students at Kent State University and killed four people. By the end of June the United States had pulled its troops out of Cambodia after having achieved only mixed results.[80] About one year later, when South Vietnamese troops conducted a similar excursion into Laos, LAM SON 719, no Americans accompanied them and the results were even more questionable.

Although the war on the ground had reached a stalemate by the latter half of 1971, the air war over Laos and North Vietnam continued. Throughout that year the North Vietnamese, with Russian support, prepared for a major campaign. The blow came on 30 March 1972 when North Vietnam launched an invasion of the South, known as the Easter offensive. With most U.S. combat forces now gone, the burden of the fighting fell to the South Vietnamese, and it initially appeared that they would be overwhelmed. President Nixon responded by ordering a resumption of sustained bombing in the North as well as the mining of Haiphong Harbor, North Vietnam's largest port. By September Saigon's forces, backed by American air and naval firepower, had broken the offensive. Although failing to bring about the collapse of South Vietnam, the 1972 invasion left the Communists in control of more territory and in a stronger bargaining position than before.[81]

In the aftermath, the stalled peace talks resumed in Paris, and National Security Adviser Henry Kissinger, who led the American negotiating team, declared that "peace is at hand." While his optimism proved premature, the fitful negotiations finally resulted in the signing of a cease-fire agreement in January 1973. According to its terms the United States would terminate all direct military support to South Vietnam while North Vietnam agreed to end its infiltration of the South. North Vietnamese and Viet Cong forces would, however, be allowed to remain in South Vietnam. The agreement also promised national reconciliation at some future date. Although North Vietnam released its American prisoners of war, thousands of men remained listed as missing in action.[82]

As the war wound down, the 1st Signal Brigade steadily decreased in size. By 1972 its strength stood at less than twenty-five hundred men. On 7 November 1972 the brigade headquarters left Vietnam and transferred its colors to Korea.[83] The 39th Signal Battalion, the first signal unit to arrive in Vietnam, became the last to leave. As its final wartime mission, the battalion supported the international peacekeeping force that monitored the troop withdrawal and prisoner exchange. The unit departed Vietnam on 15 March 1973, almost eleven years to the day after its first elements had arrived. During its long stint the 39th had participated in all seventeen campaigns and earned five Meritorious Unit Commendations.[84] By the summer of 1973 the United States had completed the withdrawal of its combat troops.[85]

North Vietnam immediately began violating the cease-fire by moving large numbers of troops into South Vietnam. Although President Nixon had pledged to President Nguyen Van Thieu of South Vietnam that the United States would enforce the Paris agreement, the Nixon administration, increasingly preoccupied with the Watergate scandal, failed to honor its commitment. Moreover, Congress sharply reduced military aid to South Vietnam and in November 1973 passed the War Powers Resolution that prohibited the reintroduction of American combat forces without its consent. The cutoff of funds also left the South Vietnamese unable to maintain the communications network the Americans had left behind. While the war-weary United States focused its attention on its domestic difficulties, which culminated in the resignation of the president in August 1974, the situation in Southeast Asia steadily deteriorated. On 29 April 1975 Saigon fell to the Communists. Among the thousands of Americans hastily evacuated before the final collapse were the remaining civilian communications technicians who had stayed behind to assist the South Vietnamese.[86]

The Communicators' War

The undeclared war in Vietnam presented a study in contrasts. While the United States conducted high-technology warfare, its opponents generally employed only the most primitive of means. Instead of the mobility offered by motor vehicles and aircraft, the Viet Cong and North Vietnamese forces traveled primarily on foot. They most often attacked at night. Lightly armed and equipped, they inflicted many casualties by ambush, mines, and booby traps, seldom engaging in set-piece battles. The United States Army, meanwhile, employed the devastating firepower of modern weapons, but lacked the ability to bring the North Vietnamese to battle, except on occasions of their own choosing.

The communications available to the two sides reflected this disparity. Into a primitive society, where electronic media had been virtually unknown, the United States Army introduced the most sophisticated signaling systems ever seen on the battlefield—the products of a century of development of military communications. American soldiers used such advanced methods as satellites, tropospheric scatter, and FM radio, items not available to the enemy. While the Communist forces communicated with telephones and AM radios supplied by their allies, particularly Russia and China, as well as with captured American equipment, such items remained in short supply and were used sparingly. Consequently, the North Vietnamese continued to rely upon couriers and such simple devices as whistles, bugles, and visual signals. Nevertheless, the overwhelming technological superiority of the U.S. Army could not provide solutions for what were basically political questions at the heart of the conflict.[87]

While considerable rancor and bitterness remain associated with the Vietnam defeat, there is little argument that the U.S. Army's communications worked well—the Signal Corps got the message through. In performing their mission, Army communicators sustained relatively heavy casualties, especially among radiotelephone operators accompanying combat operations. Their vital mission coupled with their high visibility, the telltale antennas protruding from the radio sets, made them prime targets.[88] Efficient communications helped reduce battle fatalities, however, by speeding up medical evacuation procedures.[89]

The list of signal soldiers decorated for gallantry in Vietnam includes Capt. Joseph Maxwell ("Max") Cleland, who received the Silver Star. In April 1968 Cleland, serving as the communications officer with an infantry battalion, sustained grievous injuries in a grenade explosion near Khe Sanh. After undergoing extensive hospitalization, he entered politics. Under President Jimmy Carter, Cleland became the director of the Veterans Administration, the first Vietnam veteran to hold that office. He subsequently served several terms as secretary of state of his native state of Georgia.[90]

While no members of the Signal Corps received the Medal of Honor in Vietnam, several soldiers serving as communicators earned this recognition. One of them, Capt. Euripides Rubio, Jr., communications officer for the 1st Battalion, 28th Infantry, posthumously won the award for his gallantry during Operation ATTLEBORO in Tay Ninh Province in November 1966. During an attack on 8 November, Rubio left the relative safety of his position to help distribute ammunition and aid the wounded. When the commander of a rifle company had to be evacuated, Rubio, already wounded himself, took over. Continuing to risk his life to protect his troops, he was eventually felled by hostile gunfire after tossing a misdirected smoke grenade into enemy lines. Because of Rubio's heroism, the air strike thus called for fell upon the enemy's position rather than on his own men.[91]

In addition to the end of the fighting in Vietnam, America's foreign policy underwent other transformations during the early 1970s. In 1972 Nixon had become the first American president to visit the People's Republic of China. The United States also initiated a policy of detente toward the Soviet Union, including the signing of arms control agreements, that signaled a thawing of the Cold War. The changing relationship between East and West held profound implications for world affairs during the last quarter of the twentieth century and for America's role therein.[92]

Notes

[1]On the early advisory effort, see Ronald H. Spector, *Advice and Support: The Early Years, 1941–1960*, United States Army in Vietnam (Washington, D.C.: Center of Military History, United States Army, 1983). Unless otherwise indicated, the following discussion of early Signal Corps involvement in Vietnam is based on John D. Bergen, *Military Communications: A Test for Technology*, United States Army in Vietnam (Washington, D.C.: Center of Military History, United States Army, 1986).

[2]The stratosphere lies between the troposphere and the ionosphere.

[3]In the 1940s Edwin Armstrong had experimented with this form of communication. Lessing, *Man of High Fidelity*, pp. 264–65; see also John C. Monahan, "A Step Ahead of the Future," in Marshall, ed., *Story of Signal Corps*, p. 249.

[4]The former ACAN stations (by then designated STARCOM) came under the control of the STRATCOM after its formation in 1964.

[5]Matloff, ed., *American Military History*, p. 622.

[6]See map 2 in Charles R. Myer, *Division-Level Communications, 1962–1973*, Vietnam Studies (Washington, D.C.: Department of the Army, 1982), p. 6.

[7]John B. Wilson, Divisions and Separate Brigades, draft Ms, ch. 11; John J. Tolson, *Airmobility, 1961–1971*, Vietnam Studies (Washington, D.C.: Department of the Army, 1973).

[8]As organized under TOE 11–205T (22 June 65), which remained in effect until 1971, the airmobile division signal battalion contained a headquarters, headquarters and service company and Company A. As organized under TOE 11–35E (15 July 1963), armored and infantry divisional signal battalions comprised a headquarters and headquarters detachment and three line companies. The airmobile battalion was authorized 352 officers and men; the other divisional battalions were authorized 575. A copy of TOE 11–205T is not available in DAMH-HSO, but see the unit data card and notes in the 13th Signal Battalion's unit jacket. See also Bergen, *Test for Technology*, p. 286.

[9]Guenter Lewy, *America in Vietnam* (New York: Oxford University Press, 1978), p. 42. See also William C. Westmoreland, *A Soldier Reports* (Garden City, N.Y.: Doubleday and Co., 1976), p. 154 and Thomas M. Rienzi, *Communications-Electronics, 1962–1970*, Vietnam Studies (Washington, D.C.: Department of the Army, 1972), p. 22, who both give a total of 184,000 men by the end of 1965.

[10]Bergen, *Test for Technology*, p. 144. The 41st Signal Battalion arrived in Vietnam in July 1965.

[11]Bergen, *Test for Technology*, p. 143; Myer, *Division-Level Communications*, p. 16. The disposition of signal troops in the corps tactical zones is depicted in Bergen, map 7, p. 145.

[12]Rienzi, *Communications-Electronics*, p. 36.

[13]With some dispute, see Bergen, *Test for Technology*, pp. 176–80.

[14]Ibid., pp. 141–42.

[15]A. W. Rogers and E. W. Daniel, Jr., "Hardware for the New Communications," *Army* 14 (Jun 1964): 60–68; Bergen, *Test for Technology*, p. 464.

[16]Will Harral, ed., "Without It You Have No Day...," *Army Communicator* 1 (Winter 1976): 37; Bergen, *Test for Technology*, pp. 256, 448–50.

[17]Bergen, *Test for Technology*, pp. 143, 460.

[18]Ibid., p. 162.

[19] Ibid., pp. 163–64, 186, 420–21.

[20] George C. Herring, "The First Cavalry and the Ia Drang Valley, 18 October–24 November 1965," in Heller and Stofft, eds., *First Battles*, pp. 300–326.

[21] Myer, *Division-Level Communications*, pp. 12–14, 29–30; Bergen, *Test for Technology*, pp. 153–60, 283–85; Robert S. Kellar, "The Heliborne Command Post," *Aviation Digest* 15 (Jan 1969): 14–21; Tolson, *Airmobility*, pp. 73–83.

[22] Herring, "The First Cavalry and the Ia Drang Valley," in Heller and Stofft, eds., *First Battles*, pp. 300–326.

[23] Rienzi, *Communications-Electronics*, p. 62.

[24] Bergen, *Test for Technology*, p. 420. According to Kenneth R. Grissom II, ed., *The Jagged Sword: A History of the 1st Signal Brigade* (Information Office, 1st Signal Brigade, Republic of Vietnam: 1970), "Little or no thought had been given to installing fixed communications because no permanent base camps were envisioned." (This publication has no page numbers. Copy in unit jacket, DAMH-HSO.)

[25] Rienzi, *Communications-Electronics*, p. 18.

[26] Bergen, *Test for Technology*, pp. 119–21.

[27] Richard J. Meyer, "STRATCOM is Worldwide," *Army* 16 (Oct 1966): 71–72, 86; Rienzi, *Communications-Electronics*, pp. 27–28; Battalion History, Phu Lam Signal Battalion (USASTRATCOM) (Provisional), Nov 67, copy in author's files. Other major relay stations were later installed at Nha Trang in the central portion of the country and at Da Nang in the northern portion.

[28] Rienzi, *Communications-Electronics*, pp. 25–30; Bergen, *Test for Technology*, ch. 14. In August 1965 the 2d Signal Group transferred control of the BACKPORCH and WETWASH systems (formerly the responsibility of the 39th Signal Battalion) to the newly created STRATCOM, Vietnam.

[29] Bergen, *Test for Technology*, pp. 106–15, 343, and map 25, p. 354; Rienzi, *Communications-Electronics*, ch. 7.

[30] Bergen, *Test for Technology*, pp. 124–25, 138.

[31] Interv, Maj Gen Gerd S. Grombacher with Col George W. Schultz III, Senior Officers Oral History Program Project 85–B (Carlisle, Pa.: U.S. Army Military History Institute, 1985), pp. 131, 137–38; Bergen, *Test for Technology*, pp. 467–68.

[32] Myer, *Division-Level Communications*, p. 45; Bergen, *Test for Technology*, pp. 254–57.

[33] Bergen, *Test for Technology*, pp. 199–201; Rienzi, *Communications-Electronics*, p. 124.

[34] Rienzi, *Communications-Electronics*, pp. 92–93.

[35] Myer, *Division-Level Communications*, p. 43.

[36] Bergen, *Test for Technology*, pp. 423–24; Myer, *Division-Level Communications*, chs. 7 and 8.

[37] Carroll H. Dunn, *Base Development in South Vietnam, 1965–1970*, Vietnam Studies (Washington, D.C.: Department of the Army, 1972), pp. 78–83.

[38] Myer, *Division-Level Communications*, pp. 78–79; Bergen, *Test for Technology*, pp. 476–77.

[39] Bergen, *Test for Technology*, pp. 226–34, 426; Rienzi, *Communications-Electronics*, pp. 49–51, 135; Leslie H. Taylor, "Traffic Data Collection and AUTOVON," *Army Communicator* 3 (Winter 1978): 18–21; unit jacket, 40th Signal Battalion, DAMH-HSO. The battalion received two Meritorious Unit Commendations (Army) for its work. Copies of the citations are in the unit jacket.

[40]George S. Eckhardt, *Command and Control, 1950–1969*, Vietnam Studies (Washington, D.C.: Department of the Army, 1974), pp. 52–54. The 54th Signal Battalion served with the I Field Force and the 53d Signal Battalion with the II Field Force.

[41]Rienzi, *Communications-Electronics*, ch. 3; Bergen, *Test for Technology*, pp. 183–85; Lineage and Honors Certificate, 1st Signal Brigade, copy in unit jacket, DAMH-HSO.

[42]Rienzi, *Communications-Electronics*, p. 48. The 21st Signal Group was constituted in the Regular Army on 22 June 1965 and activated on 1 September 1965 at Fort Bragg, North Carolina. It arrived in Vietnam on 9 June 1966.

[43]Rienzi, *Communications-Electronics*, ch. 3.

[44]Ibid., p. 53.

[45]Ibid., pp. 51, 125–27; Vincent Demma, "The U.S. Army in Vietnam," chapter in revised edition of *American Military History*, pp. 649–51.

[46]These units were created in mid-1962. Richard A. Baun, "Soldiers with Cameras," *Army Information Digest* 19 (Mar 1964): 51–53.

[47]Bergen, *Test for Technology*, pp. 217–18; Rienzi, *Communications-Electronics*, pp. 127–28; James S. Cassity, Jr., "MARS: The Indispensable Communications System," *Signal* 43 (Mar 1989): 41–42; William G. Mills, "Disaster...and MARS Goes To Work," *Army Communicator* 4 (Winter 1979): 44–45.

[48]Rienzi, *Communications-Electronics*, p. 84.

[49]A detailed discussion of the IWCS is contained in Bergen, *Test for Technology*, ch. 14. See also Rienzi, *Communications-Electronics*, ch. 7. According to Bergen the installation of the system cost $315 million (p. 341), while Rienzi gives a somewhat lower figure of $235 million (p. 130).

[50]Bergen, *Test for Technology*, pp. 299–304; Rienzi, *Communications-Electronics*, p. 92.

[51]Bergen, *Test for Technology*, pp. 307–09; Rienzi, *Communications-Electronics*, pp. 93–94.

[52]Bernard William Rogers, *Cedar Falls-Junction City: A Turning Point*, Vietnam Studies (Washington, D.C.: Department of the Army, 1974), p. 67; Bergen, *Test for Technology*, pp. 205–07; Demma, "Army in Vietnam," pp. 649–51.

[53]Bergen, *Test for Technology*, pp. 215–21; Rienzi, *Communications-Electronics*, pp. 117–20; Robert A. Weaver, "Up Again Down Again," *Army Communicator* 1 (Summer 1976): 25. See also William B. Fulton, *Riverine Operations, 1966–1969*, Vietnam Studies (Washington, D.C.: Department of the Army, 1973).

[54]Demma, "Army in Vietnam," p. 642; John B. Wilson, Divisions and Separate Brigades, draft Ms, table 29.

[55]Rienzi, *Communications-Electronics*, p. 53. This total does not include signal units organic to the divisions, etc. Van Harlingen succeeded Terry as brigade commander in July 1967.

[56]Bergen, *Test for Technology*, pp. 414–24, 429–30, 466–67. An unofficial signal school had been in operation in Saigon prior to that time. The South Vietnamese Army had its own signal school at Vung Tau.

[57]Bergen, *Test for Technology*, p. 168.

[58]The Tet holiday begins with the first new moon after 20 January.

[59]Westmoreland, *A Soldier Reports*, ch. 17. The official campaign dates for the Tet offensive are 30 January to 1 April 1968.

[60]Bergen, *Test for Technology*, p. 263–69, 335; Rienzi, *Communications-Electronics*, pp. 109–11.

[61]Bergen, *Test for Technology*, pp. 267–68; Rienzi, *Communications-Electronics*, p. 108; Lewy, *America in Vietnam*, p. 274.

[62]John B. McKinney, "They Communicate and Shoot," *Army* 18 (Sep 1968): 54–60.

[63]William M. Hammond, *Public Affairs: The Military and the Media, 1962–1968*, United States Army in Vietnam (Washington, D.C.: Center of Military History, United States Army, 1988), ch. 15.

[64]Lewy, *America in Vietnam*, p. 128; Westmoreland, *A Soldier Reports*, p. 411.

[65]Bergen, *Test for Technology*, pp. 277–78; Rienzi, *Communications-Electronics*, pp. 108–09, gives the soldier's name as Hankinson; Bernard C. Nalty, *Air Power and the Fight for Khe Sanh* (Washington, D.C.: Office of Air Force History, 1973), p. 92; Robert Pisor, *The End of the Line: The Siege of Khe Sanh* (New York: W. W. Norton & Company, 1982), p. 184; Tolson, *Airmobility*, pp. 165–80; Willard Pearson, *The War in the Northern Provinces, 1966–1968*, Vietnam Studies (Washington, D.C.: Department of the Army, 1975), chs. 5 and 6.

[66]Don Oberdorfer, *Tet!* (New York: Avon Books, 1971), pp. 275–83; Westmoreland, *A Soldier Reports*, pp. 429–37.

[67]A detailed discussion of the background behind his decision is contained in Lyndon Baines Johnson, *Vantage Point: Perspectives of the Presidency, 1963–1969* (New York: Holt, Rinehart and Winston, 1971), ch. 17. See also Oberdorfer, *Tet!*, chs. 7 and 8.

[68]The text of the speech is included in *Public Papers of the Presidents of the United States: Lyndon B. Johnson, 1968–1969*, 2 vols. (Washington: Government Printing Office, 1970), 1: 469–76. Lewy, *America in Vietnam*, pp. 133, 386–87; Oberdorfer, *Tet!*, pp. 332–42.

[69]Bergen, *Test for Technology*, p. 138.

[70]In his 31 March speech Johnson had indicated that the Joint Chiefs had recommended such a call-up. *Public Papers: Johnson, 1968–1969*, 1: 272. Bergen, *Test for Technology*, p. 269. Johnson had previously called up about fourteen thousand Navy and Air Force reservists to bolster U.S. forces in Korea following the *Pueblo* incident. Johnson, *Vantage Point*, p. 385. In 1967 STRATCOM's headquarters moved from Washington, D.C. to Fort Huachuca. The 11th Signal Group moved to Fort Huachuca from Fort Lewis, Washington, in November 1966. Smith, *Fort Huachuca*, pp. 322–23.

[71]Bergen, *Test for Technology*, p. 268; Rienzi, *Communications-Electronics*, p. 174; Demma, "Army in Vietnam," pp. 671–75.

[72]Abrams was succeeded by General Fred C. Weyand in 1973.

[73]Bergen, *Test for Technology*, p. 434.

[74]Demma, "Army in Vietnam," p. 676.

[75]Bergen, *Test for Technology*, pp. 346–47.

[76]Rienzi, *Communications-Electronics*, p. 144.

[77]Bergen, *Test for Technology*, pp. 346–48; Rienzi, *Communications-Electronics*, ch. 12; Jeffrey J. Clarke, *Advice and Support: The Final Years, 1965–1973*, United States Army in Vietnam (Washington, D.C.: Center of Military History, United States Army, 1988), pp. 438–41.

[78]Lewy, *America in Vietnam*, p. 144; Demma, "Army in Vietnam," pp. 678–82.

[79]Bergen, *Test for Technology*, pp. 286–90; Rienzi, *Communications-Electronics*, p. 150.

[80]Demma, "Army in Vietnam," pp. 682–83; Tolson, *Airmobility*, ch. 11. See also Keith William Nolan, *Into Cambodia: Spring Campaign, Summer Offensive, 1970* (Novato, Calif.: Presidio Press, 1990).

[81]Lewy, *America in Vietnam*, pp. 196–201; Demma, "Army in Vietnam," p. 687; Clarke, *Final Years*, pp. 481–90.

[82]Clarke, *Final Years*, p. 495.

[83]William J. McCaffrey, "Wrapping It Up in South Vietnam," *Army* 22 (Oct 1972): 59; unit jacket, 1st Signal Brigade, DAMH-HSO.

[84]Bergen, *Test for Technology*, p. 360; unit data card and Lineage and Honors Certificate, in unit jacket, 39th Signal Battalion, DAMH-HSO. The 232d Signal Company originally arrived in Vietnam on 23 March 1962.

[85]Lewy, *America in Vietnam*, p. 412.

[86]Ibid., pp. 202–22, 410–17; Bergen, *Test for Technology*, p. 364.

[87]On North Vietnamese and Viet Cong signals, see Bergen, *Test for Technology*, ch. 16.

[88]Ibid., pp. 253–54.

[89]Peter Dorland and James Nanney, *Dust Off: Army Aeromedical Evacuation in Vietnam* (Washington, D.C.: Center of Military History, United States Army, 1982), pp. 78–79; Bergen, *Test for Technology*, pp. 254–55.

[90]*Signal Corps Regimental Association Notes* 4 (Spring 1990): 8; Max Cleland, *Strong at the Broken Places* (Lincoln, Va.: Chosen Books, 1980).

[91]U.S. Congress, Senate Committee on Veterans' Affairs, *Medal of Honor Recipients, 1863–1978*, 96th Cong., 1st sess., 1979, Committee Print no. 15, p. 918; Bergen, *Test for Technology*, p. 204; Myer, *Division-Level Communications*, pp. 44–45.

[92]For details on President Nixon's role in these foreign policy breakthroughs, see Stephen E. Ambrose, *Nixon: The Triumph of a Politician, 1962–1972* (New York: Simon and Schuster, 1989).

CHAPTER XI

Signaling Ahead

Over the course of 130 years the Signal Corps evolved from a one-man oper-ation into a complex organization comprising tens of thousands of individuals. Signaling methods, likewise, underwent extraordinary changes. Myer's wigwag flags and flaming torches were replaced by radios, radar, and computers. Not only within the Army but throughout society at large, communications—or "informa-tion technology" as it is often referred to in the 1990s—had grown in size, sophistication, and influence, transforming the world into a "global village." Indeed, the pervasiveness of electronic communications is reflected in contempo-rary jargon which, for example, describes individuals as being "tuned in" or "on our wavelength." As the Army's voice of command, the Signal Corps played an active role in this transition, both influencing and being influenced by the process.

Post-Vietnam Reorganization

During the troubled years that followed Vietnam, the Army underwent a sig-nificant metamorphosis. Congress discontinued the draft in 1972, and the Army, along with the rest of the armed forces, became an all-volunteer organization the following year. Women acquired an expanded role in this new Army as their career opportunities widened. The Signal Corps opened many of its military occupational specialties (MOSs) to women and by 1976 included 7,000 enlisted women distributed among all but six of the sixty-one communications specialties. Only those jobs that might require direct participation in combat remained restricted to men.[1] In 1977 Regular Army troop strength totaled just under 775,000, and approximately 7 percent of these soldiers were women. With the discontinuance of the Women's Army Corps in 1978, women became fully assim-ilated into the Army establishment.[2]

Besides women, the military also provided opportunities for members of minority groups. On 24 March 1976 Brig. Gen. Emmett Paige, Jr., became the Signal Corps' first black general officer. From 1966 to 1968 he had been deputy project manager for the Integrated Wideband Communications System, and later he commanded the 361st Signal Battalion in Vietnam. At the time of his promo-tion, he served as commander of the 11th Signal Group (later redesignated as the 11th Signal Brigade) at Fort Huachuca, Arizona. Nearly one hundred years had passed since the Signal Corps admitted its first black soldier, W. Hallet Greene,

*Signal Towers at Fort Gordon, Georgia,
the "home of the Signal Corps"*

in 1884. Paige represented a larger trend throughout the Army and the government as a whole. In 1977 President Jimmy Carter appointed Clifford L. Alexander, Jr., as the first black secretary of the Army.[3]

With the budget tightening that has accompanied all postwar periods, the post-Vietnam Army adopted a streamlined force structure comprising sixteen Regular Army divisions, strong enough to defend U.S. interests in Europe but lean enough to reduce the strain on taxpayers' pocketbooks. Under the new "One Army" or "Total Army" concept, the Army Reserve and National Guard assumed a greater role in the nation's defense, contributing "roundout" units to the understrength regular divisions in case of mobilization. Accordingly, the Army put much of its combat support strength, to include Signal Corps units, within the reserves.[4]

In July 1973 the Army placed its branch schools under the newly created Training and Doctrine Command (TRADOC). The following year the Army began consolidating most of its signal training at Fort Gordon, Georgia. Consequently, on 1 July 1974 the Southeastern Signal School was redesignated as the U.S. Army Signal School, while the signal school at Fort Monmouth became the U.S. Army Communications-Electronics School. Shortly thereafter, on 1 October 1974 Fort Gordon became the U.S. Army Signal Center and Fort Gordon, the new "home of the Signal Corps."[5] Because the complicated transition process took some time to complete, involving the movement of personnel, materiel, and equipment, the last class in signal communication did not graduate from Fort Monmouth until June 1976. While Fort Monmouth retained its important role in research and development related to communications-electronics, the school's relocation broke up the "troika" of the post, school, and laboratories that had existed there since World War I.[6] On the other hand, Fort Gordon's southern setting made year-round outdoor training possible, and its 56,000 acres provided enough open space for deployment of full-size units. The school's relocation also saved money and facilitated the practice of "one station unit training" by enabling signal soldiers to receive their basic combat training as well as their advanced individual branch training at the same post.[7]

On 1 October 1973 the Strategic Communications Command, now located at Fort Huachuca, dropped the "strategic" from its name and became the U.S. Army Communications Command (ACC), a title that better described the broad range of its mission: from providing communications within Army posts, camps, and stations to signaling across the continents with satellites. In addition to providing the Army's nontactical communications, the ACC also had responsibility for civil defense communications and for managing air traffic control at Army airfields worldwide.[8] The ACC divided its operations among three major subcommands: the 5th Signal Command in Europe; the 6th Signal Command in the Pacific; and the 7th Signal Command in the continental United States, Alaska, Hawaii, Puerto Rico, and Panama. By 1976 the ACC comprised 30,000 military and civilian personnel in twenty nations.[9]

The Signal Corps and the AirLand Battle

Given the straitened circumstances after Vietnam, Army planners undertook a revision of tactical doctrine during the 1970s. Incorporating the lessons learned in Southeast Asia, the massive military buildup of the Soviet bloc, and the results of the Arab-Israeli war in 1973, the effort resulted in a new edition of Field Manual 100–5, *Operations*, published in July 1976. Focused upon an armor-dominated European battlefield, the new operational doctrine advocated an "active defense" that overwhelmed the enemy with massive firepower. In the face of an adversary greatly superior in strength, the strategy became one of "fighting outnumbered and winning," and victory in the first battle became all but imperative.[10] This doctrine received severe criticism, however, with its departure from the traditional emphasis on offensive warfare and its narrow concentration on Europe, and it soon fell out of favor.[11]

Events of the late 1970s, particularly the seizure of American hostages by Iranian revolutionaries in November 1979 followed by the Russian invasion of Afghanistan in December, suggested that the Soviet Union was pursuing an aggressive foreign policy in a turbulent, unstable region where important U.S. and Western European interests—in particular access to Middle Eastern oil—were involved. Suddenly the possibility of a third world war triggered by a superpower miscalculation in the region seemed very real. In this context, a different approach in the Army's warfighting doctrine became a matter of some urgency. Consequently, the Army again revamped Field Manual 100–5 and published a new edition in August 1982. With this document the Army adopted the concept of the AirLand Battle, which returned to an aggressive strategy that stressed maneuver to keep the enemy off balance. Air and ground warfare became integrated on an extended battlefield where nuclear and chemical weapons would be used if necessary.[12]

AirLand Battle doctrine, however, had no impact on the one major operation in which the Army participated during the early 1980s, Operation URGENT FURY. In October and November 1983 Army Rangers, Special Forces, and paratroopers took part in a joint operation to rescue American medical students from the Caribbean island of Grenada where a bloody revolution had broken out. Hastily planned and executed, the mission encountered a host of difficulties. Communications were seriously hampered by the absence of a joint communications plan. Consequently, no provisions were made to ensure interoperability between the systems operated by each service.[13] Fortunately, despite unexpected resistance from Grenadian and Cuban forces, the operation achieved its objective.

During the previous decade the Army had begun pursuing the development of such high-technology items as the M1 tank, the Patriot air defense missile, the Bradley fighting vehicle, and the Apache attack helicopter. AirLand Battle only became feasible because of the potential of these weapons systems. In turn, the doctrine drove the acquisition of those systems that would best assist in its implementation. At the same time, the Soviets had equaled and, in some cases, exceeded the United States in weapons technology. Budgetary constraints remained a problem until the Soviet Union invaded Afghanistan in December 1979. In the aftermath, the Carter administration initiated a massive military buildup that reached its apogee under Presidents Ronald Reagan and George Bush in the 1980s.

Modernization included communications systems designed to take the Army into the twenty-first century. For use at echelons above corps, the Army and its sister services developed interoperable telecommunications equipment through the Joint Tactical Communications Program (TRI-TAC).[14] Such equipment could alleviate the problems experienced in Grenada. At division and corps level the Army adopted new tactical communications architecture known as Mobile Subscriber Equipment, or MSE. To save time and money, the Signal Corps decided to accept a system that had already been developed rather than to design a new one.

MSE, produced by General Telephone and Electronics (GTE), was a fully automatic, secure radiotelephone switching system that could be used by both mobile and static subscribers. At a cost of over $4 billion, MSE ranked as one of the largest procurement efforts ever undertaken by the Army. It consisted of an array of electronic switching nodes, voice and facsimile terminals, and radios that replaced conventional multichannel radio systems. Housed in shelters mounted on High Mobility Multipurpose Wheeled Vehicles (or Humvees, the versatile machines that replaced the jeep as the Army's prime carrier) instead of in large vans, MSE was more mobile, required less wire and cable, and needed no large antennas like those commonly seen in Vietnam. Moreover, it was interoperable with existing U.S. and NATO tactical and strategic communications systems, including tactical satellites.[15]

Unlike communication systems then in operation, MSE was user based. The Signal Corps distributed the equipment and provided technical assistance and

Interior view of shelter housing mobile subscriber equipment

advice, but the user owned and operated it. MSE worked much like commercial telephone systems in which each subscriber received a unique directory number. Unlike commercial networks, however, the user's number in the MSE system followed that individual wherever he or she was on the battlefield. Thus, command posts could be moved without accompanying delays for rewiring—calls were automatically switched to the new location. If a node was destroyed, the system automatically rerouted messages along a new path. Just like "Ma Bell" and its competitors, MSE offered call forwarding and teleconferencing and provided facsimile transmission for record traffic and graphic materials such as maps.[16]

MSE was also distinctive because the fielding of the system occurred at the same time for both the active Army and the reserve components. The fielding was conducted on a corps-wide basis, beginning in 1988 with the III Corps at Fort Hood, Texas. Barring major complications, the Signal Corps anticipated that MSE fielding would be completed throughout the Army by the middle of the 1990s.[17]

At battalion level and below, the Signal Corps introduced new VHF-FM combat net radios. The Single Channel Ground and Airborne Radio System

(SINCGARS) was intended to replace the VRC–12 family of radios developed during the late 1950s. Available in manpackable, vehicular, and airborne versions, SINCGARS was smaller, lighter, and provided more channels than its predecessor. It also accepted both voice and data transmissions and could automatically amplify whispered messages. Moreover, it offered more secure communications because its frequency-hopping ability made it harder to locate and jam. Later models also included an integrated security device. Fielding of the sets began in 1988 with the 2d Infantry Division in Korea and was scheduled to be extended throughout the Army during the 1990s.[18]

Data systems developed as part of the modernization program included the Joint Tactical Information Distribution System (JTIDS) to be used by the Air Defense Artillery for missile fire control missions and the Enhanced Position Location Reporting System (EPLRS) that used radios to provide real-time position location, identification, and navigational information on the battlefield. Together they comprised the Army Data Distribution System (ADDS).[19]

Training soldiers in the operation of these sophisticated systems remained an essential component of the Signal Corps' mission. Moreover, as communications systems grew increasingly complex, more training became necessary. Nearly all Signal Corps training, both officer and enlisted, took place at Fort Gordon. A notable exception was photographic training, conducted at Lowry Air Force Base, Colorado. As part of its contract with the Army, GTE conducted all MSE training and operated a resident school at Fort Gordon. The Signal Corps also continued to work closely with the private sector through the Training with Industry program. This Army-wide program provided officers with education and experience applicable to their assignments by allowing them to work with civilian industry for a year. Among the participating corporations were AT&T, Boeing, GTE, and Kodak.[20] In 1984 the Signal Corps established ROTC affiliation programs at several universities, among them Rensselaer Polytechnic Institute and the Georgia Institute of Technology, in an effort to increase the recruitment of officers with technical backgrounds.[21]

Organizational changes also accompanied the Army's doctrinal adjustments. During 1978 the Army initiated the "Division 86" study to modify the ROAD configurations. Consequently, the Army designed "heavy divisions" to fight against the massive mechanized and numerically superior forces of the Soviet Army and allied Warsaw Pact armies. These restructured units would also incorporate the new weapons and equipment under development. The resulting heavy divisions each comprised six tank and four mechanized battalions, and divisional aviation assets became centralized within aviation brigades. The divisional signal battalions, however, did not differ significantly in structure from their ROAD counterparts.[22]

In addition to the heavy divisions designed to fight a conventional war, the Army in the 1980s organized light divisions for fighting limited wars wherever they might occur. Containing about eleven thousand soldiers, compared to seventeen thousand for a heavy division, these smaller units were easier to transport and thus better suited for rapid deployment.[23] To retain combat power, the divisional support elements were sharply reduced in size. The signal battalion's strength, for example, was pared from 784 soldiers to 470.[24]

In 1981 Army Chief of Staff General Edward C. Meyer approved the implementation of the United States Army Regimental System (USARS) to improve unit cohesion and esprit. As part of the new manning system, soldiers were assigned to regiments and, as originally conceived, would remain affiliated with them throughout their military careers. Within the Signal Corps and other combat support/combat service support branches, where a large portion of the soldiers served in units outside their assigned branch, the system was implemented on a "whole branch" basis. In other words, the entire Signal Corps was considered to be the Signal Corps regiment, and any soldier with a Signal MOS was automatically affiliated with the regiment upon graduation from the branch school. On 1 June 1986 the Signal Corps regiment was established as a component of the USARS with Fort Gordon as the regimental home base. Accordingly, on 3 June 1986 the commander/commandant of the Signal Center and Fort Gordon also became known as the chief of signal. Maj. Gen. Thurman D. Rodgers became the first to carry the new title.[25]

The Signal Corps tested the progress of its modernization efforts during Operation JUST CAUSE in 1989. Tensions between Panama and the United States had been building since the rise to power of General Manuel Antonio Noriega during the 1980s. Noriega's regime initiated a campaign of harassment against American civilian and military personnel, and the United States imposed economic sanctions in an effort to depose him. The situation worsened following the fraudulent presidential election of May 1989 and an unsuccessful coup attempt in October of that year. Consequently, the United States undertook extensive contingency planning for a possible intervention to protect American lives, uphold the Panama Canal treaties, and restore democracy to the country. In addition, the United States government had indicted Noriega in 1988 for drug trafficking and other crimes. Thus, as violence against Americans escalated, the stage was set for military action.

The United States launched JUST CAUSE on 20 December 1989. Early that morning the 82d Airborne Division parachuted into Panama. Members of the 82d Signal Battalion participated in this assault. The battalion's drop was somewhat off center, however, and the men landed in a swamp. Despite being burdened with up to 100 pounds of equipment each, the communicators worked quickly to establish the required communication nets.[26]

Although most of the units involved in the invasion belonged to the Army, the Air Force, Navy, and Marines also participated in JUST CAUSE. In the communications arena, this joint operation ran much more smoothly than URGENT FURY for a number of reasons. Signal Corps representatives took part in the operational planning and helped develop joint communications-electronics operating instructions. Prior to the assault, U.S. forces conducted extensive training exercises in Panama that prepared them for the actual event. Thanks to the presence of TRI-TAC equipment, interoperability did not pose a problem. Unlike Grenada, the Signal Corps could take advantage of the fixed-communication facilities already in place. Fortunately, Noriega's forces did not seriously attempt to disable the strategic communications network.[27]

On 3 January 1990 General Noriega, who had taken refuge in the Vatican embassy on Christmas eve, surrendered to U.S. officials. He was subsequently taken to the United States to stand trial. As the situation in Panama stabilized, the United States gradually withdrew its invasion forces, and Operation JUST CAUSE officially ended on 31 January 1990.

The Information Mission Area

Communications can be defined as a process or system of conveying information. In 1915 Chief Signal Officer George P. Scriven recognized this connection between communications and information when he published a manual entitled *The Service of Information* in which he outlined the scope and purpose of the Signal Corps. As Europe became embroiled in World War I, advances in the science of warfare made rapid and reliable communications increasingly valuable to the commander. As Scriven remarked: "Without information and knowledge of events and conditions as they arise, all else must fail." Moreover, "without an adequate service of information" troops would have "rather less direction and mobility than a collection of tortoises."[28]

In recent decades automation has had a tremendous impact upon communications. These two fields have become increasingly interdependent and may soon become indistinguishable. In fact, by 1978 the former chief of communications-electronics had become the assistant chief of staff for automation and communications.[29]

In accordance with this trend, during June 1983 Army Chief of Staff Meyer initiated a major realignment in the way the Army managed its information resources.[30] His successor, General John A. Wickham, Jr., carried out the detailed planning of this process. Taking a broad-based approach, he combined five information-related functions, or disciplines (communications, automation, visual information, publications/printing, and records management), into what he called the Information Mission Area (IMA). Correspondingly, the Army Communications Command became the Army Information Systems Command on 15 May 1984, incorporating the Army Computer Systems Command and several smaller elements, in order to centralize communications and the IMA under one administrative umbrella. Lt. Gen. Clarence E. McKnight, Jr., organized the new command, but led it only briefly, being assigned to the Pentagon in July 1984. He was succeeded by Lt. Gen. Emmett Paige, Jr.[31] At the same time, on the Army staff level, the assistant deputy chief of staff for operations and plans for command, control, communications, and computers (formerly the assistant chief of staff for automation and communications) became the assistant chief of staff for information management.[32]

While the Information Systems Command implemented the IMA throughout the Army's strategic systems and sustaining base (posts, camps, and stations), TRADOC in 1985 assigned to the Signal Center proponency for integrating IMA doctrine at the theater/tactical level. On the modern battlefield decisions had to be made in minutes, not in hours, and instantaneous communications made this possible. The purpose of the IMA was, therefore, to quickly give the commander the information he needed to make accurate decisions and the ability to put them into effect once they were made. The broadened scope of signal support of battlefield command and control under the IMA was outlined in Field Manual 24–1, *Signal Support in the AirLand Battle*, first published in October 1990.

General Paige

Moreover, the proliferation of automated systems on the battlefield created increasing requirements for communications. For example, the Tactical Fire Direction System (TACFIRE), which used digital computers for field artillery command and control, needed communications equipment to relay data back to the commander. It was up to the Signal Corps to integrate these automation and communication networks.

Under the IMA, photography continued to be one of the Signal Corps' primary missions, now subsumed within the discipline of visual information. This category encompassed not only still and motion photography, but also television, videotaping, and manual and computer graphic arts. The growing number of video teleconferencing centers at Army installations constituted yet another aspect of this mission.[33] Meanwhile, the Army Visual Information Center in the Pentagon continued the work begun by the Signal Corps' photographic laboratories in Washington in 1918. Although it had undergone numerous name changes and realignments during its history, including a period under Department of Defense control, the Visual Information Center (formerly the Army Photographic Agency) in 1984 found itself once again under Signal Corps auspices as an agency of the 7th Signal Command, which had its headquarters at Fort Ritchie, Maryland. To supplement organic photo support within field units, the center's Combat Pictorial Detachment, stationed at Fort Meade, Maryland, dispatched teams to document Army operations worldwide. Increasingly, joint combat camera teams performed combat photography. Composed of Army, Navy, Air Force, and Marine personnel, these units deployed during both Operations URGENT FURY and JUST CAUSE. Because the Army lacked sufficient photographic support, the Signal Corps began planning for the addition of TOE visual information units to the force structure.[34]

Probably the most difficult functions to integrate into signal doctrine were the areas of records management and publications/printing, duties traditionally performed by the Office of The Adjutant General.[35] As the Army's new records manager, the Signal Corps moved toward an electronic, paperless system. Eventually, electronic storage and retrieval of documents will be instituted on an Army-wide basis.[36] In 1988 the Army's Publications and Printing Command became a subcommand of the Information Systems Command. Its two distribution centers, in Baltimore and St. Louis, were responsible for storing and distributing the Army's forms and publications, including this book.[37] Moreover, in 1988 the Army Computer Science School, formerly a part of the Adjutant General School, moved from Fort Benjamin Harrison, Indiana, to Fort Gordon where it continued to provide training for computer programmers, operators, and managers. This transfer centralized education for both the automation and communications disciplines at one location.[38]

The development of IMA doctrine and its implementation by the Signal Corps proved to be complicated and did not occur overnight. As the Corps' history has shown, the field of military communications is constantly evolving and presenting new challenges. There is little doubt, however, that the Signal Corps will continue to adapt to changing conditions in the communications environment.

New Waves in Communications Technology

With technology changing so rapidly, the variety of communications systems and techniques that the Signal Corps had available or under development in the early 1990s seemed infinite. However, a brief look at a few of the most noteworthy suggests some of the diversity and complexity involved.

Fiber optics is one of the most notable new communication mediums that has found widespread application in the almost two decades since the end of the Vietnam conflict. Fiberoptic systems transmit information via beams of light (i.e., lasers) rather than by electrical impulses. Fiberoptic communications possess many advantages over electrical and electronic signals. Fiberoptic cables, made of glass rather than wire, are significantly smaller and lighter than coaxial cables and can carry more information. Moreover, the fiberoptic signals, which are transmitted in digital form, are not susceptible to jamming, electronic interference, the weather, or cross talk. They are also less vulnerable to the effects of the electromagnetic pulse (EMP), or power surge, that accompanies nuclear explosions and literally burns out metallic wires. The semiconductors used in computers are particularly sensitive to the EMP. Since the effects can be felt hundreds, even thousands, of miles from where a burst occurs, communications could be disrupted over an extensive area. Fiberoptics, with its immunity to such hazards, is thus highly suitable for military communications.[39] Commercial telephone systems already made substantial use of this technology by the early 1990s. Even undersea cables are now fiberoptic. Because optical fiber can simultaneously carry multiple types of signals (e.g., phone calls, television, facsimile), such fibers will likely replace the complex of wires that enter private homes as it becomes economically feasible to do so.[40]

The development of superconductors represents a promising new direction for communications. These materials offer no resistance to the passage of electric current, thus holding out the possibility of much more efficient electronic devices. Technical problems remain, but the potential is great for their use in the next century.[41]

During the Reagan administration, the military's role in space expanded under the Strategic Defense Initiative, popularly known as "Star Wars." In 1988 the Army reorganized its space efforts by creating the U.S. Army Space Command. While in the short term the Signal Corps continued to be responsible for operating the Army's portion of the Defense Satellite Communications System (DSCS), the new Space Command gradually assumed those duties.[42]

Meanwhile, on the battlefield itself, manpackable tactical satellite (TACSAT) radios became available and were especially useful for low intensity conflict and for Ranger and Special Forces units. Signal units, notably the 82d and 127th Signal Battalions, used single-channel TACSAT in Panama during Operation JUST CAUSE. These UHF signals could be easily detected, however, and the satellite readily jammed by the enemy. There was also a shortage of available satellite channels. Lightweight, multichannel TACSAT had not yet been fielded by the early 1990s, and similar high-frequency radios also awaited development.[43]

While the plethora of electronic devices used by the Army facilitate command and control, they also have introduced a host of problems. Besides crowding the frequency spectrum, such devices are extremely vulnerable to the electromagnetic pulse. Moreover, they present a serious security risk because their electronic signatures invite enemy interdiction. With the development of such items as micro vacuum tubes, that are not susceptible to the effects of the electromagnetic pulse, this danger can be reduced.[44]

Despite the sophistication of modern technology in the early 1990s, the telephone remains the Army's most commonly used medium for routine administrative and logistical communications. For the foreseeable future at least, Signal Corps "cable dogs," or pole climbers, will continue to be a familiar sight both on and off the battlefield.[45] The advance of cellular technology holds the promise that soldiers may eventually be able to communicate with something similar to the wrist radio familiar to readers of the old "Dick Tracy" comic strip.[46]

Although Army communicators of the future will be using methods unimaginable at present, they will still be doing essentially the same job as the signalmen at Allatoona, OMAHA Beach, and Phu Lam. "Rugged, reliable, and portable" signaling equipment will be as important to them as to their predecessors, and they will continue to search for the ideal field signaling device.

Signals in the Sand: The Desert War With Iraq

In August 1990 the United States launched its largest military operation since Vietnam, the deployment of over five-hundred thousand troops to the Persian Gulf. Following Iraq's invasion of Kuwait on 2 August, the United States moved quickly to protect its interests in the region. Using bases belonging to its ally Saudi Arabia the United States began the logistical buildup known as Operation DESERT SHIELD. General H. Norman Schwarzkopf, commander in chief of the U.S. Central Command, was in charge of U.S. forces. Meanwhile, the United Nations imposed economic sanctions upon Iraq, and its Security Council condemned the invasion. In addition, a coalition of approximately thirty nations joined the United States in opposition to the Iraqi dictator, Saddam Hussein.[47]

At the beginning of the conflict the U.S. military had just two leased telephone circuits and two record traffic circuits in Saudi Arabia. Automation support was nonexistent. As part of the buildup, the 11th Signal Brigade installed a state-of-the-art communications network. By the end of August the brigade was running the largest common user data communications system ever present in a theater of operations. This network enabled automated processing of personnel, financial, and logistical information. Data traffic in and out of the combat zone averaged ten million words a day. By November, when the brigade had completed its deployment to the Gulf, communication capabilities included automated message and telephone switching; satellite, tropospheric, and line-of-sight radios; and cable and wire lines. Fifteen voice and five message switches supplied communications support to more than ninety locations throughout the theater.[48]

The 11th Signal Brigade grew to include five signal battalions and two companies. In early November the brigade's assigned battalions, the 40th and 86th, had deployed from Fort Huachuca. They were joined by the brigade's 19th Signal Company, which furnished the necessary communications and electronics maintenance capability. In addition, the brigade was augmented by three other signal battalions: the 44th and 63d from Germany and the 67th from Fort Gordon. Rounding out the communications support to echelons above corps level was the 653d Signal Company, a unit of the Florida Army National Guard. It arrived in January 1991 to provide troposcatter communications.[49]

On 4 December 1990 the Department of the Army activated the 6th Signal Command at Fort Huachuca.[50] Deploying to Saudi Arabia later that month, its mission was to administer the theater communications network. The command helped to establish frequency management, which had been a problem during previous joint operations. Moreover, the Saudi government had no central office that controlled frequency assignments.[51] In March 1991 the 54th Signal Battalion was formed to provide IMA support for the theater. With headquarters in Riyadh, it comprised three subordinate companies: the 207th stationed in King Khalid Military City, the 550th in Dhahran, and the 580th in Riyadh.

To conduct offensive operations, the U.S. Army ultimately sent two corps to

Fort Huachuca, Arizona, headquarters of the U.S. Army Information Systems Command. Greely Hall is in the foreground with the Huachuca Mountains in the distance.

Saudi Arabia. The first units to be deployed belonged to the XVIII Airborne Corps, the Army's designated contingency force. Based at Fort Bragg, North Carolina, the corps was supported by the 35th Signal Brigade. Both during and after deployment the brigade maintained a permanent satellite link with Fort Bragg, allowing it to support corps assets at home as well as those in the combat theater. Providing communications coverage over an area of more than 120,000 square miles in northern Saudi Arabia and southern Iraq, the brigade installed 169 separate communications systems as well as 400 miles of wire and cable and approximately five hundred telephones.[52]

The VII Corps began moving from Germany to Southwest Asia in November 1990. Its 93d Signal Brigade encountered difficulties during deployment when its equipment was dispersed among twenty different ships. Unlike the 35th Brigade, the 93d was not trained or equipped for service in an austere environment. Once it became fully operational, the 93d supplied communications between the corps headquarters, five divisions, and an armored cavalry regiment across an area covering more than 75,000 square kilometers. To accomplish this formidable task, the brigade was augmented by the 1st Signal Battalion, the 235th Signal Company, and the 268th Signal Company.[53]

In a region with a limited telecommunications infrastructure, satellites proved essential to successful operations. They formed the backbone of both tactical and strategic communication systems, providing the connections between widely dis-

Soldier operates tactical facsimile machine.

persed units as well as furnishing circuits back to the United States. Due to a shortage of military satellites, the Army leased circuits from commercial satellites. Satellites were also used to provide information about weather, terrain, and location. The network of satellites known as the Global Positioning System (GPS) broadcast navigation, positioning, and timing signals. This information made maneuver possible in the featureless desert environment. Fortunately, the Iraqis did not, and perhaps could not, jam these vital space-based signals.[54]

The U.S. Army Information Systems Engineering Command, based at Fort Huachuca, installed an electronic mail (E-mail) system that allowed soldiers to correspond with family and friends. The system handled approximately fifteen thousand such messages each day in addition to its heavy load of official traffic. As in the past, the Military Affiliate Radio System provided its services. Commercial communications systems augmented military networks, particularly for sending messages between Saudi Arabia and the United States. Corporations such as AT&T and MCI provided facilities that allowed soldiers to phone home at reduced rates.[55]

After five months of sanctions and diplomatic efforts, Saddam Hussein had not bowed to international pressure. When the 15 January 1991 deadline set by President George Bush for Iraq's unconditional withdrawal from Kuwait passed without compliance, war became all but inevitable. On 17 January America and its allies launched offensive operations, known as DESERT STORM. On that date U.S., Saudi, British, French, and Kuwaiti aviators began bombing military targets in Iraq and Kuwait. Following six weeks of aerial bombardment, the ground war began on 24 February. It was surprisingly short, lasting just 100 hours. The coalition forces liberated Kuwait City on 27 February, and fighting ended the following day. In early March the United States began withdrawing its troops, and by midsummer most combat units had returned to their home stations.

The Gulf conflict strikingly demonstrated the power of modern communications techniques. During Vietnam television brought reports of the war into

Mobile subscriber equipment in the desert; below, *satellite antenna dish and camouflaged vans.*

America's living rooms each evening, but these news accounts lagged behind events. This time cameras took viewers directly to the action. Those tuned to the Cable News Network, for example, witnessed the bombing of Baghdad as it was happening. Even the president confessed that he received much of his information from such live broadcasts. While the military exercised tight control over the flow of information to the press, televised displays of duels between Patriot and Iraqi Scud missiles and scenes of dense clouds of smoke from burning oil wells made lasting impressions upon viewers.

While the broadcast networks kept citizens informed of the war's progress, combat cameras used the latest video technology to instantly transmit images to the Joint Combat Camera Center in the Pentagon. Still pictures could be sent electronically via transceivers in less than three minutes, but technology did not yet allow motion video to be transmitted in this manner. Instead, camera crews used commercial satellite transmitters to relay motion pictures. The rapid response time enabled local commanders and high-level decision makers to use the photos immediately for operational briefings and to make damage assessments. Video cameras aboard aircraft, for example, captured the amazing accuracy of precision-guided missiles.[56] Photos sent by courier or mail, however, did not arrive at the Pentagon for up to fifteen days. Although not timely enough to be used for operational planning, they provided valuable documentation of the conflict.

The Army remained, however, without its own photographic units, and there was a shortage of trained personnel. Moreover, the new field manual governing visual information, FM 24–40, had not yet been published. The Combat Pictorial Detachment at Fort Meade furnished combat camera teams to the theater-wide joint combat camera team (JCCT). In turn, joint combat camera detachments from the JCCT were deployed throughout the theater. At the peak of operations nearly two hundred combat camera personnel from all the services were assigned to the JCCT, with the Army contributing roughly 19 percent of the total.[57]

When the Gulf crisis erupted, the Army had not completed the fielding of MSE. The XVIII Airborne Corps had not yet received the new equipment, and the VII Corps was still in transition; only two of its five divisions had completed the MSE fielding process. The 57th Signal Battalion from Fort Hood arrived in the theater in September 1990 to provide MSE support for the XVIII Corps.[58] In Germany, the 3d Armored Division had only recently conducted field exercises with the new system. Nevertheless, the 143d Signal Battalion and its MSE were soon on their way to the Gulf. The equipment proved equal to the task, however, as it received its battle testing in the harsh desert environment. As in Vietnam, civilian technicians worked alongside the soldiers to keep the equipment functioning despite the intense heat and fine, powdery sand. Innovative communicators found that panty hose made an effective sand screen.[59] MSE played a key role, enabling commanders to stay in touch with their units even during the rapidly moving offensive phase.[60]

Due to the presence of several generations of equipment in the field, interoperability posed a potential obstacle. At echelons above corps, the TRI-TAC equipment allowed the Army to communicate with its sister services. TRI-TAC switches could also handle both analog (nondigital) and digital signals. MSE, on the other hand, had not been designed to interface with the older, analog systems still in use. Consequently, the Signal Corps sought various solutions to enable voice and data communications to be carried across the various networks. While reliable voice communications were achieved, data transmission remained problematical. Further technical challenges were presented by the equipment used by allied forces, such as the British Ptarmigan and the French RITA systems.[61]

The SINCGARS proved itself in the desert where it achieved a mean time between failures rate of 7,000 hours, compared to the 200 to 300 hours experienced by the VRC–12 radios it replaced. Patriot firing batteries used these radios for tactical communications as they defended against Scud attacks. Special operations forces employed them because of their light weight and security features. Approximately three hundred Army and four hundred Marine SINCGARS radios were in use during DESERT STORM.[62]

In addition to its traditional communication functions, the Signal Corps coped with its new responsibilities under the IMA. Because the relevant doctrine was not yet fully established, a number of complications resulted. Although Information Services Support Offices had been authorized at theater, corps, and division level to manage the duties formerly belonging to the adjutant general, they had not yet been created when the Army deployed to the Gulf.

To provide printing and reproduction support in the theater, the Corps sent the 408th Signal Detachment, an Army Reserve unit from New York State, to Saudi Arabia in December 1990. To perform its mission, the 408th took with it approximately $250,000 worth of state-of-the-art printing equipment. The 408th's personnel had not been trained to repair the new equipment, however, and they had difficulty obtaining supplies through regular channels. Therefore, the unit had to rely on local sources for support. Despite these problems, the 408th succeeded in doing its job.[63]

The Signal Corps was now also responsible for providing high-volume forms and publications, such as enemy prisoner of war tags, combat award certificates, and maintenance manuals. Without established procedures for governing this type of support, many units relied on their home station stockrooms. This procedure strained the resources of the Army Postal Office system, which was not designed to move such items to a theater of operations. Once received, distribution of the material posed further problems because no one had been assigned this duty.[64]

DESERT STORM confirmed the pervasiveness and power of electronics on the modern battlefield—not only for communications but in all aspects of combat. While high-technology weapons grabbed the headlines, the press contained relatively little information about military communications. But the very absence of such stories emphasized the fact that the signaling systems worked well enough that they could generally be taken for granted. At the end of 1992 it was still too soon for the Signal Corps to have fully evaluated all the lessons learned, but it appeared that its success in the conflict validated the changes in training, doctrine, and equipment implemented after Vietnam. In turn, the Signal Corps would apply the lessons learned in Southwest Asia toward the further refinement of its doctrine for future operations.

Looking Back to the Future

In the aftermath of victory, the Army underwent the usual postwar readjustments, but the process was magnified by the dramatic changes in the world resulting from the end of the Cold War. The era of *glasnost* and *perestroika* in the Soviet Union had led to the initiation of arms control and force reduction discussions between the Warsaw Pact and NATO even before the dramatic unfolding of events in Eastern Europe in late 1989. In November 1990 the two opposing blocs signed a history-making arms control agreement. The reunification of Germany and the subsequent collapse of the Soviet Union radically changed the geopolitical landscape of Europe. As longstanding tensions eased, the United States accelerated the pace of scheduled troop withdrawals. The need to maintain a large Army in Europe to counter the Soviet threat appeared to have greatly diminished. The VII Corps and its 93d Signal Brigade returned to Germany from their success in the desert only to be inactivated less than a year later. In 1992 the Army leadership anticipated that by 1995 the Regular Army would contain just twelve active divisions, down from eighteen, based primarily in the continental United States. Thus the Army would, they thought, spend the next decade making the transition from a forward-deployed force to one that projected power wherever needed on a contingency basis.

The Signal Corps of the early 1990s was a very different organization than that founded in 1860 by Albert J. Myer. The Army's first chief signal officer would undoubtedly find fascinating, if somewhat baffling, the evolution of signaling as he knew it to encompass telecommunications, computers, and satellites. Yet despite the changes in form, some basic similarities still existed. Myer's two-element code, for example, is amazingly similar to the binary code, the concept underlying computers. The Signal Corps' close ties with the civilian and international scientific communities and with the commercial firms that had often worked side by side with the Corps to pioneer communications technology were also similar, if more elaborate, to those that Myer had initiated during and after the Civil War.

Moreover, throughout its history the primary mission of the Signal Corps remained constant: to provide the Army with rapid and reliable communications. For many years, however, the Signal Corps' place within the Army's structure had been tenuous. Originally intended to exist only through the end of the Civil War, Congress renewed the Corps' lease on life in 1866. Nevertheless, Chief Signal Officer Myer and his successors faced an uphill battle for institutional survival. Commanders such as Sherman and Sheridan questioned the need for a separate Signal Corps during the 1870s and 1880s. Before the rise of high technology, communications was not recognized as a specialized skill. Fortunately, the Signal

Corps escaped extinction at the hands of the Allison Commission and went on to render distinguished service at home and abroad. More than ever, as its contributions to the Persian Gulf victory illustrated, the Signal Corps' status within the Army is secure at the end of the twentieth century. Every day, at locations around the globe, signal soldiers operate the communications networks, both strategic and tactical, that constitute the Army's "nervous system." These dedicated men and women preserve the Signal Corps' proud traditions and uphold its motto, *Pro Patria Vigilans* (Watchful for the Country). Whether by wigwag or radio, heliograph or satellite, flaming torch or computer, the Signal Corps gets the message through in peace and in war.

Notes

¹Gloria A. S. Olson, "Move Over Charlie's Angels, Here Comes Signal Woman," *Army Communicator* 2 (Spring 1977): 20–23.

²Bettie J. Morden, *The Women's Army Corps, 1945–1978* (Washington, D.C.: Center of Military History, United States Army, 1990), p. 397; Weigley, *History of Army*, pp. 567, 600.

³Bergen, *Test for Technology*, pp. 327–29, 339; "Paige, Emmett, Jr.," biographical files, DAMH-HSR; Barnes, "We, Too, Serve Proudly," p. 45.

⁴John B. Wilson, Divisions and Separate Brigades, draft Ms, ch. 12; Weigley, *History of Army*, pp. 573–74.

⁵Meanwhile, the Military Police School, which had been located at Fort Gordon since 1948, moved to Fort McClellan, Alabama.

⁶*Concise History of Fort Monmouth*, p. 47.

⁷Bernard I. Lewis, "Move It!," *Army Communicator* 1 (Summer 1976): 20–22; Karl E. Cocke, comp., *Department of the Army Historical Summary, Fiscal Year 1974* (Washington, D.C.: Center of Military History, United States Army, 1978), pp. 32–33.

⁸The redesignation was authorized by DAGO 31, 19 September 1973. Charles M. Rossiter and D. Jean Maire, "Air Traffic Control," *Army Communicator* 2 (Summer 1977): 52–53.

⁹Joe Whetstone, "ACC Marks Anniversary," *Army Communicator* 2 (Summer 1977): 27.

¹⁰The following discussion of the AirLand Battle is based on John L. Romjue, *From Active Defense to AirLand Battle: The Development of Army Doctrine, 1973–1982* (Fort Monroe, Va.: U.S. Army Training and Doctrine Command, 1984).

¹¹Paul H. Herbert, *Deciding What Has To Be Done: General William E. DePuy and the 1976 Edition of FM 100–5, Operations*, Leavenworth Papers no. 16 (Leavenworth, Kans.: Combat Studies Institute, 1988), ch. 8; Archer Jones, "The New FM 100–5: A View from the Ivory Tower," *Military Review* 58 (Feb 1978): 27–36.

¹²William G. Hanne, "The Integrated Battlefield," *Military Review* 62 (Jun 1982): 34–44; Weigley, *History of Army*, pp. 577–83.

¹³Earl F. Klinck II, "Improvements in C3: A Comparison of Urgent Fury and Just Cause" (Newport, R.I.: Naval War College, 1990), pp. 6–8; Stephen E. Anno and William E. Einspahr, "Command and Control and Communications Lessons Learned: Iranian Rescue, Falklands Conflict, Grenada Invasion, Libya Raid" (Maxwell Air Force Base, Ala.: Air War College, 1988), pp. 36–48; Mark Adkin, *URGENT FURY: The Battle for Grenada* (Lexington, Mass.: Lexington Books, 1989).

¹⁴"TRI-TAC and You!," *Army Communicator* 1 (Spring 1976): 34–36.

¹⁵John F. Mason, "Going Digital," *Army Communicator* 2 (Spring 1977): 14–15. MSE is based on a similar system developed for the French Army, known as RITA. RITA stands for Reseau Integre Transmissions Automatique or Automatic Integrated Transmission Network. See Remi S. Johnson et al., "RITA: A Look at the French Mobile Subscriber System," *Army Communicator* 12 (Summer 1987): 18–21. The Summer 1986 issue of *Army Communicator* is devoted to MSE. See also *Mobile Subscriber Equipment System: Reference Guide for the U.S. Army* (Taunton, Mass.: General Telephone and Electronics, n.d.); and Fred Dierksmeier, "The Impact of MSE," *Military Review* 67 (Aug 1987): 40–47.

[16]Some of the shortcomings of traditional radioteletype and teletypewriter systems are discussed in Ralph E. Herman, "Facsimile AN/GXC–7A," *Army Communicator* 3 (Spring 1978): 48–51.

[17]Author's interviews with William E. Kelley and others in the Office, Chief of Signal, Fort Gordon, Georgia, 27–30 Nov 1990. On the training of National Guard units, see Jerry L. Campbell, "Leveler Training on the Mark," *Army Communicator* 15 (Summer/Fall 1990): 38–39.

[18]Nancy S. Dumas, "Fielding SINCGARS," *Army Communicator* 13 (Winter 1988): 52.

[19]Rick Makowski, "EPLRS—More Than Just Data," *Army Communicator* 15 (Winter/Spring 1990): 12–16; Ted Filgrove, "TSM-ADDS Update," *Army Communicator* 14 (Summer 1989): 58–59; "Commander's Comments," *Army Communicator* 15 (Summer/Fall 1990), inside front cover.

[20]James E. Moffett, "Training with Industry at Boeing Aerospace," *Army Communicator* 14 (Winter 1989): 24–25.

[21]The ROTC Branch Affiliation Program was an Army-wide effort in which other branches, including the Corps of Engineers and the Ordnance Corps, also took part.

[22]John L. Romjue, *A History of Army 86*, 2 vols. (Fort Monroe, Va.: Historical Office, U.S. Army Training and Doctrine Command, 1981–1982), 1: 111, 122, and charts 17–20; see TOE 11–35J (1 Oct 1982) for the organization of signal battalions organic to armored, infantry, and mechanized divisions.

[23]Under Chief of Staff General John A. Wickham, heavy divisions had been reduced in strength from 20,000 to 17,000. John B. Wilson, Divisions and Separate Brigades, draft Ms (revised), ch. 13, p. 556.

[24]TOE 11–35J (1 Oct 1982) authorizes 32 officers and 752 enlisted personnel for a heavy signal battalion; TOE 11–45L (1 Apr 1984) authorizes 28 officers and 442 enlisted for a light signal battalion.

[25]The Signal Corps regiment was established per DAGO 21, 30 May 1986. The details of the Signal Corps' regimental plan are discussed in Kathy Roe Coker, *The Signal Corps and The U.S. Army Regimental System* (Fort Gordon, Ga.: Office of the Command Historian, Nov 1989). See also AR 600–82, *The U.S. Army Regimental System*.

[26]Campbell Cantelou, "Jumping into a 'Just Cause,'" *Army Communicator* 15 (Winter/Spring 1990): 9.

[27]For a detailed study of communications during JUST CAUSE, see Jared A. Kline, "Joint Communications in Support of Joint Task Force South During Operation Just Cause" (M.A. thesis, U.S. Army Command and General Staff College, 1991). See also William Scott Ramshaw, "Operation Just Cause Command and Control: A Case Study" (Monterey, Calif.: M.S. thesis, Naval Postgraduate School, 1991).

[28]George P. Scriven, *The Service of Information, United States Army*, Cir no. 8, Office of the Chief Signal Officer, 1915 (Washington, D.C.: Government Printing Office, 1915), pp. 10–11, 74. The author wishes to thank Col. Archie Andrews of the Computer Science School at Fort Gordon, Georgia, for pointing out Scriven's publication and his use of information terminology.

[29]There were two intervening designation changes. In 1967 the position became the assistant chief of staff for communications-electronics and, in 1974, the director of telecommunications and command and control. See chart in appendix.

[30]"The Information Mission Area and the Information Systems Command, 1984–1986" (Fort Huachuca, Ariz.: n.d.), p. 3, copy provided to the author by the command historian, Elaine M. Pospishil.

[31]Redesignation per DAGO 26, 25 July 1986. Paige retired in 1988 after more than forty years of military service. See Scott Saunders, "Lt. Gen. Paige on ISC, IMA," *Army Communicator* 13 (Spring/Summer 1988): 18–19; and Emmett Paige, Jr., "AISC: The Leap from Training Camp to Field," *Army* 35 (Oct 1985): 260–65.

[32]DAGO 26, 25 Jul 1984. In 1987 the office was again redesignated as the director of information systems for command, control, communications, and computers (DISC4), per DAGO 49, 17 August 1987.

[33]Roy Hinton, "Visual Information and the IMA," *Army Communicator* 13 (Spring/Summer 1988): 51; L. D. Manion, "A Transitioning Signal Corps: CMF 25," *Army Communicator* 15 (Summer/Fall 1990): 44–45; L. D. Manion, "A New Look for Visual Information," *Army Communicator* 16 (Summer 1991): 23–25; "The Information Mission Area and the Information Systems Command," p. 7.

[34]William E. Benner, Jr., "USAVIC Has Global Responsibilities," *Army Communicator* 13 (Spring/Summer 1988): 30–34; "Combat Cameras in Action," *Army Communicator* 15 (Summer/Fall 1990): 3–7; brief untitled history of the visual information center provided by the USAVIC, copy in author's files; Manion, "Transitioning Signal Corps," p. 44. The 55th Signal Company, a combat camera unit, was activated at Fort George G. Meade, Maryland, in November 1993.

[35]As a result of the realignment of functions, the adjutant general became a director within the Military Personnel Center, later redesignated as the U.S. Total Army Personnel Command. Terrence J. Gough, *Department of the Army Historical Summary, Fiscal Year 1986* (Washington, D.C.: Center of Military History, United States Army, 1989), p. 71; "The Information Mission Area and the Information Systems Command," p. 13.

[36]"Commander's Comments," *Army Communicator* 14 (Fall 1989), inside front cover; Carol E. Stokes and Kathy Roe Coker, *Annual Historical Review, Headquarters, U.S. Army Signal Center and Fort Gordon, Georgia*, 1989, pp. 6–7. The Information Systems Command is now the proponent for the Army's data processing units, formerly Adjutant General Corps assets.

[37]For several articles on this aspect of the Signal Corps' activities, see *Army Communicator* 14 (Summer 1989).

[38]Anon., Computer Science School, A Brief History, undated copy in author's files.

[39]Richard E. Hogue, "Fiberoptics: A Light Subject," *Army Communicator* 2 (Winter 1977): 12–14; Richard A. Cerny and Marshall C. Hudson, "Fiberoptics: A Growing Technology for Digital Systems," *Army Communicator* 3 (Spring 1978): 56–59; Robert C. Raiford, "EMP," *Army Communicator* 4 (Spring 1979): 5–10.

[40]John Burgess, "Wire War: Putting America on Line," *Washington Post*, 22 Oct 1989.

[41]Curt Suplee, "Scientists Take Big Step Toward Understanding Superconductors," *Washington Post*, 29 Mar 1991.

[42]Clayton R. Koppes, "The Militarization of the American Space Program," *Virginia Quarterly Review* 60 (Winter 1984): 1–20; Mark J. Deves, "The Slow Road to Army Space Command," *Army Communicator* 14 (Summer 1989): 48–49; Arthur J. Downey, *The Emerging Role of the U.S. Army in Space* (Washington, D.C.: National Defense University Press, 1985).

[43]Cantelou, "Jumping into a 'Just Cause,'" pp. 6–11; Thomas Armeli, "Lightfighter Communications in Operation Just Cause," *Army Communicator* 15 (Winter/Spring 1990): 48–52; David A. Barlow, "The Evolution of Tactical Satellite Communications," *Army Communicator* 14 (Summer 1989): 37–39.

⁴⁴John W. Beaver, "Tactical Radio: Threats and Alternatives," *Army Communicator* 2 (Fall 1977): 37–40.

⁴⁵Laura Hill, "31Ls Keep Abreast of Changing Technology," *Army Communicator* 14 (Spring 1989): 4–6.

⁴⁶Robert K. Ackerman, "Electronics Research Spurs Information Exchange Horse," *Signal* 45 (Aug 1991): 89. The Signal Corps had, in fact, first developed a wrist radio during the 1950s. See Michael Brian Schiffer, "Cultural Imperatives and Product Development: The Case of the Shirt-Pocket Radio," *Technology and Culture* 34 (Jan 1993): 111, n. 37.

⁴⁷Joseph P. Englehardt, comp., *Desert Shield and Desert Storm: A Chronology and Troop List for the 1990–1991 Persian Gulf Crisis* (Strategic Studies Institute, U.S. Army War College, Carlisle Barracks, Pa.: 25 Mar 1991). This study includes a list of the participating nations and the forces and/or equipment provided by each.

⁴⁸Wrenne Timberlake, "ISC Takes the Desert By Storm," *Army Communicator* 16 (Spring 1991): 18; "Gulf War Communications Quickly Fielded, Efficient," *Signal* 45 (Aug 1991): 44; Emily Charlotte Pace, "USAISC Before, During and After Desert Storm," *Army Communicator* 16 (Summer 1991): 13–17; Carol E. Stokes and Kathy R. Coker, "Getting the Message Through in the Persian Gulf War," *Army Communicator* 17 (Summer/Winter 1992): 18; Carol E. Stokes, The U.S. Army Signal Corps in Operation Desert Shield/Desert Storm, draft Ms, U.S. Army Signal Center and Fort Gordon, p. 41 (copy in author's files).

⁴⁹Lynda C. Davis, "653d Signal Company Provides Key Link in Desert Communications," *National Guard* 45 (Aug 1991): 94–95; Stokes and Coker, "Persian Gulf War," p. 18.

⁵⁰The 6th Signal Command had been inactive since 1977.

⁵¹Interv, Col Charles C. Sutten, Jr., conducted by Elaine M. Pospishil, 29 May 1991, transcript, pp. 18–19, copy in author's files; Stokes, Signal Corps in Desert Shield/Storm, draft Ms, pp. 48, 113.

⁵²Stokes, Signal Corps in Desert Shield/Storm, draft Ms, pp. 9–13.

⁵³VII Corps Public Affairs Office, *The Desert Jayhawk* (Stuttgart, Germany: Hugo Mattheas, n.d.), p. 40; "Signal Soldiers Diagnose Tangled Technical Issues," *Signal* 45 (Aug 1991): 38.

⁵⁴William A. Dougherty, "Storm from Space," *U.S. Naval Institute Proceedings* 118 (Aug 1992): 48–52; Alan D. Campen, "Gulf War's Silent Warriors Bind U.S. Units Via Space," *Signal* 45 (Aug 1991): 81–84.

⁵⁵Anthony Bell, "E-mail: Anywhere in the World in 30 Seconds," *Army Communicator* 16 (Fall/Winter 1991): 30–31; Sutten interview, p. 15; Stokes, Signal Corps in Desert Shield/Storm, draft Ms, pp. 73–76.

⁵⁶Lee E. Thomas, "Combat Camera Moves Imagery into Vital War Role," *Signal* 46 (Nov 1991): 49–50.

⁵⁷Mike Hunter and Samuel A. Barnes, "Signal Support: IMA in the Desert and Beyond," *Army Communicator* 17 (Summer/Winter 1992): 11–16.

⁵⁸Stokes, Signal Corps in Desert Shield/Storm, draft Ms, p. 96; Byron L. Burrow, "MSE Support of Corps Combat Operations," *Army Communicator* 16 (Fall/Winter 1991): 28–29.

⁵⁹Interv, Col Steven C. Harman, Jr., conducted by Elaine M. Pospishil, 18 Jun 1991, transcript, p. 12, copy in author's files.

⁶⁰Louise T. Cooper, "MSE Key to Desert Storm Communications," *Army Communicator* 16 (Spring 1991): 14–15; Bryan S. Goda and Robert M. Prudhomme,

"Communications on a Mobile Battlefield in the 100 Hours War," *Army Communicator* 16 (Spring 1991): 42–47.

[61]"Signal Soldiers Diagnose Tangled Technical Issues," pp. 37–38.

[62]"SINCGARS a 'Key Component' in Operation Desert Storm," *ITT Defense*, vol. 1, no. 3 (copy in author's files); *Congressional Study Book FY 1993*, vol. 1, Unclassified Issues, "Single Channel Ground and Airborne Radio System (SINCGARS)," paper M–2, SAIS-SDT, 9 Mar 1992 (copy in CMH files); *Army Focus*, June 1991, p. 31.

[63]Hunter and Barnes, "IMA in Desert," pp. 8–9.

[64]Ibid., pp. 9–10.

Appendix A

Chief Signal Officers and Their Successors

Chief Signal Officers
(1860–1964)

Maj. Albert J. Myer	1860–1863
Lt. Col. William J. L. Nicodemus	1863–1864
Col. Benjamin F. Fisher	1864–1866
Col. Albert J. Myer (promoted to brigadier general 16 June 1880)	1866–1880
Brig. Gen. William B. Hazen	1880–1887
Brig. Gen. Adolphus W. Greely	1887–1906
Brig. Gen. James Allen	1906–1913
Brig. Gen. George P. Scriven	1913–1917
Brig. Gen. George O. Squier (promoted to major general 6 October 1917)	1917–1923
Maj. Gen. Charles McK. Saltzman	1924–1928
Maj. Gen. George S. Gibbs	1928–1931
Maj. Gen. Irving J. Carr	1931–1934
Maj. Gen. James B. Allison	1935–1937
Maj. Gen. Joseph O. Mauborgne	1937–1941

Maj. Gen. Dawson Olmstead	1941–1943
Maj. Gen. Harry C. Ingles	1943–1947
Maj. Gen. Spencer B. Akin	1947–1951
Maj. Gen. George I. Back	1951–1955
Lt. Gen. James D. O'Connell	1955–1959
Maj. Gen. Ralph T. Nelson	1959–1962
Maj. Gen. Earle F. Cook	1962–1963
Maj. Gen. David P. Gibbs	1963–1964

Chiefs of Communications-Electronics
(1964–1967)

Maj. Gen. David P. Gibbs	1964–1966
Maj. Gen. Walter E. Lotz, Jr.	1966–1967

Assistant Chiefs of Staff for Communications-Electronics
(1967–1974)

Maj. Gen. Walter E. Lotz, Jr.	1967–1968
Maj. Gen. George E. Pickett	1968–1972
Lt. Gen. Thomas M. Rienzi	1972–1974

Directors of Telecommunications and Command and Control
(1974–1978)
(a directorate of ODCSOPS)

Lt. Gen. Thomas M. Rienzi	1974–1977
Lt. Gen. Charles R. Myer	1977–1978

Assistant Chiefs of Staff for Automation and Communications
(1978–1981)

Lt. Gen. Charles R. Myer	1978–1979
Maj. Gen. Clay T. Buckingham	1979–1981

Assistant Deputy Chiefs of Staff for Operations and Plans
(Command, Control, Communications, and Computers)
(1981–1984)

Maj. Gen. Clay T. Buckingham	1981–1982
Maj. Gen. James M. Rockwell	1982–1984

Assistant Chiefs of Staff for Information Management
(1984–1987)

Lt. Gen. David K. Doyle	1984–1986
Lt. Gen. Thurman D. Rodgers	1986–1987

Directors of Information Systems for Command, Control,
Communications, and Computers
(1987–   )

Lt. Gen. Thurman D. Rodgers	1987–1988
Lt. Gen. Bruce R. Harris	1988–1990
Lt. Gen. Jerome B. Hilmes	1990–1992
Lt. Gen. Peter A. Kind	1992–1994
Lt. Gen. Otto J. Guenther	1994–

Appendix B

Chiefs of Signal

Beginning with the implementation of the U.S. Army Regimental System in 1986, the commandant of the Signal School at Fort Gordon, Georgia, was additionally designated as the chief of signal.

Maj. Gen. Thurman D. Rodgers	1986
Maj. Gen. Bruce R. Harris	1986–1988
Maj. Gen. Leo M. Childs	1988–1990
Maj. Gen. Peter A. Kind	1990–1991
Maj. Gen. Robert E. Gray	1991–1994
Maj. Gen. Douglas D. Buchholz	1994–

Bibliographical Note

One of the major reasons for writing this book was to provide a comprehensive one-volume history of the Signal Corps. Although scholars have given some periods of the Corps' history considerable attention, particularly the Civil War and World War II, they have devoted little if any study to other periods. This volume attempts to rectify that situation. The sources consulted were largely published primary and secondary works. While the following does not purport to be a complete listing of sources about the Signal Corps, it is intended to serve as a guide for those interested in pursuing various aspects of its history.

General Sources

The records of the Office of the Chief Signal Officer comprise Record Group (RG) 111 at the National Archives. These constitute the principal primary source of information about the branch from 1860 to the 1950s. With the opening in early 1994 of the new Archives II facility in College Park, Maryland, the Archives is undertaking a major reorganization of its holdings. The Archives currently plans to house Signal Corps records that originate before World War II in its main building in Washington, D.C., while those dating after 1941 will be located in College Park. Mabel E. Deutrich has compiled a *Preliminary Inventory of the Records of the Office of the Chief Signal Officer*, Preliminary Inventory 155 (1963).

The annual reports of the chief signal officer are the single most valuable published source of information for the organization and operations of the Corps. From 1860 to 1920 these are printed as part of the annual report of the secretary of war and in some instances are published as separate volumes. In 1921, in an economy move, the War Department ceased to publish the reports by most of the bureau chiefs, although the chiefs were still required to submit them to the secretary of war. Excerpts of the chief signal officer's report appear in the secretary of war's reports of 1921 and 1922. To achieve further savings, publication of even the excerpts ceased after 1922. The manuscript copies prepared by the chief signal officer and his counterparts are located in the National Archives in RG 407 (Adjutant General), Central File, file no. 319.12. After 1937 the preparation of these reports was no longer required. Perhaps to fill the resulting information gap, the Signal Corps in 1920 began publishing the *Signal Corps Information Bulletin* (later the *Signal Corps Bulletin*), which dealt with historical and technical topics. Publication ceased in 1940. Partial or complete collections are located at the Pentagon Library; the U.S. Army Military History Institute (MHI) at Carlisle Barracks, Pennsylvania; and the National Archives.

The following secondary sources together cover most of the history of the Signal Corps:

William A. Glassford, "The Signal Corps," in *The Army of the United States*, edited by Theophilus F. Rodenbough and William L. Haskin (New York: Maynard, Merrill, and Co., 1896). This is a historical sketch written by a prominent Signal Corps officer in the late nineteenth and early twentieth centuries.

Historical Sketch of the Signal Corps (1860–1941), Eastern Signal Corps Schools Pamphlet no. 32 (Fort Monmouth, N.J.: Eastern Signal Corps Schools, U.S. Army, 1942). A reliable guide to the Corps' history prior to World War II.

Max L. Marshall, editor, *The Story of the U.S. Army Signal Corps* (New York: Franklin Watts, Inc., 1965). Contains articles by various authors on aspects of the Corps' history up to the time of its publication. This source should be used with caution as the quality of the pieces varies considerably.

Paul J. Scheips, editor, *Military Signal Communications*, 2 vols. (New York: Arno Press, Inc., 1980). A very useful anthology. The first volume of readings covers the history of military signal communications in the United States through World War II. The second volume focuses on signaling techniques.

Kathy R. Coker and Carol E. Stokes, *A Concise History of U.S. Army Signal Corps* (U.S. Army Signal Center and Fort Gordon, Ga.: Office of the Command Historian, 1991). Originally published in 1988, this revised edition expands upon the original text and includes such useful information as biographical sketches of the chief signal officers and chiefs of signal, a collection of representative photographs, and significant dates in the Corps' history.

Published unit histories are another source of much valuable information. Large collections of unit histories are maintained by the Military History Institute and the New York Public Library in New York City. In many cases these volumes may be obtained through interlibrary loan. For a guide to published unit histories, see James T. Controvich, compiler, *United States Army Unit Histories: A Reference and Bibliography* (Manhattan, Kans.: Military Affairs/Aerospace Historian, 1983). A supplement to this guide was published in 1987.

The Origins of the Signal Corps and the Civil War

The papers of Albert J. Myer, founder of the Signal Corps, are located at the U.S. Army Military History Institute, Carlisle Barracks, Pennsylvania. In addition, a small collection of his papers is located in the Manuscript Division of the Library of Congress. These collections have been microfilmed, and the U.S. Army Center of Military History (CMH) has a set of the four rolls of film. Paul J. Scheips used this material to write his invaluable dissertation, "Albert J. Myer, Founder of the Signal Corps: A Biographical Study" (Ph.D. diss., American

University, 1966), which is full of details about Myer's early career and the origins of the Signal Corps.

In addition to the Myer collection, the Military History Institute also holds papers belonging to Benjamin F. Fisher, chief signal officer from 1864 to 1866. The institute also houses the papers of several Civil War signal officers, including Luther Furst, who served with distinction on Little Round Top during the Gettysburg campaign.

The most comprehensive source of information about the Signal Corps during the Civil War is J. Willard Brown's *The Signal Corps, U.S.A. in the War of the Rebellion* (Boston: U.S. Veteran Signal Corps Association, 1896). Brown served as a signal officer during the conflict, so he knew his subject first hand. The major drawback to this work is the author's tendency to use large amounts of unattributed material. Copies of the original volume may be somewhat hard to locate, but Arno Press published a reprint edition in 1974. Unfortunately, the reprint contains neither the roster of the Corps' personnel that Brown compiled nor an index.

Among the articles that provide a general discussion of the Signal Corps during the Civil War are: George R. Thompson, "Civil War Signals," *Military Affairs* 18 (Winter 1954): 188–201, reprinted in volume 1 of Scheips, ed., *Military Signal Communications*, and Paul J. Scheips, "Union Signal Communications: Innovation and Conflict," *Civil War History* 9 (Dec 1963): 399–421.

Reports of the chief signal officer and the other signal officers in the field are scattered throughout the 128 volumes of the *War of the Rebellion: A Compilation of the Official Records of the Union and Confederate Armies* (Washington, D.C.: Government Printing Office, 1880–1901). There are, however, few published operational studies of the use of signals during the war. Among those available are Paul J. Scheips, "Signaling at Port Hudson, 1863," *Civil War History* 2 (Dec 1956): 106–13, and Alexander W. Cameron, "The Signal Corps at Gettysburg," *Gettysburg* (Jul 1990): 9–15, and "The Signal Corps at Gettysburg Part II: Support of Meade's Pursuit," *Gettysburg* (Jan 1991): 101–09. See also Cameron's *A Communicator's Guide to the Gettysburg Campaign* (Carlisle Barracks, Pa.: U.S. Army War College, 1989).

A number of Civil War signal officers later wrote of their experiences. Many of these reminiscences were published by the various state commanderies of the Military Order of the Loyal Legion of the United States (MOLLUS). The Military History Institute has these volumes among its collections, and their contents are listed in Louise Arnold, comp., *Special Bibliography 11, The Era of the Civil War, 1820–1876* (Carlisle Barracks, Pa.: U.S. Army Military History Institute, 1982). See, for example, Samuel T. Cushing, "The Acting Signal Corps," in *War Talks in Kansas: A Series of Papers Read Before the Kansas Commandery of the Military Order of the Loyal Legion of the United States*, Paper no. 5 (Kansas City, Mo.: Franklin Hudson Publishing House, 1906); Sylvester B. Partridge, "With the Signal Corps from Fortress Monroe to Richmond, May 1864–April 1865," *War Papers Read Before the Maine Commandery of the Military Order of the Loyal Legion of the United States*, vol.

3 (Portland: Lefavor-Tower Company, 1908); and Henry S. Tafft, "Reminiscences of the Signal Service in the Civil War," *Personal Narratives of the War of the Rebellion, Being Papers Read Before the Rhode Island Soldiers and Sailors Historical Society*, Sixth Series, no. 3 (Providence: Published by the Society, 1903). Other autobiographical sources include Wayne C. Temple, ed., "A Signal Officer with Grant: The Letters of Captain Charles L. Davis," *Civil War History* 6 (Dec 1961): 428–37; and Lester L. Swift, ed., "The Recollections of a Signal Officer," *Civil War History* 9 (Mar 1963): 36–54. Swift edited the writings of Capt. Gustavus Sullivan Dana.

Chief Signal Officer Myer published the first edition of *A Manual of Signals: For the Use of Signal Officers in the Field* in 1864. Subsequent editions were published in 1866, 1868, 1871, 1877, and 1879.

J. Willard Brown devotes a chapter of his book to the Confederate Signal Corps. The foremost contemporary scholar of that organization is David W. Gaddy. See his "William Norris and the Confederate Signal and Secret Service," *Maryland Historical Magazine* 70 (Summer 1975): 167–88. On the intelligence work performed by the Confederate Signal Corps, see William A. Tidwell, James O. Hall, and David W. Gaddy, *Come Retribution: The Confederate Secret Service and the Assassination of Lincoln* (Jackson: University Press of Mississippi, 1988). The Confederate Army's first signal officer, Edward Porter Alexander, gained considerable renown as an artillery commander and later became a successful businessman in Georgia. He penned his *Military Memoirs of a Confederate* (Charles Scribner's Sons, 1907; reprint, Bloomington: Indiana University Press, 1962), which is still considered a classic. The reprinted edition contains an introduction by T. Harry Williams that discusses Alexander's work with Myer in some detail. Alexander devotes more space to his early career in his *Fighting for the Confederacy*, edited by Gary W. Gallagher (Chapel Hill: University of North Carolina Press, 1989).

The two volumes of William R. Plum's *The Military Telegraph During the Civil War, with an Exposition of Ancient and Modern Means of Communication, and of the Federal and Confederate Cipher Systems...* (Chicago: Jansen, McClurg & Co., 1882) provide a full account of the operations of Myer's nemesis, the Military Telegraph. Arno Press reprinted Plum's work in 1974 as one volume with an introduction by Paul J. Scheips. Plum had been a Military Telegraph operator. Two of his colleagues who wrote of their experiences were David Homer Bates, *Lincoln in the Telegraph Office: Recollections of the United States Military Telegraph Corps* (New York: Century Co., 1907), and John Emmet O'Brien, *Telegraphing in Battle: Reminiscences of the Civil War* (Scranton, Pa.: Raeder Press, 1910).

The Post–Civil War Years (1866–1891)

The Corps' emphasis during this period was primarily on its weather activities. The chief signal officer's annual reports for these years are voluminous, sometimes comprising more than one thousand pages, and are full of interesting facts and statistics.

The National Archives removed the Signal Corps' weather-related records from RG 111 and placed them with those of the Weather Bureau, RG 27. A valuable summary of the Corps' weather activities is that by Lewis J. Darter, Jr., "Weather Service Activities of Federal Agencies Prior to 1891," the introduction to his *List of Climatological Records in the National Archives*, Special List 1 (1942). See also Harold T. Pinkett, Helen T. Finneran, and Katherine H. Davidson, comps., *Preliminary Inventory of the Climatological and Hydrological Records of the Weather Bureau*, Preliminary Inventory 38 (1952). There are also 564 rolls of microfilm that contain the *Climatological Records of the Weather Bureau, 1819–1892*, T907.

The *Monthly Weather Review*, begun by the Signal Corps in 1872 and published within the chief's annual report until 1884, is still being published by the American Meteorological Society.

A. Hunter Dupree's *Science in the Federal Government* (Cambridge, Mass.: Belknap Press of the Harvard University Press, 1957; reprint, Baltimore: Johns Hopkins University Press, 1986) discusses the Signal Corps' role in the overall governmental scientific establishment. Among the secondary works that deal with the Corps' weather duties are: Charles C. Bates and John F. Fuller, *America's Weather Warriors, 1814–1985* (College Station, Tex.: Texas A&M Press, 1986); Donald R. Whitnah, *A History of the United States Weather Bureau* (Urbana: University of Illinois Press, 1965); and Joseph M. Hawes, "The Signal Corps and Its Weather Service, 1870–1890," *Military Affairs* 30 (Summer 1966): 68–76.

The Signal Corps' work in the Arctic is discussed in John Edwards Caswell's *Arctic Frontiers: United States Explorations in the Far North* (Norman: University of Oklahoma Press, 1956). The ill-fated expedition to northern Canada, led by 1st Lt. Adolphus W. Greely during the 1880s, is well documented. In addition to Greely's two-volume official report published in 1888, *Proceedings of the Lady Franklin Bay Expedition*, he wrote a personal account, *Three Years of Arctic Service*, 2 vols. (New York: Charles Scribner's Sons, 1886). A one-volume edition was published in 1894. A. L. Todd used Greely's papers to write *Abandoned: The Story of the Greely Arctic Expedition, 1881–1884* (New York: McGraw-Hill Book Company, Inc., 1961). Although without footnotes, it is an excellent and compelling account. Todd discusses the controversial charges of cannibalism that cast a shadow over the expedition's real scientific accomplishments, such as the "farthest north" achieved to that time. The failed rescue attempt by 1st Lt. Ernest A. Garlington is discussed in Lawrence J. Fischer's "Horse Soldiers in the Arctic: The Garlington Expedition of 1883," *American Neptune* 36 (Apr 1976): 108–24. Capt. Winfield S. Schley wrote of his successful effort in *The Rescue of Greely* (New York: Scribner's, 1885). A considerable body of literature exists on Arctic exploration, many of which include the Greely expedition. See, for example, Pierre Berton's *The*

Arctic Grail: The Quest for the North West Passage and the North Pole, 1818–1909 (New York: Viking, 1988).

Just a few years after his ordeal in the Arctic Greely became chief signal officer. He headed the Corps from 1887 to 1906, the longest tenure of any chief, and he was one of the most remarkable men of his generation. Greely's papers are located in the Manuscript Division of the Library of Congress, and he donated much of his personal library to the National Geographic Society, of which he was a charter member. He also contributed a number of articles to the *National Geographic* magazine. In 1927 he published his memoirs, *Reminiscences of Adventure and Service* (New York: Charles Scribner's Sons). Greely has attracted considerable scholarly attention. He was the subject of a biography by William ("Billy") Mitchell, *General Greely: The Story of a Great American* (New York: G. P. Putnam's Sons, 1936). See also the entry for Greely in volume 21 (supplement one) of the *Dictionary of American Biography* (New York: Charles Scribner's Sons, 1944) and Charles R. Shrader's biographical essay in volume 2 of Roger J. Spiller, ed., *Dictionary of American Military Biography*, 3 vols. (Westport, Conn.: Greenwood Press, 1984).

William B. Hazen, Greely's predecessor, is less well known but not overlooked. Hazen himself wrote of his Civil War experiences in *A Narrative of Military Service* (1885: reprint, Huntington, W.V.: Blue Acorn Press, 1993). His early post–Civil War career has been studied by Marvin E. Kroeker's *Great Plains Command: William B. Hazen in the Frontier West* (Norman: University of Oklahoma Press, 1976). A biographical sketch, "William Babcock Hazen," by Paul J. Scheips appeared in the *Cosmos Club Bulletin* 38 (Oct 1985): 4–7, and Hazen is also included in volume 8 of the *Dictionary of American Biography* (1932).

The career of Cleveland Abbe is closely associated with the Signal Corps weather bureau, and he continued his weather duties with the Agriculture Department after the transfer of the function in 1891. His son Truman later published a biography of his father, *Professor Abbe and the Isobars: The Story of Cleveland Abbe, America's First Weatherman* (New York: Vantage Press, 1955), and Cleveland Abbe is the first entry in volume 1 of the *Dictionary of American Biography* (1928).

The Corps' other major activity in the post–Civil War period was the construction and operation of frontier military telegraph lines. In addition to providing communications to the frontier, these lines were also used to send weather reports. See L. Tuffly Ellis, "Lieutenant A. W. Greely's Report on the Installation of Military Telegraph Lines in Texas, 1875–1876," *Southwestern Historical Quarterly* 69 (Jul 1965): 66–87, reprinted in volume one of *Military Signal Communications*. One of the Corps' frontier operators, Will Croft Barnes, wrote an interesting account of his adventures, *Apaches and Longhorns: The Reminiscences of Will C. Barnes* (Los Angeles: Ward Ritchie Press, 1941; facsimile edition, Tucson: University of Arizona Press, 1982). Barnes was also one of the Corps' five Medal of Honor winners.

The Post–Weather Bureau Years and the War With Spain (1892–1903)

Having lost its weather functions in 1891, the Signal Corps returned to its original mission—military communications. During this period the branch began its venture into aeronautics, beginning with balloons. Tom D. Crouch of the Smithsonian Institution has written a comprehensive study of ballooning, *The Eagle Aloft: Two Centuries of the Balloon in America* (Washington, D.C.: Smithsonian Institution Press, 1983). Russell J. Parkinson's "Politics, Patents, and Planes: Military Aeronautics in the United States, 1863–1907" (Ph.D. diss., Duke University, 1963) is also an excellent source of information. He summarized much of his research in "United States Signal Corps Balloons, 1871–1902," *Military Affairs* 24 (Winter 1960–1961): 189–202. The early years of Signal Corps aviation are also discussed by two of the Army's first pilots, Charles deForest Chandler and Frank P. Lahm, in *How Our Army Grew Wings: Airmen and Aircraft Before 1914* (Chicago: Ronald Press Company, 1943).

Along with detailed information on the Corps' service in the War with Spain, the 1898 and 1899 chief signal officer's reports contain a number of photographs taken in Cuba, Puerto Rico, and the Philippines. These reflect the fact that the branch had unofficially become the Army's photographer. Other sources of information about the Corps' service in the Spanish-American War are Howard A. Giddings' *Exploits of the Signal Corps in the War with Spain* (Kansas City, Mo.: Hudson-Kimberly Publishing Co., 1900) and Adolphus W. Greely's "The Signal Corps in War-Time," *The Century Magazine* 66 (Sep 1903): 811–26. The Corps is probably best remembered for its attempt to use a balloon during the battle of Santiago. The unfortunate results are chronicled in John Cuneo's "The Balloon at Hell's Corner," *Military Affairs* 7 (Fall 1943): 189–95. The Signal Corps' work in Cuba after the war is recounted in *Report of Captain Otto A. Nesmith, Signal Corps, U.S. Army, Chief Signal Officer, Department of Cuba from July 1, 1901 to May 20, 1902* (Baltimore: Guggenheimer, Weil & Co., n.d.).

In 1900 the Signal Corps began the construction of the Washington-Alaska Military Cable and Telegraph System. Among the signal soldiers who worked on this project was Billy Mitchell, who later became well known for his views about air power. His *The Opening of Alaska*, edited by Lyman L. Woodman (Anchorage: Cook Inlet Historical Society, 1982), is fascinating reading.

The Early Twentieth Century (1904–1917)

The Signal Corps participated in a variety of activities during the early twentieth century. In 1906 alone it sent units to Cuba as part of the "Army of Cuban Pacification" and helped bring order out of the chaos of the San Francisco earthquake. The *Journal of the Military Service Institution of the United States*, the *Journal of the United States Infantry Association* (which became *Infantry Journal*), the *Journal of the United States Cavalry Association* (later *Cavalry Journal*), and *The National Guard Magazine* are good sources for articles on the

Signal Corps during this period. One of the Corps' more unusual duties was the care and lighting of the Statue of Liberty. On this aspect of its history, see Rebecca C. Robbins' "Carrying a Torch for Lady Liberty," *Army Communicator* 11 (Fall 1986): 40–43.

In 1907 the Signal Corps created an aviation section in the Office of the Chief Signal Officer. The United States Air Force traces its lineage to that organization. Maurer Maurer compiled and edited several volumes of documents relevant to the early history of the Air Force in *The U.S. Air Force in World War I*, 4 vols. (Washington, D.C.: Office of Air Force History, 1978–1979). Volume 2 is of particular interest as it covers the period under the Signal Corps' auspices. Juliette A. Hennessy's *The United States Army Air Arm, April 1861 to April 1917* (1958; reprint, Washington, D.C.: Office of Air Force History, 1985) offers a chronological study of the development of aviation and contains some useful appendixes.

In 1909 the Signal Corps purchased the Army's first airplane from Wilbur and Orville Wright. The literature on the Wright brothers and their achievement is extensive and constantly growing. Fred Howard's *Wilbur and Orville: A Biography of the Wright Brothers* (New York: Alfred A. Knopf, 1987) is an excellent study and discusses the brothers' work for the Signal Corps. Tom Crouch's *The Bishop's Boys: A Life of Wilbur and Orville Wright* (New York: W. W. Norton and Co., 1989) is also of great value and a pleasure to read. Besides Chandler and Lahm, whose volume is cited in the preceding section, another early Signal Corps aviator, Benjamin D. Foulois, wrote about his experiences. See Benjamin D. Foulois and C. V. Glines, *From the Wright Brothers to the Astronauts: The Memoirs of Major General Benjamin D. Foulois* (New York: McGraw-Hill Book Company, 1968). Henry ("Hap") Arnold also began his aeronautical career with the Signal Corps. He discusses this period of his career in *Global Mission* (New York: Harper and Brothers, 1949). See also Thomas M. Coffey's *Hap: The Story of the U.S. Air Force and the Man Who Built It, General Henry "Hap" Arnold* (New York: Viking Press, 1982).

The Signal Corps also took to the air by means of radio. An excellent study of early radio technology is found in the two volumes by Hugh G. J. Aitken, *Syntony and Spark: The Origins of Radio* and *The Continuous Wave: Technology and American Radio, 1900–1932* (both Princeton, N.J.: Princeton University Press, 1985). Eric Barnouw's three volumes on the history of broadcasting in the United States, published by Oxford University Press, are also highly informative: *A Tower in Babel* (1966) covers the period to 1933, *The Golden Web* (1968) carries the story to 1953, and *The Image Empire* (1970) completes the trilogy. Also helpful is Susan J. Douglas' *Inventing American Broadcasting, 1899–1922* (Baltimore: Johns Hopkins University Press, 1987), which emphasizes the social and cultural aspects of radio.

Edwin W. Armstrong was an early radio pioneer who worked for the Signal Corps during both world wars. Among his many accomplishments was the development of frequency-modulated, or FM, radio. See Lawrence Lessing's

Man of High Fidelity: Edwin Howard Armstrong (Philadelphia: J. B. Lippincott Company, 1956). Armstrong is the subject, along with two other broadcasting pioneers, David Sarnoff and Lee de Forest, of Tom Lewis' *Empire of the Air: The Men Who Made Radio* (New York: Harper Collins Publishers, 1991). This book was the companion to the Public Broadcasting System's documentary of the same title.

The Signal Corps' role in the Mexican Expedition is not well documented in the secondary literature, but Clarence C. Clendenen's *Blood on the Border: The United States Army and the Mexican Irregulars* (New York: Macmillan Company, 1969) provides useful background and does discuss some of the communication problems the Army faced. Foulois' report as chief of the 1st Aero Squadron in Mexico is printed in Frank Tompkins, *Chasing Villa* (Harrisburg, Pa.: Military Service Publishing Co., 1934). Foulois' memoirs, cited above, as well as Hennessy's *Army Air Arm*, also discuss aerial operations along the border.

World War I

An excellent source of information on the Signal Corps in World War I is the annual report of the chief signal officer for 1919. At over five hundred pages in length, it is full of detail, but unfortunately contains no index. Other sources include the study by the Historical Section of the Army War College, *The Signal Corps and Air Service: A Study of Their Expansion in the United States, 1917–1918*, Monograph no. 16 (Washington, D.C.: Government Printing Office, 1922), and C. F. Martin, Signal Communications in World War I [Historical Section, Army War College, August 1942]. Martin's account is among the collections of the Military History Institute, Carlisle Barracks, Pennsylvania.

The Center of Military History has reprinted, in five volumes, the *Order of Battle of the United States Land Forces in the World War* and the seventeen-volume compilation of selected AEF records, *United States Army in the World War*. Volume 15 contains the report on the Signal Corps' activities.

The Signal Corps' administration of aviation during the war became extremely controversial and led to the separation of the Air Service from the Corps in 1918. On the Air Service, see Arthur Sweetser's *The American Air Service. A Record of Its Problems, Its Difficulties, Its Failures, and Its Final Achievements* (New York: D. Appleton and Company, 1919); Edgar S. Gorrell's *The Measure of America's World War Aeronautical Effort*, James Jackson Cabot Professorship of Air Traffic Regulation and Air Transportation Publication No. 6 (Burlington, Vt.: Lane Press, Inc., 1940); and I. B. Holley's *Ideas and Weapons* (Washington, D.C.: Office of Air Force History, 1983). *Ideas and Weapons* is a reprint of the original edition, published in 1953. Another useful source of information is Lois Walker and Shelby E. Wickham, *From Huffman Prairie to the Moon: The History of Wright-Patterson Air Force Base* (Wright-Patterson Air Force Base, Ohio: Office of History, 2750th Air Base Wing, 1986).

George O. Squier, chief signal officer during World War I, was one of the first Army officers to obtain a graduate degree and the first chief signal officer to hold a degree in electrical engineering. On his career, see Paul Wilson Clark's, "Major General George O. Squier: Military Scientist" (Ph.D. diss., Case Western Reserve University, 1974). See also Charles J. Gross' "George Owen Squier and the Origins of American Military Aviation," *Journal of Military History* 54 (Jul 1990): 281–305, and his entry in volume 17 of the *Dictionary of American Biography* (1935).

Assistant Secretary of War Benedict Crowell published *America's Munitions, 1917–1918* (Washington, D.C.: Government Printing Office, 1919), which contains separate chapters on the Signal Corps and the Air Service. Robert M. Yerkes, ed., *The New World of Science: Its Development During the War* (Freeport, N.Y.: Books for Libraries Press, 1920, reprint, Appleton-Century, 1969) contains information about various aspects of the Signal Corps' activities, such as meteorology. With the advent of aviation and long-range artillery, military meteorology gained new importance during the war.

A. Lincoln Lavine's *Circuits of Victory* (Garden City, N.Y.: Doubleday, Page, and Company, 1921) is an excellent account of the Signal Corps' service on the ground during World War I. See also George R. Thompson, "Radio Comes of Age in World War I," in Marshall, ed., *Story of the Signal Corps.* Samuel A. Barnes in "Signaling Souls on the Western Front," *Army Communicator* 5 (Winter 1980): 30–35, tells the story of the 325th Field Signal Battalion, a black unit. Karen L. Hillerich's "Black Jack's Girls," *Army* 32 (Dec 1982): 44–48, is about the women who served as telephone operators in Europe for the Signal Corps. They were also known as the "Hello Girls."

Photography, though long an unofficial function, became an official duty of the Signal Corps during World War I and has remained an important aspect of its work ever since. See K. Jack Bauer, comp., *List of World War I Signal Corps Films*, Special List 14 (Washington, D.C.: National Archives, 1957).

Interwar Years

Relatively little has been published about the Signal Corps during this period. Dulany Terrett's *The Signal Corps: The Emergency*, part of the Center of Military History's World War II "green book" series, represents the only comprehensive source. Terrett's volume is the first of three volumes on the Signal Corps in World War II and covers the period up to the bombing of Pearl Harbor. It can be supplemented by the *Historical Sketch* and articles in Scheips, ed., *Military Signal Communications*, as well those in the *Signal Corps Bulletin* and other publications. On signal training during these years, see Helen C. Phillips' *History of the United States Army Signal Center and School, 1919–1967* (Fort Monmouth, N.J.: U.S. Army Signal Center and School, 1967).

During this period the Corps developed radar, one of the "wonder weapons" of World War II. On its work in this area see Harry M. Davis' "History of the

Signal Corps Development of U.S. Army Radar Equipment" (New York: Office of the Chief Signal Officer, Historical Section Field Office, 1944), in the custody of the Historical Resources Branch, CMH. On the Navy's concurrent work with radar see David K. Allison's, *New Eye for the Navy: The Origins of Radar at the Naval Research Laboratory* (Washington, D.C.: Naval Research Laboratory, 1981).

World War II

The more than seventy volumes of the series the United States Army in World War II, published by CMH and known collectively as the "green books," provide the most comprehensive history of the Army's participation in the war. Within this larger series are three volumes that specifically discuss the operations of the Signal Corps: Terrett's *Emergency*, cited above; *The Signal Corps: The Test* (1957) by George R. Thompson, Dixie R. Harris, Pauline M. Oakes, and Dulany Terrett; and *The Signal Corps: The Outcome* (1966), by George R. Thompson and Dixie R. Harris. Other volumes in the series that provided essential information for this volume include: Stetson Conn and Byron Fairchild, *The Framework of Hemisphere Defense* (1960); Stetson Conn, Rose C. Engelman, and Byron Fairchild, *Guarding the United States and Its Outposts* (1964); Stanley Dziuban, *Military Relations Between the United States and Canada, 1939–1945* (1959); John D. Millett, *The Organization and Role of the Army Service Forces* (1954); Roland G. Ruppenthal, *Logistical Support of the Armies*, 2 vols. (1953, 1959); and Mattie E. Treadwell, *The Women's Army Corps* (1954).

The Center of Military History has in its custody many of the monographs prepared as background for the green books. Among the most useful for this study were: James V. Clarke, "Signal Corps Army Pictorial Service in World War II (1 September 1939–16 August 1945)"; Sidney L. Jackson, "Tactical Communication in World War II, Part 1, North African Campaigns" and "Part 2, Signal Communication in the Sicilian Campaign"; Mary-louise Melia, "Signal Corps Fixed Communications in World War II: Special Assignments and Techniques"; and Ruth F. Sadler, "History of the Signal Corps Affiliated Plan" and "History of the Electronics Training Group in the United Kingdom (1944)." A complete list of the monographs is contained in the bibliographic note to Thompson et al., *The Test*. The Center's library also contains typescript copies of the annual reports of the chief signal officer to the commanding general, Army Service Forces, for the years 1943 through 1946.

Signal security and intelligence can be considered a separate genre of study. From 1929 to 1944 the Signal Corps operated the Signal Intelligence Service (subsequently the Signal Security Service and the Signal Security Agency, the forerunners of the current Army Intelligence and Security Command [INSCOM]), which had responsibility for codes and ciphers. Its work paid off during World War II when William F. Friedman, the Army's foremost cryptologist, succeeded in breaking PURPLE, the Japanese diplomatic code. Meanwhile, the British, with the help of the Poles, had broken the German cipher machine known as Enigma. The Allies benefited significantly from the use of the intelligence they gleaned from the Japanese (MAGIC) and the Germans (ULTRA). Most of the material regarding MAGIC and ULTRA was still classified when the green books were prepared. Since these records were declassified in the 1970s, the literature has been steadily growing. The INSCOM history office has recently produced a documentary history entitled *U.S. Army Signals Intelligence in World War II*, edited by James L. Gilbert and John P. Finnegan (Washington, D.C.: Center of Military History, United States Army, 1993). This volume gives the researcher a sample of the material long held from public view. Among those who have written works in this area are: Ronald Clark, *The Man Who Broke Purple: The Life of Colonel William F. Friedman, Who Deciphered the Japanese Code in World War II* (Boston: Little, Brown and Co., 1977); Edward J. Drea, *MacArthur's Ultra: Codebreaking and the War Against Japan, 1942–1945* (Lawrence: University Press of Kansas, 1992); David Kahn, *The Codebreakers: The Story of Secret Writing* (New York: Macmillan Company, 1967; abridged paperback edition, New American Library, 1973); and Ronald Lewin, *The American Magic: Codes, Ciphers, and the Defeat of Japan* (New York: Farrar Straus Giroux, 1982) and *Ultra Goes to War* (New York: McGraw-Hill Book Co., 1978).

The Cold War and Korea

Like the interwar years, the post–World War II period presents a research problem for students of the Signal Corps. There are two published quadrennial reports of the chief signal officer, the first covering May 1951 to April 1955 and the second from May 1955 to April 1959. Comprising about 125 pages in length each, they are not full of detail, but they do cover the major developments.

The Korean War, sometimes referred to as the "forgotten war," is not as well documented as many other conflicts. Consequently, published information about the Signal Corps' participation therein is limited as well. Some information can be gleaned from CMH's official publications on the Korean War. For specific details, told in anecdotal form by participants, see John G. Westover, ed., *Combat Support in Korea* (Washington, D.C.: Combat Forces Press, 1955). Marshall, ed., *Story of the Signal Corps*, contains one article about Korea. It describes the Signal Corps' fight alongside the marines to protect "Communications Hill" near the Chosin Reservoir in 1950.

Information about the Corps' technical achievements, such as its involvement in the space race, can be found in such journals as the *Army Information Digest* (which changed its name to *Army Digest* in 1966 and to *Soldiers* in 1971), *Signal*, and the *United States Army Combat Forces Journal* (which became *Army* in 1956). An excellent article on the development of the transistor that discusses the Signal Corps' role in the endeavor is Thomas J. Misa, "Military Needs, Commercial Realities, and the Development of the Transistor, 1948–1958," in

Merritt Roe Smith, ed., *Military Enterprise and Technological Change: Perspectives on the American Experience* (Cambridge, Mass.: Massachusetts Institute of Technology Press, 1985).

During the 1960s the Signal Corps and the other technical services were radically reorganized as a result of the reforms initiated by Secretary of Defense Robert S. McNamara. To put those changes into perspective, see James E. Hewes, Jr.'s, excellent study, *From Root to McNamara: Army Organization and Administration, 1900–1963*, originally published by CMH in 1975. The new order is also discussed by David P. Gibbs in "The Army's New Communications-Electronics Organization," found in Marshall, ed., *Story of the Signal Corps.* Gibbs was the last man to hold the title of chief signal officer and the first to be the chief of communications-electronics. He was also the son of a former chief signal officer, George S. Gibbs, who held that post from 1928 to 1931.

Vietnam

The Center of Military History has produced several publications that discuss communications in Vietnam. This volume drew largely upon John D. Bergen's *Military Communications: A Test for Technology*, United States Army in Vietnam (Washington, D.C.: Center of Military History, United States Army, 1986). Also very useful were the following monographs in the Vietnam Studies series: Charles R. Myer, *Division-Level Communications, 1962–1973* (Washington, D.C.: Department of the Army, 1982), and Thomas M. Rienzi, *Communications-Electronics, 1962–1970* (Washington, D.C.: Department of the Army, 1972). John J. Tolson, *Airmobility, 1961–1971*, Vietnam Studies (Washington, D.C.: Department of the Army, 1973) also provided important details about the development of airborne command posts.

The 1980s and Beyond

The decades since the end of the fighting in Vietnam have witnessed incredible leaps in signaling technology, particularly the explosion in digital communications. Personal computers, fiber optics, and satellites have revolutionized communications within both the civilian and military communities. Since 1983 the Signal Corps has become the leader in the Army's automation effort with the implementation of the Information Mission Area (IMA). The evolution of this doctrine is well documented through the pages of *Army Communicator*, published by the Signal Center and School at Fort Gordon, Georgia. In addition, *Signal*, the journal of the Armed Forces Communications and Electronics Association, is an excellent source of information on the latest technological innovations.

As of this writing, much of the material on the Army's recent operations in Grenada, Panama, and the Persian Gulf remains classified. Since this is a historical study, it is perhaps too soon to put these latest chapters of the Signal Corps' story into proper perspective. As more information becomes available, these episodes can be fully integrated into the Signal Corps' history as it continues to unfold. There is so much to be written about the Signal Corps. I urge those with an interest in its history to continue the exploration of the branch's past as well as to follow its journey into the future.

Glossary

AAF	Army Air Forces
ACAN	Army Command and Administrative Network
ACC	U.S. Army Communications Command
ACS	Alaska Communication System
ADDS	Army Data Distribution System
AEF	American Expeditionary Forces
AFHQ	Allied Force Headquarters
AGF	Army Ground Forces
AGO	Adjutant General's Office
AM	Amplitude modulated
AMC	Army Materiel Command
AN/TRC	Army-Navy Transportable Radio Communications
AR	Army Regulations
ARAG	Annual Report of The Adjutant General
ARMB	Annual Report of the Chief of the Militia Bureau
ARQM	Annual Report of the Quartermaster General
ARSO	Annual Report of the Chief Signal Officer
ARSW	Annual Report of the Secretary of War
ARTEP	Army Training and Evaluation Program
ARVN	Army of the Republic of Vietnam
ASF	Army Service Forces
AUTODIN	Automatic Digital Network
AUTOSEVOCOM	Automatic Secure Voice Communications
AUTOVON	Automatic Voice Network (see DSN)
C3	Command, control, and communications
C4	Command, control, communications, and computers
CARS	Combat Arms Regimental System
CCC	Civilian Conservation Corps
CCF	Chinese Communist Forces
CE	Communications-electronics
CECOM	U.S. Army Communications-Electronics Command
CMH	U.S. Army Center of Military History
COMSAT	Communications Satellite Corporation
CONARC	Continental Army Command
CONUS	Continental United States

DA	Department of the Army
DAGO	Department of the Army General Orders
DCA	Defense Communications Agency
DCSOPS	Deputy Chief of Staff for Military Operations (after 19 May 1974 the Deputy Chief of Staff for Operations and Plans)
DISC4	Director of Information Systems for Command, Control, Communications, and Computers
DMZ	Demilitarized Zone
DOD	Department of Defense
DSCS	Defense Satellite Communications System
DSN	Defense Switched Network (formerly AUTOVON)
EMP	Electromagnetic pulse
ENIAC	Electronic numerical integrator and computer
EPLRS	Enhanced Position Location Reporting System
ETOUSA	European Theater of Operations, United States Army
FCC	Federal Communications Commission
FM	Frequency modulated (also Field Manual)
GPO	Government Printing Office
GPS	Global Positioning System
HMMWV	High Mobility Multipurpose Wheeled Vehicle
HUAC	House Un-American Activities Committee
IGY	International Geophysical Year
IMA	Information Mission Area
INSCOM	U.S. Army Intelligence and Security Command
IPY	International Polar Year
IRAC	Interdepartmental Radio Advisory Committee
ISC	U.S. Army Information Systems Command
IWCS	Integrated Wideband Communications System
JASCO	Joint Assault Signal Company
JCCT	Joint Combat Camera Team
JMSI	*Journal of the Military Service Institution of the United States*
JTIDS	Joint Tactical Information Distribution System
LASER	Light amplification by stimulated emission of radiation
MACV	U.S. Military Assistance Command, Vietnam
MARS	Military Affiliate Radio System

MHI	U.S. Army Military History Institute
MIT	Massachusetts Institute of Technology
MOBIDIC	Mobile digital computer
MOLLUS	Military Order of the Loyal Legion of the United States
MOS	Military occupational specialty
MSE	Mobile subscriber equipment
NACA	National Advisory Committee for Aeronautics
NARA	National Archives and Records Administration
NASA	National Aeronautics and Space Administration
NATO	North Atlantic Treaty Organization
NBC	National Broadcasting Company
NDRC	National Defense Research Committee
NEID	New Equipment Introductory Detachment
OB	*Order of Battle of the United States Land Forces in the World War*
OCSO	Office of the Chief Signal Officer
OR	*War of the Rebellion: A Compilation of the Official Records of the Union and Confederate Armies*
OSRD	Office of Scientific Research and Development
RADAR	Radio direction finding and ranging
RCA	Radio Corporation of America
RCM	Radio countermeasures
RG	Record Group
RITA	Reseau Integre Transmissions Automatique
ROAD	Reorganization Objective Army Divisions
ROTC	Reserve Officers Training Corps
RPL	Rapid pole line
SCORE	Signal Communications via Orbiting Relay Equipment
SCR	Signal Corps Radio *or* Set Complete Radio
SHAEF	Supreme Headquarters, Allied Expeditionary Force
SIAM	Signal Information and Monitoring
SINCGARS	Single Channel Ground and Airborne Radio System
STARCOM	Strategic Army Communications Network
STRATCOM	Strategic Communications Command
SW	Secretary of War
TACFIRE	Tactical Fire Direction System
TACSAT	Tactical satellite
TAG	The Adjutant General
TDA	Table of Distribution and Allowances

TIROS	Television and Infra-Red Observation Satellite
T/O	Table of Organization
TOE	Table of Organization and Equipment
TRADOC	U.S. Army Training and Doctrine Command
TRI-TAC	Joint Tactical Communications Program
UHF	Ultra–high frequency
UN	United Nations
UNC	United Nations Command
UNICOM	Universal Integrated Communications System
USAFBI	United States Army Forces in the British Isles
USARS	United States Army Regimental System
USARV	United States Army, Vietnam
USAVIC	United States Army Visual Information Center
USMA	United States Military Academy
VHF	Very high frequency
WAAC	Women's Army Auxiliary Corps
WAC	Women's Army Corps
WAMCATS	Washington-Alaska Military Cable and Telegraph System
WD	War Department
WDGO	War Department General Orders
WWMCCS	Worldwide Military Command and Control System
YMCA	Young Men's Christian Association

Index